ECONOMICS OF INTERNATIONAL MIGRATION

ECONOMICS
OF INTERNATIONAL
MIGRATION

Proceedings of a Conference
held by the International Economic Association

EDITED BY
BRINLEY THOMAS

LONDON
MACMILLAN & CO LTD
NEW YORK · ST MARTIN'S PRESS
1958

MACMILLAN AND COMPANY LIMITED
London Bombay Calcutta Madras Melbourne

THE MACMILLAN COMPANY OF CANADA LIMITED
Toronto

ST MARTIN'S PRESS INC
New York

PRINTED IN GREAT BRITAIN

CONTENTS

v

Contents

vi

LIST OF PARTICIPANTS

Professor R. Bachi, The Hebrew University, Jerusalem, Israel

Professor F. Bastos De Ávila, Rio de Janeiro, Brazil

Professor L. Baudin, University of Paris, Paris, France

Dr. G. Beijer, Research Group for European Migration Problems, The Hague, Netherlands

Professor S. Chandrasekahr, University of Baroda, India

Dr. F. Edding, University of Kiel, Germany

Professor Howard S. Ellis, University of California, Berkeley, U.S.A.

Mr. Douglas Hague, University College, London, England

Professor W. G. Hoffmann, University of Münster, Münster, Germany

Professor E. W. Hofstee, Landbouwhogeschool, Wageningen, Netherlands

Mr. P. Jacobsen, Intergovernmental Committee for European Migration, Geneva

Professor E. James, University of Paris, Paris, France

Dr. W. Langrod, United Nations Secretariat, New York, U.S.A.

Mr. X. Lannes, International Labour Office, Geneva, Switzerland

Professor Abba P. Lerner, Roosevelt College, Chicago, U.S.A.

Professor E. Lindahl, University of Uppsala, Sweden

Professor A. Mahr, University of Vienna, Austria

Mr. J. F. Meenan, University College, Dublin, Eire

Professor G. Parenti, University of Florence, Italy

Mr. H. M. Phillips, UNESCO, Paris, France

Mr. E. Rahardt, Intergovernmental Committee for European Migration, Geneva, Switzerland

Professor H. M. Robertson, University of Cape Town, South Africa

Professor E. A. G. Robinson, Sidney Sussex College, Cambridge, England

Dr. E. Rubin, American University, Washington, D.C., U.S.A.

Professor T. H. Silcock, University of Malaya, Singapore

Professor J. J. Spengler, Duke University, North Carolina, U.S.A.

List of Participants

Professor Brinley Thomas, University College, Cardiff, Wales

Professor Mabel F. Timlin, University of Saskatchewan, Canada

Mr. R. Turvey, The London School of Economics, London, England

Dr. Hilde Wander, University of Kiel, Germany

Mr. J. Zubrzycki, The Australian National University, Canberra, Australia

PROGRAMME COMMITTEE

Brinley Thomas (Chairman)
David Glass
Austin Robinson
Alfred Sauvy

INTRODUCTION

By BRINLEY THOMAS

In the world economy, as it evolved up to 1913, international mobility of labour was an important element in economic growth ; and most of what is known about migration is based on studies of the experience of countries during that period. In the last thirty years, however, the scale and character of international movements of population have been profoundly influenced by events such as the American Restriction Act of 1924, the Great Depression of the early 1930's, and the Second World War. Not only has the environment changed but so also has the intellectual climate : the questions which used to be asked may not be the appropriate ones to-day. In order to contribute towards a new assessment, the International Economic Association decided to devote its seventh Conference to a re-appraisal of the role of migration in the international economy, and the results are given in this volume.

In view of the immensity of the subject, it was necessary to keep the programme within certain limits. A strong case could have been made for including a review of the range and quality of migration statistics — the difficulties of definition, classification, and comparability — and a critique of methods used to improve the data. While no one will deny that this is an important task, it was felt that to do justice to it would have upset the balance of the programme. For the same reason it was decided to rule out a systematic analysis of demographic aspects, *e.g.* the effect of trends in the rate of natural increase on the propensity to migrate, or the influence of migration on the population structure of sending and receiving countries. The relevant statistical problems have been well probed by the Population Commission of the United Nations and the International Labour Office, and recent work by demographers on international migration may be seen in the *Proceedings* of the World Population Conference held in Rome in 1954. Plenty of statistical and demographic matter will be found in this book ; but it is subordinate to the treatment of an economic theme, except in Part VI where social aspects are discussed and a detailed demographic analysis of the unique inflow of population into Israel is presented.

When economists speak of mobility of labour they mean movement

ix

which is the result of voluntary acts of choice by individuals. A distinction has to be drawn between this normal type of migration and the forced transfers which have been a grim feature of this century. While the determinants of these forced movements of population are clearly outside the purview of an economist's discussion, an account of their economic consequences is most relevant. No inquiry into the impact of recent migration would be adequate if it left out this aspect; attention is given to it in the analysis of Germany (Chapter 14), Eastern Europe (Chapter 16), and India (Chapter 20).

The subject-matter was broken up into five parts: the development of analytical tools for interpreting the mechanism and consequences of migration movements; a comparative study of the experience of representative countries of emigration and immigration, and the changing character of government policies; the scale and function of intra-continental migration in Europe and Asia and its possible scope in the future; social problems of assimilation; and the extent to which migration can help to relieve population pressures or contribute to the growth of some of the underdeveloped economies.

I shall not attempt to summarize the conclusions of the Conference; fortunately the main threads have been effectively brought together by Professor Howard S. Ellis in the last chapter.

One was left with a clear impression of some of the more striking contrasts between present trends and the era of large-scale intercontinental mobility. The fulcrum of world migration used to be the absorptive capacity of the United States, but this has long ceased to be true. In the nine years before the First World War, 1905–13, nearly 1 million immigrants on an average entered the United States every year, an annual rate of almost 11 per 1000 of the 1910 population; in the nine years after the Second World War, 1946–54, the inflow was only about 190,000 a year, an annual rate of 1·3 per 1000 of the 1950 population. Moreover, this recent immigration is different in character from the old, a good proportion of it consisting of displaced persons and refugees. The prospect in the United States is dominated by the great upsurge in the rate of natural increase which is expected to make the population grow from 170 million in 1957 to 220 million in 1975. There is no likelihood of any significant change in the law regulating immigration, and it was strongly argued at the Conference that a greater inflow into the United States at the present time would not raise real income per head.

The remarkable economic recovery of Western Europe since the war has reduced the need for emigration. The buoyant economy of the Federal Republic of Germany has successfully absorbed several millions of refugees, and the progress made towards integration, particularly the plan for a European Common Market, has underlined the possibilities of greater mobility of labour within the continent. If intra-European migration can become an increasingly effective substitute for outward movement, oversea countries will find it harder to attract an adequate flow of settlers.

There is often a lack of correspondence between the pattern of demand for migrants and the quality of the available supply. High levels of employment in countries of emigration have put a premium on skilled workers and highly qualified technicians, while the unskilled are not always easy to absorb in the receiving countries.

Whereas migration in Asia can do little to relieve population pressure, it can perform a pivotal function, even though the scale of movement is small, if it takes the form of diffusion of skills. In the words of Professor Silcock, '. . . the process of combining migration with cultural assimilation and organized diffusion of skills is of first-rate economic and political importance in many of the countries of Asia. One of the functions of migration in the Asian economy is to mitigate differences between the structures of different economies, and not merely to help to equalize basic levels of income per head. Training and cultural change within the areas themselves provide a substitute for migration in modifying the relative scarcities of different kinds of labour, but there are important obstacles to this training no less than to migration, and a part of the practical problem of maintaining standards of living in the area is to find methods of combining a properly controlled migration with a proper educational reform. This is the goal towards which several of the United Nations agencies and independent governments of the region appear to be converging.'

The close correlation which used to exist between foreign lending and migration has in recent times been disrupted. Since 1945 the direction of international capital movements has been greatly influenced by North American aid to Europe, and there has been only an indirect connexion between American private foreign lending and the main streams of migration. Past experience is probably an unreliable guide to future relationships in this field ; we need to know much more about capital requirements in relation to immigration under varying conditions.

In the nineteenth century it would never have occurred to anyone to suggest that a prospective relative scarcity of land in countries of immigration was a limiting factor. Conditions have changed in the present century. The development of technical inventions which are labour-saving in relation to land has the effect of increasing the relative scarcity of land, and this may become a factor strong enough to inhibit large-scale immigration.

Even though the significance of international migration may have relatively declined, the mechanism of oversea settlement has by no means lost its vitality. Ample evidence of this is to be found in the record of the Intergovernmental Committee for European Migration, and it was of great benefit to the Conference to have officers of this organization present and bringing their operational experience to bear on the discussions. A survey of the aims and achievements of the Intergovernmental Committee is given in Chapter 8. Immigration is bound to play an important part in the economic growth of countries such as Australia, Canada, Argentina, and Brazil; economic analysis has much to contribute to the interpretation of the mechanism of absorption and the uniformities and differences between the experience of various countries. For example, at this Conference we had Professor J. J. Spengler's distinction between the income and substitution effects of immigration, and Professor A. P. Lerner put forward a model in which immigration can generate a cost inflation. Much remains to be done on these lines; and perhaps the time has come for a major offensive by economists to reoccupy the territory of population analysis.

Taking as its background the past contribution of migration to economic development, the Conference tried to define the role that can be expected of it in the world as we now know it. Naturally questions of policy often came to the forefront, and, where disagreement was sharp, it was at least salutary to have to make one's value judgements explicit. The objective of the Conference, however, was not to prescribe goals for policy-makers but to elucidate current trends and to deepen our understanding of the determinants and consequences of migration movements. Any spontaneous debate is bound occasionally to stray from the main theme; nevertheless it was thought desirable to print a record of the general lines of the discussions, since much of the value of these international meetings lies in the exchange of divergent points of view which they make possible. The exacting task of recording the discussions was admirably carried out by Mr. Douglas Hague. The Indexes were compiled by Mr. J. Parry Lewis.

The thanks of the International Economic Association are due to the Intergovernmental Committee for European Migration, particularly Mr. E. K. Rahardt and Miss Silvia Baverstock, for valuable assistance in organizing the Conference. Those who took part wish to record their appreciation of the excellent work of Madame Berger-Lieser, Secretary of the Association. Finally, we would like to thank the management and staff of the Grand Hotel, Kitzbühel, for meeting the requirements of the Conference so agreeably.

PART I
ANALYTICAL SURVEY

Chapter 1

MIGRATION AND INTERNATIONAL INVESTMENT

BY

BRINLEY THOMAS
University College, Cardiff

ONE of the interesting questions raised by the period ending in the 1920's is the nature of the mechanism by which the economies of the leading countries reacted on one another. The subject has recently attracted a good deal of attention, but much work remains to be done before a satisfactory account can be given. We shall begin by examining the part played by movements of population and capital in the growth of the international economy up to 1913. Was there an automatic mechanism guaranteeing relative stability as long as migration continued? What are the main contrasts between the trends since 1945 and those of the nineteenth century? Is the rupture of the old relationship between international investment and international migration a cause of instability?

I. THE PATTERN BEFORE 1913

1. Migration and the Flow of Capital

There were two well-marked phases in the evolution of British foreign lending up to 1913. In the first phase, ending in the sixties, there was a good deal of lending to governments; about three-fifths of the £785 million of British investments abroad in 1870 were in government bonds, and much of that money had gone into military rather than economic enterprises. Another feature of the earlier part of the century was the great outburst of direct investment on the continent of Europe by British entrepreneurs, for whom it was a matter of pride as well as profit to be able to export the industrial revolution. This activity entailed the temporary emigration from the United Kingdom of technicians and other labour required to build the new capital equipment.[1]

[1] The most famous of these capital exporters was Thomas Brassey. 'He financed more than one banking house as a means to secure emergency credit. Eighty

In the second phase British loanable funds went for the most part into the purchase of securities in the underpopulated lands overseas. A clear and significant pattern may be seen in the population and capital flows of the period 1860–1913; each of the three upsurges in emigration from Europe — 1863–72, 1879–91, and 1898–1907 — was accompanied by a boom in British capital exports. That international migration synchronized almost exactly with international investment is evident from Table I.

TABLE I

PEAKS AND TROUGHS IN BRITISH FOREIGN LENDING AND
EUROPEAN OVERSEA EMIGRATION, 1860–1913

United Kingdom Net Income available for Foreign Investment *		European Emigration to Oversea Countries †	
Trough Year	Peak Year	Trough Year	Peak Year
1862		1861	
	1872		1872
1877		1877	
	1890		1891
1898		1898	
	1908		1907

Sources : * A. H. Imlah, 'The Balance of Payments and the Export of Capital of the United Kingdom, 1816–1913', *Economic History Review*, Second Series, vol. v, no. 2, 1952, pp. 234-9. † G. Sundbärg's figures in *Emigrationsutredningen*, Bilaga iv, *Utvandringsstatistik*, Stockholm, 1910, pp. 102-3.

In 1913 aggregate British foreign investment amounted to £3763 million distributed geographically as follows: 47 per cent in the British Empire, 20 per cent in the United States, 20 per cent in Latin America, and only 6 per cent in Europe. The destinations of the 24 million European emigrants in the years 1891–1914 were roughly as follows: 54 per cent to the United States, 25 per cent to Latin America, and 17 per cent to the British Empire. This simple picture of labour and capital flowing from a crowded continent to

thousand men were at one time in his employ. English schools, priests, chapels and physicians followed their migration from one contract to the next. To keep such an organization employed agents and partners roved the commercialized world seeking opportunities and concessions. At one time Brassey had railways and docks under construction in five continents. Every country in Europe possesses a specimen of this craft with the possible exception of Greece, Albania and Finland. In his thirty-five years of business life he was engaged upon one hundred and seventy different contracts, involving nearly eight thousand miles of railway.'—L. H. Jenks, *The Migration of British Capital to 1875*, Cape, 1938, pp. 136-7.

the underdeveloped sector of the world becomes more complicated when we examine the process closely.

2. *Migration and Inverse Investment Cycles*

From the 1840's to the eve of the First World War the long swings in the economic development of the United Kingdom and the United States were inverse to one another ; and this coincided with a one-way traffic of capital and labour across the Atlantic. Some of the relevant data are summarized in Table II for the period 1869–1913. We are fortunate that for these years we have for both countries fairly reliable statistics of the national income and capital formation. The long swings (with a span of about eighteen to twenty years) in home investment in the United Kingdom and the United States show an inverse relation.

The alternating phases suggest an intercontinental rivalry for resources. A wave of investment in construction did not take place on both sides of the Atlantic at the same time ; the lender gave way to the borrower and later the borrower did likewise for the lender. For Great Britain the process undoubtedly entailed relative long-run stability in the level of production, since the home construction and export sectors offset each other. This was not true of the United States, for there the magnitudes of the two sectors were different ; in the period 1869–1913 merchandise imports averaged about 30 per cent of the net national product in Great Britain and only 6 per cent in the United States. Over the long period the world's leading creditor kept putting its money back into circulation — through vigorous foreign lending in one phase and a considerable expansion in its imports of primary produce in the next phase. The absence of a chronic sterling shortage was due, not to any superior wisdom on the part of the British, but to the inner compulsions of the British economy and the relation between its growth and that of the then underdeveloped countries. Intercontinental mobility of population and capital was indispensable to the economic development of the new lands ; and the rhythmic movement of these flows was a necessary condition of the relative long-run stability in British industrial production.

The analysis suggests that, where a highly industrialized creditor country is a heavy importer of food and raw materials from an under-populated debtor country to which it exports labour and capital goods, there is a presumption that the growth of the two economies will involve inverse fluctuations in home investment and consequent disharmonious rates of economic growth.

5

Analytical Survey

TABLE II

The United States and the United Kingdom : Rates of Change in Migration, Investment, and Real Income *per capita* from Decade to Overlapping Decade, 1869-1913

Decade (Yearly Average)	United States				
	Total Immigration	Net Immigration from U.K.	Net Producer Durables	Net Construction	Real Income *per capita*
	%	%	%	%	%
1869–78	—	—	—	—	—
1874–83	+ 26·4	+ 104·0	+ 73·5	+ 39·0	+ 29·3
1879–88	+ 35·1	+ 74·4	+ 27·7	+ 53·6	+ 17·3
1884–93	– 4·4	– 18·7	– 4·2	+ 56·3	+ 5·5
1889–98	– 19·7	– 37·9	– 7·7	+ 19·7	+ 3·8
1894–1903	+ 7·2	– 29·8	+ 49·2	– 3·1	+ 12·3
1899–1908	+ 89·3	+ 41·4	+ 75·3	+ 15·8	+ 14·2
1904–13	+ 25·2	+ 4·7	+ 9·4	+ 14·6	+ 9·6

Decade (Yearly Average)	United Kingdom				
	Volume of Home Investment	Volume of Building	Balance of Payments on Income Account	Unemployment	Real Income *per capita*
	%	%	%	%	%
1869–78	—	—	—	—	—
1874–83	+ 12·8	+ 12·8	– 50·4	+ 50·0	+ 5·3
1879–88	– 4·8	– 13·5	+ 102·1	+ 44·4	+ 8·6
1884–93	+ 6·2	– 2·1	+ 46·6	– 4·6	+ 14·2
1889–98	+ 24·3	+ 23·7	– 25·4	– 29·0	+ 11·6
1894–1903	+ 26·3	+ 30·3	– 37·6	– 11·4	+ 7·0
1899–1908	+ 10·1	+ 5·2	+ 120·3	+ 10·3	+ 2·9
1904–13	– 5·5	– 22·1	+ 132·4	+ 9·3	+ 2·8

Source : Brinley Thomas, *Migration and Economic Growth*, National Institute of Economic and Social Research Study, Cambridge University Press, 1954, pp. 111-13 and references cited there.

3. *The Working of the International Mechanism*

The inverse relation between construction cycles was true not only of Great Britain and the United States but also of Great Britain and other debtor countries — Australia, Canada, and Argentina. For example, statistics of railway building and brick production in Australia reveal a prominent boom in the eighties when immigration and capital imports from Britain were heavy, a downswing in the

6

nineties corresponding to a boom in capital formation in Britain, and another upsurge in activity in the early years of this century when British funds and emigrants were again pouring in.

Any attempt to throw light on this interaction must start from the hypothesis that, to quote Professor Viner, '. . . major long-term capital movements have . . . mainly been "disturbing" rather than "equilibrating" in character'.[1] It does not go to the root of the matter to say, as Professor Cairncross does, that '. . . it was upon the terms of trade that the distribution of investment between home and foreign, as well as the course of real wages, ultimately depended'.[2] Space does not allow a discussion of this question here. Cairncross has to go out of his way to find reasons why heavy British capital exports in the eighties should have coincided with a *deterioration* in the terms of trade of the borrowing countries, for the link seemed to work so well in the nineties and the 1900's. Before we can reach a firm conclusion there is need for much more detailed analysis of the time series. The background of what follows, however, is that movements in the terms of trade are to be looked upon more as consequences than as causal forces.

A broad picture of the process can be given in the following terms. Let us envisage a simple international economy consisting of a creditor and debtor country similar to the United Kingdom and the United States in the middle of the last century. In each there is a home construction and an export sector. Over the long period the sectors within each country compete for resources, and the two countries compete for the resources of the economy which they comprise. Let C be the highly industrialized creditor country and D the underpopulated debtor country rich in natural resources.

Let us suppose that in Period 1 a large outflow of population takes place from C to D. This immigration brings about in D an induced wave of fixed capital formation (*e.g.* railways and housing) financed initially by an extension of credit; this in turn induces an inflow of loanable funds from C. D has a strong propensity to spend its borrowings on C's capital goods, so the export sector in C (which we assume to be fairly large in relation to national income) gets a boom which is at the expense of home construction. The departure of migrants has reduced the demand for housing and other fixed capital in C, and loanable funds flow out to take advantage of the marginal efficiency of fixed investment in D.

Thus in Period 1 there is a construction boom in D and an export boom in C induced by the flow of population and capital.

[1] J. Viner, *Studies in the Theory of International Trade*, Allen & Unwin, p. 365.
[2] A. K. Cairncross, *Home and Foreign Investment, 1870–1913*, Cambridge University Press, 1953, p. 208.

What happens to the price structures? Inflationary expansion (accompanied by speculation) in D sucks labour and resources into construction at the expense of D's export sector; the full effect of this is reflected in the domestic price level. The prices of domestic goods rise most; next to them come export prices; the prices of imports rise least.[1] An important determinant of the latter is the fact that C can draw factors easily into its export sector from the depressed construction sector, and so its expansion can proceed for some time without any rise in costs. Booming exports accompanied by depressed constructional activity yield a more moderate expansion than booming constructional activity accompanied by depressed exports. Thus the net barter terms of trade, *i.e.* the ratio of export prices to import prices, move against C and in favour of D.

The crucial question is: what brings Period 1 to an end? This raises all the complexities of the theory of cyclical down-turn. All we need to do here is to suggest that, if investment is a function of the relation of output to capacity, the boom in D, being of a more inflationary character, will be the first to reach its ceiling. C investors, influenced by the narrowing margin between the profitability of foreign and home investment (and the increasing risk attached to the former), switch loanable funds into home construction. The flow of emigrants reacts in sympathy.

In Period 2 we have the reverse process — an expansion in home construction in C and in exports in D, and a recession in capital and labour migration. The productive capacity of D's export sector in Period 2 is directly related to the expansion that took place in its capital equipment in Period 1; a substantial supply of primary produce is exported at falling or only slowly rising prices. Meanwhile C gets a vigorous construction boom, with a rapid increase in the volume of imports; the net barter terms of trade are now in favour of C and against D. The mechanism here is that the output capacity of primary produce in D is much increased as a consequence of the investment in fixed capital there in Period 1; whereas in C in Period 2 there is a shift away from its export sector to home construction and this tends to make its export goods relatively dearer. If farmers in the debtor country are hit by the adverse terms of trade in Period 2, that is part of the price they have to pay for having railways and houses built at a rapid rate in the previous period with the aid of men and money from abroad. One cannot expect to gain on the swings *and* the roundabouts![2] Each country, creditor as well

[1] Cf. the experience of Canada, 1910–13. See Cairncross, *Home and Foreign Investment, 1870–1913*, ch. 3.

[2] Contrast the view of P. J. O'Leary and W. Arthur Lewis: 'Whatever may have been the cause of the secular fluctuation in the export of capital, its effect

as debtor, in its home construction boom period lays the foundations for the performance of its export sector in the following period. Moreover, during export booms there is a shift away from construction investment to investment in producers' goods, the demand for which is sensitive to the level of activity in the export sector. There is, thus, an alternation of minor secular booms in fixed capital investment in the lending and borrowing countries; and it is during these booms that each country experiences its most rapid rate of growth of real income per head.

The above sketch is merely an outline of a possible interpretation of the role of capital and labour flows in the nineteenth century. It is very difficult to obtain a statistical measure of the sequence of events at the turning-points of the minor secular swings. A very rough attempt made on British data in the period 1860–1910 suggested that upturns in home construction preceded downturns in the export sector, whereas upturns in the export sector (American railway investment and/or emigration) preceded downturns in home construction.[1]

Statistical analysis of lags suggests that up to the sixties the pace of activity in the United States was conditioned by the inflow of migrants and capital from Europe, but that in the subsequent period the immigration waves were determined by the course of American investment in producer durables, while building activity continued to lag after immigration. There is ample evidence that fluctuations in the net migration balance were an important variable in the long swings in the growth of the American economy; they exercised a strong influence on changes in the rate of growth of the American population.

Some writers throw doubt on the whole idea of an interplay between the economies of Great Britain and the United States. Mr. O'Leary and Professor Arthur Lewis, intrigued by the inverse relation and sceptical of the influence of migration and capital flows, confess that they '. . . cannot even rule out the possibility that the alternation of the U.S. and U.K. building cycles was a sheer accident, springing perhaps from the different effects which the Napoleonic Wars may have had upon the progress of residential building in the two countries'.[2] This is surely to throw up the sponge too soon.

on the dependent overseas economies was deplorable from their point of view, since it transmitted to them a secular fluctuation in investment and output which was not necessarily even related to demand : on the contrary, their capacity to produce built up most during the prolonged slump in prices from 1883 to 1896. . . . If there was an automatic mechanism for stabilising the U.K. economy, by its very nature this was a mechanism for destabilising the rest of the world.'— 'Secular Swings in Production and Trade', *The Manchester School*, May 1955, p. 146.

[1] See Brinley Thomas, *op. cit.* p. 186.
[2] P. J. O'Leary and W. Arthur Lewis *loc. cit.* p. 127.

The arguments with which these authors dismiss the role of migration and investment fail to carry conviction. They contend that British lending could have had little effect on capital formation in America, because the latter's capital imports were insignificant in relation to its own savings — 'averaging between 1874 and 1895 less than a half of one per cent of gross national product'.[1] The same kind of argument is used against migration as a possible link between the economies of the United Kingdom and the United States: '. . . differences in emigration rates made less than a quarter of one per cent difference to the annual rate of growth of population, so one treats this explanation with suspicion'.[2] Obviously if you express migration and capital flows as a proportion of population growth and gross national product respectively, you will nearly always get ridiculously small percentages; but these percentages are irrelevant. It is surely the margin that counts. What we have to look at is the key industry or sector which sets the pace in each phase of rapid growth, and consider the relative significance of capital inflow to that sector. In the upswing of 1866–73 the railway mileage of the United States was doubled; this was entirely financed (directly or indirectly) through the import of 2 billion dollars of foreign funds. As L. H. Jenks pointed out: 'British, Dutch and German investors were then buying nearly half of the Civil War debt . . . to the amount of more than a billion dollars par. The railroads obtained directly only about half a billion. The purchase of government bonds by foreigners, however, released savings and bank resources for railway, industrial, and commercial promotion in the United States.'[3]

Furthermore, the impact of capital inflow must not be taken in isolation: those big inflows were always accompanied by immigration. Throughout the period 1840–1924 building activity in the United States consistently lagged a year or two behind immigration (there was only one exception — in the seventies).[4] The two together, railway construction and residential building, highly sensitive to change in the rate of growth of population, made up a large portion of current capital formation. And then, of course, there was the multiplier.[5] Mr. O'Leary and Professor Lewis have

[1] *Loc. cit.* p. 125.   [2] *Loc. cit.* p. 126.
[3] L. H. Jenks, 'Railroads as an Economic Force in American Development', *Enterprise and Social Change*, ed. F. C. Lane and J. C. Riemersma, Allen & Unwin, 1953, p. 169.   [4] See Brinley Thomas, *op. cit.* ch. 10.
[5] 'The construction moment of railway history brought an initial demand for . . . durable goods. Hence there was a chance for the innovator in the lumbering industry, in quarries, in iron mills and carriage works. Indeed these industries were hard put to keep pace with railway construction. Until the later eighties, every boom period found American factories unable to meet the demand for rails,

hardly justified their conclusion that '. . . the U.S. governed its own fortunes in the nineteenth century and if any adjustment had to be made it was made on the other side of the Atlantic'.[1] Their scepticism about the effect of emigration on the building cycle in Great Britain seems at first sight a little more plausible; but here again the simple percentage is not a very reliable guide. A slump in emigration meant (*a*) an increase in population concentrated in the house-seeking age group, and (*b*) a substantial increase in internal migration to the industrial areas stimulated by the rise in home investment; both these factors had a direct bearing on the demand for housing. Moreover, a decline in emigration was accompanied by a rise in the volume of loanable funds available at home.

II. THE PATTERN SINCE 1945

1. *Movements of Labour and Capital*

The inverse relation between long swings in the economic development of Great Britain and of the new countries overseas ceased when the era of free migration came to an end. A significant turning-point was reached when the United States introduced the Immigration Restriction Act of 1924; and by the end of the Second World War it was clear that the role of international mobility of labour and capital had undergone a profound change.

(*a*) *The Scale and Direction of Migration*

In the years 1945–52 intercontinental migration was as follows:[2]

Emigration from Europe	4,452,000
Immigration into Europe	1,150,000
Non-European migration to non-European countries	460,000
Other intercontinental migration	250,000
Total	6,312,000

and there were heavy importations from England and Wales. As late as the nineties, over one-fifth of the total output of pig iron in the United States was being rolled into railroad bars. Much of this demand for durable goods turned eventually into a demand for labor in mine and quarry and mill, into wage payment to labor. . . . Thus the initial impetus of investment in railway construction led in widening arcs to increments of economic activity over the entire American domain, far exceeding in their total volume the original inputs of investment capital.'—Jenks, *loc. cit.* pp. 166-7.

[1] *Loc. cit.*

[2] Based on 'A Survey of Intercontinental Migration in the Post-War Period', a paper prepared for the World Population Conference, Rome, 1954, by the Population Division of the United Nations.

Of the estimated total of 4,452,000 European emigrants nearly one-fourth came from the United Kingdom and one-sixth from Italy, and about 1,200,000, or well over one-fourth, were refugees. The gross oversea emigration from Europe in 1945–52 was the equivalent of four-fifths of one year's natural increase, whereas the corresponding outflow in 1900–7 was the equivalent of two years' natural increase.

The flow was distributed over the chief receiving countries as follows :

CHIEF RECEIVING COUNTRIES

	United States	Argentine, Brazil, and Venezuela	Canada	Australia	Israel	South Africa	New Zealand	Total
Immigration 1945–52 (thousands)	1104	883	726	697	526	125	75	4136
Percentage of Total	27	21	17	17	13	3	2	100

The proportion taken by the United States was 27 per cent, compared with over 50 per cent in the period 1901–13. However, North and South America together still account for over two-thirds of the total immigration; Australia took 17 per cent and Israel 13 per cent.

(b) The Scale and Direction of American Private Lending

On the average in the fifty years ending in 1913, British foreign lending was equivalent to 4 per cent of her national income ; and in the years 1905–13 it was as high as 7 per cent. If the United States now lent abroad at this latter rate, the annual sum would be no less than 20,000 million dollars. Since the end of the war American foreign investment, public as well as private, has averaged about $2\frac{1}{2}$ per cent of her gross national product. Direct foreign investment by United States companies grew by nearly 10 billion dollars between 1946 and the middle of 1954, their aggregate book value reaching 17 billion dollars, and since 1950 the annual yield of these assets has been about 2·2 billion dollars a year, after allowing for about 1 billion dollars a year paid in foreign taxes. About one-third of the earnings has been retained abroad by foreign subsidiaries, and it is estimated that 25 per cent of the aggregate exports by foreign countries to the United States consists of output produced by direct investment abroad by American firms.[1]

The direction of this flow of direct investment is shown in Table III. Latin America absorbed 38 per cent, Canada 28 per cent, and Western Europe 12 per cent; no less than 45 per cent went into petroleum and 32 per cent into manufacturing; over three-quarters of the direct investment has been in hard-currency countries or countries where dollar transfer can easily be arranged.

(c) The Character of Private Lending

A striking feature of nineteenth-century foreign lending was the large part of it that went into public utilities; the flow of private capital exports into this channel is now negligible. Whereas British investment was largely portfolio, American investment is mainly direct. In the words of a United Nations Report, 'it is precisely public utilities, the most basic and traditionally the largest investment objective, that have been deprived of . . . capital through the drying up of the two sources from which it used to flow'.[2] The place that used to be occupied by railways, the outstanding 'growth' equity of the nineteenth century, is now taken by petroleum. This is not just a difference of industry. The railway was a mighty creator of new economic space; it showered on the international economy a social product far in excess of the private return to the investors. We cannot be confident that petroleum is doing the same. Moreover, hardly any of the international investment in manufacturing has taken place in underdeveloped countries.

(d) The Rise of International Public Investment

In the nineteenth century foreign lending was overwhelmingly a branch of private enterprise. The outstanding characteristic of the postwar period is the part played by government lending; the international transfer of public long-term capital and grants in 1946–50 amounted to a gross figure of 61 billion dollars (27·8 billion dollar grants and 23 billion dollar loans), equivalent to one-quarter of the value of world exports in those years. The main receivers were Western Europe (58 per cent) and underdeveloped countries (14 per cent), and the main suppliers the United States (53 per cent) and Western Europe (24 per cent). The *net* transfer from the United States and Canada was 29 billion dollars. The 8 billion

---

[1] *Survey of Current Business*, November 1954, Washington, p. 12.
[2] *The International Flow of Private Capital, 1946–52*, United Nations, 1954, p. 38.

dollars received gross by the underdeveloped countries were offset by debt repatriation, etc., with the result that the net inflow was only 3 billion dollars.[1]

TABLE III

UNITED STATES : OUTFLOW OF CAPITAL FOR DIRECT INVESTMENT BY INDUSTRY AND REGION, 1946–51*

(millions of U.S. dollars)

Industry	Canada	Latin-American Republics	Western Europe	Western European Dependencies	Other Countries	Total
Public utilities	– 41	1	..	..	21	– 19
Agriculture	6	148	..	– 1	16	169
Petroleum †	559	1194	214	268	722	2957
Mining and smelting	207	157	2	3	30	399
Manufacturing ‡	878	587	423	12	175	2075
Trade §	96	261	88	16	97	558
Miscellaneous	117	145	73	3	58	396
Total	1822	2493	800	301	1119	6535

* The figures include reinvested earnings of subsidiaries as well as branches.
† Including refining, transportation, and distribution of petroleum and petroleum products.
‡ Not including petroleum refining and metal smelting.
§ Not including petroleum distribution.
Source : *The International Flow of Private Capital, 1946–52*, p. 14.

2. *A New Triangular Relationship*

Since the old system can hardly function under the new conditions, is it possible to discern the emergence of a new mechanism ? Why is it that the nineteenth-century pattern of oversea emigration from Europe still persists, although it seems to have little connexion with the bulk of the world's foreign lending — the 42 billion dollars of net public and private funds placed abroad by the United States between 1946 and 1952 ? The answer is that since 1945 a new triangular system has been functioning on the basis of the international flow of public capital. Part of this story is illustrated by the figures given in Table IV.

[1] The figures in this paragraph are based on M. L. Weiner and R. Dalla-Chiesa, 'International Movements of Public Long-term Capital and Grants, 1946–50', International Monetary Fund *Staff Papers*, vol. iv, no. 1, September 1954, p. 116.

The generous export of public capital from North America made it possible for European countries to maintain a good part of their exports of capital and labour along traditional channels.[1] For example, in the years 1946–50 the United Kingdom received, mainly from the United States and Canada, public loans and grants amounting to 10 billion dollars, which was six times her adverse trade balance over the period. She was thus herself able not only to make 3·7 billion dollars worth of public loans and grants but also to undertake private

TABLE IV

FINANCING OF NET IMPORTS OF GOODS AND SERVICES OF
FOUR EUROPEAN COUNTRIES, 1946–50

(billion U.S. dollars)

	United Kingdom	France	Netherlands	Belgium
Net import of goods and services, 1945–50	1·2	5·7	1·9	1·2
Financed by :				
Receipts of public long-term loans and grants	10·0	5·5	2·0	1·1
Net receipts from public capital repayments	– 0·1	0·3	0·1	– 0·2
Less public loans and grants made	– 3·7	– 1·6	– 0·8	– 1·0
	6·2	4·3	1·3	– 0·1
Drawing down of official gold and foreign exchange reserves	– 0·9	0·6	– 0·1	– 0·1
Private donations and other net capital receipts	– 4·1	0·8	0·7	1·4

Source : Weiner and Dalla-Chiesa, *loc. cit.* p. 122.

foreign investment (including short-term loans) amounting to 4·1 billion dollars, part of which helped to sustain a gross emigration of over 1,100,000 persons. Though the American private investor fights shy of Europe and the underdeveloped lands, his Government has nevertheless made it possible indirectly to promote a valuable movement of capital and migrants to the less developed sector of the world and to underpin a considerable structure of multilateral economic relations. But what will happen when this beneficent flow of public capital dries up ?

[1] See the present writer's article, ' International Movements of Capital and Labour since 1945 ', *International Labour Review*, LXXXIV, No. 3, September 1956, pp. 3-16.

3. *Conclusion*

The nexus between international migration and investment has lost the dynamic force it once had. In the nineteenth century there was a combined movement of men and money from the Old World to underpopulated countries, and the long-run rate of economic growth of the underdeveloped sector exceeded that of the leading creditor countries. This brought a diffusion both of economic power and of economic well-being. At the present time much of the underdeveloped sector is overpopulated, and direct investment funds rarely go to places where manpower is abundant. With the dice loaded in favour of the industrially advanced, the rate of economic growth in these countries exceeds that of the underdeveloped. Despite its shortcomings the international mechanism of the nineteenth century did not have that effect. It is impossible to restore the pattern of the pre-1913 era. In the last century intercontinental transfers of population were a major condition of growth : this has ceased to be true. There will, however, be an increasing need for two-way movements of labour within groups of countries such as Western Europe, Scandinavia, the British Commonwealth, Latin America, and North America; and migration — mainly internal — will have to be induced if the economic performance of the underdeveloped countries is to be accelerated. Finally, it is of the utmost importance that the indirect benefits which have resulted from the flow of public capital from the United States should become a permanent feature of the international economy.

Chapter 2

EFFECTS PRODUCED IN RECEIVING
COUNTRIES BY PRE-1939 IMMIGRATION

BY

J. J. SPENGLER

Duke University, U.S.A.

'From these heights of speculation, as from a lofty mountain,
may be obtained general views as to the directions in which
practice trends.'—F. Y. Edgeworth in 'The Objects and Methods
of Political Economy', *Papers relating to Political Economy*, vol. i.

BECAUSE of limitations of space and materials more attention is
given in this paper to the theoretical formulation of problems than
to their empirical analysis and resolution.

I. CONCERNING CERTAIN DIFFICULTIES

The preparation of essentially descriptive accounts of immigration
into particular countries, together with indications of the supposed
effects produced by this immigration, entails little difficulty. Much
difficulty, however, besets attempts to isolate and evaluate with
precision specific effects, economic and otherwise, produced in
countries of immigration by foreign-born individuals who come there
to make their homes.

Difficulties arise at both the theoretical level and the empirical
level, especially when a society is dynamic, and many of the effects
seemingly imputable to immigration are in fact attributable in whole
or in part to other agents. It is essential, therefore, that the force
of immigration be sequestered from other forces, and that the
milieu within which, or the social organism upon which, this force
supposedly operates, be carefully specified. Otherwise it is quite
possible that the force of immigration may be held responsible for
consequences produced by other forces. Even when both the force
of immigration and the *milieu* within which it supposedly operates
have been carefully defined, it remains difficult to discover and
assess what have been the concrete effects of immigration, since the

comparatively relevant data available to analysts have seldom been gathered for the purpose of testing specific hypotheses respecting such effects.

Inasmuch as the populations of most parts of the world are composed almost entirely of the descendants of individuals who immigrated into these parts, one must arbitrarily define what one means by immigrants and their descendants. For our purposes we shall define as natives those who lived in the countries of immigration prior to some specified date, say 1850 or 1800, and treat as immigrant stock foreign-born persons who subsequently came from abroad and into these countries of immigration, together with their descendants.

Because migratory movements are components of the peopling process whereby regions and countries get settled, it is essential that we distinguish between the direct effects of immigration and indirect effects which are connected with the peopling process as such. For example, if the composition of a country's native population differs significantly from that of the inflowing immigrants, the structure of this country's total population will be modified accordingly. The effect here exercised by immigration is a direct one. Immigration may, however, even if it be of the same composition as that of the native population of a receiving country, accelerate the rate at which the total population and economy of this country develops ; in consequence, it will speed up the advent of socio-economic structures whose shape and content are greatly conditioned by the size of a country's population and/or the stage of its economic development. The effect here exercised by immigration is an indirect one, produced through the medium of its direct effect upon the immigrant-receiving country's rate of population and economic growth.

II. AGGREGATIVE AND SUBSTITUTIVE MODES

For purposes of analysis of some aspects of the impact of immigration use may be made of Hicks's concepts of substitution-effect and income-effect, or of Keirstead's somewhat analogous concepts of 'aggregative mode' and 'real mode'.[1] Let us suppose that

---

[1] See J. R. Hicks, *Value and Capital*, Oxford, 1939, ch. 2. Of his concepts B. S. Keirstead writes (in *The Theory of Economic Change*, Toronto, 1948, pp. 109-10) : 'By the "aggregative mode" we mean the form or mode through which any change works its effects on the economy via its effect on aggregate income. By the "real mode" we mean the form or mode through which any change affects the economy via the alteration in the margin of substitution of one good, or group of goods, or one factor, for another good, group of goods or factor, the structure of the market, the level of real income and welfare, and the real rates of reward.' The term 'mode' denotes 'the formal channel through which a process operates'.

migrants are moving from Country A to Country B, and that the immigrants streaming into B include, besides a relatively small number of non-workers (chiefly women and children), a relatively large number of workers who fall into four occupational categories, a_1, a_2, a_3, and a_4. Let us suppose also that Country B has a very low propensity to import and export. In the event that B's labour force embraces four analogous occupational categories of workers, b_1, b_2, b_3, and b_4, the immigrant workers will be substitutable for native workers included in these categories. In consequence (abstracting from income or aggregative effects and proceeding on the assumption that the immigrant workers find employment in their occupational categories), the *relative* rates of remuneration received by native workers in these occupational categories will decline. Simultaneously the *relative* rates of remuneration received by native workers in occupational categories other than these four will rise, in part because the increase in categories b_1-b_4, which are complementary to all or most of categories b_5-b_n, elevates the schedule of demand for (and the value productivity of) workers in the latter categories. The native labour force at first will experience both real (or substitution) and complementary effects from the immigrant workers, with the substitution (complementary) effect being overriding in proportion as the relative number of workers enrolled in categories b_1-b_4 was large (small) already prior to the arrival of the immigrants.

Immigration also entails aggregative or income effects, and these will be relatively most pronounced in developing and expanding countries. The supposed influx of immigrants would almost certainly (abstracting from transient trade-cycle effects) be attended by an increase in the aggregate amount of income produced in B. This increase would be relatively greatest (*ceteris paribus*) if conditions were such that B's population was of infra-income-optimum size, since it might then be expected that (as an indirect result of immigration after the composition of B's labour force had become appropriately adjusted to the influx of the immigrant workers) produced income would increase even more than the labour force. It might be expected, in general, that absolute income per worker would rise in many of the occupations to which the economic activities of the immigrant workers were complementary, and that this rise would be relatively widespread, given that B's population had been of infra-optimum size and that the composition of B's labour force had become sufficiently adjusted to the influx of immigrant workers. It would not be likely, however, that *absolute* income per worker would rise also in occupations b_1-b_4 unless the population of B had been of infra-optimum size and a sufficient number of native workers in these occupations had transferred into occupations b_5-b_n ; *relative* remuneration in occupations b_1-b_4 would tend to be lower than it was prior to the coming of the immigrants.

The aggregative effect of immigration just described may be reinforced, even though it alone tends to be great enough to swamp the substitution effects of immigration when an economy is in the stage of increasing return ; for some consequences eventually attendant upon socio-economic changes generated by immigrants may also be aggregative in effect. When the latter type of effect is produced in an economy still in the stage of increasing return (under prevailing technological conditions), however, it is difficult to distinguish the two kinds of aggregative effect sharply. For example, when immigrants bring superior methods of production with them, the resulting improvements in production generate an aggregative effect in addition to that occasioned by their accession to the labour force and to that issuing from the economy's still being in the stage of increasing return (if that be the case).[1] This aggregative effect, whatever be its immediate source, operates in time to modify effects that initially arose from immigrant substitutability and complementarity. Again, if the coming of the immigrants facilitates (as may well have been the case in the United States) standardization of tastes, and hence the development of mass production methods, output *per capita* may increase, with the further result that aggregate income rises.[2]

Given (*ceteris paribus*) a change in the earnings structure con-

[1] Cf. A. Plummer, 'The Theory of Population : Some Questions of Quantity and Quality', *Journal of Political Economy*, vol. xl, 1932, pp. 617-37. In South Brazil, whither went over half the nation's immigrants, wages and *per capita* income are higher than elsewhere in the country ; but it is not presently determinable to what extent the force of immigration has been responsible for producing the changes underlying progress in *per capita* income in the South (where, however, wages and income remain very low by American standards). See H. W. Spiegel, *The Brazilian Economy*, Philadelphia, 1949 ; F. Bastos De Ávila, S.J., *Economic Aspects of Immigration*, The Hague, 1954, Part II. See also Mabel F. Timlin's account of the probable impact of population growth in Canada, in *Does Canada Need More People?*, Toronto, 1951, especially chs. 7-8 ; also A. Sauvy's analysis of the conflict between two aggregative effects of immigration, increase in population size and improvement in population structure, when the former operates to reduce *per capita* output and thereby offset the income-increasing effect of the latter, in *Théorie générale de la population*, Paris, 1952, vol. i, pp. 100 ff.

[2] This hypothesis remains conjectural. It rests upon the assumption that the diversity and magnitude of the immigrant stream into the United States prevented any single group from becoming ascendant and establishing an aristocratic structure of tastes that emphasized distinctive quality and differentiation rather than standardization. Of course, other conditions present in the American situation (*e.g.* relative plenty of land, fluidity of social structure) contributed to this effect. Cf. Alexis de Tocqueville, *Democracy in America* (translated by Henry Reeve), London, 1836, vol. i, chs. 2-3 ; but see also Alfred Marshall, *Industry and Trade*, London, 1927, pp. 146 ff.

sequent upon an influx of immigrants, native workers may respond variously. Those enrolled in occupational categories b_1-b_4, having had their relative and (perhaps) their absolute earnings reduced by the competition of these immigrants, may remove to less peopled parts of Country B, or even emigrate abroad ; or they may attempt to enter occupations b_5-b_n, in which event members of these occupations will experience substitutive as well as complementary effects ; or, if denied these recourses, they may reduce their net reproduction rate, thereby diminishing the potential number of recruits available for occupations b_1-b_4 15-20 years later. In each instance the savings rates of the adversely affected persons will tend to be reduced. Native workers in occupations to which the activities of the immigrants are complementary will undergo a contrary set of reactions. They will be less inclined to migrate or emigrate, less inclined to change occupation, and disposed to increase their net reproduction and/or their savings rates.

Hitherto we have supposed that Country B has a very low propensity to import and export. Let us now relax this assumption and allow Country B's economy to be open as were the leading immigrant-receiving economies of the nineteenth century ; for then, as Thomas [1] has shown, B's economy may be viewed as part of the economy of a larger meta-state community, and the influx of immigrants into B may be viewed as an adjustment of the composition of this community's labour force to the changing structure of its expanding aggregate demand. Under these circumstances the impact of immigration into B may be largely cushioned. Suppose that individuals engaged in occupations b_1-b_4 produce largely for export markets, the price-elasticity of demand for B's contribution thereto being very high. Then (assuming a sufficiency of land and other complementary inputs) the accession of immigrant workers in categories a_1-a_4 will not greatly depress the relative levels of earnings characteristic of occupations b_1-b_4, since the product of these additional workers can be sold abroad at but slightly reduced prices. The burden of adjustment will fall principally upon individuals living abroad who are members of occupations b_1-b_4. At the same time the net aggregate impact experienced by the labour force enrolled in occupations b_5-b_n will not be great since the returns from the sale abroad of the additional exports must in effect be expended abroad. In sum, when (complementary inputs being assumed available) immigrants enter export industries for whose products price-elasticity of demand is great, the effect of their coming is relatively widely diffused, the domestic economy is more easily accommodated

[1] See Brinley Thomas, *Migration and Economic Growth*, Cambridge, 1954.

to their coming, the wage structure is less affected, and conditions of full-employment-insuring balanced growth are more speedily approximated.

Thus far we have reasoned as if the substitution and the complementary effects persist through time. This may or may not be true. So long as immigration continues in significant volume and the occupational composition of the immigrant stream differs from that of the native population, both substitution and complementary effects will be experienced from the foreign-born immigrants. Even if the inflow of immigrants ceases, but the occupational composition of their descendants continues to differ from that of the descendants of the native population, elements in the latter will experience substitution or complementary effects of immigrant-stock origin. If, however, immigration ceases, and in time the descendants of the immigrants become distributed in the same manner as the natives throughout the occupational structure, the natives will no longer be sensible as formerly of substitution or complementary effects from persons of immigrant stock. When this has become the situation, therefore, the economic status of the natives may be said to be better or worse than it would have been in the absence of immigration accordingly as the amount of equipment and wealth per head, together with the level of technology, is more or less advanced than it would have been in the absence of the influx of the immigrants.

III. THE WALKER EFFECT

Inasmuch as immigration supposedly produces some of its effects indirectly through its acceleration of the rates at which the populations of immigrant-receiving countries grow, it is in order to inquire whether in fact immigration does produce such acceleration. This supposition was denied by B. Franklin, F. A. Walker, and others who suggested that immigration actually produces what may be called the Walker effect : namely, that immigrants and their descendants do not really augment an immigrant-receiving country's population, but instead displace natives and/or their descendants by disposing natives to emigrate, and/or by inducing them, together with their descendants, to make their net reproduction rates lower than they otherwise would have been.[1]

[1] Concerning this theory and its development see Corrado Gini, 'Los efectos demográficos de las migraciones internacionales', *Revista internacional de sociología*, vol. iv, 1946, pp. 351-88 ; also my 'Population Doctrines in the United States. II, Malthusianism', *Journal of Political Economy*, vol. xli, 1933, especially pp. 654-63, and *France Faces Depopulation*, Durham, U.S.A., 1938, pp. 209-10.

For purposes of exposition we may make use of a Pearl-type of logistic model, one of the various models utilized in the past to support hypotheses incorporating the Walker effect. Let K be the maximum population supportable in a given *milieu* under given cultural conditions; N, the actual population at any given time; b, the maximum potential rate of increase of which population N is capable in the absence of environmental or other resistance to population growth; and r, the per cent per year at which N actually grows. According to the logistic theory, r (which is equivalent to $b(K-N)/K$ and which approximates b when a logistic growth cycle begins) declines as N/K approaches unity. Suppose now that when N is of magnitude M in Country C there arrive H immigrants who are of the same culture and age-sex composition as N and have the same age-specific fertility and mortality patterns. Then the actual population becomes $M+H$, the growth that remains to be achieved becomes $R=K-(M+H)$, and r becomes $b(K-M-H)/K$ instead of $b(K-M)/K$. Accordingly, when Country C's population approximates K, it will be composed of $M+RM/(M+H)$ natives and $H+RH/(M+H)$ persons of immigrant stock, these persons having in effect displaced a corresponding number of natives. Under the conditions assumed, the period of time required for the actual population of Country C to approximate K in magnitude is reduced by the amount of time that would have been required for the native population to increase from M to $M+H$; but the magnitude finally attained by Country C's population is not modified.

The conclusions arrived at probably must be modified, however. It is evident that the rate of growth of Country C's total (native-plus-immigrant) population initially rises above the level at which it otherwise would have been. The coming of the immigrants may, in addition, generate a large aggregative effect and thus increase the value of K above the level initially postulated. Their coming will do this if one or several of the following conditions obtain: (*a*) their methods of production are superior to those that otherwise would have obtained in Country C; (*b*) their propensity to form capital is greater than that of the natives; (*c*) their required rates of consumption are lower than those that otherwise would have prevailed among the natives. These same conditions would cause the immigrant population H to grow more rapidly than the native population M, thus making even greater than we have supposed the proportion immigrant stock finally comprises of Country C's total population.[1] If, on the contrary, conditions (*a*), (*b*), and (*c*) hold

---

[1] It is assumed, not that the immigrant population would eventually replace the native population completely (as has sometimes happened when natives have

for the natives instead of for persons of immigrant stock, the magnitude of K will not be increased, and the proportion which persons of immigrant stock come to form of the total population of Country C will be lower than we found it to be under the conditions of the preceding paragraph.

The impact of immigrants upon the growth of a native population may be examined in terms of their substitution, complementary, and aggregative effects. Elements in the native population which feel the competition (substitution effects) of the immigrants will respond in part by migrating elsewhere or by reducing their (*i.e.* natives') net reproduction rates. The former response will improve the relative earnings of affected natives who do not migrate; but the latter response, though it reduces the pressure of living costs on the family incomes of birth-restricting natives, does not significantly improve the relative earnings of the affected natives, since a modal interval of perhaps 15-20 years intervenes between the date of an individual's birth and the date of his entry into the labour force. The disposition of natives (exposed to immigrant competition) to respond as indicated will be less pronounced in so far as the substitution effect exercised by the immigrants is cushioned by the associated increase in the aggregate income of the immigrant-receiving country. Elements in the native population to which the immigrants are complementary will respond in part by augmenting their net reproduction rates and by giving up plans to emigrate to other parts. These responses will be accentuated by such increases in aggregate income as are consequent upon the coming of the immigrants. For the time being, therefore, the rate of growth of the native population may be higher or lower than it would have been in the absence of the inflow of immigrants, accordingly as the substitution effects are or are not outweighed by the complementary effects, together with the associated aggregative or income effects.

The conclusions suggested by the preceding analysis may be summarized as follows. First, the rate at which the *total* population of the immigrant-receiving country grows will be higher, for a time, than it otherwise would have been. Second, since an abnormally large fraction of the immigrants tend to be of working age, the rate at which the labour force is augmented will be even greater than

been primitives and immigrants have possessed a superior technological culture), but that the native-immigrant population equilibrium finally achieved would include relatively more persons of immigrant stock than it did under the conditions of the preceding paragraph. Should conditions (*a*), (*b*), and (*c*) hold for the natives instead of for the immigrants, the immigrant stock as a proportion of the equilibrium population would be lower than it was under the conditions of the preceding paragraph.

that at which the total population grows.[1] Third, the maximum size (denoted by K in a logistic model) eventually approximated by an immigrant-receiving country's population may be greater or smaller than it would have been in absence of immigration, with the actual outcome dependent upon conditions (*a*), (*b*), and (*c*) described in the second paragraph preceding. Fourth, the native population will be greater than it would have been in the absence of immigration, provided that the coming of the immigrants increases the magnitude of K sufficiently; it will be less if the increase in K and hence in 'places' for individuals is insufficient to offset the tendency of immigrants to fill 'places' that otherwise might have been filled by natives.

It is not possible at present to determine with precision what effect immigration has had upon native natural increase and, therefore, upon aggregate population growth. Several estimates may be reported, however. According to Landry, immigrants and their descendants contributed about two-fifths of French population growth in 1801–1936.[2] In Table I estimates are given of the respective contributions of native natural increase, immigrant natural increase, and immigration to population growth in certain other countries; but they do not take into account the effects of immigrant age and marital composition upon natality, mortality, and socio-economic conditions which affect natural increase.[3] According to these estimates, net immigration, together with immigrants' natural increase, contributed much more to population growth in Argentina and the United States than in Brazil and Canada. Another estimate attributed 58·4 per cent of the 91,648,471 increase in the white population

[1] In the late nineteenth century the proportion of immigrants aged 15-44 exceeded by about 50 per cent the corresponding proportion of the population already resident in the United States. For this reason, and because a disproportionately large fraction of these immigrants were males, immigration was responsible for a larger percentage of increase in the American labour force than in the American population : *e.g.*, 16·2 and 10·8 respectively in 1870–80, and 30·1 and 20·1 in 1880–90. Had the age composition of the immigrants come to resemble that of the resident population, or had immigration ceased, the relative number of persons of working age in the American population would have approached that inherently characteristic of the native population. See S. Kuznets and E. Rubin, *Immigrants and the Foreign Born*, National Bureau of Economic Research Occasional Paper 46, New York, 1954, p. 45 ; V. G. Valaoras, in *The Social and Biological Challenge of Our Aging Population*, ed. Iago Galdston, New York, 1950, especially pp. 69-80 ; papers on ageing in *Population Bulletin*, No. 1, 1951, pp. 42-57, No. 4, 1954, pp. 30-9.

[2] See A. Landry, *Traité de démographie*, Paris, 1945, pp. 514-15.

[3] See G. Mortara, *Pesquisas sôbre populacões americanas, Estudos brasileiros de demografía, Monografía*, no. 3, vol. i, July 1947, pp. 298-306. On the effect of migration upon natality, mortality, and natural increase, see *ibid.* pp. 321-52. Immigrants into countries with relatively low natality tended to have higher net reproduction rates for females than did the natives, but this differential greatly diminished with the decline of gross reproduction rates in countries of emigration.

of the United States in 1790–1920 to net immigration and immigrant natural increase.[1] One must attribute nearly one-fifth of the decline in the American birth-rate in 1800–1930 to the impact of immigration if one is to suppose that, had there been no net immigration, the American population would none the less have been just as large as it was in 1930, given the recorded immigration.[2] It may be inferred, therefore, that immigration was not a predominant cause of the decline in natality in the United States.

TABLE I

COMPONENTS OF POPULATION GROWTH, 1840–1940

Country	Components of Population Growth					
	Native Natural Increase		Immigration		Immigrants' Natural Increase	
	Absolute	Per Cent	Absolute	Per Cent	Absolute	Per Cent
All America	163·0	70·87	36·0	15·65	31·0	13·48
Brazil	28·6	81·02	3·3	9·35	3·4	9·63
Argentina	5·2	41·94	3·6	29·03	3·6	29·03
Canada	8·0	78·43	1·0	9·80	1·2	11·77
United States	67·7	59·13	25·0	21·83	21·8	19·04

With the possible exception of France, which was not a developing country potentially subject to increasing returns as were most of the large countries situated in Oceania and the Western Hemisphere, immigration probably did not significantly accentuate the downward movement of natality. This downward movement of natality did not manifest itself until recently (if then) in important Latin-American countries of immigration. Immigration could not have had much influence upon native natality in Canada where, in 1851–1950, emigration exceeded immigration in five of the ten decades, the number of persons emigrating approximated nine-tenths of the number immigrating, net immigration furnished only about 4 per cent of all population growth, and the ethnic composition of the

[1] See my 'The Merits and Demerits of the National Origins Provisions for Selecting Immigrants', *Southwestern Political and Social Science*, vol. x, September 1929, pp. 149-70, especially Table III. At this time 14·5 per cent of the population was foreign-born. Corresponding percentages for other countries are: Canada, in 1921, 22·25 ; Australia, in 1921, 15·5 ; Brazil, in 1920, 5·1 (3·4 in 1940) ; Argentina, in 1914, 30.

[2] See W. S. Thompson and P. K. Whelpton, *Population Trends in the United States*, New York, 1933, pp. 308-11. See also *Income and Wealth of the United States*, ed. Simon Kuznets, Cambridge, 1952, pp. 196-204.

population underwent little change.[1] The case of the United States has already been noted. It is not likely that immigration contributed significantly to the decline of natality in Australia and New Zealand, 77 and 66 per cent respectively of whose growth in 1861–1939 was imputable to natural increase; for the population remained overwhelmingly British, and the decline lagged behind that of England, apparently having divers 'causes' not closely associated with immigration.[2]

From the fact that immigrant-receiving countries sometimes send out relatively many emigrants, it has been inferred that immigration produces a population-displacing effect in the form of induced emigration. The ratio of net to gross immigration frequently fluctuates widely and sometimes sinks to very low levels. This ratio slightly exceeded 70 per cent in the United States in 1821–1924. It approximated 54 in Argentina in 1857–1948; 74 in Brazil in 1872–1940; about 30 in New Zealand in 1853–1930, and about 19 in Australia in 1901–30; as little as 10 in Canada in 1851–1950; and even less in some small Latin-American countries.[3] In the United States the movement of departures generally paralleled that of arrivals, in part because departures were made up largely of persons who had been in the country less than five years, whilst the proportion of departures to arrivals trended upwards as the pool of potential departures rose relative to the number of arrivals. For this reason, in part, the ratio of net immigration to the number of arrivals, to total population, and to the foreign-born population fell steadily. Moreover, the percentage of intercensus population growth, attributable to increase in the foreign-born, whilst subject to great fluctuation, trended downwards.[4] Detailed analysis would reveal similar tendencies in other major countries of immigration.

[1] See Nathan Keyfitz, 'The Growth of Canadian Population', *Population Studies*, vol. iv, 1950, pp. 47-63, especially p. 62. As of 1921, 91·5 per cent of the Canadian population (compared with 95 in 1901) were of British, French, or North-western European stock. See W. B. Hurd, *Origin, Birthplace, Nationality, and Language of the Canadian People*, Ottawa, 1929, pp. 43, 53.

[2] See W. D. Forsyth, *The Myth of Open Spaces*, Melbourne, 1942, ch. 13, pp. 206-9 ; W. D. Borrie, 'Aspects historiques et contemporains de l'immigration australienne', *Population*, vol. iii, 1948, pp. 441-58, and *Population Trends and Policies*, Sydney, 1948. As Brinley Thomas observes (*op. cit.* pp. 195-7), the Anglo-Saxon countries introduced immigration restriction about the time that the poor peoples of Southern and Eastern Europe, the bulk of them without industrial skills, 'were beginning to take full advantage of international mobility'.

[3] Based on Willcox, *op. cit.* and United Nations, *Economic Survey of Latin America, 1948*, Lake Success, 1949. Mortara estimated at 64 the percentage for all of America in 1840–1940 (*op. cit.* pp. 297, 304-7). Kuznets and Rubin estimate net immigration to have been somewhat higher than the 70 per cent of gross found by Willcox. See *op. cit.* pp. 93-4.

[4] See *ibid.*, especially pp. 22-30, 39-43, 45. Of the Old-immigrant departures in 1908–10, about 77 per cent of those for whom data were given had been in the United States less than five years. For the New-immigrant departures the

Analytical Survey

It is not very illuminating to assert that aggregate immigration into a country tends to displace persons previously living therein and cause them to emigrate. This has been asserted of immigration into Canada, since Canadian emigration (one-fourth or more of which is Canadian-born) has approximated nine-tenths of Canadian immigration. It is, of course, valid to say that Canada and the United States belong to essentially the same community and that, because of their proximity,[1] potential migrants in either country are quite sensitive to relatively favourable and immigrant-attracting developments taking place in the other.[2] As has been indicated, however, substitution effects are produced by particular kinds of immigrants and are felt by particular categories of the population residing in the country of immigration. Members of categories experiencing substitution effects would be disposed to emigrate only if (a) these effects were not sufficiently counterbalanced by aggregative effects (e.g. increase in national income, increase in interoccupational mobility) consequent upon immigration, and if (b) sufficiently attractive opportunities were supposed to exist in countries whither migrants might move at sufficiently low cost. While the propensity of French-Canadians to emigrate to the United States closely resembled that of English Canadians,[3] French-Canadian emigrants working in the United States in 1910 included relatively more

corresponding percentage was 84. About 97 per cent of all departures had been in the United States less than ten years. See *Reports of the Immigration Commission*, 61st Congress, 2nd Session, Senate Document no. 682, Washington, 1911, vol. i, p. 183. Given enough information, the principle of life-table analysis is well adapted to the discovery of the determinants of the propensity to re-emigrate.

[1] Migration from either country to the other should vary directly with the number of opportunities available in the country of destination and inversely with the number available in the country of provenience, given that cost of movement, together with the rate at which opportunities in the country of destination are discounted, is the same in either direction, and that movement in one direction is no more barred by artificial impediments (e.g. laws) than movement in the other. If two countries are more removed in space, one from the other, than Canada from the United States, there will be less movement (ceteris paribus) because of the intervention of distance which here serves as a rough measure of costs of movement. Concerning some of the relevant literature see my 'Population Theory' in *Survey of Contemporary Economics*, ed. B. F. Haley, Homewood, 1952, pp. 117 ff., 122 ff. The ratio of Canadian-born persons residing in the United States to the total population living in Canada was nearly the same in 1930 as in 1870 ; and the ratio of American-born persons residing in Canada to the total population living in the United States was the same in 1931 as in 1851. The attractive force exerted by the Canadian upon the American population has increased in recent decades ; for the ratio of Canadian-born residing in the United States to United-States-born residing in Canada has fallen. For data see L. E. Truesdell, *The Canadian Born in the United States*, New Haven, 1943, pp. 10-13.

[2] E.g. see Truesdell, op. cit. ch. 2 ; Thomas, op. cit. pp. 205 ff., also 134-8 ; A. K. Cairncross, *Home and Foreign Investment, 1870–1913*, Cambridge, 1953, ch. 3 ; D. C. Corbett, 'Immigration and Economic Development', *Canadian Journal of Economics and Political Science*, vol. xvii, 1951, pp. 360-8 ; Mabel F. Timlin, 'Economic Theory and Immigration Policy', *ibid.* vol. xvi, 1950, pp. 375-82, and *Does Canada Need More People ?*, Toronto, 1951, ch. 6 ; Forsyth, op. cit. chs. 2, 4. [3] See Truesdell, op. cit. pp. 47, 60.

semi-skilled and factory workers and fewer proprietors, professional persons, and clerical personnel than did either the English-Canadian emigrants or the American population living in the states in which immigrants from Canada tended to settle.[1] It is not apparent, however, that the occupational composition of French-Canadian emigrants is to be explained in terms of the competition they experienced in Canada from immigrants.[2]

IV. SOCIAL CAPILLARITY

Immigrants of working age may be of the same occupational composition as the labour force of the immigrant-receiving country, or they may be of a different occupational composition. As a rule, in 1820–1939, they tended to enter, in disproportionately large numbers, into the lower portions of the American occupational pyramid. Immigrants might, of course, for a time tend to enter upper reaches of an immigrant-receiving country's occupational pyramid in disproportionate number.[3] The tendency of immigrants to enter the lower reaches of this pyramid has several sources. In the absence of political or religious persecution persons situated in the upper portions of the occupational pyramid of an emigrant-sending country are less likely to emigrate than are those situated in the lower portions because they have relatively less to gain and more to lose by emigrating. Furthermore, when a country of provenience is economically and technologically less advanced than a country of destination, the occupational structure of the migrants tends to be inferior to that obtaining in the immigrant-receiving country. Finally, when the cultural background of an emigrant-sending country differs significantly from that of a country of destination, this difference tends to be reflected in the immigrants, giving rise to

[1] *Ibid.* ch. 12.
[2] Quebec and the Maritime Provinces experienced considerable net emigration to other provinces as well as to the United States whereas the other provinces gained population through net internal migration. See Keyfitz, *op. cit.* pp. 50-5. In Canada in 1911 the following per cent of gainfully occupied males and females, respectively, were in certain occupational groups : manufacturing, 11·68 and 26·53 ; clerical, 3·08 and 9·25 ; labourers in non-extractive industries, 13·44 and 0·07. The corresponding percentages for Quebec are : manufacturing, 14·36 and 33·82 ; clerical, 3·12 and 5·71 ; labourers, 14·1 and 0·04.
[3] It is possible, of course, that although immigrants generally tend to enter the lower portions of the occupational pyramid, they may also enter, in disproportionately large number, into some particular sector of the upper portion of this pyramid. In the early stages of a country's settlement, in fact, immigrants may press into particular upper sectors. Thus, in New Zealand, Europeans gradually displaced the Maori from the business of supplying fresh food and wheat. (C. S. Belshaw, 'The Cultural Milieu of the Entrepreneur : A Critical Essay', *Explorations in Entrepreneurial History*, VII, 1955, p. 152).

linguistic, personality, intellectual, and other handicaps, some transient and some not entirely removable, which at least initially exclude immigrants from the upper reaches of the occupational pyramid.

Let the occupational structure of a country be represented by four categories, A, B, C, and D, into which 10, 20, 30, and 40 per cent respectively of the gainfully employed fall. Then, in the event that there arrived 10 units of immigrants culturally and otherwise identical with the natives, the 10 would tend to be distributed among categories A-D in the same proportions as the native population, namely, 1, 2, 3, and 4 units respectively. If, however, the immigrants suffered under handicaps of the sort described above, more than 4, say 8, of the 10 units might have to enter category D, and (say) 1 each, into categories C and B. In this event, one of two types of outcome would be possible. If the underlying determinants of occupational equilibrium were such as to maintain the proportions which prevailed prior to the arrival of the immigrants, there would be set in motion an upward movement of the native members of the occupational structure, eventuating (say) as follows: A, 11 natives; B, 21 natives and 1 immigrant; C, 32 natives and 1 immigrant; D, 36 natives and 8 immigrants. If, as is probable, equilibrium occupational composition changes, relative expansion would take place in the lower portions of the occupational pyramid, and there would eventuate a distribution such as the following: A, 10 natives; B, 20 natives and 1 immigrant; C, 31 natives and 1 immigrant; D, 39 natives and 8 immigrants.

The occupational composition of the children of immigrants would approximate more closely that of the natives than did the occupational composition of the immigrants themselves; and the occupational composition of the grandchildren of the immigrants would approximate that of the natives even more closely than did the occupational composition of the children of the immigrants. The rapidity with which the occupational composition of the immigrant stock approached that of the natives would depend upon how technologically and hence occupationally dynamic the country of immigration was, upon the extent and rigidity of artificial and institutional barriers which tend to prevent interoccupational movement that would otherwise take place, and upon the degree to which these barriers impeded the interoccupational movement of persons of immigrant stock even more than that of natives.[1] The rationale

---

[1] If the immigrant is of a different race than the native, and if barriers prejudicial to the occupational advancement of members of this race exist, he will be under a double handicap, but only that portion of the handicap which is connected with his being an immigrant is relevant in the context of the above discussion. On differences between the mobility of Negroes and that of sons of natives see

of the argument that in time the occupational composition of the descendants of immigrants would approximate that of the natives may be illustrated as follows. In the preceding paragraph we put at 0·4 the probability that a native would be enrolled in occupational category D and at 0·8 the corresponding probability for the immigrant. All or nearly all of the difference between these two probabilities presumably would be attributable to differences between immigrants and natives which were eliminatable in the sense that after one or several generations the descendants of the immigrants of a given period would not differ significantly from the descendants of natives of that same period. As has been indicated, however, the rapidity with which occupational assimilation proceeds through time may vary greatly between countries because both the initial spread in occupational-entrance probabilities (described above) and the circumstances conducing to the elimination of these spreads vary from country to country.

It is said that immigration tends to make a population more fluid or mobile than it otherwise would be. This result is likely under two conditions: (*a*) when the occupational (or other) composition of the immigrants differs from that of the labour force of the country of immigration, with the result that a series of substitution effects is generated; and (*b*) when the coming of the immigrants produces or facilitates fundamental changes in the technological and related determinants of the occupational structure and sets both aggregative and substitutive effects in motion. For in either instance the relative amount of movement from some to other occupational categories will increase and then remain at 'abnormally' high levels until the labour force becomes accommodated to the basic occupational structure and a model approximating that of Cairnes's and Taussig's relatively non-competing groups comes into being.[1] Initially, the upward mobility of the native population will increase in much greater degree than the aggregate mobility of the immigrant population. But, as the immigrants and their children become assimilated and hence freed of transient disabilities, their upward mobility will increase, with the consequence that natives who no longer are capable of competing effectively with the upward-moving immigrant stock will be displaced downwards. When, however, the initial occupational composition of the

Natalie Rogoff, *Recent Trends in Occupational Mobility*, Glencoe, 1953, chs. 5-6. See also P. E. Davidson and H. D. Anderson, *Occupational Mobility in An American Community*, Stanford, 1937.

[1] See, however, H. J. Davenport's criticism of this concept and the use to which it was put; in 'Non-Competing Groups', *Quarterly Journal of Economics*, vol. xl, 1925–26, pp. 52 ff.

immigrants is quite similar to that of the natives, the coming of the immigrants will produce little change in the relative amount of inter-occupational mobility, since little change will be required to permit the permanent occupational assimilation of the immigrants.

Perusal of the statistical information available suggests a number of conclusions. First, throughout much of the century preceding

TABLE II

MALE BREADWINNERS, CLASSIFIED BY OCCUPATION,
RACE, AND NATIVITY, 1900

(in per cent of total male breadwinners)

| Occupation | All Classes | Native Whites | | Foreign Born | | Other Natives |
		Native Parents	Foreign Parents	White	All Other	
Labourers (not specified)	10·5	8·0	8·6	14·4	12·1*	17·2*
Miners and quarry-men	2·4	1·5	2·3	5·1	2·0	1·3
Iron and steel workers	1·2	0·8	1·9	2·1	†	0·4
Textile mill opera-tives	1·1	0·8	1·5	2·2	0·1	0·1
Building trades	5·1	5·0	6·2	6·3	1·0	1·7
Clerks, steno-graphers, etc.	3·1	3·4	5·7	2·0	0·7	0·2
Salesmen, etc.	3·3	3·8	4·8	2·5	0·7	0·2
Professional	3·5	4·4	3·6	2·4	0·7	1·2
Farmers	22·4	28·3	13·3	14·6	3·2	25·8
Agricultural labourers	15·8	17·9	11·6	5·2	33·2	30·9
All other	31·6	26·1	40·5	43·2	46·3	21·0
Total	100·0	100·0	100·0	100·0	100·0	100·0

* Includes Negro, Indian, Chinese, and Japanese.
† Less than one-tenth of one per cent.
Source : See footnote 4, pp. 27-8.

the First World War the occupational composition of immigrants into the United States, France, and possibly Canada, but not that into Argentina, Brazil, and perhaps Australia, was somewhat inferior to that found in the country of destination, in that relatively more of the immigrants than of the natives were unskilled. Comparison of the percentages given in Table II in line 1 indicates that in 1900 14·4 per cent of the foreign-born white breadwinners and only 8 per cent of the native white breadwinners of native parentage were classified as non-agricultural labourers. In large urban centres this difference was even more pronounced.[1] As of 1930 the percentage of male native white gainful workers who were unskilled was 23·5 ; the corresponding percentage for foreign-born white and negro male gainfully employed was, respectively, 28·5 and 60.[2] Second, at any particular time, occupational composition of immigrants sometimes has varied with their ethnic origin. Thus of the 'New' immigrants (exclusive of Hebrews) into the United States in 1899–1909 who reported occupations, 46·6 per cent were non-agricultural labourers whereas only 25·6 per cent of the 'Old' immigrants were so classified. Moreover, comparatively large fractions of many of the groups making up the 'New' immigration from Southern and Eastern Europe included relatively large numbers of both non-agricultural labourers and illiterate individuals.[3] Third, many immigrants changed their occupations subsequently to admission into the United States, particularly in the late nineteenth and early twentieth century when American industry became technologically and economically adapted to the use of semi-skilled and relatively unskilled workers in place of those possessed of marked craft skill, thereby greatly

[1] This table is derived from tables in *Reports*, vol. xxviii, pp. 18–64. In 1900 the number of male breadwinners, by class, in thousands, was : all, 23,958 ; native white of native parentage, 12,014 ; native white, of foreign parentage, 4143 ; foreign-born white, 4887 ; all other foreign born, 178 ; other native, 2737. Negroes, Indians, Chinese and Japanese are included in the two last classes. See *ibid.* p. 18. For French data see my *France Faces Depopulation*, pp. 203–6. See on Argentina and Brazil, R. F. Foerster, *The Italian Emigration of Our Times*, Cambridge, 1924.

[2] See A. M. Edwards, 'A Socio-Economic Grouping of the Gainful Workers in the United States', *Journal of the American Statistical Association*, vol. xxviii, 1933, p. 385. This is based on the census of 1930. Only 3·1 per cent of foreign-born males gainfully employed were unskilled agricultural labourers ; the corresponding percentage for the native white and negro male workers was, respectively, 9·7 and 18·9.

[3] See *Reports* (cited in note 4 on pp. 27–8), vol. i, pp. 101, 173–6. Of the Portuguese immigrant workers, 6·8 per cent were reported as skilled, 7·5 per cent as farm labourers, and 46·5 per cent as non-agricultural labourers. Corresponding percentages for Spanish immigrants were 44·1, 7·8, and 20·6 ; for North Italians, 20·4, 18·7, and 47·8 ; for South Italians, 14·6, 34·5, and 42·5 ; for Hebrews, 67·1, 1·9, 11·8 ; for all immigrants, 20·2, 23·4, 35·9 ; see *ibid.* p. 101. Paul Douglas has pointed out that if one compares the 'New' with the 'Old' immigrants of the pre-1883 period, differences in occupational composition are not very marked, 38·9 per cent of immigrants with occupations in 1871–82 having been non-agricultural labourers. Unskilled 'New' immigrants had tended to displace unskilled 'Old' immigrants, causing the latter group to include relatively more skilled than before 1880. See 'Is New Immigration more Skilled than Old ?', *Publications of the American Statistical Association*, vol. xvi, 1918–19, pp. 393–403 ; also, on the New and the Old, Willcox, *op. cit.* vol. i, pp. 217–20. In 1899–1910, 12·6 and 30·6 per cent, respectively, of the Irish immigrants with occupations were skilled workers and unskilled non-agricultural labourers. Corresponding figures for the Scandinavians were 20·5 and 36·2 ; for the Germans, 30 and 19·8. See *Reports*, vol. i, p. 101. Cf. B. Thomas, *op. cit.* pp. 148–51, 268–72 ; also pp. 60–3, for data suggesting that a disproportionately large fraction of emigrants from the United Kingdom, described as non-agricultural labourers and domestic servants, went to the United States and Canada and not to Australasia and elsewhere.

facilitating the effective employment of comparatively unskilled immigrant labour, together with native workers of rural provenience.[1] Thus data relating to the occupations of returning and other immigrants in 1900–10 indicate that perhaps as many as nine-tenths of the immigrants who reported themselves as farm labourers upon entering the United States went into non-agricultural occupations; that three-quarters or more of a large sample of skilled immigrants with particular occupations abandoned them, although immigrants who on entry reported other occupations and professions apparently continued to pursue them; and that (according to a sample) about five-sixths of the foreign-born males and about two-thirds of the foreign-born females reported in manufacturing and mining had not been so engaged before coming to the United States.[2] In Argentina many, and in Brazil some, Italian immigrants experienced marked improvements in economic status.[3] Fourth, as the data in Table II reveal, the occupational composition of the children of immigrants has tended to be better than that of their parents, but not quite so good as that of natives of native parentage.[4] Fifth, immigrants tended to crowd into certain industries such as mining and quarrying, clothing, textiles, woollens and worsted mills, bakeries, meat-packing houses, car and railroad shops, silk and carpet mills, brass and rolling mills and blast furnaces, breweries, tanneries, hat factories, lime, cement, and gypsum factories, marble and stone yards, rubber

---

[1] See H. D. Anderson and P. E. Davidson, *Occupational Trends in the United States*, Stanford, 1940, pp. 53-7, 166-7, 572-4 ; also Brinley Thomas, *op. cit.* pp. 165-74, and R. T. Berthoff, *British Immigrants in Industrial America, 1790–1850*, Cambridge, 1953, *passim*.

[2] See Louis Block, 'Occupations of Immigrants Before and After Coming to the United States', *Publications of the American Statistical Association*, vol. xvii, 1920–21, pp. 750-64. P. E. Davidson and H. D. Anderson (*Occupational Mobility*, pp. 117-33, 188) found that in San Jose, California, whereas 80 per cent of the foreign-born initially had to accept unskilled and semi-skilled jobs, 26 per cent eventually improved their occupational status while only 5 per cent suffered a decline. It was largely the very young immigrants, however, who improved their occupational status, and not those who were adults already upon their arrival.

[3] See Foerster, *op. cit.* chs. 13-16 ; De Avila, *op. cit.* pp. 30-1. On France see my *France Faces Depopulation*, pp. 204 ff.

[4] See also A. M. Edwards, *Comparative Occupation Statistics for the United States, 1870 to 1940*, Washington, 1943, p. 158, Table XIII ; Davidson and Anderson, *Occupational Mobility*, pp. 130-3. Brinley Thomas (*op. cit.* ch. 9) found that British immigrants were of a higher socio-economic status and climbed the social ladder faster than did the Irish immigrants into the United States ; and that immigrant stocks tended to rise faster when they settled in cities where educational attainments could be acquired than in rural areas where these advantages were not so accessible to immigrants and their children. Rogoff (*op. cit.* ch. 7) found that, as of 1910, 'sons of foreign extraction, no matter what their fathers' occupation, had about the same chance as sons of native extraction of moving to each of the positions in the occupational structure' (but were more subject to downward mobility). By 1940, however, they were no longer in a somewhat disadvantaged position ; instead they 'received a greater share of occupational rewards than the sons of native-born'.

factories, piano and organ factories, construction and maintenance.[1]

It has been said, and it is to be expected, that the wage structure prevailing in various American industries should have reflected the occupational composition of immigrant workers and the foreign-born. Above all, it was to be expected that the relative position of the wages of unskilled and semi-skilled workers would be lower in industries favoured by immigrants than in industries not so favoured, and than in European industrial countries, the relative number of whose skilled workers had not been unduly reduced by emigration.[2] Unfortunately, however, there are not yet at hand enough comparative studies of wage structures and changes therein to permit assessment of the not easily isolated influence of immigration upon American wage structures. But data available do suggest that, between 1890 and 1914, the annual real earnings of unskilled labour fell; that real hourly earnings in all manufacturing industries rose but 1 per cent in 1893–1913, actually falling in some branches of manufacturing; and that earnings rose somewhat in coal, building, and some branches of manufacture, and appreciably in respect of farm labour.[3] The decline in the wages of unskilled labour is

[1] See A. R. Eckler and J. Zlotnick, 'Immigration and the Labour Force', *Annals of the American Academy of Political and Social Science*, vol. cclxi, 1949, pp. 92-101, especially p. 100. On the progress of the impact of immigration see, *e.g.*, Oscar Handlin, *Boston's Immigrants, 1790–1865 : A Study in Acculturation*, Cambridge, 1941 ; also M. R. Davie, *World Immigration*, New York, 1936, pp. 238-47, and D. R. Taft, *Human Migration*, New York, 1936, pp. 185-95.

[2] 'A marked peculiarity of the American labour situation during the generation preceding the Great War was the comparatively low rate of pay for the unskilled labourers. It was low, that is, in comparison with the pay of the upper stratum of the skilled labourers. . . . The differential in favour of the mechanic was greater in the United States (than in Europe) ; the unskilled were relatively cheap . . . for the American employer. The enormous influx of immigrants maintained a great supply of unskilled labour and kept down its rate of pay.' So wrote F. W. Taussig, and he pointed to such industries as the iron industry and the textile industry (especially cotton) ; and he predicted that, with the diminution in the rate of immigration, the wage differential in favour of the skilled worker would become less pronounced. See his *International Trade*, New York, 1927, pp. 58-60 ; also *Some Aspects of the Tariff Question*, Cambridge, 1915, 1931, pp. 137-8, 286, 379. See also B. Ohlin, *Interregional and International Trade*, Cambridge, 1933, pp. 308-9, 347-9, 368-9. J. A. Kleene went further than Taussig, saying that wages in the United States were determined by the price of unskilled labour which, in turn, tended to approximate the standard of living of workers in the countries whence came most of the immigrants *plus* an allowance to cover the expenses of emigration and the cost of overcoming the migration-deterring influence of distance and unfamiliarity with lands of immigration. See *Profits and Wages*, New York, 1916, pp. 63 ff. and *passim* ; and cf. H. Bernardelli, 'New Zealand and Asiatic Migration', *Population Studies*, vol. vi, 1952, pp. 39-44, 47.

[3] See Paul H. Douglas, *Real Wages in the United States, 1890–1926*, Boston, 1930, pp. 108, 135-9, 160, 177, 187, 254, 260, 267, 272, 280, 284, 288, 293, 296, 300, 304, 308, 326, 392 ff. See also W. Coombs, *The Wages of Unskilled Labour in the Manufacturing Industries in the United States, 1890–1924*, New York, 1926, ch. 5, especially pp. 119-22 ; W. S. Thompson, *Population: A Study in Malthusianism*, New York, 1915, pp. 39 ff. ; M. D. Anderson, *Dynamic Theory of Wealth Distribution*, Gainesville, 1938, pp. 129-32.

attributable, Douglas concluded, to the largeness of the volume of immigration;[1] and the decline in real wages in some branches of manufacturing, together with their failure to rise in other branches, is probably attributable in large part to the heaviness of immigration, since Net National Product per worker and per hour rose about 32 and 44 per cent, respectively, in 1884/93–1904/13.[2] The magnitude of immigration, in short, retarded the advance of wages when it did not actually produce a decline therein, most wages not moving upwards significantly until the influx of immigrants was greatly reduced by the advent of war and relatively unskilled labour was rendered scarce by military and other requirements. Immigration may be partly responsible, therefore, for the fact that the real wage rate rose relatively less in the United States in 1860–1913 than in Germany, France, Sweden, or the United Kingdom.[3] Immigration affected the course of development of American trade unionism, and this in turn may have had some effect upon the development of wage structures.[4]

Most of what has been said has had to do with the United States, whose experience has differed greatly from that of Latin America and Oceania and somewhat from that of Canada. Whereas the superiority of American over British industry had been achieved already by 1870, after which date most immigrants came to the United States, development did not come until later in other great immigrant-receiving areas.[5]

Immigration into the United States was increasingly heterogeneous, and somewhat less skilled than the American population, which had become comparatively skilled by the time of the Civil War. Of gross immigration into the United States in 1820–1930, 56·2 per cent was from Northern and Western Europe and British North America, but this fraction fell from about nine-tenths in 1820–70

[1] *Real Wages*, pp. 178–9. See also W. I. King, *Wealth and Income of the People of the United States*, New York, 1917, ch. 7 ; Colin Clark, *The Conditions of Economic Progress*, 2nd ed., London, 1951, 57–8, 458–74.

[2] See Kuznets, ed., *op. cit.* p. 71, also pp. 59, 68.

[3] See E. H. Phelps Brown and Sheila V. Hopkins, 'The Course of Wage-Rates in Five Countries, 1860–1913', *Oxford Economic Papers*, II, 1950, p. 236. Roland Wilson believes that his comparison of British and American cotton textile wages does not support Taussig's belief that the gap between the wages of skilled and unskilled workers was greater in the United States than in other countries (*Cotton Textile Wages in the United States and Great Britain*, New York, 1948, ch. 5).

[4] *E.g.* see S. Perlman, *A History of Trade Unionism in the United States*, New York, 1923, pp. 84 ff., 179, 221 ; H. A. Millis and R. E. Montgomery, *Organized Labor*, New York, 1945, pp. 14–15, 48–9, 88–90, 124, 154–5 ; also J. R. Commons, *Races and Immigrants in America*, New York, 1907 ; J. W. Jenks and W. J. Lauck, *The Immigration Problem*, New York, 1917. But see Brinley Thomas, *op. cit.* pp. 204–5.

[5] See E. Rothbarth, 'Causes of the Superior Efficiency of USA Industry as Compared with British Industry', *Economic Journal*, vol. lvi, 1946, p. 383.

to about three-eighths in 1901–20. The following rounded percentages of the foreign-born population were from North-western Europe and Germany respectively; in 1850, 64 and 26; in 1890, 47 and 30; in 1930, 27 and 12. By contrast, about four-fifths of the immigrants entering Argentina and Brazil before 1927 came from Spain, Portugal, and Italy. Moreover, coming largely after the beginning of the great Argentine boom of the 1880's and after the abolition of slavery in Brazil in the 1880's, these immigrants, though less skilled than emigrants from Britain and Germany, apparently were as skilled as, and often more skilled than, much of the native-born population. Most of the immigrants into Australia and New Zealand were of British birth, with the result that by 1930 only about 3 per cent of the population of these parts consisted of people born outside Australia, New Zealand, the British Isles, the British Dominions, and the United States. Moreover, immigrants from the British Isles, whence came most, were more skilled even than British migrants who went to the United States after 1875 and compared favourably in skill with the population already residing in Australia and New Zealand. Immigration into Canada resembled somewhat that into the United States. Between 1880 and 1930 about three-fourths of her immigrants came from the United Kingdom and the United States; and in 1931 about two-thirds of her foreign-born were from these parts. As of 1921 about nine-tenths of Canada's population was of British, French, and Northwest European stock. Immigrants into Canada from the British Isles appear to have been somewhat less skilled than those going to Australia and New Zealand.[1]

V. IMMIGRATION AND ECONOMIC GROWTH

Immigration augments the rate at which a country's Net National Product (hereinafter denoted NNP) increases and it may operate, within limits, to increase the rate at which NNP per head advances. Migration between countries takes place because the migrant expects transference of himself (and possibly his family) to the country of destination to augment the index of welfare (usually an economically dominated index) by which he guides his conduct. This index may or may not be perfectly correlated with the real income he expects

---

[1] See Willcox, *op. cit.* vol. i, pp. 196-215, 239-40, vol. ii, pp. 153, 163 ; Forsyth, *op. cit.* p. 194 ; Hurd, *op. cit.* pp. 43, 53 ; M. R. Davie, *World Immigration*, chs. 3-6, 10-11 ; U.S. Bureau of the Census, *Historical Statistics of the United States, 1789–1945*, pp. 32 ff. ; Brinley Thomas, *op. cit.* pp. 59-62, 268 ff. ; J. Lyng, *Non-Britishers in Australia*, Melbourne, 1935.

himself, or himself and his family, to receive. We shall assume, however, for the sake of expositive convenience, that complete correlation obtains in the immigrant's mind. Accordingly, migrants may be said to have moved principally because the resources used in conjunction with labour, together with the technological skill and other factors affecting the use of agents of production, gave promise of producing more income per worker in the countries of destination than in those of provenience (appropriate allowance having been made for international differences in income dispersion and stability and for costs of movement).[1] Immigration operated, therefore, to bring into being in at least some countries of immigration (*e.g.* Argentina, Brazil, Australia, and New Zealand, Canada, the United States) a better combination of available productive agents than obtained in the early nineteenth century.[2] In consequence NNP grew more rapidly than it otherwise would have done. NNP per head also grew more rapidly than it would have, so long as the population of the immigrant-receiving country remained below income-optimum size and the growth of its labour force continued to release the forces of increasing return. After this size was reached, however, immigration, although continuing to augment the rate at which NNP grew, operated to make NNP per head less high than it otherwise would have been, for it made population too dense and it absorbed capital that might have increased equipment per head of the resident population.

These tendencies were reinforced at least temporarily in several ways. First, a disproportionately large fraction of the immigrants were workers, and often, especially in the early stages of the development of immigrant countries, workers possessed of scarce skills. Second, the immigrants sometimes brought with them superior methods and approaches to production, in part because they had acquired these in the countries of provenience and in part because, as some have suggested, transmarine migration often shatters the cake of custom and inspires new frames of reference.[3] Third, the mingling of peoples of somewhat diverse cultural backgrounds may

[1] Of course, if the wage structures of two countries differ, with the result that the relative positions of earnings rates for given categories of labour differ, only certain categories of labour will be disposed to migrate from one to the other. On motivation see Brinley Thomas, *op. cit.* pp. 202-8.

[2] Cf. K. E. Hansson, 'A Theory of the System of Multilateral Trade', *American Economic Review*, vol. xlii, 1952, pp. 59-68.

[3] See Colin Clark, *The Conditions of Economic Progress*, 2nd ed., London, 1951, pp. 206-7, 245, who remarks that 'only the shock of migration to a completely new country and circumstances will suffice to shake the agriculturalist out of his less efficient traditional methods and enable him to realize the full economic potentialities of his own labour'. See also J. B. Condliffe, *New Zealand in the Making*, London, 1930, pp. 438-40 ; and A. J. Toynbee, *The Study of History*, London, 1939, vol. ii, pp. 84-100, 212-13, 291, 310-11, 315, 346 ff.

give rise to cultural heterosis, a process analogous to biological heterosis,[1] and may generate production- and competition-favouring tension. Fourth, the influx of immigrants, and sometimes the mere prospect of an influx of immigrants, into a country stimulated inflows of capital from Europe, the world's banker prior to 1914, and encouraged domestic investment of sorts. Fifth, and of far greater importance, the countries of immigration were spared much of the input-cost of producing that portion of their population which, prior to its removal to these countries, was reared abroad at the expense of the countries of provenience.[2] Sixth, so long as such meta-states as the Atlantic Community remained subject to increasing return, immigration into their underpeopled parts, by generating economic growth in these parts and thereby augmenting their demands for the products of other and sufficiently peopled parts, gave rise to further increases in return and hence to increases in *per capita* income in both the countries of immigrant provenience and those of immigrant destination.[3] Seventh, the comparative docility of the immigrant workers operated, in the United States at least, to facilitate the introduction of efficient, mechanized,

[1] To the fact that immigrants into America, being largely of working-class origin and ways of thought, continued their ways in America, but with modifications produced by the new and favourable environment of that country, have been attributed several attributes of American workers : their low propensity to save ; their disposition to look upon work as a not wholly unpleasant necessity instead of as a sacrifice ; and their rejection of extreme class-warfare. See Agostino de Vita, 'Der kapitalisierte Wert der 1820–1930 in die Vereinigten Staaten von America Eingewanderten', *Weltwirtschaftliches Archiv*, Bd. lii, 1940 (II), pp. 31-7 ; Corrado Gini, 'Apparent and Real Causes of American Prosperity', Banca Nazionale del Lavoro *Quarterly Review*, No. 6, 1948, and 'Evoluzione della psicologia del lavoro e dell' accumulazione', extract from *Moneta e credito*, No. 2, 1948, also a quarterly review of the Banca Nazionale del Lavoro. See also G. D. Snell, 'Hybrids and History, the Role of Race and Ethnic Crossing in Individual and National Achievements', *Quarterly Review of Biology*, vol. xxvi, 1951, pp. 331-47.

[2] If, as of 1930, a value of 3-10 thousand dollars is placed upon each of the 27·5 million (net) immigrants into the United States in 1821–1930, yielding a result of 82-275 billion dollars, it would appear that a large fraction of the country's accumulated wealth, 362 billion dollars in 1929, was the result of the country's having been spared the cost of rearing its net immigrants. Even if one assigns but a small value to the average immigrant and assumes that one-half to two-thirds of the resources allegedly saved are not in fact saved, the amount of capital-formation spared the United States in the nineteenth century, before the income-optimum may have been approximated, appears large. See first two papers cited in the preceding note. After the income-optimum was reached, the influx of further immigrants, if they merely represented net additions to the population, no longer operated to increase *per capita* income. Hence, even though their cost of production was incident outside the United States, their advent tended to affect the movement of per capita income adversely, by increasing the pressure of numbers upon income-producing wealth and by requiring for their equipment capital that might otherwise have been used to increase equipment per head of the resident population. Estimates of the net contribution of immigrants to a nation's capital formation must take into account both immigrant remittances and the amount of capital brought by immigrants.

[3] Cf. *Papers* of the British Royal Commission on Population, London, 1950, III, pp. 5-21.

mass-production methods, together with a consequent depreciation or dilution of craft skills and an eventual improvement of *per capita* income.[1] Eighth, the international mobility of population brought about by free migration prior to the First World War, together with such economic fluidity as it produced within affected countries, probably contributed significantly to rendering feasible the system of fixed exchange rates characteristic of a considerable portion of the pre-1913 world economy.[2]

The significance of the contribution of immigration to a country's growth turns on how one defines growth. If one concentrates upon totals, then it is evident that immigration accelerates the growth of a country's NNP and gives shape to its occupational and social structure, since immigrants tend to enter some occupations and categories in greater measure than others. If, however, one emphasizes the movement of NNP *per capita*, then the role of immigration is less easy to determine. For immigration serves to raise NNP *per capita* principally by releasing the forces of increasing return, by improving the combination of factors, by introducing new and higher order skills, and by bringing into countries new sets of values conducive to economic enterprise and the augmentation of material production.[3]

Immigration apparently has made such contributions to economic growth in Australia and New Zealand, in Canada, and in Brazil and Argentina. Thus immigration into the British dominions introduced the elements of a skilled and agricultural labour force, together with the skills requisite for economic growth. Immigration into Argentina and Brazil has introduced the rudiments of a skilled industrial and agricultural labour force, many industries, managerial skills, and the spirit of enterprise.[4]

[1] Cf. Bernardelli's argument (*op. cit.* pp. 45-54) to the effect that the comparative smallness of immigration into New Zealand has made its economy rigid and protectionist and hence retarded its development. It has been argued, however, that protectionism has stimulated immigration and population growth in Australia. See J. B. Brigden *et al.*, *The Australian Tariff*, Melbourne, 1929, pp. 84, 140. On the points of theory involved see K. L. Anderson, 'Protection and the Historical Situation', *Quarterly Journal of Economics*, vol. liii, 1938, pp. 86-104, and Marion C. Samuelson, 'The Australian Case for Protection Re-examined', *ibid.* vol. liv, 1939, pp. 143-51. On the effects of immigration into an underdeveloped country see P. T. Bauer, *West African Trade*, Cambridge, 1954, ch. 12.

[2] Cf. A. P. Lerner, *Economics of Employment*, New York, 1951, pp. 358 ff.

[3] Talcott Parsons's analysis suggests that the Latin-American type of social structure, with its emphasis upon particularism and ascription (as distinguished from universalism and achievement), is not favourable to industrial development. If this be true, it needs to be modified, probably through the influx of immigrants with appropriate values. See *The Social System*, Glencoe, 1951, pp. 198-200. Cf. L. E. Williams, 'Chinese Entrepreneurs in Indonesia', *Explorations in Entrepreneurial History*, V, 1952-53, pp. 34-60.

[4] For accounts of the contribution of immigrants see George Wythe, *Industry in Latin America*, New York, 1945, *passim*; R. Richard Wohl, ed., *Change and the Entrepreneur*, Cambridge, 1949, pp. 37-42; De Ávila, *op. cit.* pp. 18, 30-34;

Immigration made important contributions to economic growth in the United States during the first three-quarters or so of the nineteenth century when it was bringing in new skills and values, facilitating the development of industry, and releasing the forces of increasing return. Thus British immigrants brought important knowledge underlying a number of industries (*e.g.* textiles, mining, iron and steel, pottery and building and machine tools, etc.), together with many craft and professional skills. These immigrants, and immigrants of other origins who brought suitable values and skills and knowledge, greatly stimulated the development of American industry and product per head.[1] In time, however, American machinery and techniques began to depart from the British model, moving in the direction of mass-production methods suited to make use of semi-skilled and unskilled labour, with the result that craft and related skills of the British immigrants lost much of their importance except in so far as they were utilizable on the management level.[2] Presumably the history of the role of skilled immigration from other parts paralleled that of the role of skilled British immigration. If the course of the immigrants' contribution proceeded along the lines described, it is unlikely that immigration continued to accelerate the growth of NNP per head in the late nineteenth century, and it is quite possible that it decelerated it.[3] Only detailed study can reveal if an analogous stage has been reached in Australasia. Perhaps it has not yet been reached in Canada, where the forces of increasing return seem not yet to have been exhausted. It has not yet been reached in Brazil and Argentina, for there the occupational composition of the population remains one of a relatively underdeveloped country and therefore susceptible of great improvement through suitable immigration.

It may be noted parenthetically that countries of immigration

H.W. Spiegel, *The Brazilian Economy*, Philadelphia, 1949, pp. 84-9; Foerster, *op. cit. passim*. See also S. A. Mosk, *Industrial Revolution in Mexico*, Berkeley, 1950, ch. 13, J. Lyng, *op. cit.*, R. A. Lochere, *From Europe to New Zealand*, Wellington, 1951

[1] See Berthoff, *op. cit.*; also M. L. Hansen, *The Immigrant in American History*, Cambridge, 1940. Two-fifths of a sample of British alien workers in the United States in 1812 were industrial workers, with persons affiliated with textiles and textile machinery dominant. These early British immigrants carried cotton manufacturing into the factory stage and gave stimulus to woollen, linen, machine, glass, metal wares, paper, and various consumer-good industries. See Herbert Heaton, 'The Industrial Immigrant in the United States, 1783–1912', *Proceedings of the American Philosophical Society*, vol. xcv, 1951, pp. 519-27. See also O. Handlin, 'International Migration and the Acquisition of Skills', in B. F. Hoselitz, *The Progress of Underdeveloped Countries*, Chicago, 1952, pp. 54-9.

[2] See Berthoff, *op. cit.*

[3] It is possible that immigration, by holding down wages, may have increased the rate of capital formation somewhat; this rate was slightly higher between the mid-eighties and the turn of the century than earlier or later. See Kuznets, *op. cit.* p. 155. Apparently the return on capital did not rise. See *ibid.* p. 86.

eventually subject immigration to legal restriction, principally for economic reasons. While a decline in the rate of growth of *per capita* income might bring about demands for such restriction, it usually has come into being before this rate has undergone a long-continued decline. For when a country's economy and population become sufficiently developed to support a relatively strong organized labour movement, increasing pressure is put upon that country's legislators to limit immigration, it being assumed by spokesmen for organized labour that a continuing influx of immigrant labour serves to hold down wages. This pressure tends to be intensified, of course, when, as in the United States in 1885–1903 and perhaps for another decade, real wages remained virtually stationary.

The nature of the impact of immigration upon occupational and wage structures will be influenced by the provisions which countries of immigration make for the adaptation and assimilation of immigrants, for their integration into the main institutional spheres of the countries of immigration, for their acculturation, and for their surmounting difficulties associated with transplantation and adjustment.[1] These provisions are never adequate, however, to produce complete adaptation and assimilation. In consequence, there develops in countries whose immigrants are of multiple-ethnic origin what Kiser calls 'cultural pluralism'.[2] The inter-occupational and inter-industrial mobility of individuals of some ethnic origins tends to be reduced, with the result that the occupational and the wage structure of the country may be affected even in the longer run unless this reduction in mobility is compensated by an increase in the mobility of other members of the affected occupational groups.

It has been noted, particularly since the appearance of Ohlin's work,[3] that international commodity movement, which has its origin, as does international migration, in international differences in factor equipment (supplemented or modified by international differences in technology, organization, scale of activity, etc.), is a substitute for international migration, and may, under certain conditions, give rise to the same results as perfect mobility of the factors of production (including labour). Although these conditions are not realizable in practice, it remains true that, within limits, international

[1] See S. N. Eisenstadt, 'Analysis of Patterns of Immigration and Absorption of Immigrants', *Population Studies*, vol. vii, 1953, pp. 167-80, and 'The Place of Elites and Primary Groups in the Absorption of New Immigrants in Israel', *American Journal of Sociology*, vol. lvii, 1951, pp. 222-31. See also D. V. Glass, ed., *Cultural Assimilation of Immigrants*, supplement to *Population Studies*, March 1950.

[2] See C. V. Kiser, 'Cultural Pluralism', *Annals of the American Academy of Political and Social Science*, vol. cclxii, 1949, pp. 117-30. Cf. Brinley Thomas, *op. cit.* pp. 195-7.

[3] See B. Ohlin, *Interregional and International Trade*.

trade and international migration are substitutes for one another. Trade does not become a fairly effective substitute for migration, however, until the populations of labour-short economies have become sufficiently large and industrially differentiated to permit them to produce many commodities in common with labour-long countries and thus allow scope to commodity substitution. In general, then, it may be said that in the early stages of an immigrant-receiving country's history, its economy will tend to be oriented to its then comparatively simple resource endowment and hence be highly specialized, with the result that the ratio of its international trade to its NNP will be relatively high. As this economy develops, however, and it becomes large and heterogeneous enough to permit it economically to undertake the production of portions of its requirements of many commodities, the ratio of its trade to its income will fall, but its organization and its productive potentialities will come to resemble sufficiently those of many other economies to permit international commodity movements significantly to diminish wage and income differences that might have been removed by further international migration.[1]

Under certain circumstances immigration may generate inflation and forced savings, since the equipping of immigrants with industrial and residential capital requires a sufficiency of savings. A deficiency of savings is likely when the following circumstances are present : (1) domestic capital formation is relatively low ; (2) the influx of immigrants is not accompanied by an adequate amount of suitable net foreign investment in the country of immigration ; (3) there is not a sufficiency of accessible land to combine with immigrants (or those displaced by them) and thus serve as a surrogate for reproducible capital ; (4) the substitutability (or combinability) of labour for (with) available agents of production is insufficiently elastic to permit full employment unless some minimal amount of capital is formed. Given this combination of circumstances, immigration will tend to increase unemployment, or, if efforts are made to augment investment sufficiently to facilitate employment of all immigrant workers, it will occasion credit creation and inflation. (Heavy foreign investment may, of course, be accompanied by inflation and rising domestic prices.)

Immigration, by augmenting the demand for investment goods and giving rise to the multiplier effect, may increase the level of

---

[1] See S. Laursen, 'Production Functions and the Theory of International Trade', *American Economic Review*, vol. xlii, 1952, pp. 540-57, and the works of Samuelson (who has greatly refined analysis of the problem) and others cited by Laursen ; also P. A. Samuelson, 'Prices of Factors and Goods in General Equilibrium', *Review of Economic Studies*, vol. xxi, 1953–54 pp. 1-20.

employment when the immigrant-receiving country is in a state of under-employment equilibrium. It does this both directly by increasing the equipment and related requirements of the foreign-born, and indirectly by stimulating internal migration which usually serves to increase the demand for investment goods at the point of destination more than it diminishes demand at the point of departure. It is essential, however, that the increment in immigration be initially accompanied by the employment of this increment, or by a change in expectations, etc., giving rise to an increase in the demand for investment goods and eventually to the employment of this increment.

Only detailed analysis would disclose whether immigration as such has contributed to unemployment or inflation. In the United States in 1870–1910 the labour force increased 2·75 per cent per year, with the increase in foreign-born providing about one-fifth of this growth, while net foreign investment contributed only something like 2 per cent of the increase in reproducible tangible wealth. None the less, the drift of American prices seems to have been under the dominance of monetary forces rather than under that of investment, perhaps because capital was formed at a high rate and crop land continued to increase.[1] In several less advanced economies (*e.g.* Canada, Australia, Argentina), however, heavy population inflows were sometimes accompanied by investment booms and rising prices in 1870–1913, with immigration accentuating but apparently not initiating the inflationary tendencies. Apparently the long-continued upward movement of Brazilian prices was not closely associated with immigration.[2]

[1] See Kuznets, *op. cit.* pp. 78, 155, 197, 204-5, 322-3, *Historical Statistics*, pp. 29, 121. Net foreign investment in 1880–1910 exceeded 800 dollars per foreign worker added to the labour force. This amount, though much less than the amount of reproducible capital per member of the labour force, exceeded the value of equipment per worker prior to the early 1900's. The number of gainful workers in agriculture increased until after 1910, and the number of farm families until 1920. It should be noted that farm land may not be an unqualified substitute for capital, since the costs of farm-making may limit the combinability of agricultural labour with agricultural land in the absence of the necessary complementary capital. For example, see C. H. Danhof, 'Farm-making Costs and the "Safety Valve" : 1850–1860', *Journal of Political Economy*, vol. xlix, 1941, pp. 317-59 ; also P. D. Phillips *et al.*, *The Peopling of Australia*, Melbourne, 1933, ch. 9. Settlement costs are lower when the requisites of efficient agriculture are neglected (cf. Spiegel, *op. cit.* p. 166).

[2] Data on investment are given in Cairncross, *op. cit.* ; United Nations, *International Capital Movements During the Inter-War Period*, Lake Success, 1949, and *Foreign Capital in Latin America*, New York, 1955 ; Royal Institute of International Affairs, *The Problem of International Investment*, London, 1937 ; H. Feis, *Europe, The World's Banker, 1870–1914*, New Haven, 1930. See also Penelope Hartland, 'Private Enterprise and International Capital', *Canadian Journal of Economics and Political Science*, vol. xix, 1953, pp. 70-80 ; G. M. Meier, 'Economic Development and the Transfer Mechanism', *ibid.* pp. 1-19 ; Jacob Viner, *Canada's Balance of International Indebtedness, 1900–1913*, Cambridge, 1924 ; J. H. Williams, *Argentine International Trade under Inconvertible Paper Money, 1880–1900*,

VI. VARIATIONS IN MIGRATORY MOVEMENTS

The movement of migrants from countries of emigration to countries of immigration has been subject to variations of diverse kinds, ranging from those closely associated with trade-cycle movements to those having their origin in economic movements of longer duration, or in changes in secular trend, or in modifications of economic structures and of the legal conditions surrounding migration. Since the movement of migrants has usually been under the dominance of economic factors, variations therein may be examined in terms of supply and demand, supply being analogous to the so-called 'push' factor and demand to the so-called 'pull' factor. Inasmuch as these two factors operate in combination to determine what may be called the equilibrium rate of migration, students of migration seek to determine the separate influence of each by studying variations in the rate of migration, with legal conditions and costs of movement (which trended downward) given.

The supply of emigrants from Europe, whence came nearly all inter-continental migrants in 1820–1939, was affected principally by the following interrelated factors : (1) the movement of relative and absolute natural increase in Europe ; (2) the movement of surplus labour out of agricultural areas ; (3) the progress of industrialization and urbanization ; (4) variations in the rate of capital formation and in the level of aggregate non-agricultural demand for the services of labour ; and (5) the behaviour of costs of migration and of European agricultural prices and income. (1) Whilst absolute natural increase increased very little in Europe between 1820 and the First World War, it fluctuated considerably, producing corresponding fluctuations in accessions to the labour force fifteen or more years later and apparently occasioning fluctuations in the volume of emigration about twenty-five years later.[1] (2) Throughout the period covered, an excess of labour was to be found in many rural areas, ready to move on slight stimulus. (3) Industrialization and urbanization

Cambridge, 1920 ; Spiegel, *op. cit.* ch. 3. Foreign investment in Argentina exceeded 2 billion dollars in 1914 while net immigration into Argentina in 1870–1910 approximated 2165 thousand. The corresponding figures for Brazil are around 2 billion dollars and 2029 thousand ; for Australia and New Zealand, close to 2·3 billion dollars and around 882 thousand ; Canada, close to 3·7 billion dollars and 652 thousand ; United States, 3·3 billion dollars net (or 6·8 billion dollars gross) and about 13·6 million. On the subject of the above paragraph see E. A. G. Robinson's comment on this paper and A. P. Lerner's essay in this volume.

[1] See Brinley Thomas, *op. cit.* pp. 80-1, 116-18, 156-8, 218-19, 313-14. See also Arne Skaug, *Fluctuations in Migration from Norway since 1900*, etc., Norwegian Memorandum No. 1, International Institute of Intellectual Co-operation, League of Nations, Paris, (May) 1937.

proceeded relatively slowly, in many countries until the late nine-teenth century, and in some until after the First World War. (4) Capital formation, whilst proceeding at relatively high levels in Northern and Western Europe in 1870–1914, remained at very low levels in Southern and Eastern Europe, where, especially in and after the 1880's, the absolute increment in population and the labour force was rising, and where only a limited amount of foreign funds was invested in a way to give impetus to industrialization and urbanization. Britain sought to encourage emigration to Canada and Australasia, but with very limited success until after quotas were imposed by the United States in 1924 and the Empire Settle-ment Act of 1922 became effective. (5) Costs of transport fell and European agricultural prices declined as a result of agricultural expansion in these immigrant-receiving countries.[1]

British and other experience suggests that both cyclical and longer-term variations in emigration were influenced by variations *within* emigrant-sending countries in the rate of increase of persons of working age, in the rate of domestic investment, in the level of employment, and in the relative amount of capital exported. Varia-tions in emigration were accentuated when upward movements or peaks (downward movements, or valleys) in countries of immigration coincided with downward movements or valleys (upward movements, or peaks) in countries of emigration.[2]

The demand for immigrants in immigrant-receiving countries was conditioned by the progress of settlement and the accessibility of cultivable land, by domestic natural increase, by the pace of industrialization and urbanization, and by the availability of capital. Land remained available for settlement up to 1914 and after in

[1] See Brinley Thomas, *op. cit.*, especially chs. 12-13, D. Kirk, *Europe's Popula-tion in the Interwar Years*, Princeton, 1946, chs. 4-6, 8. On the progress of indus-trialization and capital formation, see, for example, Clark, *op. cit.* 9, 11 ; Dorothy S. Thomas, *Social and Economic Aspects of Swedish Population Movements*, New York, 1941, chs. 2-3 ; S. N. Prokopovicz, *L'Industrialisation des pays agricoles et la structure de l'économie après la guerre*, Neuchâtel, 1946, especially ch. 4 ; I. Svennilson, *Growth and Stagnation in the European Economy*, Geneva, 1954, ch. 4 ; K. B. Mayer, *The Population of Switzerland*, New York, 1952, chs. 9-12. As of 1914 12 billion dollars of a world total of 44 billion dollars international investment had been placed in Europe, with something like 9 billion dollars situated in Southern and Eastern Europe ; but a considerable part of these 9 billion dollars represented political and military loans. Cf. Feis, *op. cit.* The Irish potato crop failure set in motion the great migration to America.

[2] See Cairncross, *op. cit.* chs. 7-8 ; Brinley Thomas, *op. cit.* chs. 7-8, especially pp. 83-4, 96-118, 124-30. Improvements in business conditions, by making passage money more attainable, produced a similar effect in Italy and (presum-ably) other low-income countries. See *ibid.* pp. 95-6, 117. See also Harry Jerome, *Migration and Business Cycles*, New York, 1926, who found the 'pull' forces in the United States more powerful than the 'push' forces in Europe, and Dorothy S. Thomas, *op. cit.*, who found pull of the United States upon Sweden countered by cyclical upturns in Swedish economic activity. See also C. K. Hobson, *The Export of Capital*, London, 1914, ch. 8.

the major countries of immigration, though in the United States, according to Thompson,[1] the still available land was inferior in quality. The rate of natural increase fell in some countries (*e.g.* United States, Australia, Canada, New Zealand) but not markedly (if at all) in others (*e.g.* Argentina, Brazil). Non-agricultural employment was relatively high and/or increasing in the major immigrant-receiving countries other than Brazil. Considerable foreign capital flowed into the major areas of immigration, 21·3 of the reported 44 billion dollars of investment, as of 1914, having been placed in North America, Latin America, and Oceania, all underpopulated and underdeveloped regions subject to increasing return at least prior to 1914. These areas continued to be favoured after the First World War, especially by the United States, now the major lender.[2]

Heavy foreign investment appears to have stimulated immigration into a number of countries, resulting in the settling there of enough individuals to make further investment attractive. After having experienced net emigration each decade in 1861–1901, Canada experienced net immigration in an amount approximating four-tenths of its population growth in 1901–11, a period of heavy investment, and net immigration continued, though at a lower level, in the two decades following, both periods of considerable foreign investment in Canada.[3] Australia, free of proximity to the United States but distant from Britain, having exhausted the pull of the gold discoveries of 1850–51, apparently had her net immigration stimulated by foreign investment in the 1880's. For the whole period, 1871–1913, the association between capital imports and net immigration, while positive, was less marked; and the amount of correlation was still less in 1913–30. On occasion, moreover, changes in migration appear to have anticipated changes in net foreign investment.[4] In Argentina immigration first rose to great heights in the 1880's when foreign capital flowed in at the unprecedentedly

---

[1] *Op. cit.* ch. 10.

[2] Royal Institute of International Affairs, *op. cit.* ; United Nations, *International Capital Movements*; also Colin Clark, *op. cit.* pp. 512-13. As Brinley Thomas remarks (*op. cit.* pp. 199-201), the supply of funds available for foreign investment increased because, with immigration greatly reduced by quota restrictions, the equipping of immigrants no longer absorbed capital as in the past. The rate of capital formation fell somewhat in the 1920's (see Kuznets, *op. cit.* p. 155).

[3] Between 1870 and 1900 the net inflow of capital amounted to 25 to 30 million dollars per year ; in 1900-13, the corresponding figure was around 200 million dollars. Between 1914 and 1929 foreign investments in Canada increased from 3·8 to 5·9 billion dollars. See Cairncross, *op. cit.* ch. 3 and pp. 183-6 ; Hartland, *op. cit.* pp. 77-9 ; Royal Institute of International Affairs, *op. cit.* p. 256.

[4] See D. B. Copland's essay in Phillips, *op. cit.* ch. 7. See also Brinley Thomas, *op. cit.* p. 115 ; Hartland, *op. cit.* pp. 75-7 ; Cairncross, *op. cit.* pp. 183-5 ; Forsyth, *op. cit.* pp. 30 ff., 204, 209.

high rate of 85 million dollars per year.[1] Apparently foreign investment was adequate and economic growth had been given sufficient
momentum to surmount the difficulties of the early 1890's, for gross
immigration in 1901–10 reached a level slightly over double that
recorded in the 1880's. Although investment probably stimulated
immigration into Brazil, the heavy immigration of the 1890's
appears also to have stimulated French and British investment.[2]

As has been noted, immigration into the United States has been
subject to long swings as well as to cyclical influences ; arrivals,
departures, and net arrivals moved together, but with net arrivals
manifesting greatest variation. Furthermore, 'the long swings in
net immigration tended to *follow* those in gross national product per
worker, and to *precede* those in the constant dollar volume of residential construction'.[3] Conceivably an increase in net immigration,
stimulated by an increase in the rate of increase in output per worker,
gives rise in turn to an increase in the demand for housing.[4] Thomas
finds that, with one exception (1869–79), immigration preceded
building activity in the United States.[5] He finds also that, whereas
in 1844–63 increments in the rate of immigration preceded upswings
in railway construction, merchandise imports, and fixed-equipment
investment, post-1869 immigration lagged after rail construction
and (from 1899 on) after the output of coal and pig iron. Induced
investment in fixed-capital equipment fluctuated in response to
variation in population inflows. Waves of immigration, with their
origin in the European births cycle and the impact of innovations upon the European economy, were succeeded by 'minor
secular upswings in the rate of economic growth'.[6] According

---

[1] Hartland, *op. cit.* pp. 74-5. Williams (*op. cit.* p. 103) indicates that 85 per
cent of Argentina's foreign liabilities (about 923 million dollars in 1892) had been
borrowed in the 1880's. By 1914 foreign investment in Argentina must have
exceeded 2 billion dollars.

[2] French investment rose from 2 to 3·5 billion francs between 1902 and 1909.
British investment rose from an estimated 46·6 million pounds in 1886 to 148 in
1914. See Cairncross, *op. cit.* p. 184 ; United Nations, *Foreign Capital in Latin
America*, pp. 153 ff. ; Royal Institute of International Affairs, *op. cit.* pp. 272 ff.

[3] Kuznets and Rubin, *op. cit.* 27-31.

[4] *Ibid.* pp. 33-4. It is suggested (*ibid.*) that an increase in the number of
foreign-born might, in consequence of the resulting increase in communications
with persons living in countries of provenience, stimulate immigration. See also
Kuznets, *op. cit.* p. 203. Studies of immigrant settlement in southern or western
states, where immigrants were fewer and ethnically more homogeneous, might
provide a partial test of this hypothesis.

[5] Brinley Thomas, *op. cit.* pp. 102-4, 108, 112, 159-63, 174, 176-8. See *ibid.*
ch. 11, for the thesis that, Great Britain and the United States being parts of the
Atlantic community, the building cycles of these parts were inversely related, with
immigration the main connecting link.

[6] *Ibid.* pp. 159-63, 174. Brinley Thomas suggests that before 1870 population
inflows stimulated investment, immigration then being under the dominance of
'push' factors, whereas after 1870 the 'pull' factor became dominant and the
pace of investment set that of immigration (*ibid.* p. 93). Kuznets (*op. cit.* pp.

to Kuznets and Rubin, arrivals into the United States moved 'fairly consistently with business cycles'; departures tended to contract during expansions and to expand during contractions, possibly because they 'are more sensitive than the more rigidly controlled (by law) arrivals'.[1] Thomas is of the opinion that the influx of cheap, unskilled labour from Southern and Eastern Europe widened the capital structure of the United States, enabling the country 'to take maximum advantage of the technical innovations of that time, and established the basis of its modern economic power'.[2]

Immigration may affect the cyclical behaviour of immigrant-receiving economies in yet other ways. It may modify the ruling propensity to consume and the disposition to invest. It may, by increasing labour turnover, make for the preservation of a more preferred occupational balance. It may, by prolonging the period during which labour is available on satisfactory terms, increase 'the intensity of boom periods and consequently the severity of depression'.[3] It may increase the capacity of an economy to adjust its labour supply to its current needs, though usually at the expense of shifting unemployment to countries of emigration.[4] Available data for pre-1924 times suggest, however, that the ratio of years of

198-9 ; cf. Brinley Thomas, *op. cit.* pp. 195-7) notes that the 'push' factor, a concomitant of the spread of the industrial revolution, had much to do with 'the *secular* changes in the origin of American immigration' associated with the eastward and southward shift of its points of origin. Presumably, given two populations A and B, and abstracting from the presence of conditions such as gold discoveries, B must be sufficiently large and developed, in comparison with A, before it can exert much attractive force upon A. This presumption is supported by the progress in the incremental rate of immigration into countries of immigration.

[1] *Op. cit.* pp. 36-7.

[2] Brinley Thomas, *op. cit.* pp. 163-74, where he supposes that earlier heavy waves of immigration produced similar 'widening' effects. This thesis remains to be established, however. It is probably true that the docility of the immigrant workers facilitated the introduction of the newer methods. It is not clear, however, whether changes in the price structure of the factors of production, or the course of invention itself, produced such 'widening' as took place. 'Widening' did not take place in manufacturing wherein 43·4 per cent of the foreign-born whites were engaged in 1910.

[3] Jerome, *op. cit.* p. 242. Cf. G. Cassel, *The Theory of Social Economy*, New York, 1932, pp. 571-5 ; G. Myrdal, 'Industrialization and Population', in *Economic Essays in Honour of Gustav Cassel*, London, 1933, pp. 435-58.

[4] Thus Kuznets and Rubin, having noted that departures are even more sensitive to changes in the aggregate demand for labour than are arrivals, remark that 'there is something to be said for the ability of an economy to increase additions to its labour force during prosperous times and to reduce them, if not necessarily convert them into declines, during periods of contraction'. See *op. cit.* p. 37. Under these conditions migrants behave as do foreign seasonal migrants (*e.g.* Poles into pre-war Germany ; Mexicans into the United States). Such was the experience of France which, in effect, kept 'its reserve army of workers outside the country', drawing on them as they were needed and sending them back as this need disappeared. See W. Woytinsky, *Three Sources of Unemployment*, Geneva, 1935, p. 103, and my *France Faces Depopulation*, pp. 201-2.

prosperity to years of depression was not materially affected by whether or not a country experienced heavy immigration.[1]

VII. IMMIGRATION AND INTERNAL MIGRATION

The volume, the composition, and the direction of internal migration may reflect the impact of immigration if the immigrant workers are essentially substitutes for native workers. For then natives with whom immigrants particularly compete will tend to avoid areas of immigrant concentration and, if situated therein, to move elsewhere. Immigrants may become concentrated also if they enter agriculture or some other occupation in much greater relative numbers than do natives. Under some circumstances, however, both foreign and native migrants within a country may tend to move into the same areas. This will be the case if the native workers are essentially complementary to the immigrant workers; if certain areas remain subject to increasing return or are less subject than others to diminishing return; or if the influx of capital and superior technology and management into certain areas renders them highly suitable to industrial development; or if superior and accessible natural resources are discovered in certain areas. In general, especially after agricultural settlement has been completed, conditions of the latter sort appear to predominate, with the result that immigrants tend to favour many of the areas into which the native population of the immigrant-receiving countries tends to congregate.[2] This tendency may be modified somewhat by the distance factor when the countries of provenience are relatively close to some but not to all parts of the immigrant-receiving country, and by the occupational composition of the immigrants when the distribution of the markets for their labour services differs markedly from that of the markets wherein the natives sell their services.

Inasmuch as the arrival of immigrants (who are complementary to, or substitutive for natives) conditions the distribution of the native population, the comparative cessation of immigration is bound to produce changes in the distribution of the native population.

---

[1] See W. C. Mitchell, *Business Cycles*, New York, 1928, p. 410. See also Timlin, 'Economic Theory and Immigration Policy', *loc. cit.* Whether the effects exercised by immigration upon internal and external terms of trade affect cyclical tendencies significantly remains to be determined.

[2] *E.g.*, see T. L. Smith, *Brazil: People and Institutions*, Baton Rouge, 1954, chs. 10-11, 13, 17; Forsyth, *op. cit. passim*; Keyfitz, *op. cit.*; Hurd, *op. cit.*; E. L. Thorndike, 'The Causes of Inter-State Migration', *Sociometry*, vol. v, 1942, pp. 321-35. Hurd (*op. cit.* pp. 90 ff.) found that as of 1921 the ratio of foreign-born to total population was highest in the Western provinces which had experienced high growth rates in 1901–21.

For example, in the United States Negroes and foreign-born workers apparently have been substitutive for one another within a considerable range, with the result that immigrants have tended to stay out of the Southern states and Negroes have tended to move into the Northern industrial states when foreign immigration has fallen off or been greatly reduced by the quota provisions.[1] In general, however, the interstate migration of foreign-born whites was moderately correlated with both that of Negroes and that of native whites, aggregative and complementary and analogous effects having outweighed the force of rivalry between foreign-born workers on the one hand, and Negroes and natives on the other. Furthermore, the impact of the migration of foreign-born whites and of Negroes was great in a relatively few states, not always those experiencing high native-white in-migration, while the patterns and levels of interstate migration were dominated by that of the native whites.[2]

[1] See Brinley Thomas, *op. cit.* pp. 130-4. See also Dorothy S. Thomas, 'Some Aspects of a Study of Population Redistribution and Economic Growth in the United States, 1870–1950', a paper presented to the World Population Conference in Rome, 1954, as a progress report of a study being carried on by the author and Simon Kuznets. Dr. Thomas finds that in the 1870's the interstate migration of foreign-born whites was inversely associated with that of native whites and Negroes, but that later the two indices sometimes moved together.

[2] *Ibid.*

Chapter 3

IMMIGRATION, CAPITAL FORMATION, AND INFLATIONARY PRESSURE

BY

ABBA P. LERNER

Roosevelt College, Chicago

1. IN this paper I shall speak in general terms, but what I shall say is very strongly influenced by my experience in Israel during the past two years.

Its title, which was given to me by the organizers of the Round Table, suggests that inflation is synonymous with an excess of demand for goods and services over the available or potential supply, for that seems to be the meaning of inflationary *pressure*. Capital formation or investment on the one hand takes resources away from the provision of goods and services for current consumption, and on the other hand increases income, thereby creating additional demand for current goods and services. Excess demand is thus generated both by the increase in demand and by the decrease in supply. Although I have myself in past writings gone so far as to *define* inflation as an excess of demand over supply, I shall endeavour here to turn the analysis in a different direction.

2. In the first place it seems to me to be fundamental to conceive of inflation as a self-perpetuating *process*. Otherwise the inflationary pressure that tends to make prices rise could be cured by simply permitting the prices to rise to a new equilibrium level. The real trouble is that the rise in prices does not solve the problem. It re-creates the same set of conditions that led to the inflationary pressure in the first place so that there is again an inflationary pressure and the inflation continues.

This is at the core of the problem even if price controls prevent prices from rising in spite of a continuing excess of demand over supply. There is then no visible self-perpetuating process going on, and the efficiency of the economy, instead of being disrupted by the rising prices, is sabotaged by the increasingly inappropriate and irrelevant fixed or frozen prices. But the only sound justification for continuing the price control is that its removal would permit a potential self-perpetuating inflation of prices to develop into actuality, and that this would do more harm to the economic machine than is done by the condition of 'repressed inflation' under the régime of price control. Here too it is a self-perpetuating inflationary process — although only a potential one — that is at the root of the inflationary condition.

The self-perpetuating process of rising prices caused by an excess of demand, like any other self-perpetuating process, occurs because the measures taken to deal with an initial disturbance to a system are inappropriate ones. They do not remove the initial disturbance, and so the measures are repeated and the process becomes self-perpetuating. The self-perpetuating process can occur if the government, for instance, tries to draw productive resources out of consumption into investment by creating additional money for use in investment. The additional money soon finds its way into the hands of consumers whose expenditure draws the resources back again from investment into consumption. As long as the government keeps on trying to withdraw resources from consumption into investment by creating still more money for use in investment we have the self-perpetuating process.

A similar process could be the result of an attempt by the government to shift resources to any other sector of the economy by the creation of new money to be used by the favoured sector. It might be an attempt to increase consumption at the expense of investment by optimistic investors, in which case the money spent by consumers will soon reach investors who have been made even more optimistic by the inflation. It might be an attempt to increase the resources used by the government, in which case the money will soon find itself in the hands of the public bidding the factors away from the government. It might be an attempt to make faulty past investments appear profitable (via cheap credits to businesses in difficulties), in which case the money soon will reach better businesses which will bid the factors of production away from the faulty businesses. It might be an attempt to hold down the rate of interest by providing more credit, but with full employment the money soon tries to buy more goods than can be made available, prices rise, and the supply of money again appears to be inadequate to provide all the liquidity demanded at the low interest rate. In all these cases the process is self-perpetuating because a faulty response to a disturbance re-creates the initial position, including the same disturbance, so that the same response is called forth again. (In the case of *repressed* inflation the condition persists because *no* response is permitted.)

3. Immigration is one of the possible initiators of such a self-perpetuating inflationary process, but there is no *necessity* for this.

The government, seeing that additional productive equipment, houses, schools, etc., are needed, may try to provide these by spending additional new money in the hope that this will draw the necessary resources away from other uses in which they are fully employed initially. But there is no necessity for the government to adopt such a dangerous and self-defeating policy. There is no *automatic* link between immigration and inflation.

The immigrants' need for housing, etc., does not create any *demand* until the immigrants have money to spend on such items. If they get the money by earning it they thereby increase *supply* in general by the same amount and rather tend to *reduce* inflationary pressure to the extent that they use some of their earnings not to spend but to save or to build up their stocks of liquid balances.

If the immigrants are helped by others, then there would be an increase in total demand to the extent that the funds are provided not out of decreased consumption (or other expenditures) by these friends or relatives but are provided by their saving less (or dis-saving more) than they otherwise would. But such increases in the marginal propensity to consume of the old population (the friends or relatives who help the immigrants) are not likely to be large enough to create any very great difficulties for a monetary and fiscal policy that was seriously concerned to prevent inflation by preventing excess demand.

There is also an increase in demand if the immigrants are accompanied by foreign funds (whether these are their own or not). But such foreign funds permit imports to be increased and this increases supply, and in any case any excess demand could be offset by appropriate monetary and fiscal policy.

If the immigration makes domestic investments more attractive, the increase in investment expenditure might make total expenditure too great and establish the excess demand that sparks a self-perpetuating inflationary process. But here too it all depends on whether this is permitted by the monetary and fiscal policy. The monetary and fiscal authorities can prevent excessive private investment (which like any other excessive expenditure can start the inflation), just as it can decide not to undertake excessive public expenditure for the purpose of providing factories for the immigrants to work in and houses for them to live in. The inflation will not happen if the government seriously wants to avoid it.

4. I do not mean to deny the possibility or the importance of inflation due to excess demand, or even the probability that a wave

of immigration could be the initiating factor of such a demand inflation. The immigration may well induce the government to adopt, or at least to acquiesce in, a policy of excessive expenditure. What I really want to do in this paper is to draw attention to the possibility of immigration giving rise to a self-perpetuating inflationary process of quite another kind.

There can be a self-perpetuating inflationary process even when there is no excess demand. It can occur even if there is nothing like full employment or the full utilization of industrial capacity. We can have an inflationary process even if the authorities deliberately and successfully *prevent* demand from becoming excessive. In this case prices cannot be said to rise because of attempts to buy more than the available supplies of goods and services. A self-perpetuating inflationary process can go on even though business is bad and customers are hard to find.

An inflation of this type does not fit my definition of inflation as an excess of demand over supply, but that is only so much the worse for my definition. All I can do is try to save some face by the well-established tactic of re-definition. The inflation I am now speaking about is a 'cost inflation' as distinct from a 'demand inflation'.

5. In a demand inflation prices are raised because the supplier discovers that he can raise his price and still sell all that he has available. In a cost inflation prices are raised because the supplier discovers that the price he will have to pay to replace what he sells has gone up and he must raise his price if he does not want to lose money, even though raising the price will make it harder for him to sell and will reduce the volume of his trade.

The prime mover in a cost inflation is the practical acceptance by the society of a standard real wage higher than that which makes it profitable for employers to provide a satisfactory level of employment. The standard may be adopted by the immigrants from the older population, or it may be imported by the immigrants as part of their ideological equipment. In either case such an 'unrealistic' real wage is very likely where there is a heavy immigration, either because the marginal product of labour is reduced by the immigration below that of the previous population from whom the immigrants adopt the standard, or because the immigrants come from countries where the wage (and the marginal product of labour) was higher than in the country of immigration. It is strengthened if there exists an ideology which sees the maintenance (or the increasing) of the real wage not as a problem of production but as one of getting it away from the capitalists.

By an 'unsatisfactory' level of employment is meant one which moves the government to run a deficit and increase the money supply, if necessary, in order to finance additional expenditures on public works and other unemployment relief measures.

A 'satisfactory' level of employment is, therefore, one which is sufficiently acceptable for the government to refrain from incurring deficits and increasing the money supply, even though it is considerably below any desired level of full, or high, or maximum or 'really satisfactory' employment.

6. The self-perpetuating cost-inflationary process may be followed through its course, the observation starting arbitrarily at any point in a cycle (or spiral) of the inflation. Its course is as follows :

(*a*) There is an increase in costs. Although business may be very bad, sellers will not continue to sell for long at less than the replacement cost. They put up their prices. The increase in prices raises the cost of living and reduces the real wage below the 'standard'. The money wage is then raised to restore the real wage to the standard. (This may be done automatically by a cost-of-living allowance mechanism.) The increase in the wage rate raises costs and the simplest cost-inflation cycle (or spiral) is complete and can repeat itself.

This would not be a fully or permanently self-perpetuating process because, with the continuing rise in prices and costs and money wages, a constant supply of money would become less and less adequate for carrying on the same volume of business (which may be far below full employment) and in time the increasing worsening of business and increase in unemployment might break down the 'standard' real wage that is demanded. But long before this can occur the level of employment becomes 'unsatisfactory', and then :

(*b*) The government increases its expenditures, even if that means running a deficit and increasing the money supply, until the level of employment is restored to the minimum 'satisfactory' level. With practice the government will not wait until employment falls significantly below the 'satisfactory' level but will engage in financing employment-creating activities to *prevent* the level of employment falling below the minimum 'satisfactory' level. Wages will then be raised again so as to maintain the standard wage, because of price increases in the past, which operate on the money wage only with a time lag. Prices will rise because of wage increases in the past which show their effects on costs only with a time lag. (There is also some lag between cost increases and the resulting price increases.) With the government coming in, either in irregular steps to *cure* unsatisfactory employment as it develops, or in smoother action to *prevent* employment falling below the minimum 'satisfactory' level, the inflationary process can continue indefinitely.

(*c*) So far the analysis has limited itself to a closed economy. Where the economy depends on foreign trade a further cycle super-imposes itself. As the cost inflation develops the country prices itself out of the foreign market. Its exports become too expensive for the foreign market and imports become relatively more and more attractive.

The classical cure for this is, of course, a fall in money wages as a result of the unemployment caused by the decline in exports and import-competing industries and their repercussions through multi-plier effects. In the conditions we are discussing, this does not happen. The standard real wage is maintained and money wages not only do not fall, they keep on rising.

A somewhat more modern cure is to devalue the currency (or merely allow it to fall as it automatically will if it is not somehow pegged by *increasing* supplies of foreign exchange to fill the increasing gap in the balance of payments). The devaluation restores the relative position of internal and external prices, so that exports and imports can continue at about the same levels as before, the de-valuation keeping pace with the continuing inflation of domestic prices. This merely means that the domestic price of foreign currency joins all the other domestic prices in the cost-inflationary process, but the continuing devaluation, and the resulting expecta-tions of further devaluations, have an especially important place in the economic disruptions due to the inflation.

(*d*) A still further complication develops if there is an attempt to accelerate the devaluation beyond the increase in domestic prices so as to make the country more competitive in the world market and less dependent on foreign economic aid to fill the gap in the balance of payments. This does not work either, but it creates a new cycle. The devaluation of the currency *relative to the domestic price level* (or rise in the domestic price of foreign exchange *greater* than the general price rise) which is necessary for this purpose raises the (relative) price of import goods and this reduces the real wage. The maintenance of the 'standard' real wage calls for money wages to be raised so as to restore the same real wage. The increased money wages increases costs and prices again until the same relation-ship is restored between internal and external prices as before the devaluation. In other words, the devaluation is completely frustrated as an instrument of correcting the balance of payments. The only effect of the devaluation is to increase the rate of price rise and thereby to aggravate the disorganization of the economy (since price increases are just as disruptive of economic calculation whether they are caused by cost inflation or by demand inflation).

(*e*) Since the gap in the balance of payments cannot be corrected, in the conditions we are considering, either by money wage reductions or by devaluation, the gap must persist, which means that someone must be financing it. Or perhaps it would be more enlightening to say that unless someone was financing the gap the whole system would break down. The imports would not be available without which it is quite impossible to maintain the real wage or even perhaps to keep the economy going at all.

7. The problem thus shows itself in two sides, an internal side and an external side.

(i) The nucleus of the internal side is a standard real wage too high to permit even minimum 'satisfactory' employment. This is a function of the productivity of the workers. But the productivity of the workers is to a very great extent a function of the quantity of capital each worker has to work with. It is therefore conceivable that the situation could be cured by a sufficient accumulation of capital (together with other ways of increasing productivity), so as to bring the marginal productivity of labour (with the usual qualifications for monopoly, etc.) up to the standard real wage. The wage demanded would then no longer be 'unrealistic', and full (or at least 'satisfactory') employment could be provided for the immigrants without falling foul of cost inflation. If the capital needed for this solution is not available we have a *capital bottleneck*.

(ii) The external side of the problem is the gap in the balance of payments. This is the result not of the *real wage* being too high but of the *dollar wage* being too high. The money wage is too high in terms of foreign exchange, so that the country buys too much abroad and sells too little abroad and so has too great an unfavourable balance of payments and an *import bottleneck*.

8. In a sense the import bottleneck does not matter so long as someone is willing and able to finance the gap. On the contrary, the import surplus (the gap) enables the country to enjoy a higher standard of living (or a higher rate of domestic investment) than if it had to limit its consumption and investment to its own output instead of being able to use the unfavourable balance, the excess of imports over exports, in addition.

But it does matter if it is supposed that whoever is financing the gap will not continue to do so indefinitely and that the country must prepare itself, in the course of a few years, to manage without the import balance (or with a much smaller one). It is then necessary to build up enough capital, while the import balance is holding out, to raise the marginal product to the standard real wage. This will make it possible to cure the cost inflation in the long period by the liquidation of the capital bottleneck.

The liquidation of the capital bottleneck would liquidate the import bottleneck at the same time, since the increased capital and resulting increase in output per head would permit the country to compete more effectively in the production of exports and of import substitutes, thus reducing or eliminating the unfavourable balance of payments. Conversely, the elimination of the import bottleneck by an increase in the production of the exports and import substitutes would provide more employment and would thus help the increase in capital to absorb the greater population in productive work.

But this policy finds itself in conflict with the current or short-period cost-inflation problem. The short-period cost-inflation problem is alleviated by the importing of *consumption goods* (and consumption goods materials). Making such imports plentiful keeps down prices and the cost of living, and that can slow down or even stop the current cost inflation. There is thus a conflict between the competing uses of the limited import surplus. Loosening the import bottleneck for current consumption tightens the future capital bottleneck, while loosening the capital bottleneck by importing for investment involves a tightening of the import bottleneck for current consumption.

9. This conflict is clearly a part of the much more general conflict between consumption and saving, but it is proper to tie it to imports because we are concerned with a condition in which there is a general plenty of domestic resources. With respect to these domestic resources the country is an 'upside-down economy', as described in my *Economics of Employment*.[1] These factors are not really scarce, and the classical laws of economics are not really applicable, or rather are applicable only in reverse. Only imports are *really* scarce.

To put this in another way, there are unemployed resources and more of them could be used for *both* consumption and investment. Effective demand could be increased, more money could be supplied, and this would not make prices rise any more than before, since prices are rising not because of excess demand (and we are a long way from excess demand) but because of increasing costs. The only difficulty is with imports.

As effective demand is expanded, economic activity and incomes increase and there is an increased demand for imports for consumption (and for processing into consumption goods). As more of the

[1] A. P. Lerner, *Economics of Employment*, New York, McGraw Hill, 1951.

limited supply of imports are used for this purpose less, will be left for investment. Both the capital bottleneck and the consumption bottleneck thus turn out to be manifestations of the same import bottleneck.

10. The immediate cure is to export more and produce more import substitutes. Here the difficulty is that the *dollar wage* is too high and it is not possible to reduce the dollar wage without reducing the real wage; and the real wage must be maintained at the 'standard' level. (The real wage would have to be reduced much less than the dollar wage, as only the imported elements in the real wage would have to become relatively more expensive; but this does not affect the results.)

As a result of this, employment must be kept down to the minimum 'satisfactory' level as the only remaining way of holding down the volume of imports used for consumption. Without this, enough will not be left for the investment, without which it would not be possible to maintain even the minimum 'satisfactory' level of employment in a future with a smaller import surplus.

(This assumes that the import surplus, in conjunction with other measures for increasing productivity, *will* be enough, while it lasts, to provide the additional investment necessary to induce the required increase in productivity and in international competitiveness. If less than this amount of import surplus will be available there will have to be a cut in the real wage or a reduction in employment below the minimum 'satisfactory' level. On the other hand, if more than this minimum amount of import surplus will be forthcoming, it will be possible either to increase the real wage or the level of employment. There are possibilities, by various devices, of reducing the dollar wage without large reductions in the real wage, thereby increasing exports and alleviating the import bottleneck. This would permit increases in both consumption *and* investment by making use of the unemployed resources. But that would bring one outside the assumptions to which this paper is limited and which give rise to cost inflation and its accompanying problems.)

11. It is often very difficult to decide whether any actual inflation is in fact a cost inflation or a demand inflation. It is possible to argue that prices of goods are rising because the cost of producing them is rising, as well as to argue that the costs are rising because the prices of the products are rising; just as if one sees a car behind a horse and cart very close together going up a hill, one cannot see whether the car is pushing the horse and cart or whether the horse and cart is pulling the car. One has to get closer to see the pressures and tensions involved. It is nevertheless of the greatest importance

to know which it is, since in the two different situations there would be quite different results from similar disturbances. We may consider the effects in the two cases of immigrants bringing foreign capital in with them.

In the case of a demand inflation, with full employment of domestic resources, the capital import would aggravate the inflationary pressure. The capital import does permit imports to be increased by as much as the immigrant can spend. But unless he spends all his money on imports (apart from his saving) there will be an increase in the demand for domestic products. The supply cannot be increased and so the demand inflation is accentuated. The increase in the supply of foreign exchange is then greater than the immigrant's demand for imports, so that there is an improvement in the balance of payments; but this has only long-run and secondary disinflationary effects since it may be absorbed for quite a long time in improving the foreign liquidity and credit position before it is used to cheapen imports sufficiently to draw off all the increase in demand for domestic output. The improvement in the balance of payments may even induce an easing of domestic credit (hardened to check a gold-outflow) which would encourage investment and push the inflation still further.

In the case of a cost inflation where the 'standard' real wage results in capital and consumption import bottlenecks, the immigrant's increased expenditure on domestically produced goods is not inflationary because they, and the productive resources for making them, are not in short supply. He will indeed be spending some of his money on imports, which *are* scarce, but he increases the supply of foreign exchange by the *whole* amount of his capital import. There will therefore be some foreign exchange left over after supplying his demand for imports. This will permit more goods to be imported and alleviate the import bottleneck. To the extent that these additional imports are for current consumption the current cost inflation is alleviated. To the extent that they are directed into investment the capital bottleneck is loosened and the future cost inflation is alleviated.

In short, in a demand inflation the important thing is the effect on the demand for domestic products, and not the increase in the supply of foreign exchange, so that the important result is the increase in demand that aggravates the demand inflation. In a cost inflation the important thing is the effect on the supply of imports and not the increase in the demand for domestic products, so that the important result is the increased availability of foreign exchange that alleviates the cost inflation.

12. *Summary.* There is no necessary *demand inflationary* pressure induced by immigration, or by the capital formation that immigration calls for, if the government holds to a policy of preventing excess demand from developing. A 'cost inflation' can, however, develop even with the most conservative monetary and fiscal policy that is possible in practice, if 'unrealistic' real wage and income standards are strongly established. These are likely to come about where there is a large immigration.

Such a cost inflation is compatible with severe unemployment and non-absorption of immigrants into productive economic activity. It tends to establish an unfavourable balance of payments by which the unemployment and the cost inflation are aggravated in return. There is then a conflict between the measures that would alleviate these difficulties in the short run and those that are necessary for the long-run cure.

It is important to recognize whether an inflation is a cost inflation or a demand inflation because treatments that alleviate one kind of inflation may aggravate the other.

PART II

EMIGRATION COUNTRIES

Chapter 4

GREAT BRITAIN

BY

JULIUS ISAAC

London

SINCE the end of the last world war Great Britain has resumed the traditional function of the motherland of meeting the demand for immigrants from other members of the British Commonwealth. The economic, demographic, social, and political setting for the migration movements which have occurred since 1946 both in Britain and in the receiving countries is significantly different from that which prevailed in any previous period. It seems, therefore, necessary to reassess Britain's emigration potential in the new setting. This involves a brief appraisal of Britain's past experience as a country of emigration as well as an analysis of the impact of the inward and outward movements since the end of the war on the British economy.

I. THE HISTORICAL BACKGROUND

The United Kingdom's classification as a traditional country of emigration is mainly based on migration trends during the century between the end of the Napoleonic wars and the beginning of the First World War. After 1815 the cessation of production for the war effort, a number of bad harvests, and a rapid rise in population — the effect of a heavy fall in mortality and constant high fertility — caused serious population pressure and stimulated emigration to the New World. The outward movement — allowing for heavy annual changes and marked cyclical fluctuations — had an upward trend for the hundred years until the First World War.[1] It is estimated that between 1815 and 1914 over 20 million persons sailed from the United Kingdom (including Ireland) for destinations beyond Europe; about 13 million went to the United States, 4 million to Canada, and 1½ million to Australasia.[2] Until 1906 emigrants from the United

[1] Emigration from Ireland had, after the peak years between 1845 and 1852, a declining trend.

[2] N. H. Carrier and J. R. Jeffery, *External Migration, 1815–1950*, General Register Office, H.M.S.O., London, 1953, p. 33.

Kingdom went mainly to the United States. In every year since 1907 Canada and Australasia taken together have received from the United Kingdom a larger number of immigrants than the United States.

A detailed analysis of the migration trends and of their impact on the economies of sending and receiving countries is very difficult owing to the inadequate statistical information for the whole of the period, particularly for the greater part of the nineteenth century, and is subject to a considerable margin of error. A high rate of natural increase in the United Kingdom was undoubtedly an important factor determining secular migration trends. Deviations from the secular trend since the 1840's are partly accounted for by business-cycle fluctuations. Recent research [1] has stressed the great importance of 'secondary secular movements' with a span of about eighteen to twenty years, and a close correlation has been established between such cycles of economic growth and migration. While, broadly speaking, business-cycle fluctuations had an international character, secondary secular movements in the United Kingdom and the United States were inverse to one another. A rising volume of migration is associated with rising capital exports from Great Britain, with a marked rise in investment and income per head in the United States, and with economic stagnation in the United Kingdom. Diminishing numbers of emigrants are associated with a decline in capital exports and with a rise in investment activities and income per head in the United Kingdom. Nevertheless mass emigration and its concomitant, capital exports, from densely populated and increasingly industrialized Britain to the sparsely populated and underdeveloped new continents, is an essential feature of the pattern of Britain's economic growth during the century which ended with the beginning of the First World War.

British emigration during the inter-war period had three main characteristics : (1) a rapid decline in the total volume of emigration, leading in the second half of the period to a virtual cessation of emigration ; (2) a further concentration on migration within the Commonwealth ; (3) a substantial return movement of former emigrants. The result was a reversal in the net flow of migration between Britain and extra-European countries. From 1931 until the beginning of the Second World War these movements showed a positive balance. Britain had ceased to be a country of emigration. It is beyond the scope of the present paper to discuss in any detail the reasons for this reversal. Undoubtedly, the new countries were

---

[1] Brinley Thomas, *Migration and Economic Growth, a Study of Great Britain and the Atlantic Economy*, Cambridge, 1954.

hit much harder than Britain by the world depression of the 1930's; the traditional countries of immigration adopted a policy of severe restriction. Moreover the declining rate of natural increase, progress in the ageing of the population, and the prospect of a stationary or declining population must have had an adverse effect on the propensity to emigrate from Britain.

II. POSTWAR EMIGRATION FROM BRITAIN

Britain had a leading part in the revival of international migration after the end of the last war. A recent survey of the United Nations Population Division estimates the total volume of emigration from Europe in the eight years 1945–52 at about 4½ million persons. 'The country providing the largest number of emigrants was the United Kingdom with over 1,100,000 persons, or about one-fourth of the European total.'[1] The latter figure refers only to migrants travelling direct by sea between the United Kingdom and ports outside Europe and the Mediterranean Sea;[2] the corresponding figure for the ten years 1945–55 is 1,400,000. The returns do not include emigrants by air (various estimates suggest a deficit of at least 5–6 per cent due to this omission), emigrants via the European Continent to countries outside Europe, and emigrants to the European Continent and to Mediterranean ports. Statistically speaking, *i.e.* including all passengers who intend to leave the United Kingdom for at least one year as emigrants, emigration to the European Continent and the Mediterranean basin has been very substantial. But, as will be argued below, these movements were largely of a temporary nature and are balanced to that extent by a corresponding inward movement. The same applies to the movement between the United Kingdom and the Republic of Ireland. Emigration from the United Kingdom via the Continent to some extra-European countries such as Australia, India, South Africa, and Rhodesia was probably by no means negligible, but does not substantially affect the grand total. The right order of magnitude of the total gross emigration from the United Kingdom to extra-European countries over the years 1945–55 is indicated by an estimate of slightly over 1,500,000 persons.[3]

Some of the main characteristics of this outward movement have

[1] 'A Survey of Intercontinental Migration in the Post-war Period', background paper prepared by the Population Division of the United Nations for the World Population Conference, Rome, September 1954.
[2] No returns are available for 1945, but emigration from the United Kingdom was probably negligible in that year.
[3] Details are discussed in Julius Isaac, *British Post-war Migration*, National Institute of Economic and Social Research, Cambridge University Press, 1954.

to be taken into account in an appraisal of its impact on the British economy.

(1) The annual outflow fluctuated fairly narrowly around the average of 150,000 without indicating a trend. A substantial percentage of the outward movement during the first postwar years was an immediate consequence of the end of the war, and therefore did not recur in subsequent years after the completion of the adjustment. The return movement of British settlers and administrators into countries which had been occupied by the enemy during the war, and the exodus of about 100,000 war brides from the United Kingdom who married members of Dominion and Allied forces and joined their husbands, belong to this category. On the other hand, many intending emigrants had to postpone their plans for years because of the shipping shortage.

(2) A substantial proportion of the total emigration — as a rough guess possibly as much as one-third — consists of 'quasi-permanent' emigrants. They include re-emigrating aliens (about 7 per cent), re-emigrating citizens of the Dominions and British Colonies, and citizens of the United Kingdom leaving Britain temporarily, but for over a year.

(3) Over 80 per cent of the British emigrants went to destinations within the British Commonwealth. A large number benefited from various schemes of assistance, partly financed by the British Government.

(4) Comparisons with a cross-section of the population bring into relief the selective effect of emigration, particularly of assisted migration. Although the average age of the adult postwar emigrants was higher than that of the emigrants between the wars and before 1914,[1] it was markedly lower than that of the population at large. Various occupations which are in short supply in Britain were much more strongly represented among the emigrants than among the population at large.

(5) Capital exports directly associated with emigration appear to have been relatively small.

III. THE EFFECT OF EMIGRATION ON CONDITIONS IN BRITAIN

The discussion under this heading is largely theoretical, since during the postwar period population losses through emigration have

[1] It is noteworthy, reflecting the growing tendency towards family migration, that the percentage of children under 12 years of age among the emigrants appears to have been significantly higher in 1952 and 1953 than in 1912 and 1913.

been compensated to a large extent by population gains through alien immigration. The latter movement, however, is subject to controls by the British Government and has contracted in recent years. Projections of present trends indicate for the next few years a larger negative balance of migration unless immigration into Britain is encouraged or at least less discouraged.

Losses from emigration have been small in numbers relative to the total population, but they have been appreciable in certain adult age groups and relative to the rate of natural increase. Moreover, with regard to quality, the selective process operates against the sending country. The fundamental demographic changes since the peak years of British emigration in the early 1910's — in conjunction with perhaps as profound changes in her socio-economic structure — have made Britain more sensitive to even minor migratory movements, and the question arises whether a sustained negative balance of migration is compatible with the expected course of demographic and socio-economic trends in the near future.

In 1911 Great Britain's population amounted to 40·8 million (463 persons per square mile), in 1953 to 49·2 million (558 persons per square mile). In England and Wales the excess of births over deaths was over 400,000 in 1911 and over 180,000 in 1953 ; an effective reproduction rate of 1·125 in 1911 compares with 1·03 in 1953. The decline in fertility and mortality during that period is reflected in the ageing of the population. The changes are shown in the table below :

POPULATION OF GREAT BRITAIN BY AGE GROUP

	1911	1951	1972 (Estimate) *	Differences	
	Numbers (thousands)			1911–51	1951–72
0–19	15,743	14,040	13,026	− 1703	− 1014
20–44	15,739	17,785	16,842	+ 2046	− 943
45–64	6,570	11,716	13,141	+ 5146	+ 1425
65 +	2,779	5,300	7,479	+ 2539	+ 1979
All ages	40,831	49,841	50,488	+ 9010	+ 647

* Projection No. 8 of the Royal Commission on Population (Base Year 1947) assumption : declining mortality, fertility 5 per cent above 1935/38, migration nil. Bourgeois-Pichat's later calculations for England and Wales envisage the beginning of decline in total numbers as early as between 1960 and 1965 (*Population*, Jan.-Mar. 1953).

While a drastic decline in total numbers (in the absence of emigration) is not likely to occur within the next generation, population projections indicate the transition from slow growth to steadiness and slow decline in the near future. Shifts in the age composition will be marked during the period of transition.

CUMULATIVE GAINS OR LOSSES IN SELECTED AGE GROUPS

Period of Years	1952–1972 (thousands) *	
	Age Group	
	20–44	45–64
1953–1957	– 691	+ 844
1953–1962	– 984	+1232
1953–1967	– 690	+1477
1953–1972	– 320	+1293

* *First Annual Report of the Oversea Migration Board*, July 1954 (Cmd. 9261): the figures include Northern Ireland (total population in 1951: 1·3 million). Base: 31.xii. 1952, declining mortality at a rate different from that underlying the previous table.

The view is widely held that in the past emigration from Britain has been desirable and beneficial from the demographic viewpoint inasmuch as it reduced the high rate of population growth in a country which showed distinct symptoms of overpopulation. Obviously the same diagnosis does not apply to postwar Britain, with its almost negligible rate of natural increase. But is a reduction in total numbers still desirable? Would Britain be 'better off' if it were less densely populated? The Economic Committee of the Royal Commission on Population has discussed at great length the issue of stationary or declining versus increasing numbers and their effect on the standard of life and national welfare in Britain. Their verdict is: 'If we assume that employment policy is only moderately successful we are led by our analysis to conclude that for Great Britain to-day the balance of economic advantage is strongly in favour of more or less stationary numbers as compared with increasing numbers. . . . For us with our high population density, our industrial development, our dependence on overseas supplies of food and materials, and the loss of our former creditor position the considerations relating to capital and the balance of payments possess great force. From a purely economic standpoint, we have good reason, we believe, to welcome the prospect that the number of people in this island will soon cease to grow.[1] . . . There is a fairly clear presumption that a smaller aggregate of population, as such, would be advantageous from a strictly economic standpoint. On the

[1] *Report of the Economics Committee* (Royal Commission on Population, London, 1950), p. 52.

70

other hand, the process of decline, through which a smaller aggregate would be reached, would create problems and might entail net disadvantages.' [1]

In their conclusions the Committee suggest: 'So long as Britain has a birth-rate below replacement level, the maintenance of a large flow of emigration is neither practicable nor desirable. On the other hand the arguments for allowing a substantial immigration would acquire increased force if the population were tending to decline.' [2]

The birth-rate, though falling, has remained slightly above re-placement level during the whole of the postwar period. Political developments since the completion of the report and further progress in the production of nuclear weapons have given more substance to the argument in favour of emigration and dispersal on strategic grounds. Misgivings about the adverse trend of the terms of trade and about sufficient outlets for British exports appear to be justified, and emigration might be regarded as a counteracting factor. On the other hand, inflation in conjunction with over-full employment, rising levels of consumption, and inadequate internal mobility have pro-duced serious manpower shortage in essential industries and occupa-tions, which has been accentuated by emigration.

It has been pointed out above that the losses from emigration have been largely compensated, particularly during the first post-war years, through corresponding gains from immigration. Thus Britain so far has been spared the experience of a declining active population. It is hardly possible to show whether the 'law of diminishing returns' with regard to manpower input is applicable to Britain's postwar economy as a whole or — partly for different reasons — to verify the validity of the economic arguments for or against the promotion of emigration from Britain.

In theory emigration from Britain is free, *i.e.* virtually nobody who wants to leave the country for good is prevented from doing so. Nevertheless the volume of emigration from postwar Britain has been controlled to a considerable extent by government policy. Certain restrictions deal with the transfer of emigrants' funds to hard-currency countries. Available evidence indicates that relatively few would-be emigrants were affected by such measures,[3] but there can be little doubt that they were and still are necessary in view of Britain's precarious balance of payments.

Apart from these restrictive measures which affected mainly emigration to the United States and Canada, British emigration policy has been concerned with the encouragement of emigration

---

[1] *Ibid.* p. 56.   [2] *Ibid.* p. 59.   [3] See J. Isaac, *op. cit.*

within the British Commonwealth. This meant the revival of a policy which had become impracticable and had to be discontinued under the impact of the depression of the 1930's. Soon after the end of the war schemes came into operation providing free fares and priority passages to Australia for Empire ex-members of the forces and their dependants and passage assistance for other British emigrants selected by the Australian immigration authorities. The United Kingdom took full financial responsibility for the free passages and refunded to the Australian Government a varying proportion of the expenditure for the assisted scheme. So far 50 per cent of the 416,000 British postwar immigrants into Australia (up to June 1954) have benefited from these schemes. The proportion of these who would not have emigrated at all in the absence of such schemes is probably considerable.

The other Dominions did not require financial assistance from the United Kingdom for their efforts to attract immigrants from Britain, but the British Government is giving them invaluable assistance in the work connected with the recruiting and selecting of suitable applicants.[1] It set up in 1953 an 'Oversea Migration Board' as an advisory body on 'schemes of emigration from the United Kingdom to other Commonwealth countries' and similar matters.

The wisdom of this policy has been questioned, since it tends to exacerbate present manpower shortages and unfavourable features of the demographic trend. But it is held that, at a time when Australia, New Zealand, Canada, and other members of the Commonwealth are making great efforts to attract suitable immigrants, Britain cannot relinquish by default the traditional function of the motherland — the peopling of the new territories. The countries concerned by no means entirely rely on Britain for the supply of their immigrants — about 50 per cent of their postwar intake has come from non-British countries — but they have misgivings that a further contraction in the British element among the newcomers might give rise to serious problems of integration and assimilation and eventually endanger their present way of life. Such a development might adversely affect the cohesion of the Commonwealth and Britain's position as its focal point. To that extent a drastic decline in the proportion of British settlers among the immigrants to the Dominions might weaken Britain's economic and political position.

[1] As a result of this co-operation the Dominion authorities in selecting their immigrants are taking into account to some extent British requests to avoid so far as possible concentration on certain occupations and selected age groups.

IV. POSTWAR IMMIGRATION INTO THE UNITED KINGDOM

It has been suggested above that the total volume of emigration from the United Kingdom in 1945–54 amounted roughly to slightly over 1,500,000 persons. Estimates of the corresponding figure of immigration are subject to an even wider margin of error, but a figure of 1,250,000 would probably indicate the right order of magnitude. Four main categories may be distinguished.

(1) *Former British Emigrants returning to Britain.*—Outward movements as a rule generate smaller movements in the opposite direction, consisting of disappointed emigrants admitting failure, successful emigrants who prefer to return for retirement to the home country, and a large number of 'quasi-permanent' emigrants who return in accordance with their original plans. In addition to this 'normal' return movement, there was during the first postwar years the backlog from the war years. The withdrawal of British settlers, business men, administrators, etc., in connexion with political changes during and after the war from countries such as India, Pakistan, Ceylon, Palestine, Egypt, and China, has also temporarily added to the numbers in this category.

(2) *Immigrants from the Commonwealth.*—This group includes citizens of the Dominions taking up appointments in Britain or coming for study or professional training. Many return eventually to their home countries. The inflow of British subjects of non-European origin from other parts of the Commonwealth and Empire, particularly from the West Indies and West Africa, has substantially increased in recent years. An appreciable proportion are students with grants from various official sources. The majority are semi- or unskilled workers without any financial reserves. Their absorption is giving rise to some friction, although the effective demand for the type of work for which they are suitable greatly exceeds the supply.

(3) *Immigrants from the Republic of Ireland.*—An appreciable part of this movement has a 'quasi-permanent' character. The total inward movement (excluding seasonal workers) amounted on the average to about 25,000 persons a year. Domestic work and semi- or unskilled work in various industries are the main occupations of the Irish immigrants in Britain.

(4) *Alien Immigrants, mainly from the European Continent.*—This has been the main source of immigration during the postwar years. An analysis of the components shows that the admittance of the

great majority is closely connected with the impact of the war. Members of the Polish forces who had fought under British command and did not want to return to their home country account for about 115,000. A total of 24,000 German, Ukrainian, and Italian prisoners of war were allowed to stay as civilians. The British Government recruited some 90,000 displaced persons and other refugees as 'European Voluntary Workers'. Certain conditions were attached to their admission for a period of three years with a prospect of being admitted as permanent residents after the termination of their contract. A proportion of the above groups have emigrated to the United States and other 'new' countries or have returned, but it seems that the great majority have become permanently settled in Britain. Several government schemes concerned with the recruitment of Italians for work in the mines and other essential industries had to be discontinued because of the opposition of organized labour. Since 1951 the recruitment of foreign workers has been left entirely to private initiative. Labour permits of limited duration are granted to prospective employers for the employment of individual aliens provided that they can show that the vacancy cannot be filled by residents in Britain. On the average over 30,000 such permits, mainly for domestic service, are granted every year. The permits are frequently extended, but a relatively small proportion remain as permanent residents. Other groups of some numerical importance are the alien brides of members of the British forces stationed on the Continent and alien relatives of residents in Britain who are admitted on compassionate grounds.

It should be noted that the first three categories have the right of free entry, and are not subject to restrictions with regard to work or residence; only the numbers and composition of the new arrivals in the alien category are controlled by the Government.[1]

V. THE EFFECT OF IMMIGRATION ON CONDITIONS IN BRITAIN

Particularly in the first postwar years humanitarian motives played some part in British immigration policy, and to that extent the material returns to be expected from the admission of deserving would-be immigrants were of secondary importance. Nevertheless, although only about half of the total postwar intake has been selected by the receiving country and the principles of selection have been

[1] Citizens of the Republic of Ireland are not regarded as aliens.

fairly liberal, it seems that the postwar immigration of about $1\frac{1}{4}$ million immigrants (gross figure) has brought considerable benefits to Britain. From the demographic and economic point of view it offered a welcome compensation — at least partly — for the losses from British emigration to other parts of the Commonwealth. The occupational composition of the immigrants was significantly different from that of the emigrants. On balance Britain probably lost mainly highly skilled workers and members of the professions, the managerial class, etc., and may have gained unskilled and semi-skilled workers in industry and agriculture. Under the prevailing conditions of economic expansion, over-full employment and inflation, the new-comers could be fully absorbed.[1] Productivity in agriculture, transport, and other essential industries is still adversely affected by many vacancies which — partly owing to lack of internal occupational and geographical mobility — cannot be adequately filled at the present wage level without recourse to foreign labour.

VI. TRENDS IN THE NEAR FUTURE

Britain may have become less attractive as a country of immigration for European workers than it was immediately after the war ; the displaced persons have been resettled and a high rate of economic growth in Europe reduces the propensity to emigrate. It may therefore become more difficult in the near future to recruit suitable immigrants from the European Continent. But a much greater problem is whether in the long run a sustained inflow of immigrants is likely to raise productivity, standards of living, and economic and social welfare in Britain.

Unless there are unforeseeable set-backs in the economic development of the 'new' Dominions, they will welcome immigrants from Britain and, in spite of adverse demographic trends, there will be a steady, if perhaps contracting, outward movement from Britain to the Dominions. The experience of the last ten years seems to indicate that on balance a declining or stationary population trend, particularly if enhanced through a negative balance of migration, is undesirable, that the expected advantages from smaller numbers and lower density are outweighed by the advantages of slow growth. But the projection of this experience into the future is subject to important qualifications. In any case, Britain is not likely to remain

---

[1] But the 1953 recession in the Lancashire textile industry hit new immigrants harder than old residents. A minority returned to their home countries, the rest found employment in other industries.

the leading country of emigration; the Dominions, if they want to maintain or raise their present intake, may have to rely to a somewhat greater extent on non-British immigrants. In contrast to France, however, Britain is not likely to become a major country of immigration.

Chapter 5

EIRE

BY

J. F. MEENAN
Dublin

IT is hardly too much to say that emigration has been the special characteristic of the Irish economy. During the last hundred years it has outweighed all other economic factors. It has also influenced the framing of national policy since self-government was regained in 1922.

The historical background may be stated briefly. There was a considerable and continuous emigration in the eighteenth and early nineteenth centuries; at first to the Continent and to the American colonies, later to the newly created United States and to Great Britain. The causes were at first both political and economic; by the end of the eighteenth century the latter factor had become predominant. At this time, emigration did not prevent an increase of population which, beginning in the middle of the eighteenth century, continued until the 1840's. The census of 1841, the first reliable enumeration, returned the population of the present Republic of Ireland at 6,529,000. For a variety of reasons this population was heavily dependent on the land, and in particular on the potato, for its subsistence; in its turn, that dependence assisted the growth in the number of small-holdings and facilitated a further, if insecurely based, growth in the rural population. A succession of failures of the potato crop in 1845 and succeeding years undermined the basis of this society and drove its members overseas, principally to the United States, thus commencing the American emigration which was to last until the depression of the early 1930's. This emigration was on a scale hitherto unknown, and far exceeded the natural increase of population. At the census of 1851 the population was 5,112,000; by 1871 it had fallen to 4,053,000. The trend since then is shown in Table I.

Thus emigration came to be inseparably associated with the loss of population. The Irish population was the only one in Europe to decrease during the last hundred years. Emigration therefore has

rarely been regarded in Ireland as a beneficial force. Equally its
function has rarely been dispassionately assessed. In the popular
mind, its causes were soon linked with the exceptional dependence
upon agriculture and thus, by an easy transition, with the political
and other obstacles that hindered the development of other forms
of production. It was long accepted that industrialization would
reduce, if not end, emigration; that therefore industrialization should
be pursued as soon as an Irish government had the power to impose
protective tariffs. The ending of emigration, therefore, came to be
taken as the major aim of economic policy rather than the creation
of wealth or the increase of efficiency. It is only lately that these
traditional assumptions have been re-examined; that it is seen that

TABLE I

EIRE: NATURAL INCREASE AND NET EMIGRATION, 1881–1951

Year	Interval	Population	Natural Increase	Net Emigration	Decrease (−) or Increase (+) of Population
		(thousands)			
1881	1871–81	3870	318	501	− 183
1891	1881–91	3469	196	597	− 401
1901	1891–1901	3222	149	396	− 247
1911	1901–11	3140	179	261	− 82
1926	1911–26 *	2972	237	405	− 168
1936	1926–36	2968	163	166	− 3
1946	1936–46	2955	174	187	− 13
1951	1946–51 †	2960	125	120	+ 5

* 15-year period; no census was taken in 1921.
† Five-year period.

industrialization may create as many problems as it solves, and
that, above all, it is possible that emigration will continue while
the population remains stable. In Table I it will be seen that the
population has remained relatively steady since 1911 when allowance
has been made for the changes consequent on the dissolution of the
union with Great Britain in 1922. But that stability has been the
result of growth in the natural increase rather than of a fall in emigration. These matters have been greatly clarified by the findings of a
Commission on Population Trends which was set up in 1948 and
presented its report in 1954. But the removal of concepts that have
become almost instinctive is a slow business.

The principal features of Irish emigration have not changed
greatly in the hundred years since the famine of the 1840's. At all
times it has been the result of a movement from the countryside.

Statistics of comparatively recent date, covering the period 1943–51, show that 68 per cent of intending emigrants came from rural areas, 13 per cent from Dublin and its environs, and 19 per cent from the urban areas. The occupations of emigrants reflect their origin; apart from a proportion of professional workers, the bulk of the movement is composed of agricultural workers and of girls going into domestic service or, more recently, into factory work. The trend has become even more noticeable in the postwar years, which have witnessed a heavy fall in the number of people engaged on the land; thus, the number of males in farm work has fallen from 537,000

TABLE II

OCCUPATIONAL DISTRIBUTION OF PERSONS AT WORK, 1926–51

(thousands)

	1926	1936	1951	Percentage Decrease (–) or Increase (+) 1926–51
Agriculture	647	609	500	– 22·7
Industry	164	206	268	+ 63·4
Commerce and finance	114	127	144	+ 26·3
Personal service	127	122	104	– 18·1
Administration, defence	76	78	93	+ 22·4
Professions	39	44	55	+ 41·0
Transport, etc.	39	38	47	+ 20·5
Other	14	11	21	+ 50·0
Total	1220	1235	1232	+ 1·0

in 1938 to 500,000 in 1948 and to 421,000 in 1954, though the pace of this movement has been slowed down recently.

There is not, perhaps, anything unusual in these figures; the movement from the countryside to the cities, and from agriculture to industry and services, has been experienced in all countries. Historically, however, the absence of industrial development in Ireland meant that migration from the land involved emigration. People went to the cities; but these cities have been in the United States and, nowadays, in the United Kingdom rather than in Ireland. The last thirty years have witnessed an expansion in the opportunities for non-agricultural employment at home; but this expansion has been offset by the drift from the land, and the total number of people at work has remained virtually unchanged.

Other aspects of emigration have been more unusual. The vast majority of emigrants have always come from the younger age groups. This condition seems to have obtained at all times since the famine and it has not been affected by the change in the direction of emigration, in the last twenty-five years, from the United States to the United Kingdom. To take the American emigration first: in the year 1880 54·4 per cent of emigrants were aged between 15 and 24 and a further 27·3 per cent between 25 and 44. In the year 1920 the comparable proportions were 62 per cent and 26·1 per cent. The emigration to the United Kingdom shows the same characteristics. Of the men who emigrated thither between 1945 and 1951, 65·9 per cent were aged between 16 and 29, while 83·8 per cent of the women were in the same age group. In the overwhelming majority of cases, these emigrants were unmarried.

Another feature is unusual; the fact that female emigrants have normally outnumbered male emigrants. This was first remarked soon after the famine. It has continued since unchanged, except in the period of the last war. In 1920 United States immigration returns showed that for every hundred female immigrants from Ireland there were 78 males, a preponderance unparalleled in the case of any other country except Canada. More recently, in the period 1946–51, 1397 women emigrated for every 1000 men.

This has been considered to be the result of the lack of opportunity for female employment in Ireland. It also reflects the nature of Irish emigration, which has been described as 'a movement from the known to the known'. What is meant is that Irish emigrants as a body have not been pioneers into unfamiliar countries. They have tended rather to go to where their relatives had preceded them. Even when the famine of the 1840's was still in progress, it was noted that the first care of Irish immigrants in the United States was to save money to pay the passage fares of members of their families whom they had left behind. Throughout the period of the American emigration these close ties between brothers and sisters or cousins on either side of the Atlantic remained unweakened. The intending emigrant was furnished with the passage money by a relative who had already emigrated; he or she was met on arrival and speedily placed in employment. In these circumstances, emigration to New York or Boston was much less of a journey into unknown territory than looking for work in an Irish city. At the beginning of this century Sir Horace Plunkett wrote that in Ireland children are born with their faces to the west. More lately a writer in the Irish language has recounted how he proposed to make the easy journey to New York and, being frustrated by the depression, sought a living in Dublin with reluctance and dislike of going among strangers. It seems that much the same characteristics have already appeared in the emigration to Great Britain.

They are, it may be said, the results of the quite exceptional mobility of the Irish people. For the greater part of the last century and a half, they have been free to emigrate without hindrance or limitation to Great Britain, to the British dominions and colonies, and to the United States. The American quota for immigration from Ireland was not imposed until 1921. Except for war time regulation between 1939 and 1952 there has been no restriction whatever on movement between the Republic and the United Kingdom. Not even documents of identity are required.

This freedom has the paradoxical result that, in the absence of regulation, statistics of emigration are incomplete and can be checked only from a comparison of census returns. The major paradox, however, may be felt by others to be that a people who have such enviable freedom of movement, as might be thought in other countries, should account emigration as a national evil. But in this feeling there is a clear conflict between the view of the individual and that of the community. For the one, emigration offers the opportunity of enjoying a better standard of living and wider opportunities ; for the other, emigration weakens the striving after the improvement of conditions at home. It should be added that in the past emigrants to the United States did not return to live in Ireland. Whether they prospered or not, they remained in the New World. It is too soon yet to decide if the same will be true of the emigration to Great Britain; the indications are that it will be.

A further point may now be apparent : that Irish emigration has some self-perpetuating features. In each generation it is a movement of the younger sons and daughters. It is not an emigration of whole families and it never has been, except perhaps at the time of the famine. If it had been such, it might well have come to an end decades ago when the removal of families had led to a redistribution of farm holdings and the establishment of a new rural equilibrium. As things are, emigration enables those who are left to marry and rear families whose members will in their turn seek a living abroad. Certainly this is not all the story : a vicious circle is created whereby emigration causes underdevelopment, which in its turn leads to further emigration. Nevertheless, the persistence of emigration is not wholly the result of economic conditions in Ireland.

In the past, Irish economists have distinguished between the forces of 'push' and the forces of 'pull'. Under the first heading may be ranged those forces that drove people out of the country, such as the agrarian struggles of the last century with their accompaniment of evictions, or the simple lack of opportunities for employment. Under the second may be ranked such forces as close ties with those who have already found a living abroad, or the comparison of living standards with those to be found in the United States or the United Kingdom. It is not irrelevant to recall that the Irish people are placed between the two great labour markets of the world ; and they tend to take their standards of what constitutes an acceptable standard of living from what has been attained in rich and highly industrialized countries. The forces of 'push' have been greatly weakened, in modern times, particularly since the end of the struggle over land tenure in the closing decades of the last century. But the forces of 'pull' seem, if anything, to have been strengthened.

This reinforcement has taken place in spite of a vigorous policy of industrialization through protective tariffs in the last twenty-five years. It is difficult to see how this policy can profitably be pressed any further. The implication is therefore that, failing any spectacular development, the number of opportunities for employment in industry and commerce cannot be expected to increase at any comparable rate in the next couple of decades. The matter is governed by the rate of remuneration which is acceptable ; and a people that has such easy access to the British labour market does not pitch its demands low. The pace of economic development might well be quicker if the Irish people were forced to make the best of their own resources ; but that necessity has not arisen. If mobility were lost the pace of economic life would have to be quickened, but as long as it exists no one will think it wrong to emigrate in search of a better living.

In the postwar years these less obvious factors have received increasing attention ; and there is now discernible a tendency to frame economic policy in order to create wealth rather than to provide employment. There is a greater realization that if the economy is right, everything else will fall into place ; and that, even though emigration may continue, the population may be maintained on at least a stable level. It is, of course, always possible that agricultural depression in Ireland or exceptional prosperity abroad may lead to a fresh period of population loss. But at least it is now more widely understood that emigration is more deeply rooted than was assumed. 'In Irish conditions', the writer has remarked in his report on Population Trends, 'the ending of emigration is a much more complex problem than it would be in a country that simply suffered from underdevelopment. Essentially this is a small state with a comparatively high fertility rate, living (by no means as well as it might) by agricultural production. Its political and economic boundaries do not coincide. Its people have access to two great industrial countries where, with lower fertility rates, there is a demand for labour. In such circumstances it would be phenomenal if there was not emigration.'[1]

Table I shows that the present stability of population is the result of a greater natural increase rather than of any fall in emigration. In conclusion, therefore, something should be said of Irish vital statistics. These bristle with peculiarities which, however, can be explained by local conditions. In the first place the marriage rate is, and always has been, quite exceptionally low. The highest rate recorded since registration began in 1864 has been 5·91 per thousand population. This is to some extent the reflection of a predominantly rural community which, ever since the famine, has been chary of subdividing its holdings of land. Marriages have been few, and late. This tendency has persisted independently of the fluctuations of emigration. Irish birth control, it might be said, is achieved by celibacy. In recent years, however, there has been some change. The average annual marriage rate was 4·8 in 1921–30; it has been 5·3 in 1950–54. In the main, this seems due to growing urbanization. It must also owe something to the fact that the fall in the numbers on the land has occurred in the category of 'assisting relatives', thus leaving the owner of the holding more free to marry at an earlier age.

If the marriage rate is exceptionally low, the fertility rate is exceptionally high. It has indeed fallen by some 19 per cent since its peak in 1910–12. But it is by far the highest in a table drawn up by the Commission on Population Trends which includes eighteen European and five extra-European states. The contrast is most striking. As the Commission goes on to remark: 'The combination of the two extremes — high fertility per married woman and low proportion of married women — tends to give for the population as a whole a birth-rate which is about the general average'.[2] It also has increased in recent years; from an average of 19·3 in 1931–40 to 21·3 in 1950–54.

The result, when coupled with a falling death-rate, is to augment the natural increase. This natural increase, it is recognized, may in its turn lead to an increased emigration in the later 1960's. But it is now better realized than before that the low rate and lateness of marriage is at least as great a demographic weakness as the loss of population through emigration. An improvement in the marriage

---

[1] *Reports of the Commission on Emigration and other Population Problems,* Dublin Stationery Office, 1955, Pr. 2541, Second Minority Report, par. 11, p. 371.

[2] *Ibid.,* Majority Report, par. 198, p. 92.

rate should create a happier and more confident society; it should also supply the missing incentives to economic improvement. Possibly more families and more children will mean more emigrants hereafter; but their existence may provide the conditions for a stable and later an expanding population.

These questions are for the future to answer. It cannot be claimed that the demographic problems which Ireland inherited from the nineteenth century are yet within sight of solution. But, as we hope, they are now perhaps better understood than they were; and that is the first step in progress.

Chapter 6

ITALY

BY

G. PARENTI

Florence University

I

OFFICIAL statistics on emigration have existed in Italy only since 1876. The data available, however, are rather unreliable because of the uncertain definition of the term 'migrant' and because of the rough methods of collection. There are no data on emigrants returning prior to 1902, and only from 1921 on emigrants returning from Europe and from the Mediterranean area (continental migration).

It is not possible here to analyse the technical aspects of Italian migration statistics; [1] it will suffice to draw the reader's attention to the approximate nature of the data in Table I. They show clearly a steadily rising trend from 1876–80 to 1911–15, both for continental migration and, to a greater extent, for migrants overseas.

A notable feature of this trend is the increasing proportion of migrants from the southern provinces, rising from 22 per cent of the oversea movement in 1876 to 70 per cent in 1913. This reached a peak in 1909–13 of 33·6, 33·5, and 29·1 per thousand inhabitants respectively from Calabria, Abruzzo-Molise, and Basilicata. Continental migration, which is for the most part temporary or seasonal, comes mainly from the northern provinces, particularly from Veneto, which has consistently sent to Europe over twenty per thousand inhabitants, with peaks of thirty to thirty-five per thousand.

The First World War halted this development. After two prominent peaks in 1920 and 1924 there was a steady decline until the eve of the Second World War. This fall is less noticeable in the annual averages in Table I because of a slight peak for the years

[1] For a fairly detailed analysis of the methods by which statistics of Italian migratory movements before 1927 were established see *International Migrations*, vol. ii, National Bureau of Economic Research, New York, 1931, pp. 440 ff. Since 1928, when the special emigrant's passport was abolished, those considered as emigrants were those who went abroad with a work contract or who were invited by relatives already resident in a foreign country and in employment in that country. A similar criterion, although a little less restrictive, was also applied after 1946. I.L.O., *Year Book of Labour Statistics*, 1949.

Emigration Countries

1936–37 and the beginning of the transfer of Italian workers to Germany under the Axis policy (almost 300,000 in the years 1940–41). Between 1876 and 1900 emigration was made up of individual

TABLE I

ITALIAN EMIGRATION, 1876–1954 *

Years	European	Overseas	Total	Per 1000 of Population	
				Emigrants	Emigrants returning
1876–80	82,201	26,596	108,797	3·90	..
1881–85	95,146	58,995	154,141	5·36	..
1886–90	90,694	131,005	221,699	7·43	..
1891–95	109,067	147,444	256,511	8·31	..
1896–1900	148,534	161,901	310,435	9·72	..
1901–1905	244,808	309,242	554,050	16·82	4·14 †
1906–10	257,594	393,694	651,288	19·09	5·89 †
1911–15	243,535	305,077	548,612	15·46	5·55 †
1916–20	95,754	121,247	217,001	5·96	1·30 †
1921–25	172,360	130,904	303,264	7·87	3·72
1926–30 $\{(a)$	137,645	89,768	227,413	5·66	3·70
1926–30 $\{(b)$	122,872	89,373	212,245	5·28	3·29
1930–35	63,447	28,181	91,628	2·19	1·60
1936–40	64,472	19,729	84,201	1·92	1·44
1946	53,709	7,076	60,785	1·32	0·13
1947	82,605	60,143	142,748	3·11	0·53
1948	89,038	110,146	199,184	4·31	0·71
1949	60,529	154,083	214,612	4·62	0·57
1950	19,114	140,198	159,312	3·41	0·66
1951	64,491	135,296	199,787	4·24	0·83
1952	57,530	131,625	189,155	4·00	0·53
1953	31,483	106,880	138,363	2·91	0·63
1954	22,562	138,744	161,306	3·38	0·71

* The figures for 1876–1940 are yearly averages.

Up to 1913 those who in general left in adverse conditions were considered as emigrants ; from 1914 to 1946 manual workers (and from 1928, also intellectual workers) and those who went to join relatives who had already emigrated ; from 1947, those who went abroad to follow a profession, art, or trade or to establish their residence there.

Continental migration includes movements to countries in Europe and in the Mediterranean area.

Up to 1925 the data were compiled on the basis of passports issued to those who had expressed their intention of emigrating ; from 1927 to 1946, for European countries on the basis of emigration coupons collected at the frontier posts, and for oversea countries on the basis of ships' manifests completed through the coupons. From 1947 on, data recorded in this table were compiled for oversea migration from the ships' manifests ; for continental migration from figures estimated by the Ministry of Foreign Affairs on the basis of data relating only to assisted emigration to European countries with which Italy has emigration agreements ; these figures do not include seasonal migration.

Statistical records of emigrants returning from European countries have only been kept since 1921 ; after 1946 the remarks concerning emigrants also apply to those returning from these countries.

† The percentages of emigrants returning refer only to oversea migration.

(*a, b*) Because of varying criteria for collecting data after 1927, separate annual averages are given for the periods 1926–27 (*a*) and 1928–30 (*b*).

and family movements which were free and unplanned, though encouraged by shipping companies and private recruiting agents through propaganda which was often deceitful. In 1901, with the establishment of a General Emigration Agency, Italy adopted a policy of sponsorship and assistance for migrants. After the First World War every effort was made to encourage as many as possible to emigrate, in spite of the backlog resulting in some areas from the sudden interruption of migration to the United States which had followed the Immigration Acts of 1921 and 1924; in 1927 the Emigration Agency was abolished, and there was a tendency to discourage emigration, particularly to oversea countries. The Government suspended its activities in the field of migration, aiming rather to protect national communities already existing abroad in order to make them aware of their origin and to strengthen their links with the mother country.

II

The first movements to be resumed after the paralysing effects of the Second World War were those of continental migration. In Italy productive activity was slow to recover, whereas in other European countries reconstruction and the need to meet the pent-up demand for capital and consumer goods, and the difficulty of re-directing national manpower to certain heavy jobs after the war, helped to create a demand for labour which could not be satisfied internally. Reconversion of industry in these countries, however, had caused some frictional unemployment which, in view of housing and food difficulties and the prevailing policies of trade unions, did not allow them to open their doors to uncontrolled immigration. This resulted in a strictly selective policy, which tended to admit into the country only workers who were essential — or were so considered — to the smooth development of productive activity. Like other emigration countries which needed to find new fields of employment for an increasing population, Italy had to submit to that policy; she was even led actively to foster it by establishing Ministry of Labour machinery (pre-selection procedures, emigration centres, etc.), to assist the work of the foreign recruiting missions. This made it possible, in some instances, through the good relations established with these missions, to direct recruitment towards localities or industries where a reduction of manpower was essential for economic development or the resumption of normal productivity.

The statistics show a general increase in continental migration up to 1948, followed by a decline which continued until 1954 (see

Table I). These data are approximate and relate almost exclusively to what is termed 'organized migration', carried out with the active participation of the Italian government authorities [1] and nearly always under bilateral agreements (as in the case of France, Belgium, and, on a small scale, Luxembourg, the Netherlands, Sweden, Czechoslovakia, and Poland) or under administrative arrangements (as in the case of the United Kingdom).

To the figures in Table I should be added those for seasonal migration, mainly to Switzerland, which in the years 1947–54 were as follows : [2]

1947	108,360		1951	141,858
1948	140,800		1952	163,542
1949	91,512		1953	175,853
1950	93,150		1954	153,104

A characteristic of postwar continental migration — which is partly due to the selective policy followed by immigration countries in granting labour permits — is the small number of emigrants who return to their home country ; this is particularly true of movements to countries which promote plans for family reunion ; these plans are frequently carried out with financial aid from the immigration country (France, Belgium), or with the assistance of the Italian Ministry of Labour (in the case of the United Kingdom). In France, out of a total of approximately 170,000 non-seasonal migrants (1946–1954), about 17,000 families, totalling about 46,000 persons, were assisted in resettlement. In Belgium and England in the period 1953–54 there were respectively 3340 and 2325 migrant workers and 8025 and 1774 assisted dependants.

Among the features of postwar continental migration are the following : a slight but steady increase in the proportion of workers migrating from the south, and in particular from Umbria, Marche, Abruzzo, and Puglie ; and a relatively large number of agricultural and construction workers — except for the period 1946–47, during which haphazard reconversion in Italy resulted in the emigration of a number of metal engineering specialists who are very scarce.

It is interesting to note how the occupational pattern of migration

[1] As far as possible, the data also include the 'regularization' of clandestine migrants who, in some countries and under certain circumstances, are granted the same administrative status as normal 'organized' migrants. It is possible, however, that the data given in Table I for continental migration are lower than the actual figures.

[2] The data shown in the text are supplied by the Ministry of Foreign Affairs ; in the cases of France and Austria (only 300 individuals), these are assisted migrants recruited under seasonal contracts through the office of Italian emigration centres ; in the case of Switzerland the data were collected when the Italian Legation in Bern validated the labour contracts.

movements to European countries — and overseas — varies both according to the region of origin and according to the region and country of destination. Space does not allow a detailed analysis of this aspect of the problem and we shall merely refer to Table II, which shows the distribution of emigrants by occupational groups and by regions of origin. That table relates only to 'emigrants for the first time' (see note at the foot of Table II) ; thus the totals do not correspond to those given in Table I.

As regards the countries of destination it may be said that, of approximately 250,000 emigrants to France during the period 1946–1954, the largest groups were for the farming and cattle-raising industry (about one-fifteenth), the building industry (about one-eighth), mining (one-tenth), and engineering (about one-fifteenth) ; of 177,000 emigrants to Belgium, nearly all went to work in the coal-mining industry : the 38,000 emigrants to Great Britain were mainly skilled and unskilled labourers for a wide range of manufacturing industries, from textiles to chemicals, from engineering to construction industries. As regards seasonal migration, in the case of France this relates mainly to the agricultural sector (in particular beetroot-growing), whereas Switzerland mainly takes workers for the building, agricultural, and hotel industries.[1]

III

Oversea migration began to recover in 1947 and a peak was reached in 1949. After that year the number of migrants to Argentina, which in 1947–49 had absorbed more than half the total outflow, began to decline, partly because the capacity of the numerous Italian communities in Latin America to take in new settlers became exhausted and partly because of a deterioration in economic conditions. After 1949 other currents became more marked ; migratory movements to Venezuela, Australia, Canada, and Brazil, which in the five years 1950–54 reached an annual average of nineteen, eighteen, nineteen, and thirteen thousand persons respectively, came to account for more than half of the total emigration overseas.

Unlike continental migration, only a small proportion of oversea migration can be considered as 'organized' ; with the exception of a small number of recruited workers who emigrated to Argentina and Brazil under agreements concluded respectively in 1948 and 1950, only the 'assisted' migrants under the agreement between

[1] The data for France were provided by the Office Nationale d'Immigration (ONI) ; in the case of the other countries the figures were estimated by the Italian Ministry of Labour.

Emigrants aged 14 and over (Emigrating for the First Time)

(a) to European countries.

Region		Agricultural Workers	Workmen and	
			Total	Miners
Piemonte	a	739	3,775	137
	b	699	2,283	18
Valle d' Aosta	a	47	2,096	14
	b	—	37	—
Lombardia	a	9,131	24,035	1,387
	b	940	2,892	49
Trentino A. Adige	a	416	4,646	47
	b	192	1,346	16
Veneto	a	47,124	32,150	4,935
	b	3,966	9,853	152
Friuli-V. Giulia	a	5,969	13,228	1,423
	b	2,092	6,565	71
Trieste	a	10	164	8
	b	31	265	—
Liguria	a	207	1,888	123
	b	269	1,444	6
Emilia Romagna	a	7,785	11,393	1,925
	b	782	3,597	15
Toscana	a	1,177	5,044	375
	b	712	3,689	28
Umbria	a	219	2,353	430
	b	134	925	94
Marche	a	458	5,067	1,480
	b	2,245	2,634	11
Lazio	a	1,112	3,784	496
	b	4,893	8,386	70
Abruzzi & Molise	a	3,678	11,572	2,012
	b	18,122	19,147	107
Campania	a	5,549	6,078	359
	b	14,637	15,904	87
Puglia	a	1,832	8,089	2,745
	b	3,478	8,803	44
Basilicata	a	413	687	410
	b	3,488	3,087	50
Calabria	a	2,222	2,661	621
	b	22,823	13,094	211
Sicilia	a	1,427	5,962	1,862
	b	11,190	13,731	125
Sardegna	a	183	2,514	53
	b	329	280	11
Not indicated	a	13	38	1
	b	10	25	—
ITALY	a	89,711	147,223	20,843
	b	91,032	117,991	1,165
Total		180,743	265,214	22,008

Source : Central Statistical Institute (unpublished data). Data given in the table refer to persons emigrating for the first time ; they are collected on the basis of statistical coupons included in passports since 1950 and detached by the frontier police. A detailed classification such as that given in this table can only be com-

(b) To oversea countries.

raftsmen		Contractors, Managers and Employees	Non-professional Persons*	Total	
Masons	Mechanics			No.	‰†
941	343	405	690	5,609	1·59
308	518	541	2,151	5,674	1·61
10	4	6	32	2,181	22·95
2	7	2	28	67	0·70
6,362	1,174	1,091	3,911	37,568	5·72
414	615	446	2,288	6,566	1·00
212	51	127	662	5,851	8·02
60	91	62	469	2,069	2·83
5,722	650	599	6,005	85,878	21·95
1,949	1,758	682	7,245	21,746	5·56
7,592	478	266	5,622	25,085	27·03
3,321	1,201	344	5,043	14,044	15·13
20	32	102	192	468	1·57
13	53	80	305	681	2·29
378	325	189	390	2,674	1·71
220	318	370	1,585	3,668	2·35
1,440	656	359	2,141	21,678	6·12
705	1,077	514	2,780	7,673	2·17
1,021	154	244	1,332	7,797	2·47
450	518	404	2,733	7,538	2·39
521	57	48	453	3,073	3·83
149	264	68	481	1,608	2·00
1,465	53	53	882	6,460	4·74
1,040	463	209	2,536	7,621	5·60
1,495	141	476	1,979	7,351	2·19
3,621	1,482	748	5,511	19,538	5·83
6,681	94	117	2,938	18,305	10·87
4,703	2,051	1,098	13,550	51,917	30·84
2,562	199	424	2,806	14,857	3·42
3,841	2,478	1,391	12,831	44,763	10·31
1,192	102	100	1,581	11,601	3·61
2,063	1,214	430	4,571	17,286	5·37
201	17	8	236	1,344	2·14
764	536	247	3,021	9,843	15·67
1,342	62	59	1,307	6,249	3·06
4,843	1,293	733	16,612	53,262	26·07
1,698	133	198	4,072	11,659	2·61
3,152	1,508	969	16,207	42,097	9·43
1,107	19	27	447	3,171	2·49
54	50	49	302	960	0·75
2	7	19	54	124	
1	4	8	30	73	
41,964	4,751	4,917	37,132	278,983	5·93
31,673	17,519	9,395	100,279	318,697	6·78
73,637	22,270	14,312	137,411	597,680	12·71

* Including occupations not specified.
† Per thousand residents, according to the 1951 census.
piled from the first coupon in the passport. These data do not include subsequent
departures in cases where the initial departure took place in 1950 or later.

Italy and Australia (a total of a little over 6000) went through selection and movement procedures similar to those provided for in agreements with European countries. In the great majority of cases, occupational selection by the immigration countries was limited to the refusal of landing-permits to workers in certain trades which were already saturated or to workers who were too old; oversea migration as a whole has therefore a more normal demographic and social structure than that of migration to European countries.[1] This also results from the large number of people in the non-professional category shown in Table II; about one-third of all those emigrating for the first time to oversea countries, as compared with 13 per cent for emigrants to European countries.

Table II also shows the distribution of oversea migrants by region of origin and by occupational group; this cannot be examined in detail in this brief study. It may be noted, however, that, as in the past, oversea migration continues to come mainly from the south of Italy, and in particular from Abruzzo and Molise, Campania, Calabria, and Sicily; the totals of those emigrating for the first time from those areas in the four years 1950–53 are thirty-one, ten, twenty-six, and nine per thousand inhabitants respectively. From those four regions, which account for about one-quarter of the population of Italy, have come almost half of all oversea migrants and, among them, over two-thirds of the agricultural workers and two-thirds of the non-professional migrants.

IV

The location of emigration currents in particular regions —and within those regions in certain provinces or even in certain municipalities — is a characteristic phenomenon which stems less from demographic conditions or the prevailing local economic structure than from a tradition which continues to have a powerful influence.

In the case of 'organized' continental migration, most of the recruitment is based on 'individual' contractual offers to persons suggested by workers who have already emigrated; and even when recruiting occurs on the basis of 'anonymous' offers of work, preference is frequently given to workers from a region from which others

[1] The abnormal structure is less marked in more recent years because migration 'for work' to some countries (*e.g.* Argentina) was discontinued and the family reunion schemes organized by the Intergovernmental Committee for European Migration (ICEM) have tended to increase the percentage of women and children. A study made in the autumn of 1953 of ICEM'S embarkation lists shows that of 'assisted' migrants to Argentina 48 per cent were children under 13 years of age, and three-quarters of all migrants over 13 years of age were women.

have come who have proved their value abroad. On the other hand, a large proportion of oversea migration, with the exception of a few movements of selected workers as mentioned above, results from invitations from relatives or friends, who supply a very rough assessment of prospects in the labour market of the country where they have settled.

Some light is thrown on this aspect of the problem by the data given in Table III, in which the figures in the first two columns headed 'For Employment' include all migrants who went in order to fill a particular job. Of a total of 396,050 emigrants going overseas for the first time in the four years 1950–53, 296,286 were 'invited' as

TABLE III

EMIGRANTS (FOR THE FIRST TIME) CLASSIFIED BY AGE
AND MOTIVE FOR EMIGRATION (YEARS 1950–53)

Age in Years	For Employment		Invited by Friends		Total	
	European Countries	Oversea Countries	European Countries	Oversea Countries	European Countries	Oversea Countries
Under 14	—	—	15,464	76,881	15,464	76,881
14–30	160,665	77,841	16,532	113,257	177,197	191,098
30–50	81,129	45,348	10,424	62,143	91,553	107,491
50–65	6,380	3,058	2,529	12,267	8,909	15,325
Over 65	709	517	1,018	4,738	1,727	5,255
Total	248,883	126,764	45,967	269,286	294,850	396,050

Source : Central Statistical Institute (unpublished data). To interpret the data contained in this table, see note to Table II. Emigrants 'for employment' are those who leave to fill a specific post which has been offered to them ; the 'invited' are those who are sponsored by relatives or other persons who provide a guarantee.

against 126,764 'for employment' ; of 294,850 migrants to European countries, on the other hand, only 45,967 were 'invited'. A sample inquiry carried out in 1953 [1] into the number and characteristics of potential migrants revealed that at that time about 1,800,000 persons expressed a desire to emigrate and had already taken some action, *e.g.*, applications, passport requests, requests for information from the authorities or relatives, etc. About half of them had relatives who had emigrated from Italy since 1945, and of those 49 to 73 per cent, depending on the country to which their relatives had emigrated, frequently received letters from them ; and 21 per cent were confident that travel funds would be advanced to them.

[1] See Ministry of Foreign Affairs *Notiziario dell' emigrazione*, March 1953 (supplement).

The sample also threw light on the motives which lay behind the desire to emigrate. It indicated that 23 per cent of those wishing to emigrate were actually unemployed and 41 per cent under-employed. But as to the reasons given for their intention to move, only 13 per cent cited unemployment, whereas 12 per cent mentioned the difficulty of finding the first job, 43 per cent the desire to improve their material situation, and 21 per cent the search for stable and sure employment.

We must be content with these data about potential migrants, since there is no corresponding information about actual migrants; facts are nevertheless available which indicate that the causes of recent migration do not differ greatly from those noted above. Reference may be made to the findings of foreign recruiting missions in Italy, according to which the majority of selected migrants had some form of activity before emigrating, and it is well known that emigration takes place out of occupations in which there is a shortage of labour in Italy. A typical case is that of certain construction workers; the activities financed in several provinces by the Cassa del Mezzogiorno were hindered by the difficulty of finding, for instance, masons (in twenty-one provinces), carpenters (in nineteen provinces), smiths (in twelve provinces), stone workers, cement workers, scaffolding workers, and workers in other subsidiary trades.[1] Men in these categories have emigrated in fairly large numbers overseas and to other European countries, and even to countries in which the average wages for those trades are not very much higher than in Italy — for example, to France, which still succeeds in recruiting specialized construction workers, particularly from southern Italy, though offering wages which are almost the same as those in Italy but with prospects of regular work, even in the winter season.

V

The foregoing comments on the influence of traditional factors on migration movements are not meant to exclude economic factors. On the contrary, if we leave out border regions from which migration takes place for special reasons and areas near growing cities which offer an outlet, there is a fairly well defined inverse relation between *per capita* income and the rate of emigration in the various regions of Italy. It is the economically backward regions — with the highest rates of natural increase — which provide most of the emigration, particularly to oversea countries. It is precisely in those regions that,

[1] See Cassa per il Mezzogiorno, *Relazione al bilancio, 1952–1953*, p. 41.

owing to limited resources and the large proportion of the population engaged in agriculture, an increase of *per capita* income would be difficult without a transfer of population to other areas. Migration thus makes a definite contribution to the country's economic development, especially in the south, except where it causes a hold-up in key sectors of the economy or where an excessive outflow entails wasteful depopulation.

In order to prevent these harmful results, it would be appropriate if a larger proportion of migrants could be 'organized' by the Italian authorities and requests for labour were directed to areas most likely to benefit. It must nevertheless be recognized that at present — both in Italy and in the immigration countries — the 'organized' migrants find it much more difficult to adapt themselves than do the 'invited' migrants, and this frequently results in failures, followed by costly repatriation. Thus the economic advantage of greater control over the location of the recruitment could be lost in other ways. There have, however, been several successful attempts to carry out 'anonymous' recruitment in places or industries suffering from a surplus of manpower, and there is one project now in progress — as a joint undertaking by the Italian authorities and ONI — to prevent a glut of agricultural labour in regions where land reclamation is being carried out.

Another economic consequence of migration is the flow of remittances from migrants. This is no longer on the same scale as it was in the era of free migration; in several countries there are now restrictive regulations which prevent an emigrant from transferring his own savings. On the eve of the First World War Coletti estimated at about 100 million dollars annually the amount of remittances from migrants, after deducting sums taken out by the migrants themselves;[1] at that time, that sum was enough to cover almost half the adverse trade balance of Italy. In the present postwar period, according to data supplied by the Italian Exchange Office, remittances have reached the following amounts, in millions of dollars:

1946	45·3		1951	69·5
1947	32·2		1952	102·5
1948	70·4		1953	118·8
1949	90·8		1954	114·1
1950	72·2			

These sums, although considerable, represented only one-fifth of the deficit in the balance of trade in the five years 1950–54.

[1] See F. Coletti, *Dell' emigrazione italiana*, Milan, 1912.

95

Chapter 7

NETHERLANDS

BY

E. W. HOFSTEE

Wageningen

SINCE the Second World War relatively important oversea migration has been one of the noticeable features of social life in the Netherlands.[1] As Fig. 1 shows, the total number of emigrants and the emigration surplus — Indonesia and the Dutch oversea territories excluded — in several years after the war were much higher than at any time since 1865.[2] If we divide international migration to and from the Netherlands — Indonesia and the oversea territories excluded again — during the period since the war into migration to and from European countries and migration to and from other countries (Fig. 2), we see that the relatively high emigration surplus has little to do with intra-European migration.[3] After some years of rather high migration from and to European countries, which can be considered as a demographic readjustment to postwar conditions, intra-European migration sank to a low level. As a whole, the years 1946–54, as regards intra-European migration, show an *immigration*

[1] There is an extensive literature in the Dutch language on postwar emigration from the Netherlands, but as a result of the activities of the Research Group for European Migration Problems (REMP), some of the best studies are published in English. We mention : G. Beijer and J. J. Oudegeest, *Some Aspects of Migration Problems in the Netherlands*, Publication No. 3, R.E.M.P., The Hague, 1952 ; William Petersen, *Some Factors influencing Post-war Emigration from the Netherlands*, Publication No. 6, R.E.M.P, The Hague, 1952 ; Willem Steigenga, *Industrialization/Emigration, the Consequences of the Demographic Development in the Netherlands*, Publication No. 10, REMP, 1955.
An important study is William Petersen's doctorate thesis, 'Holland, Canada and International Migration', which was at the author's disposal in manuscript.
[2] The high figures for emigration during the Second World War (see Fig. 1) are not reliable, because conditions during the German occupation made it impossible to make the normal differentiation between those who left the Dutch municipalities for an unknown destination and those who left to migrate to a foreign country. Besides, emigration, so far as it took place, was for the most part abnormal.
[3] On intra-European migration from the Netherlands see E. W. Hofstee, 'De functie van de internationale migratie' (The Function of International Migration), *Tijdschrift voor economische en sociale geographie*, 1949, pp. 10-22 ; T. van den Brink, 'Les Pays-Bas et la migration intra-européenne', *Études européennes de population*, Paris, 1954, pp. 251-65 ; Sj. Groenman et E. W. Hofstee, 'Chances de succès d'une émigration hollandaise à l'intérieur de l'Europe', *Études européennes de population*, Paris, 1954, pp. 266-76.

surplus. Oversea migration, on the other hand, still at a low level in the first years after the war, shows a rapid increase till it comes to a peak in 1952. In the following years it shows some decline, but still remains on a relatively high level. Oversea migration permanently shows an important outward balance.

FIG. 1

EMIGRATION FROM AND IMMIGRATION INTO THE NETHERLANDS, 1865–1954
(INDONESIA AND DUTCH OVERSEA TERRITORIES EXCLUDED)

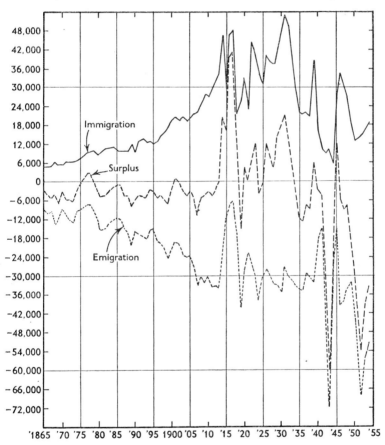

In the Netherlands the people and the Government are very much interested in this postwar oversea migration. In thousands of families the possibilities of migration are discussed. In newspapers and periodicals articles on the subject are frequent and the Government stimulates the outflow as much as possible. It charters ships for transport of migrants, it subsidizes the movement of emigrants to the oversea countries, it organizes migration by means of a special government agency, it employs special migration officers in the most important immigration countries, it endeavours to make arrangements with all countries which offer some possibility for Dutch settlers, and it gives information to would-be migrants through the employment offices. Farmers' unions and other private organizations put out migration propaganda, churches occupy themselves seriously

FIG. 2

NETHERLANDS EXTERNAL MIGRATION, 1946–54

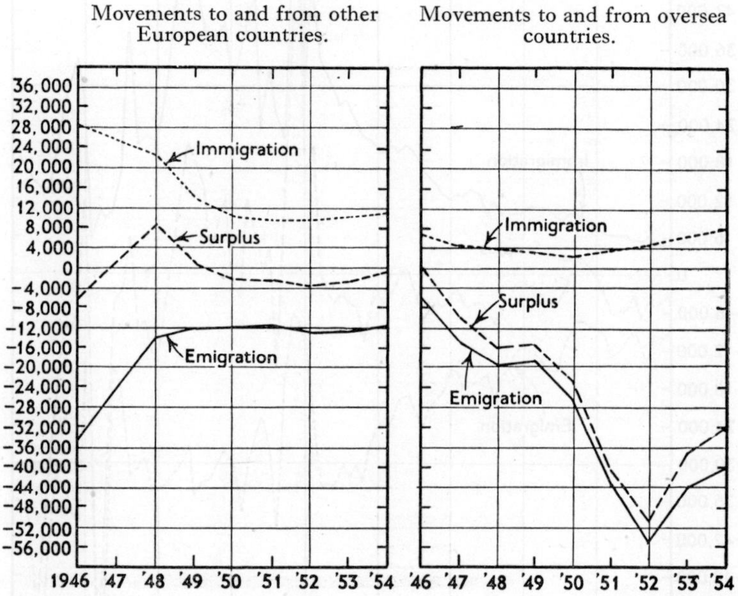

Movements to and from other European countries.

Movements to and from oversea countries.

1946 '47 '48 '49 '50 '51 '52 '53 '54   '46 '47 '48 '49 '50 '51 '52 '53 '54

with the problem of migration, scientists study the possibilities and the consequences of migration; almost everyone and everything in the Netherlands is in some way touched by these activities.

For many, Dutchmen as well as foreigners, who were interested in this postwar migration, the development seemed natural. Thinking of the high density of population and the high surplus of births in the Netherlands and of its limited natural resources, they saw it as a clear case of emigration as a result of overpopulation in the economic sense. In the following pages we hope to show that this view is a far too simple one. It is by no means easy to explain this phenomenon; on the contrary, it is very remarkable from an historical as well as from a demographic and economic point of view.

Historically the Netherlands never was a real emigration country. Fig. 1 shows that before the First World War the Netherlands normally had an emigration surplus, but only a very small one. Seldom was it higher than 5000–10,000 a year. Between the two wars there was mostly an immigration surplus. During the period from 1865 to 1940 as a whole, emigration was practically counter-balanced by immigration, so that until the Second World War the influence of migration upon the total number of the population of the Netherlands was almost nil. It is a pity that Dutch migration statistics before the Second World War do not permit one to divide the emigrants according to the country of destination, but probably the majority — if we again exclude Indonesia and the Dutch oversea territories — went to European countries. In 1930 in North and South America, South Africa, and Australia together there lived about 160,000 people born in the Netherlands, and at the same time in Europe outside the Netherlands there lived about 178,000 people of Dutch nationality.[1] Probably in Europe there was a further unknown number of people born in the Netherlands who had changed their nationality. Special statistics of those who left the Netherlands for permanent settlement in oversea countries — migrants in the more restricted sense — show that their number was seldom higher than a few thousand a year. These special statistics are not very reliable and the number may have been somewhat higher, but there is no doubt that the contribution of the Netherlands to the white population of oversea territories prior to the Second World War was a very modest one, if we compare it, for example, with the contributions of Great Britain, Sweden, Germany, etc.

From the demographic point of view the development of the migration movement after the Second World War was remarkable because in this period the young people appearing for the first time on the labour market were born at the beginning of the thirties, when the crude birth-rate and the surplus of births were at a lower level than ever before or since, so that the supply of labour after the war was certainly not abundant. From the economic point of view the development of this migration was rather surprising, because in the postwar period the demand for labour in the Netherlands was higher than it had been for decades. Apart from a slight recession in 1951 and 1952, the years after the liberation were a period of full employ-ment, which culminated in 1954 and 1955 in a definite shortage of labour.

[1] Dudley Kirk, *Europe's Population in the Inter-war Years*, League of Nations, 1946, Appendix III, Tables 3 and 4.

After the war many believed that the rupture of political ties with
Indonesia would have serious direct and indirect influences on
economic development in the Netherlands. Fig. 3 shows one aspect
of the direct influences ; in the postwar period there was an important

FIG. 3

THE NETHERLANDS : EMIGRATION TO AND IMMIGRATION FROM INDONESIA
AND DUTCH OVERSEA TERRITORIES, 1865–1954

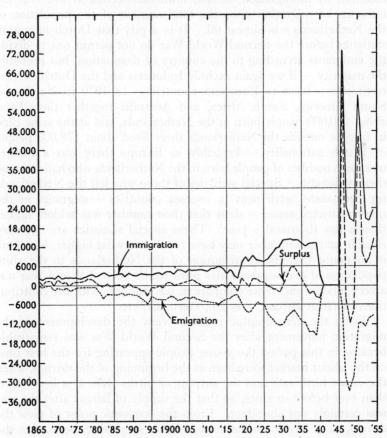

immigration surplus from Indonesia because many who had been
working there returned to the Netherlands. But neither the direct
nor the indirect consequences of the changes in the relations between
the two countries, as is shown by the development of economic life in
the Netherlands in general and by the development of employment
in particular, meant a serious setback. There is no direct relation

between the immigration from Indonesia and the increase of emigration from the Netherlands to other oversea countries ; only relatively few of those who returned from Indonesia emigrated afterwards.

Perhaps the objection will be made that in the foregoing only short-term tendencies have been discussed and that probably the long-term trend will show a discrepancy between the increase of the population and the development of employment, so that those who migrate now rightly anticipate a situation to be expected in the near future.

The problem of long-term economic development in relation to emigration has been discussed at length in the Netherlands in recent years. As was mentioned above, the Government displays great activity in the field of emigration. At first this activity was hardly more than an expression of the general feeling in the Netherlands that migration was necessary, but afterwards the Government tried to base its migration policy on an insight into its bearing upon future economic conditions in the Netherlands. Consequently many studies were made of emigration from this point of view, and their results served as a basis for Government policy. It must be said that the economic motivation of the Government's policy has never been very convincing, and now, in the light of the development of the economy of the Netherlands, it has become practically obsolete.

In the first years after the war, shortage of capital was stressed and calculations were made to show that every emigrant meant the saving of an important investment. This was only a short-term motive which could not be a starting-point for a long-term emigration policy. Shortage of capital was a temporary postwar phenomenon, and nowadays capital is once more abundant in the Netherlands.

Later the attention of the Government shifted to the long-term problem of the balance of payments. It was pointed out that the Dutch economy was already heavily dependent on international trade and that the natural increase of the population, combined with the shortage of natural resources in the Netherlands, would mean — assuming that a fair standard of living and full employment had to be maintained — that imports and exports had to develop to such an extent that it would be virtually impossible to reach that goal. It is, of course, far beyond the scope of this paper — even if the author were qualified to do so — to discuss here at length the problem of the Dutch balance of payments. The table on page 102 gives a picture of the relative importance of imports and exports in the economy of the Netherlands. It certainly shows a high degree of dependence on international trade. But does this mean that the economic problems of the Netherlands in the future can be solved only if an important part of the natural increase of the population emigrates, since a further expansion of Dutch foreign trade, as a consequence of this increase, will soon bring it near certain limits which cannot be surpassed ? Foreign trade as a percentage of the national income is not very much higher now than it was during boom periods in the twenties, notwithstanding the fact that the population increased from 6,900,000 to 10,000,000 between 1920 and 1955. These figures are not a definite refutation of the opinion mentioned above, but they show that a relatively enormous increase of population, combined with rapid industrialization, can take place without seriously disturbing the traditional ratio between national income and foreign trade.

IMPORTS AND EXPORTS IN 1951 AS A PERCENTAGE OF THE
NATIONAL INCOME IN DIFFERENT COUNTRIES

Belgium and Luxembourg	85·2	United Kingdom	58·2
Denmark	61·8	Sweden	50·0
Germany, Western	32·5	Switzerland	54·4
France	33·6	United States	9·4
Italy	30·2	Australia	53·2
Netherlands	100·7	New Zealand	73·8
Norway	96·0	Canada	46·7

Source : United Nations, *Monthly Bulletin of Statistics.*

The econometric approach of Isaac and van den Beld [1] to the problem of the desirable number of emigrants from the Netherlands, from the point of view of the economic development of the country, has already shown that a relatively unimportant change in the volume of international trade will lead to a relatively important change in this desirable number of emigrants. This means that a slightly more optimistic view of the possibilities of development of exports from the Netherlands in the future would lead to the conclusion that there is no necessity for emigration, which, according to the estimates of Isaac and van den Beld, had to have a volume of about 30,000 to 45,000. The development of Dutch foreign trade in recent years justifies the optimistic view *and so at present long-term calculations show hardly any need for emigration.*

Thus neither conditions in the postwar period nor long-term

[1] Julius Isaac and C. A. van den Beld, *The Effect of European Migration on the Economy of Sending and Receiving Countries*, Report by the Research Group for European Migration Problems, The Hague, 1953. According to their conclusions, an increase of 1 per cent in the expected volume of exports from the Netherlands leads to a reduction of the desirable volume of emigration by 5000 persons.

expectations as to the economic development of the Netherlands seem to give an economic basis for Dutch oversea migration and the emigration policy of the Government.

Is, perhaps, this postwar migration nothing but a temporary phenomenon, caused by an abnormal socio-psychological situation in which the war left the Dutch people ? Are the activities of the Dutch Government nothing but an over-hasty reaction to these attitudes towards emigration after the war ? And are these activities of the Government perhaps already like a machine which, once set in motion, cannot be stopped, because it has already become an end in itself ?

It cannot be denied that there are facts which seem to support this assumption. In many respects the conditions in the first post-war years created a socio-psychological climate which favoured emigration. The following points may be noted :

(1) After the war there was a strong feeling in the Netherlands, perhaps like that in other European countries, that it was impossible to make a normal society again out of the immense chaos in which the war had left Western Europe.

(2) This feeling of facing a hopeless situation was strengthened in the Netherlands by the political events in Indonesia, which meant the separation of the Netherlands from a territory which formerly played such an important role in the economic and social life of the country.

(3) The war and the German occupation and, in another way, the economic depression already experienced in the thirties, caused in the Netherlands strong feelings of frustration and an almost physical feeling of oppression. Many, after the war, felt a need of expansion and of more space, physically and mentally.

(4) For the plundered, starved, and impoverished Netherlands, the prosperity in the oversea countries of immigration was very attractive.

(5) For many the fear of a new war and of a possible Russian occupation made emigration more attractive.

(6) Friendly relations with the Canadian soldiers who liberated the Netherlands and remained in the country for some time after the war created strong ties between the Netherlands and Canada which were afterwards maintained by the 'war brides' and which played a very important role in the de-velopment of emigration to Canada.

(7) Partly because of the very high birth-rates in the Netherlands

after the war, which caused many controversies in newspapers and periodicals about the demographic situation, the Dutch people have become much more conscious of population problems than ever before, and even the man in the street has become convinced that the country is 'over-populated'.

There is no doubt that all the factors mentioned above had an important influence on the development of emigration after the war. Without this influence there would perhaps not have been the beginning of a migration trend of any importance. Once it had begun, the success of those who went first stimulated others, while in the meantime the efforts of the Government to facilitate migration became more effective.

The recession in 1951 and 1952 influenced the propensity to migrate, and hence in 1952, the peak year, 55,368 people left for oversea countries (see Fig. 2). But gradually the socio-psychological factors which inaugurated and stimulated postwar migration disappeared. It is evident now that the Netherlands can prosper again in postwar Europe, even without Indonesia. People take the cold war more or less for granted and the feeling of oppression has disappeared.

Is it not to be expected that the postwar emigration wave from the Netherlands will come to an end within a short time? Is not the decrease in the number of emigrants since 1952 the beginning of the end? Is it not perhaps the active policy of the government agencies alone that keeps emigration still going?

After the foregoing it seems logical to predict a rapid end of Dutch oversea migration. Yet probably everyone in the Netherlands who has some knowledge of the subject is convinced that oversea migration will go on; in all classes of Dutch society there is still a strong and active interest in emigration. It cannot be denied that government activities in this field have become an important factor in keeping up the present volume of migration, but the Government is not compelling people to leave their country; it is only paving the way for those who are inclined to go. When the fear of a serious depression disappeared after 1952 the number of migrants did indeed decrease, but in spite of all, even in 1954, a year of definite shortage of labour, oversea migration remained on a relatively high level.

What is the reason for this seeming contradiction? We must admit that we are not able to give a clear and complete answer to this question. It is a pity that a thorough study has not yet been made of the real motives inducing the migrants from the Netherlands to make their decision, so that we have to rely on general impressions and hypotheses. But there is hardly any doubt that the most general reason given by the migrants is lack of opportunities at home for themselves and for their children. How can this feeling of lack of opportunities, now and in the future, be reconciled with what is said above about the economic prospect in the Netherlands ?

A rapidly growing population entails the creation of new jobs, and this means that many people have no opportunity to follow the same trade and to live in the same conditions as their parents did, even if they wish to do so. A clear example of this situation is found in agriculture. The farmers in the eastern and southern parts of the Netherlands still tend to have rather large families. Many farmers' sons are brought up as farmers on the parents' farm, but will never have an opportunity of getting a farm of their own because there is no more land available. These young farmers can certainly find jobs as unskilled labourers in industry but consider such work to be socially inferior.

For many ambitious young people conditions in the Netherlands, which result from the high birth-rate and the high density of population, bar the way to a higher position on the social ladder. In the Netherlands the chances for a farmhand to become a farmer are practically nil, because land is scarce and he has to compete with a multitude of farmers' sons who bid desperately for a farm. In some oversea countries land is still abundant and, as the history of Dutch migration to Canada after the war shows, a migrant there gets a chance to become an independent farmer in a few years. For young craftsmen and skilled labourers the chances of getting some kind of business of their own are few in the Netherlands ; in Australia and Canada the opportunities for good craftsmen to become their own master are much better.

These few examples, to which many could be added, go to show that in a country with a dense and rapidly increasing population there is not only the problem of the total number of jobs available ; the problem of the quality of the opportunities that are open for the active population is far more urgent. The number of jobs that are offered may be sufficient, but often these jobs will not be suitable from the economic, technical, or socio-psychological point of view for those who are looking for work which gives them satisfaction.

There is still another indirect relation between the propensity to emigrate and the intensity of population growth which is often forgotten. As was mentioned above, even if the total number of jobs offered in a certain country is adequate, a rapid increase of the population makes the process of bringing the man and the job together far more difficult than in countries where the population is increasing very slowly or not at all. The new opportunities will be concentrated in certain areas, industries, and occupations; and in a country such as the Netherlands the transfer will involve for many people a breaking of ties with the geographical, social, and psychological environment to which they are accustomed. In other words, in a country with a high natural increase, finding a job means for many that they have to cover a considerable 'social distance'. Consciousness of this fact makes people less afraid of the changes in environment which are inherent in emigration. Generally speaking, we can say that a modern society with a rapidly growing population will be a dynamic society, and in a dynamic society the resistance to changes in personal life, including those arising from emigration, will be less than in a society in which social life is changing only gradually.

Before the war, and certainly before the economic depression of the thirties, there was a resistance to rapid changes in personal life and in society. The influence of the First World War was superficial, and it might be said that the nineteenth century ended only in 1930 in the Netherlands. The economic depression of the thirties, the development of Nazism, and the Second World War had a profound effect on the Dutch people. These events shattered a picture of the world which the Dutch had made for themselves during the nineteenth century and the beginning of the twentieth. The feeling of living in a world where people are safe, where a man can form a picture of his future life when he is 20, where things are going well and will certainly go better in the future, has gone. Perhaps the Dutch, and especially the young people, have become more sceptical; they have certainly become more restless, more mentally mobile and active, more inclined to take chances when they offer themselves, without thinking too much of the petty problems of the near future and of the past, and less afraid to burn their boats. This postwar mentality is more compatible with emigration than the former one.

Thus we come to the conclusion that the relation between the economy of the Netherlands and postwar emigration is not as self-evident as many seem to believe. There are probably certain relations between emigration and economic-demographic conditions, but perhaps these relations are more indirect than direct. A more intensive study of them is needed.

The motivation of the migration policy of the Dutch Government after the war was not very convincing. This does not mean that this policy as such was not right. In addition to the importance of emigration for the solution of the special socio-economic problems of separate individuals and families, of certain regions and professional groups, there are non-economic problems which make a limitation of population growth by means of emigration desirable. Recreation, modern traffic, and military training, for example, face ever-increasing problems of space. The Netherlands are simply becoming too crowded.

Chapter 8

THE INTERGOVERNMENTAL COMMITTEE FOR EUROPEAN MIGRATION

BY

PIERRE JACOBSEN
Deputy Director, ICEM, Geneva

I. THE SITUATION WHICH LED TO THE ESTABLISHMENT OF ICEM

IN the postwar years the Western countries were very much concerned with the economic and political dangers arising in Europe from surplus population and the influx of refugees. The population problems of countries of relatively high birth-rate,[1] such as Italy, Greece, and the Netherlands, had been made acute by the damage and after-effects of the war. Not only had these countries suffered severely from war damage, but oversea migration, which had provided a safety valve for their increasing populations, had ceased altogether during the war years. Political changes had reduced their ability to absorb their growing populations and increased the extent of the problem by causing groups of their nationals who had been established elsewhere to return home, frequently as refugees. For example, the loss of Indonesia considerably weakened the power of the Netherlands to absorb its increasing labour force and at the same time added to its population some 260,000 Dutch citizens who returned from Indonesia during the years 1946-54. Italy also lost the colonial outlets for its population as well as part of its European territory, and at the same time received over 400,000 refugees from these former possessions. In Greece the disasters of the war were followed by civil war which rendered between 600,000 and 700,000 persons homeless. In addition, some 50,000 refugees entered Greece from the Communist states of the north, almost four-fifths of whom were from the Greek communities which had been established in these countries for generations.

[1] Although the Italian rate of natural increase was 11·4 per thousand in 1948, it had fallen to 7·4 per thousand by 1953. In 1954 it recovered, however, and the excess of births over deaths was not far short of the high annual average recorded during the period 1946–50.

The war created population problems also in countries of low rates of natural increase in which population had previously been relatively stable. Western Germany, for example, received vast waves of refugees, chiefly of German ethnic origin, from the eastern countries, the territories east of the Oder-Neisse line, and the Soviet Zone. By 1951 the number of these refugees had reached about 9·5 million, with the result that, in spite of heavy war losses, the population of the area was 20 per cent greater than it had been in 1939. Austria had to bear a similar influx, although on a much smaller scale. Even so, the number of refugees in Austria in 1947 was almost 10 per cent of the total population.

International effort was at work on one segment of this problem. The International Refugee Organization had been established in 1947 to deal specifically with the problem of displaced persons and refugees resulting from the war, although refugees within their own country were not within its mandate. Although IRO gave assistance in some form or other to over 1,600,000 refugees, and succeeded in resettling over one million of them, its operations were due to come to an end on the completion of its programme for 1951.

It is not surprising, therefore, that the statesmen of the West were very much disturbed by this politically explosive situation. When the Foreign Ministers of the United States, France, and Great Britain met in London in May 1950, they referred to it in the following terms : 'In the course of their discussions, the Foreign Ministers have recognized that the excess of population from which several countries in Western Europe are suffering is one of the most important elements in the difficulties and disequilibrium of the world. They also believe that the systematic exploration of opportunities for greater population mobility can contribute significantly to the solution of this problem.' (Communiqué No. II, relative to European emigration, issued by the three Foreign Ministers after their meeting in London, May 11/13, 1950.)

During 1951 there were several international gatherings to consider the problem. A Committee of Experts on the Problem of Refugees and Surplus Population was convened by the Council of Europe, and included representatives from fourteen European countries with observers from the United States, OEEC, and interested United Nations Agencies. This Committee described the situation it found as follows : 'There are at present within the territories of the Member States . . . owing to the influx of 11,000,000 refugees in the widest sense of the term — including both those enjoying normal rights of citizenship and those coming under the protection of the United Nations — some 4·5 million refugees, who have neither finally nor temporarily been absorbed into the economy of their country of residence. The halt in migration since 1930 and the economic destruction and dislocation caused by the war, moreover, contributed to the accumulation in certain European countries of surplus population which cannot rapidly be absorbed as a result of improved domestic economic conditions, but which, consequently, calls for special measures to be taken, particularly as the influx of refugees has not yet stopped.' [1]

The Committee of Experts, accepting the definition of OEEC that overpopulation may be said to exist in cases where the lack of national resources or capital prevents work being given to the unemployed persons within a reasonable time and under reasonable economic conditions, 'estimated that the surplus population in certain European countries amounts to several million workers'. [2]

When they came to consider solutions to these problems, the experts stressed the need for re-establishing the traditional stream of emigration from Europe, and pointed out that the capacity of immigration countries appeared to be considerably greater than could be utilized by potential emigrants from Europe unless ways could be found of providing the latter with financial aid for their transport. It was also significant that the experts considered that when the question of transport and its costs had been solved, any future substantial increase in migration overseas would have to depend on the increased economic development of the under-developed countries of immigration. Another matter of interest touched upon in the report and which was later to have some bearing on the establishment of ICEM was the need for a 'decision whether the smooth working, technical operational machinery set up by the IRO' should be maintained or dissolved.

Another meeting of considerable importance which took place in this year was the conference held at Naples in November under the auspices of the International Labour Office. The ILO had been preparing some very useful groundwork to focus the problem of over-population and to lay down the standards and conditions which should govern any large-scale migratory movements. Although the Naples Conference closed without establishing any international organ to deal with the problem of surplus population, it could point to several substantial achievements in the technical field and did serve to underline the urgency of the problem. Within a month,

[1] *Committee of Experts on the Question of Refugees and Overpopulation, Final Report*, Strasbourg, 8 October 1951, CM(51)69, p. 2.
[2] The Report of the Committee of Experts contained the following note : 'On the basis of available sources the figure of 5 million would seem to indicate the amplitude of the problem'.

therefore, on the initiative of the United States and Belgium, a conference of interested governments took place in Brussels to consider whether some way could not be found of using the operational machinery of IRO to deal with the greater problem of refugees and surplus population as a whole after that organization's mandate had come to an end.

At this conference in December 1951 the organization which later became known as the Intergovernmental Committee for European Migration was set up. Whilst the conference was largely preoccupied with European problems and recognized the necessity of 'an increase in European emigration to countries overseas', it did consider at length the requirements of the immigration countries. The conference emphasized the 'close relationship (which) exists between economic development and immigration', and, pointing out that 'international effort to increase European migration should stimulate the creation of new economic opportunities in countries lacking manpower', laid upon the new organization the dual task of alleviating population pressure in Europe and helping to supply shortages overseas.[1]

II. THE WORK OF ICEM

A person who wishes to migrate has three essential needs which must be met if he is to have a chance of success : first, he must have an opportunity in an immigration country for which he is fitted ; secondly, he must have transport ; and thirdly, he must have money to pay for it. When ICEM first began operations, several thousands of persons did in fact already have an opportunity to emigrate but could either not find the transport or could not pay for it if it could be found.[2] The immediate tasks were therefore to arrange transport and to meet the costs where available resources, either from the would-be migrants themselves or from the governments concerned, were insufficient. It was first thought that if these two essentials were provided the flow of migration would expand to the volume which the problems in Europe and in the developing countries seemed to warrant. It was not long, however, before it became clear that if the volume of migration was to be expanded sufficiently, many more opportunities would have to be found or developed and much would have to be done to prepare the prospective migrants to

---

[1] See Enabling Resolution of the Brussels Conference, 5 December 1951.

[2] These were chiefly persons given visas during the lifetime of IRO under schemes for Displaced Persons and ethnic German refugees. It was thought also that the existence of an international organization with financial and transport resources would stimulate the flow of migrants under existing bilateral agreements.

take advantage of them. Thus, during the brief period of its existence, ICEM, whilst not losing sight of the essential task of transporting migrants efficiently under satisfactory conditions and at economical cost, has tended more and more to concentrate its efforts on developing new immigration opportunities in the oversea countries and on ensuring the success of the migrants by proper selection, language, and vocational training, and the provision of satisfactory information regarding the countries to which they want to go. It is therefore convenient to review the work of ICEM under three headings : (1) the provision of transport and its financing, (2) the improvement of the technical machinery of migration, and (3) the development of new migration opportunities.

There is, however, another factor of considerable importance in reviewing the value of ICEM's work ; that is, the type of migrant which it moves. The constitution of ICEM applies a certain negative criterion in so far as it authorizes the organization to give its assistance only to those persons who could not migrate without it. But there is an important positive element which must be considered also. One of the goals of ICEM is to alleviate population problems which are retarding the economies of both emigration and immigration countries, and thus to help raise the general standard of living. Therefore, while ICEM contributes manpower to exploit the resources of the developing countries, it must be careful not to take excessive numbers of qualified workers [1] from the emigration countries nor to disturb their demographic structures. These matters are not entirely within the control of the administration of ICEM, as it is specifically recognized in the constitution that standards of admission and numbers of immigrants to be admitted are matters of domestic jurisdiction of member states and that in carrying out its operations ICEM must conform to the policies of the emigration and immigration countries. Nevertheless, within these limitations ICEM tries to ensure that its movements are well balanced demographically and in terms of skilled and unskilled workers. Its political structure, which combines European governments as well as the governments of oversea immigration countries, and its operational responsibilities, well qualify it to do so with some measure of success. It will therefore be useful later in this paper to review the information available regarding the type of person whom ICEM has been able to assist.

---

[1] This problem of satisfying the needs of receiving countries for skilled workers without creating manpower shortages in certain trades in the sending countries is one of the most difficult that ICEM — or any agency attempting to organize migration — must face. The answer may be found in vocational training, which should produce qualified workers to emigrate if they so wish or to replace on the labour market of the sending country those skilled workers who do wish to migrate.

1. *The Provision of Transport and its Financing*

The essential problem in the transport of migrants arises from the difficulties which this type of traffic creates for commercial shipping. It is a traffic subject not only to seasonal fluctuations but also to change and dislocation at very short notice, and its volume is always difficult to estimate in advance. In general, migratory movements are of a one-way nature and the problem of finding adequate return traffic is considerable. Fares must also be low. Thus it is a difficult trade for which to establish a sound long-term programme and, although the improvements natural to competitive trade are taking place, commercial shipping tends to be unable to meet peak periods of migration movement and to be slow to provide transport when a new migration flow develops. The need therefore is for shipping, freed from these commercial considerations, to be available for peak periods and to operate new routes until their commercial feasibility has been demonstrated.

The relations of ICEM with governments of countries of emigration and immigration, its liaison and operating offices in these countries, and the agreements it has with governments to effect the movement of migrants under specific schemes, assure it the extensive and detailed knowledge of short-term migration trends which is essential if transport of this character is to be provided.

Ships of commercial lines are used by ICEM up to the extent that space is available under satisfactory conditions and at an appropriate price. In general, only third or tourist class accommodation is taken and, where possible, special price arrangements are agreed between the Committee and the Shipping Conferences. Where adequate commercial space is not available, ICEM arranges transport either by guaranteeing a high proportion — usually 95 per cent — of a ship's capacity, or by taking vessels on time or round trip charter. In the latter case, price adjustments are made when the owner earns return revenue.

ICEM is also making increasing use of aircraft. By the end of 1954 it had transported nearly 15,000 migrants by air, 5880 of them during 1954. Air transport has many characteristics which make its operation well adapted to the movement of migrants. It is very easy to suspend or re-direct the movements of aircraft, and this operational flexibility accords well with the fluctuations of the migration programme. Aircraft are very useful to cover a peak period of movements when workers are wanted urgently in the immigration country; for example, for work on the harvest. Immigrants can be flown quickly at short notice and disembarked inland in very close proximity to their eventual place of work. Furthermore, the speed of air transport avoids a loss of working hours and also the psychological hazards of a long voyage.

ICEM usually charters the aircraft which it uses and the cost per migrant does not normally exceed that of ocean transport. Air transport has proved particularly useful in moving migrants to the United States, but has also been invaluable in supplementing sea transport on the much longer route to Australia.[1]

ICEM initially pays the costs of the transport it provides from funds contributed by governments, either as free grants towards its general operations or as *per capita* payments based on the number of migrants assisted by ICEM from or to the country concerned. Additional contributions towards the costs of transport may be received from some of the following sources after — and sometimes even before — the movements have taken place; from governments or from migrants when ICEM has agreed to provide transport on a fully reimbursable basis only; from sponsors or migrants as partial prepayment or partial reimbursement of costs; from voluntary agencies in connexion with movements partly financed on the passage-loan principle and for which the voluntary agencies collect repayments from the migrants; and from certain special sources such as the United States Escapee Programme.[2] ICEM has already introduced the principle that migrants should prepay or reimburse part of their passage costs when they are in a position to do so. It is believed that these arrangements should be progressively extended, so that more and more of the costs are met by the migrants themselves.

The Development of Migration.—There are two major factors which restrict the development of oversea migration. The first is the relative inadequacy of essential migration services in some emigration and immigration countries, and the second stems from temporary limitations in the capacity of oversea countries to absorb immigrants. These limitations are advisedly described as temporary because it is clear that many oversea countries are destined eventually to carry much larger populations than they do today, and in several instances their statesmen have expressed their intention to accelerate the process of development by receiving as many immigrants as may be satisfactorily absorbed.

[1] By 31 December 1954, ICEM had transported 143,324 migrants on commercial sea transport and 1553 on commercial aircraft; 127,155 had been transported on chartered ships and 13,143 on chartered aircraft.
[2] This is a United States Government scheme to assist the re-establishment of persons escaping from persecution or the threat of persecution in Eastern European countries.

One of ICEM's most important tasks has therefore been to try to combat these restrictive factors by assisting governments to improve the technical services of migration and by seeking ways of helping oversea countries to develop their absorptive capacities.

2. *The Improvement of Migration Services*

The 'essential migration services' concern chiefly the selection and documentation of migrants before they embark, their reception and placement in employment in the immigration country, and the provision of such training, orientation, and information as they may need in order to take proper advantage of the opportunities which await them overseas. The aim of these services should be to ensure that full advantage is taken of every opportunity to place well prepared migrants in jobs overseas where they will be successful and productive.

ICEM has tried to gather precise knowledge of the problems met by European countries in facilitating the emigration of their nationals and by oversea countries in receiving and placing immigrants, and hence to adapt its activities and services to the particular needs in each country. In some instances ICEM has co-operated with the appropriate government departments in order to improve or expand existing services, whilst in other instances the organization has undertaken to provide with its own staff the services required. Where this has been necessary, it has been understood that ICEM provides the necessary services on a temporary basis until such time as the Government can itself provide them.

One of the most important elements in the success of organized migration, that is, migration carried out under formal bilateral agreements or administrative arrangements accepted by the two countries concerned, is the existence of adequate services for the pre-selection, documentation, and final selection of the migrant, functions which are generally known as 'processing'. Efficient processing services speed up the rate of movement, reduce its cost and, by ensuring that the general quality of the persons who migrate is high, help to increase their number. ICEM has therefore made a special effort to improve processing arrangements, although the detailed action taken has depended on each emigration country's particular need. In Greece ICEM has assumed full responsibility for these services, whilst in Germany and Austria its staff has worked with the national services in setting up procedures and has helped their smooth working.

An interesting development in this sphere has taken place in

Italy. The Italian Government often expressed its wish to receive help in improving processing and selection services, and in 1953, therefore, a programme was carried out by the Government, ILO, and ICEM jointly to instruct two travelling teams of Italian pre-selection officers in the most satisfactory methods and to assist those teams when they visited the regional labour offices to pre-select from applicants. This programme, which lasted six months, was successful and was repeated in the first half of 1954. The improved selection methods which these two programmes made possible were so successful in reducing the rate of rejection at the final selection stage and in diminishing costs of pre-selection that the Government asked ICEM to continue its co-operation in pre-selection operations, and the establishment of a joint service — the Selection Assistance Service — was agreed upon. In addition to assisting the Italian administration, this service has simplified the task of the selection missions of immigration countries by ensuring that only candidates who have been thoroughly pre-selected under professional and medical criteria and whose documentation is in order are presented to them.

In oversea countries which do not have comprehensive man-power and employment services — and this is the case in several countries of Latin America — it has been useful for ICEM to improvise special arrangements to seek out opportunities for the employment of immigrants and to place them in work after arrival. Immigrants are attracted by the major cities, where suitable jobs may not be available for them, while at the same time advantage is not taken of many opportunities in the interior owing to the lack of placement services to assess manpower needs and place immigrants in employment. In trying to meet this deficiency ICEM has sought, *inter alia*, to make the utmost use of the sponsorship possibilities of established immigrants, ethnic groups, or religious organizations.

However, not every person desiring to migrate is suitable for the opportunities that can be found : would-be migrants with no very high standard of vocational skill and no language but their mother tongue find opportunities overseas very limited. Training facilities are therefore needed to enable them to improve the skill they possess and learn the rudiments of the language of the country to which they can migrate, so that they may have a real chance of selection and of living successful lives in the immigration country.

These training programmes can also help immigration countries to obtain the type of migrant needed without draining excessively the skilled manpower of emigration countries; they are becoming increasingly necessary as the availability of skilled workers for migration decreases.

ICEM has advised and assisted governments to establish special training schemes for potential emigrants or to divert a portion of their existing training services to this purpose. Language and vocational training schemes have been set up in Italy and Greece, but so far their value has been more to demonstrate what can and should be done rather than substantially to influence the volume of migration.

3. *The Creation of New Opportunities for Migration*

While it cannot be doubted that the improvement of the technical services of migration will increase its volume, there are clearly limits to the increase such improvements will achieve. If migration is to be expanded beyond these limits more fundamental action will be necessary: in addition to full advantage being taken of existing opportunities for migration, new ones must be found.

New areas to which European migration may be directed are limited. Countries which are not members of ICEM — or have but recently joined — may perhaps increase their intake of migrants, although movements are not likely to be large.[1] However, when considering new outlets the attention turns first to Africa. Political obstacles to the expansion of the small stream of European migration to Africa are considerable, but there are signs that more immigration opportunities may be forthcoming. Movements are not yet likely to be substantial but they may nevertheless make a positive contribution to solving Europe's problems, and the potentialities for the future may be greater.

The search for new opportunities for European migrants in countries which have received considerable numbers in the past leads to the inescapable conclusion that the necessary action is to bridge the gap between the potentialities of those countries to carry greater population and their present absorptive capacities. The number of migrants permitted to enter a country is usually determined by a judgement regarding the rate at which increased population can be satisfactorily absorbed into the economic and social life of the country while standards of living are at least maintained. Migrants must be put to work, housed, their children educated, and so on: thus the maintenance of a steady or increasing rate of immigration ultimately involves the provision of more farms, factories, houses, and schools. No matter how efficient the services of migration may be, immigration will not increase beyond a certain point unless the

---

[1] At the Second Session of the ICEM Council in May 1955 the applications of New Zealand and the Federation of Rhodesia and Nyasaland for membership were accepted.

essential economic and social capital can be obtained. It follows that, if migration is to be expanded, consideration must be given to what can be done to help immigration countries to provide these essentials.

The activities of ICEM in this field have so far been limited to the encouragement of land settlement, which, in spite of its many difficulties, is sometimes a particularly appropriate method of creating migration opportunities. It gives migrants the means of utilizing a major production factor, the uncultivated land, and provides them with the housing, welfare, and social amenities with which their non-working life is occupied. Normally it makes provision for marketing their produce. As a medium of immigration it has many advantages ; it helps to expand agricultural production and raise nutritional standards ; it increases population with a most desirable type of migrant, and it tends to correct the drift from land to town. Further, in certain European countries, particularly the Netherlands, Italy, and Greece, farmers and farm workers make up a substantial part of the population surplus. Land settlement is one way of creating opportunities for these people.[1]

Land settlement provides opportunities for immigration in one sector of the economy only, although it does give rise to secondary opportunities in the services which modern agricultural communities require. Large development schemes in the power, transport, and industrial sectors have often needed immigrant technicians and workers in the past and will no doubt do so again.[2] There is clearly a very close relationship between immigration and general economic expansion in the developing countries ; an increased immigration will provide part of the technical skill and manpower required by development projects and will create a larger internal market for industrial and agricultural production, and thus in turn stimulate the general process of economic development. ICEM therefore sets great store on its relations with international and national planning bureaux and international institutions for financing development, in order that its work may be closely co-ordinated with theirs.

Recent initiatives in the international world give grounds for hoping that additional funds will become available for the financing of economic development. The decision to establish an International Finance Corporation, the discussions in the Economic and Social

[1] Land settlement experts or technical missions recruited by ICEM have been active in Argentina, Bolivia, Brazil, Chile, Costa Rica, and Venezuela.

[2] Australian experience in this connexion is interesting ; by the end of 1950, 53 per cent of former displaced persons were working in the investment industries, building, building materials, metals, engineering, and national undertakings. About 70 per cent of the technicians and even more of the labourers employed on the Snowy Mountains Hydro-Electric projects were immigrants.

Council of the possibility of establishing a Special United Nations Fund for Economic Development, and the project to set up an Inter-American Development Bank with a capital of 200 million dollars, are all examples. Progress towards establishing these and similar institutions will inevitably be slow ; but if they do begin operations, much-needed funds will be available to enable immigration countries to make the investments which are necessary before greater numbers of migrants can be absorbed.

4. *The Type of Migrants Moved*

By September 1956, 498,696 persons had been able to migrate with the assistance of ICEM. Table I gives a breakdown of this number by country of origin and country of destination.

The type of migrant assisted by ICEM is perhaps as interesting as the total number of migrants moved, and statistics are available for the year 1954, during which 121,222 persons received ICEM's assistance, showing the age, sex, and family status of the migrants and those who migrated as workers or as dependants. It has previously been mentioned that although the policy regarding migration is in the hands of the national governments concerned, ICEM does its best to encourage a balanced migration which is beneficial to both sending and receiving countries. An examination of the statistics for 1954 will give some idea of the results of its efforts.

The following are the figures regarding workers and non-workers :

	Total	Male	Female
Persons who migrated as workers	48,636	40,503	8,133
Persons who migrated as non-workers	72,586	22,169	50,417
	121,222	62,672	58,550

Thus 40 per cent of the total migrants transported by ICEM were workers and 60 per cent non-workers. The comparable figures regarding all immigration — assisted and unassisted — to Australia were 44 and 56 per cent, and to Canada 55 and 45 per cent. Total emigration from Germany in 1953 comprised 58 per cent workers and 42 per cent non-workers.[1]

Table II compares ICEM-assisted migration, by age group, with total migration (assisted and unassisted movements included) in respect of certain sending and receiving countries. This table shows

[1] Comparable statistics regarding emigration from Germany in 1954 are not yet available.

TABLE I

PROVISIONAL ANALYSIS BY COUNTRY OF EMIGRATION AND IMMIGRATION OF THE NUMBER OF MIGRANTS WHO DEPARTED FROM EMBARKATION OR EMPLANEMENT CENTRES OR OTHER PORTS OF EMBARKATION

1 February 1952–30 September 1956

Area of Emigration	Total	Country of Immigration											
		Argentina	Australia	Brazil	Canada	Chile	Israel	New Zealand	Rhodesia and Nyasaland	United States of America	Uruguay	Venezuela	Others
Austria	47,130	151	10,974	1,796	9,743	89	181	76	14	22,004	17	162	1923
Germany	154,467	231	37,256	3,172	54,835	950	266	32	12	55,010	142	694	1867
Greece	40,106	314	27,804	4,027	2,776	61	55	98	377	3,963	32	117	482
Italy (including Trieste)*	164,405	59,470	24,508	38,075	6,462	2802	273	28	927	7,385	4347	18,178	1950
Netherlands	36,438	17	31,344	1,136	837	2	102	2179	480	298	10	..	33
Hong Kong	7,249	49	1,498	2,925	247	154	351	3	..	236	..	27	1759
Others	48,901	482	19,132	1,053	6,216	184	5780	34	23	14,553	102	213	1129
Total	498,696*	60,714	152,516	52,184	81,116	4242	7008	2450	1833	103,449	4650	19,391	9143

* Reports for cases moved under the Revolving Fund arrangements are incomplete for the month of September 1956 and therefore totals are subject to minor adjustment.

TABLE II

MIGRANTS IN 1954 BY AGE GROUP

(shown as percentages)

Age Group	In ICEM-assisted Movements	Emigration Italy Total	Italy ICEM	Germany * Total	Germany * ICEM	Netherlands † Total	Netherlands † ICEM	Immigration Australia Total	Australia ICEM	Canada Total	Canada ICEM	Argentina Total	Argentina ICEM	Brazil Total	Brazil ICEM
0–19	41·4	39·6	49·5	32·2	36·8	35·2	46·1	38·6	40·7	28·8	33·1	—	40·5	26·2	28·8
0–17												41·1			
0–21															
20–59	55·6	57·5	46·0	66·3	62·2			58·5	58·7	69·2	65·9		53·2	71·5	68·6
18–59												51·8			
22–60						64·1									
20–64							53·5								
60+	3·0	2·9	4·5	1·5	1·0			2·9	0·6	2·0	1·0		6·3	2·3	2·6
61+												7·1			
65+						0·7	0·4								
	100·0	100·0	100·0	100·0	100·0	100·0	100·0	100·0	100·0	100·0	100·0	100·0	100·0	100·0	100·0

* The statistics regarding emigration from Germany are for the first nine months of the year only.
† The differences between total emigration and ICEM movements are not significant, as ICEM assisted only 1274 Netherlands migrants in 1954.

Sources : *Bollettino mensile di statistica*, Istituto Centrale di Statistica, Rome. *Statistische Berichte, Die Aus- und Einwanderung im 1., 2., 3. Vierteljahr 1954*, Statistisches Bundesamt, Wiesbaden. *Maandstatistiek van de bevolking*, April 1954–Mart 1955, Centraal Bureau voor de Statistiek, Utrecht. *Statistical Bulletin No. 14*, April 1955, Department of Immigration, Canberra. *Statements for the Calendar Year 1954*, Immigration Branch, Department of Citizenship and Immigration, Ottawa. *Síntesis estadística mensual de la República Argentina.* Departamento Nacional de Imigração, Brazil.

that in relation to total migration ICEM moved more young persons of 19 years and below and fewer persons of normal working age. The percentage of migrants above the age of 60 was not significant except in regard to emigration from Italy and immigration to Argentina. The composition of the migratory flow between these two countries was greatly influenced by the ICEM Family Reunion Programme which reached its peak in 1954 when 28,756 persons were moved from Italy to join their family heads in Argentina. The following figures illustrate the effect of this programme on the age-group breakdown of Italian oversea emigration in 1954.

EMIGRATION FROM ITALY IN 1954 : AGE GROUPS OF EMIGRANTS
(given as percentage of the total)

Age Groups	Total Emigration Overseas	Emigration assisted by ICEM	Emigration without ICEM Assistance
	%	%	%
0–19	39·6	49·5	34·1
20–59	57·5	46·0	63·9
60 plus	2·9	4·5	2·0
	100·0	100·0	100·0

These figures suggest that although ICEM movements may not help to check the trend in Europe towards ageing populations, the organization's services do permit a higher percentage of old persons to emigrate than would otherwise be possible.

The tendencies illustrated by the 1954 statistics result from the fact that organized migration as carried out by ICEM concentrates on family movement and, on the whole, moves workers for whom definite employment opportunities are available. One of the characteristics of spontaneous migration, on the other hand, is that the breadwinner often moves ahead of his family without any definite employment offer, in the hope that he may quickly settle down and be able to pay for his family to join him. In the postwar years these hopes were often illusory. In 1954 ICEM transported a total of 33,197 families, comprising 100,212 persons. Of this number 12,375 were complete family units while 20,822 were families migrating for reunion with their breadwinners. Those persons assisted by ICEM who were migrating for employment normally fell into one of three groups. Either they were sponsored and had an individual job offer, or by virtue of their occupation they were considered easily placeable in the immigration country by the government or ICEM placement officers, or they were selected for employment under a government immigration scheme.

The combination of family migration and the careful selection and placement of workers, while it may result in a higher proportion of dependants to workers in assisted movements, does go far to ensure the success of migration and reduce the number of returnees. The comparative tables suggest that, in 1954 at least, ICEM tended to work to the advantage of emigration countries by moving proportionally fewer workers and more dependants, but tended to strengthen the immigration countries demographically by moving proportionally more persons under 20. It seems, therefore, that the organized and assisted migration effected by ICEM tends to reconcile the conflicting interests of sending and receiving countries and tends towards a type of movement giving the greatest measure of advantage to both. More analysis of migratory movements, particularly with regard to the occupations of migrants, will be necessary before this can be stated with assurance.

III. THE EXPERIENCE OF THE MIGRATION COMMITTEE AND FUTURE PERSPECTIVES

The early paragraphs of this paper referred to the refugee and surplus population problems of postwar years which led to the establishment of ICEM with the dual task of attempting to ameliorate the European situation and at the same time contributing to a solution of the manpower shortages in the developing countries overseas. Since that time the situation in Europe has changed considerably.

The most striking change has, of course, been the ability of the Federal Government of Germany to find employment for its vast refugee population. The expellees and refugees have been integrated into the economy of Western Germany; jobs have been found for them, although not necessarily the jobs for which they were trained or experienced. The annual average of unemployment has been steadily diminishing and it reached 651,000 at the end of June 1955. The winter unemployment figures have not shown a similar decline and peak unemployment has continued to be in the region of 1,800,000 each year.[1] Unemployment of refugees also fluctuates seasonally, but the percentage of the unemployed who are refugees has been decreasing. There are, however, still relatively more refugees unemployed than permanent residents, although the difference is small. Refugees and expellees represent some 21·5 per cent of the total

[1] The figure for February 1955 was 1,815,000.

population, but they accounted for 24·7 per cent of all persons unemployed in May 1955 ; 27 per cent of the male unemployed were refugees.

It should not be forgotten that many of the refugees in employment have had to accept work under conditions which compare unfavourably with those to which they were accustomed. It has been estimated that about one-quarter of the refugees in employment are working in occupations other than those for which they have been trained. The following paragraph from the report of M. Pierre Schneiter, Special Representative of the Council of Europe for National Refugees and Overpopulation, explains this situation very clearly.

'My attention was drawn to two aspects of integration : first, that it was achieved at the cost of a considerable fall in the social standing of the refugees. Whereas 40 per cent were independently employed before their expulsion, only 10 per cent were able to re-build their lives on an independent basis. Although there is no prospect of settling all refugees in their various occupations, since they represent the total population of vast areas, it is true to say that they should be found reasonably satisfying employment in order to avoid tensions which might be a threat to social peace. The second aspect is that even successful cases of integration are vulnerable to new fluctuations in the international markets. Where refugee industries have been established they suffer from a dangerous lack of reserves. Wholesale dismissals would be unavoidable in the event of the slightest disturbance.'[1]

The situation described by M. Schneiter is particularly evident with regard to those refugees formerly engaged in agriculture. Among the refugees and expellees from the East were about 300,000 farm families who had formerly worked their own land. The Government has made great efforts to settle many of these families on the land in Western Germany, efforts which have involved a change in the country's agricultural structure and very considerable expenditure — the equivalent in 1954 of 150 million dollars. Very many farm families have turned to other ways of earning their living and are probably lost to agriculture for ever. There are, however, some 60,000 families comprising at least 200,000 persons who are determined to return to the land. There is little or no hope of settling them in Western Germany and immigration opportunities should be found for them.

[1] 'The Problem of National Refugees and Overpopulation in Europe', a Report presented to the Committee of Ministers in pursuance of Resolution (53) 35, by M. Pierre Schneiter, Strasbourg, October 1954, CM (54) 178, p. 10.

The population situation in Germany no longer requires mass emigration, but a need for emigration remains with regard to certain groups and categories of persons for whom there are no satisfactory places in the economic and social life of the Federal Republic. Such persons include the expellee farmers, the stateless aliens and foreign refugees who remain, and probably certain groups of unskilled workers.

The situation in Austria is now very similar. Emigration schemes designed to meet the situation of the refugees — particularly those whose mother tongue is not German, — or schemes including substantial quotas for refugees, would greatly help Austria with some of its social problems and assist the economic rehabilitation and development of the country.

The economic improvement of the last few years has not, however, greatly modified the population situation in the Netherlands. Full employment is enjoyed, but the labour force increases by some 40,000 to 50,000 per annum, and if emigration were to cease the total population would rise from some 10·6 million in 1954 to some 14·3 million in 1981 — provided, of course, that present demographic trends continue. In a country which must import most of the raw materials for its industry, the task of absorbing such a population increase is almost insuperable. The situation is most serious in the agricultural sector. The agricultural population is increasing at a greater rate than the population as a whole and the opportunities for absorption in agriculture are practically non-existent: the agricultural labour force has increased by only a little over 1 per cent since 1909, and the amount of arable land per inhabitant is already by far the lowest in Europe. Emigration thus remains essential for the Netherlands and the emphasis must be placed on migration of the surplus agricultural manpower.

Economic improvement in Italy and Greece has perhaps made the population problems of these countries a little less acute, but it has scarcely changed their character. In Greece the recent natural disasters have been a retrogressive factor. Under-employment remains very serious in the agricultural sector and is believed to be equivalent to some 800,000 to 900,000 persons unemployed. It has recently been estimated by the Ministry of Welfare that nearly 25 per cent of the entire population is classifiable as destitute. The Greek Government is striving to develop the country's productive equipment and exploit its natural resources but, in the words of OEEC, if it were 'to finance the investment programme from its own resources and at the same time maintain equilibrium in its balance of payments it would have to reduce consumption to a point which would be quite unacceptable'.[1] It is clear, therefore, that in addition to the continuation of foreign aid some of the manpower surplus must be removed by emigration if the standard of living is not to fall even below its present level.

In Italy unemployment has remained in the region of 1·7 to 1·9 million since 1947, but the recent economic improvement has almost certainly resulted in a reduction of the number of under-employed; under-employment was estimated in 1951 to involve as many as 2 million persons, mostly working in agriculture. Nevertheless increasing economic strength has enabled Italy to plan to absorb much of its surplus manpower during the next ten years. In the Vanoni Plan [2] it is estimated that this surplus manpower will total 4,800,000 during the period 1955–64, but that some 4 million additional jobs will be created. This does, however, presuppose a net emigration of at least 800,000 workers, making with their dependants a total of perhaps 1,500,000 persons. Much of this emigration will have to take place during the early years of the Plan.

Thus, although there has been improvement in the European situation since 1950, there is still a need for large-scale emigration. The general improvement in economic conditions has led to a change in the type of persons available for emigration — or rather the type of persons whose emigration would contribute most to alleviating population pressure. It is clear that the problem now concerns agricultural workers and semi-skilled or unskilled workers rather than surplus workers as such. Geographically the emphasis has passed to Southern Europe. With the exception of the Netherlands, the main surplus population problems of Europe are in Italy and Greece.

There have been great changes also in the immigration countries. In the immediate postwar years countries such as Argentina and Australia were able to receive large numbers of immigrants from Europe without too much regard for the types of skill they had to offer. This situation no longer applies. In Latin America the high rate of natural increase has made the demographic need for migrants much less, but has increased the need for immigrant workers of a reasonable standard of skill, who would contribute to a rise in the present low levels of productivity and thus help to accomplish the immense task of absorbing a growing population at improved living standards. Furthermore, wage levels in Latin America are such as to make it unwise to send immigrants who do not have definite skills to exercise. In Australia, although unskilled immigrants can be

[1] *OEEC Fifth Annual Report*, 1954.
[2] 'Study of the Development of National Income and Employment during the Period 1955–64', presented by M. Ezio Vanoni, Minister of the Budget.

employed at living standards higher than those they could find in many European countries, the number of them which can be placed depends very largely on the number of skilled immigrants received each year. Further, in many of the traditional immigration countries, industrial development during and since the late war has outstripped agricultural development and tended to unbalance the national economies. Thus there is a need for immigrants who can be employed in the agricultural sectors and who will remain on the land. While opportunities exist in countries of the British Commonwealth for the placement of agricultural workers in dependent employment at good wages, it is only possible to place European agricultural workers in Latin America satisfactorily if arrangements are made whereby they own, or will eventually own, the land on which they work.

This changed situation has had its effect on the general orientation of ICEM's policy and operations. Without losing sight of the special problems in Germany and Austria, and while increasing its assistance to the Netherlands, ICEM is concentrating upon the expansion of emigration from Italy and Greece. This means it must try to effect the migration of farm workers and urban workers at present unskilled. Opportunities must be found for these people and they must be helped to qualify themselves for the opportunities that exist; the key programmes are therefore vocational training, placement, and land settlement.

ICEM is encouraging European governments to develop extensive vocational training schemes for potential emigrants and is advising them on the types of training and the trades which will give the trainee the best chance of successful emigration. ICEM has not now the resources to undertake a vocational training programme of the size the situation demands, but, in co-operation with governments, it is carrying out certain experimental and demonstration projects which it is hoped will lead governments to embark on the large-scale training programmes required. The need of vocational training to raise the level of competence of Europe's large mass of unskilled and semi-skilled workers is generally recognized, and it is the Committee's hope that, as the necessary programmes are initiated, a reasonable proportion of the training resources will be set aside for those persons who wish to emigrate. The orientation, information, and language training programmes of ICEM also have an essential part in these efforts to make the European migrant more qualified for the place which awaits him overseas.

In the immigration countries, particularly in Latin America, ICEM is steadily expanding placement networks to find employment opportunities and to place European immigrants in them. It realizes that its work in this connexion is of an emergency nature and will become unnecessary when these countries have comprehensive employment services of their own. It therefore works very closely with Technical Assistance experts who are helping the Latin-American countries to establish such services.

ICEM is also pushing ahead with its work to help governments to establish sound agricultural colonies which will provide outlets for some of Europe's surplus agricultural workers and will contribute to developing the primary production of the immigration countries. Here the problem is largely financial and the solution appears to be an equitable division of the investment requirements between the country in which the settlement will be located, the country which will send the immigrant settlers, and external sources aware of the potential value of immigrant land settlement. Some of the interested governments have recently given indications which suggest that even this difficult problem will gradually be overcome.

What, then, are the future prospectives? It seems reasonable to predict that although ICEM must try to raise the annual level of its own movements and of total emigration from Europe, the future emphasis of its work will be on quality rather than quantity. It must do its best to solve the difficult dilemma of reducing population pressure in Europe without draining away too many of the workers needed for strengthening the European economy, while at the same time providing the type of immigrant that the developing countries overseas require. If it is to solve this dilemma, it is fairly clear that the emphasis of ICEM's work in the future must be increasingly on improving the techniques of migration and helping to develop the absorptive capacities of immigration countries.

It might be useful at this stage to attempt some estimate of the magnitude of the problem with which ICEM has to deal. That such an attempt must be tentative and must risk being proved inaccurate by time is demonstrated by the progress made by Western Germany in absorbing its refugee population during the last five years. Nevertheless, ICEM believes that migration from the European countries with which it is chiefly concerned, Germany, Austria, the Netherlands, Italy, and Greece, should average some 340,000 per annum during the period 1956 to 1960. Of this number it would appear that 180,000 should come from Italy, 60,000 from the Netherlands, and 30,000 from Greece, whereas some 55,000 per annum may be expected to leave Germany and 15,000 to leave Austria. Probably no more than half of these migrants will need financial assistance from ICEM and many of them will need no assistance at all. However, if this average is to be reached and maintained it is reasonably clear that ICEM's work towards developing migration opportunities and improving migration machinery must be considerably developed.

This emphasis on the promotional side of ICEM's work, which does not of course mean any neglect of the transport aspects, will serve an additional purpose. It will create the conditions which will permit a free flow of migration, organized on the basis of international co-operation and in conformity with modern standards of social welfare, even after the need for an international operational agency has ceased to exist. As ICEM works to raise the level of migratory movements it will help to develop the national institutions and the habits of international co-operation in migration matters which will enable future movements to continue on an appropriate level and in a satisfactory manner.

PART III

IMMIGRATION COUNTRIES

Chapter 9

UNITED STATES

BY

ERNEST RUBIN

American University, Washington, D.C.

INTRODUCTION

BETWEEN 1790 and 1950 the population of the United States increased from 4 million to 151 million; during these 160 years the gross national product (in constant 1947 dollars) rose from an estimated 1 billion dollars to 300 billion dollars. Table I gives the growth of the United States population, gross national product, and *per capita* gross national product. The gross national product figures prior to 1910 have been derived, with certain adjustments and conversions, from the studies of Kuznets and Martin and will be used primarily to indicate magnitudes and trends.

Since the primary purpose of this paper is to examine the relationships between immigration trends and the growth of the American economy, I shall consider those economic periods that appear to be fairly homogeneous. These homogeneous periods are in fact arbitrarily selected long-term intervals which appear to possess, at least to a reasonable degree, the property of economic homogeneity. I have chosen three broad periods which may be briefly described as follows:

(1) *Period 1790 to 1870.*—During this interval of eighty years the United States may be characterized as an underdeveloped country, with little technology and little capital and heavily oriented in its economy toward agriculture. Until 1865 a large part or region of the country, the south, depended upon slave labour. Estimated gross immigration to the United States between 1790 and 1870 amounted to about 7·6 million, of which 6·6 million came between 1845 and 1870.

(2) *Period 1870 to 1914.*—In the period between the end of the Civil War in the United States and the beginning of the First World War in Europe, the United States became an industrial nation. During these years Europe made large capital investments in the United States, stimulating large-scale industrial development in oil,

coal, and steel and large-scale transportation, primarily in the railroads. At the same time various inventions, *e.g.* in the electrical and automotive fields, contributed to the economic impetus. The economic organizations that arose in this period were the trusts, the cartels, and the modern corporations. Between 1870 and 1914

TABLE I

THE GROWTH OF THE POPULATION AND OF THE GROSS NATIONAL PRODUCT OF THE UNITED STATES, 1790–1955

Year	Population (millions)	Decennial Increase (millions)	Gross National * Product (billion 1947 dollars)	Decennial Increase (billion 1947 dollars)	Gross National Product *per capita* (1947 dollars)
1790	3·9	—	1·0	—	256
1800	5·3	1·4	1·7	0·7	321
1810	7·2	1·9	2·2	0·5	306
1820	9·6	2·4	2·5	0·3	260
1830	12·9	3·3	3·2	0·7	248
1840	17·1	4·2	5·0	1·8	292
1850	23·2	6·1	8·4	3·4	362
1860	31·4	8·2	14·0	5·6	446
1870	39·8	8·4	13·0	– 1·0	327
1880	50·2	10·4	25·0	12·0	498
1890	62·9	12·7	38·5	13·5	612
1900	76·0	13·1	54·0	15·5	711
1910	91·8	15·8	86·1	·32·1	938
1920	105·7	13·9	102·1	16·0	966
1930	122·8	17·1	135·2	33·1	1101
1940	131·7	8·9	171·6	36·4	1303
1950	150·7	19·8	264·7	97·1	1756
1955	165·0 †	14·3 †	330·0 †	55·3 †	2000 †

* Gross national product for the years 1790–1900 is based, in part, on the sources cited below. For the years 1910–50 the *National Income*, 1954 edition, was used.
† Provisional estimates.

Sources : Robert F. Martin, *National Income in the U.S., 1799–1938*, National Industrial Conference Board, New York, 1939, pp. 6-15 ; Simon Kuznets, *National Product since 1869*, National Bureau of Economic Research, New York, 1946, pp. 86, 88 ; U.S. Department of Commerce. *National Income*, 1954 edition, Washington, 1954, p. 5 and pp. 216-17.

the human capital investment in the form of (gross) immigration amounted to 25 million persons. During these years the economy of the country shifted from an agricultural to an industrial orientation. The economy of the country was better balanced, preparing the way for a more rapid utilization of national resources.

(3) *Period 1914 to 1954.*—Primarily as a result of the First

World War the status of the United States in the world economy changed from a debtor to a creditor nation. During the four decades since 1914 the economic rise of the United States has been phenomenal; as a result of two world wars the expansion of industry was tremendously accelerated. (The estimated *per capita* gross national product (Table I) appears to have doubled between 1790 and 1880, *i.e.* over a period of ninety years; however, in less than half that time, *i.e.* in the forty years between 1914 and 1954, the *per capita* gross national product doubled.) Various estimates place the United States share of world national income (as of 1951) at about 40 per cent. In the last thirty years, *i.e.* 1924–54, immigration to the United States has changed drastically. From 1914 to 1954 gross immigration amounted to 8·9 million. Since the present quota system went into effect in 1924 the aggregate immigration amounts to 4·1 million.

I. THE PRE-INDUSTRIAL PERIOD, 1790–1870

For the years 1790 through 1820 a series of immigration data on an annual basis is not available. According to early writers on immigration it is estimated that 250,000 immigrants came to the United States between 1783, the close of the Revolutionary War, and 1820 when immigration statistics were first collected and published on an annual basis. It is my impression that this figure did not include the non-white population, primarily slaves, who were legally imported from Africa until 1808 and for many years thereafter smuggled into the country.

In Table II the foreign-born and total population of the United States are shown for the period 1790–1955. For the years prior to 1850 the figures for the foreign-born are only provisional estimates based on (1) immigration estimates for 1790–1819, (2) immigration data for the years 1820–50, and (3) various assumptions as to foreign-born mortality and emigration. It will be noted that the foreign-born for 1790 are estimated at one-half million (of which 300,000–350,000 were non-white). Although the foreign-born population slowly increases in the fifty years 1790–1840, the ratio of foreign-born to total declines from about 13 per cent in 1790 to 8 per cent in 1840.

Immigration to the United States, as officially reported, between 1820 and 1845 amounted to 1·1 million, but actual immigration was in fact greater. (For the period prior to 1870 it is necessary to re-examine the immigration statistics carefully, since there are many inaccuracies in these data, including under-reporting.) The introduction of steam vessels greatly augmented immigration. From

1845 onwards immigration exceeded 150,000 annually, except for a few recession years, 1858–59, and the Civil War years 1861–62.

The characteristics of the immigration to the United States prior to 1870 are well known and may be briefly summarized here. First, the immigration is almost entirely from the United Kingdom and the German States. The largest single group came from Ireland,

TABLE II

THE TOTAL AND FOREIGN-BORN POPULATION OF THE
UNITED STATES, 1790–1955

(millions)

Year	Total United States Population	Total Foreign-born	Foreign-born as Percentage of Total
1790	3·9	0·5*	12·8*
1800	5·3	0·6*	11·3*
1810	7·2	0·8*	11·1*
1820	9·6	1·0*	10·4*
1830	12·9	1·2*	9·3*
1840	17·1	1·4*	8·2*
1850	23·2	2·2	9·5
1860	31·4	4·1	13·1
1870	39·8	5·6	14·1
1880	50·2	6·7	13·3
1890	62·9	9·2	14·6
1900	76·0	10·3	13·6
1910	92·0	13·5	14·7
1920	105·7	13·9	13·2
1930	122·8	14·2	11·6
1940	131·7	11·6	8·8
1950	150·7	10·3	6·8
1955	165·0*	10·0*	6·1

* Provisional estimate.

Source : U.S. Bureau of the Census, *Historical Statistics of the United States, 1789–1945*, Washington, 1949, p. 25, and U.S. Bureau of the Census, *Statistical Abstract of the United States, 1954*, Washington, 1954, p. 40.

2·5 million or about one-third of all the immigrants who came in the period 1790–1870. Other parts of the United Kingdom furnished 1·6 million. Almost as many came from Germany as from Ireland — about 2·3 million in this period. These areas furnished about 85 per cent of the immigrants during this eighty-year interval. In the main this immigration consisted of agricultural and unskilled labourers. The demographic characteristics of the immigration for the period 1820–70 are : between three-fifths and two-thirds of the immigrants were males; the median age of the immigrants was under 25 years, the males being on an average slightly older than the females. Of importance is the point that almost all the female immigrants were in the child-bearing period.

The population of the United States grew steadily during the period 1790–1870; in eighty years the population had increased ten times from 3·9 million to 39·8 million. This increase was the result of native fertility strongly assisted by immigration and the fertility of the immigrants. Between 1790 and 1870 estimated gross national product rose from 1 billion dollars to 13 billion dollars. The decade 1860–70 included the extremely destructive Civil War, during which time the economic growth of the United States reversed. The *per capita* gross national product for 1870 reflects the decline, compared with 1860, and is only slightly higher than that of 1790. The rise in the *per capita* gross national product during the pre-industrial period was slow, *i.e.* between 1790 and 1860 the rise from 256 to 446 dollars *per capita* gross national product was at the rate of only seven-eighths of 1 per cent (compounded annually). The contribution of immigration was to provide part of the labour needed for the recovery and expansion after the Civil War.

II. THE RISE OF AMERICAN INDUSTRY, 1870–1914

Recognition of the value of immigration to the United States appears to come in years of war crisis. The only piece of Congressional legislation to encourage immigration and actually allocate funds for this purpose was signed by President Lincoln in July 1864. The agency that was set up to encourage immigration lasted until 1868. Since 1868 the United States has passed legislation that either prohibits or restricts immigration, except during the First World War and the Second World War when special Acts were passed to obtain foreign labour from countries in the Western Hemisphere.

Between 1870 and 1914 the volume of immigration increased tremendously; at the same time the composition of European immigration to the United States changed considerably. Of the 25 million that arrived in this forty-five-year period, the principal immigrant groups were: 4 million Italians, 4 million Austro-Hungarians, 3·3 million Russians, 3·2 million Germans, 2·4 million British, 2 million Irish, and 2 million Scandinavians. This immigration supplied the unskilled and semi-skilled labour that was needed in the new mines, factories, railroads, steel plants, etc. It also supplied some capital, but it is difficult to estimate the amount of liquid capital that was brought or transferred to the United States from Europe by the immigrants.

The population of the United States increased from 39·8 million in 1870 to an estimated 99 million in 1914, or an increase of about 250 per cent in forty-four years. In the forty years 1870 to 1914 the gross national product rose from 13 billion dollars to 91 billion dollars — about a sevenfold increase.

During the half-century following the end of the Civil War in the United States there existed a unique combination of factors that provided for this spectacular accelerated rate of growth in the American economy. Advances in technology, heavy European investment in the United States, large areas of fertile land and natural resources, together with a population sufficiently large to exploit and to develop these potentials, provided the conditions for this rapid growth. The role of population was very important as one of the factors in this development because unskilled and semi-skilled labour was required in great numbers. Advancing technology had begun to substitute machine for hand operations, but this development had only begun.

Although the nationality composition of European migration had changed, shifting from north-west to south-east origins, the basic demographic characteristics were consistent with those of the immigrants who came prior to 1870. The median age of immigrants was under 25 years, and about two-thirds of the immigrants were males.

After 1840 the foreign-born proportion of the total population rose almost steadily until 1910 (Table I). For the years 1870, 1890, and 1910 this component exceeded 14 per cent of the national population. A more accurate estimate of the importance of the foreign-born in the economy of this period may be formed in terms of labour-force participation. Although there are no breakdowns to show the foreign-born in the total labour force we do have an indication of the labour-force participation by this group in terms of the age and sex distribution.

According to Census returns, the age group 0–13·9 years of the foreign-born averaged 5 per cent of the foreign-born population during the period 1870–1914. In 1910, *e.g.*, the median age of the foreign-born was about 38 years compared with 24 years for total population. We also know that the foreign-born women participated to a higher degree in the labour force than native-born women, and we also know that among the foreign-born the sex ratio averaged 120, *i.e.* 120 males to 100 females. Although the foreign-born averaged about 14 per cent of the total population in the years 1870–1914, an estimate on the conservative side would place the foreign-born at more than one-third of the national labour force. Of a total population in 1910 of 92 million, native-born under 15 years amounted to 28 million of a total native population of 78 million, *i.e.* native-born 15 years and over amounted to 50 million compared with 12·5 million foreign-born 15 years of age and over. On this basis adult foreign-born stand in a relation of one to four to the adult native-born population. In view of the other known facts the foreign-born participation in the labour force exceeded this 25 per cent level, which would be a lower bound set by demographic conditions.

TABLE III

NATIVE WHITE POPULATION OF FOREIGN PARENTAGE IN
THE UNITED STATES, 1890–1950

(millions)

Year	Both Parents Foreign	One Parent Foreign
1890	8·1	3·4
1900	10·6	5·0
1910	12·9	6·0
1920	15·7	7·0
1930	17·4	8·5
1940	15·2	8·0
1950	14·8	8·8

Source : U.S. Bureau of the Census, *Statistical Abstract of the U.S.*, *1954*, Washington, 1954, p. 40.

In addition to examination of direct participation in the labour force by the foreign-born, a separate examination is required regarding their contribution to the population by way of children. This is an important residual effect of immigration, contributing substantially to the economic growth of the country. Table III gives the native-born white of foreign or mixed parentage over the years 1890 to 1950. We consider the population contribution, shown in Table III, to consist of the total for 'Both Parents Foreign' and one-half for 'One Parent Foreign'. Note that for the years 1890, 1900, and 1910 this would amount respectively to about 10, 13, and 16 million as the increment of the foreign-born by way of parentage, or an amount somewhat greater than the foreign-born population in those years (see Table II), *i.e.* 9·2, 10·3, and 13·5 million respectively. The children of the foreign-born, 14 years and older, should also be considered in terms of labour-force participation. In

1910 children of foreign parentage over 14 years amounted to about 8 million. The foreign-born and their children born in the United States probably accounted for 40 per cent of the labour force during the major part of the period 1870 to 1914.

III. THE DOMINANCE OF AMERICAN INDUSTRY, 1914–54

In the four decades from 1914 to 1954 the United States became the dominant industrial power of the world. This period embraced two world wars in which the role of the United States was that of an arsenal for the Western powers. Partly as a result of these wars, the industrial growth, as shown by the gross national product (Table I), spurted at an accelerated rate. And after each of these wars, particularly after the Second World War, the United States helped to reconstruct areas of widespread destruction in Europe and elsewhere.

Although the United States found it necessary to import temporary labour from Western Hemisphere countries in the First and Second World Wars, and proportionately more in the Second World War, important restrictive immigration legislation was passed over Presidential veto in 1917. This legislation imposed a 'literacy' test requirement — the main purpose of which was to provide a method of exclusion. After the end of the First World War the first Quota Act went into effect in 1921. This set up the temporary quota, which was replaced by the Immigration Act of 1924, setting up a permanent quota system. Though modified several times since 1924, most recently by the McCarran Act of 1952, the essentials of the 1924 Quota Act are in operation to-day. Special legislation after the Second World War was passed to facilitate the entry of war brides, displaced persons, and other refugees.

Of particular interest are the changes in the composition of immigration to the United States that have taken place since 1924 and the effects of those changes on the population. (Immigration during the Second World War was small and need not be considered here.)

During the period 1900 to 1954 net immigration contributed approximately 13·6 million to the United States population. Between 1 July 1924, the effective date of the present quota system, and 1 July 1954 net immigration amounted to 2·9 million. Thus net immigration in the thirty years 1924 to 1954 accounted for only one-fifth of the entire net immigration since the beginning of the century. As was to be expected, the quota system sharply reduced the pre-First World War volume of immigration. In fact the reduction of immigration was not from a fixed level, but rather the pre-First World War migration had increased over the years, *i.e.* an upward trend is readily apparent for the period 1875 to 1914. Had the legislation (and the Second World War) not intervened, it would appear that the immigration volume would have continued the upward climb except for the periodic falls with recessions and depressions.

The effect of the reduction of the volume of immigration is directly reflected in changes in the foreign-born population. Table IV shows the changes in the foreign-born population since 1900.

TABLE IV

FOREIGN-BORN WHITE POPULATION OF THE
UNITED STATES, 1900–55

(millions)

Year	Foreign-born White	Percentage + or −	Percentage of Total Population	Percentage of Total White Population
1900	10·2	—	13·4	15·3
1910	13·3	+ 30·7	14·5	16·3
1920	13·7	+ 2·8	13·0	14·5
1930	14·0	+ 2·0	11·4	12·7
1940	11·4	− 18·3	8·7	9·7
1950	10·1	− 11·1	6·7	7·5
1955*	9·7*	− 3·0	6·0	6·7

* Estimated on basis of migration data and on the assumption of 250,000 annual mortality.

Source : U.S. Bureau of the Census, *Statistical Abstract of the U.S., 1954,* Washington, 1954.

Changes in the size of the foreign-born population are also associated with changes in the age and sex composition of this population. During the periods of 'free' immigration, *i.e.* immigration unaffected by restrictive and quota legislation, the median age of the foreign-born was 37·1 years in 1890, 38·5 years in 1900, and 37·2 years in 1910. The First World War cut down the volume of immigration and the median age rose to 40 years ; thereafter the quota system has been in effect, with the result that the median age of the foreign-born rose to 44 years in 1930, 51 years in 1940, and 56 years in 1950. The reasons for this increase in median age of the foreign-born are directly traceable to changes in the age distribution of the immigrants who came after 1924.[1] An indication of this change is shown in Table V. The years 1951–54 reflect in part the admission of special groups, *i.e.* displaced persons, orphans, and refugees.

TABLE V

PER CENT DISTRIBUTION OF IMMIGRANTS TO THE UNITED STATES
BY AGE, 1 JULY 1900–1 JULY 1954

(age in years)

Years	Under 16	16–44	45 and over
1901–10	17·0	78·1	4·9
1911–20	16·3	76·7	7·0
1921–30	17·6	73·7	7·4
1931–40	16·6	66·4	17·0
1941–50	15·6	66·9	17·5
1951–54	22·6	62·1	15·3

Source : U.S. Department of Justice, Annual Reports of the Immigration and Naturalization Service.

Not only has the age composition of the foreign-born changed markedly, but also the sex ratio as well. In 1910 there were 129 white males to 100 females in the foreign-born white population. By 1950 the sex ratio had declined to 102 for this group, and as of

TABLE VI

SEX RATIO OF IMMIGRANTS TO THE UNITED STATES, 1900–54

Year	Sex Ratio
1900–9	229·1
1910–19	186·4
1920–29	128·2
1930–39	80·8
1940–49	63·4
1950–54	86·9

Source : U.S. Department of Justice, Annual Reports of the Immigration and Naturalization Service.

1 July 1955 I estimate it at 100. As in the case of the age distribution, the change in the sex balance was primarily the result of the immigration that came to the United States since 1924 (Table VI).

The immigration during the period 1924 to 1954 was small in

[1] For a discussion of how the immigration law of 1924 affected the demographic characteristics of immigration after 1924, see E. Rubin, 'Immigration and Population Trends in the United States : 1900–1940', *American Journal of Economics and Sociology*, vol. vi, no. 3, April 1947, pp. 345-62.

volume, and from a demographic-economic standpoint was less beneficial to the country than the 'free' type of immigration. By this I mean that the recent immigration (*a*) accentuated the ageing of the foreign-born instead of going counter to this trend in the native population and (*b*) also accentuated the imbalance in the native sex ratio which the immigration prior to 1924 had offset. These remarks refer to the quantitative aspects of the situation ; nothing is implied, however, as to any qualitative differences between 'old' immigration, *i.e.* prior to 1924, and the 'new', *i.e.* since 1924.

IV. IMMIGRATION SINCE 1945 AND FUTURE PROSPECTS

Migration to and from the United States for the years 1946–54 is shown in Table VII. As in many previous peace-time years since 1924, the annual quotas of approximately 150,000 immigrants were

TABLE VII

MIGRATION TO AND FROM THE UNITED STATES, 1946-54

(thousands)

Fiscal Year ending June 30	Aliens admitted			Aliens departing			Excess of Admissions over Departures	
	Total	Immi-grants	Non-immi-grants	Total	Emi-grants	Non-emi-grants	Total	Immi-grant over Emi-grant
1946	312	109	203	204	18	186	108	91
1947	514	147	366	323	23	301	190	125
1948	646	171	476	448	21	427	198	150
1949	636	188	447	430	25	406	206	164
1950	676	249	427	457	28	429	219	222
1951	671	206	465	473	26	447	198	180
1952	781	266	516	509	22	488	272	244
1953	656	170	486	545	24	520	111	146
1954	775	208	567	600	31	569	175	177

Source : U.S. Department of Justice, Annual Report of the Immigration and Naturalization Service for the fiscal year ended 30 June 1954, Table 11.

frequently not filled. Under certain arrangements, such as that provided for in the Displaced Persons Act of 1948, many immigrants were charged to future annual quotas. The reason for this procedure goes back to the quota set-up, which prevents the transfer of quotas from one country to another or from previous years to a current year. In effect the quota part of the immigration law operates to limit immigration in three ways : (*a*) by the setting of a total world quota; (*b*) within the total world quota, total country quotas are set and the unused quotas are not transferable to other countries in a current year ; and (*c*) unused quotas are not treated as a credit that may be drawn upon at some future time. For the thirty-year period 1924 to 1954, the total possible quota was about 4·7 millions. During this time only 2 million quota immigrants came into the United States, *i.e.* there were about 2·7 million unused quota numbers. Because the quota is set on a national origins basis, the quota is almost always oversubscribed for some countries and undersubscribed for others. In recent years several countries entitled to large quotas have not used them. Nor does the quota system make allowances for emigrants who were admitted as quota immigrants. Such emigrants might be treated as if they had entered the United States as non-quota immigrants or as non-immigrants on an extended stay. Statistics are not available to indicate the size of this group.

Immigration to the United States since the end of the Second World War is the result of many factors — economic, political, humanitarian, national security, etc. It is perhaps the most artificial type of immigration to the United States that has come since the founding of the country. The fraction of immigration that is responsive to cyclical movements in the American economy is scarcely discernible. Refugees, displaced persons, orphans, and war brides account for a sizable proportion of the immigrants admitted since 1945. In the six years 30 June 1948 to 30 June 1954, 405,000 immigrants were admitted in the displaced persons' category out of 1·7 million immigrants admitted in this period. Immigrant war brides (and their children) exceeded 100,000 immigrants after the Second World War.

The postwar immigration policy as embodied in the McCarran Act of 1952 is subject to increasing criticism in the United States, from many standpoints. From the economic side, what must be explained to the legislators and to the public is that the economy of a country is not a static entity or whole. The popular but mistaken view of immigration is that the more people there are to share the economic pie, the less each person gets. The idea of an expanding pie, *i.e.* of a growing economy wherein the total national product and the *per capita* national product increase simultaneously, is an alien notion to the natives. During the Congressional session that ended in August 1955, legislation that would provide for additional refugee admissions was not acted upon. Since the end of the Second

World War the immigration policies have become part of the American political scene — perhaps more so than at any time since the First World War.

Although it is not part of the permanent immigration set-up, attention must be called to the imports of labour during both world wars, as well as for certain years after the Second World War. From an economic standpoint it may be argued that this type of immigration, as well as the entire immigration since 1924, has been of only marginal significance. In periods of crisis the economic margin takes on special importance.

Part of the immigration picture, in the economic sense, is the move of United States citizens from Puerto Rico. This internal migration is in substance equivalent to immigration to the United States, although not considered as such. Essentially the immigration from other parts of the Western Hemisphere (as well as Puerto Rico) consists of unskilled or semi-skilled labour that is replacing to some extent the immigrants from South-eastern Europe. A major part of the immigration from the Western Hemisphere is non-quota.

It is doubtful whether there will be any basic change, that is, liberalization of the current immigration policy. Although the United States could assimilate twice the present quota, in addition to eligible non-quota migrants, I am not too hopeful that such legislation will be forthcoming soon. On a comparative basis the liberalization of trade is a simpler matter than the liberalization of immigration. Judging from the progress in the trade field along these lines, which appears to move in an up-and-down fashion, it will take longer to accomplish creditable ends in this area. Perhaps what is needed is a GATT organization in the field of international migration that will give direction to reasonable ends and will help towards achieving an optimum use of the resources of the world.

Chapter 10

CANADA

BY

MABEL F. TIMLIN
University of Saskatchewan

I

A NATION which follows a selective immigration policy finds its intake of migrants for any period determined by the relation between its own principles of selection, the numbers it is prepared to take in specified categories, and the availability of candidates from preferred sources whose health and character make them acceptable to the receiving country. Up to 1914 Canadian policy in general gave priority to the immigration of farmers and farm workers and domestic servants from the British Isles, the United States, and continental Europe. As unoccupied arable land disappeared, particularly in areas accessible to transportation and in climatic ranges where agricultural production for the market was under current technologies feasible, the character both of policy and of emigration forces altered. In the 1920's immigration became to a greater extent than before an immigration of workers for industry rather than for agriculture. In the period since the Second World War this tendency has been greatly strengthened.

Thus in the postwar period although (apart from dependants) farmers and farm workers have formed the *second* most important group of immigrants, skilled workers have formed the largest class of entrants among workers. The differences in size between the two groups would be even larger if entrants could be classified, not by *intended* occupation at the time of landing, but by *actual* occupation one to two years later. In spite of the large-scale entry of agricultural labour the working force in agriculture has fallen not only relatively but absolutely during the postwar period.

Since the Second World War, although Canadian policy has grown increasingly generous in broadening terms of admissibility, it has become more self-consciously selective, not only for economic but also for other reasons. Before an account is attempted of the nature of the principles of selection and their origin, however, it

146

appears advisable to set up for reference data respecting the growth of the Canadian population, first for the total period since 1851 and second for the postwar period.

Table I below is just what its title implies. It is a careful reconstruction, made by Mr. Nathan Keyfitz, of the total population changes for census periods over the last century. Table II has been constructed from Table I and exposes three aspects of the total record which are worth noting. The first is the extraordinary variability in percentage rates of change from one census period to another. The second is the evidence that this variability has been

TABLE I

A RECONSTRUCTION OF CANADA'S POPULATION RECORD, 1851–1951

Census Period	Births	Deaths †	Immigra-tion	Emigration	Population at End of Decade
		(thousands)			
–1851	—	—	—	—	2,436
1851–1861	1,281	611	209	86	3,230
1861–1871	1,369	718	187	377	3,689
1871–1881	1,477	754	353	439	4,325
1881–1891	1,538	824	903	1110	4,833
1891–1901	1,546	828	326	505	5,371
1901–1911	1,931	811	1782	1067	7,207
1911–1921	2,338	1018	1592	1330	8,788
1921–1931	2,414	1053	1195	967	10,377
1931–1941	2,291	1070	150	241	11,507
1941–1951*	3,205	1216	548	380	14,009
Total 1851–1951	19,390	8903	7245	6502	

* Including Newfoundland from 1949, an estimated 345,000.
† Including 36,000 oversea casualties of the Second World War.

due principally to changes in the rate of net migration. The third is the tendency for net migration to be negative in the latter half of the nineteenth century and positive in the twentieth. A corollary is that the periods of heavy emigration were also mainly periods of heavy immigration, especially in proportion to the size of the population.

It is probably only a coincidence that the tendency towards negative net migration ran so largely parallel to the Great Depression of the nineteenth century. Heavy emigration started earlier than that depression and is probably related to the disappearance of free or cheap land of good quality and location east of the Canadian

Shield. The first transcontinental railway, the Canadian Pacific, was completed only in 1885, and differences between American and Canadian homestead and land settlement policies, as well as simple ignorance respecting the qualities of the new areas and their productivity under what were regarded as sub-arctic conditions, account probably in large part for the further delay in active settlement of the prairie region until 1896 and after.[1]

The single census period in the twentieth century, namely 1931–1941, that showed negative net migration had also certain institutional characteristics which emphasized the effects of economic

TABLE II

DECENNIAL NATURAL INCREASE AND NET MIGRATION
IN CANADA, 1851–1951

Census Period	Natural Increase	Net Migration	Population Increment for Decade	Percentage Change from Previous Census
	(thousands)			
1851–1861	670	+ 123	794	32·6
1861–1871	651	− 190	459	14·2
1871–1881	723	− 86	636	17·2
1881–1891	714	− 207	508	11·8
1891–1901	716	− 179	538	11·1
1901–1911	1120	+ 715	1836	34·2
1911–1921	1320	+ 262	1581	21·9
1921–1931	1486	+ 103	1589	18·1
1931–1941	1221	− 91	1130	10·9
1941–1951*	1989	+ 168	2502	21·7 (18·6)

* Population increment includes an estimated 345,000 for Newfoundland, which does not appear therefore in natural increase or net migration. If Newfoundland is excluded the percentage change is 18·6.

Note.—Table I is Mr. Nathan Keyfitz's revision of Table 11 contained on p. 62 of his article, 'The Growth of Canadian Population', *Population Studies*, vol. iv, No. 1, June 1950, pp. 47-63.

factors. In the fiscal year ending 31 March 1931, Canada received 88,223 immigrants. Thereafter Order in Council, P.C. 695, passed by the Bennett Government on 21 March 1931, and interpretations made under it, virtually limited entry to close relatives of Canadian residents. The immigration of the 1930's was therefore predominantly feminine and the number of immigrants for the census period 1931–41 was the lowest in the century covered by Table I.[2]

[1] John W. Dafoe, *Clifford Sifton in Relation to his Times*, Toronto, Macmillan, chs. 5 and 11.
[2] Report of the Department of Mines and Resources, Fiscal Year ended 31 March 1948, Table I.

The level of emigration was raised by heavy deportations from Canada, particularly during the first five years. At that time a change of government apparently brought a change in policy. It is at least a tenable hypothesis that the rising rate of industrialization in Canada which has been in part the product of two world wars has tended toward a positive net migration. In the period since the Second World War the whole non-agricultural sector of the economy has grown at the expense of the agricultural sector. Thus the August Labour Survey figures for 1946 show 73·1 per

TABLE III

POPULATION CHANGES IN CANADA, 1945–54

Year	Total Population	Gain	Percentage Gain from Preceding Year
	(thousands)		
1945	12,394	—	—
1946	12,622	228	1·8
1947	12,888	226	2·1
1948	13,167	279	2·2
1949	13,447	280	2·1
1950	13,712	265	2·0
1951	14,009	297	2·2
1952	14,430	421	3·0
1953	14,781	351	2·4
1954	15,195	414	2·8
Total (9 years)		2801	22·6

Source : United Nations, *Monthly Bulletin of Statistics*, December 1954, p. 1. For 1951, census figure ; for others mid-year intercensal estimates. Figures for 1945 through 1948 have been adjusted to include Newfoundland so that they may be comparable with later figures.

cent of all workers with jobs in the non-agricultural sector and 26·9 per cent in the agricultural sector. Thereafter over the whole period to August 1953 the figure for the non-agricultural sector rises continuously, and for that month and year it is 82·4 per cent. Even the extensive unemployment in the non-agricultural sector of August 1954 brought the percentage down only to 81·2 per cent of all workers with jobs.[1]

Tables III and IV are included to give the population and immigration record for the postwar period. Fiscal rather than

[1] Dominion Bureau of Statistics, *The Labour Force, November 1945 to January 1955*, Reference Paper No. 58, Ottawa, Queen's Printer, 1955, pp. 30-2.

calendar years have been used in Table IV because the former give the shorter lag between the immigration figures and the mid-year

TABLE IV

IMMIGRATION INTO CANADA, 1946–54

Fiscal Year ending 31 March	Total	Oversea	United States
1946	31,081	23,627	7,454
1947	66,990	55,580	11,410
1948	79,194	70,160	9,034
1949	125,603	118,297	7,306
1950	86,422	78,762	7,660
1951	85,356	77,348	8,008
1952	211,220	203,450	7,770
1953	144,692	134,748	9,944
1954	174,154	164,860	9,294
Total	1,004,712	926,832	77,880

Sources: For 1946–49, Annual Reports of the Department of Mines and Resources, Ottawa.
For 1950–54, Annual Reports of the Department of Citizenship and Immigration, Ottawa.

population estimates. For the period June 1946 to March 1954 total emigration has been estimated at 444,000, and for the more limited period June 1951 to March 1954 at 158,000.[1]

II

The classic statement outlining postwar immigration policy was given by the late Mr. W. L. Mackenzie King to the Canadian Parliament on 1 May 1947.[2] The long-term policy was stated to be the building up of the Canadian population by immigration as well as by natural increase. Short-term policy was defined as an intention to bring in immigrants only at the rate at which they could be absorbed. Moreover, the Prime Minister stated that it is not a 'fundamental right' of any alien to enter Canada, and that he was sure there would be general agreement 'that the people of Canada do not wish, as a result of mass immigration, to make a fundamental alteration in the character of our population. . . .'

[1] These figures are taken from a revised table furnished by the Economics Branch of the Bank of Nova Scotia to replace Table 2 of the *Supplement* to the *Monthly Review* of the Bank for July 1954. Figures were supplied by the Dominion Bureau of Statistics.
[2] Debates of the House of Commons, 1947, pp. 2644-7.

Under current regulations, for non-Asians there are two broad groups of admissible classes. Group I may enter without regard to special trade qualifications. Group II must qualify for admission on the basis of trade or occupation. Under Group I come British subjects by birth or naturalization in the United Kingdom, Australia, New Zealand, or the Union of South Africa, citizens of Ireland, citizens of the United States, and citizens *born* in France or in the islands of St. Pierre or Miquelon. All these may enter provided they have sufficient means to maintain themselves until they have secured employment and provided they are not otherwise barred by the provisions of the Immigration Act [1] defining classes prohibited under medical, social, and security causes. In this group come also relatives of Canadian citizens and legal residents in direct line of relationship. Sponsorship is also accepted in cases of immigrants of exceptional merit. These include immigrants bringing in capital to start businesses of their own, or with outstanding qualifications whose entry is in the public interest, compassionate cases, and cases where employers sponsor admission of persons known to them whose services are deemed essential. In Group II (under which the bulk of workers have entered) a prospective immigrant must carry on some trade or occupation for which there is a shortage of qualified Canadian labour. Families of these immigrants are also of course admissible subject to the provisions of the Act.

With respect to Asiatic immigration, except for India, Pakistan, and Ceylon, landing is limited to the wife, husband, and unmarried children under 21 of any Canadian citizen resident in Canada in position to receive and care for dependants. For Chinese, exceptions have sometimes been made to permit entry of unmarried children up to the age of 25. Since the Chinese Immigration Act was repealed in May 1947 more than 11,000 Chinese have entered Canada under these provisions. With Asiatic members of the Commonwealth the Canadian Government has made agreements, concluded in 1951, under which in addition to relatives of degrees admissible from other Asiatic countries 150 nationals of India, 100 of Pakistan, and 50 of Ceylon are admissible annually.

No account, however brief, of Canadian immigration policy could be complete without some discussion of the provisions which give Canadian policy its extraordinary flexibility and at the same time lodge an extraordinarily wide area of discretion to regulate entries, both with respect to source and numbers, in the hands of the Minister in charge, and with officials of the Immigration Branch of the Department of Citizenship and Immigration. Section 20 (4) of

[1] *Revised Statutes of Canada, 1952*, ch. 325.

the consolidated Immigration Regulations set up under the 1952 Act reads as follows :

> Subject to the provisions of the Act and to these regulations the admission to Canada of any person is prohibited where in the opinion of a Special Inquiry Officer such person should not be admitted by reason of
>
> (*a*) the peculiar customs, habits, modes of life or methods of holding property in his country of birth or citizenship or in the country or place where he resided prior to coming to Canada ;
>
> (*b*) his unsuitability, having regard to the economic, social, industrial, educational, labour, health or other conditions existing, temporarily or otherwise, in Canada or in the area or country from or through which such person comes to Canada ; or
>
> (*c*) his probable inability to become readily assimilated or to assume the duties and responsibilities of Canadian citizenship within a reasonable time after his admission.

It is evident that under these provisions almost anyone can be barred and that changes in policy, particularly under subsection (*b*), can be made overnight !

III

Only the briefest account is possible here of factors determining policies set out above. Yet that account is necessary since on the nature and permanence of these factors rest future trends in Canadian immigration.

An understanding of Canadian policy requires in the first place the knowledge that Canada is not only a federal but a bi-cultural state, with two official languages, two different systems of civil law, and two basic racial stocks living sometimes in an uneasy compromise. The French-Canadian minority, about 30 per cent of the population, historically has opposed immigration which tends to change the ethnic balance of population in favour of the predominantly Protestant English-speaking majority. High rates of natural increase among French-Canadians have promised them in time a victory in the 'battle of the cradle', and any immigration policy understood by French Canada to increase the preponderance of the English-speaking section of the population must always take opposition from French Canada into account. French-Canadian attitudes have been modified to a degree in the postwar period on compassionate grounds through the influence of the Catholic Church and probably by the fact that Italian and other continental immigration has brought into Canada a large number of Roman Catholics. But a government of the day which follows a policy contrary to French-Canadian convictions must have strong convictions of its own supported by a strong majority.

Convictions reached in Canada respecting the assimilability of various ethnic groups must also be recognized. Troubles have occurred at various times because of expansion of organized religious groups living in collectivized communities and because of the tendency of racial groups, particularly Oriental, to concentrate in certain geographical areas. But origins of preferences lie more generally in certain statistical studies respecting rates of assimilation, based on the relations of origins and nativity to inter-marriage with native stocks, use of the English and French languages, illiteracy and school attendance, and crime.[1]

The parallelism between immigration and emigration which appears in Table I has led to the development in Canada of certain hypotheses respecting causal relations between the two magnitudes related to the Pearl-Reed theories of population growth.[2] These theories hold that immigration leads to emigration, and, if exit is impeded, to periods of unemployment. When depression threatens, these theories begin to take on importance. Allied with them is the concern felt in Canada over the size and highly professional character of emigration to the United States.[3]

Tables V and VI are included to show some of the effects of selection in the postwar period. Table V has been divided into two sections because of differences in the character of the two movements owing to transportation difficulties and movement of servicemen's dependants in the earlier period, the effects of the sterling crisis of 1949, modifications of Canadian policy made in 1950, and new classifications of immigrants introduced in the year 1949–50. Racial origin rather than nationality has been used because of the nature of the data available over the series of years.

Table VI is introduced because it covers the class of entrants where the nature of Canadian policy and preferences, public and

---

[1] See, for example, the study published by the Dominion Bureau of Statistics and based on the Census of 1921, entitled *Origin, Birthplace, Nationality and Language of the Canadian People*, Ottawa, King's Printer, 1929.

[2] M. C. MacLean, *Analysis of the Stages in the Growth of Population*, Ottawa, King's Printer, 1935 ; *Census of Canada, 1931*, vol. i, pp. 99-132 ; W. Burton Hurd, 'Some Implications of Prospective Population Trends', *Canadian Journal of Economics and Political Science*, vol. v, November 1939, pp. 492-503 ; and 'Demographic Trends in Canada', *Annals of the American Academy of Political and Social Science*, vol. 253, September 1947, pp. 10-15.

[3] Leon E. Truesdell, *The Canadian Born in the United States*, New Haven, Yale University Press, 1943.

TABLE V

RACIAL ORIGINS OF MAIN GROUPS OF POSTWAR IMMIGRANTS TO CANADA

Fiscal Year	Oversea						Percentage of Oversea Movement	Total Oversea	United States	Grand Total
	British	Dutch	Italian	Polish	German	Total 5 Origins				
1945–46	20,162	97	58	528	234	21,079	89·2	23,627	7,454	31,081
1946–47	47,976	2,365	142	336	338	51,157	92·0	55,580	11,410	66,990
1947–48	44,788	4,264	204	4,269	530	54,055	77·0	70,160	9,034	79,194
1948–49	40,015	9,866	5,207	15,420	4,785	75,293	63·6	118,297	7,306	125,603
Sub-total	152,941	16,592	5,611	20,553	5,887	201,584	75·3	267,664	35,204	302,868
1949–50	19,198	8,372	7,230	10,884	4,807	50,491	64·1	78,762	7,660	86,422
1950–51	15,429	9,514	9,766	6,535	7,487	48,731	63·0	77,348	8,008	85,356
1951–52	36,000	19,908	28,402	13,440	36,053	133,803	65·8	203,450	7,770	211,220
1952–53	40,152	19,530	18,016	3,360	26,590	107,648	79·9	134,748	9,944	144,692
1953–54	48,592	20,617	27,477	3,268	34,516	134,470	81·6	164,860	9,294	174,154
Sub-total	159,371	77,941	90,891	37,487	109,453	475,143	72·1	659,168	42,676	701,844
Total	312,312	94,533	96,502	58,040	115,340	676,727	73·0	926,832	77,880	1,004,712

Sources : Through 1948–49, Annual Reports of the Department of Mines and Resources.
1949–50 through 1953–54, Annual Reports of the Department of Citizenship and Immigration.

TABLE VI

RACIAL ORIGINS OF MAIN GROUPS, PROFESSIONAL CLASS, FISCAL YEARS 1949–50 THROUGH 1953–54

Fiscal Year	Oversea						United States	Sub-total 7 Origins	Percentage of Grand Total	Total Grand
	British	Dutch	French	German	Hebrew	Polish				
1949–50	690	45	56	31	115	72	466	1,485	82·0	1,812
1950–51	521	55	84	90	77	69	530	1,426	76·8	1,856
1951–52	1,556	192	150	608	240	251	693	3,690	79·9	4,867
1952–53	3,285	250	156	543	239	207	1522	6,202	88·7	6,996
1953–54 *	5,109	530	225	523	202	215	1039	7,843	87·9	8,924
Total	11,161	1072	671	1795	873	814	4250	20,646	83·4	24,455
Percentage of all entries in class	45·6	4·3	2·7	7·3	3·6	3·3	17·3	83·4		100

* In the fiscal year 1953–54 a new category of entrants appears in the statistical record of the Department of Citizenship and Immigration. This category is called 'Managerial (Owners, Managers, Officials)'. The class of professionals may therefore have been somewhat reduced by the appearance of this new category. Entrants numbered 1604, of whom 1490 came from the seven origins of Table VI. Numbers were as follows :

British	600	German	40	Polish	10
Dutch	67	Hebrew	78	United States	670
French	25				

Total : 1490 or 92·9 per cent.

Source : Annual Reports of the Department of Citizenship and Immigration.

private, is likely to operate with most effect in determining the ethnic origin of entrants. The growth in professional entrants is not an evidence of change in policy at the political level, but rather of shortages in supply in Canada of members of the engineering professions, designers and draughtsmen, teachers and nurses and other professional groups for whom expanding demands have been outrunning changes in supply.

The last aspect of policy is connected with rates of change in natural increase. While Canada has not in the past geared immigration explicitly to these, there are at least implications of a possible shift in policy. The opinion has been advanced that a 25 per cent increase in a decade is a 'very high rate of increase, compared with past Canadian and American experience', and further, 'Whether . . . it would be wise to grow by more than one-fourth, or 25 per cent, during the years 1951–61, leaves room for quite serious misgiving'.[1] Table III shows recent rates of growth when both natural increase and net migration are included. Table VII shows the demographic changes which have determined the rates of natural increase over the past thirty-four years. These rates must be taken into account in any consideration of possible future trends in immigration.

IV

Economic assessment is made difficult by the nearness of the migration inflow. The main assessment of effects must for the present rest on a consideration of the effects of the inflow of workers and their dependants. With respect to the group taken as a whole, indications are that postwar immigrants have been swift to copy the Canadian standard of living. Tables 122 ff. in the Census of 1951 gave early evidence of this. The effects upon the internal market in an economy only too 'open' should be healthy.

An estimate of the Department of Citizenship and Immigration for the period to the end of 1953 indicates that approximately 53 per cent of the total inflow have been workers. Skilled workers numbered about 132,000; managerial and professional groups about 33,000; trading about 22,000; and clerical about 35,000. Semi-skilled and general labourers were reckoned at about 12 per cent of the total inflow of workers.[2] Immigrants have been going

---

[1] Press Release, Department of Citizenship and Immigration, 18 August 1953. Address given by Mr. Jean Boucher, Special Assistant to the Deputy Minister, at the 1953 Couchiching Conference Round Table on Immigration Policy.

[2] Press Release, Department of Citizenship and Immigration, 7 May 1954. Address given by Mr. E. B. Reid, Chief of Information Services, at a meeting of the Association of Canadian Advertisers.

Table VII

Canadian Vital Statistics, 1921–54 *

Year	Live Births	Deaths	Natural Increase	Marriages	Rates per 1000 Population			
					Births	Deaths	Natural Increase	Marriages
Average 1921–25	254,524	104,925	149,599	67,558	27·4	11·3	16·1	7·3
Average 1926–30	243,277	112,609	130,668	73,517	24·1	11·2	12·9	7·3
Average 1931–35	235,039	107,244	127,795	70,302	21·6	9·8	11·8	6·5
Average 1936–40	236,405	113,195	123,210	99,031	20·7	9·9	10·8	8·7
Average 1941–45	286,124	118,825	167,299	116,903	23·7	9·8	13·9	9·7
1946	342,765	118,358	224,407	137,155	27·2	9·4	17·8	10·9
1947	371,740	121,050	250,711	130,228	28·8	9·4	19·4	10·1
1948	358,941	122,492	236,449	125,924	27·3	9·3	18·0	9·6
1949	366,139	124,047	242,092	123,877	27·3	9·2	18·1	9·2
1950	371,071	123,789	247,282	124,845	27·1	9·0	18·1	9·1
1951	380,101	125,454	254,647	128,230	27·2	9·0	18·2	9·2
1952	402,527	125,950	276,577	128,301	27·9	8·7	19·2	8·9
1953	416,825	127,381	289,444	130,837	28·2	8·6	19·6	8·9
1954 †	438,000	123,000	315,000	128,000	28·8	8·1	20·7	8·4

* Exclusive of Yukon and North-west Territories. Figures for 1921–48 have been adjusted to include Newfoundland. That Province joined Canada in 1949 and the adjustment has been made to make the earlier years comparable with the recent ones. † Estimated.

Source : Figures supplied to the Economics Branch, Bank of Nova Scotia, by the Dominion Bureau of Statistics.

157

mainly to those areas of Canada where the rate of industrialization has been highest and where internal migrants have been going also. More than half have gone to Ontario, with Quebec a poor second, and British Columbia and Alberta third and fourth.[1] Even agricultural immigrants have gone in the largest numbers to these same geographical areas, replacing farmers and farmers' sons who have joined the rural-urban trend. The Department of Citizenship and Immigration estimates that farmers and farmers' sons have been leaving Canadian farms for urban centres at a rate approximating 60,000 a year. The Department also estimates at about 10,000 the farms operated by immigrants as owners or under purchase options at the end of 1953.[2] Capital brought in by all postwar immigrants was estimated at 415 million dollars at the end of the same year.[3]

Since 1945 the Canadian economy has undergone a substantial expansion. Table VIII below gives index numbers showing changes in the constant dollar volume of the national income calculated from the National Accounts of Canada.

TABLE VIII

NATIONAL REAL INCOME IN CANADA, 1946–54

Year	Index No. 1946 = 100	Percentage of Previous Year
1946	100·0	. .
1947	101·3	101·3
1948	104·3	103·0
1949	107·5	103·0
1950	114·3	106·3
1951	120·5	105·5
1952	128·8	106·9
1953	131·9	103·8
1954 *	127·9	96·5

* Preliminary.

The fall in the national income in 1954 gives an indication of the flexibility of immigration policy and also of the importance of a maintained expansion if Canada is to be willing to maintain an inflow of immigrants. For the calendar year 1954 immigration was only 9 per cent below 1953. But the first months of the year were months of large inflow. Inflows began to decline in the month of

[1] *Annual Reports*, Department of Citizenship and Immigration.
[2] Press Release, Department of Citizenship and Immigration, 27 April 1954. Address given by Lt.-Col. Laval Fortier, Deputy Minister, to the Agricultural Institute of Canada. [3] E. B. Reid, *op. cit.*

Timlin — Canada

June, and for the last three months of the year were 40, 38, and 25 per cent respectively below inflows of the preceding year.

A rate of expansion approaching that indicated in Table VIII requires an expanding labour force. Tables IX and X below, provided by the Department of Labour, indicate some of the pertinent relations between immigration and the size of the postwar labour force. Preliminary checking of the new Labour Force Survey paper published in 1955 by the Dominion Bureau of Statistics indicates that the relations hold in the revised figures, though population in that publication is reckoned on the non-institutional population rather than the total civilian population.[1]

TABLE IX

CIVILIAN POPULATION AND LABOUR FORCE OF CANADA, 1947–54

Date	Civilian Population aged 14 and over	Civilian Labour Force	Percentage of Population
	(thousands)		
1947 : June 1	9,170	4907	53·5
1948 : June 1	9,302	4979	53·5
1949 : June 1	9,657 *	5141 *	53·3
1950 : June 1	9,790	5130	52·4
1951 : June 1	9,882	5179	52·4
1952 : June 1	10,108	5279	52·2
1953 : February 21	10,272	5194	50·6
1953 : June 1	10,285	5353	52·0
1954 : February 20	10,432	5230	50·1

* Newfoundland added.

The causal connexions between immigration and emigration and between immigration and labour-force participation are largely unknown. But the writer believes that there is sufficient evidence to make it a tenable hypothesis that the effects of postwar immigration on the structure and size of the labour force and on the expansion of the internal market have been active factors in the expansion of the Canadian economy in the postwar period, and that this expansion has been a retarding force in emigration, particularly in management and professional groups. It is nevertheless necessary to remember that the maintenance of expansion for an economy as open as the Canadian economy depends, and will depend for a long time to come, on activity in the export industries and on the international balance

[1] Dominion Bureau of Statistics, *The Labour Force, November 1945 to January 1955*, Reference Paper No. 58, Ottawa, Queen's Printer, 1955, pp. 30-2.

of payments. Short-run factors determining intake of migrants will depend in turn again mainly on changes in these and on the effects of past population changes. It has been the position of this paper that immigration into Canada will depend upon a combination of

TABLE X

IMMIGRATION AND THE CIVILIAN LABOUR FORCE
IN CANADA, 1946–53

Year	Civilian Labour Force June 1 each Year	Increase during preceding 12 Months	Estimated Immigrant Workers during preceding 12 Months	Increase in Labour Force without Immigrants
		(thousands)		
1946	4813	..	..	..
1947	4907	94	32	+ 62
1948	4979	72	51	+ 21
1949	5141	57 *	69	- 12
1950	5130	- 11	45	- 56
1951	5179	49	56	- 7
1952	5276	97	115	- 18
1953	5353	77	73	+ 4

* Not including an increase of 105,000 due to the addition of Newfoundland.

political, social, and economic factors, but the economic factors are the crucial ones. It may be the long-run aim of the Government of Canada to build up the Canadian population through immigration as well as through natural increase, but it has become axiomatic that long runs are made up of series of short runs.

NOTE

An important development, which has occurred since the foregoing paper was written, deserves to be noted. A decision of the Supreme Court of Canada, made under date of February 9, 1956 (1956, S.C.R., p. 318), has limited greatly the degree of discretion permitted to Immigration Officers and Special Inquiry Officers of the Department of Citizenship and Immigration. It was held by the Court in that decision that the Governor-General-in-Council has no power to delegate his authority to such officers, and that what Parliament had in contemplation in passing Section 61 of the Immigration Act of 1952 was 'the enactment of such regulations relevant to the named subject matters, or some of them, as in His Excellency-in-Council's own opinion were advisable and not a wide divergence of rules and opinions ever changing according to the individual notions of Immigration Officers and Special Inquiry Officers.'

As a consequence it became necessary to amend the immigration regulations originally set out in P.C. 1953–859 (see also P.C. 1954–1351) referred to in the above paper. The most important change replaces Section 20 of the former regulations by a new section which defines positively the admissibility of persons to Canada. Conditions for the admission of British subjects, French citizens, and United States citizens stand substantially as they were before, although one important change respecting entry of American citizens to Canada as landed persons will be noted below. Applicants for landing in Canada from other countries are divided into three groups. In the first group, citizens by birth or naturalization of Austria, Belgium, Denmark, the Federal Republic of Germany, Finland, Greece, Iceland, Italy, Luxembourg, the Netherlands, Norway, Portugal, Spain, Sweden, or Switzerland, or refugees from a country in Europe, may be admitted if such persons undertake to come to Canada for placement under the auspices of the Department of Citizenship and Immigration or, if the Department has given its approval, for establishment in a business, trade or profession, or in agriculture. The second group provides for the entry of a rather wide category of relatives of Canadian citizens or of persons legally admitted to Canada, if the applicants for admission are citizens of any country in Europe, a country in North America, Central America, or South America, or from Egypt, Israel, Lebanon, or Turkey. The sponsor in each case must be in position to receive and care for such persons. All other countries come into the third category. Here sponsorship is also required but sponsors are limited to Canadian citizens and kinship must be of the first degree. It is also required that children admitted shall be unmarried and under 21 years of age. Where parents are admitted, the father must be over 65 years of age and the mother over sixty. A child may not be landed in Canada from these countries unless his father or mother as the case may be is landed concurrently with him. Under Section 21, exceptions are made from these provisions to provide for the landing of 150, 100, and 50 persons annually from each of India, Pakistan, and Ceylon, in accordance with agreements previously made with these governments. These persons are in addition to the persons qualified for admission within the close degrees of kinship otherwise permitted. In all groups, of course, permission to enter Canada is subject to the requirements of the Act of 1952, and any other provisions contained in the regulations.

The Supreme Court decision resulted in the quashing of a deportation order which had been issued against an American citizen. To prevent the occurrence of such cases in the future, Section 18 of the regulations has been replaced by a new section which includes among other provisions the requirement under subsection (9) that a citizen or legally admitted person in the United States, coming to Canada directly from the United States or from Alaska, may not be admitted to Canada as a landed person 'unless he is in possession of a letter of pre-examination in the form prescribed by the Minister'. The intent seems to be to limit the acquisition of legal residence as landed persons to those who can qualify under the Immigration Act and regulations and thus to fortify the validity of deportation orders which may be taken against other persons. The nature of movement both ways across the 'undefended border' between Canada and the United States makes deportations from time to time inevitable, but they are often attended both by legal difficulties and by considerable unpleasantness.

The changes in regulations are all embodied in Order-in-Council P.C. 1956–785. Immigration policy under the new regulations remains flexible and selective, but in conformity with the ruling of the Court, regulations must now be positive and changes in them have become explicitly the responsibility of the Cabinet. The new regulations appear to have been framed with the object of maintaining the character of former selection principles and to give continuity to policy in spite of the new limitations on the discretion to be exercised by immigration officers.

Chapter 11

AUSTRALIA

BY

W. D. BORRIE

Australian National University, Canberra

THE Australian Government welcomed the millionth postwar immigrant to Australia in 1955. This represents the most substantial inflow of new settlers in any decade of the nation's history. The balance of immigration and its relative significance in the total rate of growth is summarized in Table I.

TABLE I

THE BALANCE OF IMMIGRATION, 1947–1954

Year	Permanent Arrivals	Permanent Departures	Net Immigration	Percentage Rate of Growth	
				Net Immigration	Natural Increase
1947	31,765	19,579	12,186	0·14	1·44
1948	65,739	17,271	48,468	0·72	1·31
1949	167,727	18,457	149,270	1·90	1·34
1950	174,540	20,855	153,685	1·86	1·37
1951	132,542	22,180	110,362	1·32	1·32
1952	127,824	30,370	97,454	1·09	1·39
1953	74,915	32,032	42,883	0·49	1·38
1954	104,014	35,449	68,565	0·75	1·32
1947–54	879,066	196,193	682,873		

In composition as well as in volume this postwar flow of immigration has been unique in Australia's history, for slightly more than half the permanent new arrivals have been non-British, and many of the non-British have represented national groups who have previously been little known in Australia (*e.g.* Poles and Latvians). The diversity of nationalities amongst the immigrants is summarized in Table II. The majority of non-British before 1952 were displaced persons from Europe, some 170,000 of whom came to Australia. Since then the Government has consciously sought a considerable proportion of the total annual immigration target from Europe, particularly from Germany, Holland, and Greece. The most significant national group has, however, been the Italians, most of whom have been sponsored by earlier Italian settlers in Australia rather than by Government.

A third feature of postwar immigration has been the extent to which the flow has been primed by direct government assistance.

TABLE II

DECLARED NATIONALITY OF PERMANENT NEW ARRIVALS,
OCTOBER 1945 TO DECEMBER 1954

Nationality	Numbers	Percentage of Total
British	439,400	48·8
Non-British		
Italian	100,400	11·1
Polish	71,700	8·0
Dutch	64,100	7·1
German	36,400	4·0
Yugoslav	26,000	2·9
Greek	24,400	2·7
Russian	20,400	2·2
Latvian	19,800	2·2
Hungarian	13,900	1·5
Czechoslovak	11,600	1·3
Lithuanian	10,100	1·1
American	9,800	1·1
Estonian	6,200	0·7
Others	46,500	5·3
All Nationalities	900,700	100·0

The principle of state assistance for British immigrants selected to meet economic requirements is not new : it goes back for more than a century and has represented the price Australia, with its great distance from the migrant sources, has had to pay to compete with the nearer countries of North America. From approximately 1850 until the end of the century assisted immigrants accounted for almost half the total net gain from immigration. Similarly, for the period 1901–40, when the total net gain from immigration was 593,000, 421,400 assisted immigrants arrived in Australia, almost all of them British.

New features in the policy since 1945 are the organization of immigration through a separate Minister and Department of the Federal Government, the vigorous search for immigrants in many Western European countries as well as in the United Kingdom, and the extensive assistance given to non-British immigrants. The contribution of State-assisted and other immigrants to the total flow since the war is summarized in Table III.

What then has been the effect of immigration of this quantity and composition upon national development?

In one sense the answer is simple. Without immigration the industrial and technical developments which have occurred in Australia since 1945 could not have taken place: there would not have been enough Australians to do the work. Whether or not

TABLE III

CATEGORIES OF PERMANENT NEW ARRIVALS,
OCTOBER 1945 TO DECEMBER 1954

British Immigrants		Non-British Immigrants		Total Permanent Arrivals	
Assisted	229,798	Displaced Persons	170,846	Assisted	481,748
Unassisted	209,615	Other assisted	81,104	Unassisted	418,965
		Unassisted	209,350		
Total	439,413	Total	461,300	Total	900,713

those developments have established higher living standards than would have been the case without immigration is a more difficult question. Nor should the matter be considered in this way. The significant point is that Australia ended the war committed by a Labour Government to a long-term and extensive programme of economic development and this objective has been fully carried over into the policy of the present non-Labour Government. Large-scale immigration, with a considerable proportion of the inflow assisted by the State, was originally and still is an integral part of that programme. The assumption has been that immigration and development will lead ultimately to improved living standards, but it has been recognized that forcing the pace will create short-term stresses and strains.

The precise stresses and strains which have been created in the Australian economy as the direct result of a net 'permanent' immigrant gain of 683,000 persons by December 1954 are not easily

165

identifiable; but that this immigration did increase the pressure of demand upon resources, and was a significant factor in the inflationary spiral which occurred between 1949 and 1953, seems incontrovertible.[1] Against this may be argued that even had there been no immigration there would have been considerable inflation in Australia. For example, at the end of the war Australia had to face heavy investment in capital works and housing to catch up back-logs created by the war; and sharp price-rises overseas, difficulties in obtaining imports because of inadequate shipping and shortages in the export countries themselves, together with excess demand arising from booming wool prices, all helped to create an inflationary situation before the immigration programme began to show really substantial results in 1949.

Without immigration and its associated objective of development, the inflation caused by these factors might have been of relatively short duration. Price-rises in imports would have been a problem; but against this a much higher level of imports *per capita* would have been possible to overcome lags in Australian production, for the income from primary exports (which was essentially a matter of price-rises and not of increased production, certainly before 1952) would not have been greatly reduced compared with actual figures attained with a net gain of almost 400,000 immigrants by the end of 1951. But while caution in regard to migration may have added in the short run to the material comforts of 'Old' Australians, events after 1948 really moved faster than the planners — and there are probably few 'Old' Australians who now regret it. The original objective of those who planned the migration policy was an average annual increase from immigration of 1 per cent a year. This rate of growth, it was felt from historical evidence, could be absorbed without undue economic or social strains. But the sudden easing of the shipping position in 1948, the desire of so many to emigrate from Europe and the remarkable success of the International Refugee Organization in handling the Displaced Persons soon enabled Australia to double the target. In 1949 and 1950 immigration increased the Australian population at the rate of some 1·9 per cent a year.

The initial immigration was required to overcome labour shortages and excess demand in the economy; but the short-term effect was the opposite. In 1949 and 1950 the estimated employment vacancies in Australia increased as the immigrant flow increased. The system was growing by what it fed upon; excess demand

[1] See, for example, P. H. Karmel, 'The Economic Effects of Immigration', in *Australia and the Migrant*, Australian Institute of Political Science, Sydney, 1953, pp. 82-112. Also *The Impact of Immigration*, Commonwealth Bank of Australia, 1950, particularly the article by H. Arndt.

required more labour in the form of immigrants, immigrants created new demands, and so on. Public and private investors were planning to increase their stocks of capital to levels sufficient to meet current demand and also to meet the demands expected from the planned increase in population. However, the immigration flood of 1949 and 1950 had one significant aspect which could be considered dis-inflationary: a high proportion of the immigrants (*e.g.* Displaced Persons and many of the other 'assisted' immigrants) could be directed for two years into sectors of the economy (*e.g.* extractive industries, housing) which could help to break 'bottlenecks' and to gear the economy quickly to higher production levels of consumer goods both for internal use and for export.

To some extent this did occur in relation to internal factors, as for example in coal, iron and steel, and housing. But much of the capital investment was still of the long-term variety (*e.g.* hydro-electric schemes) which was not likely to yield quick returns in increased foodstuffs or consumer goods. Development was still capital-absorbing, and events to 1952 had increased rather than reduced dependence upon exports to pay for imports. Most articles 'manufactured' in Australia still had a high proportion of imported raw or partially processed materials. Further, the immigrants them-selves brought heavier consumption demands than probably the planners had anticipated. Certainly public statements of the time usually referred to immigrants as *workers* and seldom as *consumers.* True, a somewhat higher proportion of the immigrants (approxi-mately 70 per cent) were breadwinners compared with the non-migrant population (66 per cent), but because of the low level of the birth-rate in Australia after 1930 the numbers of Australians entering the work force in 1949 and 1950 were comparatively slight. The 'natural increase' of the non-migrant work force [1] at this time was only about 0·4 per cent. Immigration lifted this figure to 2·8 per cent, but at the same time the increase in the total population (*i.e.* natural increase plus net immigration) was above 3 per cent. Calcula-tions based on an assumed annual increment of immigration each year at the 1949 level and of the same age and sex composition show that the sector of the Australian population available for the work force (*i.e.* aged 15-64) will still fall from 66·9 per cent in 1947 to 62·9 per cent in 1957 and that it will not regain the 1947 level until approximately 1970.[2]

The net gain of over 300,000 immigrants in 1949–50 was not,

[1] Here defined as all males and one-third of females, aged 15-64.
[2] See W. D. Borrie, 'Economic and Demographic Aspects of Post-War Immi-gration to Australia', *R.E.M.P. Bulletin*, January–March 1955, pp. 1-9.

however, considered to be the conclusion of the immigration side of planned development: it merely represented initial success in the long-term concept of development. Success was breeding success. The conclusion of a dollar loan in 1950 and booming export prices encouraged public authorities to step up their capital works programme. Government expenditure on new works and maintenance rose from £218 million in 1949–50 to £308 million in 1950–51.[1] This again increased in 1951–52 to £415 million, or 11 per cent of the gross national product compared with 8 per cent in earlier years. The optimism in the private sector of the economy was evidenced in the similar increase (both in absolute terms and as a proportion of the gross national product) in the investment in fixed capital equipment from £433 million (16 per cent) in 1949–50 to £735 million (19 per cent) in 1951–52.[2] The stimulus to inflation implied in this level of total investment (30 per cent of the gross national product in 1952–53) was offset to some extent by higher levels of imports, which rose in value from £653 million in 1949–50 to £1274 million in 1951–52, although a considerable proportion of this increase represented price rises in the items imported. This high level of imports had been rendered possible by the favourable prices for Australian exports (and particularly wool) from which receipts rose to £1048 million in 1950–51, compared with £660 million in the previous year. But the import spree of 1951–52, accompanied as it was by a fall in the receipts from exports to £746 million and a decrease in the balance of payments of more than £500 million forced the Government to clamp on import controls and other fiscal measures to restrict investment demand (*e.g.* capital issues control), and to increase taxation in the 1951–52 budget.

These internal measures, together with continued favourable prices for exports and relative stability in the prices of imports, helped to bring a respite from inflation after 1952.[3] Other factors favourable to greater stability were also operating. The inflow of immigrants had slowed down considerably as a result of the greater caution by the Government which had reduced the annual 'target' from 200,000 in 1949–50 to 80,000 in 1952–53, the increased difficulty of securing migrants with the required skills from the United Kingdom and Europe, and the increase in 'permanent departures'

---

[1] Compared with £118 million in 1947–48 and £154 million in 1948–49, and £408 million in each of the years 1952–53 and 1953–54.

[2] Compared with £247 million in 1947–48 and £318 million in 1948–49, and £657 million in 1952–53 and £700 million in 1953–54.

[3] Inflation was also probably checked in some measure by abandoning automatic wage adjustments based upon quarterly changes in the retail price index.

from Australia.[1] The net gain of 153,000 in 1950 fell sharply to less than 43,000 in 1953, followed by a rise again to 68,600 in 1954 (Table I). In addition, as the migrant inflow diminished after 1951, the capital investment of earlier years began to show positive results in increases in volume of production. Compared with 1938–39, the volume of production in the fiscal year 1953–54 had increased by some 25 per cent in foodstuffs, by over 60 per cent in iron and steel and by 64 per cent in tiles, compared with an increase in population of approximately one-quarter.

Do such figures, together with the relative stability of prices in Australia in 1953 and 1954, mean that the demands created by the immigrant flow after 1947 have been substantially met? An estimate frequently used in Australia to gauge the capital requirements of immigrants is to apply the formula that the stock of capital required by an industrial society is approximately four times the value of annual national production, so that each increase of 1 per cent in population through immigration will create a capital requirement equivalent of 4 per cent of the value of current annual production.[2] On this argument an investment programme of 6 to 8 per cent of current annual production would have accounted for the needs of immigrants between 1949 and 1954.[3] With public and private capital investment running at some 25 per cent of gross national product, this leaves a substantial margin for overcoming the backlogs in capital equipment arising from the war, as well as for the natural increase. But against this, the industrial expansion of Australia since the war has not reduced dependence upon imports, and herein lies the crucial factor in regard to a sustained migration inflow.

Thus, while it would seem reasonable to conclude that some of

[1] The increase in 'permanent departures' (*i.e.* Australian residents going abroad for a year or more) was substantially in relation to emigration to the United Kingdom and to other British countries :

	1953	1954
Total permanent departures	32,032	35,449
Permanent departures to British countries	25,295	27,609
Permanent arrivals from British countries	33,772	43,309

Departures in 1953–54 should, however, be considered against arrivals in earlier years as much as in the same years. A considerable proportion of the permanent departures to the United Kingdom would also be Australians going abroad for a year or two without any intention of settling permanently overseas.

[2] See, for example, P. Lawler, 'Meeting the Needs of Migrants' in *The Impact of Immigration, op. cit.*, and P. Karmel, *loc. cit.*

[3] There may, however, be some grounds for arguing that a net gain from immigration requires a higher short-term capital outlay than a corresponding gain from natural increase, since immigration is frequently associated with development of new areas and industries. For example, the Snowy Mountain Hydro-Electric Scheme required entirely new capital in the form of extensive additions to communications, new towns, schools and other service industries.

the major problems associated with the demands created by postwar immigrants and war-time back-logs have been overcome, a substantial increase in immigration in the immediate future at a higher rate than the comparatively low net intake of 1953 and 1954 will not be without its difficulties. The problem now lies less in the nation's stock of capital or back-logs in consumer goods, than in its capacity to meet higher imports from the revenue from exports. As already emphasized, while Australia has greatly expanded the volume of finished articles produced internally, these contain a high imported content in the form of raw and partly finished materials, and while oversea reserves remain at a fairly high level (some £400 millions), these have been running down to some extent in 1954–55 as imports have again been climbing (*e.g.* from £676 million in 1952–53 to £841 million in 1953–54). There seems little chance of Australia enjoying the windfall of booming prices for wool and other primary exports which so greatly helped to finance the investment requirements of population increase before 1954. Further, primary production has so far done little more than keep pace with population growth. Applied science has worked wonders in some aspects of primary production (*e.g.* myxomatosis in exterminating the rabbit, and trace elements in improving fodder crops), but an immediate and great increase in primary product surplus to the needs of an already rapidly growing Australian population cannot be expected. Nor is Australia yet ready to earn substantial income from the export of manufactured goods, quite apart from the problem of reducing costs of production to compete with traditional large-scale exporters such as the United States and the United Kingdom.

In other words, although the national economy may have broadened, the sheep's back is still very much the key to Australian population growth. The economy is still brittle and the success of an immigration programme in the immediate future still depends upon the export of a narrow range of primary products.

But rightly, for reasons of security and of the ultimate advantages which will accrue through economies of scale to an Australia with double the existing population of 9 million, the present Government is determined to push forward with its immigration programme. In terms of 'permanent' arrivals the official 'target' of 110,000 in 1954–55 was reached, and the confidence of the Government in its policy of development is again implied in the 'target' for 1955–56, which was raised to 125,000.

The attainment of this new target may prove more difficult because of external as much as internal economic factors. The marked economic recovery in Western Europe and in the United

Kingdom, the return of relatively full employment, and even the acute labour shortages developing in some areas as a result of war losses, have all rendered the recruitment of immigrants much more difficult. For example, while two years ago substantial emigration was expected in Australia from Western Germany, economic recovery there has prevented this. It is from some areas of Southern and Eastern Europe that recruitment is easiest (*e.g.* Italy and Greece), but the problem here is to secure immigrants with the required skills.

Nevertheless the determination of the Government to press on with development and migration, and to comb Europe as well as the United Kingdom for immigrants, implies not only determination to attain the long-term economic objectives laid down after the war, but also a new and broader approach to the question of the assimilability of immigrants. While the policy aims to recruit as high a proportion of British immigrants as possible, for the first time in their history Australians have witnessed and acquiesced in the granting of extensive State assistance to non-British immigrants. In a total of 900,700 total permanent arrivals over the period 1945–54, 461,300 (of whom only 209,400 were *unassisted*) were non-British and 439,400 were British. The diverse national composition of the inflow can be gauged from Table II.

The study of problems associated with the integration in Australia of these immigrants of diverse national, cultural, and social patterns raises questions of a non-economic character which may not be strictly relevant to a Conference of the International Economic Association, but it is significant that *so far* the absorption of these people has been achieved with remarkably little friction. In the writer's view, this lack of friction can be explained substantially, again *so far*, in economic terms : full employment which has prevented competition for jobs. So long as this can be maintained, the content of common interests and tolerance between 'New' and 'Old' Australians will gradually be enlarged. But integration at social and cultural levels has still so far to go that it may be unwise to press the immigration programme to the point that it can jeopardize economic stability.

This raises again the question of exports and their continuing importance in internal economic organization in Australia. In the absence of any real prospect of 'windfall gains' of price such as Australia enjoyed after the war it has become all the more necessary that immigrants shall be chosen in the immediate future with qualifications that will help to expand the volume of exports — and in the immediate future this means the export of primary products. Such an approach does not necessarily imply a rapid increase in the population engaged in primary production, so much as better capital equipment on farms, the development of such rural amenities as housing, more power and irrigation, improved road and rail transport and port facilities to increase the efficiency of marketing. A million immigrants in ten years has been a fair mouthful for Australia to take, and a few years of carefully selected settlers of the right *quality* to strengthen the weak points of the economy might do more than too much immediate emphasis upon *quantity* to preserve what has been laid, and so to facilitate the attainment of the ultimate goal of 20,000,000 people.

The key to the success of immigration in the immediate future certainly lies in the volume of exportable surpluses, and particularly of primary exports.[1] Pointers to the need for a reasonable degree of caution have been the fall late in 1954 and early in 1955 in oversea reserves and a 15 per cent cut in import quotas imposed by Government in March 1955, together with a further tendency to internal price increases and a rise in the cost of imports (*e.g.* increased shipping freights). But there seems no justification at the moment for assuming that Australia cannot reasonably aim at the 'target' of the original planners of the immigration policy, namely an annual net inflow equivalent to 1 per cent of the population.

Nor is there any indication at the moment that immigration is likely to be left again to the vagaries of *laissez-faire* principles. Planning for immigration as an integral part of national development is still an important platform of the present Government and has not been seriously questioned by the Labour opposition. The acceptance of this view by both Labour and non-Labour is essentially a new aspect of public policy since the war, as indeed is the view that non-British as well as British have a part to play in this nation-building. These attitudes may not yet be deep-rooted, but the roots go deeper every year 'Old' and 'New' Australians work side by side in a fully employed economy.

---

[1] For a useful survey of trends in rural production since the war and of targets required to meet future immigration sustained at recent levels, see J. N. Lewis and E. A. Saxon, 'Agricultural Output Requirements for Future Population Growth in Australia', in *R.E.M.P. Bulletin*, January–March 1955, pp. 9-15.

Chapter 12

SOUTH AFRICA

BY

H. M. ROBERTSON

University of Cape Town

INTRODUCTION

It may be true that there is always something new from Africa. But there is often much that is not new. Most African (or at any rate South African) problems tend to contain important common elements which may not be found elsewhere, but which are never absent from our country. Our King Charles's head of colour (and all that is connected, actually or in imagination, with colour differences) is the constant feature which has to be borne in mind when discussing the role of immigration in the South African economy.

To tackle it straight away I shall borrow from Mr. Leo Marquard more expressive words than I could probably have chosen as my own.

'South Africa is a country of contrasts and contradictions. White and Black, European and non-European, wealth and poverty, science and superstition, education and illiteracy, Christianity and heathendom, live side by side in the same towns and villages and on the same farms. . . . It lacks skilled workers, but limits immigration and legislates to prevent the majority of its population from acquiring skill. . . . Perhaps the strangest contradiction, and the one that explains a good deal of what is happening in South Africa, is that this union of four former colonial possessions has become itself a colonial power, with all the problems that face those European states that hold dominion over non-European people.

'This fact is obscured by the circumstance that colonial possessions are traditionally oversea possessions. . . . South Africa is at once motherland and colony. . . . The European South African is in daily contact with his colonial African subjects. . . . In these respects South Africa's problems differ radically from those of other colonial powers.' [1]

This way of looking at South Africa requires a real effort of the imagination, but once its implications have been appreciated it

[1] L. Marquard, *The Peoples and Policies of South Africa*, Oxford University Press, 1952, pp. 238-40.

becomes a key to the understanding of many of the apparent puzzles of South Africa's development and South Africa's policies. Certainly it helps to explain the fundamental factors in the history of immigration into South Africa.

I. ORIGINS OF THE SOUTH AFRICAN POPULATION

Up to the 1840's, the Cape of Good Hope was the only European colony in Southern Africa. Until the very end of the eighteenth century it had been a possession of the Dutch East India Company, and, not being a source of any valuable articles of commerce, it was of comparatively small account in that Company's vast commercial Empire. European immigration was only fitfully encouraged and, indeed, for the greater part of the eighteenth century it was more often actually discouraged. In 1793 the returns of the non-official white population gave a total of 13,842.[1] They were mainly of mixed Dutch, French, and German descent (the German element being greater than the pioneer historian G. M. Theal was willing to admit), and this small number provided the major, though not the exclusive, source of the Afrikaans-speaking section of the white population of the South Africa to-day, some 1,400,000 out of a total white population of 2,400,000.[2] The stream of nineteenth-century immigration has not swamped this group whose forefathers were settled in South Africa in the seventeenth and eighteenth centuries.

The only type of immigration which was regularly conducted in the days of the Dutch East India Company was the import of slaves — from East and West Africa, from Madagascar, from Bengal and the East Indian Archipelago. Even this was on a small scale. In 1793 privately owned slaves numbered 14,747,[3] not many more than the Europeans (though the adult male slaves outnumbered the adult male whites by more than two to one), while aboriginal Hottentots had perhaps dwindled to some 4000, according to contemporary estimates of doubtful reliability.[4]

By this time various Bantu-speaking tribes, in the course of migration southwards, had long been in occupation of those districts where they are still thickest, Natal and Zululand, the Native Territories of the eastern Cape, Swaziland, and the Northern Transvaal.

---

[1] C. Beyers, *Die Kaapse Patriotte*, Cape Town, Juta [1930], p. 249.
[2] Figures for 1946. Population Census, May 1946, vol. iv, U.G., No. 18 of 1954, p. 54.
[3] C. Beyers, *loc. cit.* In his *Memorandum of the Cape*, 1803, Commissary J. M. de Mist, however, for the same year gives a total of 16,767 for white labourers (a handful) and slaves. *Van Riebeeck Society Series*, vol. 3, Cape Town, 1920, p. 175. The slave trade was abolished in 1807.   [4] De Mist, *op. cit.* p. 193.

In the area immediately north and east of modern Port Elizabeth there was common interpenetration by, and growing conflict between, European stock-farmers spreading outwards from the Cape and Bantu pastoralists still seeking new land for settlement as their fluid political systems gave rise to constant tribal fission.

II. IMMIGRATION AND THE WHITE POPULATION IN THE NINETEENTH CENTURY

The capture of the Cape by the British during the Napoleonic wars ushered in a period of more rapid economic development [1] and brought with it a steady trickle — at times broadening into a significant stream — of migrants from the United Kingdom. In 1820 the first big government-aided scheme of settlement added 4000 British immigrants. This scheme had four main objectives: [2] (i) through emigration to relieve distress in the agricultural districts at home; (ii) to divert existing currents of emigration which went from the United Kingdom to the United States, towards a British colony which still had only a minority of inhabitants of British origins; (iii) to develop the agricultural potentialities of the eastern districts of the Cape; and (iv) to interpose a barrier of compact arable farms between the expansive groups of Dutch stock-farmers on the one hand and Xhosa [3] stock-farmers on the other hand, *i.e.* to check that interpenetration of black and white which has proved since then to be the most important pattern of migration affecting Southern Africa. Of these objectives, the only one which proved directly successful was the dilution of an almost wholly Dutch-speaking white population with an appreciable admixture of British settlers, and the extent to which this took place was also, in part, a consequence of the Great Trek of the 1830's which denuded parts of the eastern Cape of its Dutch-speaking inhabitants, who became the founders of the Transvaal and Orange Free State republics. The whole plan for closer agricultural development was a failure. Yet the 1820 settlement itself must be regarded as an outstanding success; but only after the settlers had regained their individual initiative in the choice of occupation and the opportunity to create openings for themselves in the occupation of their choice.

From the capture of the British Colonial Office's interest in the 'systematic colonization' plans of E. G. Wakefield in the 1830's,

[1] C. G. W. Schumann, *Structural Changes and Business Cycles in South Africa, 1806–1935*, London, Staples Press, 1938, pp. 37 ff., 45 ff. and 63 ff.
[2] Cf. I. E. Edwards, *The 1820 Settlers in South Africa*, London, Longmans, 1934. [3] The southernmost tribal group of the Bantu-speaking peoples.

attempts were made in the South African, as in other British colonies, to make use of the capital value which unoccupied Crown lands only acquired when there was sufficient labour to bring them into production, as a source of funds from which the cost of the immigration of that labour could be defrayed.[1] This brought in about 5000 British immigrants to the Cape between 1846 and 1850, while schemes undertaken by the Colony itself, after achieving self-government in 1854, brought in nearly another 10,000 between 1857 and 1863, plus German immigration of more than 3500 in 1857–58 to the newly annexed frontier province of British Kaffraria.[2]

Yet the first proper census, held in 1865, disclosed that of a total white population of 181,600 only 26,300 had been born in Europe.[3] Moreover the next census, held in 1875, showed a rise in the white population to 236,800, but of these only 29,100 had been born in Europe.[4] Even if one includes the Province of Griqualand West which was only incorporated in the Cape Colony in 1880, but which, being the seat of the diamond discoveries of Kimberley and district, was a magnet both for internal migration and immigration from abroad, the impression of the relatively minor part being played by immigration in the growth of the population of European stock persists. A census held in this territory in 1877 gave a European or white population of 12,400,[5] more than half, no doubt, having been born in neighbouring parts of Africa.

Even the 1891 Census of the Cape reported: 'It is very disappointing that there has been so small an advance in the percentage of European-born persons in the Colony to the total population of all races during the long interval that has elapsed since the last census was taken.' . . . Out of a total white population of 377,000 there were now some 50,000 whose birthplace was in Europe — a very large increase from 1875 — yet 86 per cent of the white population in 1891 was born in the Cape itself or neighbouring territories. Significantly enough, however, over 28 per cent of the white male population of Griqualand West was European-born.[6]

In the Transvaal one not very successful enumeration, confined

---

[1] See H. M. Robertson, 'The Cape of Good Hope and "Systematic Colonization"', *South African Journal of Economics*, vol. v, no. 4, December 1937.
[2] *Loc. cit.* pp. 383-4, 387-401.
[3] *Census of the Colony of the Cape of Good Hope, 1865. Cape Parlt. Papers*, no. G.20 of 1866. [4] *Ibid. 1875*, no. G.42 of 1876.
[5] *Cape Blue Book* for 1880, Section V, p. 27.
[6] *Results of a Census of the Colony of the Cape of Good Hope, 1891. Cape Parlt. Papers*, no. G.6 of 1892, para. 167 ; and Part II, Tables IV, V, VI. The Report also stated (para. 84), 'In the absence of a system of Registration of Births & Deaths and of complete records of arrivals in and departures from the Colony during the last sixteen years, it has been found impracticable to determine the extent to which emigration and immigration and births and deaths have respectively affected the population during that interval'.

to the European population, was held in 1890. It disclosed a population of 113,700 with a high masculinity ratio (63,600 M. ; 50,100 F.)[1] which is indicative of substantial immigration. But much of this immigration was from other parts of Southern Africa, particularly the old Cape Colony.[2] The gold discoveries were too recent to have made the Transvaal as yet a significant magnet for oversea immigration.

In the next decade immigration into the Transvaal developed so far as to create grave political difficulties which ultimately led to war. In the absence of a further census or any register of immigration and emigration it is impossible to obtain accurate estimates ; but an unrepentant C. J. Rhodes at the Jameson Raid inquiry, in 1897, insisted that the 'Uitlander' section of the population comprised 80,000 men in their prime of life as against 60,000 of both sexes and all ages of the original Transvalers, and was being reinforced by fresh immigrants at the rate of 25,000 a year.[3]

On the not unreasonable assumption that the majority of oversea immigrants to South African ports was headed for the Transvaal to match the £24 million of new capital invested in the gold mines from 1895 to 1899,[4] Rhodes's last estimate may be no overstatement. The Guide-book of the Union Castle Line said : 'During 1895 some 26,000 emigrants left England for South Africa and during 1896 the number increased to 36,000. Of these 5751 and 11,246 respectively were foreigners from Europe. During the years 1893-96 the emigrants to South Africa have outnumbered those to Australia, and during 1895 and 1896 they exceeded the departures to British North America by 3600 and 13,250.'[5]

During the nineteenth century the Orange Free State held two censuses. According to the first, in 1880, its European population was 61,000, and this had grown to 77,700 in 1890.[6] This was largely a home-grown population which had also drawn heavily on the old Cape Colony.[7] The white population of Natal, from small beginnings,

[1] *Results of a Census of the Transvaal Colony and Swaziland on 17 April 1904*, p. vi. The original census returns of 1890 are most inaccessible.
[2] There were 56,800 born in the Transvaal itself, 42,400 born elsewhere in Africa (of whom 29,600 were born in the Cape) and 14,500 born outside Africa. (Calculated from the figures in the 1904 Census, p. vii, and the 1891 Cape Census, p. xxxi.)
[3] *Second Report, S.C. on British South Africa.* H. of C. Paper 311 of 1897, Minutes of Evidence, Qq. 1298-1303, 1566-77.
[4] S. H. Frankel, *Capital Investment in Africa*, Oxford University Press, 1938, p. 95.
[5] Quoted in W. Bleloch, *The New South Africa*, London, Heinemann, 2nd edn. 1902, p. 203.
[6] *Census Report of the Orange River Colony, 17th April 1904*, p. iv.
[7] *Ibid.* p. xi. In 1880 70 per cent of the population was born in the Orange Free State, 25 per cent in the Cape Colony, and 3·2 per cent in Europe. In 1890 the proportion of European-born had remained almost stationary (3·3 per cent), while 67 per cent had been born in the Orange Free State and 27 per cent in the Cape Colony.

had by 1891 (partly as a fortunate by-product of a most unfortunate speculative immigration scheme)[1] grown to 46,800.[2]

III. THE NON-EUROPEAN POPULATION

Comparative figures for the European and the non-European population of the Cape in the second half of the nineteenth century are:

	European	Non-European
1856	115,700	151,300 *
1865	181,600	314,800
1875	236,800	484,200
1891	377,800	1,150,200
1904	579,700	1,830,000

* The 1856 figures, given for comparative purposes in the 1865 Census report, are estimates of doubtful reliability.

In Natal the Census of 1891 disclosed 497,000 non-Europeans as against 46,800 Europeans. In the Orange Free State, in 1890, there were 129,800 non-Europeans to 77,700 Europeans. In the Transvaal, in 1904, there were 972,700 non-Europeans to 297,300 Europeans.

These figures — especially the longer Cape series — are deceptive unless full account is taken of the extension of colonial boundaries throughout the nineteenth century to include, piecemeal, the most thickly populated African tribal areas. By about the middle of the century the Cape Colony had in stages annexed the districts south of the River Kei; between 1877 and 1894 the populous Transkei was added. In 1887 Zululand was annexed to Natal, which itself was a colony formed forty years earlier of an area well supplied with black inhabitants. On these figures, one might agree that South Africa was a land of limited immigration from Europe in the nineteenth century, because the need of population was met firstly by what Leroy-Beaulieu called 'la fécondité de cette remarquable population de Boërs',[3] and secondly by what De Kiewiet described as '. . . an immigration from within. Her immigrants were black.'[4]

[1] H. M. Robertson, 'The 1849 Settlers in Natal', *South African Journal of Economics*, vol. xvii, nos. 3 and 4, September and December 1949. Cf. A. F. Hattersley, *The British Settlement of Natal*, Cambridge University Press, 1950.
[2] *Natal Blue Book, 1890–1*. The sources of the population are not given.
[3] P. Leroy-Beaulieu, *De la colonisation chez les peuples modernes*, Paris, 1891, Guillaumin, pp. 609–10.
[4] C. W. de Kiewiet, *A History of South Africa, Social and Economic*, Oxford, Clarendon Press, 1941, p. 87.

Moreover, one might gain the impression that these black 'immigrants' came in through the extension of frontiers to envelop them. There is truth in this view, but not the whole truth. The expansion of European rule — even of European land-ownership for the more extensive forms of land use — did not break down the economic self-sufficiency of African life. The traders did this first, but until the 1870's there was no great capital investment in Southern Africa for employing labour to earn profits for employers. There was no concentration of labour demands into particular occupations or particular districts. Until the era of diamonds there was no force strong enough to create mobility amongst African labour, to make a reality of 'an immigration from within' by focusing internal African migrations on the growing points created by European enterprise.[1] Had this not been so, another chapter in the story of immigration into South Africa, the assisted immigration of Indians to provide steady labour in the Natal sugar plantations from 1860, would not have been added.[2] Nor would the Chinese labour experiment on the Rand gold mines from 1904 to 1910.

Special measures for the 'recruiting' of African labour in the tribal areas had, therefore, to be resorted to, owing to the sudden intensity of demand for native labour in the diamond fields or on railway construction far from any reservoirs of existing indigenous populations. These were later systematized into the widespread network (which still exists, controlled by the Chamber of Mines of the Transvaal and Orange Free State) for drawing African labour to the gold mines, with its ramifications into the Central African Federation as far north as Nyasaland, into the Portuguese province of Mozambique, and into Basutoland, Bechuanaland and Swaziland, as well as in the Union itself.[3]

In the Cape, in the 1890's, there was a strong desire to stimulate an inflow of African labour, coupled with an indifference to an immigration of white labour (except for female domestic servants).[4] On the other hand, in the Transvaal, after the war, when the gold mines were still unable to work at full capacity, it was argued that inability to obtain sufficient supplies of 'crude labour' was rendering

[1] See, in general, H. M. Robertson, '150 Years of Economic Contact between Black and White', *South African Journal of Economics*, vol. ii, no. 4, vol. iii, no. 1, December 1934, March 1935. S. T. Van der Horst, *Native Labour in South Africa*, Oxford University Press, 1941.

[2] L. M. Thompson, 'Indian Immigration into Natal (1860–1872)', *Archives Year Book for South African History*, 1952, vol. ii, Cape Town and Pretoria, Government Printer, 1952, especially ch. 8.

[3] H. M. Robertson, '150 Years of Economic Contact', *South African Journal of Economics*, March 1935, pp. 9–18.

[4] *Report of the Labour Commission, 1893–94*, vol. iii. Cape Parlt. Papers, no. G.3 of 1894.

ineffective the capacity of the mining industry to 'tap the whole world' for skilled labour, brains, and capital.[1] More plentiful African or unskilled labour was being envisaged as necessary to the creation of the economic conditions in which a flow of white immigrants could be successfully established.

By the Census of 1946 some 2,000,000 Africans out of 7,800,000 enumerated were in towns or on mines, sugar plantations, etc., more than 2,000,000 were on European-owned farms, and only 3,250,000 were in native areas. Well over half a million (and this is likely to be too low) were from outside the Union's borders.[2] It is clear that the black 'immigration from within' has become a major force in the development of the South African economy.

IV. MORE RECENT IMMIGRATION AND IMMIGRATION POLICY

Lord Milner placed his main reliance for the political reconstruction in the Transvaal after the war of 1899–1902 on an immigration of British settlers so massive as to outweigh the Afrikaner element of the population.[3] But it is not easy to control men, to direct human migration or natality, so as to suit the calculations of political arithmetic.

At the end of that war immigration into South Africa was feverish; but in November 1903 an ominous break started in the landings at Cape ports. 58,600 passengers from ports outside South Africa landed from February to December 1903, and only 35,300 in the whole twelve months of 1904.[4] In the Transvaal, Milner saw a British immigration at the rate of 2245 a month up to November 1903 drop to 800 a month, which was probably less than the number leaving the colony. For this inability to attract and keep white immigrants he blamed an economic depression which he ascribed to a shortage of black labour.[5]

In contrast with the general course of events outside, South Africa (particularly the two coastal provinces) suffered a severe depression between 1903/4 and 1909/10. Although unwilling to commit itself

[1] *Reports of the Transvaal Labour Commission, 1904. British Parlt. Papers,* Cd. 1896.

[2] *Official Year Book for the Union of South Africa, No. 27, 1952–53,* p. 465. The figure of 556,807 for non-Union natives was supplied by the Union Department of Census and Statistics.

[3] C. Headlam (ed.), *The Milner Papers,* London, Cassell, 1933, vol. ii, pp. 279-80 and *passim.*

[4] *Report on the Working of the Immigration Act, 1902, Cape Parlt. Papers,* no. G.63 of 1904, pp. 6-7. Cf. *Report on Immigration and Labour,* G.4 of 1906, p. 3.

[5] C. Headlam (ed.), *op. cit.,* vol. ii, pp. 523-4.

to figures, the Union's Bureau of Census and Statistics suggests that emigration exceeded immigration of Europeans from 1904 to 1910,[1] while the incomplete figures available suggest a further net loss through emigration up to 1918.[2]

Although it is not possible to separate figures for immigration and emigration from the general arrivals at and departures from Union ports until 1924, it would appear that there was a marked spurt both in gross and in net immigration in 1920 and 1921, started by the postwar boom and falling rapidly till past the trough of the depression in 1923. The five-year period 1925–29, one of recovery to the height of a boom, presents the following picture :

	Immigration	Emigration
Average, 1925–29	6700	4000
Highest	7900 (1929)	4500 (1925)
Lowest	5400 (1925)	3600 (1929)

The succeeding five-year period covers a steep decline into depression and a rapid recovery. The figures are :

	Immigration	Emigration
Average, 1930–34	4200	2700
Highest	5900 (1930)	4600 (1930)
Lowest	3000 (1933)	1800 (1934)

One or two points may be noted here. In this rather more chequered period it is not surprising that both gross and net immigration should have been lower than in the previous one. But that immigration was highest in 1930 (during the downward movement of the business cycle) and lowest in 1933 (a year of strong recovery) is perhaps to be explained not only by time-lags but by the passage in 1930 of the *Quota Act* for restraining within a narrow quota immigration from eastern European countries. This caused a drop of 1800 immigrants from restricted countries between 1929 and 1931. The steady decline in emigration throughout the period is due to a drop from 2700 to 400 in emigration to Southern Rhodesia, no doubt

---

[1] *Official Yearbook No. 27*, p. 1099.
[2] *Statistics of Migration, 1935*, U.G. no. 38 of 1936, pp. v–vi. The subsequent discussion is based on material in this report, in *Statistics of Migration, 1948*, U.G. no. 19 of 1950 and in the *Monthly Bulletin of Statistics*, vol. xxxii, no. 1, January 1953, and vol. xxxiv, no. 3, March 1955. Professor Schumann has already (*op. cit.* p. 140) drawn attention to the way in which other considerations have reinforced the influence of South African economic conditions on immigration.

largely to be ascribed to the severe economic depression there and to the introduction of more stringent immigration regulations.[1]

In the period of prosperity, 1935–39, the average annual European immigration rose to 7800, with a peak of 10,800 in 1936 and a low point (6300) in the year in which the war broke out. Emigration averaged 3200, but, with fewer than 500 emigrants to Rhodesia in 1935, and 1200 in 1938, the high and low points were reached in 1938 (4000) and 1935 (1900).

In the six war years, 1940–45, emigration averaged 2500 per annum and immigration only 1700 per annum, dropping to 900 in 1943. For the postwar years a year-by-year discussion is appropriate. The relevant figures are:

Year	Immigration	Emigration	Of this, Emigration to the Rhodesias comprised	+ Net Immigration – Net Emigration
1946	11,300	9,000	5,100	+ 2,200
1947	28,800	7,900	5,500	+ 20,900
1948	35,600	7,500	6,100	+ 28,100
1949	14,800	9,200	7,200	+ 5,600
1950	12,800	14,600	11,200	– 1,800
1951	15,200	15,400	13,000	– 100
1952	18,500	9,800	7,600	+ 8,700
1953	16,300	10,200	7,000	+ 6,000
1954 (Provisional)	16,400	11,300	8,100	+ 5,100

Towards the end of the war the problems of reabsorbing South Africa's own ex-servicemen into civil life were regarded as posing a big problem of finding jobs for men, not of finding men for jobs. Immigration did not figure in the Government's White Paper of 1944, *Outlines of Post-War Reconstruction*. But the unexpected ease with which demobilization was accomplished led the Government into bold plans of mass immigration. In August 1946 General Smuts announced a radical change in immigration policy, to meet demands for development which the Union's human resources were too small to meet. He set up active missions in different parts of Europe to hunt for suitable emigrants, and voluntary Immigration and Employment Committees at various centres throughout the Union based on the highly successful Demobilization Committees.

[1] For a brief contemporary survey of Rhodesia's economic position see *The Round Table*, vol. xxiii, December 1932, pp. 211-16. Following upon several Government Notices in 1931 and 1932, designed to ensure the exclusion of immigrants likely to be unable to support themselves, a more stringent Act, no. 23 of 1933, was promulgated in the middle of the next year.

Two 20,000-ton liners were set aside solely for the transport of immigrants under government guarantee. Immigration was running at the highest rate ever known in South Africa's history. To the opposition, this was just Milner's plan again — designed to drown the Afrikaner people and the Nationalist Party in an Uitlander flood. By it, Dr. Malan complained, 'immigrants by tens of thousands are being invited . . . while for thousands of South Africa's own sons . . . the door to apprenticeship and wage-earning labour remains closed'.

The change of government brought this massive immigration policy to an abrupt end. The ships were returned to their owners, the committees disbanded, and the whole scheme was wound up by the end of 1948. Instead, a stricter screening of immigrants was instituted. By 1949 net immigration had been cut by four-fifths. By 1950 there was a net emigration of 1800. 11,200 persons left the Union to settle in the Rhodesias alone, and a large exodus to the Central African Federation seems likely to persist for many years.

There were inconsistencies in the ill-starred United Party policy. For some members of the party European immigration on a large scale was regarded as essential to making fuller use of the non-European labour supply as a co-operant resource and enabling non-European workers more rapidly to progress in skill; but for others the main attraction was a strengthening of the white population to ensure the continuance of white political supremacy, and to reduce the economic dependence of the smaller white group on the non-Europeans. But, if some United Party support for large-scale immigration arose from an unacknowledged predilection for *Apartheid* and if Nationalist opposition to it took no account of the need to import *unskilled* white labour to take the work over from blacks if *Apartheid* became a reality, Nationalist attitudes have also shifted from the uncompromising hostility of 1947 to 1949.

By April 1950 the Minister for Lands — Mr. Stijdom, now Prime Minister — was calling for Dutch immigrants, while at a party congress in October the Minister for the Interior, Dr. Dönges, first spoke of the need of immigration to help fill a lack of 25,000 skilled workers. Gradually, in fact, immigration formalities were relaxed, government departments themselves sent out recruiting missions, much of the discarded machinery of the United Party immigration drive was silently reintroduced, though on a minor scale. But special encouragement was given to settlers from Western Germany and from the Netherlands, whose Government chartered three ships for the special purpose of carrying emigrants to South Africa.

The hopes of some who had seen, in an immigration drawn from these sources, a chance to operate a Lord Milner's policy in reverse have in some measure been disappointed. Many of the Dutch immigrants have found that they fitted in more easily with the traditions of English-speaking South Africa than with the rather narrower Afrikaner traditions, and there have also been murmurings over the relatively large proportions of Catholics or Freethinkers amongst them.

On all counts, it seems unlikely that any large increase in immigration into South Africa will occur in the near future. This is not solely a matter of policy, though it is policy which has made Asiatic immigration insignificant, and which was responsible for the sudden change in European immigration after the elections of 1948. But it is not only that conditions in South Africa were exceptional in 1947 and 1948, and that the doors are unlikely to be thrown open so wide again, for as far as one can see ahead. 'Full employment' seems to have been reached in several countries which appeared to have redundant populations then, so the pressure from outside is also reduced. The most significant flows of population in Southern Africa are still likely to be the movements of black migrants — either those flows which will be set in motion by the first whole-hearted attempts to implement *Apartheid* on a grand scale, or those set in motion by the dispersed initiatives of individuals, not conforming to the plans of political arithmetic, but cumulatively so irresistible as to break *Apartheid*.

Chapter 13

BRAZIL

BY

PADRE FERNANDO BASTOS DE ÁVILA, S.J.

Rio de Janeiro

THIS paper is an attempt to study the experience of Brazil in the field of immigration since 1924, and to bring up to date the analysis made by Ferenczi and Willcox.[1] The first part contains factual information on migratory movements to Brazil; the second discusses the factors which have influenced this influx; and the third part is an attempt at an interpretation of these movements, so as to obtain some idea of possible trends during the coming years.

I. THE FACTS

Except for a few sporadic fluctuations the period 1924–54 is characterized by two distinct stages : a period of decline in immigration and a period of recovery. The movement has followed a parabolic curve, the bottom of which coincides with the war years.

Let us consider the details. Immediately after the First World War immigration showed an upward tendency, but the peak of the postwar period (118,686 in 1926) was much lower than the preceding maximum figures (190,333 in 1913 and 215,239 in 1891). In fact, as early as 1929 — the date is significant — a decline set in which, in spite of short-lived recoveries in 1932 and 1936, brought immigration to almost zero. (Table I and Fig. 1 on following pages.)

Immediately after the Second World War the figures show a modest but steady rise with a slight fall in 1947. This situation continued until 1953, and then in the following year there was a more substantial decline. This raises the question whether this was a purely seasonal phenomenon or whether it was part of a depression within an unavoidable cyclical movement. We shall deal with this later in this paper.

[1] I. Ferenczi and W. F. Willcox, *International Migrations*, National Bureau of Economic Research, New York, vol. i, *Statistics*, 1929 ; vol. ii, *Interpretations*, 1931.

Immigration Countries

An analysis of immigration to Brazil by country of origin reveals much diversity. While the number of Portuguese is as high in the 1950's as it was in the 1920's, German, Italian, and Spanish immigration fell from a peak at the beginning of our period, only to recover

TABLE I

ANNUAL ARRIVALS OF MIGRANTS IN BRAZIL
BY COUNTRY OF ORIGIN, 1924–54

	Total	Germans	Spaniards	Italians	Japanese	Portuguese	Russians	Others
1924	96,052	22,168	7,238	13,844	2,673	23,267	559	26,303
1925	82,547	7,175	10,062	9,846	6,330	21,508	756	26,870
1926	118,686	7,674	8,892	11,977	8,407	38,791	751	42,194
1927	97,974	4,878	9,070	12,487	9,084	31,236	616	30,603
1928	78,128	4,228	4,436	5,493	11,169	33,882	823	18,097
1929	96,186	4,351	4,565	5,288	16,648	38,879	839	25,616
1930	62,610	4,180	3,218	4,253	14,076	18,740	2699	15,444
1931	27,465	2,621	1,784	2,914	5,632	8,152	370	5,992
1932	31,494	2,273	1,447	2,155	11,678	8,499	461	4,981
1933	46,081	2,180	1,693	1,920	24,494	10,695	79	5,020
1934	46,027	3,629	1,429	2,507	21,930	8,732	114	7,686
1935	29,585	2,423	1,206	2,127	9,611	9,327	29	4,862
1936	12,773	1,226	355	462	3,306	4,626	19	2,779
1937	34,677	4,642	1,150	2,946	4,557	11,417	52	9,913
1938	19,388	2,348	290	1,882	2,524	7,435	19	4,890
1939	22,668	1,975	174	1,004	1,414	15,120	2	2,979
1940	18,449	1,155	409	411	1,268	11,737	17	3,452
1941	9,938	453	125	89	1,548	5,777	23	1,923
1942	2,425	9	37	3	—	1,317	—	1,059
1943	1,308	2	9	1	—	146	—	1,150
1944	1,593	—	30	3	—	419	20	1,121
1945	3,168	22	74	180	—	1,414	2	1,476
1946	13,039	174	203	1,059	6	6,342	28	5,227
1947	18,753	561	653	3,284	1	8,921	18	5,315
1948	21,568	2,308	965	4,437	1	2,751	1342	9,764
1949	23,844	2,123	2,197	6,352	4	6,780	36	6,352
1950	35,492	2,725	3,808	7,342	33	14,739	59	6,786
1951	62,594	2,858	9,636	8,285	106	28,731	103	12,875
1952	84,720	2,326	14,082	15,254	261	40,561	140	12,096
1953	80,070	2,149	17,010	16,379	1,255	30,675	496	12,106
1954	72,248	1,952	11,338	13,408	3,119	30,062		12,369

Source : *Anuário Estatístico de Brasil, 1954*, p. 59.

slightly after the Second World War. For the other nationalities the curves are similar, except for Japan, whose peak coincides with the trough of the other curves. A considerable inflow from Japan began about 1910 under strong demographic and economic pressure. After being stopped by the war of 1914, it started again immediately after the

Armistice and continued until 1935 when Brazil introduced the annual quota system, following the example of the United States of America. After the First World War, Germany and Italy started a vigorous emigration period ; but the number of emigrants diminished as these countries developed nationalistic movements. Since these countries were seeking to develop their power to a maximum, their interest lay in preventing emigration so as to build up their resources of manpower.

FIG. 1

IMMIGRATION INTO BRAZIL BY COUNTRY OF ORIGIN, 1924–54

(in thousands)

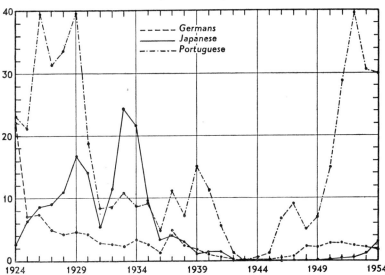

Thus the factors influencing migration currents pull in different directions. While in some places the expulsive forces are predominant, in others the forces that retain migrants are more powerful. This leads us to a first conclusion : the overall results of population movements are determined mainly by conditions in the receiving countries. This principle applies to all countries where immigrants arrive from a variety of sources, as in the case of Brazil.

II. THE INFLUENCES

Let us now examine the conditions which have influenced immigration to Brazil during the period under review.

In receiving countries the main consideration which influences the migrant is whether he can attain a certain standard of living. On the other hand, immigration countries tend to accept or to reject immigration according to the view they hold as to the effect it will have on the standard of living. Thus population movements are determined by economic factors, particularly in the receiving country.

It is important to note that in new countries the concentration of wealth gives great economic power to those who control the sources of production for export. In those countries that power is often associated with a political power which succeeds in subordinating the administrative forces to the immediate interests of the current economic situation. Thus, in order to understand the problem of Brazilian immigration during the past thirty years, it is necessary to examine briefly the development of the Brazilian economy during that period.

At the beginning, Brazil was still living under the régime of a semi-colonial economy. Primary products, particularly coffee, were exported, while most of the manufactured products and equipment required in the country were imported. The whole Brazilian economy was thus dependent on the price of coffee on the international market. In view of the leading position of Brazil as a coffee-exporting country, the coffee producers enjoyed a kind of natural monopoly, which enabled them, up to a certain point, to play a determining role in the fixing of international prices. The situation was favourable and the producers tried to take advantage of it. During prosperous years they accumulated profits, and in difficult periods their losses had to be borne by the community.

Let us now further consider this movement because it gives us a picture which helps us to understand the development of new countries. During periods of prosperity part of the profits was either used up or was taken out of the economic circuit through imports; another part was saved in order to be reinvested in coffee plantations. In times of depression the collapse of prices on the international market led to a fall in the income of the planters and in the revenue of the State. The latter met the situation by issuing inconvertible notes which meant a fall in the value of money and in the purchasing power of wages. Thus the losses were borne by the community; that is to say, they were distributed among the masses of consumers. The situation can be best illustrated by a few figures. Let us suppose that a planter sold one bale for 25 dollars, which brought him 200 cruzeiros, at the rate of 8 cruzeiros to the dollar. In times of slump the value of the product declines, say by 40 per cent; the bale is sold for 15 dollars. The exchange rate is then readjusted and the dollar which used to be worth

8 cruzeiros goes up to 12. Thus the 15 dollars of the planter will procure him not 120 but 180 cruzeiros. His loss which, in terms of foreign currency, amounted to 40 per cent is reduced to 10 per cent in terms of national currency.[1]

The existence and the development of a coffee-growing monoculture did not depend on the creation of an internal market, on a progressive increase of the revenues, and of the purchasing power of the community. The transactions were in fact carried out in warehouses, at the terminal point of a trading line originating outside the country; and the market was not an organism living in its own economic environment. This observation is an important part of the interpretation of an underdeveloped economy.

Under these circumstances immigrants arrived on their own initiative when there were good prospects of making profits on coffee. Immigration was even stimulated as an aid to more economical production. The contrary occurred during bad years. Fluctuations in coffee prices determined wage levels and, through them, influenced the course of immigration. This phenomenon was all the more conspicuous as the influences were working in one direction; wages influenced immigration, while the latter had no substantial repercussions on the wage level. This can be readily understood if it is borne in mind that this system functioned with an under-employed reserve of labour and that coffee monoculture was expanding rapidly.

If we take a fairly long period we notice a positive relationship between the course of immigration and the level of economic activity. Let us adopt as an index of the economic situation the movement of the terms of trade. This index seems appropriate in view of the type of semi-colonial economy which we have already described. If we take intervals of five years, so as to allow for the necessary adjustments, we obtain Table II in which Column 1 shows the development of the terms of trade and Column 2 the number of immigrants.

One striking fact which is immediately apparent is the very close correlation between the immigration figures and the terms of trade.

However, a new era in the Brazilian economy began between 1930 and 1940. The expansion of monoculture called for an increasing population and led inevitably to a redistribution of income in the form of wages. Thus the internal market expanded under the influence of coffee and was already strong enough to cause difficulties for the financial policy which had hitherto been applied. If a decline in the value of the cruzeiro was favourable to the exporters in periods

[1] See Celso Furtado, *A economía brasileira*, Rio de Janeiro, 1954, p. 103.

of crisis, it also helped the development of national industries, owing to the artificial rise in the prices of imported manufactured goods. Such goods could be produced by national industries at a lower cost, and the demand kept growing during prosperous years.

The importance of this factor in the development of the Brazilian economy should not be underestimated. It meant a transition from a system independent of the internal economic situation to a system of internal marketing on which the country began to depend more and more. New forces emerged that were less rigidly tied to the fluctuations of the international market in one single commodity. At the same time a redistribution of the national income was bringing into being a new class, namely the industrial *bourgeoisie*. From

TABLE II

DEVELOPMENT OF THE TERMS OF TRADE AND OF THE NUMBER OF IMMIGRANTS

(1901–5 = 100)

	Column 1 Terms of Trade	Column 2 Immigration
1901–5	100	100
1906–10	120	140
1911–15	136	219
1916–20	54	67
1921–25	85	138
1926–30	104	161
1931–35	87	65
1936–40	50	37

Sources : For Column 1 : H. W. Spiegel, *The Brazilian Economy*, Philadelphia, 1949, p. 128. For Column 2 : *Anuário estatístico do Brasil, 1954*, p. 59.

now on, this new class was going gradually to exert its influence on the financial policy which hitherto had had only one objective : to protect the coffee market. The implementation of this new policy raised extremely delicate problems, and this explains the trials and errors of the last few years.

It was realized, in the light of the 1929 crisis, that a new situation had to be faced which can now be described as follows : the creation of an internal market sufficiently important to allow the industrialization process to be started ; the appearance of a new type of middle class, consisting of urban industrialists whose interests are different from those of the big planters ; a realization by the community that it was possible to go beyond the stage of a semi-colonial, *i.e.* an underdeveloped economy.

In the light of these explanations we can now interpret the immigration movement to Brazil during the past thirty years and evaluate its possible trends during the next few years.

III. INTERPRETATION

The period which we have chosen is of particular interest, because it covers the end of one stage in the development of the Brazilian economy and the beginning of another.

In the first of these two stages the economy was mainly based on the export of a single commodity which strongly influenced the immigration curve. If we examine the relationship between the annual average prices of coffee and the annual immigration figures, we note that 29 times out of 40 (1914 to 1954) a rise in coffee prices was followed by an increase in the volume of immigration, and that the volume decreased when coffee prices went down. Moreover, the immigration curve is much more elastic than that of prices, since small changes in the price of coffee on the international market are followed, a year later, by violent fluctuations in immigration. Finally — and this is the most important aspect — that curve has for very many years shown a downward trend; the maximum was attained when the coffee market reached saturation point and when the expansion of an extensive monoculture reached its geographical limits.

The second stage, although still under the influence of a coffee-protection policy, saw the birth of new interests which are beginning, in their turn, to exert a certain pressure on immigration policy. This policy is characterized by a slow, but steady, expansion. Gradually immigration becomes less dependent on fluctuations in coffee prices and more on the increase in absorptive capacity. This is a new fact which opens entirely new prospects for immigration. Brazil has enormous underdeveloped resources; the frontier of pioneer settlement is slowly moving towards the west; thus new areas offering tremendous possibilities are gradually brought within the economic system. In this way the economic system carries within itself the factors capable of generating expansion.

There is every reason to believe that during the next few years immigrants will have to co-operate with national forces to start a chain reaction; the growth of the economic system resulting from more immigration will increase the absorptive capacity of the country, and so on. Under such conditions immigration offers more guarantees of stability and progress.

However, an internal phenomenon of great importance, namely

internal migration, will have to be taken into account. During the past fifteen years there have been two main currents — migration from rural areas and the movements of population from the North to the South. The former takes place in the form of a capillary process : people abandon their farms to join the nearest small rural centre ; from there they move to the 'vila', which is the seat of the district authorities, from there to agglomerations of a more urban character, and finally to the big cities. The second movement, *i.e.* from the North to the South, has increased since 1940, in spite of the transport difficulties due to the war. Between 1940 and 1950, 410,000 Brazilians settled in the Federal District, *i.e.* about 50 per cent of the population that lived there at the beginning of that period. During the same decade 700,000 Brazilian workers went through the migrant hostels of the capital of São Paulo.

Thus the Census of 1950 shows that 5,206,316 persons, *i.e.* 10 per cent of the Brazilian population, moved away from their State of origin : 661,846 settled in the Parana district, 929,846 in the Federal District, and 1,064,009 in São Paulo. These are the territorial units which offer at present the best opportunities for foreign immigrants.

These internal migrants are heading towards the pioneer zones in the South or towards the urban centres, particularly in the building trades. To-day, with the expansion of the road network, this manpower is cheaper than foreign labour. It is also less exacting because of its simpler and more primitive standard of living, and it therefore strongly competes with the immigrant workers at the unskilled levels of employment. This fact precludes the possibility of foreign mass immigration. On the other hand, however, it offers prospects for immigrants in three important sectors : specialized industries, trades, and land settlement.

In conclusion it may be said that foreign immigration and the national effort to emerge from the stage of a semi-colonial economic system are complementary to each other. This is in the interest of the country. Brazil, which has vast territories available for development, need not fear the ultimate results of a steadily increasing immigration, based on progress towards economic integration.

Of course the implementation of such a programme raises certain difficulties. Those due to internal migration are a problem the importance of which I do not wish to conceal. Nevertheless I am convinced that all obstacles can be overcome provided two conditions are fulfilled : first, those who are called upon to co-operate in the solution of these problems must be fully conscious of their human responsibility. Often the background of big decisions on which the fate of millions of human beings depends remains obscure. It seems clear that decisions about immigration to Brazil in the past were dictated by the economic interest of small groups. However, the problem with which we are dealing involves the fate of millions of individuals ; it is high time that it were given the attention it deserves. The second condition is that reasonable risks and sacrifices, which are the price of any undertaking of importance, must be accepted in a spirit of courageous optimism. Exaggerated protectionism sometimes hampers the most constructive efforts. I hope that Brazil will show itself worthy of its possibilities and that it will not jeopardize such a hopeful future.

PART IV

INTRA-EUROPEAN MOVEMENTS

Chapter 14

MIGRATION AND THE GERMAN ECONOMY

BY

HILDE WANDER

Institut für Weltwirtschaft, Kiel University

GERMANY is generally regarded as a country with a tradition of
emigration, but this description has for many years ceased to apply
to the territory of modern Germany. The idea is mainly based on
the experience of the nineteenth century, when millions of Germans
were leaving their home country under the pressure of a rapidly
growing population in order to enjoy better opportunities overseas.
Since that time there has been a fundamental change in the demographic, economic, and social conditions in Germany and overseas ;
this has brought about a simultaneous change in the volume, structure, and economic significance of migratory movements. If
Germany is still looked upon as a characteristic country of emigration, this is largely because there has been much public interest in
oversea settlement even during periods when Germany or important
parts of Germany had a big inward balance. Until recently there
were only statistics on oversea emigration but hardly any showing
the volume and structure of oversea immigration, of intra-European
migration, and of internal migration in Germany. These various
movements are closely connected with one another ; their economic
consequences cannot be considered separately. This chapter will
describe the interdependence of these movements from the historical
and economic points of view, and it will attempt to explain present
and future movements on the basis of that interdependence. However, mainly for statistical reasons, the analysis will have to be
confined largely to the Federal Republic of Germany, so far as it
deals with recent developments.

I. HISTORICAL BACKGROUND

The decisive factor in the migration balance of the whole territory
of Germany during the past century was undoubtedly migration to
oversea countries. Germany, which was predominantly agricultural

197

up to the eve of the foundation of the Reich, was unable to offer enough opportunities to her growing population. Under those circumstances emigration to oversea countries was a means of alleviating strong population pressure and social crises. It started from the territories of south-western Germany, where estates are divided between the heirs of the deceased owner, and spread more and more into the region of the large estates in the east and in the north. Both forms of property made it difficult to absorb a growing population. Already during the seventeenth and eighteenth centuries and beginning of the nineteenth these systems of property had caused a considerable intra-European migration to Russia, Hungary, and Roumania. Those parts of Germany where skilled trades and handicraft played a more important role supplied relatively less migrants or soon made up for their emigration losses through immigration.

Between 1843 and 1910 more than 5 million Germans emigrated to oversea countries, mainly to North America. The fluctuations of these migratory movements corresponded to the political and economic conditions in Germany and in the receiving countries. The German migrants, who were equipped with agricultural and technical knowledge and accompanied by an ever-growing flow of capital from Europe to oversea countries, contributed to the development of the receiving countries. They produced raw materials which after being processed in Europe found ready markets overseas. This give-and-take between receiving countries and sending countries, which meant a better geographical distribution of labour, land, and capital, is the most significant feature of nineteenth-century oversea migration. It led to an intensified exchange of goods throughout the world, thus contributing to general well-being in the receiving countries as well as in the emigration countries. The losses of population and of capital invested in the training of the migrants, although considerable in terms of figures, were of little significance in comparison with the benefits which Germany derived from emigration. Without oversea migration such a quick industrialization and absorption of the growing population of Germany would have been impossible. Towards the end of the nineteenth century the German economy was able, for the first time, to absorb not only its natural increase but also an immigration balance which resulted mainly from the exchange of manpower with other European countries.

On the whole, intra-European migration had relatively little influence on the migration balance of Germany before the First World War. In fact, a comparison between the number of oversea emigrants and the total migration balance (Table IA of Appendix, p. 212) suggests that during the period 1843 to 1910 Germany gained only a few hundred thousand persons from intra-European migration. This small balance does not prove that only a few migrants crossed the German borders. To-day we are no longer in a position to ascertain the volume of these movements, but many factors seem to indicate that they were quite substantial. However, their significance differed from that of oversea migration. Whereas oversea migration, in view of the distance and the difficult and expensive communications, was mostly one-way, leading to a new geographic distribution of large populations, intra-European migration sometimes meant a reciprocal temporary exchange of manpower owing to the close economic interdependence of neighbouring countries. German technicians, scholars, and merchants lived abroad in European countries, while an equal number of foreigners had settled in Germany. Towards the end of the nineteenth century, at a time of increasing industrialization, a considerable outflow of population from German rural areas towards the big cities and the industrial areas coincided with a growing influx of foreign agricultural and industrial workers. This immigration, which was largely seasonal, became more intense the more oversea migration decreased.

Internal migration in Germany was closely connected with the movements across the border. This must be mentioned here, because it contributed so much to the development of the territories west of the Oder which now comprise the Soviet Zone of Occupation and the Federal Republic of Germany. From that area 1·65 million persons emigrated to oversea countries between 1871 and 1910. The net positive migration balance for the same period was 942,000. The loss of oversea migrants was therefore offset by a net gain of 2·6 million persons through other migratory movements, mainly within Germany.

At every census since 1871, and even probably for some time before, the other German territories situated east of the Oder had a net outflow which largely exceeded the number of oversea emigrants. In view of their economic structure, which was predominantly agrarian, they could sustain only part of their rapidly increasing population. Those who were seeking a higher living standard left these territories, thus facilitating the employment of cheaper labour from the neighbouring Eastern European countries. Between 1871 and 1910 the total loss of population through migration (3·2 million) was equal to about 50 per cent of the excess of births over deaths during the same period (6·5 million). Since the number of oversea migrants was only about 1 million, a net total of 2·2 million persons must have been received in the other parts of Germany. As a result of these internal migratory movements the territory which is now the

Federal Republic lost its position as a characteristic emigration territory about 1890, and that of the Soviet Occupation Zone, including Berlin, as early as 1871 (Tables IA and IB of Appendix, pp. 212, 213).

The First World War brought to an end the period of free migration. From that time onwards the German migration balance, irrespective of the area, was strongly influenced by political decisions which restricted the freedom of movement of the migrants. The considerable surplus of immigrants recorded in Germany, for example between 1910 and 1925, in spite of war and defeat, was due, on the one hand, to the influx of expellees from the lost territories and colonies and, on the other, to immigration restrictions overseas which sometimes kept the number of migrants below the level which it would probably have reached under identical economic and political conditions if migration had remained free.[1] Foreign manpower from other European countries was therefore not in great demand.

Meanwhile, since the beginning of the century, the demographic and economic conditions in Germany and overseas had changed in such a way that the volume of free migration was reduced. With a rather sharp decrease in the birth-rate and a death-rate which declined only very slightly, the natural increase of the German population was slackening. The older and less mobile groups bulked larger. The war losses of about 2 million men, mainly middle-aged, accelerated that process. As a consequence of the war the German economy was impoverished. Germany had lost her position as a country from which capital was exported. Overseas, especially in the United States, very efficient industries had developed, and there was a limited but more specialized demand for foreign workers. German oversea migration had lost its impetus. It is true that between the two wars a considerable number of persons wanted to emigrate; this was due to the economic and political position. In so far as these persons were successful in realizing their desire, these movements were largely of a temporary nature, concentrated particularly on European countries. The actual number of oversea migrants remained very small, with the exception of the period 1923 to 1928. The quotas for German immigrants fixed by the United States were hardly ever fully used. On the other hand, many Germans returned from overseas at the beginning of the world economic crisis.

---

[1] Between 1919 and 1928 492,000 Germans emigrated to oversea countries. During the same period almost 800,000 persons applied to the German Migration Agency (Reichsstelle für Auswanderung) for information on emigration possibilities. Together with their families, which are not covered in the statistics, the number of persons who actively demonstrated their willingness to emigrate may be estimated at a total of 1·2 million.

II. MIGRATORY MOVEMENTS SINCE THE
SECOND WORLD WAR

It is extremely difficult to obtain a clear picture of German migratory movements after the Second World War. The lack of adequate statistics for the Soviet Occupation Zone makes it impossible to give an accurate description of overall German migration and its economic consequences. However, as there has been no free direct migration between the Soviet Zone and other countries, statistics for West Germany may be considered valid for the entire German territory. In the Federal Republic, statistics of immigration and emigration comparable to those of the pre-war period and conforming to established international usage have been available only since 1953. In addition there are statistical data on the entries and departures across the Federal boundaries since 1950, based on police records of arrivals and departures. Information on movements in previous years can be obtained only from population statistics according to residence at the beginning of the war and from the migration balance computed from total population minus excess of births over deaths.

The large inward balance of migration in West Germany (Table III of Appendix, p. 214) throughout the postwar period is no proof that migrants were attracted by economic expansion. It is mainly the consequence of the expulsion of Germans from the German provinces beyond the Oder and the Neisse and from the countries of Eastern and South-Eastern Europe, and of the still continuing influx of refugees from the Soviet Zone. On the day of the census of 1946 there were 7·1 million persons in West Germany whose residence at the beginning of the war had been outside the present Federal frontiers. By the time of the census of 1950 this group of persons had grown by another 2·5 million. It must therefore be assumed that between September 1939 and September 1950 there was a net immigration of 9·6 million persons.[1] After 1950 the influx of expellees from abroad and from the East German territories dwindled, but immigration from the Soviet Zone continued. Statistics on arrivals and departures across the Federal borders show that between October 1950 and the end of 1954 this category grew by another 1·2 million.

---

[1] Accurate data concerning residence at the beginning of the war were of course available only for those who were born before 1 September 1939. The children of expellees and refugees born subsequently were included in these statistics according to their fathers' former residence. The aforementioned figures are therefore somewhat too high. For the expellees in West Germany they include an estimated surplus of births of 200,000.

Only the 4 million expellees who came from abroad can be considered as migrants in the sense now generally accepted. However, in this connexion the remaining 6·8 million whose pre-war homes were in the Soviet Zone, in Berlin, or in the East German territories now under foreign administration must also be taken into account. Their immigration has influenced the economic and social structure of West Germany and has thus directly or indirectly determined the volume of the other movements across the border.

The heavy inflow and the difficult economic and political situation in postwar Germany produced a strong propensity to emigrate. It is not possible to express this pressure in the first few years in terms of figures. It is probable, however, that the result would have been considerable emigration if it had been authorized by the Occupation Powers and if the immigration countries had opened their doors to the Germans. As conditions in Western Germany improved, the number of people who wished to emigrate declined. Nevertheless, the tremendous influence of the recent expulsions and refugee movements on the emigration pressure can still be seen from the fact that in 1954 65 per cent of those who sought information from the Migrants' Advice Bureaux had their pre-war residence outside the Federal Republic and 61 per cent indicated political and economic instability as the main reason for wanting to emigrate.

Both the volume and the structure of the actual movements during the postwar years have been determined not so much by supply of prospective migrants as by the attitude and the requirements of the immigration countries. Emigration did little to alleviate population pressure. Between 1945 and 1948 about 30,000 Germans succeeded in breaking the immigration barriers and in settling overseas.[1] Only after 1948, when the attitude of other countries towards Germany had changed, and particularly when many countries had achieved full employment, was there a growing interest in obtaining German immigrants. Since 1951 at least 60,000 persons per year, or 12 per 10,000 of the total population, have left the Federal Republic. Although this outflow seems small in comparison with the still considerable influx from the Soviet Zone, it is nevertheless large in comparison with migration during the past forty years. In West Germany this figure was reached or exceeded only in 1923, when 22 per 10,000 of the population settled overseas, and during the period of mass migration before 1894 (Table II of Appendix, p. 214). These movements are particularly significant if both parts of present-day Germany are considered as one unit. Since 1950 the entire

---

[1] *Wirtschaft und Statistik*, Statistisches Bundesamt, Wiesbaden, vol. vi, New Series, 1954, p. 276.

German territory has had a net migration loss, but in demographic and economic terms this is not comparable with the outflows of the nineteenth century (see Sections IV and V). The fact that in 1953 and 1954 the proportion of expellees and refugees among the total number of migrants (45 and 40 per cent) was much lower than the proportion of these categories among the persons willing to emigrate (67 and 65 per cent) shows how little the structural composition of emigration corresponded to the existing needs.

As previously, the main destination was the United States of America, which took over 50 per cent of all the Germans who emigrated to oversea countries between 1945 and 1954. Another 36 per cent went to Canada and 10 per cent to Australia. The number of persons who emigrated permanently to European countries was insignificant in comparison with oversea migration. In 1953 and 1954 these groups totalled only 2124 as against 120,251 oversea migrants. It is true that in recent years a relatively large number of Germans have gone to Great Britain, France, Sweden, and Switzerland under employment contracts. However, in most cases their stay in other countries was authorized only for a limited period. According to the statistics on arrivals and departures in 1954, for example, 54,040 persons went to other European countries while 83,690 arrived in the Federal Republic from other European countries. The latter included only 39,961 foreigners. The rest were Germans returning to the Federal Republic. If incoming foreigners only are taken into account, West Germany's temporary migration balance, with particular reference to the exchange of workers, has so far been negative *vis-à-vis* all the countries of Western Europe.

III. DEMOGRAPHIC ASPECTS OF GERMAN MIGRATION

From the demographic point of view, free migratory movements have a selective effect. Since the majority of migrants are young and middle-aged persons, the receiving countries gain new population not only directly but also potentially; on the other hand, the emigration countries suffer a corresponding loss which varies directly with the relative size of the emigrating age groups. This observation, however, does not apply to the expulsions of the war and the postwar years. The expellees who came to Germany were entire populations whose sex and age structure was only a little more favourable than that of the native population. In spite of the absolute gain of millions of people, the ageing of the German population continued rapidly. The proportion in the age group over 50 which was 16 per cent before the First World War, has risen to about 29 per cent in present-day Germany, while the proportion of those under 20 has gone down from 44 to 30 per cent. These changes in the age structure, which were accelerated by the heavy war losses of middle-aged men among both the native population and the expellees, differentiate present migration from Germany from that of the nineteenth century. If during the nineteenth century emigration could be considered as a means of adjusting the growth of the population to the economic capacity of Germany, it can no longer

TABLE I

AVERAGE ANNUAL EMIGRATION FROM GERMANY PER 10,000 OF
POPULATION, BY SEX AND AGE GROUP, 1893–94 AND 1953–54

Age Groups	1893–94 *	1953–54 †		
	Total	Total	Male	Female
Under 20	10·8	13·0	12·9	13·0
20 to 24	29·1	32·3	35·4	29·1
25 to 29	18·9	28·1	29·9	26·4
30 to 49	11·0	12·4	14·4	10·8
50 and over	4·8	2·5	2·2	2·6
Total	12·2	12·4	13·6	11·4

* German Empire within its boundaries prior to the First World War.
† Federal Republic of Germany.

Source : *Statistik des Deutschen Reichs*, published by Kaiserliches Statistisches Amt, vol. 240, Berlin 1915, p. 79 ; *Statistik des Deutschen Reichs*, published by Statistisches Reichsamt, Vol. 360, Berlin 1930, p. 231 ; *Statistische Berichte*, published by Statistisches Bundesamt, Wiesbaden, no. viii/26/5-9 and no. viii/7/37.

fulfil that function. A substantial loss of inhabitants through the emigration of about 60,000 persons from the Federal Republic during the past few years has already had more significant demographic consequences than it would have had previously. In 1893–94, for example, the German Empire had an average annual emigration rate of 12 per 10,000 of the total population, *i.e.* a rate which is roughly equal to that recorded in the Federal Republic during 1953–1954.[1] However, there are great differences between the age composition of the two outflows.

These differences are due to the fact that with the ageing of the population the proportion of middle-aged persons among the

[1] Population in 1893 : 50,100,000 ; in 1953 : 49,300,000.
Emigrants, 1893–4 : 124,000 ; 1953–4 : 122,000.

migrants has increased. In 1893–94 54 per cent of the migrants were between 20 and 50 years of age, whereas in 1953–54 that age group comprised 63 per cent of all the migrants. The demographic losses through emigration which the Federal Republic has suffered during the past few years have been more than offset quantitatively and qualitatively through immigration from the Soviet Zone.[1] It was mainly the younger and more mobile persons who got into trouble with the communist régime or decided to leave the zone because they were attracted by the better living conditions in the West. The age and sex structure of these migrants was more favourable than that of the West German population and corresponded approximately to that of the emigrants. However, the Federal Republic's gain was a loss for the Soviet Zone. Ever since 1950 Germany as a whole has no longer received a sufficient number of immigrants to offset the number of departures.

IV. ECONOMIC AND SOCIAL ASPECTS OF GERMAN MIGRATION

From the economic point of view free migratory movements help to adjust the labour force to changes in the other elements of production. The decisive factor in this process is not so much the volume of the movements but the optimum co-operation of all economic forces. Internal migration is generally considered to be an indispensable instrument to balance demand and supply of manpower. At least in the Western world there is a strong belief that the free choice of place of work and residence are important prerequisites if productivity and the standard of living are to be raised. Migratory movements between countries can also bring these advantages if they adapt themselves to the absorptive capacity of the receiving countries and if immigrants are able to work more productively than previously, thus adding to the overall supply of goods and services. To the extent that these movements promote prosperity in one country they create new markets in other countries and thereby contribute to the development of international economic relations.

At the outset the immigrants whom Germany had to receive after the last war did not serve that purpose. The newcomers were neither volunteers nor had they been selected; their number, too, greatly exceeded the economic possibilities that existed in Germany

---

[1] *E.g.* in 1953 and in 1954 the net number of arrivals from the Soviet Zone amounted to 583,000.

at that time. The capital which had remained in Germany at the end of the war was not even enough to cover the needs of the indigenous population. At first emigration seemed to be more adapted to circumstances than immigration. For the millions of expellees, who no longer had any means of production of their own, new jobs had to be created, a task which called for a development of industrialization and an expansion of foreign trade. The restrictions on production which were imposed in Germany immediately after the war, the division of the country into several zones, and the keen shortage of capital made this process of adjustment very difficult. Moreover, the occupational and social structure of the expellees as well as their geographical distribution did not correspond to the requirements. Many of them were too old to start a new life and to maintain themselves in a labour market characterized by very severe competition. Others were not sufficiently qualified for industrial jobs since they had been either farmers or small business men. They often had to be occupied at a lower level and their professional skills were inadequately used. A distribution of the population according to effective demand was difficult because of the housing shortage in the towns. This state of affairs resulted at first in lower productivity and in structural unemployment and there was only little hope that conditions would become normal again within a reasonable period of time.

The rapid recovery of Western Germany was due partly to direct and indirect foreign aid and partly to the fact that for years the German people accepted a relatively low level of consumption whilst working very hard, thus making possible a steady increase of capital formation. Last but not least the determination of the expellees and refugees to re-establish themselves contributed decisively to that recovery. The misery among the new arrivals gave rise to a drive for achievement which proved a real stimulant to the whole Germany economy.[1] Some of the immigrants introduced new industries and production methods which created new export possibilities. Above all they promoted a spirit of competition which had a beneficial effect on productivity. Some figures may illustrate recent developments in West Germany. On the basis of 1936 prices gross national product per head in 1950 was still 6 per cent below that of 1936; in 1954 it had exceeded that level by 25 per cent.[2] The rate of net investment was 60 per cent higher in 1954 than in 1936,

---

[1] Friedrich Edding : 'Die Flüchtlinge als Belastung und Antrieb der westdeutschen Wirtschaft' (The refugees as a burden and a stimulus to the West German economy), *Kieler Studien, Forschungsberichte des Instituts für Weltwirtschaft an der Universität Kiel*, Nr. 12, Kiel, 1952.

[2] 4 per cent higher than in 1938.

although investments in housing, transport, educational institutions, etc., were still well below the needs of population growth. During the same period industrial productivity rose by almost 30 per cent. The labour force which, in spite of the considerable immigration, had increased very slowly during the early postwar period, showed an expansion of 2·4 million between September 1950 and September

TABLE II

SOCIAL AND ECONOMIC STRUCTURE OF THE WEST GERMAN LABOUR
FORCE, 18 MAY 1939 AND 13 SEPTEMBER 1950

(Percentages)

Social or Economic Group	Total Labour Force		Expellees	Rest of the Labour Force *
	1939	1950	1950	1950
Social Structure				
Self-employed	14·4	14·8	5·2	16·5
Unpaid family workers	17·8	14·4	1·8	16·7
Government officials	5·0	4·0	3·7	4·0
Employees	16·0†	15·9	14·1	16·3
Wage-earners	46·8	50·9	75·2	46·5
Total	100·0	100·0	100·0	100·0
Economic Structure				
Agriculture	26·2	23·2	13·5	24·9
Industry and mining	40·5	42·3	48·6	41·2
Commerce and transport	16·6	15·6	12·0	16·2
Service industries	16·7	18·9	25·9	17·7
Total	100·0	100·0	100·0	100·0

* Predominantly natives.
† Including soldiers and persons in working camps (Reichsarbeitsdienst).
Source : *Statistische Berichte, op. cit.* no. viii/8/2, 18 and 28.

1954. Since then it has continued to increase; simultaneously unemployment has fallen to less than 4 per cent of the dependent work force. More than one-fifth of the increase in the labour force was due to the refugee immigrants who kept coming in from the Soviet Zone; more than two-fifths were re-activated 'reserves', including a high proportion of expellees who had been admitted before 1950. These previously idle workers were absorbed into employment because of a growing shortage of manpower in various occupations, and particularly because of an increasing rate of internal migration which was partly sponsored by the government.

Although all classes of the population benefited from the increased prosperity in West Germany, the average income of the expellees and refugees is still lower than that of the native population. Owing to this relative disadvantage, many still wish to emigrate. Apart from certain exceptions, however, there are only few groups with chances to emigrate who would not also find good opportunities in Germany. The majority of those who used to be independent farmers or craftsmen cannot be adequately absorbed in Germany. Some of them could improve their economic situation overseas but even there the possibilities of setting up and maintaining an independent business are limited. Language difficulties, different working methods and unfamiliar customs often make their competitive power abroad weaker than it is at home and offer adequate chances only to the best qualified among them. Many of those who are still socially dissatisfied are no longer in a position to meet that challenge. A large number have now become too old, or have lost the spirit of enterprise after long periods of distress and disappointment, so that they would have great difficulty in adapting themselves to new conditions abroad. The number of potential emigrants is therefore much lower than the number of discontented persons; and even those who are eligible for emigration will only find opportunities if their professional qualifications are in demand in the new country. There is scope for skilled industrial workers, specialized technicians, and agricultural workers, *i.e.* categories which are also in demand in Germany. Therefore, the widely held opinion that, in view of the growth of its population, Germany could provide large numbers of emigrants is erroneous.[1]

Recent emigration has been in the interests of receiving countries but not of Germany. It has contributed little to the solution of the economic and social problems caused by the expellees and refugees. Of the working people emigrating in 1953 and 1954 about two-fifths were technicians or metal or building workers, *i.e.* members of trades which require long training. Only relatively few of them had been unemployed in Germany, and it was difficult to fill the resulting vacancies. Vocational training courses and an increased regional exchange of workers became necessary.

In spite of these drawbacks emigration as it is at present need not be an economic danger to Germany. Of course the capital

[1] See, for example, Michael P. Fogarty, *Economic Control*, London, 1955, p. 197 : '. . . The postwar problems of refugees from Eastern Europe, and especially of the refugee population of Germany, has had to be solved very largely by emigration.'

invested in the training and the education of the migrants must be regarded as a loss. However, inasmuch as it helps to raise the productivity and the purchasing power of the receiving countries, it indirectly benefits the German economy as well. It is difficult to determine to what extent postwar emigration from Germany has had this effect. Selective controls and various forms of discrimination applied in the receiving countries have certainly hampered this prosperity-promoting effect. It will be all the more necessary in the future to ensure that, whenever migration agreements are concluded, the immigrants are given an opportunity to make full use of their skill and knowledge.

Recognition of the advantages of individual freedom has had a stronger influence than the manpower situation on the emigration policy of Western Germany. It is true that propaganda in favour of emigration is subject to supervision by the government, which tries to keep the outflow of skilled workers within reasonable limits. Likewise, the *per capita* contributions stipulated in the agreement with the Intergovernmental Committee for European Migration are now granted only for persons whose departure does not weaken the German labour market. The individual, however, is free to decide whether he wants to emigrate or not. In Western Germany emigration is not legally restricted in any way. On the contrary, anyone wanting to emigrate can obtain accurate information about living and working conditions in the country of destination from the Migrants' Advice Bureaux which have been set up in all the Federal States; the prospective migrant can thus find out whether his plans are practicable and whether he can expect good economic and social opportunities in the new country.

V. PROSPECTS

There is nothing in the demographic or the economic conditions in Germany and the relevant immigration countries to suggest that large migratory movements across the German borders may be expected or would be necessary in the future, if present trends continue. They certainly could not alleviate the age-specific demographic pressure in Germany. The encouragement of immigration for the purpose of improving the age structure would not be appropriate, and a substantial outflow of population from the higher age groups is not possible. From the economic point of view the demand for specialized manpower, which varies with business fluctuations, sets limits to larger movements of a permanent nature. The present scale of movement to oversea countries reflects an emigration pressure which had been banked up in previous years rather than a genuine economic necessity. There have always been, and there will always be, people who wish to emigrate, and it is right that they should be allowed to do so.

Recent trends in the West German economy suggest that there is an effective demand for immigrants. This demand is for the present largely satisfied by the influx from the Soviet Zone and from Berlin, but the picture changes completely if both parts of Germany are considered as one unit. The continuous emigration of production workers from central Germany has already led to a considerable shortage of manpower in that area. Under normal political circumstances that area would probably not be losing population. The attracting power of the industrial areas of Saxony and Berlin-Brandenburg has been so considerable, ever since the foundation of the Reich in 1871, that it much more than offset emigration from central Germany. If the Soviet Zone were liberated there would probably be a considerable reflux of the population which had fled to Western Germany, and this repatriation would then reveal the gaps in the manpower resources of the reunified territory.

In spite of immigration from the Soviet Zone labour keeps getting scarce in West Germany. During the coming years the natural increase of the West German labour force will decline, and at times the expected gains of young workers will not even be enough to offset losses due to the ageing of the population. The reserve of unemployed is already largely exhausted; as a reservoir for the labour market the inactive population will yield much less than during recent years. This problem will be particularly acute when, in the course of rearmament, several hundred thousand young men will have to be continuously available for military service, quite apart from the secondary manpower requirements of the armed forces.

The question whether there should now be increased immigration of foreign workers is largely a problem of economic policy. In the light of national considerations it may be deemed more appropriate, for the time being, to extend the employment of women, to postpone the retiring age of elderly persons, especially skilled workers, or to speed up the employment of young people. Moreover, the possibilities of a rational use of manpower through vocational training and regional transfers are by no means exhausted. The efficiency of these measures and their effect on productivity would have to be separately ascertained in each industry. In this way detailed information could be obtained about the volume and character of immigration which might be necessary to raise productivity still further.

The results of such investigation will be different according to whether West Germany or the entire German territory is considered as a unit or as a future part of a larger integrated territory. Whatever the future development, it may be assumed that the traditional industrial centres will continue to attract people. Though the future structure of demand cannot be foreseen, it may be assumed that these areas will mainly need skilled immigrants, particularly after the reunification of the two parts of Germany which are now separated. The demand for skilled workers precludes large-scale migration. Skilled workers are, on the average, older than the unskilled, and more attached to their families, homes, and workshops ; they also run a greater risk of losing important social benefits provided by industry. When they move across the border they are also apt to lose social security benefits granted by the State. The reports of the High Authority of the European Coal and Steel Community on the movement of workers show how difficult it is, even in an economically integrated area, to ensure adequate migration of skilled labour. It will be easier to promote flexibility through two-way movements of temporary migrants across national frontiers.

TABLE Ia

GERMAN MIGRATION BALANCE AND GERMAN OVERSEA MIGRATION BY AREA OF ORIGIN, 1843–1950

(thousands)

Period *	Years	Months	Excess of Immigration (+), of Emigration (−)				Oversea Emigration			
			Total Germany	Western Germany†	Middle Germany‡	Rest of Germany§	Total Germany	Western Germany†	Middle Germany‡	Rest of Germany§
			Boundaries of 1910 (excluding Alsace-Lorraine)							
1843–52	9		− 624	− 593	− 3	− 28	669	..	..	..
1852–61	9		− 682	− 536	− 102	− 44	857	..	..	..
1861–71	10		− 932	− 508	− 23	− 401	872	..	..	225
1871–80	9		− 604	− 180	+ 92	− 516	548	244	78	225
1880–90	10		− 1240	− 413	+ 249	− 1077	1334	621	185	528
1890–1900	10		− 329	+ 253	+ 254	− 836	525	250	84	191
1900–10	10		− 85	+ 316	+ 371	− 772	274	137	51	86
			Boundaries of 1934							
1910–25	14	6	+ 330	+ 75	+ 376	− 121	320	211	72	37
1925–33	8	11	− 234	− 218	+ 285	− 300	332	236	57	38
1933–39	5	11	+ 504	+ 250	+ 425	− 171	106	69	25	12
			Boundaries of 1950							
1910–25	14	6	+ 457	‖ 73	¶ 384	—	..	=	¶	—
1925–33	8	11	+ 72	− 214	+ 286	—	..	..	..	—
1933–39	5	11	+ 727	+ 252	+ 475	—	..	..	..	—
1939–46	7	5	+ 9532	+ 6790	+ 2742	—	..	..	..	—
1946–50	3	11	+ 2665	+ 2005	+ 660 **	—	..	64 **	..	—

* Period between two population censuses.

† Total of the following provinces or states within their boundaries of 1934: Schleswig-Holstein, Hanover, Westphalia, Hessen-Nassau, Rhine-province, Hohenzollern, Bavaria, Württemberg, Baden, Hesse, Hamburg, Oldenburg, Braunschweig, Bremen, Lippe, Schaumburg-Lippe. This area can be compared with that of the Federal Republic of Germany.

‡ Total of the following provinces or states within their boundaries of 1934: Berlin, Berlin-Brandenburg, Province of Saxony, Saxony, Thuringia, Mecklenburg, Anhalt. This area can be compared to some extent with that of the Soviet Zone of Occupation and Berlin.

§ Rest of Germany comprises mainly the eastern provinces of Germany.

¶ Area of the Soviet Zone of Occupation and Berlin.

‖ Area of the Federal Republic.

** Partly estimated.

Source : See Table II.

TABLE Ib

GERMAN MIGRATION BALANCE AND GERMAN OVERSEA EMIGRATION BY AREA OF ORIGIN, 1843–1950

(per 10,000 of mean population)

Period*	Length of Period		Excess of Immigration (+), of Emigration (−)				Oversea Emigration			
	Years	Months	Total Germany	Western Germany†	Middle Germany‡	Rest of Germany§	Total Germany	Western Germany†	Middle Germany‡	Rest of Germany§
			Boundaries of 1910 (excluding Alsace-Lorraine)							
1843–52	9		− 188	− 341	− 4	− 33	201	..	..	..
1852–61	9		− 192	− 296	− 126	− 48	242	..	..	..
1861–71	10		− 245	− 266	− 26	− 401	229	..	..	..
1871–80	9		− 145	− 87	+ 92	− 479	132	118	78	209
1880–90	10		− 271	− 180	+ 216	− 951	292	271	160	467
1890–1900	10		− 64	+ 98	+ 189	− 698	102	97	63	159
1900–10	10		− 14	+ 105	+ 240	− 586	47	45	33	65
			Boundaries of 1934							
1910–25	14	6	+ 55	+ 22	+ 219	− 139	53	62	42	42
1925–33	8		− 37	+ 59	+ 158	− 329	52	64	32	42
1933–39	5	11	+ 75	+ 65	+ 226	− 181	16	18	13	13
			Boundaries of 1950							
1910–25	14	6	+ 89	= 21	¶ 223	—	..	=	¶	—
1925–33	8		+ 13	− 59	+ 158	—	..	..	..	—
1933–39	5	11	+ 127	+ 66	+ 250	—	..	..	..	—
1939–46	7	5	+ 1537	+ 1617	+ 1371	—	..	..	..	—
1946–50	3	11	+ 398	+ 434	+ 319	—	..	14	..	—

Footnotes * † ‡ § ‖ ¶ see Table 1A.

Source : *Statistik des Deutschen Reichs*, published by Statistisches Reichsamt, vol. 451/1, Berlin 1935, p. 66 ; Population census returns of 1925, 1933, 1939, 1946, and 1950, *Statistik des Deutschen Reichs, op. cit.* vol. 360, Berlin, 1930, pp. 232 ; *Statistisches Jahrbuch für das Deutsche Reich*, published by Statistisches Reichsamt, Berlin, vol. 1922–1940/41.

TABLE II
GERMAN OVERSEA EMIGRATION, 1871–1954
(average annual emigration)

Period	Western Germany *		Middle Germany †	
	Number	Per 10,000 of Mean Population	Number	Per 10,000 of Mean Population
1871–1880	28,696	13·8	9,181	9·1
1881–1890	62,116	27·1	18,521	16·0
1891–1900	25,000	9·7	8,445	6·3
1901–1910	13,715	4·5	5,098	3·3
1911–1920	3,737	1·1	1,478	0·9
1921–1930	38,844	10·8	10,894	6·2
1931–1939	10,429	2·7	3,567	1·9
1945–1954	32,443 ‡	7·2‡	..	..
1950	35,000	7·3	..	..
1951	61,000	12·7	..	..
1952	59,000	12·2	..	..
1953 §	60,814	12·4	..	..
1954 §	61,614	12·4	..	..

* See footnote †, Table Iᴀ. † See footnote ‡, Table Iᴀ.
‡ See footnote ‖, Table Iᴀ. § Including emigration to European countries.

Sources : *Statistik des Deutschen Reichs, op. cit.* vol. 360, Berlin 1930, pp. 332 f. ; *Statistisches Jahrbuch für das Deutsche Reich, op. cit.* vol. 1922–1940/41 ; *Wirtschaft und Statistik,* published by Statistisches Bundesamt, Wiesbaden vol. vi (new series), 1954, p. 276.

TABLE III
COMPONENTS OF POPULATION GROWTH AND OVERSEA EMIGRATION FROM WESTERN GERMANY, 1946–54

Period *	Population Growth				Excess of Immigration over Emigration		Oversea Emigration	
	Total Growth		Excess of Births over Deaths					
	1000	Per 10,000 of Mean Population	1000	Per 10,000 of Mean Population	1000	Per 10,000 of Mean Population	1000	Per 10,000 of Mean Population
1946	3406	802	175	41	3231	761	8	1·9
1947	1105	247	223	50	882	197	9	2·0
1948	1143	249	292	64	851	185	12	2·6
1949	760	162	313	67	447	95	15	3·2
1950	654	138	279	59	375	79	35	7·4
1951	458	95	250	52	208	43	61	12·7
1952	403	83	255	53	148	30	59	12·2
1953	569	116	221	45	349	71	61 †	12·4
1954	485	98	264	53	221	45	62 †	12·4
1946–54	8983	221 ‡	2272	56 ‡	6712	165 ‡	322	7·9 ‡

* 1 January–31 December. † Including emigration to European countries.
‡ Average annual rate.

Source : *Wirtschaft und Statistik, op. cit.* vol. 1-7 (new series), 1949–55.

Chapter 15

REGIONAL ASPECTS OF IMMIGRATION
INTO FRANCE

BY

XAVIER LANNES
International Labour Office, Geneva

BETWEEN 1 July and 31 December 1954 the National Immigration Office in France sponsored the arrival of 393,154 foreigners, comprising 306,139 workers and 87,013 dependants, under the Family Immigration Scheme. This figure does not include all the immigrants who entered the country during the period under review, as the monopoly of the National Immigration Office applies only to wage earners; but it certainly covers the part of the influx which had economic significance.

Like internal migratory movements, the immigration of foreigners results from the fact that economic growth in certain areas is more rapid than in others. In this study we shall give a quantitative estimate of the regional distribution of immigrants and the internal shifts of population since the war, and we shall attempt to interpret the bearing of these movements on the economic development of France.

The analysis is based on the following statistical data:

Statistics on the immigration of workers and dependants between 1946 and 1954 (National Immigration Office);
Census of 1946 and 1954 (National Institute for Statistics and Economic Studies);
Statistics on the acquisition of French citizenship from 1946 to 1953 (Ministry of Justice);
Statistics on North African workers employed in France between 1948 and 1954 (Ministry of Labour and Social Security).

I. STATISTICAL DATA

(1) *Geographical Distribution*

Table I shows the distribution of immigrant workers over the various areas of France between 1946 and 1954.

The majority of the immigrants were absorbed by undertakings situated in the eastern half of the country. Two-thirds of them were concentrated in only fifteen Departments, particulars of which are set out in Table II.

It is in these fifteen Departments that the most important mining and heavy industries are located, particularly in the north and the east. The statistical data supplied by the National Immigration Office do not give details by Department of the branches of industry for which foreign workers were recruited. All that is available — and this only since 1949 — is a classification of workers recruited for agriculture

TABLE I

REGIONAL DISTRIBUTION OF IMMIGRANT WORKERS
IN FRANCE, 1946–54

	Number	%
Northern area (Nord, Pas-de-Calais, Somme, Oise, Aisne, Ardennes)	54,447	17·7
Paris area (Seine, Seine-et-Oise, Seine-et-Marne)	25,992	8·5
Eastern area (Meuse, Meurthe-et-Moselle, Moselle, Bas-Rhin, Haut-Rhin, Belfort, Vosges)	75,685	24·7
Area of Lyon (Rhône, Loire, Saône-et-Loire)	19,932	6·5
Jura-Alpes (Haute-Saône, Doubs, Jura, Ain, Haute-Savoie, Savoie, Isère, Hautes-Alpes, Basses-Alpes)	39,962	13·1
Mediterranean area (Alpes-Maritimes, Var, Bouches-du-Rhône, Vaucluse, Drôme, Ardèche, Gard, Aude, Hérault, Pyrénées-Orientales, Corse)	27,032	8·8
Remainder of France	63,089	20·7
Total	306,139	100·0

and for industry. However, as immigration has declined since the middle of 1955, this information loses a great deal of its interest.

The main facts may be summarized as follows :

(*a*) The bulk of the immigration into the *Northern area* was in response to the needs of the coal-mining industries in the Nord and Pas-de-Calais Departments, which were considerable until 1949. The remainder went into the building trades. Few agricultural workers were placed in that region, since it is customary to call on seasonal Belgian workers and, in recent years, Italians.

(*b*) In the *Paris area*, those recruited were mainly building workers, skilled mechanics, and unskilled industrial labourers, with only few permanent agricultural workers.

(*c*) In the *Eastern area*, while there was appreciable recruitment into agriculture, the major immigration Departments, Meurthe-et-Moselle, Moselle, and Haut-Rhin, absorbed mainly industrial labour such as building workers, and the Department of Moselle, particularly until 1949, took unskilled labourers for the iron and steel industry.

(*d*) In the *Lyon area* the immigrants went chiefly into the building and steel industries.

(*e*) In the *Jura Alpes area* foreign manpower was required in agriculture (especially in the Departments of Doubs and Isère),

TABLE II

DEPARTMENTS RECEIVING MORE THAN 5000 IMMIGRANT
WORKERS EACH, 1946–54

Department	No. of Immigrant Workers	% Share of Total Immigration	Immigration as % of 1946 Occupied Population
Moselle	37,382	12·2	14·9
Nord	36,772	12·0	4·6
Seine	19,792	6·5	0·9
Meurthe-et-Moselle	13,462	4·4	6·2
Savoie	11,463	3·7	9·0
Isère	10,617	3·5	3·6
Haut-Rhin	9,615	3·1	4·5
Pas-de-Calais	8,822	2·9	1·9
Loire	7,756	2·5	2·5
Bouches-du-Rhône	7,113	2·3	1·7
Bas-Rhin	6,976	2·3	2·3
Rhône	6,677	2·2	1·5
Haute-Savoie	6,137	2·0	4·3
Saône-et-Loire	5,499	1·8	2·1
Doubs	5,107	1·7	3·8
Total	193,190	63·1	

wood-cutters (particularly in the Departments of Savoie and Haute-Savoie), and building workers for public works (mainly in major projects of the Électricité de France).

(*f*) In the *Mediterranean area* immigrants were mostly agricultural and building workers.

(*g*) In other areas foreign workers were rare, with the exception of some industrial Departments in the *South-West* (Aveyron, Tarn, Haute-Garonne, and Gironde).

Annual figures show that the summer of 1949 was the end of a three-year period during which immigration had been heavy; but from 1950 on, with the exception of a modest recovery in 1952, the intake was generally much lower. If the territory of France is taken as a whole, 70 per cent of the postwar immigrants arrived between 1946 and 1949; in Departments where industrial workers were in greatest demand the proportion even exceeded 80 per cent.

(2) *Net Foreign Immigration by Area*

By comparing the figures of the Census of 1946 with those of 1954, it is possible to calculate the net foreign immigration into each Department. The estimate can only be approximate, since it does not take into account the natural increase of the foreign population and there is doubt whether the foreign population was recorded accurately in some Departments.[1]

For the metropolitan area of France the apparent excess of foreign immigrants over the number of foreigners who left the country, between the Census of March 1946 and that of May 1954, was about 85,000, and the 'real' excess about 160,000.[2] This total errs on the low side, but we are interested less in the aggregate figures than in the comparisons between different areas. The figures for each area are as follows:

Area	Apparent Excess of Inward over Outward Movement(+)
Northern	− 31,000
Paris	+ 39,000
Eastern	+ 53,000
Lyon	+ 5,000
Jura Alpes	+ 27,000
Mediterranean	− 16,000
Remainder of France	+ 8,000
Total	+ 85,000

[1] *E.g.* in the southern part of the country, particularly in the Departments of Alpes-Maritimes and Bouches-du-Rhône.

[2] The apparent excess is arrived at as follows:

Foreign population on 10 May 1954	1,451,752
Number of persons who acquired French citizenship in the Metropolitan Departments	376,534
	1,828,286
Foreign population on 10 March 1946	1,743,670
Net immigration 1946–54	84,616

However, in 1946 about 75,000 nationals of the Union Française were included in the foreign population. To-day they are no longer considered as foreigners and are consequently not included in this calculation. Thus we reach the 'real' figure of 160,000.

This table shows that the three areas which are still absorbing a substantial number of foreigners are the Eastern, the Jura Alpes, and the Paris areas, and that elsewhere recent immigration did not offset the outflow. There is a considerable discrepancy between net immigration and gross immigration which suggests that the flow of foreign labour since 1946 has shown little stability.

(3) *Algerians employed in the Metropolitan Territory*

In June 1954 the Ministry of Labour counted 150,222 North Africans employed in the Metropolitan Territory, as against 113,326 in June 1951 and 84,620 in July 1948. There are also wide variations in the regional distribution of these workers. For the areas already mentioned the figures are as follows :

Area	Number of Algerians	Percentage
Northern	21,751	14·5
Paris	51,376	34·2
Eastern	24,571	16·4
Lyon	16,508	10·9
Jura Alpes	9,607	6·4
Mediterranean	13,104	8·7
Remainder of France	13,305	8·9
Total	150,222	100·0

The regional distribution of Algerians is different from that of foreign immigrants. North African labour is predominantly industrial and there is a large concentration of it in the Paris area. These workers are quite free to take any employment wherever they like, and they tend to settle in a small group of important centres which offer the greatest variety of jobs. In fact 107,333 North Africans, *i.e.* 71 per cent of the total, were registered in the following eight Departments :

Seine	43,802
Nord	15,489
Moselle	13,282
Rhône	9,613
Seine-et-Oise	6,976
Bouches-du-Rhône	6,422
Meurthe-et-Moselle	5,994
Loire	5,755
Total	107,333

(4) *Main Internal Migration Currents* [1]

Between the Census of 1946 and that of 1954 extensive migration movements took place within the metropolitan territory. They can be roughly estimated if we compare the 'natural movement' of the population during the period under consideration with its 'general movement'. Between these two dates 72 Departments out of 90 experienced a net loss of population in favour of the other 18 which are listed below. For each Department the excess of immigrants compared with the total population in 1946 is expressed as a percentage.

	%		%
Alpes-Maritimes	13·4	Haut-Rhin	2·6
Seine-et-Oise	13·3	Meurthe-et-Moselle	2·5
Moselle	11·7	Vaucluse	2·4
Seine-et-Marne	5·0	Loire-Inférieure	1·6
Belfort	4·6	Savoie	1·4
Var	4·3	Seine	1·1
Bouches-du-Rhône	4·1	Nord	0·9
Isère	3·8	Charente-Maritime	0·7
Ardennes	2·9	Seine-Inférieure	0·5

These percentages do not represent what is usually termed 'internal migration', but they show the total balance of all migratory movements. In order to obtain the balance of internal migration, the excess of North African immigration should be deducted from the figures showing the net total of immigration or emigration, and then the balance of foreign immigration should be either deducted or added, as the case may be. Such a calculation would be too complicated to be included in this study, whose purpose is to bring out the most important general features.

The two main centres of attraction for internal migrants were the Paris area, particularly, and the Mediterranean area. The Eastern area, at least its industrial Departments, and the Isère and some other coastal Departments (Seine, Loire-Inférieure, and Charente-Inférieure) were of secondary importance. A net outward balance was recorded in the West and the Massif Central, and many rural Departments outside these regions, particularly in the South-West, also had a migration deficit.

[1] See *Études et conjoncture*, January-February 1955, pp. 17 ff., and June 1955, pp. 503 ff.

II. TENTATIVE INTERPRETATION OF THE STATISTICAL DATA

(1) *Postwar Migration and Economic Development*

Recent migratory movements are an adaptation to new conditions arising from three basic factors, namely, demographic pressure, technical change and economic development.

Demographic pressure, *i.e.* a permanent excess of able-bodied individuals over the number of jobs, has continued in a number of agricultural areas, particularly in the West and in the centre of the country where the birth-rate has remained high. This has resulted in a persistent rural exodus. Overpopulation in the three Algerian Departments raises a still more acute problem which has a direct bearing on the French economy, since the Algerians enjoy complete freedom of access to the Metropolitan Territory.

The modernization of equipment and of methods of production has been systematically pursued since the liberation, under the impulse of the Commissariat Général au Plan de Modernisation et d'Équipement. This has been an important aspect of the economic progress achieved during the past few years. Wherever productivity increased more quickly than production, workers were dismissed, particularly the least skilled grades in agriculture and extractive industries. The modernization drive therefore resulted in a structural decline in the demand for labour in certain sectors, expressing itself chiefly in a slackening or cessation of new recruitment. On the other hand, new developments in other sectors had the opposite effect, since they entailed an increase in the manpower required in secondary and tertiary industries. Another factor contributing to this expansion in employment was the relative increase in public administration resulting from the activities of the State.

Thus the 'push' and 'pull' factors affecting the migratory movements as a whole were, on the one hand, rural overpopulation and technical modernization and, on the other, industrial expansion and the spread of tertiary industries. The fact that the French economy was able to provide employment not only for the rural surplus but also for North African and foreign workers does not prove either that the internal migration of the past few years has completely solved the demographic problem in the rural areas or that there has been considerable economic development. What it proves is that the stimulating effects of industrial development have on the whole more than offset the displacement due to modernization. In other words, the number of new jobs created through the expansion of existing factories or the building of new ones was larger than the number lost through technical rationalization.

The unequal development of industries in the various regions and the differences in their resources of manpower explain the nature and trends of migration within the country. In the Western half there was enough labour to meet the needs of an industrial development which was confined to a few centres such as Nantes or Le Mans; but in the Eastern half, where most of the country's capital equipment and sources of energy are situated, economic development outpaced the local labour supply and it was necessary to recruit foreigners and North Africans. Economic development is mostly accompanied by quick promotion inside each trade, so that the vacant jobs which attract immigrants are at the bottom of the scale; French experience in recent years shows this to be strikingly true of the influx of North Africans and foreigners.

On the whole, recent migratory movements do not indicate a high rate of economic development. Hampered by an inadequate volume of investment, the level of employment has not risen very much, especially when one remembers that after the war there was a shortage of labour due to casualties and the departure of a number of former immigrants (Poles, Yugoslavs, and Spaniards). It would have required a much more rapid rate of economic growth to induce a large influx of immigrants under the regulations which have prevailed since 1945.

(2) *The Role of Foreign Immigration within the Total Migratory Movement*

In order to understand the role of foreign immigration in postwar economic development the following two factors should be considered. First, ever since the liberation foreign immigration has been subject to severe restrictions. Immigrants were not allowed to compete with French nationals, and they were confined to those sections of the economy where there was a shortage of manpower (agriculture, mining, building trades, steel production, and domestic service). They could not even compete with North Africans, since they were not allowed to accept unskilled work. Foreign immigration was thus directed into certain channels, and the authorities tried to keep it down to a minimum. Second, the bulk of recent foreign immigration, *i.e.* that between 1946 and 1949, served to replace workers, mostly foreigners, of whom the French economy had been deprived immediately after the war. Thus the admission of new foreign workers does not necessarily imply a higher degree of employment.

In the light of these considerations an attempt can now be made to assess the role of foreign immigration in each area.

(*a*) In the *Northern area* immigration served mainly to fill vacancies in the coal mines resulting from the departure of Poles and German prisoners of war. Though the influx here, particularly of North Africans, was substantial, this could not be regarded as a symptom of a growing volume of employment. The Northern area, which has a birth-rate higher than the average, seems to have reached an equilibrium, in which the pace of its development no longer requires the regular addition of foreign manpower.

(*b*) In the *Paris area* in-migration from the Provinces and North Africa has been more important than foreign immigration.

(*c*) In the *Eastern region* foreign immigration has played a much bigger part than in the north, and this has continued to be so since 1949. A relatively large number of agricultural immigrants were required to replace workers attracted into industry. The remarkable progress of the iron industry in the Lorraine area has been and continues to be the most noteworthy element in a general industrial development which has had repercussions far beyond the boundaries of that area.

(*d*) In the *Lyon area* immigration has lost its significance since 1949.

(*e*) In the *Jura Alpes area* vigorous economic development has given rise to a substantial current of immigration as well as in-migration. The mountain area in the South-East is no longer over-populated; it has become an area of attraction for the natural reservoir of manpower in neighbouring Italy.

(*f*) In the *Mediterranean area* and the *South-West* the inflow of foreigners has declined.[1] Once the needs resulting from the war had been satisfied, there were hardly any new immigrants except those who arrived on individual contracts arranged through relatives or friends who had already settled in France.

III. CONCLUSIONS

(1) A regional study shows clearly that the two stages of post-war immigration, *i.e.* before and after 1949, differ not only quantitatively but also qualitatively. Most of the immigrants who entered

---

[1] North African immigration has not been considered in the Mediterranean area in spite of geographic proximity.

France during the early postwar years came to replace workers, mostly foreigners, who had left the country. Those who came in more recent years were generally called upon to occupy new jobs arising from economic development. Therefore immigration since 1949, in spite of its modest scale, is a more genuine criterion of economic development than the relatively considerable inflow of the preceding years.

(2) A study of foreign immigration cannot by itself provide a reliable guide to the trend and speed of the economic development of each area. The influx of North Africans and internal migration cannot be separated from the general currents of immigration in an analysis which must deal with the overall movement of labour. As foreign workers are introduced only in trades which have been abandoned by the native population, but which are nevertheless essential, foreign immigration seems to be associated with certain forms of economic development which particularly affect the lower strata of the labour market.

(3) A general study of migratory movements brings out a geographical disequilibrium in the French economy. On the one hand, there are areas of advancing productivity and high standard of living, which attract immigrants; on the other hand, there are underdeveloped areas labouring under demographic pressure. The spontaneous migration currents increase this disequilibrium instead of reducing it. The only solution would be a policy aiming at balanced development.

Chapter 16

MIGRATION AND THE ECONOMY OF EASTERN EUROPE

BY

J. ZUBRZYCKI

Australian National University, Canberra

THIS study aims at analysing some of the striking changes in the demographic and economic structure of five East European countries which now lie within the Soviet sphere of influence, namely, Bulgaria, Czechoslovakia, Hungary, Poland, and Romania.

During the first three decades of this century these countries provided about a quarter of the oversea emigration from Europe and more than a half of intra-continental migration in Europe. To-day emigration of nationals is prohibited on political and economic grounds. The countries of Eastern Europe are undergoing rapid industrialization on the Soviet pattern and are suffering from an overall shortage of manpower. The ambitious long-term plans of economic development are likely to remain a drain on manpower for decades to come.

The study falls into four parts. In the first section an attempt is made to give a wide demographic background for the area as a whole. Section II analyses population changes during the period of the Second World War and the three years of economic reconstruction. Section III gives an account of the pattern of demographic development in Eastern Europe in the period 1948–54. Section IV discusses the pattern of economic evolution and the volume and intensity of internal migrations.

The analysis of changes in the demographic and economic structure of the Satellite countries is hampered by lack of published statistical data comparable with what is available for most of the industrialized countries outside the Soviet orbit. The Iron Curtain of concealment was lowered for Eastern Europe at the time when absolute Communist control over the five countries was finally established. From 1948 to 1949 the publication of statistical information on population movements, industry, and trade ceased almost completely. The flow of periodical reports was reduced to a mere trickle consisting of items such as percentage indices of output changes, volume of transactions, and changes in vital rates. The latest Satellite country to hold a population census was Poland (December 1950), and the only published results of this census included a table giving the enumerated total population tabulated by sex and by urban/rural residence. Information on the age structure and other vital characteristics was withheld. The example of Poland is typical of all the Satellites. The only statistics bearing on population trends are found from time to time in official speeches published at the time of Communist Party Congresses with the intention of eulogizing the achievements of Communist régimes in bringing about an improvement in public health or an increase in the rate of population growth.

Finally there is also the problem of changes of political frontiers brought about by the Yalta and Potsdam agreements (chiefly affecting Poland and Czechoslovakia) and a number of intra-orbit agreements.[1] These territorial changes make comparisons with the state of affairs before the Second World War very difficult.

I. DEMOGRAPHIC BACKGROUND

The pre-war position in Eastern Europe was analysed by W. E. Moore in his *Economic Demography of Eastern and Southern Europe*. He pointed out that the populations of Western Europe were entering a period of stability or decline whereas those of Eastern Europe were still expanding rapidly. The growth of population in Eastern Europe was not accompanied by a corresponding increase in the rate of utilization of economic resources. Throughout the area numbers were going up at an annual rate of approximately 1·5 per cent, or three times as fast as in Western Europe. With the sole exception of Czechoslovakia (which inherited the industrial arsenal of the Austro-Hungarian Empire), the countries of the area had some notable economic and demographic features in common. At least four out of every five persons lived in rural areas, and about two-thirds of the working population earned its living in agriculture. An army of almost ten million 'hidden' unemployed depressed the living standards of the rural population of some forty million; birth-rates remained largely uncontrolled, and gradually falling mortality made for high rates of natural increase.

The only available outlet for the surplus population was emigration.

[1] For a summary of population transfers and boundary changes see J. B. Schechtman, 'Postwar population transfers in Europe', *Review of Politics*, Notre Dame U.S.A., April 1953.

226

The countries of Eastern Europe have been a traditional source of manpower for the West since the turn of the twentieth century. First, there was migration within Europe, chiefly from the over-populated regions of German and Russian Poland to Germany where the growing industrial centres of the Ruhr and Westphalia offered special attractions.[1] Secondly, a far more powerful flow of migrants went across the Atlantic; five million Poles, Czechs, Slovaks, Serbs, and Magyars entered the United States during the twenty-five years ending in 1925.

In the inter-war period, particularly after the imposition of immigration restrictions by the United States, transatlantic emigration from Eastern Europe was lower than it was in the first quarter of the century. France was the main country of immigration, followed by the United States, Canada, Brazil, Argentina, and Palestine, and Poland contributed the largest contingent of some 1,100,000 emigrants.[2] In addition to these movements of the indigenous populations of Eastern Europe there was a westward transfer of ethnic Germans following the boundary changes after the First World War, the result of which was an influx of about a million into Germany from the territories lost by the Reich.[3]

II. POPULATION CHANGES : THE SECOND WORLD WAR AND ITS AFTERMATH

During the Second World War the demographic structure of Eastern Europe was drastically changed by two factors: mass extermination and mass expulsion.

Table I shows the pre-war and postwar population in Eastern Europe. According to the projections made by the office of Population Research of Princeton University,[4] the population in 1948 would have risen to 82·3 million : [5] in fact it fell to 68·4 million.

[1] There was also considerable *seasonal* emigration, chiefly to Germany, Denmark, and Latvia in the inter-war period ; see J. Zubrzycki, 'Emigration from Poland in the Nineteenth and Twentieth Centuries', *Population Studies*, March 1953.

[2] Of those 622,000 went to France, 54,000 to the United States (1925–38), 116,000 to Canada, 185,000 to South America, and 85,000 to Palestine. The return movement of Polish emigrants which started in the late twenties was caused by the world economic depression, and it affected chiefly Polish emigrants in France of whom some 198,000 returned to Poland (1926–38). (Source : Office Central de Statistique de la République Polonaise, *Petit Annuaire statistique de la Pologne 1939*, Warsaw, 1939.)

[3] E. M. Kulischer, 'Population Changes in Eastern Europe', American Academy of Political and Social Science, *Annals*, vol. 271, September 1951.

[4] *The Future Population of Europe and the Soviet Union: Population Projections, 1940–1970*, League of Nations, 1944.

[5] Projections now adjusted to the present borders.

TABLE I

POPULATION OF EASTERN EUROPE

(millions)

Country (Present Territory)	1939 (1)	Projected 1948 * (2)	Actual 1948 (3)
Bulgaria	6·3	6·8	7·1
Czechoslovakia	14·7	14·9	12·3
Hungary	9·2	9·4	9·2
Poland	32·1	34·0	23·9
Romania	15·8	17·2	15·9
	78·1	82·3	68·4

* Not allowing for the war.

Source : Columns (1), (3) : United Nations, *Demographic Year Book*.

The following components of the total deficit of some 14 million can be distinguished : (1) deficit of births ; (2) excess military and civilian mortality ; (3) losses arising out of population transfers.

(1) *Deficit of births*

War-time confusion and the temporary disruption of vital registration make it impossible to present an accurate estimate of the influence of the war on birth-rates. Postwar estimates, however,

TABLE II

Country	Years	Pre-war Years	Birth Rate % Change	Death Rate % Change	Natural Increase % Change
Bulgaria	1941–45	1936–40	− 3·4	− 1·5	− 6·7
Czechoslovakia	1941–45	1936–40	15·7	12·8	24·4
Hungary	1941–43	1936–40	− 5·5	13·5	− 51·5
Poland	1941–45	1936–38	− 17·4	21·3	− 66·1
Romania	1941–42	1936–39	− 28·7	2·1	− 83·3

Source : Henryk Zieliński, *Population Changes in Poland: 1939–1950*, Mid-European Studies Centre, New York, 1954, p. 7.

suggest that the decline was not as pronounced as during the First World War. For instance, in Poland the greatest relative decline in birth-rate during the Second World War was of the order of 22 per

228

cent in 1943 (1938 = 100). During the First World War birth-rates declined by 40 per cent in 1917 (1913 = 100).[1] Czechoslovakia was the only exception among the East European countries, with a live birth-rate in 1944, 32 per cent in excess of the 1938 level.[2]

Percentage changes in crude rates of natural increase for the area in comparison with the pre-war period were calculated by Henryk Zieliński and are quoted in Table II.

(2) *Excess Military and Civilian Mortality*

Losses under this heading were estimated by Frumkin[3] at 7·1 million, of which military losses amounted to nearly 1 million. It will be seen from Table III that the civilian victims of the war were mainly Jews.

TABLE III

MILITARY AND CIVILIAN EXCESS MORTALITY IN EASTERN EUROPE
DURING THE SECOND WORLD WAR

(thousands)

Country	Civilian victims of Political Persecution	Military Losses	Jews Killed	Total
Bulgaria	—	10	10	20
Czechoslovakia	75	200	140	415
Hungary	50	140	240	430
Poland	2500	100	3200	5800
Romania	—	300	160	460
Totals	2625	750	3750	7125

(3) *Losses arising out of Population Transfers* [4]

The country most affected by population transfers was Poland. They were of three kinds : movements of refugees, deportations by the Occupying Powers, and transfers arising from changes of political frontiers. The number of refugees who fled the German occupation (chiefly in 1939 to Lithuania, Hungary, and Romania) was about 300,000 (including some 70,000 soldiers interned in the border states). Most of these people never returned. About a million

[1] 'Contribution to Vital Statistics in Poland in 1946 and 1947', *Statystyka Polski*, Series D, No. 10, Warsaw, 1949, p. 28.
[2] *Zpravy*, vol. xxx, nos. 12-14, Prague, 1949.
[3] G. Frumkin, *Population Changes in Europe since 1939*, London, 1951.
[4] For population transfers the sources used are Eugene M. Kulischer, *Europe on the Move*, 1946, and G. Frumkin, *op. cit.*

Polish citizens were deported to the interior of Russia before the German invasion in 1941. The Nazi régime, too, was responsible for the policy of mass displacement. About 2·5 million Polish slave labourers and prisoners of war were found in Germany at the end of the war, of whom some 400,000 chose not to return. Finally, transfers arising out of frontier changes included the loss of the bulk of the non-Polish population of the Eastern Provinces annexed by the Soviet Union and the expulsion of the German population to the Oder-Neisse Territories.[1]

In Czechoslovakia there were no transfers comparable to the movements of refugees, deportees, and expellees in Poland. The main group affected were the Sudeten Germans, about 2·6 million of whom were expelled from Czechoslovakia in 1945–47. In Hungary there was a big influx of Hungarians from border states ; these groups included 170,000 who left South Transylvania and other Romanian territories and 75,000 repatriates from Czechoslovakia. Romania lost the whole of Bukovina with a population of 3 million to the Soviet Union, and at the end of the war 200,000 Germans were expelled from Transylvania. About 225,000 Turks were re-settled in Turkey from Bulgaria and Romania during the Second World War.

III. THE PATTERN OF POSTWAR DEMOGRAPHIC DEVELOPMENT

All the East European countries considered here have already passed or are now reaching the peak of their revolution in population structure. In Hungary, Romania, Bulgaria, and Czechoslovakia the birth- and death-rates reached a postwar peak a few years ago and have now entered the phase in which the population is increasing, but at rates far lower than in any comparable period of the last forty years. Poland is an exception ; there the birth-rate continues to increase while the reported death-rate is fairly constant. In all East European countries the proportion of urban population is higher than ever before and is on the increase.

Table IV illustrates some of the striking changes in the rates of population increase in Eastern Europe over the past three decades.

The rates of population increase follow the expected demographic pattern in Eastern Europe. With the exception of Poland, all East European countries are in the downward phase of the vital revolution. The rise in the rate of population growth in the

---

[1] See below, p. 233.

postwar period is a phenomenon common to most of the European countries which experienced a 'compensatory' increase lasting about four to six years, mainly as a result of voluntary and involuntary postponement of births during the war. The postwar increases in Eastern Europe are by no means high in relation to what is happening in other parts of Europe. Here are some other European rates (1948–53): France, 4 per cent; Sweden, 4·2 per cent; Italy, 4·4 per cent.[1]

It is somewhat surprising that Romania did not experience the 'compensatory' process; in fact, Romania, which in pre-war years was one of the most prolific countries in Europe, had in 1948–53 a

TABLE IV

RATES OF POPULATION INCREASE IN EASTERN EUROPE

(five-year periods in percentages)

Period	Bulgaria	Czechoslovakia	Hungary	Romania	Poland
1920–24	10·0	4·6	4·4	7·2	9·7
1925–30	7·9	4·4	4·2	6·9	6·7
1930–35	6·4	2·1	3·8	6·7	7·0
1935–40	3·9	2·0	3·3	5·0	5·3
1949–54	5·1 *	3·2	4·0	4·0	9·9 *

* Known figures 1949–53 ; extrapolated to 1954.

Sources : Figures for 1920–40 from United Nations *Demographic Yearbook*, 1952. Figures for 1949–54 based on official government sources.

rate of increase lower than that of some West European countries (*e.g.* Sweden). The reason must be extremely poor economic conditions.[2]

Table V give rates of natural increase for East European countries for selected periods over the last three and a half decades. (Unless otherwise stated the figures are from the United Nation's *Demographic Yearbook, 1953.*)

The pattern of growth of the East European populations is much as we would expect. Falling birth- and death-rates, with a declining rate of increase, indicate an advanced stage in the demographic revolution. Although the lack of published statistics makes it impossible to compare the experiences of East European countries in the most recent five-year period (1949–54), it seems certain that the postwar increase in rates of natural increase, common to most of Europe, is probably a temporary reversal of the long-run trend.

[1] The comparable figure for the United States is 8·0 per cent.
[2] See Note ‡, Table V.

Poland seems to be an exception, as the official figures indicate. This is probably due to several factors, of which the pro-natalist policy of the Communist Government is the most important. However, in the long run the assumption that fertility rates (but not death-rates) are likely to decline seems a safe one. It will be shown

TABLE V

CRUDE RATES OF NATURAL INCREASE IN EASTERN EUROPE

(per 1000 of population)

Period	Bulgaria			Czechoslovakia			Hungary		
	B.	D.	N.I.	B.	D.	N.I.	B.	D.	N.I.
1920–24	39·6	21·3	18·3	26·7	16·5	10·2	30·2	20·9	19·3
1935–39	24·2	13·9	10·3	17·8	13·3	4·5	20·1	14·3	5·8
1946	25·6	13·7	11·9	22·7	14·0	8·7	18·7	15·0	3·7
1947	24·0	13·4	10·6	24·2	12·1	12·1	20·6	12·9	7·7
1948	n.a.	n.a.	n.a.	23·4	11·5	11·9	19·1	11·2	7·9
1946–49	n.a.	n.a.	n.a.	23·4	13·1	10·3	20·0*	13·2*	6·8
1953	n.a.	n.a.	n.a.	n.a.	n.a.	n.a.	n.a.	n.a.	n.a.

	Period	Romania			Poland		
B = Crude Birth-rate.		B.	D.	N.I.	B.	D.	N.I.
D = Crude Death-rate.	1920–24	37·6	24·0	13·6			
N.I. = Crude rate of Natural In-crease.	1935–39	30·2	20·0	10·2	25·3	14·1	11·2
	1946	19·6†	20·0†	0·4†	25·9	15·0	10·9
n.a. = not available.	1947	23·4	22·0	1·4	26·6	11·5	15·1
	1948	n.a.	n.a.	n.a.	29·3	11·2	18·1
	1946–49	n.a.	n.a.	n.a.	n.a.	n.a.	n.a.
	1953	24·0‡	11·7‡	12·3‡	30·1	10·2	19·9§

* *Statisztikai Szemle, 1950*, p. 376. † 1954 figure.
‡ *Probléme Economice*, June 1954. These figures quoted from an official source are probably false and indicate the halving of the Romanian death-rate over a period of some six years : a natural increase rate of 12·3 per thousand per year would mean an annual increase of about 195,000 (based on the 1948 population), or nearly one million for the years 1948–53. In fact, however, as official statistics indicate, the total increase for the years 1948–53 was about 627,000 (approximately 125,000 per year), and certainly much smaller than it would have been if official birth- and death-rates were correct.
§ *Przeglad Zagadnien Socyalnych*, August-September 1954.

in the next section that in all East European countries rapid industrialization will call for further concentration of the labour force in industry, and this is almost certain to lead to increased urbanization. The experience of West European countries suggests that a combination of increased urbanization and industrialization has been accompanied by decreasing fertility. Assuming that mortality will not be reduced still further, the strong emphasis on industrialization in Eastern Europe seems likely to bring about a decrease in rates of natural increase. Thus, given present political factors, the emigration potential of Eastern Europe is likely to remain negligible.

IV. INDUSTRIALIZATION AND INTERNAL MIGRATION

(1) *The Phase of Reconstruction* (1946–49)

At the end of the war Soviet Russia was too much preoccupied with the problems of her own economic recovery to engage in any long-term planning in Eastern Europe where she had suddenly become the dominant power. The planning of reconstruction was left to the governments of the countries which found themselves in the Soviet orbit. The year 1947 saw the beginning of two-year plans in Czechoslovakia and Bulgaria and of three-year plans in Poland and Hungary; in Romania economic conditions were too unsettled for any but the most provisional programmes.

These plans covered only large-scale industry; the targets set for the other sectors of the economy were more like general directives with provision for appropriate fiscal and credit policies. Even in the field of industry, governments' powers were by no means absolute. The 'commanding heights of the economy', to use Lenin's phrase — viz. heavy industry, transport, banking, and foreign trade — had been seized, but, except in Poland, large segments of industry remained in private hands during the first stage of the reconstruction period. Throughout Eastern Europe these postwar programmes, while giving full weight to the increased output of industrial goods, were on the whole intended to achieve reconstruction rather than industrialization. For this reason there was little rural-urban migration. The process of rapid urbanization belongs to the second and more recent phase of development on Soviet lines.

Most of the internal migration in the postwar period was due to changes of national frontiers; the countries particularly affected by these transfers were Poland and Czechoslovakia. In Poland the expulsion of two-thirds of the German population of the territory ceded to her under the Potsdam Agreement (henceforth referred to as Western Territory) left large areas temporarily denuded of population. Between the German Census of 1933 and the Polish Census of 1946 the Provinces of Zielona Gora, Szczecin, and Olsztyn had lost up to two-thirds of their population.[1] Heavy migration into the areas vacated by expulsions occurred in 1946 and after.

[1] U.S. Bureau of the Census, *The Population of Poland*, by W. P. Mauldin and D. S. Akers, International Population Statistics Reports, Series P. 90, No. 4, Washington, 1954, p. 57.

Most of the Poles repatriated from the Soviet Union were settled in the Western Territories, and every encouragement was given to displaced Poles returning from the West to settle there. The Polish Ministry for the Recovered Territories estimated that by November 1946, when the repatriation programme was nearly complete, there were 1·7 million repatriates in the Western Territories. In the next three years some 1·5 million moved into that area from Central Poland, and most of them went into urban centres.[1] Finally, the majority of the 1·2 million 'returnees' from the Eastern Territories ceded to the Soviet Union under the Yalta Agreements were offered homes and land in the Western Territories.[2] The total number of migrants into these territories can thus be estimated at just over 4 million persons.

In Czechoslovakia the vacuum created by the expulsion of some 2·6 million Germans from the Sudeten region was only partly filled by the migration of Czech farmers from Moravia, Bohemia, and Slovakia. According to published Czech statistical reports, some 1,460,000 persons moved to the border areas in the years 1945–47.[3]

No comparable shifts of population occurred in the other Satellite countries during the postwar period. The only two known instances can perhaps be classified as deportations which took place in the summer of 1950 and affected the population of regions bordering on Yugoslavia. The first was the transfer of some 16,000 peasants of German, Romanian, and Serbo-Croatian origin from the Romanian Banat to the Baragan area, north-west of the Danube; this was presumably a 'security measure against Titoist influence"[4] The second was a deportation of some 75,000 peasants from the southern frontier area in Hungary. The official *Szabad Nép* admitted in its issue of 4 July 1950 that the deportations had actually taken place, but justified this move by saying that those who were affected were 'well-known Fascists, Arrow-Crossists, kulaks, and notorious bandits who until now have supported the Titoist provocations'.[5]

(2) *The Development Plans of 1950*

After the reconstruction period and the consolidation of political power by the Communists, the governments of the five Eastern European countries were able to plan more ambitiously and comprehensively than hitherto. Economic planning was dictated by

---

[1] *Ut supra*, p. 62.
[2] *Rocznik Statystyczny, 1949* (Statistical Yearbook for 1949), Warsaw, 1950, p. 26.　　[3] See below, p. 235.
[4] *News from behind the Iron Curtain*, February 1955, p. 34.
[5] 'Report of the Social Committee', quoted in *Assembly of Captive European Nations*, New York, 1954.

political considerations such as the priority given to creating a large industrial proletariat and eliminating the remnant of the rural and urban *bourgeoisie*. Consequently special attention was given to developing heavy industry, creating agricultural collectives, and nationalizing private enterprise. These were the objectives of the plans launched in 1949 and 1950. Except in Poland, where a six-year plan was introduced, five-year plans, modelled on the Soviet pattern, were announced throughout the area. As in the Soviet Union, planning was focused on investment and production, while such important questions as the manpower budget for industry and agriculture, the volume and value of domestic consumption and of foreign trade, were treated in a rather cursory fashion. Few absolute data were made known and most targets were expressed as percentages of a base which was frequently undisclosed.

The main result of these economic policies has been a major shift of population from rural to urban occupations. Rapid collectivization and mechanization of agriculture tapped the reservoir of 'disguised' unemployment, which had been the curse of the pre-war situation. Industrialization meant the construction of new centres peopled mainly by migrants from the countryside,[1] and the population of existing urban centres increased so much that there was an acute shortage of housing which has never been denied by the Satellite governments.

The areas affected by internal migration were the densely populated agricultural regions of Slovakia, South-eastern Poland, and Dobrudja. The experience of Slovakia is illuminating since it illustrates two distinct phases : westward migration to the existing industrial centres of Bohemia and Moravia and, after about five years, a return movement to the newly constructed industrial undertakings in Slovakia. According to a Czech textbook of economic geography :

. . . The centre of gravity of [internal] migration is in the Czech provinces, although in Slovakia migration is on the increase as well. There has been considerable migration of Slovaks to the Czech provinces but since 1948 many of them are returning again to Slovakia.[2] Slovakia's migration balance is passive.

[1] These new industrial centres are now household words in Eastern Europe. They include Nowe Huta (population 100,000 in 1953) and Nowe Tychy in Poland, Sztalinvaros (population 30,000 in 1954), Komlo in Hungary, and Dimitrovgrad in Bulgaria.

[2] The cause of a reversal in the flow of migration must be sought in the forced collectivization of agriculture and partly also in the drive to recruit manpower for industry under the Five-Year Plan. Farmers from the poorer parts of Southern Bohemia and Slovakia who had hoped to find better conditions in the more fertile lands bordering on Germany preferred to move back home when the Communist-dominated government began to force them to give up the ownership of their newly acquired farms and join the kolkhozes.

At present the migration is mostly into large cities and industrial regions, in Slovakia, mainly to its Western provinces. The majority of the Slovak migrants in the Czech provinces will probably return home after the Five-Year Plan is fulfilled and will find work in the new factories being built there.

The main losses by migration are to be found in the agricultural regions, especially in the densely populated agricultural regions in Slovakia. The migration from the newly resettled border regions is relatively high. The direction and extent of migratory movements are governed by the development of the rapidly growing industrial production, which needs more and more man-power. Among the expanding regions since 1950 is Ostrava. Prague has a lower absorptive power.[1]

The same source gives some statistical evidence of outward migration for a number of Slovak provinces in 1950, indicating a considerable passive balance. For example, in the province of Banks Bystrica the yearly excess of emigration over immigration was 8 per thousand; in the province of Nitra it was 10·9 per thousand.

Detailed analysis of rural-urban migration is not possible owing to the lack of published statistical material. Even where fairly recent figures are available, a comparison with the pre-war position may be misleading for two reasons. First, in Poland the urban population during the war suffered greater inroads than the rural because of the Nazi policy of mass extermination of the intelligentsia and the Jews, most of whom lived in towns. The restoration of urban-rural ratios after the war meant that many people from rural areas moved to the cities for the first time. Thus the actual volume of rural-urban migration was greater than would appear from a comparison of the pre-war and postwar proportions.[2] Another reason for rejecting a comparison in terms of urban-rural ratios can be illustrated for Hungary where, according to an official source, in 1953 the proportion of the population depending on agriculture was 45 per cent while the proportion classified as rural was 58·8 per cent.[3] This difference arises because industrial workers and dependants *reside* in rural areas and travel to work in towns. The decentralizing of industrial enterprises, drawing on workers who live in the surrounding countryside, is a particular feature of Satellite policy.

It should also be borne in mind that the notable increase in the proportion of non-agricultural population has taken place in the relatively short time during which the Communist governments of

---

[1] Miroslav Blazek, *Hospodarska Geografie Ceskoslovenska*, Prague, 1953.
[2] In the case of Poland 27·4 per cent in 1931 (Inter-war Territory) as compared with 35·8 in 1950.
[3] *News from behind the Iron Curtain*, February 1955, p. 29.

Zubrzycki — Migration and the Economy of Eastern Europe

Eastern Europe have been carrying out their plans of intensive industrialization.[1] For this reason the economic and social impact of the mass exodus to industry and other urban pursuits must have been very pronounced. The whole of Eastern Europe, except Czechoslovakia which had already been industrialized before the Second World War, is rapidly losing its rural character. It seems safe to conclude that, given the existing political, economic, and demographic trends, the countries of Eastern Europe will not contribute to the volume of international migration.

[1] The Romanian economic publication, *Probléme Economice*, February 1954, gives the following index of the population growth of all Romanian cities : 1938, 100 ; 1949, 120 ; 1953, 173   1960 (Plan), 221.

Chapter 17

INTRA-EUROPEAN MIGRATION AND THE PROSPECTS OF INTEGRATION

BY

FRIEDRICH EDDING
Institut für Weltwirtschaft, Kiel

I. EUROPEAN MIGRATION IN THE NINETEENTH AND TWENTIETH CENTURIES

INQUIRIES into the economic and general significance of intra-European migration were regarded as unimportant until recently, when interest began to be aroused in European integration and in the redistribution of population within the continent as an alternative to oversea migration. This is not a criticism of previous work in this field. First of all, mention must be made of the chapters in Dudley Kirk's study, *Europe's Population in the Inter-War Years* (League of Nations, 1946). It is not easy to think of an idea on the subject which is not to be found in that book. No synthesis based on recent research has been published ; years of co-ordinated study by many scholars will be required before any new generalizations can be formulated concerning the history and future possibilities of European migration. The present paper is intended merely as an outline for discussion and a stimulus to further work.

For detailed statistics of intra-European migration reference may be made to the above-mentioned book by Kirk and the study by Ferenczi and Willcox,[1] as well as to the many publications of the International Labour Office and the Manpower Committee of OEEC. For the present paper, which is chiefly concerned with the prospects of intra-European migration, statistics of past trends have only limited significance.

There is a close interrelation between various forms of migration. The inadequacy of our knowledge of movements within Europe may be partly due to the fact that oversea migration has hitherto attracted greater attention. The effects of a gross outflow of about 60 million are clearly visible. Emigration is part of the dramatic

[1] *International Migrations*, vols. i and ii, National Bureau of Economic Research, New York, 1929 and 1931.

history of exploration and pioneering in distant continents; it was long surrounded by an aura of romance, and promised more space, freedom, and independence and better prospects of advancement than Europe could offer. From the end of the eighteenth century emigration helped to alleviate the misery caused by rural over-population, and it coincided with extensive oversea investment of European capital. The savings of migrants and the profits of capital which they helped to make possible were for many decades important items in the balance of payments of European countries. Last but not least, these migrants opened ever-widening markets, thereby permitting the expansion of European industries and services. Opportunities within Europe were improved by the additional pro-duction, income, and oversea demand. This was the most important contribution of emigration to the welfare of European countries.

In the circumstances of the nineteenth century and down to the outbreak of the Second World War, large-scale inter-continental migration seems to have had great advantages both for countries losing and for those receiving migrants. But one important pre-requisite was that migration coincided with free movement of goods and capital. The obstacles to other economic exchanges between the continents were so small that the benefits of migration for all parties were hardly questioned.

Intra-European migration was affected by very similar con-siderations before the First World War. The movement of goods, capital, and labour was largely unrestricted; the industrial revolu-tion created a constantly increasing demand for labour as well as great shifts in location. During the early stages of this revolution intensive migration was an important factor in securing a balance of demand and supply on the European labour market. Differences of opportunity within Europe may in general have been less than those between Europe and the New World. On the other hand, movement was made easier by smaller distances, lower transport costs, and the advantages of remaining in familiar surroundings and often within the same linguistic area (as where there was movement between Switzerland and her neighbours, Germany, Austria, Belgium, and France). The risks of intra-European migration were smaller, as it was easier to return home.

The full dimensions of intra-continental movement, which was necessarily correlated with industrialization, are only revealed if migration within national boundaries (particularly the rural exodus) and permanent migration from and to European countries are added together. The total of all these movements was always greater than the volume of oversea migration. Though little is known of trans-frontier migration in Europe, census data suggest that it had comparatively little influence on the density and structure of populations.[1] Between 1830 and 1950 density in the Netherlands almost quadrupled; in Western Germany, Great Britain, and Denmark it trebled; in Italy, Spain, and Belgium it doubled; while in France the population increased by only one-fifth.[2] Voluntary migrations between the countries of Europe have contributed very little to their development; population density in the various countries is primarily a result of natural increase.

Seasonal migration and frontier movements within Europe were far more important than permanent emigration. In the decades before the First World War seasonal shifts took between 1 and 2 million annually across national frontiers. They came mainly from Poland, Austria, Hungary, Italy, and Spain, and they went in the first instance to France, Germany, and Belgium. Between the wars this temporary migration remained important, though the depression and numerous restrictions[3] caused a decline after the 1920's. Temporary movements since the Second World War are not comparable with those of earlier periods, because of the large numbers of prisoners of war and refugees; in recent years temporary migrants have gone mainly to countries of full employment, *e.g.* Switzerland, Great Britain, and Sweden.

The past and possible future effects of trans-frontier migration on the structure of European settlement become clearer when their relations with internal migration are analysed. Internal migration is unquestionably the chief factor in redistributing population. The complex problem of agglomeration and deglomeration and its influence on European economies and populations have been comparatively neglected. Migration research has an important contribution to make towards its clarification.

II. PRESENT PROBLEMS

All integration programmes claim to promote the general welfare. This may be merely an attempt to state in a simple form the rational

---

[1] Kirk, *op. cit.* p. 126 : 'In the middle of the inter-war period some 10 million inhabitants of Europe west of the Soviet Union were resident outside the country of their birth. By contrast, as many as 75 million were living outside their native province or department and at least one-third of all Europeans were living outside the commune or locality of their birth. Prior to the war at least 150 million had moved from their native communities.'

[2] The only example of an absolute population decrease in Europe is provided by Ireland.

[3] See *Analysis of the Immigration Laws and Regulations of Selected Countries*, ILO, Geneva, 1954, vol. i.

economic aim ; but it is possible that the implication is wider. If the objective were to raise average real income more rapidly than would be possible without integration, migration would have to be considered only as a means towards an economic end. Considerations of this kind, however, are remote from reality. If, for instance, income *per capita* in Western Germany were to increase at an unusual rate as a result of the integration of displaced persons, this would certainly not justify similar shifts of population in other parts of Europe.

If welfare includes elements other than the purely economic, different points of view can arise in regard to migration. The widest possible freedom to move around and accept employment might be looked upon as an intrinsic value, a basic human right, quite apart from the question whether or not this freedom is an economic advantage. Moreover, to remain in a certain community and enjoy familiar associations might yield more satisfaction than the benefits to be got through migration. In what follows, the emphasis will be on the economic aspect of migration, but we shall not overlook the fact that welfare is something more than the maximization of income.

The arguments used against free migration within Europe, though seldom made overt in official negotiations, are similar to those used against oversea migration. Emigration is held to have the following harmful affects : the loss of the social capital 'invested' in the emigrants, a deterioration of the age structure, the loss of key workers, and the strain in the labour market under full employment. Immigration, on the other hand, is feared for the following reasons : the inflow of unselected immigrants tends to depress income per head ; unemployment might increase ; undercutting in the labour market leads to frictions, and competition might become severe in the independent trades and professions. To these must be added religious, political, and racial factors.

People seem to be willing to accept the fundamental principle and at the same time resent its practical implications ; this is because it is assumed that the approach to the ideal of free movement should be accompanied by the integration of various factors of the national economies. As our illustration we shall take the experience of Western Germany, where there have been extensive shifts of population since 1949. We may be able in this way to throw light on the problem of the continent as a whole, though it is to be hoped that what has happened in Germany will remain an exception.

The course of events in Western Germany after the war showed that, by itself, internal mobility of labour and capital was not able to solve the problem of structural unemployment in certain areas. An excessive supply of labour could not bring about a regional decline in wages because of the tariff wage system, and therefore private capital was not induced to move into the areas worst hit by unemployment. At the same time there was an inadequate outflow of surplus labour to regions where capital was available. Many people in the depressed areas had previously been uprooted through expulsion or flight, and they were reluctant to move on again to other areas. Powerful incentives were needed to produce a voluntary redistribution of the population.

Areas losing people through out-migration found compensation in a more effective combination of factors or production. It is true that they were depriving themselves of potential future wealth, but the relief to their budgets was felt immediately. These areas of out-migration experienced an increase in product per head, partly through a rise in productivity and partly by participating in the growing wealth of the receiving areas. Since these prosperous districts were part of the West German economy, the sending areas received a transfusion of strength via the circular flow of incomes. This might not have been evident in the short run, but the benefits were generally acknowledged when there had been time for the process to work itself out. Four elements in the economic gain of the sending areas may be noted. Migrants who had left their families behind sent back remittances; the rapid increase in the supply of commodities due to the employment of immigrants lowered the prices of many goods; the increase in consumption associated with the additional income of the migrants improved the sales prospects of firms in the out-migration areas; and the increase in Federal tax revenue made it possible to compensate the weak areas for the distortion of their age structure. The social burdens assumed by the Federal Government entailed the investment of Federal funds in the interests of the losing areas. Thus despite the *laisser-faire* bias in the economic policy of Western Germany, the migration of labour to the centres of effective demand was accompanied by government-sponsored migration of public capital to the depressed areas.

The task in the receiving areas was to raise product per head under conditions of rapidly growing population. It is true that they had the advantage of an established industrial and commercial tradition, but it would be a mistake to think that these districts could have raised output per head merely by receiving an addition to their population. Other opportunities were open to them, and there had been strong objections to in-migration. But once the new population had arrived, the new labour force set in train a dynamic expansion which expressed itself in unusually high rates of increase in the national product. In a few years real income per head had risen above the pre-war level. This achievement owed much to ERP credits and the liberalization of trade in Western Europe. The rise of unemployment due to resettlement was temporary and local. Wage tariffs generally made undercutting impossible, but there was a slight weakening in the bargaining position of trade unions. In so far as new labour made competition more severe, this was to the benefit of productivity.

A large number of workers moved without help from public funds. As the West German economy approached a state of full employment the protests of districts and firms losing manpower grew louder. The Government, however, adhered to its principles of free competition ; according to this view individuals change their jobs in order to gain higher incomes, and this mobility should be fostered in the interests of a productive and flexible economy. The improved working conditions are believed to correspond with higher productivity, so that the interests of both the individual and the public are alike promoted ; but this point of view is not usually held in regard to international migration.

The above argument in favour of internal migration would also apply to a great extent to an integrated community of nations. The question is : how advanced must this integration be to allow the economic advantages of free migration to take full effect ? Theoretically a complete union would no doubt be the ideal. If Europe were organized like the United States of America, the economic objections to free intra-continental migration would disappear. Free movement of workers as well as of other factors of production, and a unified economic, financial, and social policy would give a powerful stimulus to economic growth in Europe. The looser the degree of union, the stronger will be the resistance to free migration and the smaller its effect on the rate of increase of income per head. The more sovereign States assert themselves, the more difficult it is to calculate the gains and losses experienced by sending and receiving countries. Where integration is incomplete each government is likely to prefer to negotiate each case separately with other governments.

III. MIGRATION PROSPECTS IN AN INTEGRATED EUROPE

Even in the event of complete integration it is highly improbable that there will be intra-European movements on the scale of the pre-1913 period when restrictions were comparatively few. That period is often cited as a norm by which to assess the effects of European integration; but circumstances have changed considerably since then. We shall refer only to the most striking of these changes.

The demographic situation in Europe now is entirely different from what it was at the beginning of this century. The rate of population growth has slackened, and the pressure of numbers characteristic of many countries before 1914 is seldom found at the present time. Remedies other than emigration are now more apt, and the course of natural increase will soon relieve pressure where it is still felt. Changes in age distribution have reduced the size of the mobile groups and they are likely to shrink further.

In earlier decades a large contribution to intra-European migration was made by the efflux from countries of Eastern Europe induced by political upheaval and low wages. Since the Second World War the political and industrial revolutions in Eastern Europe have created a completely new situation. Rural overpopulation, formerly characteristic of Eastern Europe, is no longer acute, and is likely to disappear as a determinant of emigration. It is true that the considerable difference between average real incomes in the East and West might still provide an inducement for a substantial outflow; however, an integration which would include Eastern Europe is improbable as long as the level of incomes there remains below the Western level. Moreover, totalitarian rule in those countries makes free migration impossible.

In the past, intra-European migration was largely an affair of unskilled labour. As a result of increasing mechanization the demand for unskilled labour is relatively declining, while at the same time nations seek to prevent the emigration of skilled craftsmen. The trend of demand differs considerably from grade to grade; this is a question which calls for far more thorough research than has been devoted to it hitherto. To judge by current trends, the large supply of unskilled labour from the less developed areas of the Mediterranean and the dependent territories of some European countries may no longer expect to meet a corresponding demand in the more developed European countries. It may soon become impossible, for social and political reasons, to direct this supply into those occupations in which the native-born are reluctant to work. Thus a further stream of migration will lose much of its significance.

Other developments which have strongly influenced the rate of migration are the Welfare State, the system of collective bargaining under which wages seem to be adjustable only in an upward direction, and the introduction of industrial pension schemes which have the effect of attaching a nucleus of workers to particular firms or factories. Migration has very little effect on wages. Differences in real wages, which might at present promote trans-frontier migration, would be narrowed under active integration. The social services furnished by States and employers and the conditions governing benefits vary so much from country to country and are so difficult to unify that there would be little incentive for young people to emigrate, even though full integration were achieved. A title to social service benefits is quite as great an impediment to mobility as the ownership of real property. There is wide scope for co-ordinated research into the conditions determining mobility in the various European countries. The smaller the mobile fringe in the population, the more necessary it is to study its attitudes.

The importance of the State as planner and investor has increased, particularly since the Second World War. In the East as well as in the West national development programmes absorb workers who would otherwise emigrate. It must remain an open question whether the capital resources of an integrated Europe or major changes in sources of energy would set in motion development schemes which would revive intra-European migration. Whether the unemployment which will be caused by technological change will be solved by international planning coupled with trans-frontier migration or by national investment policies will depend on political decisions which cannot possibly be foreseen.

In recent years much has been said about the unequal distribution of wealth among the countries of Europe. Free migration was sometimes regarded as a remedy and sometimes as an aggravating factor. Such arguments are misleading. There are no countries in Europe where population is not big enough to use the natural resources to the full. The economic development of a country or area depends partly on natural resources ; but the decisive element is the productive mind (creative gifts, will-power, talent for organization, perseverance) and the training or immigration of persons with this quality. Up to the present these factors have been the chief reason for international and interregional differences in density of population and concentration of capital, and there is every sign that they will become more so in the future. Natural resources as a determinant of the location of industries will probably become even less important in the atomic age than they are to-day. If we are to assess the volume and character of the migration movements to be expected in an integrated Europe, there must be more thorough research into the process of agglomeration, its evolution in the past, and the conditions likely to affect it in the future.

The expectation of large-scale migration movements in an

integrated Europe is often based on the idea that a large number of firms will be eliminated as soon as the political advantages of their location are removed. There can be no doubt that the free interplay of factors over a wide area would threaten the life of many enterprises which now owe their prosperity to national protective measures. Nevertheless, the probability is that extensive re-location will not occur, partly because of the expected decline in the propensity to migrate and partly because of the imperfect mobility of capital. Where plants would have to be closed down owing to integration, it would not usually be necessary for displaced workers to move across national boundaries. In the course of normal economic growth many firms are started and liquidated every day and as a rule redundant labour is absorbed in the same area.

In 1952–53 OEEC sent a *questionnaire* to important industries in several countries to find out what results they expected from economic integration. The replies showed that the leaders of industries anticipated that the advantages would outweigh the disadvantages and that no striking change in the conditions governing location would emerge. The impression given by the reports was that integration would simply accelerate trends already in existence — tendencies towards a higher optimum size of plants and increasing specialization.

If the transition resulted in the creation of 'depressed areas' the remedy would be resettlement within national frontiers or planned investment. There is plenty of practical experience in this field which could be studied. Average incomes in the Mediterranean countries are below those of Central Europe; political and social considerations, even in an integrated Europe, would favour adjustment through national economic development rather than international movements of population. The concentration of European financial resources in a central investment bank would make it possible to improve conditions in the underdeveloped parts of Europe without much intra-continental migration.

IV. FREER MIGRATION AS A STEP TOWARDS INTEGRATION

The argument so far has suggested that, in an integrated Europe, free migration, even on a large scale, could bestow economic benefits on both the receiving and the sending countries, but that the volume of migration which would in fact occur would be relatively small unless unforeseen technical changes took place. Migration, however, is indispensable if the European labour market is to be as flexible as it ought to be. By easing the process of competition and industrial adjustment, it helps to increase productivity. Free movement is also desirable in the interests of international understanding and education, and, from a psychological point of view, the citizen derives satisfaction from the knowledge that he has this freedom, whether he takes advantage of it or not. For these reasons all efforts to make migration freer are to be welcomed, even though the economic circuit linking the countries of the continent remains broken at many points. We may thus consider what kinds of migration are practicable and desirable during the stage when Europe is moving in the direction of integration.

Countries have certain common interests which can be promoted through migration, *e.g.* where the increased productivity in the receiving countries confers on the sending countries advantages which at least offset the disadvantages of the loss of manpower. Moreover, all countries benefit from the enlargement of individual opportunity and the lessening of social friction. Attempts have been made to measure the advantages and disadvantages by applying econometric methods.[1] If, however, the quantitative value of international migration is insignificant as compared with other variables in the system of equations, the procedure might prove inaccurate. Moreover, a method which takes into account many rapidly changing variables is not well fitted to handle permanent migration.

The econometric method may well be useful when applied to temporary migration of homogeneous labour. The risk entailed in this kind of migration is negligible for all parties ; both the receiving and sending countries may be expected to gain. This is particularly true of districts forming an economic unit through which a frontier runs. In such areas the economic facts call for a considerable two-way traffic of labour, and this would take place easily, if there were no national boundary. As things are, a great deal of commuting is possible ; but integration would be carried much further if the commuting zone were extended on both sides of the frontier and work permits were more liberally granted. In view of the great length of political frontiers in Europe and the widespread use of motor-cars, such measures might easily pave the way for a considerable volume of migration.

Distance has an important bearing on labour mobility. It is not just a question of transport: the degree of knowledge of

[1] G. Beijer and C. A. van den Beld, 'Effects of Migration on the Economic Situation of selected European Countries of Emigration', *R.E.M.P. Bulletin*, Den Haag, July-September 1954.

conditions and prospects in the labour market is a crucial factor. In view of the great variety of wage regulations, social services, and taxes in the countries of Europe, knowledge of labour conditions in a zone both sides of a frontier will clearly be much more accurate than over long distances. In such areas, too, people tend to be bilingual. Thus it seems probable that free movement in Europe would have as its main result a quickening of migration within these frontier zones; here the removal of restrictions would entail the minimum of risk, and promise considerable success.

Measures for the freeing of migration have already been applied in the Iron and Steel Community, the Benelux Union, Scandinavia, and member countries of OEEC, but these have not yet yielded any far-reaching results.

PART V

THE FAR EAST

Chapter 18

MIGRATION PROBLEMS OF THE FAR EAST

BY

T. H. SILCOCK

University of Malaya

I. POPULATION PRESSURES

INTERNATIONAL migration in the Far East is in part the normal movement from areas where land is scarce in relation to population to more empty areas where the factors complementary to labour are more abundant. There are, however, special complications in the pattern of migration in the Far East which result partly from the impact of an external administration and economic pattern, and partly from the wide differences in culture and technical skill of the peoples inhabiting this area.

The distances over which movement has to take place are comparable with those of the migrations of the Western world, and in relation to the prevailing standards of living in the Far East the capital costs of moving over these great distances are high. The statistics of migration, like many other statistics of Asia, are very inadequate, and this paper makes no pretence of supplementing the limited statistical information available by any special investigation or new techniques of estimation. Its purpose is rather interpretation in economic terms of some of the movements that have taken place, and an attempt to survey some of the social and economic implications.

The feature of the population of the Far East which is probably best known is its great expansion in recent times. Sensational estimates are frequently quoted, anticipating the population of India or China within a fairly limited period of years, or indicating with alarm the rate of growth of the rice-eating peoples in relation to the available potential rice areas. We are all fairly well aware that the population of India is expanding so fast that its development plans and enormous economic effort barely suffice to keep pace with it. The political implications of the rate of growth in the populations of Japan and China have been widely advertised, with emphasis sometimes on manpower and sometimes on the need for economic adaptation. The population pressure on the island of Java is perhaps slightly less well known internationally, but there is probaby a general awareness that one of the major economic problems of the Indonesian Republic is the more even distribution of its population over its outer territories so that these less crowded lands can be colonized by inhabitants from the overcrowded heart of the Republic.

It is no part of the purpose of this paper to attempt to controvert these popular ideas or to minimize the importance of the Malthusian devil in the economies of the Far East. Those of us who work there are only too well aware that, while nationalist politicians talk of raising standards of living to levels more comparable with those of the West, it will in practice be necessary to put forward stupendous economic efforts to prevent the standard of living in most of these areas from falling rapidly and drastically below its existing, grossly inadequate level.

It is, however, probably worth while to draw attention to the fact that the rate of population growth in the Far East appears actually to be much greater in the smaller and less populated territories (*e.g.* Malaya, Thailand, Ceylon, and Korea) than in the great centres of population to which reference has been made above. This is not simply a matter of available empty land, though this may be a part of the explanation of the apparently high rate of growth of the population in the Federation of Malaya, Thailand, and Ceylon. The highest rates of all, however, appear to be in already crowded territories such as Taiwan, Hong Kong, and Singapore, showing the almost unparalleled rate of natural increase of more than $3\frac{1}{2}$ per cent per annum in some instances. These rapid rates of growth appear to be rather an example of Malthusian conditions interpreted in slightly less orthodox terms of modern medical knowledge and public health techniques. The standard of medicine and public health appears to be related in some degree to the level of national income per head; and death-rates have been successfully reduced in those areas where the administrative problem is relatively simple and the standard of wealth per head is sufficient to pay for an adequate supply of skilled medical knowledge. With the great expansion of education now taking place in some of the less prosperous areas, a further expansion in the population may be expected.

The process of provision of doctors, public health workers, etc. is at first extremely expensive when the general level of education is low. The cost of the necessary professional workers is high and they are spread very thin in all but the wealthiest countries. Only in such countries, at first, can the really spectacular reductions in mortality be achieved. But though the process of expanding the educational system takes time, the margin of earnings for professional workers in comparison with the basic standards of living of the wage earners of the country can be reduced as the volume of education is increased, particularly if a secular process of inflation eases the process of adjusting the relative levels of earnings. The possibility of providing educated village-level workers in the community development programmes, and educated agricultural extension workers throughout large areas of rural India, indicates a further potential improvement in public health at no great cost which may be expected to increase the population still further. The temporarily higher rates of expansion in the more prosperous countries, which at present are able to import a more adequate supply of professional workers from elsewhere, may therefore be matched in the fairly near future by similar rates of expansion in the poorer countries.

It is by no means certain that the expansion of population in Asia during the last two hundred years is mainly the result of improved medical knowledge or relatively peaceful conditions. The problem confronting Asia, however, is not one of the continuation of the trend of natural increase of the past two centuries, even though this alone has been sufficient to offset much of the technical progress that has taken place. Rates of growth of $1\frac{1}{2}$ per cent make a significant difference to communities which find difficulty in raising the level of capital formation above about 6 per cent of the national income ; [1] but the prospect which must be faced is one of a rate of natural increase throughout most of Asia of over 3 per cent in the fairly near future, and rates of growth of this magnitude make it almost literally impossible to provide the necessary capital from local sources to prevent a decline in the standard of living.[2]

If we contemplate the fantastic pressure of population now developing in the Far East and the very great differences in density between, say, Bengal and Burma, Java and Sumatra, or South China and Borneo, it seems natural to think of the migration movements that have taken place in Asia as primarily movements of a more or less orthodox economic kind — a result of large differences in the earnings of labour as a mobile factor, arising from the abundance or scarcity of complementary factors, and chiefly of land. At first sight the movements that have actually taken place appear to support such a comparatively straightforward interpretation.

[1] Cf. H. W. Singer, 'The Mechanics of Economic Development', *Indian Economic Review*, August 1952.
[2] Cf. Rockefeller Foundation, *Public Health and Demography in the Far East*, ch. 1.

II. GENERAL CURRENTS OF MIGRATION

We may consider briefly the direction of oversea migration from the main areas of congested population in China, India, Japan, and Java. The Chinese have migrated during the present century and the latter half of the nineteenth century both to the comparatively unpopulated areas in Manchuria and to the areas collectively known to the Chinese as Nanyang or South Seas.[1] Migration to Manchuria was, in the earlier years, a relatively short-journey migration of farmers from overcrowded to more empty lands, as a result of some weakening of the Manchu Government's ban on migration to the area coupled with a weakening of governmental authority at home, and hence some pressure from internal disorganization in China itself. Later, the industrial development of Manchuria provided an additional magnet for population. This appears to be a comparatively orthodox migratory movement, though it has one interesting feature — that the strictly economic conditions favourable to migration were not new, and that one of the chief causes of movement was a breakdown of previous moral and legal forces tending to restrain movement.

The movement of the Chinese to the South Seas was also a movement from an area of high population density to one where population was much sparser, and where, in fact, economic prospects were considerably better in consequence. The migration here, however, is of a more mixed character, mainly on account of the fact that all migrations had to cross the sea. Though there are Chinese farmers in some of the more empty lands to the south and south-west, notably in Malaya, the main movements of Chinese were either those of merchants or of people who were transported virtually as merchandise. The two classes cannot now be clearly separated, as many of those who were transported as indentured labour have acquired money of their own and passed into the very large trading class.

From India the migrations to Burma, Malaya, and Ceylon, as well as the interesting movement to Fiji, have been mainly movements of human merchandise, although the effects of political control have made the transactions less frankly commercial between these areas. There have, of course, been other movements of Indians: merchants from Bombay or Calcutta, money-lenders from Southern India and the various, more specialized professional or occupational categories such as clerks for the government services or the railways,

[1] Cf. B. Lasker, *Asia on the Move*, New York, 1945, chs. 2, 7, 8.

and Sikh Police; but the main movements of Indians have been movements first of indentured Indian labour for use in plantations or public works and later of labour recruited under government-sponsored schemes, which were designed to secure an adjustable flow of cheap and willing labour, allocated fairly between the different estate owners who contributed to the cost of moving.[1]

From Japan the organization of movement has been almost wholly a deliberate political effort consciously designed to relieve overcrowding as well as to consolidate Japanese influence.[2] Colonization of the Pacific Islands was mainly done under government control, and the Japanese peasants have in fact proved rather unwilling to move to other areas without some government pressure. A large part of the migration has taken the form of movement of educated Japanese to take up responsible positions in other areas, in undertakings both private and government-sponsored. In this respect the movement of the Japanese to Korea, Taiwan, and later to ports of China was more similar to the movement of Europeans to the Far East, which will be discussed later in this paper, than to the normal population movements from other overcrowded areas.

It has been frequently pointed out that the Japanese, though anxious to emphasize that their population pressure calls for outlets for migration, in fact have not been eager migrants. The defeat of Japan in the war and the return of the greater part of the oversea Japanese to Japan provides some statistical evidence of the limited scope of Japanese migration.[3]

In the Malay archipelago there is evidence of a good deal of unassisted movement of population from areas of greater pressure to areas of less pressure, and many of the Malaysian settlements in Malaya, Sumatra, and Borneo, etc. appear to have been of this form. There have also been quite substantial colonization schemes organized before the war by the Dutch and since the war by the Indonesian Government to encourage a transfer of population. Malays have been rather mobile along the rivers and over the narrow stretches of sea in this region, and the movement that has taken place, while it has not been adequate to keep up with the rate

[1] Cf. Lennox A. Mills, *British Rule in Eastern Asia*, Oxford, 1942, pp. 219-29.

[2] Cf. I. Taeuber, 'Migration and the Population Potential of Monsoon Asia' in *Postwar Problems of Migration*, Milbank Memorial Fund, New York, 1942.

[3] Returned Japanese migrants from Asia, including the Kurile, Ryukyu, and other islands, numbered only 5·5 million according to the *United Nations Demographic Year Book, 1949–50*. These included 2 million from China, 1 million from near-by islands and South-east Asia, 0·9 million from Korea, and 0·6 million from Manchuria.

of expansion of population, appears to have resulted in some redistribution in accordance with the basic pressures of population on land; [1] though cultural and political features have also been of great importance.

III. ROLE OF SPECIALISTS IN MIGRATION

This general approach in terms of the overcrowded sources and the more empty areas into which migration has flowed can provide a beginning to the analysis, but it has obvious limitations. It leaves out of account some of the most economically significant population movements and does not adequately explain the direction or method of movement. It pays little attention to the changing structure of the economies of Asia and does not explain the occupational specialization of migration which is one of the important social and economic problems arising from migration in Asia.

It may be natural for a European who earns his living in Asia to attach excessive importance to the statistically insignificant group of migrants from the West whose direct effect on the population statistics of Asia has been negligible. There are, however, lessons to be learned from surveying the role of the European in the different Asian economies, because some of the economic characteristics of European migration apply also to migrants within Asia between regions with widely different economic structures. Though they are scattered very thinly over Asia there are Europeans living more or less permanently in most of the main trading centres and also in mining and plantation areas. These Europeans have come from countries where the basic standard of living is considerably higher than in any part of Asia, and they are found not only in politically dependent territories, but also in areas like Thailand, which have never been subject to European rule, and in the newly independent states.

Though these individuals are commonly in competition, in business or the professions or in technical posts, with a few locally educated people of similar qualifications or capacities, they are attracted to these underdeveloped countries mainly because there is a wider relative spread in incomes than in Europe between those who have these capacities and the bulk of the population.

Certain kinds of enterprise are scarce in Asia.[2] One could

[1] Cf., on this and other migration movements, map and discussion in E. H. G. Dobby, *Southeast Asia*, London, 1950, pp. 390-94.
[2] This has been discussed briefly in T. H. Silcock, *The Economy of Malaya*, Singapore, 1954.

describe such enterprise briefly as the capacity to play a role in relation to a system of assets and ensure by economic and psychological incentives that others also play an assigned role. Certain kinds of professional and technical competence are also scarce, mainly those related to the application of organized academic study in practical life. The skills generated by apprenticeship with a substantially formal content, and some of the junior executive skills, are also very scarce and have to be substituted by costly alternative methods of organization. Those who possess these special skills have been able to make very considerable profits.

The causes of these scarcities are of course related to the cultural impact of Europe on Asia, but it is important to realize that the greatly increased facilities for transport which have resulted from Western technologies have also led to impacts on one another of countries with social classes widely different in their relative suitability for roles within the currently emerging economic system. There are important common characteristics between the movement of the English public-school-trained business man out to Asia and the movement of the Chinese retail shopkeeper, the Indian clerk or lawyer, and the Japanese industrial manager, to other areas in Asia ; and the occupational specialization of migrants that results is something that no doubt characterizes migrants elsewhere in some degree, but appears particularly significant in the economy of Asia.

It is fairly well known that there are scarcities of experts in various skills in different parts of Asia which make it profitable for Europeans to migrate to these countries notwithstanding the much lower general standard of living that prevails ; though it is not always realized that similar scarcities have attracted various classes of specialized migrants from one Asian country to another. It is also fairly well known (since Asian students can rarely for long avoid discussing this question) that the payments made to non-Asians sometimes exceed those made to Asians doing work which is generally similar, and that there are sometimes restrictions which profess to be based on standards, but which actually discriminate in favour of oversea applicants and limit local entry to certain well-paid posts. The disparities in salary that result, the barriers that are imposed, the measures taken to break down these barriers, and local salary disputes often appear to be trivial ; but they have made up an important part of the politics of Asia because of the social prestige of those involved. The pattern of diffusion of skill from the migrant community is therefore worth a little attention.

IV. DIFFUSION OF SKILL

The theoretical pattern might be held to be a migration of a limited number of skilled workers followed by instruction of local unskilled workers, who would at first be paid less, while they were learning, but would subsequently be paid at the same high rate as the immigrants. As these in turn were employed to train new local people, the occupation would become over crowded at the existing salary, and rates of earning would fall and would tend to go on falling until the return to be achieved from the sums invested in training corresponded with the return attainable in similar investments in training for any other occupations. Where the initial premium for the skill was high, and the time taken in training relatively short, the fall in earnings would be rapid, but where the initial disparity was not so great, and the time required for training was long, there might be no appreciable fall, provided the general standard of living of the community was rising. Different occupations would have different speeds of adjustment depending on initial premiums and training times.

This basic pattern is subjected to a number of strains that can be regarded as automatic, and others that depend on political and cultural factors. First we must bear in mind that in the pattern of organization which prevails in most Western communities there is a good deal of rigidity in salary scales. It would be a reasonable approximation to the long-run economic pattern for the immigrants to be paid on a high scale with short-run contracts and for the local trainees, even when their training was completed, to be paid at a lower scale that would correspond to the long-run situation after the immigrants had ceased to practise this occupation. This would be, for example, a normal situation and unlikely to be seriously resented where training was being given by an expatriate artisan in some scarce but important craft which it would certainly not be profitable for an immigrant to practise once an adequate number of local people were trained. In other cases the standard of qualification appropriate in a wealthier country might be inappropriate in a poorer Asian country, and it might be desirable to lay down a lower standard of training for locally recruited staff as a long-run measure, and adopt differential salaries even where the training period was fairly long, on the ground that ultimately the immigrants would cease to practise the profession.

In these instances separate scales of earning at all times would be natural. A somewhat similar pattern arises when institutions (*e.g.* banks, hospitals, legal firms) are designed for carrying on skilled occupations in such a way that immigrants retain one role and local people are trained for a subordinate role on a more or less permanent specialized basis. It is doubtful whether this specialization could persist if it were not reinforced by important cultural factors, one of which is the much greater difficulty of making appropriate selections based on character when dealing with people of another culture. It is also a fact worth observing that some of the institutions appropriate to Western business and professional techniques are not easily fitted into the framework of Asian cultures ; the same applies to Chinese retailing in non-Chinese Asian communities, and perhaps also to the Japanese. It may be genuinely much more difficult to assimilate the local population to the immigrant institution, or to assimilate the institution to the local population, than to maintain a permanent specialization.

The fact must, however, be faced that one of the most important reasons for continued specialization is that a small group of immigrants develops a special public opinion which opposes any change and favours the perpetuation of the immigrants' advantage even to the disadvantage of the oversea owners of the business. Similarly in government a group of immigrants may frustrate the policy which is designed to secure increasing local participation in the technique of governing.

The methods adopted include the use of technical expertise to insist on qualifications which may not be essential or appropriate, but are much more easily acquired by immigrants. They also include a more or less unconscious incorporation into the practice of skilled occupations, or social habits which are very difficult for a local population to acquire. These social habits then tend to perpetuate themselves, the difference in income and the different conventions reinforcing one another in the manner made familiar by Veblen. The latter type of exclusiveness appears to be practised even more successfully by the Chinese than by the Europeans, and probably accounts for the extraordinary tenacity with which the Chinese retain their superiority in retail and wholesale trade even in the face of considerable political opposition.

More conscious and deliberate manipulation of the market to maintain differentials is found where migration is financed as a business venture. The indenture system which became widespread after the abolition of the slave trade contained frank penal sanctions to bind the indentured labourer to the person who had imported him for a period of years, and for years after the decline of the system public opinion regarded it as immoral for one employer to 'crimp' the labourer imported by another employer. Highly restrictive contracts, binding the immigrant to work for a particular employer, are still frequently used at the higher business and professional levels. There are also attempts made to limit the economic effects of diffusion of skill by tying those trained in any particular skill to work for a particular employer (generally the government) for a long period of years as a condition of obtaining training.

These restrictions and manipulations of the market are much resented and have accentuated the tendency to a rigid system of paper qualifications in all employment with substantial salary differentials, and a consequent excessive desire to secure meaningless and often irrelevant certificates and degrees. There can be no doubt that this has gravely aggravated the shortage of technical manpower in countries such as India and Ceylon. The process of assimilating foreign economic techniques and devising institutions (related to the local culture) which can apply them is seriously hindered by the conscious and unconscious reactions of migrant groups; so that the process of combining migration with cultural assimilation and organized diffusion of skills is of first-rate economic and political importance in many of the countries of Asia.

One of the functions of migration in the Asian economy is to mitigate differences between the structures of different economies, and not merely to help to equalize basic levels of income per head. Training and cultural change within the areas themselves provide a substitute for migration in modifying the relative scarcities of different kinds of labour, but there are important obstacles to this training no less than to migration, and a part of the practical problem of maintaining standards of living in the area is to find methods of combining a properly controlled migration with a proper educational reform. This is the goal towards which several of the United Nations agencies and independent Governments of the region appear to be converging.[1]

V. SPECIALIST MIGRANT GROUPS

The class of migrants which most clearly has played a specialist role in the economies to which it has travelled is that of the Chinese small trader. The role of the Chinese in retailing is almost ubiquitous in South-east Asia, and Chinese retail stores are found in Sarawak, North Borneo, the Philippines, Indonesia, Malaya, Thailand,

---

[1] Cf., for example, Report of the ECAFE/ILO/UNESCO Inter-Secretariat Working Party on Trained Personnel for Economic Development, United Nations Economic Commission for Asia and the Far East, Committee on Industry and Trade, Sixth Session, 1954.

Cambodia, Vietnam, and Burma.[1] In many of these countries the Chinese have also played the role of a subordinate executive, acting as intermediary between the colonial power and the local population. In both these roles the Chinese have specialized cultural aptitudes which give them a great advantage over the local populations. In most of these territories the advent of European enterprise extended the range of a money economy into regions where specialization had previously not gone very far. In South China there were large numbers of petty traders, hawkers, and others with even less stake in the social system, who had the traditions of hard work, thrift, and specialization of China behind them and were able, with the weakening of the checks exercised by the Chinese Government on migration, to move overseas. Many of those now owning small retail businesses are probably descended from Chinese who were transported as indentured labourers to the various countries of the South Seas, but who subsequently built up a position of independence by their social talents, their thrift, and their extraordinary capacity for work.

The Chinese respect for learning also led the oversea Chinese to be among the first to acquire a Western education of which the native populations were often suspicious. This has given them a special position as clerks and managers on behalf of European business men, particularly in Malaya but also in other territories of the South Seas.

In some of the countries of the South Seas the proportion of the Chinese who have come to occupy these special positions, either as traders or as junior executives in Western-run businesses, is high. In Malaya, however, the Chinese community, although it provides most of the traders and junior executives, is also extended over a greater range of occupations. This is partly because a greater proportion of the Chinese there came as indentured labourers, and partly because many settled on the land, mainly illegally during the great depression and the Second World War. But another cause was the extensive immigration of Chinese women [2] during the decade before the Second World War, which resulted from Japanese pressure in China and the Malayan Government's selective policy of encouraging female immigration.

A somewhat similar position was occupied by the Indians in

---

[1] Cf. V. W. W. Purcell, *The Chinese in South-east Asia*, Royal Institute of International Affairs, Oxford, 1951, and G. W. Skinner, *Report on the Chinese in South-east Asia*, Cornell University Data Paper, 1951.

[2] Cf. M. V. del Tufo, *Census of Malaya, 1947*, London, 1949, and T. E. Smith, *Population Growth in Malaya*, Royal Institute of International Affairs, London, 1952.

Burma [1] and to a lesser extent in Malaya also. This was a result of earlier British rule in India and the availability of comparatively large numbers of Indians with a higher level of education in the English language than prevailed in Burma and Malaya themselves. The Indians were sought more as clerks and in other positions requiring some education, and were less important in retail trade; though a substantial number of South Indian money-lenders played a part in the development of a money economy in Burma and Malaya. Substantial numbers of Indians in Malaya, however, are labourers on estates and in the government services who were recruited first under the indenture system and later under a system of assisted migration.

The development of this system is an interesting example of the provision of a specialized class, and of arrangements to ensure the permanence of this class in the economy of the country. Originally Indian labour was imported by recruiting agents of the estate owners themselves. The system of government control was introduced partly because of abuses such as misrepresentation in India of conditions prevailing in Malaya,[2] but perhaps mainly because of the difficulty of preventing labourers from leaving one employment and taking up another. When this happened, the estate which secured the labour would pay a rather higher proportion of what the labourer was worth but would save itself the expense of recruiting and bringing him from India. The scheme of assisted migration was therefore financed by a levy on all employers of Indian labour, and was used to bring in labour in accordance with the prevailing demand so as to maintain in key areas in the country a standard rate of wages based on an approved standard of living, and to repatriate labourers to India whenever the demand for them fell off. This system persisted until 1938 when it was discontinued by the refusal of the Indian Government to allow unskilled labour in these categories to migrate. By far the greater proportion of the Indians in Malaya, however, are still agricultural labourers or unskilled workers in the government service.

Another example of specialized migrant groups is provided by the oversea Japanese. In the second, third, and fourth decades of the present century their much higher educational standard enabled large numbers of them to occupy positions as managers and other executives not only in official positions, but in business of all kinds in Korea and Formosa. Similar examples of status based on earlier

[1] Cf. J. Russell Andrus, 'Three Economic Systems Clash in Burma', *Review of Economic Studies, 1935–6* ; *Burmese Economic Life*, Stanford, California, 1947.
[2] Cf. Lennox A. Mills, *op. cit.*, and Rt. Hon. V. S. Srinivasa Sastri, 'Report on the Conditions of Indian Labour in Malaya, 1937'.

acceptance of Western education can be found in India, where many of the Hindus occupy such positions in the predominantly Moslem areas, and in Sarawak, where, until after the Second World War, the Malays held (with the Chinese) a virtual monopoly of education.

VI. MIGRATION PROBLEMS: SHORT PERIOD

The significance of the specialist position of migrants in the area of South and South-east Asia can be seen if we consider some of the special problems of migration that have attracted attention since the war. The most significant migrations have been those resulting from war and civil war, particularly the return of large numbers of Japanese from the former Japanese Empire, the large influx of Chinese into Hong Kong, and the exchanges of population between India and Pakistan following the partition. Other Asian problems related to migration are the changing position of the Chinese community in many areas in South-east Asia and of the Indian community in Ceylon, and also the economic problems confronting the Indonesian Government in organizing its transmigration programme.

From the point of view of Japan itself, the return of large numbers of Japanese colonists from Korea and Taiwan merely added to the greatly aggravated population problem, which was already severe because of the large numbers of returned soldiers and colonists from the South Seas. This population problem was made more serious by the destruction of productive equipment in the latter part of the war and by the continuing high rate of Japan's natural increase of population. Certainly Japan experienced some surplus of trained and educated workers, and the standard of living of the middle classes was depressed, but this was not a special feature of the post-war Japanese economy. Japan had, before the war, already largely overcome the shortage of graduates, technicians, and artisans of all kinds which is such a marked weakness of most other Asian countries; [1] and this fact, combined with the low basic standards which resulted from the high population density, had made the middle classes one of the most depressed in the world. The political implications of this before the war were well known, but it is perhaps not always appreciated that depressed middle-class standards are still an important feature of the economy.

The significance of the return of the Japanese to Japan has been

[1] Cf. United Nations Economic Commission for Asia and the Far East, *Economic Survey of Asia and the Far East, 1954* [Chapter on Japan].

more marked in Korea and Taiwan themselves. Though Korean comment itself emphasizes the disruption of the economy, mainly in terms of the loss of supplies and markets, it is apparent that one of the important causes of disorganization in Korea has been the loss of nearly all the skilled industrial direction and technical ability previously provided by the Japanese.[1] This is by no means the only economic problem of the South Korean economy, but it is probably one of the reasons why the other problems have not been more successfully tackled. A vast amount of work has had to be put in by the United Nations Korean Reconstruction Agency, and also by the Korean Civil Assistance Command in collecting information and planning reconstruction, much of which was probably chiefly necessitated by the absence of the experts and technicians, who could have responded in a piecemeal fashion to the new scarcities of the postwar period if they had been available.

It is fashionable in Korea to blame this situation on the unwillingness of the Japanese to train the Koreans for responsible positions. No doubt there is some truth in this charge, but by colonial standards in most other countries Japan's record does not appear to have been especially bad. Both in Korea and in Burma (where large numbers of Indians as well as British business men have left the country) the sudden change in the political situation has aggravated the difficulties of solving problems that would have been difficult enough even without this loss of specialist personnel.

In both Korea and Burma the situation has been met by a large part of economic development being undertaken by the government. In Burma this accords with national ideology, in Korea it does not. Ideology, however, seems rather unimportant in this field. It is also noteworthy that in both countries foreign business firms have been employed not only to advise on the economy as a whole but also to run individual industries, virtually with monopoly powers, and under contract to train local staff to take over. In other respects, of course, both ideology and the structure of the government service make the economies very different, but these differences will not be discussed here.

In Hong Kong the influx of large numbers of Chinese from the mainland, while it has caused exceptional problems in the provision of municipal supplies and social services, appears to have stimulated a remarkable development of industry. While the immigrants into Hongkong are racially similar to those already in the colony, this situation may be yet another example of a specially selected group

[1] Cf. R. Nathan and Associates, *A Plan of Economic Development for Korea*, United Nations Korean Reconstruction Agency, 1954.

of migrants, since it is likely to have been mainly the entrepreneurs who became refugees from Communist China.

One of the severe economic problems confronting the Government of Pakistan as a result of the forced exchange of populations that followed the partition has been the loss of a substantial proportion of the educated and professional classes. This is of course primarily a result of stronger resistance by the Moslems than by the Hindus to Western education in earlier decades. Occupational specialization appears to have caused special difficulties in assimilating the refugees on both sides of the frontier, since several Indian industries have been handicapped by loss of Moslem artisans; but it must be admitted that the sheer numbers involved have been large enough to make the problem an important one even if no occupational specialization had aggravated it.[1] Some 15 million people have been involved altogether — a number that no reasonably practicable measures could be expected to absorb completely. On the whole the superior educational and economic status of the refugees returning to India, though it undoubtedly accentuated individual suffering, probably made it easier for India than for Pakistan to plan successful rehabilitation schemes. It is probable that serious loss of skill through specialization now no longer appropriate has caused India to lose more effective manpower than Pakistan has gained, and that the converse is true for Pakistan.

VII. MIGRATION PROBLEMS: LONG PERIOD

In the more long-term problems which are now occupying attention because of the need for large numbers of recent migrants to change their political status, the same theme of economic specialization is again significant. Probably the two countries in which the changing status of the Chinese is of most importance are Malaya and Thailand. In both of these countries, though in very different ways, the special economic functions of the Chinese have seriously aggravated the social and political difficulties.

Thailand, until comparatively recent times, was probably one of the countries which had been most successful in assimilating Chinese immigrants. The situation was one in which religion provided no barrier to intermarriage, while the monarchical structure and the very different cultural pattern built around it made it much more necessary for the Chinese to assimilate themselves to the local

---

[1] Cf. discussion on the Refugee Problem in C. A. Vakil, *Economic Consequences of Divided India*, Bombay, 1950, chs. 2 and 3.

population. It was partly the dominance that Chinese traders had secured over export of rice and other important trades in the country that led to sharper differentiation of the Chinese by the Thai people themselves. Political and cultural factors related to the growth of the Kuomintang, and the spread of Chinese education no doubt aggravated this tendency, but it would be misleading to neglect the economic specialization of the Chinese as one of the important causes of distrust between the Thais and Chinese in spite of their widespread cultural interaction and intermarriages. The family and guild structure of Chinese society reinforces trade links and makes for exclusiveness; and the specialization in trade reinforces the cultural separation.

In Malaya the most significant feature of Chinese migration was the large-scale migration of women during the decade before the Second World War, and the consequent foundation of large numbers of families which have since been cut off from return to China by the war and the civil war and have now become bound to Malaya by economic and social ties that were never intended but cannot now be severed. The sociological and political consequences of these migrations — which range from fashion changes to new patterns in education — would be sufficient for a paper by themselves. It is, however, significant that one of the principal causes of difficulty in fusing Malays and Chinese into a single nation capable of conducting its own affairs has been the economic specialization of the Chinese immigrants. It is because the Chinese are overwhelmingly stronger in the towns, and because they control the trade and most of the professions of the country, that the Malays have feared that any equality of status of the Chinese would result in their dominating the country through their predominance in all the controlling positions and in the economic life of the country. It is mainly because the Malays have feared this dominance of the Chinese that they have resisted common citizenship and obstructed other concessions that might have made it easier for the Chinese to identify themselves with Malaya.

In the early days of the Communities Liaison Committee, which attempted to provide sufficient contact to make the Federation agreement work, the basis of future development was agreed as an improvement in the political status of the non-Malays and of the economic status of the Malays.[1] It has, however, proved far more difficult to raise the economic status of the Malays than to improve the political status of non-Malays, and though greatly improved

---

[1] This is briefly discussed by the author and Ungku A. Aziz in W. L. Holland, *Asian Nationalism and the West*, Institute of Pacific Relations, 1952, p. 327.

political harmony has been at least superficially achieved, the under-lying economic specialization largely remains, and will probably cause many more difficulties in future.

There is still far more specialization by community in Malaya than appears to be compatible with the degree of identity of interest that would be necessary to form a united nation. The prevalence of large numbers of Indians in the plantation and industrial labour of the country has made trade unionism a sphere dominated by Indians, and the greater awareness by the Indian professional classes of the techniques of mass leadership has also led to disproportionate influ-ence of the Indians in political life, though this may be expected to wane in the near future with the growing power of the Alliance between the United Malays National Organisation and the Malayan Chinese Association. So far as it goes, Indian influence is a factor making for national unity, since the Indians, as the smallest of the main communities, appear to see their future mainly in terms of a united Malayan nationality, while both the Malays and the Chinese are partly looking to their economic advantage and to improving the relative position of their own race. While it seems probable that the Alliance, to which reference has been made, will secure control of the government in the forthcoming elections, it is difficult to see how economic conflicts of interest between the two races will be reconciled when actual policy decisions have to be taken.

The position of Indians in Ceylon is also one of the migration problems of Asia to which attention has recently been given in the discussions between the Governments of the two countries. Here, again, occupational specialization is a part of the problem because of the predominant role of the Indian labourer on the tea estates. Many of the Indians who have migrated to Ceylon have done so as part of a similar system of organized supply of labour for a European plantation industry, and in principle their sojourn in Ceylon was intended to be temporary.[1]

The estates naturally organized their life on a pattern which was made up partly of the requirements of the estate itself and partly of their own traditional habits. There was little opportunity for linguistic or cultural assimilation or intermarriage. India is not as far from Ceylon as from Malaya and contacts were maintained by visits and by remittance of funds. When political organization began, the Indian labourers were naturally organized as an extension of the Indian Congress Party. All these things have tended to make assimilation and acquisition of Ceylon citizenship more difficult.

The largely English-educated middle-class nationalists who rule

[1] Cf. Sir Ivor Jennings, *The Economy of Ceylon*, Oxford, 1951, ch. 4.

Ceylon resent the almost complete dependence of their economy on exports of plantation-grown tea, coconuts, and rubber which make possible their essential imports of food and clothing, but cannot do without the estates in spite of their tendency to remit profits to the United Kingdom and savings to South India. Thus in Ceylon the problem of assimilation is not, as in Malaya, a result of demographic changes, but rather of a change in the status and working of the plantation industry as a result of the transfer of political power. It is not a question of Indian labour being assimilated by circumstances but not accepted politically; rather it is a question of large numbers of Indians who are felt, and probably feel themselves to be, alien to the ordinary life of the country, but who cannot, for economic reasons, be driven out or excluded from its life. The need for decisions on citizenship is something that has been introduced by the political change, and the degree of economic specialization makes it difficult to secure an agreed solution.

VIII. ABSORPTION OF CAPITAL IN MIGRATION

The problem of financing and organizing an adequate flow of migrants from Java to the outer islands in Indonesia is one which does not introduce the same pattern of occupational specialization. Both the former Dutch Government and the present Indonesian Government have been chiefly concerned with moving people in large numbers from an overcrowded territory to lands that are less crowded and sometimes seriously short of manpower. The chief problem is simply one of the capital cost and administrative difficulty of moving people in sufficiently large numbers to cope with the demographic problems that confront the small island of Java.

Many of the tropical lands are fairly empty, and available for migration, simply because they are areas that need substantial public expenditure on clearing the ground, on malaria control, on the construction of highways, etc. to make them fit for occupation. In addition, the sheer cost of moving, while low by European standards, is high in relation to the average standard of living of a peasant in monsoon Asia. It is estimated that the cost of moving an average family of five from Java even to the neighbouring island of Sumatra works out at Rps 10,000, which is probably more than half the amount of capital that would be required (on the average) for setting an additional wage earner in industry and removing pressure on agricultural land in this way. The Dutch Government [1] never

[1] Cf. H. de Meel, 'Demographic Dilemma in Indonesia', *Pacific Affairs*, 1951.

succeeded in moving more than about 200,000 people in the five years up to 1940. The present Government [1] plans to move half a million people a year within the next few years; but a cost of a thousand million rupiahs annually represents a considerable development expenditure, and the net outflow from Java, even if this target is achieved, would be less than three-quarters of the annual rate of increase in the island, and would therefore contribute nothing towards alleviation of the position but merely act as a palliative against further deterioration.

There is some evidence that in colonization schemes of this kind too little attention is usually given to the need to create a new kind of community.[2] The Indonesian Government is aware of the need for avoiding the reproduction of the agrarian evils of Java in the new countries, and some of the new colonization is being planned in relation to new industrial projects. It is desirable also that not only should the area per head be large but the pattern of community development and trade be such as to prevent excessive population growth and fragmentation of holdings in future. There is far too little study, by sociological and anthropological techniques, of the factors that determine the development of these new colonies of migrants.

The Indonesian problem brings home another fundamental economic difficulty of the demographic future in Asia and also underlines the function which migration can perform and the relation of migration to the other needs of the region. The expanding population of these areas is generating increased pressure on the agricultural land. There is other agricultural land in the region which is available and could be used to absorb the population if political difficulties could be overcome. The occupation of this land, however, would involve a use of capital resources both for moving the population and for clearing the land and making it available for occupation, and it is not certain that the pattern of rapid population growth with a new fall in standards of living would not soon be repeated.

It has been often emphasized that the demographic problems of Asia need for their solution a transformation of the economies of the region leading to new social patterns which will not in future generate the same excessive population pressure. This transformation of the economies, however, demands very large supplies of capital, and it is doubtful whether a use of the limited supplies of capital in

---

[1] Cf. United Nations Economic Commission for Asia and the Far East, *Economic Survey of Asia and the Far East, 1954*, Part II, ch. 8.

[2] Cf. the brief comments in International Bank for Reconstruction and Development, *Report on a Mission to Ceylon*, and in other International Bank Mission reports.

colonizing new lands by methods not widely different from those used on the old lands will contribute materially to the problem.

IX. MIGRATION AND TRAINING

Capital will need to be invested not merely in factories and cities, but in human beings. Indeed, the training of efficient tax collectors, administrators, managers, and teachers must be enormously expanded if much more public capital formation is to take place. The creation of a suitable class of entrepreneurs, accountants, foremen, etc., is almost equally necessary if private capital formation is to expand very greatly. For either public or private capital formation foreign aid will be needed, but without a large investment in human beings the limits to the provision of foreign capital are probably so narrow that no important improvement can take place.

It is in this connexion that the role of migration must be considered. Migration in Asia has in the past helped to overcome or at least diminish some of the significant shortages that have emerged in developing a specialized economy. Migration can often meet a need for a specialized class much more quickly than the training of the local population; and some migration, if only of a temporary kind, is an essential part of any training. Migration on a large scale may be expensive, but in the early stages is almost always less expensive for the more difficult types of specialization than local training. In the past, however, this migration has not been accompanied by the sociological investigations that may be necessary to plan successful assimilation; and the social and political forces that commonly help assimilation have often been inhibited by colonial rule. In many instances there are political obstacles to migration and also political obstacles raised by former migrant classes to the necessary training of the local population. The problem of planning to overcome the scarcities of skills, in the short run by migration and in the longer run by training related to the migration, are by no means easy of solution.

Probably cultural assimilation of the specialized immigrants to the local population would contribute to the diffusion of the new skills. Such assimilation is hardly possible with the European migrants who come from countries of a much higher basic standard of living and are attracted mainly by the greater scarcity of trained personnel and consequent large differentials in earning. European immigrants are likely to continue to have a vested interest in keeping the provision of such skill limited, and if the skill becomes very widely diffused they are likely to return to their home countries. For this reason it is probably undesirable to encourage the growth of a class of European settlers, who are likely to acquire considerable power through their superior education and oversea contacts, and to have a very strong inducement to resist diffusion of skill. Some of the migrations between different Asian communities, however, would appear to have permanent economic value if they could be combined with deliberate planning of assimilation and diffusion of technique. One of the essential conditions would appear to be that the initial standard of living of the migrants should not be so high that assimilation would involve considerable economic loss.

The cultural obstacles to any such programme are immense. Most of the international agencies are planning their training programmes on the basis of a purely temporary migration of highly paid experts or the sending overseas of small numbers of picked personnel from the countries themselves. This fact, however, seriously limits the range of training that can be given. It also often ensures that the immigrant specialist has no interest in the culture of the community that he is visiting and no capacity to adapt his knowledge to the local *mores*.

The trained personnel who are sent overseas are inevitably isolated in the process from many of the problems of their community, and only the outstandingly able ones can overcome the combined stress of social readjustment to their own community and adaptation of their knowledge to its local problems. The scarcity of people with the necessary talents is by no means an indication of inferiority in the Asian populations. It is extremely unlikely that any known population would produce a higher proportion of people with these exceptional talents. The scarcity, however, generates feelings of frustration and often of superiority on the part of those who are trying to organize suitable programmes of training.

Specialist migrations that occurred during the colonial period suffered from many of the well-known difficulties of colonial rule. They developed in response to economic motives, and only the minimum social adjustments which these economic motives required took place. The existence of a small, highly qualified class of foreign officials led to inadequate attempts by the populations themselves to solve the resulting social problems, and a vested interest among the ruling group in delaying the substitution of local training for migration. Nevertheless these migrations made possible a degree of economic development which the scarcity of various special human factors of production would otherwise have inhibited altogether. The bias is now all in favour of autarky in the supply of human resources; and this, though it has been probably pushed too far by nationalist politicians, may be a useful corrective; but it is important to recognize that in building up human capital the role played by imports is a good deal less simple than in the building up of material capital. It is not possible to shut out the imports altogether, and it is undesirable to approach the problem merely in terms of limitation of quantity.

There are several fields in which a proper assessment of the relations between migration, linguistic and cultural assimilation, and diffusion of technique may yield fruitful results. There may still be developments that could be fostered by making use of Chinese enterprise, industry, and thrift, the widespread English education of India and the Philippines, and the abundance of technical skill at the lower levels in Japan in the planning of economic development in Asia; but the patterns of migration which can usefully exploit these resources to overcome the most critical shortages in Asia will not come about of their own accord.

The migrations will certainly not be allowed to occur unless they are clearly integrated with programmes of training and diffusion of skill; and the migrants would be unlikely to qualify for highly paid posts as United Nations experts. Indeed it would largely undermine their position if they were paid United Nations salaries and induced to live in a largely Western style. Money would have to be spent on them to assist them in their task rather than given to them — always a much more difficult undertaking.

The problems that need to be overcome are primarily economic problems. The obstacles are political, cultural, and linguistic. The techniques needed for investigating what needs to be done appear to be those of the sociologists and the anthropologists. There is much hope in the awakening interest of the academic world in the intellectual problems involved in the economic development of Asia; in particular, the growing interest shown by American universities, with their vast resources both in manpower and in finance, is an encouraging sign. One of the problems that will need further investigation is the role of specialist migration, and the special techniques needed to enable it to lead rapidly to a culturally acceptable situation in which the principal shortages have been overcome.

Chapter 19

MIGRATION AND THE ECONOMY
OF INDONESIA

BY

NATHAN KEYFITZ
Ottawa

MOVEMENT of peoples and of the cultures that they bear characterizes from its earliest history the archipelago that now makes up
the Republic of Indonesia. To go only as far back as the end of the
Stone Age, which in this area occurred about 300 B.C., it appears
that immigration of people from South China brought about the
use of bronze and iron. We have no direct information on the
movement of people, but the record of archaeology shows Han
pottery in Java well before the Christian era. The Han objective
was to develop the sea route to India, and this was probably not the
first of many contacts that the archipelago owes to its location on
this route. Ptolemy's atlas of the second century B.C. shows the
outlines and seaports of the archipelago: since India was a trans-
shipment point for goods moving between the Mediterranean and
East Asia, Ptolemy probably got his information from Indian sailors.
Images of the Buddha found in Java seem to date from the second
century of our era. About that time writing was introduced from
South India, and many words of Sanskrit and Indian vernacular
languages came into the speech of Indonesia.[1] Tales of the Ramayana
were incorporated into the shadow drama, which is very much alive
in present-day Javanese culture.

A succession of Indianized states dominated Indonesia and the
neighbouring mainland, starting in the seventh century when Srivajaja
spread its power from the river port of Palembang and continuing
through to Modjopahit's pre-eminence eight hundred years later.
The Javanese kingdoms tended to be based on agriculture — on the
uniform surplus produce by the wet rice cultivation of East and
Central Java. The states that arose in Sumatra and Malaya, on the
other hand, were more concerned with trade.

Hinduism by the fifteenth century was a lost cause in the

[1] Sundoro, *Sedjarah Indonesia*, Djakarta, 1953.

273

archipelago, and when the trade in spices was taken up by the Moslem Gujerati, who established themselves first in the ports of Malaya and Sumatra and then came to the cities of the north coast of Java, they were not effectively opposed. With the ideological tolerance that characterizes this part of the world, Islam did not seek to wipe out the earlier cultures but rather became assimilated to them in a process of settlement and intermarriage.

Almost contemporaneously with the Gujerati and other bearers of Islam came the Europeans, who also combined trade and religious missions. First to arrive were the Portuguese, who developed their own route round the Cape of Good Hope early in the sixteenth century, secured command of the Indian Ocean, and captured Malacca. But Portuguese settlers and occupation forces were too few, and after a century gave way to the Dutch, who put large amounts of capital into shipping and the construction of factories. The English also proved too few to withstand in the face of the Dutch; Jan Pieterzsoon Coen, appointed Govenor-General in 1618, took decisive steps towards establishing the Netherlands as a power in the Far East for three centuries to come. The Dutch administrators and settlers were to have a major effect on the economies of all the islands, starting from the seaports of Java, and especially Jacarta, which the Dutch made their capital, changing its name to Batavia.

The new-comers attempted to close the Moluccas and other parts of the Indies to foreign trade and immigration alike, with a few exceptions such as the bringing in of African, Indian, Philippine, and other slaves for the work which commerce required. To close all the ports was, however, beyond their powers, and Achin in North Sumatra was visited by English, Portuguese, Gujeratis, and Chinese throughout the eighteenth century; perhaps the sharpest traders of all were the Indian Moslems. It was not until the end of the nineteenth century that the Netherlands consolidated its hold on the archipelago. At first the Dutch were interested in commerce only (and in fighting the Portuguese) and except in the Moluccas they did not intervene in government. The number of settlers they required increased when they started to open up the interior of Java, even though the system of indirect rule was adopted. Deliveries of coffee, pepper, and indigo — this last aided by the import of indigo workers from the Coromandel coast of India [1]— brought the villages into the world market and helped to spread the 'dualistic' [2] economy. On the political side the rulers became regents for the Dutch interest,

---

[1] Brian Harrison, *South-East Asia*, London, 1954, p. 129.
[2] J. H. Boeke, *Economics and Economic Policy of Dual Societies as exemplified by Indonesia*, New York, 1953.

and were strengthened *vis-à-vis* their subjects by their affiliation to the foreign power.[1]

There had been some Chinese in the archipelago from very early times, but their numbers increased greatly under the wing of European power. Java in particular was settled by large numbers of Chinese from Fukien, of whom by 1720 there were said [2] to be 100,000, with 80,000 in the neighbourhood of Batavia. They lived culturally separate from the Javanese and the Dutch ; though they often took wives from among the Javanese and perhaps forgot their own language, they always recognized themselves as Chinese ; unlike other immigrants for a thousand years, they converted their neighbours to no foreign religion. At one time they began to overflow the niches that existed for them as intermediaries between colonial power and Indonesian, and a massacre took place in 1740 in which some 10,000 Chinese were killed.

After the English interregnum in Java during the Napoleonic wars the native rulers were restored to power, and the culture system initiated about 1830 rapidly expanded commercial agriculture and increased the significance of Java in world trade. During this period, and even more during the liberal period which followed it when private enterprisers were permitted to open estates, the number of Dutch in the country steadily increased. The 1860 Census counted 44,000 Europeans in the archipelago, the 1905 Census 95,000 ; in the present century the average rate of increase was even greater so that the number of Europeans increased to 240,000 by 1930.

The 1930 Census gives in a cross-section form the cumulative result of all the long history of migration into the area which is now Indonesia. Of a total count of 60,727,000 people the number of Europeans was 240,000, of Chinese 1,233,000, and of other foreign Asians 116,000.[3] The remainder of the population was classified as 'native' and shown in some fifty culture groups.

Of the Europeans 208,000, or 87 per cent, were Netherlanders, 7000 Germans and Austrians, and an equal number of Japanese. The breakdown of the Chinese into culture groups shows that almost half (555,000) were Hokkiens, followed by 201,000 Hakkas. Also reflecting the long history of the archipelago to which we have briefly referred above is the breakdown of Other Foreign Asians — 71,000 Arabs, 30,000 Indians, 4000 Malays from Malacca. Rates of increase between the 1920 Census and that of 1930 show a much more rapid increase for the foreigners than for the natives : thus

---

[1] George M. Kahin, *Nationalism and Revolution in Indonesia*, Ithaca, New York, 1952.   [2] Brian Harrison, *op. cit.* p. 135.
[3] Centraal Kantoor voor de Statistiek, *Netherlands Indian Report, 1939*, vol. ii, *Statistical Abstract for the Year 1938*, Batavia, 1938, p. 116.

while the Indonesian population increased by 2 per cent per annum, the Europeans increased by 3·6 per cent, the Chinese by 4·3 per cent, and the other foreign Asians by 5·7 per cent. Of the total European population 170,000, or 70 per cent, were born in the archipelago, and even if we consider men of working ages, the number born there is almost equal to the number who were born away. This reflects partly the fact that Indonesia had become home to the Dutch, who included many permanent settlers (*blijvers*), partly the fact that many of those legally classified as European were Eurasians.

The census, incidentally, reflects the division of labour which had sprung up between Europeans, Chinese, and Indonesians. Thus of 85,000 Europeans exercising an occupation 21,000 were in government service and 11,000 were in the liberal professions. Of 470,000 Chinese negligible proportions were in government and professions, but 172,000 were in commerce and 98,000 in industry, mostly making food, drink, and tobacco or else articles of wood and bamboo. Among Indonesians themselves some were in government service, for of 20,280,000 exercising an occupation there were 492,000 in government, over half in the service of the *desas*. Some 11,997,000 were in native agriculture; this group roughly defines those who were relatively unaffected by the foreign sector of the economy, and to them might be added some of the 677,000 in textile manufacture. On the other hand, the 529,000 workers on sugar estates were in some degree part of the export economy, though in capacities which were not very remunerative. The large number — 724,000 — of sellers of food and tobacco indicates a high degree of effort going into petty trade.

If the colonial state can be fairly described as 'forced cultural diffusion', then the administrators and others who migrated from Holland were the agents of that diffusion. The ways of doing things that developed in Netherlands India, while having some similarity to those that the administrators and business men had learned in Holland, also had a style of their own, not Dutch and not Indonesian. Administrative methods were modified to take account of the surplus of unskilled clerical and manual labour and the dearth of highly skilled labour. In regard to style of living, houses and furnishings, clothing, food and when and how meals are served, a very pleasant way of doing things that is neither Dutch nor Indonesian, called 'Indisch' in the Netherlands, arose; it seems a permanent contribution of the Dutch to the inheritance of the new Republic, along with many Dutch words in the fine and growing Indonesian language.

The declaration of independence on 17 August 1945, and the transfer of sovereignty at the end of 1949, changed greatly the situation of Netherlanders, and this is probably not yet stabilized within the new Republic. Many whose skills are valued remain and have important positions — academic, business, and government. Those who have come since the war seem best able to meet the new conditions of social intercourse; all are recognized as making needed contributions to reconstruction and to new construction.

The colonial administration counted as citizens of the mother country all registrations of children of mixed marriage and of those born out of wedlock who were acknowledged. The Indos, as they were called, found a place for themselves in the ranks of the civil service, which positions were said to belong to them just as the soil belongs to the nobility under feudalism.[1] Since the revolution these positions, as also to some extent those with private business,[2] have been lost to the majority who did not opt for Indonesian citizenship. Many have gone to Holland, but the 100,000 still remaining [3] face real difficulties; there is a strong opinion in Holland that they are likely to prove unassimilable if they move to that country.

Among the foreigners who have come to Indonesia during past centuries, the Chinese to-day by far outnumber all others together. They had traded from earliest times, and then settled into the sugar industry, where they received particular support during the term of Governor-General van Diemen (1636–45). Numbers were brought in as construction labourers by the East India Company. Later they came to work in the tin mines of Banka, and in the plantations of Sumatra. However, they soon moved into other spheres of work, including even the collection of taxes. The collection of native tobacco, maize, kapok, copra, coffee, rubber, dried cassava, gums, resins, wood, fruit, was largely in the hands of Chinese.[4] The moneylender who came to the door of the ever-impoverished *tani* each week, either to offer a loan or to collect the instalment on one previously given, was generally a Chinese. He sold clothing and other goods wholesale on his way to the village, and often another Chinese retailed them in the village. In all this activity the close connexions with other Chinese in a variety of complementary businesses gave him an important advantage (in market information, for example) in competition with Indonesians. The concentration of the Chinese in trade and small industry is reflected in the high proportions they showed in the cities in 1930: thus of Batavia's 533,000 population

---

[1] Amry Vandenbosch, *The Dutch East Indies*, Berkeley, California, 1944, p. 10.
[2] Paul W. van der Veur, 'The Eurasians of Indonesia : Castaways of Colonialism', *Pacific Affairs*, vol. xxvii, no. 2, June 1954, p. 132.
[3] W. F. Wertheim, 'Changes in Indonesia's Social Stratification', *Pacific Affairs*, vol. xxviii, no. 1, March 1955, p. 49.
[4] J. H. Boeke, *op. cit.* p. 115.

79,000 were Chinese, and of Surabaya's 342,000 population 39,000. Because the Chinese had a superior status in colonial times, he never assimilated to the Indonesian community, even when he was both by descent and culture very largely Indonesian.

Under the Republic the Chinese do not have the role that they had as ancillaries to the colonial power, and their commercial interests have changed. This writer's observation in certain *desas* of Java suggests that the money-lending function has gone underground; the itinerant Chinese money-lender has given place to arrangements among neighbours. Kahin[1] also reports that better-off Indonesians took the place of the Chinese who fled the villages in the revolution. The effect of inflation and revolution was to wipe out indebtedness and sometimes the money-lender himself. But on the whole the Chinese has re-established himself.[2] He has extended his activities in wholesale trade, in the manufacture of such consumer goods as ice, soft drinks, and furniture; Chinese own cinemas and work in European banks and trading houses.

With an economic role in some ways resembling that of the Chinese, and a versatility almost equal to theirs, the Arabs do not share the unpopularity of the Chinese. Because they are the carriers of a pure Islamic faith, and because also the Arabs of Indonesia rallied to the Republic immediately Independence was declared, their standing is high despite trade practices that make some of them very wealthy. Like the Chinese they marry Indonesian women, but, at least in Java and Sumatra, they retain a sense of being separate from the Indonesian community.[3]

Immigrants registered during the year 1938 are given as 16,821.[4] This was a decline from 19,282 of the preceding year, which in turn represents the peak of a steady rise from a trough of 9280 in 1933. During the more prosperous twenties the numbers had been far higher, and in both 1920 and 1930 over 40,000 persons entered. During the whole of this period two-thirds of the entrants had been Chinese, and the Dutch numbered from 2000 to 5000, the larger number being reached when business conditions were brisk. These figures do not, however, include those Dutch who came on government service and their families, who needed no permit; during most of the years of the thirties about 8000 persons in this group entered, and 6000 or 7000 left, children included.[5]

Indonesia is listed on this programme of the International

---

[1] *Op. cit.* p. 327.   [2] W. F. Wertheim, *op. cit.*
[3] Justus M. van der Kroef, 'The Arabs in Indonesia', *The Middle East Journal*, vol. 7, no. 3, Summer 1953.
[4] Centraal Kantoor voor de Statistiek, *Netherlands Indian Report 1939*, vol. ii, *Statistical Abstract for the Year 1938*, Batavia, 1939.   [5] *Ibid.* p. 49.

Economic Association as a country of immigration, but in fact its attitude towards immigration is a complex one. Over the course of history the Chinese, so useful as labourer and as middleman between the colonial power and the mass of its subjects, has only been welcome at certain times and was for long not allowed to settle on the land. The entry of Europeans, including Netherlanders, was limited until 1870 to the military and those filling administrative posts, for to the East India Company and its successor, the culture system of the nineteenth century, there was no place for competition. In the era of liberalism, however, the archipelago was opened up to foreigners, and the government took some mild steps to protect Indonesians against new-comers. An indication of the attitude towards immigration is an act passed by the Volksraad in 1937 which limited immigrants to 12,000 per year, and of these the number of any one nationality except Chinese and Dutch was to be no more than 800.

The limitation on immigration has been continued by the Republic, which regards as one of its foremost responsibilities the protection of its subjects against outsiders. For 1953, and again for 1954, the number of immigrants was fixed at a maximum of 8000. Less than half of this number — 3500 — were admitted in 1953. Of these 1500 were Dutch, followed by Chinese, Americans, Indians, and Pakistanis.[1]

It will be useful also to bring together the Netherlands figures giving the movement between Indonesia and the Netherlands; these are shown in the table on page 280. The much larger totals of the Netherlands statistics undoubtedly result from different definitions of migration. Thus the Indonesian immigrants apparently include only those who have come for the first time and intend to stay six months or more. The total traffic was much greater; in 1952[2] 47,626 foreigners entered Indonesia, the majority Dutch and Chinese, while 52,232 left; in 1953 some 40,628 entered and 38,833 left. From the Netherlands record of migrants it appears that about 128,000 more left Indonesia than entered in the eight years 1946 to 1953; over half of the Netherlanders present before the war have apparently left.

One aspect of the feeling that immigrants must be watched is the drive towards a registration of foreigners. Thus the head of the Central Immigration Office is quoted[3] as saying that this registration,

---

[1] 'Djumlah Orang Asing ke Indonesia th. 1953', *Warta Imigrasi*, vol. iv, no. 12, December 1953, p. 32.
[2] '20 Djuta orang Asing di Indonesia', *Warta Imigrasi,* vol. v, no. 2, February 1954, p. 37.
[3] *Ibid.*

suspended since 1940, is the only way of controlling the illegal entry of foreigners.

As far as an outsider can see, Indonesia is not likely to seek immigrants in the near future. She feels, indeed, that her own people must be educated up to Western standards, and some foreign educators are participating in this programme, to which an enormous amount of effort is being devoted and which is securing remarkable results. Once this educational plan has attained its goal, Indonesia will be able to look after her own needs for technicians and specialists of all kinds. The entry of essential specialists of many kinds is

POPULATION MOVEMENT SINCE THE SECOND WORLD WAR
BETWEEN NETHERLANDS AND INDONESIA

Year	Immigration to Netherlands from Indonesia	Emigration to Indonesia from Netherlands
1946	69,225	5,339
1947	21,989	23,382
1948	17,628	28,976
1949	16,513	23,150
1950	55,909	9,160
1951	30,352	8,775
1952	16,221	8,919
1953	14,232	6,348
Total, 1946–53	242,069	114,049

Sources : 1946–49, Central Bureau voor de Statistiek, *Jaarcijfers voor Neder-land 1947–50.*
1950–53, United Nations *Demographic Yearbook 1954.*

accepted as a necessity in the period of transition, and it is clearly recognized that foreign investors, in oil and other industries, must bring their own technicians. What dominates the official attitude is its unwillingness to place its Indonesian subjects, economically and educationally weak for the moment, at the mercy of economically strong foreigners, be they from the East or the West. The fostering of an Indonesian middle class has been a goal of all Governments since Independence, and the control of immigration is one of the instruments towards that goal.

Note on Internal Migration

At one time international migration served the purpose of developing new lands on the one hand and on the other of lightening the burden of countries whose population had expanded beyond the resources which their technology allowed them to draw on, or which their productivity permitted them to obtain by trade. With the growth of nationalism both in the East and in the West, the adjustment of rates of natural increase, population numbers, resources and standards of living is less and less permitted to occur by the movement of people across international frontiers. Many reasons are given for the closing of the doors of immigration; Eastern countries, like Western ones, cite arguments of maintaining their standard of living, of refusing to be a dump for the unemployment of other countries.

The growth of nationalism, and the arguments which support it, close the doors between countries and help to open them among the territories of any one country. If population growth is unequal, a country can effectively increase its agricultural resources, and therefore its standard of living, by redistributing its people. Indonesia has shown through the colonial period, and continues to show at the present time, a remarkably uneven distribution of population. Estimates made by the author in 1953, which agree fairly well with the count for the election applying to about the same point of time, give the population of Java as about 53 million, and that of the whole of Indonesia about 80 million, both of these figures being minimum. The rate of Java's increase can only be surmised, but some evidence is available to indicate that 2 per cent per annum, or a million persons for the island, is not unlikely for the near future. Vice-president Hatta gives 40 million as Java's optimum population.[1] A population problem threatens Java despite whole-hearted and effective work on the part of the Indonesian Government to improve the productivity of agriculture by better seed varieties and the use of fertilizers.

To say simply that Java, with its two-thirds of the population of Indonesia, contains only one-fifteenth of the land area, is to exaggerate the difference in effective density, for the average productivity of the soil in the Outer Islands is not equal to that of Java. However, parts of Sumatra and other islands are unquestionably fertile.

The Indonesian Government plans to move some 2 million persons during the next five years.[2] If those moved are largely young adults this will reduce the increase of Java to negligible proportions, and will at the same time open up areas in the Outer Islands that will produce that surplus of foodstuffs so essential to economic development. However, a very substantial effort is implied

---

[1] Mohammed Hatta, *Beberapa Fasal Ekonomi*, Balai Pustaka, 1951.
[2] 'Transmigration in Indonesia', *Indonesian News Bulletin*, Ottawa, Embassy of the Republic of Indonesia, vol. i, no. 2, September 1954, p. 6.

in a movement such as this. The largest number of movers during the colonial period was some 60,000 persons in 1940.

The transmigration programme includes, for each area of potential migration, soil tests, plans for irrigation works, surveys by health specialists so that necessary action can be taken against disease and particularly malaria, legal action for acquiring land, planning of roads, and surveys of lots. In order to hold down cost the use of paid labour for clearing of the forest and building of roads and houses prior to the coming of the settlers should be kept to the minimum. Studies made in the migration areas and elsewhere reveal that much can be done by the settlers themselves. As far as willingness of the Javanese to move is concerned, observation by the author in the villages of the crowded portions of Central and West Java shows that these villages contain many peasants who have no legal connexion with the land and little claim on the produce of the land; they seek nothing better than an opportunity to build a heritage for themselves and their children. This motivation, far stronger than the desire for money wages, will permit a very large-scale effective investment in expansion of the agricultural domain of the Republic. It will produce the food surplus which everywhere has been the necessary condition of industry.[1]

[1] N. Keyfitz and Widjojo Sunarti, *Soal-Soal Penduduk dan Pembangunan Indonesia*, Djakarta, 1955.

Chapter 20

THE IMPACT ON INDIA OF POPULATION TRANSFERS IN 1947 AND AFTER

P. R. BRAHMANANDA
University of Bombay

I. THE MAGNITUDE OF THE DISPLACEMENT

THE partition of undivided India into India and Pakistan was followed by one of the greatest mass transfers of population in history and involved about 16 million, *i.e.* more than twice the population of Australia and more than the entire population of Canada.[1] The suddenness of this event made all attempts towards a planned exchange of population impossible. Large-scale migrations have taken place in different countries in the past for reasons such as political dissatisfaction, religious persecution, racial hatred, and economic insecurity; but the migrations of India and Pakistan are unique in that at one stroke millions in either country found themselves as aliens in lands where they and their forefathers had earned their livelihood for centuries. A substantial part of the transfer had to be completed within less than a year. In view of the suddenness, the magnitude and the speed of the migrations, they can rightly be called the Great Displacement. This paper will deal with the economic impact of the transfer on the Indian economy.

II. ECONOMIC SIGNIFICANCE OF THE POPULATION TRANSFER

From the economist's point of view, it may be noted that this is perhaps the first instance of an underdeveloped economy with a very low rate of growth being called upon to make immediate adjustments

[1] See C. N. Vakil, *Economic Consequences of Divided India* (and references cited therein), 1950; H. Alexander, *The New Citizens of India*, 1951; J. B. Schechtman, *Population Transfers in Asia*, 1949; V. K. R. V. Rao, 'Economic Reviews of Refugee Rehabilitation in India'. Studies of Faridabad, Rajpura, Tripuri Townships and Kingsway Camp; C. N. Vakil and P. H. Cabinetmaker, 'A Study of the Socio-Economic Conditions and Attitude of Displaced Persons',

283

arising out of a substantial population transfer. The Indian economy had hardly recovered from the strain due to the war, and had to spend large amounts in relief and rehabilitation at a time when funds were scarce and were badly needed for capital formation. Innumerable delicate administrative problems had to be tackled while the administrative structure was undergoing changes because of Independence. The process of transfer itself was a heavy burden on the overworked transport system; everything from foot-travel to the aeroplane was used. As the Moslems who left India had specialized in a number of vocations, there was a gap in the occupational structure. Those who left the country were cultivators and artisans; they were specialized in weaving, leather-working, tailoring, trade in provisions, meat and fish, etc. They formed a large part of the semi-skilled labour in the woollen industry, hosiery, engineering, metalworks and jute textiles, and on railways. Their migration caused an acute shortage of skilled artisans. On the other hand, most of the immigrants who came from Pakistan had no aptitude for these vocations. As will be seen later, a number of them belonged to the trading and professional classes and they could not pursue their original vocations in the areas to which they had migrated because these occupations were already overcrowded. The immigrants were mostly accustomed to intellectual work and could not adapt themselves easily to manual labour in India. Most of the agricultural immigrants had been large landowners in West Pakistan; they had been pioneers of agricultural development and had been accustomed to cultivating superior lands, well equipped with irrigation services. When they came to India they had to be satisfied with inferior land, and even this was not plentiful. Such were the main features of migration in the west.

Most of the immigrants from East Pakistan belonged to trading and professional classes, and many of them concentrated in the city of Calcutta and the surrounding urban areas. An interesting fact about the displacement is that it intensified the rural character of Pakistan and increased the degree of urbanization in India. This is because the Hindus and the Sikhs had mostly stayed in the urban areas before the transfer. As we shall see later, a sudden rise in the degree of urbanization may not be beneficial to an economy which is not growing at a fast rate.

1953 ; Government of India, Annual Reports of the Ministry of Rehabilitation ; Census of India, Paper No. 4, 'Displaced Persons', 1951 Census ; P. Pant, 'Survey of Faridabad Township', National Sample Survey No. 6, 1954 ; D. Y. Lakdawala, 'An Enquiry into the Conditions of the Refugees in Bombay City', *Journal of the University of Bombay*, 1951–52, vol. lviii, 1948, and 'Resettlement and Rehabilitation of Displaced Personsi n Pakistan', *International Labour Review*, vol. lxviii, 1952.

III. A STATISTICAL PICTURE OF THE DISPLACEMENT

It may be interesting to give a brief idea of the statistical features of the Great Displacement in so far as it affected India. The information has been compiled from several official sources. The total number of displaced persons in India enumerated in the 1951 census was 7·3 million, of whom 3·9 million were males and 3·4 million females. Since 1951 there has been some spasmodic immigration from East Pakistan, estimated by the Ministry of Rehabilitation, Government of India, at 0·8 million to the end of March 1955. Thus the total number of displaced persons amounts to 8 million, that from West Pakistan being 4·7 million, and that from East Pakistan 3·3 million, or about 2·2 per cent of the total population of the country. In certain States like Delhi and the Punjab they constitute respectively about 40 per cent and 23 per cent of the total population; in West Bengal the proportion is 10 per cent. Displaced persons from West Pakistan have been concentrated in North-West India except for those from Sind in Bombay; whereas the displaced persons from East Pakistan have gone mostly to West Bengal. According to the census of 1951, out of a total of 4·7 million displaced persons from West Pakistan about 3 million, or roughly two-thirds, had to be transported during the three months August to October 1947. Of the displaced persons from East Pakistan, roughly half or 1·3 million persons out of a total of 2·5 million (enumerated at the time of the census) came during 1950. Out of the total of 7·3 million, 3·6 million were counted in North-West India, 2·6 million in East India, a little less than 0·5 million in North India, 0·4 million in West India, and 0·2 million in Central India. The number in South India is hardly 17,000.

Of the 7·2 million of the displaced persons for whom figures of rural-urban distributions are available, 3·3 million are in villages and 3·9 million in towns. The rural-urban ratio for the economy is 83 : 17, whereas among the displaced population it works out at 46 : 54. There are 871 females per 1000 males among the displaced persons in India, as against 946 per 1000 for the general population in India. The figure is 872 among arrivals from West Pakistan; this is distinctly higher than the corresponding number (833) among the Hindus and Sikhs of the Punjab and Sind in 1941. Among the arrivals from East Pakistan the females number 871 per 1000 males, which is lower than the corresponding 1941 figure (930) for that part of Bengal which is now in East Pakistan. A higher proportion of females among the migrants from West Pakistan may perhaps be explained by the fact that during the Second World War this area, which normally contributed substantially to military personnel, must have suffered heavy casualties. In Eastern India there is a higher ratio of males among the migrants from East Pakistan, probably because migration here appears to have been a result of immediate

TABLE I

ANALYSIS OF DISPLACED PERSONS BY OCCUPATION, 1951

Occupation	General Population (exclusive of Displaced Persons)	Displaced Persons
Agricultural Class	%	%
1. Cultivators of land wholly or mainly owned and their dependants	47·7	5·6
2. Cultivators of land wholly or mainly unowned and their dependants	8·7	18·0
3. Cultivating labourers and their dependants	12·7	4·3
4. Non-cultivating owners of land, agricultural rent receivers, and their dependants	1·6	0·9
	70·7	28·8
Non-Agricultural Classes		
Persons (including dependants) who derive their principal means of livelihood from :		
5. Production other than cultivation	10·5	11·8
6. Commerce	5·6	24·0
7. Transport	1·6	4·3
8. Other services and miscellaneous sources	11·6	31·1
	29·3	71·2

Source : *Census of India, 1951*, Paper No. 41.

political and other disturbances and may perhaps be considered to some extent as short-term in character. The age structure of the displaced persons is practically the same as that of the general population, except that there are fewer infants and young children among displaced persons (children under 4 years number 13·5 per cent in the general population and 6·4 per cent among the displaced persons). Out of every 1000 persons in the general population (excluding

286

displaced persons) 441 are unmarried, 470 are married, and 89 are widowed or divorced. Among the displaced persons, for every 1000 persons 451 are unmarried, 469 are married, and 60 are widowed or divorced. The proportion of unmarried is higher among the displaced persons, particularly in Bombay.

Table I on page 286 provides interesting information on the occupational structure of the general population (excluding displaced persons) and that of the displaced persons.

It is easily seen that the majority of the displaced persons belong to the non-agricultural classes whose livelihood depends largely upon tertiary activities. The percentage of literates among displaced persons is 37·3 (males 46 per cent and females 27 per cent), whereas of the total population exclusive of displaced persons the percentage is 16 (males 24 per cent and females 8 per cent).

IV. THE ECONOMIC FEATURES OF THE IMMIGRATION

From the above it is clear that most of the immigrants have tended to settle in areas similar to the environment to which they were accustomed, and in places as near as possible to the points of immigration. This explains why very few have gone to Southern India. As the urban element among the displaced persons was high the movement was naturally towards the cities ; this was also influenced by the superior economic opportunities there. Since the degree of literacy is high among the displaced persons as compared with the population as a whole, the problem of adjustment would tend to be more difficult. The differences between the economic and social status of the immigrants and that of the rest of the population in the areas in which they are now situated, as well as the contrast with their position before transfer, have caused much bitterness and resentment. The fact that the proportion of the unmarried among the displaced persons tends to be higher, particularly among those from Sind, shows that there must have been serious obstacles to marriage, perhaps because of the system of dowry. No wonder that a good many of the young immigrants, both men and women, have been forced to seek jobs at a tender age.

V. THE ROLE OF THE STATE IN REHABILITATION

It is creditable that the Government of India took upon itself the main burden of relief and rehabilitation. The incoming refugees who arrived in such large numbers and at such short notice had to be furnished with consumption goods and accommodation. There was considerable overcrowding, and medical and sanitation facilities had to be provided. The displaced persons had to be assisted with doles. Gradually the problem shifted to that of rehabilitation. This involved the granting of loans and credits direct by the Governments as well as through the Rehabilitation Finance Corporation. Plans had to be devised for starting new constructional activities so that appropriate accommodation might be supplied on a permanent basis. Children and young men were given facilities for education through fee concessions and scholarships, and some new educational institutions had to be opened. The Government also set up a number of training centres and promoted new industrial establishments and trading estates. Displaced persons were given priority in public employment. The governmental authorities concentrated on speeding up economic development in the border States like the East Punjab and Pepsu in North-west India and West Bengal and Assam in East India; for example, a number of electricity and irrigation projects have been undertaken. In some of the States the displaced persons were provided with lands reclaimed through governmental action. Compensation to the displaced persons was sometimes arranged by taking into account the pool of evacuee property left by the Moslems who went back to Pakistan, the amount being supplemented by contributions from the Government. The authorities also settled a large number of displaced persons in new towns in which assistance was furnished in the form of new economic activities.

By the end of 1954–55 the Central Government had spent a sum of Rs 2237 million in the relief and rehabilitation of displaced persons. If we include the provision of Rs 653 million for 1955–56, the total expenditure on displaced persons by the end of March 1956 would have been a little less than Rs 3000 million. About 0·9 million have been settled on the land (of this, 0·56 million are from West Pakistan and 0·35 million are from East Pakistan). Rs 205 million have been advanced as rural loans to different State Governments for disbursement to displaced persons. By March 1955 about 200,000 houses had been built or were under construction for displaced persons from West Pakistan, and about 303,000 for displaced persons from East Pakistan. About 223,000 had found work through employment exchanges (181,000 from West Pakistan and 42,000 from East Pakistan); about 103,000 had received or were receiving technical and vocational training. About 67,000 business or industrial premises had been made available to immigrants from West Pakistan, 38,000 of which were new shops and stalls. The State Governments had been advanced a loan of Rs 241 million by the Central Government for the purpose of rehabilitation. A special body created for the purpose, called the Rehabilitation Finance Administration, had sanctioned loans to the extent of Rs 128 million by the end of March 1955, the total number of people benefiting being about 17,000. Besides the above, 177,000 displaced persons were receiving relief from the Government by the end of March 1955.

To displaced persons from West Pakistan 199,000 acres of land had been allotted as compensation together with Rs 110 million in cash. It was estimated that the total value of the evacuee property left behind by the displaced persons in the areas from which they migrated was approximately Rs 5000 million, and the assessed area of land involved was 0·9 million acres. This does not give the complete picture because it covers only the verified claims by displaced persons on the properties that were left behind. Surveys of the income of displaced persons show that their economic status has deteriorated considerably.

VI. THE WELFARE IMPLICATIONS OF THE DISPLACEMENTS

The economic impact of the displacement cannot be fully appreciated if we concentrate on the number of net immigrants. As noted earlier, those who came differed from those who went out, and this involved a number of short-term and long-term problems. The country finds too many in certain jobs and too few in others; and the problem of adjustment looms large from the point of view of the individual as well as the community.

The welfare implications of a displacement involving a change in occupational structure as well as in income and social status can be considered in terms of the concept of producer's surplus. Let us assume that the immigrants into India have been to some extent forced to adjust themselves to the new environment. There are three classes of producers. First there is the negligible group which has become relatively better off as a result of the transfer. As the economy was already producing to the limits of capacity, some of the local producers would have reaped windfall gains. The second class consists of those immigrant producers who are just as well off as before, and these too can be neglected. The third class, *i.e.* those who are worse off in the process, is the most important. It includes a large number of immigrant traders, business men, lawyers, doctors, teachers, clerks, landlords, and agricultural labourers. To make good their loss, one would have to give them the equivalent of the employment, income, and status which they enjoyed before the displacement. Since there was previously a certain balance between the different occupations, the immigrants who overcrowded into certain types of occupations naturally had to accept lower earnings. They are difficult to absorb because the native producers resent the overcrowding. Thus, on the whole, there is a net loss in welfare. As the capital assets left in Pakistan by those who came to India were more valuable than what was left in India by emigrants to Pakistan, it may be said that on balance the mass migration was detrimental to the welfare of India.

Some idea of the implications of displacement may be obtained by considering the rural settlement in East Punjab. It was found that the land vacated in East Punjab totalled 5 million acres, whereas the corresponding total in West Punjab was 6·7 million acres. Excluding uncultivated land, about 4 million acres were available for resettlement and redistribution among the immigrants. Perennial irrigation was less prevalent in these areas than in West Punjab. The land was therefore smaller in area and inferior in quality. Schemes of proportionate reduction in holdings became necessary, ingenious calculations of the value of the different types of land were made, and a 'standard acre' was worked out. A policy of graded cut was applied, and some type of resettlement was accomplished. The outcome was not as satisfactory as could be desired, because nearly all the displaced persons, particularly agricultural labourers, were worse off than they had been when they were living in West Punjab.

VII. IMMIGRATION AND CAPITAL FORMATION

What were the effects of the Great Displacement on aggregate output, employment, and capital formation ? Whether this immigration, on balance, increased or lowered the rate of growth of the economy is a crucial issue. As noted earlier, the displacement distorted the occupational structure of the economy, and in a number of fields output declined. The fall in earnings in overcrowded occupations had some effect on the rate of capital formation ; the contribution to savings from distribution, trading, and services would have been larger had not the average level of earnings been brought down by keener competition. Secondly, the displacement involved large-scale expenditure on relief and rehabilitation by governmental authorities, and most of this was avoidable expenditure which could otherwise have contributed to the building up of the economy. Thirdly, as the displacement involved no substantial transfer of real capital and other fixed resources, the effects on the economy were bound to be adverse. The displaced persons, particularly from Sind, could transfer a large part of their movable properties. This implied an increase in the supply of money. The inflow of money, unaccompanied by real assets, would have a tendency to push up the price level.

VIII. CONTRIBUTION TO INFLATIONARY PRESSURE

If the economy could safely take in a certain degree of deficit financing, the net inflow of currency might perhaps lead to a larger volume of employment and, possibly, a higher rate of capital formation. But the Indian economy, at the time of the displacement, had very little excess productive capacity. In fact, most of the plant and fixed equipment in the different factories had been over-utilized during the war and badly needed renewal and replacement. In agriculture there was little margin of immediately utilizable land; and the level of agricultural output could not be increased. Moreover there was considerable inflationary pressure in the economy, partly because of a pent-up demand for consumption goods, short-falls in total output, and deficit financing by the Government. Partition coincided with the country's Independence and, as decisions were being taken about the respective sphere of public and private enterprise, investment was handicapped by uncertainty. Any cash brought by displaced persons would tend to promote inflation; their immediate expenditure was mainly on consumption goods, buildings, estates, and shop sites.

It is difficult for those who have been accustomed to a high standard of living to accept a sharp reduction in it when their incomes go down; in such circumstances dis-saving is inevitable. The additional expenditure by the displaced persons would not have added much to inflationary pressure if they had been able to bring with them adequate supplies of co-operating factors. We have already noted that most of the immigrants had enjoyed a higher social status before displacement, while the emigrants from India were, on the whole, poorer. The transfer of population involved some inflow of liquid resources; the burden was mainly felt in the States in which the displaced persons were concentrated, particularly in cities like Delhi, Calcutta, and Bombay.

IX. IMMIGRATION AND URBANIZATION

An important effect of the Great Displacement was the increase in the degree of urbanization. When this happens as a result of the growth of industrialization, it is a welcome feature; but it is not necessarily a blessing when not accompanied by an increase in economic activity. The balance of the economy is such that, given the extent of industrialization and pattern of production of goods and services, a certain number of persons can be maintained in the cities. A sudden addition to the population of towns calls for an immediate increase in the supply of social capital such as public utility services, sanitation, and health facilities. As many of the displaced persons wished to be employed in trading and distribution services, and as the necessary increase in the level of activity had not taken place, the overcrowding resulted in a marked reduction in earnings, which created bitterness among those already in these occupations. The flow of goods to the cities was inadequate, and so the prices of a number of consumption goods rose sharply. Housing accommodation was very scarce, and the establishment of new factories was hindered by inadequate supplies of electricity and technical skill. The whole process entailed a number of frictions between the local inhabitants and the immigrants.

X. THE NEW TOWNSHIPS

The Government sought a way out by spending lavishly on the development of training centres in order to bring about vocational readjustments. The training and education of displaced persons were heavily subsidized, and loans were given to those wishing to embark on new industrial activities. The most ambitious step which the Government took was to set up a number of townships to provide employment; some of them were started through the initiative of the displaced persons themselves. While the townships were being built, there was plenty of employment; but once they were constructed, difficulties arose. The fact that they were planned to provide a variety of jobs did not ensure full employment. Townships by themselves do not produce all that they consume; they have to depend for their food, raw materials, and investment goods on the outside world. Unless these new centres could be merged into the general pattern of growth in the economy, the experiment could not be successful. In a rapidly developing economy, adjustments would be easy to bring about, but experience in India has been quite different. The factories in the new townships were kept going for some time through purchases of goods by the State and co-operative organizations, but this could not go on indefinitely. A number of surveys have shown that, as soon as the period of construction had come to an end and outside assistance ceased, a serious problem of unemployment appeared.[1] The problem of rehabilitation points to the need to bring about a more rapid rate of economic development.

XI. THE PROBLEM OF ECONOMIC AND SOCIAL MOBILITY

Part of the solution depends on increasing the degree of mobility of the displaced persons themselves. With the completion of the major irrigation projects in various parts of India, it should be possible to settle in these areas some of the immigrants who are now subsisting on very low incomes. A readjustment on the part of the State as well as in the mental attitudes of the displaced persons is necessary for the success of any policy of resettlement. The aim should be to distribute the displaced persons over different regions of the economy instead of permitting concentration in a few areas only. There are a number of obstacles to economic and social mobility, *e.g.* differences of language, customs, conventions, social status, and way of life. Since the displaced persons form only about 2 per cent of the population of the country as a whole, it should have been possible to spread them more evenly over the economy.

XII. CONCLUSION

The chief economic feature of the displacement is the nature of the difficulties that an underdeveloped economy with a low rate of growth has to face when it has to adapt itself suddenly to a higher degree of urbanization and relatively more employment in the tertiary sector. From this we may draw a moral. Many Indians now living abroad are members of the business and professional classes, and if a number of these people were to return to India they would create a problem similar to the Great Displacement. Since such immigration cannot be ruled out, the experiments in the

---

[1] Mr. Pant's survey of the Faridabad Township reveals that during the period March–April, 1954, nearly 15 per cent of the migrant population had been living on doles ; about 5 per cent of the population were wholly unemployed.

settlement of the displaced persons provide a significant lesson. This paper perhaps sounds a note of pessimism. Fortunately, however, planned economic development is now being undertaken in India. Following on the First Five-Year Plan, it is hoped that the Second Five-Year Plan will bring about an appreciable rise in the rate of economic growth; it is in this context that the prospects for a permanent resettlement of the displaced persons appear to be bright. Every displaced person is not a net burden on the community. Once the rate of growth has been increased, the business and entre- preneurial talent possessed by a number of displaced persons will be a strong asset to the community. We can thus say that some of the growing points in the economy have been strengthened by the immigration, and the extent to which the economy can utilize these talents will depend upon the possibility of creating conditions under which a higher rate of economic growth is possible. No such state- ment can be made about the problem of assimilation in the regions where the new-comers are located. This calls for major sociological changes. In view of the impoverishment which many displaced persons have had to endure, and the social difficulties of adjustment in a strange environment, assimilation is bound to be a slow and difficult process.

PART VI

SOCIAL ASPECTS

Chapter 21

PSYCHO-SOCIAL ASPECTS OF MIGRATION

BY

ALFRED SAUVY

Paris

IMMIGRATION, by bringing into contact two populations previously apart, causes the deepest perturbations and creates serious social and political obstacles which hamper international mobility. This analysis is divided into two parts:

1. Fears caused in a receiving country by the prospective immigration of aliens;
2. Adaptation and assimilation of immigrants to their new surroundings.

I. FEARS CAUSED BY IMMIGRATION

Immigration gives rise to feelings of two kinds: those caused by immigration as such and those caused by the immigrants considered as persons or groups of persons.

Discrimination

Discriminatory attitudes against certain peoples are found in every country. Such attitudes spring either from purely racial or physiological considerations such as the colour of the skin or hair or from considerations based on customs, habits, and education. Generally speaking, populations most distant from one another fear each other most (though exceptions might be mentioned and political or religious affinities also play an important part).

As these discriminatory phenomena are fairly well known and have often been described, we shall leave them aside and consider the fears caused by alien immigration as such, even when the newcomers are fairly akin to the receiving population, for instance Italians in France, or English people in the United States.

As the analysis is based mainly on experience recorded in France, its application to other countries might require some amendment.

Self-interest and Xenophobia

Sometimes foreign workers are welcomed because they happen to fill a gap, for example, mine-workers in France after the First World War, but such circumstances are exceptional. As Tucker pointed out as early as 1780, such 'gaps' are seldom permanent in any community; the arrival of skilled aliens usually disturbs the social machinery. When the receiving population is intolerant or indifferent, the phrase 'arrival of foreigners' is always associated with social trouble, so that the attitude of the nationals tends to be unsympathetic; foreigners bring about changes which may be either favourable or unfavourable, but people pay more attention to the latter. They feel — and reason has nothing to do with it — that the aliens are going to 'take' something from the community. If, for instance, there is a housing shortage the unavoidable impression is that aliens will take the place of nationals.

Thus not only will each organized group be against immigration but the whole population will tend to adopt a similar attitude. Logically, workers in one occupation should be in favour of immigration into other trades, for their interest lies in increasing the number of consumers; but their point of view does not leave room for such reasoning. In 1945 investigations which took place in France showed that in all occupations there was a large majority against any kind of immigration: 89 per cent in the professions, 79 per cent in the iron and steel industry, and 68 per cent in the building industry. At that time the possibility of unemployment within the next five years did not affect public opinion, as the replies to this question were 65 per cent 'No', 24 per cent 'Yes', and 11 per cent 'uncertain'.

Xenophobia is keener the less people are concerned with development; there is a widespread belief that the number of jobs is limited and that employment is a sort of common property to be shared out. The irrational nature of such an attitude is shown by the change in reply when the wording of a question is altered. In 1949, in a public opinion poll in France, the following question was asked: 'Generally speaking, are you in favour of a number of foreigners being settled in France?' In a second *questionnaire* identical with the first, the word 'settled' was replaced by the weaker word 'admitted'. In the first case 67 per cent were against immigration and in the second 59 per cent; out of 41 not opposing, 8 had changed their attitude as a result of this change of wording.

Pure xenophobia is mainly a phenomenon of collective psychology. The word 'foreigners' tends to excite more opposition than 'a foreigner', as the former is associated with an idea of force or even invasion. The departure of nationals or even of foreigners previously settled does not necessarily create the reverse impression, *i.e.* that the community's wealth can henceforward be shared between a smaller number of persons : on the contrary, there is the feeling that men belong to the community, such feeling being naturally stronger in dictatorial countries. Thus the Soviet Union tries, sometimes violently, to reunite all its nationals inside its borders, even claiming refugees from other countries ; but it does not admit any real foreign immigration.

II. ASSIMILATION OR ADAPTATION OF MIGRANTS

Assimilation is achieved when a former immigrant or his descendants can no longer be distinguished from nationals and are no longer conscious of their original characteristics. It is necessary to draw a clear distinction between the *individual* and the *group*.

The Individual in His New Surroundings

Studies carried out during the last few years and investigations made in several countries have clearly shown the various stages in the assimilation of individuals.

The three main stages can be defined as follows :

Settlement, Adaptation, and Assimilation

(1) *Settlement* is completed when an individual has adopted habits and obtained permanent accommodation and employment or, at least, permanent employment opportunities. His living is then secured. This first stage, a vital one, can be reduced to a minimum where jobs and housing are provided for the immigrants in advance. Only material needs, however, are met in this way.

(2) *Adaptation* to surroundings has a physical as well as a cultural aspect. The individual has to get used to the climate ; he has to learn how to dress, how to keep warm, how to adapt himself to varying conditions, by following the example set by nationals. In order to become adapted to new social surroundings it is necessary to know the language ; it takes several months, at least, before an immigrant is able to express himself in the language of his new country. An effort is involved, and he may be hampered by a feeling of pride and timidity or discouraged by the gibes and smiles of the nationals. Nowadays individuals seldom have to change their

religion; but when it is different from that of the receiving country, they find it more difficult to adapt themselves and the Church does not try to make it easier.

It is sometimes hard to become accustomed to new ways of cooking. It is reported that Italians in New York who, after several generations, speak English only and have adopted most American habits, nevertheless keep their ancestors' way of cooking. Other aspects of social life must also be mentioned, for example, entertainment (sports, films, concerts, etc.) and societies (trade unions, orchestras, sports clubs) create ties which can develop a feeling of pride and self-confidence.

Adaptation can be achieved by partly re-creating the original surroundings. A foreigner has found friends, relatives, or they have sent for him; he goes to coffee-houses or joins associations where he meets his fellow-countrymen. Sometimes whole villages have been transferred, complete with priests and schoolmasters; in such cases the cultural surroundings remain unchanged and we have to deal with groups rather than individuals. In this way things are made easier for the new-comer, but it is prejudicial to the following stage, which is assimilation.

(3) *Assimilation* cannot be attained in the course of the first generation unless the immigrant was very young when he first entered the country. The attitude and behaviour of an immigrant are influenced by the attitude of nationals towards him. Accent and pronunciation, certain details of his dress and, in a village, the well-known origin of a foreigner, are sufficient reasons for nationals to keep away from him.

Naturalization is merely a legal act which is not necessarily accompanied by assimilation. However, it is sometimes the acknowledgment of an advanced stage of assimilation and it can put an end to the inferiority complex from which the immigrant may have suffered since his arrival.

The main factors of assimilation are the *dispersion of immigrants*, *schools*, and *mixed marriages*. Schools must of course be national and include only a small proportion of foreign children of the same origin. Children of mixed marriages are easily assimilated even when their parents are both foreigners but of different nationalities.

Groups : Coexistence of Two Populations

When immigration is carried out by groups of families with their own leaders, we then have an example of a population brought into contact with another population; it is a case of coexistence of two populations. Even more than in the case of individuals, the question of reciprocal relationship arises. Segregation may become more or less permanent, through the fault either of the immigrants themselves or of the native inhabitants who, owing to their unsympathetic attitude, may compel the members of the immigrant group to live among themselves. Between two populations 'a neighbourhood arrangement' is achieved when coexistence goes on without too serious conflicts, such as, *e.g.* Swiss people speaking different languages, Jews, Arabs, and Christians in the Middle East, and Chinese and Malayans in Malaya. Assimilation may be indefinitely delayed even when no obstacle lies in its way, but usually the line of demarcation between the group of immigrants and the native population is not so sharply defined.

'Assimilation' does not mean that the children of immigrants become identical with nationals. The national population itself is not homogeneous, and changes may take place in the old population, as assimilation can be reciprocal. In order to avoid any possible misunderstanding, the word 'amalgamation' should be used.

Let us deal first with physical characteristics. If we consider the case of a white population receiving black immigrants (or the reverse), assimilation does not mean that the population will finally be white, not even that the population will finally have a definite complexion. It means that, between a pure white man and a pure negro, there will be a whole colour scale and graduated shades, in such a way that no clear line of demarcation could be drawn. The physical features of the new population will no longer be so well defined, but a sort of amalgamation will have taken place. The physical differences between populations (complexion, height, etc.) are apparent characteristics due to the diversity of genes, so that mixed marriages give intermediate characters without discontinuity. The problem would be different if, for instance, men could recognize one another by their outside aspect and keep away from one another, according to their blood group.

When we come to cultural characteristics, intelligence and natural abilities do not come into question; the scale is so large that a great deal of overlapping is bound to occur. On the other hand, conventional characteristics may be more definite, particularly with language and religion.

An immigrant population, even a minority, may impose its language, or at least obliges the native population to modify its own language (for instance, the Normans in England); but nowadays the immigrant population usually adopts the language of the receiving country. In such circumstances there is no new language or bilingualism ; as long as the immigrants retain their original language there is no real assimilation.

As people are more tolerant to-day than they were in the past, the immigrant population can retain its religion. However, if religion does not play an important part in social life and chiefly, or if between extremes there is a whole range of non-believers or indifferent people, there is a sort of amalgamation, even when wide differences still exist. What is essential is that the border-line is actually altered.

General Pattern

We can now summarize the various possibilities in the following chart:

ARRIVAL IN THE TERRITORY

Individual adaptation to the new surroundings		Individual adaptation through reconstitution of the original surroundings		Non-adaptation	
Assimilation	Non-assimilation	Coexistence of two populations	Overall assimilation	Returnees	Permanent conflict

This chart is applicable only to the first generation.

Final Result

When assimilation is attained, the resulting population may differ from the original one. We know very little about this question. Theoretically it is almost impossible to solve. If we proceed empirically, we meet with considerable difficulties in view of the number of factors which play a part in national evolution and the diversity of historical situations. But the consequences should be noted. Confronted with an immigration of individuals who become assimilated, some people express their concern and even speak of degeneration. Whether justified or not, this state of mind may give rise to feelings and attitudes hostile to assimilation, and for this reason it finds its place in this study.

Chapter 22

SOCIAL PROBLEMS OF ABSORPTION SINCE 1945

BY

WITOLD LANGROD
United Nations Secretariat, New York

THE object of this survey is to examine the experiences of representative immigration countries since the Second World War from the social rather than the economic point of view. The scarcity of reliable data on the magnitude, composition, and effects of migratory movements in a number of countries has made it impossible to deal with the subject with scientific precision. An attempt will therefore be made to provide an empirical background as a basis for discussion.

The following countries,[1] which received about 75 per cent of all permanent immigrants in the postwar period, have been selected as being representative: Argentina, Australia, Brazil, Canada, France, and the United States.[2] Seasonal and internal movements have been excluded.

I. POLICY AIMS AND PRINCIPLES

At the end of the Second World War the governments of a number of countries announced their return to active immigration policies. The stated or implied motives were economic, social, and political: e.g. increasing the size of the population in order to reinforce the economic and defence potential of the nation (Australia); reconstruction of war-devasted areas and industries, and filling gaps created by war casualties (France); enriching social and cultural life by bringing in elements considered beneficial to the nation (some

[1] Detailed statistical data on intercontinental immigration to selected countries during the period 1945–54 are set out in the Appendix on p. 312. Unfortunately there are no reliable comparable data on *net* immigration in various countries.

[2] The two other countries with important immigration movements—Israel, with roughly 800,000 (including 250,000 continental), and the United Kingdom with about 650,000 — have been left out. The unprecedented achievement of Israel in this field cannot, in view of its special political background, be taken as typical ; and in the United Kingdom the balance-sheet of migration for the postwar period suggests net losses (cf. Julius Isaac, *British Post-War Migration*, p. 205).

303

Latin-American countries); carrying out ideological commitments by resettling refugees and displaced persons, and helping to solve the difficulties of other countries by absorbing part of their 'surplus' populations (primarily the United States). The diversity of these aims and the contrasts between the populations of the receiving countries resulted in wide variations in the volume and timing of migration movements.

In the United States, while immigration continued to be regulated by the quota system, the Government took the major responsibility for helping to solve the problem of refugees and displaced persons in Europe. Legislation provided for the admission of about 155,000 quota immigrants per year,[1] 400,000 displaced persons,[2] and an additional contingent of 209,000 refugees. The policy was based on the assumption that the expanding economy of the country was able to absorb the newcomers without difficulty.[3] In order to ease the social integration of the immigrants, preference was given under the quota system to those national or ethnic groups whose members were expected to assimilate easily; but strict security regulations were applied.

In Canada the Government wanted immigration at a rate corresponding to the growth of industries based on natural resources; the numbers admitted were regulated according to the absorptive capacity of the labour market and the varying demands for skilled and semi-skilled workers, and there was a preference for people from English-speaking countries and from France.

The Government of Australia has pursued an ambitious programme, introduced in 1946, designed to strengthen national security and expand the economy. Australia is also one of the countries which has opened its doors liberally to refugees under the auspices of the International Refugee Organization. As in Canada, the inflow was adjusted to the estimated absorptive capacity of the economy. The movement of more than half of the migrants was facilitated by the assisted passage scheme. Although preference was given to people of British stock, 50 per cent of the immigrants were non-Britons of European descent.

The interest of Latin-American countries in organized immigration springs from the need to develop sparsely populated regions

---

[1] In particular the Immigration and Nationality Act of 1952, the Displaced Persons Act of 1948, and the Refugee Relief Act of 1953.

[2] The displaced persons falling within this category were charged to 50 per cent of the quotas of their nationalities for as many years ahead as would absorb the number.

[3] As an exception to the general rule, however, heads of families and single adults entering under the refugee scheme are required to have employment assured in the United States before immigration.

favourable to land settlement, to secure a balance between the industrial and agricultural populations, and to raise productivity and standards of living by admitting skilled immigrants. In Argentina, for instance, over one thousand million pesos were allotted under the five-year plan for the establishment of new land settlement centres, part of which was to be reserved for European settlers. Similar projects were put in operation in Brazil.

In France immigration policy was shaped on the one hand by long-term demographic needs and, on the other, by the current requirements of the labour market. The demographic needs were officially estimated at a minimum of 5 million immigrants.[1] The prevailing policy followed the pre-war pattern of limiting the inflow according to the current manpower requirements of industry and agriculture; entry regulations linked admission of foreign workers with the jobs available, proven in each case by a pre-established contract of work.

II. SOCIAL CONSEQUENCES OF IMMIGRATION

What have been the effects of postwar immigration on the economy and social structure of the receiving countries? A substantial difference may be noted between those countries which have on the whole achieved their aims and those in which the programme was only partially successful. Immigration made an important contribution to the economic growth of the receiving countries only when it was introduced (*e.g.* in Canada and Australia) as an integral part of the process of economic expansion. Where economic expansion was not already under way, the effects of immigration in this respect were negligible. Australian experience leads to conclusions which may be of general validity. 'The extent to which migration provides an expansionary force in an economy depends very much on the economic climate into which the migration is injected. In conditions of high employment or full employment or inflation, migration unquestionably provides an expansionary force. . . . The implication of the fear that migration may lead to unemployment is the fear that governments cannot prevent unemployment in the absence of migration anyway.'[2]

The effect of immigration on the demographic structure of

[1] A. Sauvy, 'Évaluation de besoins de l'immigration française', *Population*, January-March 1946, and 'Besoins et possibilités d'une immigration en France', *Population*, April-June 1950.
[2] P. H. Karmel, 'The Economic Effects of Immigration', in *Australia and the Migrant*, Australian Institute of Political Science, Sydney, 1953, p. 90.

various countries since the end of the war does not seem to have been substantial; this is true even for Australia,[1] which had the greatest influx of new-comers in relation to local population. Where the role of immigration was important was in contributing to the growth of the labour force. In the United States recent immigrants included a high proportion of people in their productive years, with an adequate level of education and skill;[2] in Canada, without immigration the labour force would hardly have increased at all.[3] Immigrant labour made an important contribution to industrial expansion, particularly in Australia.[4] In general, immigration countries found it difficult to obtain the necessary number of skilled industrial workers and farmers required for the development of their resources. Pre-emigration professional training, organized with good results in certain European countries, was therefore valuable; such training was sometimes organized in immigration countries, even for agricultural immigrants.[5]

As the assimilation of immigrants is a lengthy process, the assessment of which presents serious difficulties, no attempt will be made here to do justice to the results obtained in this field in postwar years. Experience shows that present-day problems of assimilation differ considerably from those brought about by mass immigration in the past. Fears expressed on many occasions that large-scale migration would inevitably create in the receiving country an alien community, living apart and unable to identify itself with the rest of the society, have not, on the whole, been substantiated. While assimilation may require more than one generation to be fully achieved, there is evidence that postwar immigrants to Australia, Canada, and the United States have settled more easily in their new environment than their predecessors did. There appear to be several reasons for this.

[1] W. D. Borrie, 'Australia's New Population Pattern' in *Australia and the Migrant*; and W. D. Borrie and K. Jupp, 'The Economic Demography of Immigration to Australia', Papers of the World Population Conference, Rome, 1954.

[2] George Minton, 'Integration of Displaced Persons into United States Economic Life', *Monthly Labor Review*, December 1952.

[3] D. Corbett, 'The Economic Objectives and Achievements of Immigration Policy in Canada since 1946,' Papers of the World Population Conference, Rome, 1954.

[4] More than 70 per cent of the technicians and labourers employed on the Snowy Mountains Hydro-Electric project were immigrants. Immigrant labour has also contributed to the development of the railway system and to the steel works of the Broken Hill Company. It has been estimated that of the Australian national income of £A3572 million for 1952–53 some £A322 million, or 9 per cent, resulted from the productive efforts of immigrants.

[5] In Argentina the Government, in co-operation with ICEM, established a pilot farm school where migrants are trained in Argentinian farming methods for about six months; at the end of this training they are allotted a piece of land in a land settlement centre, or are placed in agricultural employment.

In the first place, there has been a marked change in the character of the migrants. The majority of pre-war and earlier migrants were peasants and unskilled labourers, with a high proportion of unmarried males. Many intended to return to their homeland; they were willing to work for low wages and tended to concentrate in groups where they could follow their traditional ways of life. The assimilation of those who stayed permanently was slow, imperfect, and often spaced over several generations. In recent years two new factors have had a profound influence — the large-scale movements of refugees and the end of the emigration of peasants from Eastern Europe. The new migrants have included a high proportion of professionals, intellectuals, and white-collar workers, as well as of women and young children. Few planned to return to their native country; the vast majority intended to settle permanently in their adopted home and to make the best possible adjustment to the new environment.[1] They were better able than their predecessors to fit into the occupational structure of the new country; in particular, the immigrants of the professional class have on the whole made 'remarkable progress towards the goal of integration'.[2]

Secondly, the methods of selection used by the immigration countries should not be underestimated. In Australia and Canada preference was given to skilled or semi-skilled workers and precautions were taken to avoid flooding the labour market with wage-earners who could not be placed in productive employment without a longer period of training. A preponderance of males was avoided, and women were admitted equally with men; if possible, family groups rather than individuals were encouraged to migrate. The process of assimilation was seriously handicapped whenever (for instance in Argentina and, in the past, Australia) preference was given to workers without families.

A third factor (particularly in the United States and France) which appears to have eased the absorption of postwar new-comers has been the changing ethnic structure of the immigration countries. As the earlier ethnic groups became assimilated they lost many of their original characteristics and ceased to persevere as socially self-contained and alien bodies; increasingly they became 'cultural' minorities by their ethnic origin rather than by their ways of life. Instead of insulating the later immigrants from the rest of the

---

[1] Maurice R. Davie, *Refugees in America*, Report of the Committee for the Study of Recent Immigration from Europe. New York-London, Harper, 1947, pp. 37 ff.

[2] Donald Peterson Kent, *The Refugee Intellectual*, Columbia University Press, New York, 1953, p. 241.

society, they have provided a mechanism which protects the new-comers from the initial shock and paves the way for their gradual assimilation.

Long-term planning to ensure social conditions favouring assimilation is far more important than the characteristics of the immigrant stock. This is particularly evident in countries such as Canada or Australia which have recently adopted policies of large-scale immigration. They have to prepare for the absorption of the newcomers without the help of former ethnic minorities or without counting too much on the spontaneity of the assimilation process. The experience of these two countries shows clearly that even the most favourable conditions of employment are no guarantee that large numbers of immigrants can be successfully assimilated. The new-comers cannot settle happily in their jobs unless they are socially at ease; this is not so much a problem of individual life but of the development of new communities in which the migrants become firmly established through personal, family, and neighbourhood ties.

There are three elements to be considered in social planning for the orderly adjustment of immigrants to their new environment. First, the incipient immigrant communities have to be provided with adequate social services and amenities to prevent a lapse in their standard of living below the average in the country at large. Housing, education, and health services as well as other institutions of communal life may add much to the initial expense of immigration, but to provide enough of them at the right time is cheaper than the ultimate costs of maladjustment.

Secondly, it is desirable for the immigrants to participate actively in organizing their individual and collective life in new conditions. Keeping alive a part of their cultural tradition may be as important as their ability to develop new interests and aspirations and their willingness to adjust themselves to a strange environment. The immigrants, brought together by accident, may at first be just an amorphous social body, bound only by a common cultural pattern. They are more likely to feel at home in their adopted society if no attempt is made to impose on them a new pattern to the complete exclusion of the old cultural tradition.[1] This policy is now part of the programmes of Australia and Canada, and it has a long tradition in the United States. The policy of rather forceful assimilation is still being followed in some other countries, *e.g.* in Brazil.

Finally, an indispensable condition is that immigrants should

[1] *On putting Down Roots. The Integration of Migrants into the Life of their Countries of Resettlement*, International Conference of Organizations Interested in Migration, June 1954; see also Jean I. Craig, 'The Social Impact of New Australians', in *Australia and the Migrant*, pp. 66-7.

have equal status with other members of society. The experience of many countries has shown that measures which discriminate between citizens and aliens, and curtail the social and economic mobility of the immigrants, serve only to retard the process of adjustment.[1] The World Population Conference of 1954 drew attention to the fact that wherever the receiving country allows the migrant to be mobile and thus enables him to attain a status in line with his qualifications and past experience, the psychological stresses to which he is inevitably exposed are lessened.[2]

III. SOME PROBLEMS OF ORGANIZATION

The way in which policy has been carried out in certain countries has often resulted in keeping immigration at a low level even though it was considered economically and socially desirable. The complicated procedures of admission, the numerous documents required, their cost, the delays in approval by administrative authorities and the lack of uniformity in the requirements of various governments, have not only created hardship for the persons involved but have also seriously handicapped the immigration programmes.[3]

In many countries since the Second World War the rules governing the admission of aliens, *e.g.* about security or physical fitness, have been made more selective and are being more rigidly applied. In some countries migrant workers are admitted only if their jobs have been secured in advance (in France and, in varying degrees, in Australia and some Latin-American countries). Experience has shown that the long delays between the time that a specific vacancy arises and the time that it is actually filled by a foreigner reduce the volume of immigration, even when demographic necessity calls for mass immigration.[4] The example of countries like Canada demonstrates that the national labour market does not suffer if the categories of migrant workers are adjusted to its needs but no compulsory advance hiring for specific jobs takes place.[5]

[1] Cf. René Lautier, *Les Étrangers et les lois sociales en France*, Lyon, 1951.

[2] Cf. *International Migration with Special Attention to Areas of Immigration* (preliminary draft report submitted to the World Population Conference), Part III.

[3] United National Economic and Social Council, *Simplification of Formalities and Reduction of Costs for Migrants*, Report by the Secretary-General.

[4] Lannes, *L'Immigration en France depuis 1945*, Research Group for European Migration Problems, The Hague, 1953, p. 66.

[5] The following statement of the Canadian Minister of Citizenship and Immigration may be quoted : '. . . No policy of immigration can be operated on a stop and go basis. We cannot possibly develop that policy on a plan that calls for one specific immigrant for one specific opportunity. We must be prepared to work.' (Canada, House of Commons Debates, 4 July 1952, p. 4268.)

In some countries, particularly those which require the engagement of new-comers in advance, immigrants who have completed their first contract are not allowed to take another job without a governmental authorization, and the number of aliens employed must not exceed a certain proportion of the number of nationals in the same enterprise. Sometimes there are also rules about choice of residence by immigrants ; in Argentina they are not allowed to reside within a certain radius around the capital. Such regulations involve a vast and costly administrative machinery of licensing and enforcement. We do not know enough to draw conclusions about the success of these restrictions ; doubts have been expressed as to their effectiveness, particularly in preventing immigrants from adopting the habits of the local population, *e.g.* by moving from rural communities to the cities.[1]

Inter-war and postwar experience proves that immigration, particularly when it has to play a formative role in an underdeveloped country, does not achieve its objective, or does so at a disproportionate cost in time, effort, funds, and human suffering, if it is not an integral part of a development programme. The big repatriation movements from Argentina, Brazil, and Venezuela may be taken as characteristic. Migrants of to-day are more aware of their social and economic rights than their pre-war counterparts, and migration streams tend to dry up if the legitimate interests of migrants and their families are not sufficiently protected.[2]

In certain countries serious obstacles to a long-term programme seem to result from a lack of co-ordination between the activities of different governmental agencies concerned with various aspects of immigration. Moreover, the work of these agencies is not always properly supplemented by that of voluntary bodies. It is true that the action of non-governmental agencies in promoting the development of immigration policies and the welfare of immigrants has been extended in the United States, Canada, Australia, France, and some

[1] The following opinion on the suggestion that measures be taken in Australia to ensure that immigrants remain in rural areas may be noted : '. . . there is no good reason to believe that, even if we select our immigrants from the rural population of Europe, these same people will want to be rural dwellers here. . . . They will be increasingly subject to the influences which affect the Australian population as a whole, and which, up to the present, have encouraged the expansion of the metropolises to the detriment of the rural areas. It is important to keep out of our thinking any idea that immigrants can, or should, be manipulated any more readily or justifiably than Australians.'—Jean I. Craig, 'The Social Impact of New Australians', in *Australia and the Migrant.*

[2] 'The Italian is a free man with a home and country to return to, if his emigrant's status in a foreign country is unsatisfactory. And if he is really unhappy, not only will he break his contract and get home by hook or by crook, but he will tell others not to embark on that particular emigration.'—*Manchester Guardian,* 1 March 1951.

other countries;[1] but in several countries, particularly in Latin America, such agencies are scarce, their possibilities are limited, and their efforts fail to influence migratory movements.

Finally the co-operation of immigration countries with international organizations should be mentioned. During the inter-war period, the assistance given by inter-governmental agencies — in addition to protection of refugees — consisted mainly in the setting up and promoting of minimum standards to be applied in this field. War-time destruction, impoverishment, and the displacement of populations have heightened the need for a more comprehensive international programme. As a result of various inter-governmental conferences there is a concerted international programme[2] covering the following: research on migration in relation to population and social and economic factors; provision of information; technical assistance for the various stages of organization of migratory movements; protection of immigrants in their capacity as workers and as aliens; assistance to families of migrants; and social and cultural integration of immigrants. An entirely new type of international assistance is the provision of transportation for migrants.[3] It is true that this programme is still inadequate to deal with the complexities of the immigration problem, even given its present restricted scale. Nevertheless, it has not only facilitated immigration and contributed to the success of some movements, but has also paved the way for more comprehensive planning, which may be expected to influence the migratory movements of the future.

[1] An important beginning has been made for inter-agency planning through periodical sessions of the Conference of Non-Governmental Organizations Interested in Migration, sponsored by the United Nations and the International Labour Organization with the active co-operation of other intergovernmental organizations, particularly ICEM.

[2] International Labour Office : Report of the Preliminary Migration Conference, Geneva, April–May 1950 (CPM/1/45/1950) ; see also United Nations Programme of Concerted Practical Action in the Social Field of the United Nations and the Specialized Agencies, Geneva, 1953 (E/CN.5/291/Rev. 1), paragraphs 667-716.

[3] Provided by the International Refugee Organization, followed by ICEM ; from 1952 to 1954 the latter organization provided transportation for about 300,000 migrants.

APPENDIX

INTERCONTINENTAL IMMIGRATION, SELECTED COUNTRIES, SINGLE YEARS 1945 TO 1954

Country	Total	1945	1946	1947	1948	1949	1950	1951	1952	1953	1954
A. Immigration, mainly of aliens:											
Argentina †	742,259	989	4,422	38,632	119,201	149,764	134,933	106,499	76,506	49,567	61,746
Australia *	868,768	5,752	15,759	28,634	61,898	163,640	169,612	127,986	124,202	71,669	99,616
Brazil ‡	413,252	2,889	12,852	18,652	21,421	23,713	34,458	62,229	84,720	80,070	72,248
Canada †	1,027,243	11,793	57,071	51,161	114,387	86,370	65,535	185,675	154,055	158,216	142,980
Israel * ¶	547,520	12,398	20,525	19,049	106,567	167,586	112,073	70,897	16,742	7,517	14,116 ¶
New Zealand * §	131,581	3,011	5,960	7,812	9,550	14,386	14,372	20,563	22,725	18,922	14,240
S. Rhodesia † **	55,512	...	3,071	6,904	10,550	6,340	4,885	6,846	8,566	5,139	3,211 **
United States †	1,444,806	14,116	106,854	126,756	127,148	209,534	165,542	196,022	158,109	114,972	225,753
Union of South Africa ‡	153,212	2,100	9,074	25,307	32,532	13,352	11,787	14,257	17,108	14,438	13,257
Venezuela ||	150,000	...	...	...	...	...	...	...	...	...	...
B. Immigration mainly of nationals (return of former emigrants):											
Italy †	142,450	...	525	9,128	15,323	16,319	28,826	28,567	18,946	10,422	14,394
Netherlands *	334,133	...	79,183	28,966	25,847	22,841	60,870	35,715	24,202	25,239	31,270
Portugal †	42,613	1,704	5,367	7,963	10,235	8,508	3,784	1,423	1,047	1,209	1,373
Spain *	106,205	2,591	5,107	6,288	6,148	6,888	9,626	11,630	19,471	19,815	18,641
C. Immigration of nationals and aliens:											
United Kingdom *	668,760	...	67,051	62,780	73,746	64,792	71,932	76,295	82,072	77,764	92,328

* Nationals and aliens. † Nationals only. ‡ Aliens only. § Fiscal year ending 31 March of the following year.
|| Estimated. ¶ The figure for 1954 refers to both intercontinental and continental immigration to Israel.
** In 1954 ten months only.

Source : The data in this table have been taken from *A Survey of Intercontinental Migration in the Post-War Period* (Background Document prepared by the Population Division of the United Nations for the 1954 World Population Conference), Table III. Data for 1953 and 1954 have been added and, in the case of Argentina, data for 1947–52 were revised on the basis of recent information obtained from the International Labour Office.

Chapter 23

IMMIGRATION INTO ISRAEL

BY

R. BACHI

Hebrew University and Central Bureau of
Statistics, Jerusalem

I. JEWISH IMMIGRATION TO ISRAEL (1882–1954) [1]

(1) *Jewish Immigration to Israel as a Distinct Part of Modern Jewish Migratory Movements*

The destruction of Jerusalem by the Romans in the first century led to a gradual movement of the Jewish population of Palestine towards the countries of the Dispersion (Diaspora). Only a dwindling number of Jewish inhabitants remained in Palestine under the Romans, Byzantines, Arabs, Crusaders, Mamelukes, and Turks. This population was reinforced from time to time — throughout the Dark Ages and the modern era — by Jewish immigrants who, singly or in groups, returned under the impulse of Messianic hopes or in order to worship the God of their fathers in the Land of Israel and to be buried there. However, it seems that bad economic conditions, lack of personal security, poor health standards, re-emigration, and high mortality greatly reduced the demographic influence of these movements. By the middle of the nineteenth century only some 12,000 Jews were to be found in Palestine; and even during the second half of that century, after contacts with Europe had increased, the Jewish population of Palestine consisted of some 24,000 souls only (1882).

Since that year a continuous inflow has taken place. Over a period of approximately seventy years, $1\frac{1}{4}$ million immigrants have entered the country and built up to-day's Jewish population of Israel (1,526,000 at the end of 1954).

---

[1] In this paper the Jewish population of the former territory of Palestine, and of the present territory of the State of Israel, is often referred to in an abridged form as 'Jewish population of Israel'. The territory of the State of Israel includes about 77 per cent of that of Palestine under the Mandate. In Mandatory days the Jewish population of Palestine was concentrated almost solely in those areas which are included to-day in the State of Israel. Most of the data quoted and some of the graphs used in this paper are taken from the publications of the Central Bureau of Statistics of Israel.

This influx into Israel was a part of the huge migratory movement which has, in modern times, driven millions of Jews out of their traditional countries of residence, and it can best be interpreted within the framework of the changing distribution of the Jewish population throughout the world (I (2)). Immigration to Israel was also influenced by special factors which gave it the distinct features examined in I (3) to (7).

(2) *The Jewish Exodus from Former Countries of Residence and the Changing Size and Distribution of the Jewish Population throughout the World*

Although estimates of the total Jewish population throughout the world are to be regarded, at best, as rough guesses, there can be no doubt about its very remarkable growth during the nineteenth and the first part of the twentieth century. The estimates show an increase from some 2·5 million at the beginning of the nineteenth century to 6 million at about 1860, 10·5 million about 1900,[1] and 16·6 million on the eve of the Second World War.[2] The Nazi massacres reduced the number of Jews in the world by 5·8 million; in 1947 only some 11·3 million were left. To-day world Jewry is estimated at some 11·9 million.

This tremendous fluctuation in the size of the Jewish population was accompanied by a major change in its geographical distribution. In 1880 the overwhelming majority still lived in Eastern and Central Europe, especially the Russian, Austro-Hungarian, and German Empires. From that period onwards, 4½ million Jews emigrated overseas. They departed — before the First World War — mainly from anti-Semitic Russia, Romania, and Austrian Galicia. After the First World War the countries of exodus were mainly Poland and later, as a consequence of Nazi persecutions, many countries of continental Europe. This migratory stream was directed towards the United States, Argentine, Canada, Brazil, other American countries, and South Africa. The mass destruction of European Jewry and the emigration to Israel caused further changes in geographical distribution. To-day less than 25 per cent of Diaspora Jewry remain in Eastern and Central Europe; the majority of them (19·7 per cent) are living within the closed borders of the U.S.S.R., whilst the Polish, Hungarian, Romanian, German, and Austrian communities constitute less than 5 per cent. On the other hand,

---

[1] Ruppin, *Soziologie der Juden*, Berlin, Jüdischer Verlag, 1930.
[2] *American Jewish Yearbook, 1947–8*, Jewish Publication Society of America, Philadelphia.

the various American Jewish communities have increased from 3 per cent of the Diaspora in 1880 to over 57 per cent at the present time.

(3) *Size and Characteristics of Immigration to Palestine during the Final Turkish Period (1882–1914)*

Table I shows the size of Jewish immigration to Israel from 1882 to 1954, in absolute numbers as well as in proportion to (i) the Jewish population of the countries of origin (Diaspora Jewry) and (ii) to oversea Jewish migratory movements. Fig. 1 shows absolute data and rates of immigration from 1919 to 1954.

Fig. 1

IMMIGRATION TO PALESTINE AND ISRAEL, 1919–54

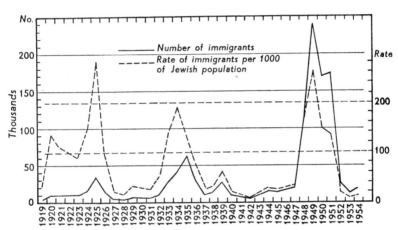

It will be noticed that in Turkish times Jewish penetration into Palestine was very slow; during the first phases of immigration only just over 1000 persons per annum entered the country. Immigration during 1904–14 was only about 3000 yearly, even after renewed persecutions in Russia gave new impetus to emigration and systematic colonization work was undertaken by the Zionist Organization. Only some 3 per cent of the Jews who left Europe in 1882–1914 went to Palestine, but this small group deserves mention because it laid the foundations of modern Israel. Many of these people were attracted towards Palestine not so much for reasons of economic advantage or personal safety: they came for ideological reasons to seek a solution to the collective Jewish problem. Three kinds of

Table I

Jewish Immigration to Israel, 1882–1954

Administration	Period	Absolute No. of Immigrants		No. of Jewish Immigrants to Israel for every 1000 Jews in the Diaspora	Average Annual No. of Jewish Immigrants to Israel for every 1000 Oversea Jewish Immigrants	Approximate Average Annual Immigration to Israel per 1000 of its Jewish Population
		During the whole Period (round figures)	Annual Average			
Final phase of Turkish régime	1882–1903	20,000–30,000	909–1,364	0·12	about 29	26(?)
	1904–14	35,000–40,000	3,182–3,636	0·27	about 29	42(?)
	1882–1914	55,000–70,000	1,667–2,121	0·17	about 29	31(?)
British Mandate	1919–31	117,000	8,984	0·58	150	86
	1932–39	225,000	28,098	1·81	462	95
	1940–14 May '48	111,000	13,170	0·99	372‡	24
	1919–14 May '48	453,000†	14,125	1·03	300‡	71
Israel's independence*	15 May 1948–51	687,000	189,186	18·09	788§	192
	1952–54	54,000	18,197	1·77		12

* Including tourists who were permitted to settle.
† Including all types of 'illegal immigrants'. The total immigration for the Mandatory period may be estimated as 485,000 (see Sikron report, etc., quoted below).
‡ See Sikron Report on Immigration to Israel, 1948–53 (Falk Project for Economic Research in Israel, in preparation). The total is for the period 1920–47.
§ 15 May 1948–52. See B. Gil, *The Immigration to Israel*, Jerusalem, Institute for Zionist Education, 1954 (in Hebrew).

ideological influence may be mentioned: religion, which influenced European immigrants and to a large extent Yemenite and other Oriental immigrants; nationalism, which acquired new character and strength with the development of the various movements which coalesced in the Zionist organization; socialistic aspirations, which were brought mainly by immigrants of Russian origin after 1904.

The implementation of national and socialist ideals was not easy; the new immigrants, even when inspired by them, had to fight a hard battle in a poor and backward country, with no help from a Turkish administration which was often unfriendly. Frustration and re-emigration during the period 1882–1914 were therefore not infrequent.

Nevertheless, on the eve of the First World War, some 85,000 Jews were established in Palestine. Apart from the 'holy cities' of Jerusalem, Tiberias, Safad, and Hebron, they had gained a strong foothold in the growing seaports of Jaffa (of which Tel-Aviv was then a small new suburb) and Haifa, and in 47 agricultural colonies.

(4) *Size and Characteristics of Immigration into Palestine during the British Mandate (1919–48)*

The First World War brought immigration to a standstill. Expulsion and emigration of citizens of the Entente Powers and of Zionists, and epidemics and shortages of food, brought about a reduction of the Jewish population. On 2 November 1917 the British Government expressed its sympathies with Zionist aspirations through the 'Balfour Declaration', and a period of recovery followed. Immigration under the British Mandate may be roughly divided into three epochs: (*a*) 1919–31; (*b*) 1932–39; (*c*) 1940–48.

(*a*) During 1919–31 the need for Jewish emigration from Eastern Europe, mainly from Poland, continued to be strong, while the restrictions on immigration in the United States of America and in other countries made it more difficult to find an outlet. During this period Palestine absorbed a considerable proportion of Jewish oversea migration (15 per cent). Immigration was not entirely free; limits were fixed periodically by the Mandatory Power according to the country's absorptive capacity. Immigration was thus on a selective basis and it included a large proportion of young pioneers. A big part was also played by the influx of persons with capital, mainly from Poland. This developed into a 'boom' in 1924–25, but the economic crisis which followed led to some re-emigration.

(*b*) The pressure in Europe increased when Nazi propaganda and persecutions endangered the political and economic rights and, ultimately, the very lives of Central-European Jews. Between 1932 and 1939 Palestine absorbed some 46 per cent of all Jewish oversea migration. The inflow from Central Europe brought to the country new skills and capital which contributed greatly to its technical and industrial development. A new 'boom' in immigration took place in 1934–36, and the Jewish population of Palestine reached 384,000 by the end of 1936.

(*c*) The increase of the Jewish population of Palestine by immigration was, however, slowed down by the Arab riots of 1936–39 and the consequent change of policy by the Mandatory Power. In 1939 the British Government imposed a 'political ceiling' for Jewish immigration into Palestine during the next five years and declared that 'after the period of five years no further Jewish immigration will be permitted unless the Arabs of Palestine are prepared to acquiesce in it'.[1]

In the meantime the mass murder of European Jews by the Nazis caused the pressure to leave Europe to become desperate. Severe restrictions on immigration to Palestine at that time and even after the end of the war — when masses of Jewish survivors were homeless — resulted in open and heated conflicts between the Jews of Palestine, the Arabs, and the Mandatory Power. By the end of 1947 the United Nations Organization acknowledged the principle that Palestine should be partitioned; Britain abandoned the Palestine Mandate, and by May 1948 the British administration was dissolved. The State of Israel was established in those sections of Palestine then in Jewish hands. The Arab States invaded the country and the resulting war ended with the Rhodes Armistice.

(5) *Size and Characteristics of Immigration to Israel after the Establishment of the State* (*1948–54*)

Immigration to Israel after the establishment of the State may be roughly divided into two periods : 15 May 1948 to 1951 ; 1952 to date.

15 May 1948 to 1951. The establishment of the State was immediately followed by the abolition of all restrictions on Jewish immigration, which was announced in the Declaration of Independence and afterwards found its full legal expression in the 'Law of the

[1] Command Paper No. 6019, May 1939.

Return' (1950). Immigration between 15 May 1948 and 31 December 1951 reached an annual average of nearly 190,000 persons and made Israel the country absorbing the largest number of Jewish oversea immigrants. For the first time in the history of Zionist immigration there was a steady decrease in the number of Diaspora Jews. The total number of immigrants who entered the country in this period was 687,000 and the Jewish population of Israel was thus more than doubled, rising from 650,000 in May 1948 to 1,404,000 in December 1951 (see Fig. 4).

Three factors were chiefly responsible for this large influx: (*a*) the evacuation of European 'displaced persons' camps; (*b*) organized immigration of what was left of Jewish communities in Eastern Europe and the Balkans; and (*c*) immigration from certain Asiatic and African communities, under the slogan of 'the In-gathering of the Exiles'.

From the Yemen, Iraq, and Libya Jewish communities were transplanted to Israel almost in their entirety, leaving behind only small remnants. Those movements comprised, respectively, 45,000, 123,000, and 31,000 persons during the period 1948–51. Immigration from Turkey (34,000), Morocco, Tunisia, and Algeria (45,000), Egypt, and Iran were also considerable.

Various factors influenced these migratory movements, which were organized mainly by the Jewish Agency. Immigration for religious and Zionist reasons had ancient traditions in some of the above-mentioned countries. Changing political conditions in countries with Arab majorities created a sense of insecurity among their Jewish communities; the intensification of the Arab national sentiment, the increasing tension between the Arabs and Israel, the outburst of anti-Jewish riots in some countries, and a surge of Jewish national feeling after the attainment of independence by Israel acted as further stimulants to immigration.

1952 to date. Immigration came almost to a standstill at the end of 1951; an appreciable amount of emigration began to develop (see I (7)), so that in 1953 the balance became negative.

This change was mainly due to: (1) the end of the evacuation of 'displaced persons' camps; (2) the ban on emigration by some Communist countries of Central and Eastern Europe; (3) the economic difficulties caused in Israel by the absorption of the mass immigration of 1948–51.[1]

---

[1] While the doors of Israel were kept open to any Jew willing to come there, the Jewish Agency decided at the end of 1951 that, apart from rescue immigration and the immigration of people with independent means, encouragement through economic help and free transport should be given only to immigrants selected according to age, health conditions, etc.

During 1954 and 1955 improved conditions in Israel and renewed pressure, mainly in French North Africa under the impact of the growing Arab national movement, have resulted again in a considerable influx of immigrants.

(6) Immigration to Israel from Various Countries of the World

In order to compare the years since independence with previous periods, we have tried to relate the size of immigration to Israel to that of the Jewish population of the various countries of origin. The analysis shows that five areas of the world saw a large part of their Jewish population transplanted to Israel in the years 1948–51, namely, the Balkans (75 per cent), Asia (66 per cent), Eastern Europe (43 per cent), Africa (15 per cent), and Central Europe (10 per cent).

On the other hand, very low proportions of Jewish population emigrating to Israel are found in the following three areas.

(a) The Soviet Union. Whereas immigration from Czarist Russia to Palestine was large, this movement was brought almost to a standstill when the Soviet Union closed its frontiers.

(b) Northern and Western Europe. Immigration to Palestine was continuous but very limited during the British Mandate, and increased only moderately just after Independence. A more detailed analysis shows considerable rates of immigration among the Jewish population of the Netherlands and Italy during and after Nazi persecution. Rates of immigration from France, the United Kingdom, and other European countries was very low between 1919 and 1954.

(c) Even lower were the immigration rates from the comparatively new Jewish communities of the Americas and Oceania. Of all the countries considered the United States had the lowest rates; during the whole period immigration from America to Israel may be roughly estimated as of about 50 per annum per 1,000,000 Jewish population, as compared with 2800 per annum per 1,000,000 Jewish population living in all other parts of the world.

(7) Emigration from Israel (1948–55)

Like previous immigration waves, the mass movement of 1948–1951 produced, with a certain time-lag, a wave of emigration which reached its peak in 1952 and afterwards receded. This interpretation is suggested by the following facts. About 71 per cent of all emigrants in 1948–52 were found to be new immigrants (who entered Israel after the establishment of the State) or their children; only 21 per cent were old residents and 8 per cent Israel-born. Emigration during 1948–54 amounted to about 8 per cent of the immigration during the same period.

II. THE INFLUENCE OF IMMIGRATION ON THE SIZE AND DISTRIBUTION OF THE POPULATION OF ISRAEL

(1) *Size of Population*

The Jewish population of Palestine and Israel under the impact of the first waves of immigration grew from 24,000 in 1882 to 85,000 in 1914 (see Fig. 2), and it decreased to 56,700 in 1916–18. With the

FIG. 2

JEWISH POPULATION OF ISRAEL, 1881–1954

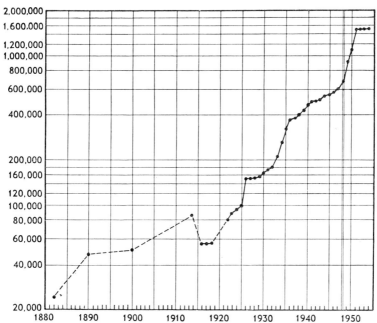

return of some of the emigrants and the beginning of the new immigration, it reached 83,790 at the time of the Census of 1922. During the period of the Mandate between 1922 and 15 May 1948 the population grew to 650,000, 71·2 per cent of the increase being due to the surplus of immigrants over emigrants, and 28·8 per cent to natural increase. Between 15 May 1948 and the end of 1951 it increased to 1,404,392, 88·3 per cent of the increase being derived from net migration and 11·7 per cent from natural increase. Between 1952 and 1954 the increase was slower (up to 1,526,000), of which only 16·6 per cent was due to net immigration and 83·4 per cent to excess of births over deaths.

(2) *Country of Birth*

In the first phase of the Mandate most of the immigrants (as during the Turkish period) came from Eastern Europe. During 1932–48 the influx from Central Europe also contributed a large part of the total. On the other hand, in recent years Asiatic and

FIG. 3

PERCENTAGE DISTRIBUTION OF JEWISH POPULATION OF ISRAEL
BY BIRTHPLACE, 1916/18–1953

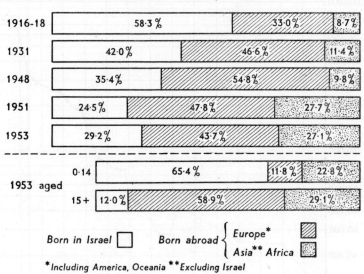

African migrants have been in the majority; they comprised 76 per cent of the total in 1952–54 as compared with 10 per cent in 1919–47.

The composition of the Jewish population of Israel changed accordingly (see Fig. 3). With the higher rate of inflow the proportion of persons born abroad went up from approximately 42 per cent of the Jewish population in 1916–18 [1] to 58 per cent in 1931, 64·6 per cent in 1948, 75·5 per cent at the end of 1951, and 70·8 per cent at the end of 1953. The proportion is even higher among adults, whilst the percentage of locally born is substantial only among juveniles and children (Fig. 3).

Persons born abroad come from many countries, a variety accentuated by every new wave of immigration. Before the First World War, among persons born abroad those from Czarist Russia were the largest group. In 1931 persons of Eastern European origin (including the Soviet Union) formed 72·6 per cent and Polish-born alone made up 35·4 per cent. By 1948 the proportion of Eastern Europeans had dropped to 58·6 per cent and by 1953 it was only 42·8 per cent. The proportion of Jews born in Central Europe, which increased from 3·1 per cent in 1931 to 18·5 per cent in 1948, has now fallen again to 10·9 per cent. On the other hand, the proportion of Jews born in Asia and Africa, which had been 19·6 per cent in 1931 and 15·1 per cent in 1948, rose to 36·9 per cent in 1951 and 38·3 per cent in 1953.

(3) *Sex*

As immigration to Israel is generally a permanent movement and not a temporary displacement for economic reasons, the surplus of males over females is, on the whole, rather small. Among 1,160,000 immigrants between 1919 and 1954 for whom data were available, males constituted 51·5 per cent. When economic or political conditions were very severe the percentage of males was higher (63·2 per cent in 1919–23, because of the return of Jewish inhabitants expelled during the First World War and pioneer immigration). This percentage remained rather high in 1924–31, and increased even more in the periods in which 'illegal immigration' was considerable (1939–45, 56·9 per cent; 1946–14 May 1948, 55·4 per cent). On the other hand, it was low during periods of larger and less restricted immigration (1932–38, 49·0 per cent; 1949–54, 50·1 per cent).

The distribution of the population by sex changed in a similar way but to a smaller extent. This was due also to the fact that emigration included a larger proportion of males, and this to some extent corrected the effects of the slight surplus of males among immigrants. The proportion of males among the population changed from 52·3 per cent in 1922 to 50·5 per cent in 1931, 50 per cent in 1936, 50·5 per cent in 1940, 51·8 per cent in November 1948, 50·9 per cent in 1951, and 50·8 per cent in 1954.

[1] Not including Jerusalem.

(4) *Age*

The age structure of the immigration and the population is shown in Table II. During the period of the Mandate immigrants included a very high proportion of persons in the younger productive age groups. Thus, for instance, 54·2 per cent of the immigrants in 1928–38 and 59·3 per cent in 1938–14 May 1948 were aged 15–34. This was due mainly to the selective character of immigration originating from populations in which the proportion of young age groups was far lower. In the periods in which 'pioneer' or 'illegal immigration' was predominant the proportion of youth was even larger, and it was lower in periods in which 'capitalists' and 'dependants' were a larger element.

On the whole, the productive age groups 15-64 constituted some four-fifths of total immigration during the period of the Mandate. Old people (65 and over) comprised only 3·9 per cent and 2·1 per cent, respectively, in 1928–38 and 1939–14 May 1948, whereas children made up only 18·5 and 16·1 per cent.

Immigration after the establishment of the State had a different age structure, for the following reasons. First, the age distribution of people of European origin was largely affected by that of the survivors of Nazi extermination ; thus, for instance, among European immigrants in 1948–49 it was found that persons aged 5-9 constituted only 3·2 per cent, those aged 10-14 4·5 per cent, those aged 15-19 6·2 per cent, as compared with 14·2 per cent aged 0-4 and 11·4 per cent aged 20-24, thus reflecting low birth-rates and high child mortality before and during the Second World War. Secondly the age distribution of people of African and Asiatic origin was much more normal — reflecting that of the transplanted oriental communities which are very fertile and have a high proportion of children.

The age structure of the Jewish population of Israel has changed a great deal with the passing of time, under the impact of the following factors. Birth-rates which were high in the first phases of the Mandatory period fell to a minimum at the beginning of the Second World War. The proportion of children in the population decreased accordingly ; but the 'baby boom', the stronger influence of oriental elements on the general birth-rate, and the immigration of a large number of children born in Asia and Africa reversed the trend.

As the large number of young immigrants who entered Palestine during the first phases of the Mandate grew older, and as the proportion of young age groups amongst the immigrants was reduced, the proportion in the age groups 15-24 and 25-34 — and, latterly,

TABLE II

AGE STRUCTURE OF IMMIGRATION AND POPULATION

	Percentage, aged			Total	Among those aged 15-64	
	0-14	14-64	65 and over		15-34	35-64
Jewish immigrants to Israel						
1928–38	18·5	77·6	3·9	100	54·2	23·4
1939–14 May 1948	16·1	81·8	2·1	100	59·3	22·5
15 May 1948–51	28·3	67·5	4·2	100	36·5	31·0
1952–54	36·0	59·9	4·1	100	34·7	25·2
Jewish population of Israel						
1926	31·8	64·0	4·2	100	42·9	21·1
1939	27·5	68·1	4·4	100	38·7	29·4
1948	28·7	67·5	3·8	100	34·3	33·2
1954	32·8	62·7	4·5	100	31·0	31·7

	Percentage, aged			Total		
	0-14	15-59	60 and over			
Jewish population of Israel						
1948	28·7	65·1	6·2	100		
1954	32·8	60·1	7·0	100		
World estimate, 1947 *	36	57	7	100		
Estimates for selected world regions, 1947						
North-West-Central Europe	24	62	14	100		
U.S.A.–Canada	25	64	11	100		
Oceania	28	62	10	100		
Southern Europe	30	59	11	100		
Eastern Europe	34	59	7	100		
Near East	40	54	6	100		
Africa	40	55	5	100		
Latin America	40	55	5	100		
South Central Asia	40	56	4	100		

* United Nations, *Demographic Yearbook, 1949–50.*

also 35-44 — became smaller, while the proportion in the upper age groups rose. The exceptionally large productive age groups, which were a political and economic asset for Israel during the first phases in the Mandatory period, exist no longer. To-day the population of Israel has an age structure not very different to that of Eastern European countries and other countries occupying a middle position, as shown by Table II. The proportion in the productive ages is only slightly larger than the estimated world average. On the other hand, among people in dependent ages old persons are still relatively few, whilst the increase in the proportion of children promises a large influx into the productive young age groups in the future.

III. SOME ASPECTS OF THE LIFE OF IMMIGRANTS IN ISRAEL

We shall now deal with certain aspects of the problem of how immigrants adapt themselves to life in Israel. We shall examine their distribution by area, occupation, and language, to what extent they intermarry with other nationalities, and how far they maintain demographic and health habits acquired abroad.

(1) *Urban and Rural Distribution*

In almost all countries Jews have a rather strong tendency towards urban life. Up to the beginning of modern immigration, the Jews of Palestine lived almost exclusively in towns. The first modern attempt at rural settlement was made in 1878 by Jews from Jerusalem who founded the colony of Petah Tiqva. In the course of time the idea of rural settlement gained momentum and it became one of the foremost aims of the Zionist movement to create an independent Jewish agricultural society. Great difficulties were encountered, *e.g.* the need to buy land from Arab owners, malaria, and lack of essentials such as capital, water, proper communications, and agricultural skill.

At first there was a tendency to create a class of Jewish peasants owning their land and living in villages (*moshavot*). Later on the necessity for a united effort to overcome difficulties, and the strong influence of socialistic ideals, led to the development of new types of settlement. In the communal settlement (*kibbutz* or *kvutza*), a large, mixed farm is run in common by all members, earnings are pooled, and a common household is kept (common kitchen, dining-room, children's house, etc.). Then there are settlements in which farmers keep independent households but co-operate to some extent, such as the collective smallholders' settlement (*moshav shitufi*), the co-operative smallholders' settlement (*moshav 'ovdim*), and the smallholders' settlement (*moshav*).

The immigration which came after the founding of the State stimulated the creation of other types of settlements (such as the rural immigrant settlement and the work village) and of temporary settlements (such as the transitional settlement (*ma'barah*), and the work camp).

The development of the Jewish rural population during the periods 1882–1914, 1914–48, and 1948–54 may be seen from Table III.

TABLE III

RURAL SETTLEMENTS AND POPULATION *

	Communal Settlements (*Kibbutzim*)	Smallholders' Settlements (*Moshavim*, etc.)	Villages (*Moshavot*)	Rural and Temporary Immigrant Settlements	Others	Total
			Number of Settlements			
1882	—	—	5	—	—	5
1914	4	3	32	—	8	47
1948	177	104	34	—	11	326
1954	223	314	39	74	59	709
			Population			
1882	—	—	500	—	—	500
1914	180	400	11,000	—	410	11,990
1948	54,208	30,142	24,160	—	2121	110,631
1954	76,115	112,278	60,110	106,651	6628	361,782

* Col. 1 includes *kibbutzim* and *kvutzot*; Col. 2 includes *moshavim, moshavey ovdim*, and *moshavim shitufiyim*; Col. 4 includes 'rural settlements', 'work camps', 'independent *ma'barot*; Col. 5 includes mainly educational institutions and farms. Former villages, which in the course of time became towns, are not included in the data for 1948 and 1954 (Col. 3).

During the Mandatory period people who settled in rural localities and turned to agricultural occupations were mainly of European, often urban, origin. Many of them changed their occupation or trained themselves for agriculture under the impulse of Zionist ideals; among them there was a strong tendency towards collective settlement.

After 1948 there was a marked change in the situation. On the one hand, with the exodus of the larger part of the Arab rural population, the need to settle a large number of Jews on the land and to increase agricultural production was acutely felt. This was made possible by the existence of large tracts of agricultural land and by the receipt of financial aid from abroad, which could be used for soil reclamation, afforestation, and irrigation.

On the other hand, the proportion of the immigrants entering Israel in 1948–51 who had received adequate pioneer training was much lower than in previous immigration waves. The proportion of persons willing to live in communal settlements was also much smaller than previously. New immigrants from Asiatic countries were generally not prepared for socialist ideals as expressed in the life of communal settlements. Many European immigrants who had been in Nazi camps and in displaced persons' camps longed for privacy and disliked the life of communal settlements. A number of new immigrants on arrival joined communal settlements. However, there was a high rate of turnover in these settlements and many of the new-comers as well as a number of the older members left.[1] Although the settlements could now dispose of more land than before, and the prospect of expansion was better, their population nevertheless did not grow much between 1948 and 1954 (Table III).

A much larger proportion of immigrants of the 1948-51 wave, as compared with former immigration waves, settled in rural localities other than communal settlements. This may often have been due simply to the need to accept accommodation or work wherever offered, rather than to ideological motives. The consequences were, however, far-reaching.

The population in rural settlements increased even more rapidly than the urban population, so that the proportion in rural settlements amounted to 24 per cent in 1954 as compared with 16 per cent in 1948; within the rural population the proportion of persons living in communal settlements has declined; and, although only a tiny minority of the new immigrants had previous agricultural experience,[2]

[1] Communal settlements not belonging to left-wing socialist movements have therefore employed hired workers to a considerable extent.

[2] The Labour Force Survey of 1954 found that people working in agriculture who had been gainfully occupied abroad were distributed as follows according to former occupation abroad :

PREVIOUS OCCUPATION

	Agriculture	Industry or Building	Commerce	Liberal Professions	Managerial or Clerical Workers	Others
Per 100 persons who arrived in 1948 or later	7·4	41·6	37·4	1·9	6·5	5·2
Per 100 persons who arrived before 1948	17·5	35·3	22·6	10·4	11·4	2·9

the drift to agricultural work was considerable. Agricultural production increased and the proportion of persons of Asiatic and African origin exceeded by far the proportion of Europeans living in rural settlements.

(2) *Occupational Distribution*

In order to do justice to the problem of the occupational distribution of immigrants, we should examine:

(*a*) The occupational distribution of the communities from which the immigrants came;

(*b*) The occupational distribution of the immigrants in countries of origin;

(*c*) Changes of occupations by the immigrants after arriving in Israel;

(*d*) Occupational distribution in Israel of the various waves of immigrants and of Israel-born, and the resulting overall occupational distribution of the population of Israel.

There is a great deal of statistical material on this subject; but owing to wide differences in classifications used in various countries and at different times, the fragmentary character of some of the data, and the inaccuracies and bias affecting statements on previous occupations given by immigrants on arrival, an adequate appraisal of the sources would need much more space than is available here.

(*a*) *The occupational distribution of the Jewish communities from which the immigrants came.* The occupational distribution of Jews all over the world shows certain common characteristics, such as: (i) a very low proportion of people occupied in agriculture; (ii) a large proportion engaged in commerce; (iii) a concentration in specific branches of industry and handicraft; (iv) in countries where political conditions were favourable (*e.g.* in Western and Central Europe before the Nazi domination, United States, etc.) a relatively large number in the liberal professions, in clerical work, and in the middle classes; (v) in some of these countries a strong concentration among proprietors, managers, and business men; and (vi) a better standard of living than in many other population groups. On the other hand, vast masses of Jews in Eastern Europe lived, both under the Czarist rule and in the period between the two world wars, under very precarious economic conditions.

(*b*) *The occupational distribution of immigrants in countries of origin.* The Zionist movement considered it one of its major aims to build in Israel a self-supporting Jewish population having a more 'normal' structure than that of Diaspora Jewry, with a broad foundation in agriculture. Proper selection of prospective immigrants, agricultural training abroad before immigration, vocational training of youth and adults in Palestine, encouragement of agricultural settlement and of employment in selected branches — these were among the means chosen to achieve the end.

During certain phases of the Mandatory period, the occupations of young immigrants coming to Palestine were by no means representative of the Jewish communities from which they came. A relatively large number said that they had had previous experience in agriculture or as unskilled labourers; relatively few had been in commerce, finance, and liberal and clerical professions.

The influx into Palestine in the later phases of the Mandatory period and the mass immigration to Israel after the creation of the State had an occupational structure more akin to that of Jewish communities in the countries of origin. As shown by detailed data by countries of origin for 1948–52,[1] agriculture was the previous occupation of a small minority of immigrants (excepting Yemenite males, 16 per cent of whom reported a former occupation in this branch). The most important branches were crafts and industry (in particular the clothing industry, which accounted for over half of the gainfully occupied oriental women), trade (mainly among Asiatic males), liberal professions (mainly among Central Europeans); administration and clerical professions.

(*c*) *Changes of occupations by the immigrants in Israel.* Data comparing the actual occupations in Israel with the previous occupations of the immigrants or their fathers abroad were collected by the workers' censuses of 1922, 1926, 1937, by the census of rural population in 1941–42, and by the survey of immigrants of 1948–49 taken in 1950–51. These statistics show a marked shift from commerce (and during early periods also from some free professions) to manual labour in agriculture and industry, and more generally from lighter to heavier work. More recent data, furnished by the Labour Force Survey in 1954, are summarized in Tables IV and V for persons who had been gainfully occupied abroad and were gainfully occupied in Israel at the time of the survey. Occupational changes, as shown in Table IV, appear to have been very extensive,[2] and more frequent

---

[1] See Sikron Report quoted above.

[2] Indices evaluating the tendency to continue in Israel the same occupation followed abroad are given in Table V. They show that among Europeans this tendency was most pronounced among people who belonged to free professions, among the small group of people who were already engaged abroad in agriculture, etc. The index — capable of varying between 0 and 1 — is calculated by taking the ratio between (i) excess of actual number of people working in Israel in occupation followed abroad, over the number 'expected' in case of random distribution and

among the new immigrants than among old residents, among Asians and Africans than among Europeans, among men than among women.

Table V compares for the same group the occupational distribution abroad and in Israel. The major changes are the impressive decrease in percentages of people working in commerce ; the decrease in percentage of industrial workers and the large increase in the percentage of persons working in agriculture, mainly among new immigrants from Africa and Asia (see III (1)) and the increase in the percentage working in building.

TABLE IV

PERCENTAGE OF IMMIGRANTS WORKING IN ISRAEL IN AN
OCCUPATION DIFFERENT FROM THAT IN WHICH THEY
WORKED ABROAD *

Sex	Born in		Total
	Europe, America	Asia, Africa	
Males			
Old settlers	45·4	54·2	46·8
New immigrants	52·4	69·9	60·1
Total	49·6	67·7	56·0
Females			
Old settlers	40·8	— †	41·6
New immigrants	46·0	— †	44·6
Total	43·5	51·6	46·8

* Labour Force Survey 1954, people aged 14 or over. People included are subdivided into occupational classes. 'Old settlers' indicates people who arrived before 1948, 'New immigrants', those who arrived from 1948 onwards.
† Number of cases too small to calculate the percentages.

(*d*) *The occupational distribution of the various waves of immigrants and of the whole population of Israel.* The changes which have taken place in Israel have created a labour force whose occupational distribution is very different from that of Diaspora Jewry.

According to the Labour Force Survey of 1954, the proportion of persons working in agriculture and industry in Israel is considerable and the proportion in trade does not exceed that found in many other countries. The percentage of persons working in public and personal services is, however, very high as compared with that found in most other countries.

(ii) the excess of people working abroad in the occupation considered over the 'expected' number. The index becomes 1 when all people continue in Israel to hold the occupation followed abroad.

Social Aspects

TABLE V

OCCUPATIONAL DISTRIBUTION OF ADULT MALE IMMIGRANTS ABROAD AND IN ISRAEL (1954)

(sample including only people already gainfully occupied abroad)

Occupational Groups	Born in Europe, America				Born in Asia, Africa			
	Old Settlers		New Immigrants		Old Settlers		New Immigrants	
	Abroad	Israel	Abroad	Israel	Abroad	Israel	Abroad	Israel
Agriculture	3·4	7·0	2·1	10·3	1·5	10·0	2·0	30·8
Industry and Craft	31·1	29·8	31·8	29·1	34·0	24·2	39·0	17·8
Building	4·0	7·7	6·2	19·5	12·0	24·9	7·4	27·1
Transport	1·8	3·5	2·4	3·4	1·5	1·9	2·9	1·8
Trade	26·7	15·8	33·2	13·1	35·3	19·7	31·3	8·1
Services	1·5	4·8	2·5	6·5	0·7	8·5	3·1	5·7
Liberal and technical professions	13·1	10·5	7·0	5·5	6·0	2·6	3·5	2·6
Managerial	3·5	5·0	3·2	1·8	0·7	1·4	1·9	0·3
Clerical	14·9	15·9	11·6	10·8	8·2	6·6	8·9	5·8
Total	100·0	100·0	100·0	100·0	100·0	100·0	100·0	100·0

Occupational Groups	Differences in the Percentage in Each Occupational Group Abroad and in Israel				Indices of Tendency to Remain in Same Occupational Group	
	Born in Europe, America		Born in Asia, Africa		Born in Europe, America	
	Old Settlers	New Immigrants	Old Settlers	New Immigrants	Old Settlers	New Immigrants
Agriculture	+3·6	+8·2	+8·5	+28·8	92·7	(50·5)
Industry and craft	−1·3	−2·7	−9·8	−21·2	54·9	52·5
Building	+3·7	+13·3	+12·9	+19·7	39·2	42·4
Transport	+1·7	+1·0	+0·4	−1·1	33·6	49·5
Trade	−10·9	−20·1	−15·6	−23·2	22·6	15·7
Services	+3·3	+4·0	+7·8	+2·6	64·0	54·0
Liberal and technical professions	−2·6	−1·5	−3·4	−0·9	63·2	62·9
Managerial	+1·5	−1·4	+0·7	−1·6	26·6	11·9
Clerical	+1·0	−0·8	−1·6	−3·1	42·5	41·2
Total	—	—	—	—	44·6	36·1

Source: See Table IV.

332

The enormous growth in population as a result of mass immigration during 1948-51 did not have much effect on the distribution by economic group. In comparison with figures for 1948, there was a small increase of the proportion of persons working in agriculture, in electricity, water, and sanitary services, in transportation and in services, a sharp increase in building (which was at a standstill in 1948 and developed greatly with immigration), a decrease in industry, no changes in other branches. The data for 1954 show that there are no great differences in the distribution of various immigrant waves by economic group; outstanding differences are the large proportion of new Asiatic-African immigrants in agriculture (see II (1)) and their low proportion in commerce as compared with that of old residents of the same origin.

It should not be concluded, however, that the various waves of immigrants penetrate in equal proportions into each industry, occupation or social group. On the contrary, interesting differences are shown by data taken from the Labour Force Survey of 1954, the manpower survey of 1950, and a sample taken in 1948, in which a breakdown is given by occupational status and occupation for immigrants from each country of birth classified by length of stay.

The Labour Force Survey of 1954 also threw light on the proportions gainfully employed and unemployed. Both among new immigrants and old residents, Asiatic- and African-born males were found to enter active life at younger ages than European and Israeli-born. At ages 25-44 the proportion in the civilian labour force was large among males in all population groups. At higher ages, and mainly above 55, the percentage in the civilian labour force was lower among new immigrant males (mainly Asiatic and African origin) than among old residents. It would appear that people arriving in Israel at ages over 55, if they have not a special skill or profession, have greater difficulty in re-entering active life. Unemployment was higher among new immigrants than among old residents in upper age groups. Among females the percentage in the civilian labour force was found to reach a maximum of about 50 per cent in the age groups 20-24 among Israeli-born and old residents of European origin, and to decline slowly with age. This percentage was somewhat lower in all age groups among European new immigrants as compared with old residents. Among Asiatic and African females — both old residents and new immigrants — the maximum is found at even lower ages (14-19), and the percentages fall rapidly (probably because of the increasing proportion of married women and large families).

(3) *Language*

The majority of the population of Israel (and the large majority of the adult population) are foreign-born. As among Diaspora Jews, the use of specifically Jewish languages (Yiddish,[1] 'Ladino',[2] etc.) is now generally declining, whilst the use of local national languages is large and increasing. Immigrants have brought with them into Israel an amazing variety of languages. This could have been a serious obstacle to cultural development if a common language — Hebrew — had not been revived.

The revival of Hebrew began at the end of the nineteenth century, when the majority of immigrants still had the Yiddish language in common, whilst other communities generally spoke Ladino or Arabic. The first steps were due more to national idealism than to a desire to meet practical needs. At first many technical difficulties had to be overcome owing to the inadequacy of the vocabulary and differences in pronunciation; a long struggle to modernize Jewish schools in Palestine took place.

In the last years of the Turkish régime Hebrew had not succeeded in penetrating the very orthodox population of the 'holy cities' of Hebron, Safad, and Tiberias. On the other hand, it had won over one-third of the adult immigrants of the modern sections of the population in Tel-Aviv and the rural settlements, and it was already on its way to winning over the new generations in those places (where three-quarters of the younger people already spoke Hebrew).

During the Mandatory period Hebrew improved from a technical point of view, gained acknowledgment as an official language, and established itself in the expanding school system of the Jewish community. By the end of the Mandatory period almost all persons born in Israel spoke Hebrew; the few still using foreign languages were mainly elderly people. Persons born abroad who reached Israel under the age of 20 were found to use Hebrew almost as much as the Israel-born, owing to the influence of kindergartens, contacts with other children, and Hebrew schools and youth movements. This group adopted Hebrew very rapidly. The number of persons using Hebrew as their only or main language was found to have reached 511,000 by 1948, as compared with some 34,000 in 1914 (75 per cent of the population aged 2 years or over compared with about 40 per cent in 1914).

The establishment of the State strengthened still further the place of Hebrew in public life, where it became the main official

---

[1] German, mixed with Hebrew and other words, and written in Hebrew letters.
[2] Spanish mixed with Hebrew and other words.

language. In fact politics and administration are conducted almost entirely in Hebrew; in educational and cultural life Hebrew has kept or achieved a predominant position (schooling for Jewish pupils from the kindergarten to the University is exclusively in Hebrew; books and newspapers appearing in Israel, radio talks, theatre performances, and public lectures are mainly in that language).

Despite the large volume of immigration, the process of assimilation to Hebrew of *children* of immigrants' families seems to have continued unabated. With the coming of compulsory education, nearly all children have been absorbed into schools.

An inquiry in 1954 gave the following indices for the use of Hebrew [1] among children under 14:

(i) born in Israel (*a*) to families whose head was born in Israel, 94·6; (*b*) to families whose head had arrived before 1948, 96·0; (*c*) to families of new immigrants from Europe or America, 77·8; (*d*) to families of new immigrants from Asia and Africa, 69·6;
(ii) born in Europe or America, 71·6;
(iii) born in Asia and Africa, 61·6.

The child population, though over twice its size in 1948, registered only a slight fall in its index — from 90·9 to 80·5 per cent.

Among adult immigrants of the 1948–51 wave the percentage of people who knew Hebrew abroad was much lower than it had been in previous waves.[2] According to a sample taken in 1950–51 of adult immigrants who entered in 1948–49 only 31 per cent were found to have had some knowledge of Hebrew before they came; knowledge of reading, writing, and speaking was found only among 16 per cent, and actual use of Hebrew abroad among only 0·4 per cent.

The extent of the use of Hebrew in the first year or two after arrival in the country varied according to the type of need to be satisfied. As shown by data from the sample of new adult immigrants taken in 1950–51, the use of Hebrew was still very limited in family life (between husband and wife 3·7 per cent; with children 16·7 per cent; somewhat wider in social life, where Hebrew was used in 14·9 per cent of contacts with other people; in the cultural

---

[1] Calculated by weighting by 100 per cent the number of people using only Hebrew, by 75 per cent the number of those using Hebrew as an additional language, by 0 per cent the number of those using only foreign languages.
[2] Previous knowledge of Hebrew was found to be a very important factor in facilitating the introduction of this language into the immigrants' daily life. Statistical data show that the percentage of use of Hebrew in family life, in social contacts, at work and in reading newspapers and books, increases from people who had no knowledge of Hebrew abroad, to those who had some knowledge, and to those who before immigration were already able to speak, read and write.

field some 27 per cent were found to be able to read Hebrew news-papers, whereas only 18 per cent were actually accustomed to read them and only 12 per cent were accustomed to read Hebrew books. On the other hand, Hebrew was used already in 38·7 per cent of contacts taking place at work.[1]

The number of people speaking Hebrew increased from 511,000 in 1948 to 679,000 at the end of 1950 and 861,000 in June 1954; but the proportion using Hebrew as their only or first language decreased from 75·1 per cent in 1948 to approximately 60·9 per cent in 1954. It is common for people to speak two or more languages. In 1954 only 31·3 per cent used one language only (17·4 per cent Hebrew, 13·8 per cent a foreign language); 43·0 per cent used two languages; 25·9 per cent three languages or more. Children and youths take to the mother tongue easily. Since Hebrew is becoming for them what Spanish is for Spaniards or French for Frenchmen, the future of the language is firmly assured.

(4) *Social Contacts by New Immigrants*

In 1950–51 a sample was taken of immigrants who entered Israel during 1948–59, in order to obtain information on cultural assimila-tion and other aspects of the life of new immigrants.[2] The adults included (numbering over 8000) were asked — among other things — to say whether they met at work or after work (*a*) with old residents, (*b*) with new immigrants, and to indicate the country of origin of the persons in question and the language in which conversations were held. Whilst the somewhat vague character of the questions is admitted [3] the data thus obtained may nevertheless be of some value.

The main conclusions which may be drawn from these data (not reproduced here) are as follows :

(*a*) The majority of contacts recorded are with other new immi-grants (62 per cent of the cases); 38 per cent of those report-ing contacts indicated that they were made with old residents. Since this percentage is far lower than that for old residents in the country, it suggests a tendency towards seclusion. In interpreting this, however, we must remember that at the time of the inquiry many new immigrants lived in settlements

---

[1] See III (4).

[2] This sample was partly taken with the help of UNESCO (an unpublished report was submitted to this institution in 1953 on 'The revival of Hebrew and the cultural assimilation of immigrants in Israel'. Thanks are due to UNESCO for allowing this material to be used in this paper.

[3] Moreover, no account was taken of 'frequency of contacts' by people report-ing contacts ; nor of 'length of meeting' or 'number of persons met', etc.

and urban quarters where the proportion of old residents was not high.

(*b*) The proportion of contacts with old residents is higher at work than outside work. Time spent earning a living brings more contacts with the 'outside world' than do leisure activities.

(*c*) Of the old residents with whom contacts are established, the majority are of the same country of origin as the new-comer.

(*d*) Contacts with other new immigrants are mainly with persons from the same country of origin.

(*e*) Hebrew is the language used in 57 per cent of meetings with old residents at work, in 29 per cent of meetings with old settlers after work, in 24 per cent of meetings with new immigrants after work.

(*f*) On the whole, Hebrew already holds an important position, and is used in some 39 per cent of the contacts at work and 15 per cent of all social contacts reported. The language of the country of origin is, however, still the main language for social purposes, and other languages are subsidiary.

(5) *Intermarriage*

Various attempts have been made by the Central Bureau of Statistics and the author to study the extent of intermarriage between Jews who have come from different countries or between those who reached Israel during different immigration periods. Indices of 'attraction' between people from the same country of origin or belonging to the same community have been calculated, according to a formula proposed by Benini which, although inadequate for refined work, may be used in a first approach to the problem of endogamy.

The index is obtained by calculating the ratio between: (i) the excess of the number of marriages contracted by persons belonging to the same group over the 'expected' number of such marriages (if all marriages were concluded at random); and (ii) the maximum possible value of such an excess. The index becomes $+1$ when all men of the group marry women of the same group or all women of the group marry men of the same group. It becomes 0 when the actual number of marriages between persons of the same group is equal to the 'expected' number. If the actual number is less than the expected number, an index of 'dislike' is calculated (which varies between 0 and -1) by taking the ratio between (i) and the 'expected' number.

337

Whilst it is impossible to quote here all indices which have been calculated, a few averages may be mentioned, together with some general conclusions reached in the study of detailed indices. In 1952–53 indices of endogamy according to country of birth of husband and wife averaged 0·60. From this average it is seen that on the whole the different Jewish groups in Israel have a strong tendency towards endogamy. A detailed analysis for countries of origin shows that the indices vary and that the differences are due to the following factors :

(a) The size of the group. Small groups usually have the lowest indices.

(b) The character of the group. Indices of endogamy between people born in the same country are higher for people of Asian and African origin than for people of European origin.

(c) Length of stay in Israel. Other things being equal, endogamy decreases with length of stay. Table VI shows that where both husband and wife are new immigrants the indices are high [1] and very high for certain countries (for instance, Yemen, 0·97 ; Iraq, 0·95 ; Libya, 0·92). Lower indices are found in marriages where husband *or* wife only are new immigrants.[2] When *both* husband and wife are old residents, endogamy is lowest.

(d) Place of residence. Indices of attraction are lowest in communal settlements where, in various fields of life, a quick process of assimilation and standardization is taking place. On the other hand, other rural localities largely inhabited by new immigrants show very high indices of endogamy.

As far as can be judged from the comparison of the data of 1938–1940 and 1945, endogamy was declining before the mass immigration of 1948–51. This process has continued among groups which have not been reinforced by that immigration. On the other hand, mass immigration has brought about an increase in endogamy in most Asiatic and African communities and among certain European groups. However, it is likely that with the lower rate of immigration endogamy will again become less prevalent and intermarriage will increase. The direction in which intermarriage is developing is

[1] New immigrants marry extensively among themselves, whilst old residents born abroad and people born in Israel have a comparatively high proportion of intermarriage.

[2] Indices are higher for marriages in which the wife is a new immigrant than for those in which the husband is a new immigrant. This can be explained probably by the fact that the new immigrant females have less contact outside the restricted circle of people of the same origin and are under stronger family influences than new immigrant males.

338

shown by detailed indices of 'attraction' or 'dislike' between people belonging to different countries. From this analysis some general conclusions may be drawn.

Intermarriage, as shown by indices of attraction or mild dislike, is found mainly among the following categories:

(*a*) Persons coming from neighbouring countries. This is often due to the fact that changes in frontiers in European and

TABLE VI

AVERAGE INDICES OF ENDOGAMY BY COUNTRY OF BIRTH OF HUSBAND AND WIFE ACCORDING TO LENGTH OF STAY IN ISRAEL

(marriages 1952)*

Country of Birth	Marriages between			
	Husband New Immigrant : Wife New Immigrant	Husband Old Resident : Wife New Immigrant	Husband New Immigrant : Wife Old Resident	Husband Old Resident : Wife Old Resident
Asiatic countries	0·90	0·73	0·54	0·39
African countries	0·82	0·66	(0·39)	(0·13)
East European countries	0·82	0·59	0·42	0·36
Balkan countries	0·76	0·58	0·42	0·35
Central European countries	0·36	0·32	0·28	0·24
Other countries in Europe and America	0·40	(0·20)	(0·42)	—
Israel (by communities)	—	—	—	0·48
Average	0·80	0·56	0·41	0·37

* Indices based on less than 20 cases are given in brackets.

Middle Eastern countries have separated formerly united Jewish groups.

(*b*) People coming from countries where Jews live under more or less similar cultural, linguistic, or social conditions, such as Eastern Europe — Russia, Poland, former Baltic States, part of Romania; Central Europe — Germany, Austria, Hungary, Czechoslovakia, Romania (partly); Yugoslavia (partly); European Sephardic communities — Greece, Turkey (partly); Bulgaria, Yugoslavia (partly); Turkey (partly);

Syria, Lebanon, Egypt (partly), Libya; Iran, Iraq (partly); Yemen, Aden.

(c) Persons from European countries in general. Recent data seem to show that 'Eastern Europeans' and 'Central Europeans' intermarry quite frequently.

(6) *Demographic Habits and Health Standards*

The question of how far immigrants from European and Oriental countries are changing their demographic habits and health standards in Israel (as a result of mutual contact, passage from the *milieu* of the Diaspora to new surroundings, or partial settlement on the land) is the object of research now in progress at the Central Bureau of Statistics and the Demographic Department of the Hebrew University. The results of this work cannot be anticipated. Here we shall draw on the results of previous investigations.

Immigrants coming to Israel may or may not have been a representative sample of their community of origin. In any event, they brought with them different demographic habits and health standards, largely influenced by those prevailing among Diaspora Jews. Some of these habits are maintained in Israel; some underwent considerable change.

In the past a high rate of, and low ages at, marriage seem to have been prevalent in many Jewish communities. Among Jews in Europe and mainly in Central Europe these characteristics have largely disappeared. On the other hand, they are still found among Asiatic and African Jews coming to Israel. In Israel Oriental Jews have a very high marriage rate. Their marriage age on the average has remained low, but there are symptoms showing delay of marriage among the higher social classes of Oriental communities. European Jews in Israel have lower proportions of unmarried people than those found in various Jewish communities in Europe. However, these proportions are higher than those found among Oriental Jews in Israel. Average age at marriage remains higher among the European Jews in Israel than among Asiatic and African Jews. Incidentally marriage is much more prevalent among the population as a whole than it is among the Jewish population in the Diaspora.

Wide variations in fertility are found among the various communities in Israel. It is very high among certain Asiatic and African groups (such as the Yemenites, Persians, Iraqis, etc.), lower among Sephardi and Eastern European groups, lowest among persons of Central European origin — thus reflecting the geographical distribution of fertility prevailing among Jewish Diaspora communities.

There are signs that oriental Jews are assimilating the European habit of birth control. The evidence is found among Asiatic and African persons belonging to higher urban classes, and among Asiatic and African people in communal settlements, where there is a general tendency towards standardization of fertility habits. Thus the fertility differences between persons of oriental origin, according to types of occupation, are considerable (agricultural and lower urban classes having a high fertility), whereas those differences are slight among persons of European origin.

The scanty data available on mortality indicate that children from families coming from Asia and Africa used to have higher death-rates than children of families from elsewhere. During the Mandatory period the differences became less marked. The big waves of immigration from Asia and Africa during the first years following the establishment of the State brought about a new differentiation, but in the course of a few years the infant mortality among new immigrants has fallen to a level much nearer that of old residents. This process has taken place at an extraordinary speed and it is to be ascribed mainly to such factors as large-scale medical services, voluntary health insurance by the majority of the population (including new immigrants), the exceptionally large number of physicians per head of the population, the supervision extended to the majority of children and mothers, and the readiness of Oriental immigrants to avail themselves of the health services.

All this can be interpreted more generally as follows. Oriental immigrants are rapidly passing through the phase of demographic evolution characterized by falling mortality, while fertility still remains high. On the other hand, European immigrants, who already had a low age-specific mortality and low fertility abroad, have succeeded in Israel, despite environmental difficulties, in keeping mortality low and even reducing it further. The marriage rate is higher than it was abroad, but birth control is widespread. After a prolonged period of 'baby boom', fertility is once again on the decline.

On the whole, however, under the influence of the high fertility of Asiatic-African families,[1] the Jewish population of Israel has achieved high reproduction rates (in 1951–53 a gross reproduction rate of 1·92 and a net reproduction rate of 1·79).

[1] PER 100 BIRTHS IN ISRAEL

	1949	1951	1953
To mothers born in Europe	65·3	45·9	38·5
To mothers born in Asia and Africa	19·6	43·0	49·9
To mothers born in Israel	15·1	11·1	11·6

IV. CONCLUSIONS

The analysis of the immigration of 1¼ million Jews to Israel during the past seventy years reveals the following general characteristics :

(1) Immigration has been continuous, mainly during the past thirty-five years.

(2) There have been several waves of immigration.

(3) In the course of time the *absolute* size of migration waves has increased. However, the relative size, *i.e.* in proportion to absorbing population, has not changed (Fig. 1).

(4) Rates of absorption per 1000 population are extremely high as compared with those found in other immigration countries.

(5) Immigration has a cosmopolitan character. There is virtually no Jewish community in the Diaspora which is not represented in it.

(6) Participation of the various countries has varied a great deal, ranging from an annual flow of 50 per 1,000,000 American Jews to the movement of almost the entire Jewish populations of Libya, the Yemen, Bulgaria, and Iraq.

(7) Immigration is, in general, permanent; the outward movement is low; and the participation of both sexes in immigration is roughly equal.

(8) Immigration has been largely influenced by the political condition of the Jews in countries of emigration and ideological factors of a religious, national, or socialistic character.

(9) The cyclical aspect and the varying direction of migration seem to be mainly due to the interplay of changes in :

    (*a*) the political and economic conditions of Jews in the various countries ;

    (*b*) the ideological factors mentioned under (8) above ;

    (*c*) immigration policies in Palestine — Israel and other countries absorbing Jewish immigration ;

    (*d*) policies of emigration (restriction of emigration with or without property) in various countries.

    (*e*) economic conditions in Palestine-Israel.

(10) In the case of mass immigration (1948–51 and to some extent 1932–36) the distribution of the immigrants by age, occupations, etc. tends to resemble the corresponding distributions in Jewish communities of origin. In the case of selected

immigration, divergences from corresponding distributions in Jewish communities of origin tend to be larger.

(11) Immigration has brought to Israel a substantial number of Jews and has succeeded in creating an autonomous Jewish society.

(12) This society — though formed by a variety of people from all over the world who brought to Israel many different languages and cultures, an anomalous occupational structure, and a very large percentage of persons of urban origin — is striving in the face of many difficulties to achieve a more normal balance of urban and rural occupations, a common language, a common educational system, a closer contact between people of various origins, and a larger degree of intermarriage among them. At present the population — particularly the part which is of oriental origin — has a high fertility rate and a low and decreasing death-rate.

(13) As immigration to Israel is strongly influenced by political factors, its future is unpredictable. The following considerations may be suggested :

    (*a*) In four out of five of the regions which in the past have contributed largely to immigration to Israel (Eastern and Central Europe, the Balkans, and Asia), the Jewish population has greatly decreased. In the first three regions this was due both to mass extermination and to immigration to Israel. Emigration from Communist countries is at present restricted.

    (*b*) In the fifth region — North Africa — which has already made a big contribution to immigration to Israel, there are still over half a million Jews ; and there is a considerable urge to emigrate. It is likely that this area will in the near future be one of the main sources of migrants for Israel.

    (*c*) The majority of Diaspora Jews are now to be found in countries in which their political conditions are not unfavourable ; 5,918,000 live in communities established in America and Oceania by Jewish emigrants from Europe ; 881,000 live in Western and Northern Europe. Emigration from these countries is unrestricted, and there is a small but steady outflow.

In the long run the course of immigration to Israel will depend on the extent to which ideological factors will promote immigration from America, Oceania, and Northern and Western Europe, and on economic conditions in Israel. Average living conditions in Israel are not likely to become better than those of most Western Jewish communities, and so the purely economic incentive can be disregarded. However the narrowing or widening of differences in standards of living will help to determine the effectiveness of ideological factors in influencing immigration. Unpredictable political changes, for example, in the emigration policies of the Soviet Union or the People's Democracies may open up new sources of immigrants for Israel.

PART VII

CONCLUSION

Chapter 24

ARE THERE PREFERABLE ALTERNATIVES TO INTERNATIONAL MIGRATION AS AN AID TO ECONOMIC DEVELOPMENT?

BY

HOWARD S. ELLIS
University of California

I INTERPRET the question which has been posed as pertaining to alternative ways to achieve higher *per capita* incomes; and I use 'economic development' as a short phrase to designate this objective, without, of course, implying that other elements, such as a lessening of inequality, may not also be involved commonly in the concept of progress. The test of the behaviour of *average per capita* income somewhat simplifies the further question 'to whom preferable' by ignoring the conflicting interests of groups within a national economy. But if migration raises average *per capita* incomes in one country and lowers them in another, the conflict of economic interest cannot be ignored and can only be resolved by the automatic working of the market or by some supra-national authority.

The following analysis attempts to take account of divergences of interest wherever they obtrude conspicuously, but the main concern of the analysis is not with these divergences. Consequently, the question might be rephrased to read: 'Are there more *efficient* methods of achieving economic progress than migration?' Either as recast or in its original form, the question is one of breath-taking generality, though not necessarily an inappropriate question to confront in a conference devoted to migration.

Accepting the question as legitimate on a high level of generality, I am disposed to the belief that migration is not to-day one of the most promising lines of action — either as emigration from over-populated areas or as immigration into underpopulated areas — to achieve economic development, however magnificent a bearer of progress it has been in the past. In expressing this judgement, I do not mean that the role of migration is limited because migration is itself limited by legal barriers. I mean rather that the role itself is relatively limited, compared to other sources of development. Even

Conclusion

in those conspicuous cases, such as Canada, Australia, Brazil, and South Africa, where immigration still bids fair to raise *per capita* incomes, this factor recedes in importance relatively to other factors in growth.

I. STATIC EQUILIBRIUM ANALYSIS

A beginning upon the answer to the question can be made, and some propositions of even ultimate consequence can be drawn, from static equilibrium analysis. If labour enjoys a lower marginal productivity in country A than in country B, migration from A to B will raise the wages of the migrants and of labour in A, and — if 'increasing returns' obtain in B — of labour in B also. This harmony of interest seems to have characterized most of the great migrations of the nineteenth century. The gain was enhanced by a parallel movement of capital, which undoubtedly increased profits in both A and B, helped to maintain wages in the immigrant country, and, by cheapening imported foodstuffs and raw materials in the emigrant country, tended to raise real wages there even above the level attained through a reduced working population.

Economic theory has always recognized that international commodity trade is, within certain limits, an economical substitute for migration of labour. Historical illustration of this point, however, is generally precluded by the facts that trade has followed lines of greatest profit (so far as permitted by tariffs, etc.) with *given* factor endowment, and that migration has probably — even in the absence of legal barriers — seldom risen to the rate which would be given by a comparison of cost of transfer and the increase of labour earnings *over a lifetime*. The classical theory does, however, point to the fact that to-day, when the limits to the movement of labour are drawn more narrowly by political obstacles than by economic costs, the role of international commodity trade in the economic progress of both more and less developed countries is greater than if migration were not limited by law.

Political obstacles to the movement of factors arise from divergent economic interests or from cultural reasons. Migration from A to B may raise the wages of the migrants and the labourers remaining in A ; but if diminishing returns on labour begin to make themselves felt sufficiently in B, the labourers in B may secure legal enactments restricting immigration into B, even though the total national product of B, to say nothing of *per capita* incomes in A, would be raised by further migration. Furthermore, from a cultural angle, there is the very real danger that the presence of large numbers of A labourers in

348

B may reduce standards of living, increase natality, and eventually result in both A and B labourers 'sharing equally in poverty'.

Still remaining within the framework of stationary equilibrium analysis, we discover other cases where harmony of interests does not prevail and where therefore we cannot answer the question which constitutes my title, without specifying to *whom* 'preferable'. Country A may be characterized by lower wages than B but by relatively still lower interest rates. Exportation of capital from A might thus, from the angle of national income, be even more preferable than emigration, although capital export alone — while preferable to the capitalists — would not only prevent labourers from realizing higher wages through emigration, but would also lower their productivity in home employment. If the national policy were dictated by an interest in raising real wages and employment even if this entailed less than optimum capital earnings in the long run, labour would be allowed to emigrate but not capital ; and this seems to have been the policy espoused by Keynes in the interwar period.

In present-day England, however, capital earnings at home compete on equal or superior terms with most foreign investment, and the same is true in greater degree for the United States and other potential creditor countries. To the degree to which this is true, capital export is not an eligible device for raising national income in potential creditor or debtor countries ; and by the same token it ceases to be an 'alternative' to migration in those cases where migration is economically possible. High income countries may, of course, desire to export capital by *public* loans or grants on political or humanitarian grounds, or on the basis of long-run economic benefits which elude the private profit motive.

II. MOVING CAUSES IN ECONOMIC DEVELOPMENT

The optimum allocation of factors, which is the essence of the static equilibrium analysis, is indeed crucial for economic progress, whether we think of the less or the more developed economies, and I shall return to this theme again. But the optimum allocation of resources is commonly regarded as one of the essential *conditions* of progress rather than as a *moving cause*. Although the distinction between passive and active elements is difficult to maintain with any rigidity, the dichotomy often seems to be illuminating and is in many cases clearly applicable. Before the alternatives to migration can be appraised for their role in economic growth, we should survey the factors which appear to be most commonly the great prime movers.

Conclusion

In our present-day preoccupation with aggregative and especially objective and measurable variables, we have — I fear — too often ignored the humble fact that the individual's desire to win a livelihood from day to day is fundamentally the same as the urge to *improve* his material lot. Granted that this, the really basic economic motive, is sometimes almost smothered out by religious taboos or by ill health and hopelessness, or frustrated by adverse conditions of tenancy, and the like, is it not the most nearly ubiquitous *active* force lying behind economic growth? By the middle of the eighteenth century, prior to the great agricultural and industrial revolutions, the level of living in most Western European countries had advanced to several multiples of the level obtaining for the masses of the presently underdeveloped areas; and this achievement was largely due to a slow accretion through hard work, saving, trading, and venturing, with only a modicum of what we now think of as improvements in technique. Even the great thrust towards development which currently makes itself felt in those countries having recently achieved political independence or having cast off oppressive internal régimes does not come into operation, even in communist régimes, without in some way appealing to the individual desire for improvement.

Lying very close to the motive of improvement is the motive to accumulate. Some of the economic historians, such as Cairncross, Gerschenkron, and Habakkuk, have indeed concluded that capital formation has more frequently been pulled along from the demand side than pushed onwards from the side of savings. I should not like to question this generalization even though occasional exceptions may appear, for example, in the English mercantilist writers' envy of the flourishing state of Dutch commerce, which they ascribed to the low rates of interest in the first instance and ultimately to the greater frugality of the Dutch populace. My point would be, rather, that saving, rising income, capital formation, and greater saving work in a mutually accumulative process in which cause and effect are difficult to unravel. I shall therefore not hesitate to regard capital accumulation as a basic factor in economic progress and to count international capital movements as a potential alternative to migration.

No significant doubt seems to attach to improved techniques — in the broad inclusive sense of Schumpeter's 'Durchsetzung neuer Kombinationen' — as an active cause of progress. We have, of course, to take account of the sombre warnings of Professor Frankel and the cultural anthropologists that the sudden introduction of modern technique into primitive economies may cause intense social disruption, which has, in any sensibly inclusive concept of progress, to be set against a mere increase of conventionally measured gross

350

national product. Even so, if we bear in mind that not all primitive folkways turn out to be really desired if modern alternatives are available, and if the 'new combinations' are *appropriate* to the new environment, technical improvement is the great bearer of progress in underdeveloped economies. And there can be no doubt that it is the great prime mover for the more advanced nations. In either case it must be interpreted, as Schumpeter insisted, to include not merely improved industrial machinery, but also more productive breeds and strains in agriculture, better transportation and communication, new consumer goods or services, improved credit and marketing facilities, more efficient business and managerial methods, etc. In a broad interpretation of economic development, it may even be extended outside the field of private profit-making to the improvement of facilities for education, public health, etc.

Finally, I come to changes in population, including migration, as a factor in economic progress. Underpopulated areas may be described as areas in which an increase of *per capita* income is associated with, and partly ascribable to, an increase of population, and overpopulated areas may be described as areas in which an increase of population would, other things being equal, produce a decline in *per capita* income. The condition of being underpopulated need not derive from the static equilibrium analysis, but may arise from dynamic elements such as capital accumulation and technological improvement. Furthermore it need not imply exclusively one-way causation. Increasing *per capita* incomes may induce population increases, augment the demand for population-sensitive investment, increase capital formation, and thus increase gross national product. Increasing population and the dynamic elements often associated with it must, however, be positively correlated in some significant degree with a rise in *per capita* income if 'underpopulation' exists.

The industrial West in general seems to fall into the first category, and the painstaking researches of Simon Kuznets have clearly established the positive correlation, with a certain lag, between increasing population and rising *per capita* incomes for the United States, the United Kingdom, Sweden, and other countries. Underpopulation seems also to characterize most of Africa with the exception of Egypt, large parts of continental South America, Australia, and New Zealand. The rest of the world, with certain exceptions, is overpopulated on the test of the definition. Increasing population in this vast area retards the increase or produces a positive decline in *per capita* income.

Migration can take place from one underpopulated area to another with a gain to the migrants, and indeed this has accounted for the great movements from Western Europe to North and South America in the nineteenth century, though increasingly the outward movements shifted to the non-industrial and overpopulated parts of Europe, such as Italy and south-eastern Europe.

Emigration may at first glance seem to be a purely passive element in the economic development of the country of origin — a safety-valve, or a mere reduction of the denominator in the fraction by which income *per capita* is found. But this would neglect the strong *income effect* which the increase of output overseas has indirectly upon the home economy. It was, indeed, this income effect which accounted for the fact that industrial Europe could, at one and the same time, gain both from an increase of home population *and* from emigration. Later on, as the rate of increase of domestic income slowed down, the amount contributed by the income effect of oversea development proved to be too small to prevent a fall of *per capita* income, and emigration — as in Ireland to-day — became important simply as a reduction of the denominator of the fraction.

Immigration into underpopulated regions, as Professor Spengler and other participants in the round table have clearly set forth, contributes more than simply man-hours: the breaking down of castes and of customs adverse to economic advance, the transfer of capital, the supplying of scarce managerial and labour skills, etc., and perhaps most importantly, the introduction of genuine entrepreneur-ship and new techniques.

Nevertheless, despite the indubitable gains of both emigration and of immigration, I find significant grounds for believing that the contribution of migration to economic growth is nowadays less important than in times past as a matter of *potential* magnitude, and not simply as consequence of legal and other impediments.

III. THE LESSENED SIGNIFICANCE OF INTERNATIONAL MIGRATION

(1) *The Demographic Factor*

The basic differences between the population situation of the nineteenth century, particularly the first half, and the second half of the twentieth century, in which we now find ourselves, are: (1) that a much larger part of the world outside the economically more advanced nations is overpopulated; and (2) that many of the under-populated nations are much less underpopulated or are even approach-ing conditions of overpopulation. I will not pause to present statistics in support of these propositions, for the facts are familiar. It may suffice to point to Indonesia, the Caribbean and Central America, Egypt, south-eastern Europe, southern Italy, and much of the Near East as examples of transfer from the category of under- to over-populated. As for the second category, the United States, Canada, New Zealand, Australia, and South Africa have grown to 'developed economies' in the 'unoccupied' continents, and in some cases reveal quite brisk rates of population increase themselves. And in Latin America generally, which has remained relatively underdeveloped, populations have increased very greatly and rates of population increase surpass all other large regions.

The results of these changes for migration are two. In the first place, though the possibility of profitable transfers of man-hours is still no doubt significant both from over- to under-populated regions and within each of these categories, the geographic range of profitable migration is considerably narrowed down by the filling up at the receiving end. But in the second place, those gains which accrue to the labour-receiving country aside from simply man-hours — cultural stimulus, new techniques, etc. — also accrue to a smaller area, since some of the most advanced countries now occupy areas which a century ago were nearly 'unoccupied'. This point is further elaborated under (3) below.

(2) *Labour-saving Techniques*

The great increase of labour-saving techniques in industry and agriculture in recent decades probably enhances the importance of labour movements in one dimension and reduces it in another. Occupational mobility takes on added significance in each national economy, and this probably implies a parallel need for rural-urban migrations, since some of the great labour-saving improvements in agriculture have been of relatively recent origin. But the movement of man-hours to the relatively underpopulated regions of the earth means less to the receiving country the more widespread are labour-saving techniques.

(3) *New Techniques and Migration*

It may be objected, however, that this kind of argument neglects the aspects of migration which are not embraced in mere man-hours ; more specifically, it may be said, it overlooks the innovations in techniques, the cultural fructification, the supplying of entrepreneurial functions, and the transfer of capital which may attend immigration.

But it is precisely on these heads that we nowadays observe a growing divorcement between the transfer of labour and the transfer of these older complements to migration. Techniques may be conveyed from one region to another by labour, or they may be conveyed by capital, or they may be conveyed alone. In times past, when techniques meant in large measure labour skills, they were imparted to apprentices and journeymen by the master craftsman. In some measure this still obtains. Increasingly, however, techniques are scientific procedures which are embodied in apparatus, and the movement of the apparatus moves the techniques. The skills appropriate to the new apparatus can frequently be imparted by skilful instructors in a few weeks of intensive training. Outstanding examples are afforded by the British and American oil companies in the Near and Middle East.

Even more dramatic is the almost complete divorcement of the transfer of techniques from labour migration, and even from capital transfer, in the Technical Aid programmes of the United Nations, the United States, and certain colonial powers such as Belgium. Beginning with humble matters, such as breeds of chickens, livestock, maize, grasses, etc., and simple agricultural implements, this adaptation of technological improvements runs through the whole gamut of the modern industrial process. It extends also to business administration, and to the various departments of central and local government. No longer are immigrants necessary to this evolution, which has been called 'non-Schumpeterian innovation', in the newly developing areas.

Nor is the capital of the migrant of much import. In the heyday of British and other European private investment, as Ragnar Nurkse has recently set forth, capital and emigrants moved together into relatively 'unoccupied' territories or into regions culturally and politically sympathetic to the new-comer and his wealth. Conditions nowadays seldom favour the migration of labour *cum* capital: exchange controls block the outward flow of funds and, more significantly, persons of any means seldom expose their property to the vicissitudes of nationalistic discriminations. Most foreign private investment in the underdeveloped areas is the direct investment of corporations in foreign plant and equipment. Any association of international capital movements with labour, as in the case of Israel, is the exception proving the rule.

(4) *The Lessened International Flow of Capital*

While capital and labour are frequently substitutes in particular industries, there can be little doubt that for an economy as a whole they stand in a complementary relation. This implies that, if less capital moves from one country to another, there is a corresponding reduction in the differential advantage in moving labour. Latin-American economists with whom I have spoken have not infrequently stressed the reduced flow of international private investment as an important reason why even an underpopulated country such as Brazil cannot employ new European immigrants on the scale once possible. This particular reason for reduced migration might dis-solve if the present impediments to international private investment were removed, or if public international sources of funds for develop-ment took over in sufficient volume. Neither of these appears to be in immediate prospect, however.

IV. ECONOMIC PROGRESS IN UNDERDEVELOPED AREAS AS AN INDIGENOUS PROCESS

The thesis of the present section is that the potential rise of *per capita* incomes in the vast underdeveloped areas, comprising two-thirds of the world's population of 2·5 billions, depends fundamentally upon indigenous factors. The bare statement of this truth is not apt to convey its profound importance without some embellishment, except perhaps to economists who have first-hand acquaintance with the problem.

Lack of capital, because it is ubiquitous in underdeveloped countries, whether under- or overpopulated, may afford a con-venient starting-point in the maze of vicious circles of low pro-ductivity and low incomes. With the great mass of the population at subsistence or near-subsistence levels, voluntary saving does not hold forth much hope. Where surplus labour exists in agriculture, as in large portions of Asia, a potential source of capital exists in creating non-agricultural employment. Voluntary local self-help undertakings offer promise, but require a long sustained effort at organization and some capital ; and the beginning, from the con-struction of local sanitation facilities, roads, or irrigation or drainage projects, is slow and laborious.

The painful process of deriving capital for development from within these impoverished economies themselves suggests foreign capital as the *deus ex machina*. But the presently underdeveloped countries afford a quite different prospect from that of the United States, Canada, New Zealand, and Australia in their early histories, for then the foreigner occupied the land with his own nationals and his own culture. Even nowadays United States private capital moves first into Canada, next into Latin America, and last of all into the least developed economies where cultural and legal barriers are too formidable and risks are too great. Even when these barriers are overcome, foreign capital generally moves into production for export, without greatly affecting the domestic economy. Investment in the domestic economy of underdeveloped countries is frequently less attractive than investment abroad to the nationals of these countries themselves.

This dearth of saving and of investment rests fundamentally upon the lack of domestic markets, rather than upon any perversity of private capitalism. In its successive annual reports the Bank for Reconstruction and Development, designed to be a solvent but not necessarily a profit-making institution, has complained of the *paucity* of prospectively self-liquidating projects even in the midst of the capital scarcity of underdeveloped areas. But why are markets so limited when, on the one hand, there exists a wealth of unexploited modern productive techniques, and when, on the other hand, there are empty stomachs and human backs and brawn in abundance ? The answer lies in the lack of mass purchasing power.

Consider the typical peasant household of the economically under-developed countries. The structure — whether mud, brick, or wattle — comprising a single room, usually with one opening, houses a sizable family and often its contingent of livestock. It boasts neither floor nor light after dark, and only a few pieces of rude furniture. Ordinarily the supply of water for human consumption originates in a near-by pool, canal, or river, which also serves for washing, bathing, and the disposal of night soil. Endemic and debilitating disease is widespread, and life-expectancy at birth may be as low as 27 years in India, 30 in Egypt, and 37 in Chile, compared with 68 in Sweden, 66 in the Netherlands, and 64 in the United States. High rates of mortality in the early years of life mean that the working population must, in most of Asia, Africa, and Latin America support 40 per cent of the total inhabitants in the unproductive ages under 15, compared to 24 per cent in Western Europe. Beside this source of frustrated saving, further wastages may arise from seasonal unemployment or chronic surpluses of labour in agriculture. Birth, death, and population-increase rates are typically high ; and the 'prudential restraint' is generally weakened by the social prestige and old-age insurance afforded by large families, by religious beliefs, and by the lack of any known contraceptive which is at once safe and cheap enough for subsistence income receivers.

Such a populace does not present an auspicious *milieu* for increasing production and raising *per capita* incomes by the techniques of Western industrialism. Illiteracy must be reduced from its prevalent levels of 40–90 per cent in the underdeveloped areas, compared to 4–8 per cent in the West. Endemic diseases must be brought in check and infant mortality rates reduced. Before industry can sell its products, the farmers must be able to increase their output through simple improvements in agriculture, reform of tenancy laws, improved marketing facilities and credit arrangements, and possibly also through land reclamation projects. Manufacturing industry generally requires a complement of public utilities before it can progress far — roads, railways, harbours, power, housing for its employees, waterworks, sewage disposal plants — much of which must be financed by the government from taxation or foreign borrowing.

Well has it been said that the increase of output depends upon 'balanced growth' — upon judicious investment guided by present or prospective marginal productivities, supplemented perhaps by the more refined technique of linear programming. The domestic market is called into being by production : production creates its own vent, according to the profound insight of Jean-Baptiste Say. Explanations of this sort do indeed contribute to the rationale of economic development and offset the frequent tendency to find in some one dynamic element, such as foreign capital, the immigrant, or technological innovation, a *deus ex machina* to break the numerous and intractable interdependencies of low productivity and low income. But general principles are no substitute for the piecemeal and laborious assault upon all obstacles to material progress along its entire front.

Unfortunately, however, the role of national governments in guiding and fostering economic development, in any event a crucial component, cannot always be assumed to be intelligent or even beneficent. In Latin America, the prevalence of personal government takes a heavy toll upon economic progress. Tax systems are frequently archaic and inefficiently or dishonestly administered ; producers are compelled to seek security through 'mordida' or bribery ; ordinary life is interrupted by palace or popular revolutions.

But aside from political abuses and uncertainties, public policy is frequently most inimical to economic development. The four horsemen of this economic Apocalypse are chronic inflation, a bias against imports and against exports of primary products, ostentatious or ill-conceived public projects, and finally, a tendency to succumb to popular demands for welfare expenditures exceeding budget capacities.

As in the industrial nations of the West, inflation often occurs less as a deliberate policy and more as the simple arithmetic result of the failure of the legislative body to agree upon taxes. But in many of the countries now aspiring to rapid development there seems to prevail a certain faith in the capacity of inflationary finance to force the pace of capital formation. W. Arthur Lewis has recently expounded a formal theory according to which, in countries endowed with surplus labour, forced saving through inflation automatically raises incomes until the surplus labour is employed and voluntary savings equal investment. But for this remarkable automaton to operate requires : (1) that forced transfers by inflation be in no part consumed ; (2) that this saving be productively (and not speculatively) invested ; (3) that inflation produces no adverse effect on voluntary saving; or (4) upon the allocation of resources in general. The admirable record of the Government of India in conducting its economic development programme over the past several years without appreciable inflation seems to show that not all statesmen are persuaded of the force of Professor Lewis's argument. But this achievement is nearly unique among the newly developing countries.

It seems highly probable that many of these countries are inhibiting their economic growth by autarkic policies regarding foreign trade. On the side of import restrictions, the least harmful are those designed to increase domestic saving by prohibitions or quotas on luxury imports. The probability seems strong that the protection thus afforded to home-produced luxuries largely negates any net gain in saving. But at worst the result is nil. This cannot be said of infant-industry protection, where, as in the recent history of Mexico, it falls victim to political log-rolling. Influential economists in underdeveloped countries, such as Paul Prebisch, the director of ECLA, should not lose sight of the character of Latin-American politics when they dwell upon the potential external economies of industrial development under restrictive import devices. The autarkic strain of thinking shows itself also in a resentment by the less developed countries of their dependence upon exports of primary products. Whether primary producers have suffered through a deterioration in the terms of trade — a questionable proposition at best — the fact remains that a diversification of the domestic economy and of exports should rather be an eventual end achieved by economic progress, not one of its first stages. To be able to command imports of machinery and basic equipment for industrialization, the raw material producers have to maintain, and possibly even, for a phase, augment exports of this character.

Dictatorial régimes are prone to ostentatious expenditure on public buildings, stadia, super-highways, and other dubiously productive installations in order to court the public favour; but the cost in terms of progress may be dear. Many writers have pointed to the tendency of low-income countries to aspire to standards of consumption achieved by other nations only after many decades of solid economic growth. In the sphere of public policy this may mean, as in Argentina, acceding to excessive wage demands by labour parties or, as in Turkey, imposing social security taxes of 13-15 per cent on pay-rolls, surely too onerous for a country at an early stage of development.

What all of this means — all the interrelated elements of public health, cultural factors, demographic problems, scarcities of capital and skills, organizational difficulties, and pitfalls of public policy— is not that economic progress is impossible in the underdeveloped world. By spurts, at least, growth rates of gross national product of 6–8 per cent annually have been realized as, for example, during the immediate postwar years in Mexico, outstripping even the near 3 per cent annual increase of population. What it does mean, however, is that *economic progress is much more indigenously conditioned* than it was in the relatively 'unoccupied' areas of the New World and in the much more open, uncontrolled, and less autarkic societies of the nineteenth century. While foreign capital, entrepreneurs, and immigrants still play a role, it is much more nearly true that each indigenous society sets its own pace of development.

V. CONCLUSIONS REGARDING MIGRATION

During the golden age of migration from the Old to the New World ending in the 1930's, it is scarcely possible to doubt that immigration into unoccupied territories was to be counted as one of the great — occasionally the greatest — prime movers in economic development. It supplied not only the scarce factor of man-hours, but also special skills, technological innovation, and entrepreneurs, and — because the culture of the receiving country was sympathetic — also a fructifying flow of capital. The relatively highly developed European countries of origin experienced a rise of *per capita* income caused partly, of course, by other great prime movers of economic progress. In so far as it related to emigration, the effect was two-fold. In the first place it generated a powerful income effect upon the Old World through its contribution to the rise of incomes abroad. In the second place, by reducing the supply of labour in Europe it raised wages ; as Professor Spengler points out, this factor probably accounts for the more rapid rise of real wages in several countries of Europe than in the United States from 1860 to 1913.

Conclusion

If the argument developed here is correct, the *income effect of emigration* — over the world generally and specifically also for Europe — is nowadays greatly attenuated. This does not, of course, imply that the presently developed economies will not experience favourable, and conceivably even strong, income effects if the aspirations of presently underdeveloped economies are realized. But there are, as I have argued, two reasons for supposing that this income effect will not be significantly related to migration. First, the economic development of underdeveloped economies chiefly depends to-day upon endogenous factors, of which the most important are those bearing most directly upon the creation of mass purchasing power and the expansion of domestic markets. Second, in so far as development does depend on exogenous factors, the immigration of labour plays a lesser role because of new labour-saving processes, because of the transfer of techniques through equipment or even independently of either labour or capital, because of the reduced international flow of complementary capital, and because of rapid rates of population increase in the underdeveloped world.

What I have been saying sums up to the generalization that migration is ceasing to be a major factor in the rise of *per capita* incomes, not because of legal barriers to movement but because of its reduced economic significance. For the advanced countries this is traceable to the decline of the income effect of emigration, and for the newly developing countries it is ascribable to the lesser significance of immigration *per se* and to the greater significance of endogenous factors.

So far as concerns the Country Papers prepared for this conference, the most striking confirmation of my hypothesis seems to appear in the cases of the United Kingdom, Ireland, Germany, and Holland, which, according to the findings of the investigators, would not be benefited by general emigration. Economic progress, defined in terms of *per capita* income, depends upon other things than migration. (I would strongly suspect that this might be the finding for Belgium, Switzerland, and the Scandinavian countries.) Indonesia seems to accord with the hypothesis on the side of receiving countries, though the indifference of the authorities to immigration may partly be political and partly due to preoccupation with the problem of moving the excess population of Java to the Outer Islands. But Mr. Keyfitz himself stresses the greater significance of education and the provision of technicians from within the economy — an example of endogenous evolution.

The kind of intra-Asian migration treated so perceptively by

Professor Silcock seems bound to continue with mutual advantage to originating and receiving countries — the 'migration of a limited number of skilled workers followed by instruction of local unskilled workers'. My argument draws attention to the words 'limited number'.

Substantial immigration, according to the respective Country Papers, would be advantageous to Canada and Australia; and this is not surprising in view of the fact that the limitational factors on immigration stressed in Part IV are less strong in these countries. For two other countries — South Africa and Brazil — for which the particular investigators state or imply a generally favourable potential effect of immigration but in somewhat qualified terms, the kinds of limitation emphasized in Part IV assume greater importance. Furthermore, with respect to Canada and Australia, their large land areas should not conceal the fact that they are relatively small economies supporting populations, even after decades of relatively free migration, of 15 and 9 millions respectively. This applies in some measure also to South Africa with its $12\frac{1}{2}$ million inhabitants. Immigration may eventually reach large aggregate numbers, but the absorption rate is held down by the size of the economies.

Most of the Country Papers add to the strength of my hypothesis in a further way not alluded to in the argument developed in this paper. The types of immigrant most sought after are the trained technician or agriculturalist and the relatively skilled labourer; but, unfortunately for the prospective future volume of marginal adjustment of relative labour supplies, these are the very types of manpower for which the economic, social, and political pressures to emigrate are least strong.

PART VIII

REPORT ON THE PROCEEDINGS

SUMMARY RECORD OF THE DEBATE

BY

DOUGLAS HAGUE

THE DISCUSSION ON PROFESSOR THOMAS'S PAPER

First and Second Sessions, 3 September 1955

Professor Lindahl suggested that as an introduction to the problem of migration he might put Professor Thomas's paper into perspective by outlining a scheme of types of migration. First, there was forced migration. For instance, one had the slave trade, and cases where, by government order, British convicts had been sent to Australia. Such questions had not been discussed in Professor Thomas's paper. Second, there was free migration. Here, too, there were two possibilities; there were 'push' forces and there were 'pull' forces. Both the push and the pull forces might be either economic, for example abundant natural resources plus capital and technique, or political, like encouragements to emigration or restrictions on immigration.

In the nineteenth century the main migration flow had been from overpopulated countries to those with unused land. For instance, people had moved from Europe to the United States, Australia, and so on. These migrants could obtain *land*. This was the pull. At the same time, however, there was the special characteristic that the migrants had to bring their own capital with them, so that capital movements also took place. This special phase was not over. In theory one might argue that, whilst it lasted, it need have caused little disturbance. But the nineteenth century had strong business cycles in addition to this movement of labour and capital. What were the combined effects of these two tendencies, one long-run, the other cyclical?

A priori, one would suppose that when there was unemployment there would be most movement. But was this true of capital as well as people? Professor Thomas had said that capital would follow the population movement, but a little after it. He had argued that there would be a rise in American imports if a slump in Britain drove people, from Ireland especially, to the United States. The migration would cause a building boom in America, financed in part by capital imports. This was reasonable enough, but not so Professor Thomas's argument about the terms of trade. He had argued that the terms of trade would not move in favour of England, whose exports were rising, but in favour of America. Was this, asked Professor Lindahl, a necessary part of the theory, or was it mere sophistication?

365

Nor was Professor Thomas convincing in his criticisms of Professor Lewis, for example in the footnote on pp. 8–9. Professor Lewis had said that the nineteenth-century cycle was bad for Britain. This was true. An even flow was needed. It was hard to judge Professor Thomas's material. In Table II the upswing in immigration in 1879–88 increased the output of producer durables in the United States, whilst there was a slump in Britain. In 1884–93 the situation was the opposite. But could one be sure how significant these figures were, since the periods overlapped? What did the *yearly* percentage change mean?

Professor Thomas answered that Table II compared the rate of change in one period with that in the previous period. The figures were given in this form only because they were not available in any other form in the original source which he had used, namely, the figures given by Professor Kuznets.

Professor Lindahl still wondered if there was enough support for Professor Thomas in this statistical material. He felt others would agree that the question still remained open.

Mr. Rubin said that Professor Lindahl's categories represented extreme cases, like slavery, and that in practice one had mixtures. Nor need one have both push and pull forces. There was often only one.

Mr. Robertson agreed that the schema was incomplete, ignoring 'half-way houses' like indentured labour. However, he took issue with Mr. Rubin over his suggestion that one did not need both push *and* pull. With free migration, he suggested that migrants' expectations of the new environment *did* matter. A push would be ineffective, unless they thought the new environment would be better; though one might have a pull without a push. Economically, this type of migration was the most beneficial, since it used human resources to best advantage.

Professor Lindahl said he had not meant to imply that push and pull factors must work in the same direction. He had merely given a systematic account of the possibilities, and other participants could combine these as they wished.

Professor Hoffman asked a question about Professor Thomas's contention that unemployment led first to migration and then to a capital flow. He felt that this argument needed the support of a theoretical explanation. How else could it have occurred in unorganized nineteenth-century markets? Second, he wondered what would have happened in England without migration? The United Kingdom at the end of the nineteenth century was experiencing a diminishing rate of economic growth. What did emigration mean in these conditions? Would there have been a higher rate of growth without emigration on this scale?

Professor Lerner suggested an alternative classification. One should consider conditions in the country *from* which people moved and those in the country *to* which they went. Then one need not have push factors in the country losing population, and pull factors in the gaining country. After that, one could separate economic from other factors.

Professor Silcock argued that on the economic side there had to be a difference between conditions in the two countries if there were to be movement. He thought that if the movement were regular, it did not make sense to say that there was either a push or a pull. If the movement was irregular, however, push or pull factors might be responsible. He felt that it was the *difference* between conditions in the countries concerned that was significant with regular movements, and *changes* in conditions where migration was irregular.

Professor Spengler asked Professor Thomas to clarify his argument on the terms of trade. Surely the price-reducing factors in England were stronger than the price-raising influences in the United States. Why, then, did Professor Thomas give this particular answer ?

Professor Thomas replied that in the United Kingdom, which exported both capital and labour, a boom in the export sector drew factors from fixed capital construction to the production of portable goods for export. To begin with, this would not cause a rise in costs of production. Export prices might well remain constant, or even fall. Factors of production were easily obtainable, and consequently the goods sent to the United States were comparatively cheap. Towards the end of the export boom one would have sharp rises in export prices. Therefore his argument about the terms of trade assumed that factors of production were readily available to the United Kingdom export trades. In the United States, on the other hand, there was a building boom. Domestic prices rose sharply, and goods were sucked into the construction sector. *Professor Timlin* confirmed that this was also true in Canada up to 1914.

Mr. Turvey asked whether Professor Thomas meant that in the United Kingdom, when there was an increase in emigration, a building slump *preceded* the rise in exports to the United States.

Professor Thomas said that it was difficult to answer this. He was using yearly figures, which made it hard to study lags. This answered Professor Hoffman also. One could not say whether the construction or the export boom came first.

Mr. Turvey still felt that the argument required that the building slump should come first.

Professor Lerner could not see why the proposition about the direction in changes in the terms of trade was relevant to the remainder of Professor Thomas's argument. More than this, he could not see why they should change in the way Professor Thomas postulated. Empirically, he thought Professor Thomas was right, but it did not seem to follow from his analysis. One could easily say that the higher demand for exports raised the price of labour. He would, however, be happy to see this shown in terms of *costs* rather than *demand*, because he could not see whether the boom caused migration, or migration caused the boom. Perhaps a third thing caused both. One got the same result with a depression in the United Kingdom. Migration then changed the terms of trade, as described, with capital that was not now needed in Britain being exported. Yet, in the paper, the change seemed to be the other way.

Professor Thomas denied this. Exports only enjoyed a boom whilst construction was languishing. In *total*, trade union figures for employment showed a relative depression in the United Kingdom.

Professor Lerner persisted that sometimes migration came first, and, as a result of fewer people remaining in Britain, less housing was needed. Then would come greater exports and a movement in the terms of trade against the United Kingdom. If the terms of trade moved in favour of Great Britain, this fitted in with the theory that the depression in the United Kingdom caused *both* the slump in the United Kingdom *and* migration from the United Kingdom.

Professor Timlin felt that one should think of the great movement of capital to Canada which built the Canadian Pacific Railway in the middle of a British depression. This capital movement had been a spur to later migration from about 1896 until 1930, though not to concurrent population movements. Migration was made possible only because of the earlier capital movement, but it later became the *main* expanding force in Canada up to the 1930's and drew in further capital. Professor Viner had shown that, in the early part of the century, the Canadian price level was higher than the price level in the United States, which exported to Canada. Therefore synchronization was not close.

Professor Thomas stressed the fact that one could not determine from the statistics whether the labour flow preceded the capital movement or vice versa. But did it matter ? One could start with emigration from Ireland, where the potato famine represented a push, pure and simple, resulting from an exogenous factor. Then one had first the labour flow and later the Lerner sequence. After that, as the United States grew in attractiveness, it was the rate of growth of producer durables in America which was significant. In America, first one had the boom, with capital flowing in. Then, as labour flowed in, the housing boom began, after a short lag. There were, if one liked, two models : first, the Irish case, with exogenous causal factors and large-scale migration ; second, the usual model which showed the labour movement as second or third in the sequence.

Professor Timlin added that in Canada migration represented one source of secondary investment to carry the economy over slumps.

Professor Spengler said that speakers so far had been concerned with short-run differences during slumps, but there might also be persistent differences.

Professor Robinson was surprised by Professor Thomas's contention that there had been a boom in British exports at the same time as a depression in construction. This seemed somewhat paradoxical to those familiar with the Hicks-Harrod models of economic fluctuations. Professor Thomas conceived a British economy which simultaneously displayed conditions of unemployment and of full employment. Professor

Robinson found this confusion between full employment and unemployment hard to apprehend, and asked Professor Thomas to clarify his position. Was it that we were always so near full employment in the nineteenth century that many of the phenomena experienced were those of full employment rather than those of a violently oscillating economy ? Professor Robinson said his point was simply that he was puzzled why the export boom led to so little capital construction. Was it something in the structure of the economy ? For example, with a country like New Zealand, with a relatively large export trade, would one get different results from those in the United States ?

Professor Thomas did not agree that there was confusion. It was true that, in any theoretical model, an export boom would have an income effect, and lead, through the accelerator, to increased construction. But one must distinguish short and long cycles. His argument ignored short cycles and concentrated entirely on the 'Kuznets cycle'. Two points needed emphasis. First, whatever one did with the statistics, one got long swings. Second, the inverse relation between the long swings in the United States and the United Kingdom was undeniable.

To clarify the position for Professor Robinson, Professor Thomas pointed out that Professor Kuznets had shown that one could distinguish between capital formation which was 'population sensitive' and that which was not. Kuznets had suggested that these types of capital formation were inversely related, and had confirmed that the net migration balance was a *primary* variable in the economic growth of the United States up to 1913. Professor Thomas thought the distinction between population sensitive and population non-sensitive investment was important. When British exports boomed there was a derived demand for the construction directly required by the export industries ; but capital formation not connected with exports (*e.g.* housing) languished. One should therefore distinguish between export-sensitive and export-non-sensitive capital formation. A combination of an upswing in the export sector and a downswing in export-non-sensitive construction produced a milder expansion in income and employment than the opposite combination — an upswing in export-non-sensitive construction and a downswing in exports.

Professor Lerner asked whether this meant that construction was larger than exports. Professor Thomas had said that construction was more important. Either fluctuations in exports were greater, or else construction accounted for more than 30 per cent of all activity. Why were fluctuations in building more important than those in exports ? Professor Lerner suspected that in fact the opposite was the case.

Professor Thomas replied that when there was a major boom in the construction of fixed capital at home, the effect on income was greater than with a boom in exports.

Professor Robinson wondered if the words 'boom' and 'slump' were misleading. This was a question of *long*- and not short-term swings.

The economy was fairly fully occupied throughout the period, yet we were using words denoting short-period changes in the level of activity.

Professor Timlin said that the difference in rates of expansion between the two economies in question was fundamental. In Canada capital flows and migration depended on the rate of expansion at home. When the United States was expanding faster, Canada lost population to the United States and vice versa. It was not so much a question of a boom in one economy and a slump in the other, as of differing rates of expansion in each country.

Professor Lindahl thought the distinction between long and short cycles was important. By his long cycle Professor Thomas suggested one lasting, say, twenty years, and therefore equal to two short cycles. One could make no inference about the terms of trade in long-term cycles, for the terms of trade were not relevant in the long run. Nor was Professor Thomas very explicit about the effect of migration on the short cycle. It was important to apply the analysis to the short cycle, when one could stress other aspects. If there were a depression in the United Kingdom, with much emigration, Britain would export her unemployment and there would not nowadays be a boom in the United States. But in the nineteenth century there would have been a boom in America, since the inflow of labour would have caused an expansion. How would the cycle in Britain be affected? The unemployed would leave Britain and find jobs in America. British exports would rise, the terms of trade would move in Britain's favour, and the export boom would shorten her depression.

Professor Hoffman supported Professor Thomas in his stress on the importance of a 20-year cycle; there were many facts to justify this assumption. This was true not only for the United Kingdom, or for the building industry; it applied also to all capital goods industries. The figures given for the United Kingdom by Professor Thomas started in the 1870's, but railways and canals came earlier. This early investment was extensive. After 1870 there was capital intensification. This might well explain the change in the export quota as well as the corresponding changes in the terms of trade. If one looked at exports of manufactured goods and imports of raw material, one might well find the explanation.

Professor Lerner recalled that Professor Robinson thought there might have been shifts between the production of capital and export goods, and not changes in the level of activity. Professor Lerner was surprised that Professor Thomas agreed with this. For Table II, which showed changes in unemployment, seemed to show a secular population movement from Europe to a booming United States. Migration could be attributed to the fact that the rise in real income was greater in the United States, though the rate of increase was falling in both countries. But this steady process was interrupted in 1894–1908. There was an investment boom in the United Kingdom and a consequent fall in migration. This led to a fall in the volume of construction in America in 1884–93 and 1889–98. After that the process was renewed. Therefore, Professor Thomas was studying a 50-year movement with an interruption in the middle.

Mr. Turvey wondered whether, if one considered the Juglar cycle, there was a positive correlation, in the short run, between the level of investment in the two countries.

Professor Thomas replied that there was.

Mr. Turvey then suggested that, since we were dealing with 10-year moving averages, the question was not one of a decline in *levels* of activity so much as one in rates of growth. For example, in 1874–83 not only was unemployment up, employment was up too. He also pointed out that if the British investment industries were shifting from building railways and houses, there would be a more rapid turnover of capital. Did the rate of interest then change, so that during the 10-year periods of high export and low housing construction there was a high rate of interest in the United Kingdom ?

Professor Thomas replied that when Britain was investing in the United States rates of interest in the United States were generally higher, and vice versa in the next period. In building, the rate of interest would obviously have an effect.

Professor James thought Professor Thomas was right so far as migration between the United Kingdom and the United States in the period 1860–1900 was concerned. Professor Thomas ended with the optimistic theory that a country with unemployment could export unemployment without exporting its employment, because the receiving country could benefit from a high rate of growth. But should one generalize this theory ? It seemed correct if one supposed that migration of population always accompanied capital movements, but this hypothesis might not always be justifiable. One could have migration without any accompanying movement of capital, for example from Ireland to the United States. If this happened, dare one be so optimistic ? Professor James did not think so. He raised three questions on this point. First, could we agree that, when men moved, capital always moved too ? Second, if migration were not accompanied by capital movements, how far was Professor Thomas's theory right ? Third, when the movement of capital *followed* migration, was the optimistic theory still valid ?

Professor Thomas replied that where migration was accompanied by a capital movement, as in case 3, it made no difference whether the population moved before the capital or after it. It was Professor James's second case that caused trouble. If capital stayed at home when population moved, there would be a different effect on the home construction industries. If all investment depended on home activity, the mechanism would surely be upset. The supply of funds at home would differ, and so presumably would the rate of interest. There might not then be an inverse relationship. This was, however, an interesting situation, though he himself had not worked it out.

Professor Timlin felt that emigration should make the depression shorter and the boom longer in the population-losing country.

Professor James wondered what happened in the receiving country, to which *Professor Thomas* replied that, since it received many migrants, the process of credit creation and inflation would be exaggerated. This was, in essence, the problem of the underdeveloped areas, where rapid natural increase of population meant 'immigration via the birth-rate'.

Professor Lindahl said that Professor Thomas had omitted to mention that the losing country was not always the same country as the source of capital. Sweden, for instance, had emigration at the same time as she was *importing* capital. This complicated, though it did not upset, the theory.

Professor Rubin thought one could speak of migration movement irrespective of capital movements. Migration itself was a form of capital movement. He pointed out, first, that labour in the nineteenth century brought much money capital with it. Second, he reminded the conference that one had to 'decapitalize' to allow for the immigration of children. Children did not enter immediately into the labour force, but adults did. One, therefore, had a double 'capital export' with grown labour, quite apart from the traditional notion of capital.

Professor Thomas inquired whether, in Professor James's case 2, there was *no* capital movement, only the migration of pure labour.

Professor James said this was so. He thought, for instance, of movements from Algeria to France now, and also from Ireland to the United States in the nineteenth century.

Professor Thomas said that, if one relaxed this assumption slightly, one could study the relation between the rate of migration and the inflow of remittances to losing countries from the United States. Migration would then become a function of American income growth. Italy was a good example of this. Italians were able to migrate because of money sent from the United States, and a higher level of income in the United States made it possible to send more money back.

Professor Rubin added the point that each immigrant was a 'magnet' for further potential migration. Not only did he send money back home; he also sent descriptions of the new country.

Mr. Meenan pointed out that the migrant could also find jobs in the new country for his relatives at home. Of course, there was much migration that was quite independent of capital movements. With an agricultural society, disintegrated as in Ireland, people would emigrate whether they had money or not. It might be hard to build up capital in the losing country. Even in the last forty years much of the saving in Ireland had gone into capital formation in England. The lack of investment in Ireland was the result of a long period of emigration.

Professor Robinson said Professor Lindahl had claimed that emigration helped recovery at home and thus smoothed out the short cycle. But the rate of population growth at home was important too. He was surprised that Professor Lindahl thought emigration favourable to diminishing cyclical movements. Experience in Ireland surely illustrated this point very clearly.

Mr. Phillips, commenting on Professor James's case 2, said that immigration could bring about a better use of existing capital in under-developed countries by making up gaps in skill. For example, in the case of public transport in Latin America it was noticeable that the proportion of vehicles out of action in garages was generally higher than in Europe. This was caused by the shortage of skilled maintenance workers, and a relatively small intake of skilled workers might allow existing capital to be used more effectively.

Professor Thomas had contended that it did not matter whether capital followed or preceded migration. Yet, if too many immigrants arrived in advance of the construction of public utilities, serious bottle-necks would result which would hold back production. This had been the experience with power supplies in Argentina. It was often important that capital should arrive first. Again, there were great variations in the types of capital needed by migrants. The original migration to the Western Hemisphere had needed little capital, and later migrants used the capital accumulated by earlier ones. He thought these points should be borne in mind in analysing the relationship between population movements and capital movements.

Professor Silcock suggested that if one treated the United States and the United Kingdom as a *single* economy and assumed a long-term difference in income between them, unemployment in the short run might accentuate the willingness to move, and labour would move towards resources in the place where the latter were more productive. Therefore unemployment could create a situation where the fundamental improving force, that of getting labour to the right place, would work. Similarly, migrants moving to unexploited natural resources might create conditions in which capital would move.

In modern underdeveloped areas, however, the effects of natural increase were the opposite of those of migration. Rapid natural increase led to a high demand on the education system, and that was a negative factor in development, leading to a large demand for 'social' capital where such capital was already short. But where migrants moved to the United States or Latin America they were not only adults but also well trained. This was an important difference between migration and natural growth.

Professor Thomas replied that he wondered if it was overpopulation that caused the problems of underdeveloped countries. Was it not rather that, because of the high infant death-rate, much of a backward country's small capital was used up in wasteful ways, for instance, in rearing children who never reached the point of producing at all ? Was not this the problem, and not overpopulation ? When the United States received migrants the United States grew. If population growth was

good for underdeveloped countries in the nineteenth century why was
it bad now ? The answer, surely, was that it would not be bad *if* these
countries had the same demographic structure as their counterparts in
the nineteenth century. The need was to ensure that children did grow
up and become producers. However, Professor Thomas did not think it
made any difference to his theory whether the extra members of a country
were adults or children.

Professor Silcock did not agree that infant mortality was the cause of
the trouble. Nor was the 20-year lag between birth and coming on to the
labour market irrelevant to the question whether underdeveloped countries
had enough capital. He pointed out that education *was* expensive, and
in underdeveloped countries it absorbed much scarce capital.

Mr. Turvey suggested that the relationship between capital movements
and migration depended on the character of migrants. For example,
the Irish moved to America without capital and went to urban areas,
forcing down wages and raising the marginal efficiency of investment in
manufacturing industry. The Swedes, on the other hand, often took
enough money to live for a year whilst making a farm. But they *did*
require previous investment of a large amount of fixed capital in railways,
etc., while the immigration of the Irish made it profitable to build new
factories in which they could work.

Professor Thomas agreed with Mr. Turvey's view on types of migrant
and his distinction between the Irish and the Swedes. He thought the
point to remember was that in the early migration to the United States
the amount of capital coming from the United Kingdom was important;
for example, British purchases of American railroad securities, as well as
purchases by Dutch and Germans. In each upward phase of the long
cycle there was a crucial sector of the American economy into which
the incoming capital flowed. The immigrants' own money represented
mere driblets compared with the volume of securities bought by foreign
investors. An upswing in the United States enabled the Irish to send
cash home, but that upswing received much of the impetus from purchases
of American securities by Europeans.

Professor Hoffman had asked about the 20-year cycle. Was it merely
a result of skilful doctoring of statistics ? Professor Thomas did not
think so. Nor was it a result of the fact that some Juglars were strong
and others weak. The long swing was evident in many series. Professor
Thomas referred to the many examples of this which had been given by
Mr. O'Leary and Professor Lewis. It was not just a question of different
intensities of the Juglars. There must be some variation at the heart of
the system, and he thought this was the building cycle. Economists had
concentrated too much on the Juglar. What was needed was a thorough
analysis of the 'construction cycle'. It was not clear what caused the
inverse U.K.-U.S.A. relationship. Was it to be explained by the theory
of the building cycle, by 'cobwebs', or by the reinvestment cycle ? The
really interesting point emained : why should the period be twenty

years ? Building was 30 to 40 per cent of national capital in many countries, and therefore had a great effect on the economy as a whole.

Professor Hoffman emphasized that it was the 20-year cycle which we were considering. A crisis might force migration or capital movements, but how could it explain a 20-year cycle ? Was the cause a lag before reinvestment ? He thought the data might justify this idea for the 20-year cycle, but *not* for the short cycle. Both Britain and the United States had used similar techniques until the 1860's, after which the superiority of the United States began to emerge. On the other hand, if one tried to answer the question by combining the effects of different cycles in the United Kingdom and the United States, saying that the boom or the crisis was responsible, how did one decide which ?

Dr. Edding felt that both short and long cycles were important. Jerome had been concerned with the short cycle, as had, for example, Beveridge. All said the business cycle was an *international* phenomenon, and this was undeniably true in the short run. Sir Dennis Robertson would speak of simultaneous hiccups. He himself was interested in a longer, 20-year cycle. There was no inconsistency between simultaneous business cycles and inversely-related construction cycles. Jerome had been led to unfortunate conclusions, and the United States anti-migration laws reflected Jerome's view that migration exacerbated the United States unemployment position. Yet, taking a longer view, during the years when most immigrants went into the United States, income grew fastest.

Professor Rubin pointed out that Jerome wrote in 1925, just when the United States was restricting the influx of migration and when the public was interested in the question. This had been one of the few books published by the National Bureau of Economic Research which 'took a position'. America still held to the fallacy that migration was bad during a recession.

Professor Thomas commented that politicians had short time-horizons because of elections. Even in an upswing recessions were feared, and in a recession it was thought that migration caused unemployment for home workers. It was an 'overhead social cost' if one let in these workers. Yet it was a cost which the economy should be glad to bear, since, in the long run, it encouraged rapid development.

Professor Lindahl wondered if Professor Thomas was not limiting the value of his theory by applying it only to the 20-year cycle ? Professor Thomas had said that his theory did not apply to the Juglar ; but had he really distinguished between nineteenth-century and twentieth-century cycles ? Professor Thomas might try to apply his theory to the nineteenth-century business cycle, because the expansionary trend was so very strong in the United States that she could resist the influence of European cycles.

Professor Rubin thought it important to remember that, when Jerome wrote, the importance of long cycles was not so widely acknowledged as it was later.

Professor Ellis wondered if Professor Thomas's argument rested on his statement that fluctuations in construction were greater than fluctuations in imports. What he was uncertain about was the theoretical justification for this view.

Professor Thomas said his argument was that when one was building, say, railways, roads, or docks, the income-generating effect was stronger than when one was producing portable export goods.

Professor Lerner, however, could not see why construction should be more effective in raising the level of incomes than a corresponding volume of exports. If exports in England represented 30 per cent of national income, and construction less than 30 per cent, why did one get this result ? If the fluctuations were of the same order of magnitude in both sectors, then the results would be the reverse of Professor Thomas's. Was the relative size of the construction fluctuations bigger ?

Professor Thomas replied that he could see Professor Lerner's problem, but the facts were otherwise.

Mr. Turvey said that it seemed to be agreed that in some periods exports were going up faster than construction, while at other times the opposite was happening. Over a long period, however, must not the share of construction in the national income have risen ?

Professor Lerner was prepared to acknowledge that the facts were against him. But how did Professor Thomas's model work ? He said that there had been an explanation of the inverse cycles in terms of *given* resources moving from one sector to another. But the same model was used to explain fluctuations in employment by assuming that there were bigger changes in construction than in exports. Why should this be ? Was there a general explanation ? Why should construction generate bigger multipliers ?

Professor Thomas replied that he was firmly convinced that when the switch to exports took place, the overall rise in employment was weaker than when the economy was engaged mainly on making fixed capital for use at home.

Mr. Turvey said that the greater import content of exports as opposed to construction would not in this case be a refutation of Professor Lerner's criticism, because British construction involved much timber and other imported materials. Besides, the size of both construction and exports should be reckoned *net* of imported materials.

Professor Spengler felt there was an empirical puzzle. He asked Professor Thomas whether the statistics of unemployment in Great Britain showed this shift of labour from exports to construction, via the 'third sector'. Since the third sector represented 50 per cent of the British national product, it could not be ignored, even in a simple model.

Professor Thomas replied that in the Great Depression loud cries came from the exporters and yet, at the same time, the builders did not complain. There must have been considerable labour mobility in Britain during such periods.

Professor Robinson said that at the period in question most British exports were textiles. Women in Lancashire did not move directly to construction, though there might have been a step-by-step movement.

Mr. Rubin felt there were too few facts to justify even this notion.

Professor Thomas agreed that one could not draw a precise borderline between sectors. Nevertheless the difference between exports and home construction remained important.

Professor Lerner was bothered by a 'chicken and egg' problem. Did investment rise and fall before migration, or after it? If some other factor made people think the United States was not so attractive, both migration and capital movements could fall off.

Professor Thomas wondered what might do this. Was not Professor Lerner introducing a *deus ex machina*?

Professor Lerner said he did not know what this other factor might be. But if there were some psychological reason which prevented expansion in America and therefore stopped migration, the effects on exports from Britain might be smaller than on activity as a whole. Perhaps the real answer was not that *construction* fluctuated more than exports, but only income.

Dr. Edding wondered what was the implication of Professor Thomas's paper for the present. Short-run cycles could be smoothed out by government action. Professor Thomas had said that long cycles must go on, but could not even long swings be ironed out by a correct economic policy?

Professor Thomas said that if it were true that nowadays the inverse construction cycle did not exist any more, then if all countries experienced their building cycles at the same time one might have a major general boom or slump. For the offsetting effect in the nineteenth century might now have been removed; but he did not like to speculate on this.

Dr. Beijer returned to the relation between capital exports and emigration. The export of capital from the United Kingdom had been based on capital accumulation in foreign countries. At the same time, much of what was called British migration had really been Irish. If the same parts of Britain had lost both capital *and* migrants, the situation might have been very different. The model helped to show a migration country that it should be careful whether it sent capital or migrants.

Professor Thomas stressed that one ought to relate the flow of capital from London to the flow of people from *Europe*. The two were complementary from the viewpoint of the receiving country. Nevertheless, from the senders' point of view, migration from the United Kingdom was relevant. When it fell off, more houses were built at home. Once the downturn in the export of both capital and people was passed, however, loanable funds were available in the United Kingdom. It was not only migration and construction which had to be considered in explaining the problem.

Professor Lerner returned to the question of his 'exogenous cause'.

There was no reason, of course, why this should not be an endogenous factor, in which case Professor Thomas's reasoning would apply. He noted that there was a reference to the proposition that Britain was a 'better' creditor nation in its time than the United States. Why was this view held ?

Mr. Turvey suggested that the relation of migration to construction must have been unique. Was part of the answer that in Ireland there had been an absolute fall in population, so that no houses were demanded ?

Professor Robinson wondered if Irish migration should be related to Irish or United Kingdom construction. Irish navvies were used all over Europe, and by 1860 were moving to the United States.

Mr. Meenan agreed about the great mobility of Irish labour. In the railway age, in the mid-1840's, Irish labour moved to England, France, and even Algeria. There was tremendous movement in response to pressures from outside Ireland.

Professor Rubin suggested that, in the absence of restrictions after 1918, migration from Europe to the United States would have gone on, but capital movements would not. It was only because of the Quota Act that both ended simultaneously.

Professor Silcock commented on the comparison between a growth in population caused by immigration and the increase of population in underdeveloped areas caused by improved health measures. The problem was not so much the size of the population as its demand on capital resources. Professor Thomas had said that the important thing was that the young died before becoming productive. His own impression was that it was not in the age group 2-15 that the death-rate was so high in underdeveloped countries. If there were any demographic causes at all, the main one was that so many people died after a very short working life. An exogenous factor, the advent of Western medicine in recent years, also meant that there were more young people. The significant difference, therefore, was that in backward countries the rate of natural increase was a burden on domestic capital resources, though it might be held to be a stimulating factor which could lead to increased investment by other countries in underdeveloped areas.

In the Atlantic area a high marginal efficiency of capital had existed over a long period. The position was not the same in underdeveloped areas, because the lack of education there meant there were not enough specialists available to use capital assets. So it was not easy now to move in capital. Professor Silcock referred again to the statement that capital did not seem to move voluntarily to underdeveloped areas. This seemed true enough, and that was why he had mentioned the need for developing new skills rapidly, and the way in which at present this caused a drain on capital resources. If one could attract private capital on a large scale to the underdeveloped areas, one might have the same kind of stimulus to growth in underdeveloped areas as one had experienced in Britain and America during the nineteenth century.

Professor Thomas agreed on two points. First, the average working life was very short in underdeveloped areas. Second, *private* savings might not be very low as a percentage of national income, but so much of them was consumed unproductively. The shortage of capital might therefore be exaggerated.

Professor Silcock agreed that, to some extent, capital was used in ways that turned out to be inefficient, though he thought that to some extent this was due to imperfect capital markets. Even so, he did not think private and public savings in backward areas exceeded 5 or 6 per cent of national income. They only reached 10 per cent in an exceptional boom. Perhaps one needed to *use* such fluctuations to get more capital.

Professor Ellis wondered whether, in fact, many production resources were used in rearing children who did not work for long, if at all.

Professor Silcock replied that few people died before the age of 15, though, as he had said, many people had only a short working life.

Professor Robinson thought that, so far, the older people had been ignored. *Prima facie*, the fact that the old died off early lightened the burden. Looking at East Africa, where most mortality occurred in the first few years, its cost was not high. He did not think there were more 'passengers' in underdeveloped areas than elsewhere.

Professor Lerner inquired whether the percentage of population working was different in backward areas.

Professor Silcock said it was hard to compare accurately. He suspected, however, that the proportion of the population that was working was a little lower in backward areas. With the rapid population increase there were more people below working age.

Professor Lerner thought that a poorer country had a greater percentage of its population working longer.

Professor Robertson said that we must make up our minds what to blame the medical profession for. Was it for keeping too many people alive, or was it for not reducing infant mortality enough ?

Professor Silcock did not think one should blame the medical profession for reducing mortality at high ages. He did not think the structure of population was at fault. So far as there was any demographic cause, it was because people's working lives were not long enough.

Professor Thomas thought Professor Lerner vulnerable on this point. He had forgotten disguised unemployment in backward areas.

Professor Silcock said that was another problem. The real question here was how many people were available. He did not think that whether women worked or not was a demographic factor. Apart from that, he doubted whether the nature of the working population in underdeveloped areas was much different from that elsewhere.

Professor Spengler suggested that, in an underdeveloped country, the number of people of working age might be several per cent lower than elsewhere because of the high rate of growth of population.

Professor Robinson pointed out that the Indian census figures showed that, with varying rates of growth, the size of the central working-age group was very little different. He did not think rapid growth would seriously affect the proportion of workers to total population.

Professor Lerner suggested that it was a *change* in the rate of growth, which had not yet been worked out, which led to our problem.

Mr. Turvey noted that Professor Robinson had said that different net reproduction rates did not make much difference to the population structure. But if two countries had the same net reproduction rates, and one country had a much higher *gross* rate, then there could be differences in the population structure. Mr. Turvey asked three questions. First, he wondered if money spent on the education of those who died early was important. Second, since technicians were trained after the age of 15, could it be argued that much money was wasted in training them? Many would have died already. Third, were not the best-trained people those with the highest living standards and therefore the least likely to die off?

Professor Silcock said that when a large percentage of the working population was engaged in training the young, the wastage was important. For example, this was the case in Malaya and other South-east Asian countries.

Professor Rubin felt that in India the greatest problem, up to 1975, was likely to be how to attain a high rate of capital formation per head. It was right to keep coming back to the burden of expenditure on training; but disguised unemployment was also important. In India and Malaya there was considerable confusion because medicine had cut the death-rate precipitately. He did not know the age distribution of those who had lived longer because of medical advances, but it was certainly going to be difficult for India to maintain a high rate of capital formation.

Professor Robinson returned to the relation between capital movement and migration. Two sources of capital had been suggested: (*a*) capital taken by migrants; (*b*) savings in the receiving country. Surely (*c*) agricultural migrants created capital themselves by 'living thin' while creating their farms. In much of American and also of Canadian settlement this was very important. Was it not always an important factor when agricultural areas were opened up? Professor Timlin thought it might be, but pointed out that much capital came in afterwards.

Professor Robinson admitted this, but wondered if, even so, we did not underestimate the importance of this other source; for example, of capital created in developing the land.

Professor Thomas did not think that, in fact, it was very important, whilst *Professor Ellis* regarded it as a past factor, which was now endogenous.

Professor Lerner said he was concerned with the need to supply just as much capital as was needed to maintain the new migrant and enable him to start to save. After that, he could progress by himself.

Dr. Edding noted a secular shift in importance from land and machinery to 'brain' capital. This was shown by comparing the cost of education in 1900 and now. Germany, for example, had recently received 10 million migrants, without risk capital. Much capital for them had been created out of 'forced savings' and a policy favouring self-financing, but he himself had calculated in 1950 that the refugee-immigrant needed at least the same capital as he had had before; that was to say, on average, 6000 Reichsmarks per person. On this basis, capital worth 100,000,000,000 Deutschmarks would have been needed before a 20 per cent larger population could be fully used. Yet, in fact, these people had been used much sooner. So he concluded that the capital invested on the education and training of the migrants should be given more weight in calculations such as his.

THE DISCUSSION ON PROFESSOR SPENGLER'S PAPER

Third and Fourth Sessions, Sunday, 4 September 1955

Professor Robinson opened the discussion. He said that Professor Spengler's paper emphasized the effects of migration on the receiving countries. One could say that there were (*a*) aggregate and (*b*) substitution effects, and that the attitude of every native population to migration was the result of both of these. With powerful 'lobbies', and with the need to placate minorities, people might ignore the aggregate effects and concentrate attention on the substitution effects. The latter would then have a disproportionate effect on migration policy.

Professor Robinson said that he would begin with the substitution effects. The simplest case would arise if one added a 'block' of migrants with similar occupations, skills, and social classes, to an existing population. There would then be no substitution effects; only problems of scale. In practice, however, there was always the danger that some of the migrants' skills would be competitive with those of natives. On the other hand, it would be advantageous if some of the migrants had skills that were complementary to those of the natives. The question was, who was likely to benefit from migration and who would suffer. In general, Professor Spengler seemed to say that any given group of migrants would be likely to have more unskilled workers, more members of the lower social classes. This was convincing in the case of the United States; but was it general ?

The push to migration was twofold. Among economic factors, there was the push of poverty and of unemployment (which had perhaps been over-emphasized so far), but there was also the pull of opportunity, which depended on there being different real rewards for skill in various countries. One could distinguish two cases. First, there was the movement of the unskilled to Australia, New Zealand, and perhaps South

America. Second, there was the movement of the skilled to where they had greater opportunity. Europeans moved to South, East, and West Africa and parts of Asia. Indians went from India to East Africa, and to other areas where Indians possessed skills not possessed by the indigenous population, for example, to Burma before 1939. There were, here, two patterns and not one. One was where the migrants were less skilled and of a lower social class than the native stock. The other was where they were the reverse.

Professor Robinson said that one should distinguish these two cases, especially in their political effects. In the United States type of migration the upper classes benefited, though the unskilled might be damaged and might resist. In East Africa the pattern was that the unskilled benefited from higher employment and wages. The skilled were unlikely to, or at least they thought so. Even if one took the United States pattern, was it really so simple? Were we not treating as homogeneous a 'block' of many parts? Around 1900 the movements to the United States were of the kind Professor Spengler had noted. If large-scale immigration happened again, the results would be similar. But what about the recent smaller-scale moves? Were not the migrants now highly qualified technicians, competitive with the top classes in the United States, and not with the bottom: for example, trained chemists from England? This had interesting consequences on the distribution of income. If unskilled workers were now less mobile internationally, professional incomes after tax must be more equal internationally than the earnings of unskilled workers. Did it follow that one needed a bigger spread of incomes in under-developed areas than at present in order to keep their relatively few qualified workers at home?

Professor Robinson then turned to the aggregate effects of migration. Professor Spengler had said that the rate of growth was increased by migration. But was that increase an increase per head? The answer, Professor Spengler said, was that it depended on whether one had increasing returns in the receiving country. This was true; but was it the whole answer? Professor Spengler had quoted the *Economic Journal* article by Rothbarth, explaining the greater productivity of the United States. Lord Keynes had argued, in describing this article, that it was largely because of migration that the United States economy was always growing rapidly and outstripping capacity. There was consequently less risk in undertaking investment, and capital formation was larger, more rapid and more confident. Because of this high rate of investment, the American economy was always tending to outstrip its resources, and was near to full employment (and consequently short of labour) more of the time than the losing countries. Therefore, more labour-saving devices were installed, and this further aided growth.

Conversely, in population-losing countries, some of the effects of migration were almost exactly the opposite. It was harder to export unemployment than Professor Thomas's paper seemed to suggest. First, those who emigrated were not normally the unemployed. Second, if one lost, say, 100,000 workers' output, and at the same time their effective demand, did not these cancel out ? Indeed, if the consumption of unemployed workers had been maintained by government grants, would not emigration actually reduce effective demand ?

Professor Spengler said that America experienced the kind of differences in labour mobility that Professor Robinson had mentioned. Because of differences in mobility, one had a greater dispersion of income in the Southern States than in the North.

Professor Bachi said that Professor Spengler had indicated that forced migration took place for economic rather than political reasons. This was true for the cases discussed in the paper. But it was not true of all migration, for example of migration from Greece to Turkey after 1918, and of some Jewish migration. Was Professor Spengler's model of the effects of migration applicable to such politically induced migration ? Or did we need to modify the general scheme ?

Professor Spengler felt that one should distinguish (1) forced immigration, as in the Turkey-Greece case, where migrants were told where to go, and (2) forced emigration where migrants could choose where to go. The second case fitted his analysis, being similar to what had happened since 1945. The first case, however, was complicated by government intervention.

Professor Parenti raised several points on the analysis of the aggregate effects of migration. Professor Robinson had explained that emigration could remove bottlenecks when growth required a change in the structure of the economy. This would increase the aggregate mobility of labour. So, in other sectors, where there was no real bottleneck, resources would be better used. If one considered the United States, big relative changes in employment there had not, except in agriculture, meant any *absolute* reduction in the employment in any sector because the labour force as a whole had increased rapidly. So capital was not wasted. In a country like France one did get absolute falls in employment in some sectors, and previous investment was wasted. Immigration would allow this surplus capital to be used.

Professor Spengler thought the argument on bottlenecks was valid, since other papers before the Conference made the same point. He himself had neglected this point, though it was clearly important. He agreed that in the United States the labour force had changed without absolute falls in employment. But the numbers in any industry could fit themselves to demand through normal wastage. At least 2 to 3 per cent of employees left in any year because of retirement, etc. A 25 per cent reduction would occur in about five years, and the loss of 'personal' capital was therefore not so great as it might seem at first sight.

Speaking of the 'Walker Effect', *Professor Parenti* said he had never found any evidence for it. He had mainly considered the problem from the emigration side, though his study had been for other purposes, to see if the effect was visible in the losing country. But even the use of modern techniques showed no evidence of the action of the law. Did Professor Spengler agree with the theory ? Was there any statistical basis for it, or any deductive model explaining it ? Professor Spengler had talked of the displacing effect of immigration, and of the possibility of induced emigration. In Europe, Switzerland's statistics, for example, showed that she was a receiver and also sent migrants. Yet the occupations of immigrants and emigrants differed. Emigrants were in the higher occupations and went to less developed areas. Immigrants were in the lower occupations and went to occupations other than those of the emigrant group. Thus the Walker effect was not plausible. Perhaps, however, one had emigration to the United States from Canada to complement some movements to the United States from Europe.

Professor Spengler said that he had used logistic methods to study the Walker effect and thought immigration had little effect on birth-rates. The effect on birth-rates was negligible, though migration might even have increased birth-rates. It was also hard to find factual support by studying migration. The strong movement from the United States to Canada about 1900 was hardly explainable in terms of displacement. There might be some movement owing to an upset in the occupational or social structure, though this was purely a question of labour mobility. Indeed, he thought most displacement was to be considered as labour mobility rather than migration. So, he preferred to deal with Switzerland in terms of labour mobility plus peculiarities in the social structure.

Dr. Wander asked whether, when he said that the Walker effect caused birth-rates to decline, Professor Spengler meant that an indigenous population had a lower birth-rate in any case, because of its age structure.

Professor Spengler said it was true that the age structure differed.

Dr. Wander wondered about the sex structure. How was intermarriage taken account of ?

Professor Spengler said that where there was intermarriage with migrants to the United States, the number of children per mother was higher than where both parents were American, reflecting the European pattern. The number of children per mother was low with immigrants from the United Kingdom or France, and high if the immigrants were from Eastern Europe. Where foreigners married Americans, the birth-rate was a little lower than in Europe, though higher than in the United States. In the second generation this was still true. In the third generation there was little difference between the migrant and the American birth-rate. Therefore, some cultural element assimilated migrants into the American population. It was said by Walker that after heavy immigration to the United States the rate of population growth declined, Americans having fewer children than they would have done without immigration. Professor Spengler did not agree.

Professor Timlin said that the character of migration within North America was an element which needed to be considered. For example, women were more attracted by cities than men were, and men might be arriving in Canada as inter-continental migrants while women might be the chief migrants leaving Canada for American cities. Students of both sexes often went to graduate schools in the United States and then found jobs there. The shortage of graduate schools in Canada was therefore an institutional factor influencing migration. It was also doubtful whether the statistics on United States-Canadian movement were reliable. Perhaps some people just slipped over the border. In addition, the administration of visas was probably not always efficient enough to distinguish visitors from immigrants. Because of the relatively free character of movement across the United States-Canadian border, perhaps the United States authorities often did not or could not know which Canadians were permanent immigrants and which were not.

With immigration into Canada, the development of principles of selection had affected the character of migration. When the first Immigration Act was passed in 1869, Canada's main concern was that if the migrant were a pauper, the transportation companies should pay his fare to his destination. After 1896 selection was introduced and a closer check kept on the occupation of immigrants. At that time, movement from the United States was quite free. American immigrants usually had the right qualifications, usually went to the West, and were given favoured treatment to encourage them to come. From Britain and the Continent selection principles aimed at encouraging agricultural immigrants only. Over a portion of the period selection was sufficiently successful for it to have been estimated in 1906 that more than $99\frac{1}{2}$ per cent of immigrants from Hamburg, the main port of embarkation from the Continent, were agricultural. The Western land settlement movement in the early part of the century created the wheat economy with its exports and customers for Eastern Canada.

In 1921 the Dominion Bureau of Statistics studied the relation between the racial origins of immigrants and intermarriage, language-learning speed, criminality, etc. Preference was then given to settlers who would be likely to intermarry. This might mean that in Canada the impact of migrants on natives was conditioned by selection. This sort of institutional effect would alter the value of Canada as a model.

Professor Rubin commented on the Walker 'fallacy'. La Place, a French mathematician, had related the geometric progression to the growth in the population of the American colonies between 1750 and 1800. Every twenty-five years or so the population doubled. In 1816 Elkanah Watson used more data and made projections which proved correct up to 1860, the date of the Civil War. After that date, however, Watson's estimates became increasingly incorrect. Walker argued that it was the large flow of immigrants after 1865 that distorted Watson's estimates. On Watson's calculation, for example, the population in 1900 should have been 160 million. It was a classic case of mistaking numbers for facts, in a neo-Pythagorean manner, and arguing as though numbers ruled the

Report on the Proceedings

universe. The growth of cities, for example, had been ignored by Walker. Professor Rubin did not think one needed to take Walker too seriously.

Dealing with the sex and age distribution, Professor Rubin pointed out that before 1914 women had higher mortality at the child-bearing age, though mature migrants replaced women who died and many farmers married more than once. More recently, the quota system favoured some groups rather than others, for example professors and farmers. Before 1924 (except for the Chinese Exclusion Act, 1872) there was no exclusion at all.

Professor Spengler did not think one should call the Walker effect a fallacy. There were conditions where one could get the Walker effect; there were others where one did not. In the empirical world one found no manifestation of the Walker effect, though the ethnic composition of a population *was* altered. But one should not dismiss the idea too readily in the light of only a hundred years' experience.

Professor Robertson did not think Professor Robinson had damaged Professor Spengler's case. He thought that his own paper supported Professor Robinson's view on South Africa. Were Indians and Europeans of superior economic status to the natives ? Yes, even though the first Indians in Natal in 1860 were only superior because they were willing to work continuously. Indeed, they had to, owing to the terms of their indentures. Local labour did not. The later Indians were attracted by the presence of indentured Indians and came to trade with them. The usual Hindu/Moslem relation was reversed. The indentured labourers were largely Hindus from Madras ; the traders were mainly Moslems.

The changed pattern of development after minerals were exploited needed an adjustment by both black and white in South Africa. One had to remember that European farmers, as well as Africans, now had to work for the first time in a market economy. The farmers in the North were self-sufficient and did not adapt themselves rapidly enough to changed conditions. Railways were direct routes to the coast, and let in agricultural supplies from the rest of the world. When the farmers did not learn quickly enough, this led to the long-lived problem of the 'poor white', a problem similar to that in the southern part of the United States. To keep down white poverty, restrictions were imposed on the entry of immigrants without means. There was also the 'civilised labour policy', which reserved unskilled work for poor whites and helped to keep up their standards of living in relation to the rest of the community. Now all poor whites had been absorbed, not because of these measures, but only because of rapid industrial development and the growth of service industries in the towns. After 1945 the door to white immigration was opened wide, but the fear that the absorption of poor whites might be reversed by large-scale immigration was partly responsible for the change in immigration policy in 1948.

The effects of immigration on the native Africans were not simple. There was little doubt that the substitution effect was most noticeable with the coming of indentured Indians. The Zulus of Natal had remained amongst the poorest Africans. But the favourable aggregate effect was nevertheless predominant. Rapid development led to a bigger national product, and to more earnings all round. The marginal product of unskilled labour had risen, and, though the difference between the wages of skilled and unskilled labour was high in South Africa, it had diminished since the 1870's. Thus immigration and capital imports had been to the advantage of unskilled Africans. Had the rise of African unskilled labour to skilled status been delayed ? One could not yet give a plain yes or no. But if it had, then the beneficial effects of immigration on African incomes would have been offset.

Professor Lerner said that comment on the tendency for highly skilled people to leave the underdeveloped areas made him hark back to his elementary economics. If they moved, their higher income showed they were more productive. What was the answer to this conflict ? Was this movement a burden to backward areas, or were the people in question of more use to the world elsewhere ?

Professor Silcock wondered how far, in studying such a problem, the institutional structure should be taken as given. How far did it reflect basic scarcities ? Within the underdeveloped areas, there might be good reasons against allowing the income distribution to be fixed on a basis which would later (one hoped) become inappropriate. If specialist salaries were raised to the world level, only inflation could remove the future income-differentials problem for the governments of backward areas when more specialists were available. Yet if salaries were below the world level one would lose specialists. Internal mobility differed from country to country, but existing scarcities, leading to a given income structure, could influence the social structure and modify it as the scarcities changed. One should take the existing structure neither as given, nor yet as wholly conditioned by economic factors. So how did we stand in making policy recommendations ? How far could we alter the social structure by economic means ?

Mr. Zubrzycki said it was necessary to remember that one had to allow for institutional and social factors, both in the receiving and in the sending country. For example, there was the case of Polish and East European emigrants to Latin America in the late nineteenth and early twentieth century. There were too many peasants in East Europe and too few in Latin America. The Latin American governments wanted to attract Poles, and there was, for example, the rumour in Poland that the Pope had asked Brazil to give land to Poles. This was not true ; but the Brazilian Government was prepared to give land under certain conditions. Landless peasants went, not to the United States as unskilled industrial workers, but to Brazil as independent farmers. Therefore one had to emphasize the interplay of institutional forces at both ends.

Professor Robinson felt one should remember the important fact that professional classes were usually remunerated according to salary scales, and not according to marginal net products. There were people in control in industry who might either save or lose £1 million per week; yet they were not paid their marginal net product. In most countries, the rewards of the professional classes could rarely equal their marginal net product, either in industry or in the civil service. In the civil service administrations of the world, countries related civil service salary scales to average incomes in those countries. In the past, civil service salary scales in the East had represented the cost of persuading Europeans to go to these countries, but as countries had taken over their own civil services this scale of payment had given way to the present scales related to local incomes. A valuable administrator in Pakistan or India would be better off in the World Bank, the International Monetary Fund, the United Nations Organisation, and so on, than at home. One should remember that, in an underdeveloped area, the marginal net product of an able person was high; but one could not pay this marginal net product very easily.

Professor Ellis suggested a complementary consideration. It was often said that in underdeveloped areas specialists' rewards, though *potentially* great, were not actually high. For example, there was the perverse movement away from the underdeveloped areas. With skilled chemists, their rewards, both in the United States and in underdeveloped areas, might conform to what the price mechanism would suggest they were worth. For though their potential contribution in backward areas might be very great, their actual contribution might be quite small.

Mr. Turvey pointed out that if one assumed that skilled labour moved to obtain a higher real income, one must remember that real product and real wage were not the same. A man might produce chemical research, but he consumed food, clothes, etc. Thus the same marginal product in terms of chemical research might give a higher real income in some countries because their consumption goods were cheaper. On the face of it, this should redound to the benefit of the underdeveloped areas. For example, domestic servants should be cheaper, even though imports were dearer. In the United States, however, some goods could be bought which were just not obtainable elsewhere. Therefore, even though one's marginal product might be higher in parts of East Africa, if one were paid one's marginal product one might nevertheless have a higher standard of living in a developed country.

Professor Lerner could not see why, if a worker's marginal product was higher in an underdeveloped area, and the cost of living was also lower, he should go to the United States. He felt that this was a serious problem which applied to capital too. The higher potential marginal product mentioned by Professor Ellis might be an ideological illusion, like the preference for agriculture in Israel. He did not know the real answer. Ordinary skilled people, who were paid their marginal product, still went to the United States. Was their marginal product in fact higher in the United States?

Dr. Edding said that this was a case of 'to him that hath shall be given'. It had been said that people went where they had the highest marginal product. This was not true. He felt that people went for the highest income, and this was not always the same thing. Where wealth was, there genius was found too. If there were a 'free circular flow of incomes' between countries, all would be well; but in present conditions the poorer countries were in danger of falling progressively further behind.

Professor Timlin thought that the underdeveloped areas raised a special problem. One's marginal product meant producing not only current output, but also the acquisition by the native population of technical skill. For example, in Nigeria, if a plant superintendent came from Britain, he was probably paid more than he currently earned. He had to be paid not only to produce goods, but also to train others to do his job. To the value of his physical product one had to add the discounted value of the future usefulness of his trainees. So, the marginal product of a person coming in this way was higher than his effective marginal product in the plant.

Mr. Turvey said that this was a question of the estimated economic value of creating skilled labour. In Pigovian terms, the marginal social product of the trainer was greater than his marginal private product.

Professor Parenti pointed to two important limitations on the flow of professional men and technicians from underdeveloped areas. First, there was the language problem. It was not difficult for Britons to go to America or to move within the Empire, but it was hard for Italians, say, to go to countries with different languages, to fill technical or professional posts. Second, it might be true that for institutional reasons salaries in underdeveloped areas were low, but this was only true of the basic salary. For instance, in Italy, or Brazil, or India, a professor had a low salary compared with a professor in the United States or the United Kingdom, but he had other advantages. In Brazil (or India) no one who was skilled had only one job, so that a man's total income might equal his marginal product. In Italy a professor had a lower salary, but greater prestige, than in America.

So far as competition from migrants for the unskilled worker was concerned, Professor Parenti felt there would be damaging results for individuals. But to unskilled workers as a class, immigration gave the opportunity of moving up the social scale more quickly, as Professor Spengler's paper showed.

Professor Lerner thought the fact that professional workers in these countries had 'side jobs' showed an unsatisfactory state of affairs, and gave part of the answer. He still felt that the marginal produce of an entrepreneur was very high in underdeveloped areas. This was not only a question of need versus effective demand. There really was a greater social produce. The difficulty was an institutional one. Professional men could not be given the pay they deserved, so they took on other jobs. This was just one of a long list of cases where the price mechanism did not work. Therefore one did not use it, and yet still proceeded to criticize it for being inadequate.

Professor Robinson said that he agreed with much of what had been said, but his own point was a different one. He was worried about the effects on the mobility of the professional class, which arose from differences in their incomes in various countries. What he had said was that, since 1939, the professional classes had become more mobile. First, they possessed skills needed in other countries. Second, the cost of moving them was relatively small as a percentage of their marginal product. What he had wished to argue was this : if one did reward professional people in accordance with their marginal net product in whatever country would pay them best, then the underdeveloped areas would be obliged to have a bigger income spread than the advanced countries. Thus, if marginal net products determined rewards, and one paid high salaries in underdeveloped areas, there must be a moral about one's hopes for narrowing the spread of incomes in any country. For example, countries with highly progressive tax systems would tend to lose professional people to other countries. Given the greater postwar mobility of such people, one could not hope to keep them unless the tax system at home were made less progressive.

Professor Silcock stressed the point that the marginal social product did not exceed the marginal private product for imported technicians only. Local technicians also passed on their skills, indeed they were often not only more skilled but better able to transmit skill. Their marginal social product was greater than their marginal private product, and that marginal private product was declining as skills were diffused. Salaries were rigid and tended not to fall rapidly enough. Objections to higher incomes for expatriates were accentuated by political feelings, but this might not be in the best interests of the dependent countries. All turned on how rigid the structure of the labour market was. If labour scarcities were changing rapidly, and salaries were rigid, it might be possible and desirable to pay the local technician, temporarily, even less than his marginal private product. But such a payment would fall even further below his marginal social product.

Professor Rubin did not think that American professors had such high incomes that they needed no extra-curricular jobs. In Italy a professor had a 'prestige product', whereas in America the professor was an 'unsuccessful man'.

Professor Thomas felt that what Professor Lerner had said was that if the price mechanism worked, the problem of developing backward areas would be solved much more easily. The analogy with the British communities in Australia made him want to challenge that. Land was cheap, the emigrant got a plot and became an entrepreneur, and so there were many entrepreneurs and few labourers. Since the aim was to found balanced communities, the 'Wakefield Plan' was to sell land above the market price so as to keep new immigrants landless, and thus promote an induced inflow of capital. This policy was designed to interfere with the price mechanism. As it happened, however, it was the discovery of gold which did most to stimulate the growth of Australia's population and provided a large labour force.

Professor Lerner did not see why, even here, the price mechanism would not solve the problem. If there were too many entrepreneurs and too few workers, profits would fall, wages would rise and the necessary readjustment would then take place.

Professor Ellis suggested that the contrast between the marginal social product of a scarce type of worker, say a teacher, in an under-developed area and his marginal private product was a particular equilibrium concept. Perhaps the Government should subsidize him. But in the aggregate, the current marginal social products of all workers could not exceed the current national income. In practical terms, then, one might subsidize workers in particular industries, but one could not have a *general* subsidy.

Dr. Beijer complained that so far the words 'migration' and 'immigration' had been used in a loose sense. Should permanent and temporary migration be distinguished, since their economic effects were not the same ? Temporary movements might have great effects, so perhaps speakers would state which they meant.

Mr. Turvey thought that the main instance of temporary migration was when there were seasonal swings in employment offsetting each other, for example migration from Italy to her neighbours. Both countries experienced a pure gain.

Professor Robinson found it hard to interpret the statistics because he did not know what migration meant in all the countries concerned. Was an Englishman working in Geneva a migrant when he went there and a migrant when he returned home ?

Professor Thomas said the convention was that if his declared intention on moving to a country was to stay in residence for one year or more he was a permanent migrant. If less, then he was temporary. The figures given in his own paper covered only permanent migrants. Diplomatic representatives were specifically *excluded* from all migration statistics.

Mr. Lannes explained that the United Nations definition included among migrants not only members of the family *accompanying* the head of the family, but also those who came to join him.

Father Ávila said the permanent/temporary distinction was not so crucial as the need for a migrant to do work. 'Permanent-temporary' migration had the same effects, economically, as did migration that was defined as permanent.

Professor Robertson explained that Father Ávila was considering a situation where a large number of migrants remained in a country. For example, in South Africa a labour force of a constant size would come from Portuguese East Africa. But the individuals making up that labour force would be continually changing.

Dr. Langrod warned against basing research on, and drawing scientific conclusions from, the definitions of immigration and emigration used by the various nations. These definitions were by no means uniform, and they reflected only administrative criteria connected with the types of visas accorded to immigrants. So, in France, most entrants were classified as temporary, and yet probably the majority arrived with the view of a permanent settlement and, as a matter of fact, remained in the country indefinitely. An acceptable definition would be that seasonal immigrants existed in cases where the law of the country enforced the return of immigrants after the end of the season to the country from which they had come. This was the case, for example, with the pre-war seasonal immigration of agricultural workers to Germany.

Mr. Zubrzycki considered the relation between the substitution effect and seasonal migration. One should not underestimate the significance of such migration in the nineteenth and early twentieth centuries. A book by an English writer, Tucker, had introduced the concept of the economic vacuum created by an outflow of factors of production. In the nineteenth century such a vacuum was often filled, with no difficulty, by seasonal migrants. Prussia was fed annually by about $1\frac{1}{4}$ million Polish, Czech, and Bohemian workers who came each year just to work at harvest time. They filled the vacuum created by the movement of population to industrial areas.

Professor Spengler pointed out that seasonal migration often happened because more men were needed by an industry at some times than at others. For example, the cotton-growing industry would not experience such large seasonal fluctuations in employment if operations were mechanized.

Dr. Wander said that the inflow of Poles to Rhine-Westphalia had been mostly seasonal, because the Government sent them out again after one year. Often they wanted to stay, but government regulations usually prevented this.

Dr. Langrod said that, in effect, the movement of Polish industrial workers to Westphalia was permanent; after the First World War a substantial number of these workers and their families moved to France. With Polish agricultural workers moving to Germany the migration was seasonal. They were obliged to go back to their country, at the latest in December, with the possibility of immigrating to Germany again in February-March for a new season.

Professor Parenti suggested that, in Europe, there had been a large reduction in the volume of seasonal migration because, except for sugar beet growing, harvesting was now mechanized. But this was true only of agriculture. Seasonal migration still existed in building, in the tourist industry, and so on.

Professor Robinson said he wished to return to the aggregate problem in Professor Spengler's paper. What had the aggregate effects been in receiving countries? This was a central problem. He wanted to argue that we needed to consider dynamic problems and their effects. Was there a chain of causation from a higher rate of growth to more investment, more labour-saving machinery, etc.? What did Professor Spengler say? Did migration accelerate capital formation and technical change?

Professor Spengler said it would be hard to test Professor Robinson's hypothesis, though he thought he might be right. Eventually the process would 'blow out'. But perhaps not in the nineteenth century, so that during the major part of the century before 1920 there might have been much to be said for it.

Professor Robinson suggested that where there was rapid growth the average age of industrial equipment would be lower. For example, one could contrast the United States and Eire. A stable or declining economy had less reason to replace old machines, and was landed with obsolete equipment.

Mr. Meenan said this was true of Ireland's railways. They had been planned to serve a population of 8 million. The population was now much smaller, so that drastic writing-down of capital had been needed.

Professor Lerner said he had often wondered about the 'scale argument', namely that because America was big it could produce cars on a large scale, and more efficiently; then again, was not growth rather like destruction? With earthquakes and wars people were made poorer *per capita*, and therefore needed to invest more. But wars were not good.

Mr. Turvey instanced the case of San Francisco. Perhaps it would have been better if the earthquake had not been in 1906 but in the 1930's. Yet while the present town might have been better, that would have been no consolation to the inhabitants in the 1930's.

Professor Robinson said that Keynes argued that out of the rapid growth of America came the American spirit of enterprise.

Mr. Turvey suggested that migration might have added more to the demand for labour than to the supply, and thus given a stimulus to the use of labour-saving machinery.

Professor Thomas said he wished to sharpen the difference of opinion. Professor Robinson said that in the nineteenth century, as migrants came into America, labour-saving devices were used. If one million migrants came in each year, one could hardly talk of labour shortage. The immediate impact must surely be that of a free gift of labour. Most of these workers were unskilled and could not speak English, and the entrepreneur's problem was how to use them. That difficulty was solved by the installation of foolproof automatic machinery. As Professor Domar had shown, the 'widening' of capital in the United States was far more notable than 'deepening'.

Professor Spengler did not agree about capital widening, except in terms of the construction of railways, etc. In manufacturing, his impression was that there had not been much change. But techniques changed, and America had shown little resistance to changes in technology.

Professor Robinson asked how Professor Thomas defined capital widening, to which *Professor Thomas* replied he meant that the capital/ output ratio was constant or falling *per head*, though not in aggregate.

Professor Lerner said that, in other words, it meant more capital of the same general kind. He agreed with the views of Professor Thomas and Professor Spengler about American readiness to accept new ideas. But the need to 'widen' capital was a burden rather than otherwise. It used up capital, and could only help in terms of challenge and response.

Professor Thomas felt it was curious that in those phases when immigration had been most rapid, real income *per head* had gone up fastest.

Professor Robinson suggested that the inflow of migrants meant more capital in aggregate, though it would imply a constant amount per head, and this led to inflation, full employment and labour shortage.

Professor Ellis suggested that we were back at a 'chicken and egg' problem. Professor Robinson had argued from an increase in population to a growth in income. Professor Kuznets had gone the other way; an increase in income led to immigration, to increased investment and finally to increased income. In fact one could argue either way, or even both ways at once.

Professor Lindahl said it seemed implicit in Professor Spengler's paper that, at present, immigration to the United States would not raise income per head. We could take this as a hypothesis. Reasons in favour of it were, first, the land had now nearly all been used; second, more capital in the form of housing, etc. was now needed to cope with a population influx. In Sweden, for 100 million kroner paid in wages, one needed at least 10 or 15 times as much capital. So, the amount of extra capital needed to maintain the present level of *per capita* incomes was greater than the income which could be produced by immigrants. Third, the United States was now exporting capital herself. There was no foreign source of capital for her. None of these propositions had been true in nineteenth-century America. Then there had been much land, there was less need for capital, and capital had been imported from Europe. So, whilst immigration might have caused a rise in income per head up to a certain date, that date was now past.

Professor Silcock felt that the crucial factor might well be that immigration could make available capital from abroad. One could have an expanding economy without major disturbances through factor disproportions. If one had Professor Lindahl's situation, where immigrants made big demands on existing capital, that was a strain. But the immigration also helped to supply capital that could make for expansion. An important factor in America had been the early predominance of immigrants of British stock and the amount of British capital coming in with them. Later migration was made simpler because essential links, for example between British lenders and American borrowers, were already in existence.

Dr. Edding felt that there was no statistical evidence for this discussion. Yet it was certain that without the 60 million Europeans who had gone abroad the world economy would be less prosperous than it was. Their marginal productivity in their new countries was higher, and the redistribution of population thus added to world output and to economic welfare. So far as the receiving countries were concerned, he did not see why Professor Spengler distinguished some periods in which it seemed more certain than it did in others (there being no evidence for the latter) that migration aided growth. Similarly, Professor Spengler said that where the population was of 'income optimum size' further migration was harmful. What did Professor Spengler mean by this term ? Again, Dr. Edding asked what were the countries of increasing returns. State-created Israel ? Germany since the war ? Entrepreneurs could be sure that consumers would increase in numbers, and that was quite different to the atmosphere where there was a decrease. Again why, on page 49, had Professor Spengler quoted Professor Thomas. Did he agree ? Surely the quotation contradicted Professor Spengler's own view.

Professor Spengler said that he had quoted Professor Thomas ; but did not agree with him. He did not think the capital/labour ratio in the whole nation went up much. Something did happen, but it was a change in the nature of the labour force rather than a widening of capital. Professor Spengler thought there were three ways in which the rise of income per head was increased. First, skilled labour came in. Second, there was a change in the climate of opinion, though he did not know how big. Third, there were the 'increasing returns' associated with largeness. The labour force became more diversified as it grew. How long did this go on ? He thought the third force was now spent. But now there were technical improvements instead. One could either use more capital per head or spread it more thinly. The exhaustion of the 'increasing returns' process seemed important. There was now expenditure on, for example, arms to prevent large political changes, but the forces favourable to immigration seemed to have worked themselves out. Nevertheless, one could justify it on political grounds. In terms of welfare the answer might be different, for, eventually, surely more migration would mean lower welfare per head.

Dr. Edding suggested that immigration to the United States was perhaps not needed for growth in America, but it was necessary for the welfare of the migrant.

Mr. Turvey commented on Professor Thomas's contention that non-English-speaking workers needed automatic machines. The *Proceedings* of the 1954 meeting of the American Economic Association included a paper by Marvin Frankel. He cited two reports of the 1850's, showing that the contrast between American and British industry was much the same as to-day. In American industry, the manufacturing principle was carried further, with more labour-saving devices and more specialization. The phenomenon had therefore been noted long before non-English immigrants came to the United States. Professor Robinson had said that immigration had raised the demand for labour more than the supply. But surely high wages in American manufacturing were possible only because of the high transfer earnings obtainable in agriculture, so long as the frontier remained open.

Professor Rubin explained that in his own paper he had shown that, between 1870 and 1914, there had been a unique combination of circumstances leading to a more rapid rise in income. Since it was a *combination* of factors which had existed, one did not need to argue about which came first.

Professor Ellis said that Professor Spengler was suggesting that at some times there was a flow of capital, techniques, etc. which made immigration favourable; at other times it was lacking. Would Professor Rubin go further ?

Professor Lerner said that both Professor Spengler and Professor Rubin had said that things went well in a particular way. Professor Spengler gave some specific reasons why these conditions did not exist now.

Professor Rubin said that in 1952 Louis Beau had shown, in Congressional Hearings, that if there had been no laws restricting immigration, America would have had a bigger labour force and a bigger *per capita* income. He himself did not like this approach; one could not *prove* whether immigration was good or bad.

Mr. Turvey said that Professor Spengler had talked of 'optimum population'. What was it, other than the population which gave maximum real income per head ? Was it not a term implying circular reasoning ?

Professor Spengler said it was really a question whether one spoke of income or some other criterion. It was not just maximizing something. If one had a set of circumstances, and population was an independent variable, income per head reached a 'plateau', and then fell, as population rose. He thought one could argue that the United States population was now 'big enough', ignoring certain dynamic factors. He did not think that, in the nineteenth century, America had had a big enough population to make the best use of its resources. Perhaps, in the future, techniques would change, and make the population too small once again.

Professor Thomas said this was a 'point of time' optimum, not proving anything. Perhaps it was better to think in terms of the rate of population growth, namely that rate which gave an optimum rate of increase in national income.

Professor Spengler said that in those terms he would say that a zero or negative rate of growth was best now, since no major changes in technique were in prospect.

Professor Robinson asked if Professor Spengler meant a zero rate of increase, assuming full employment, or that a zero rate of population increase would give full employment. A marked *change* in the rate of growth might lead to unemployment.

Professor Spengler said that one could not rely on population growth to solve the problem of how to keep full employment. Ultimately one had to face this problem. Why not solve it now ?

Professor Lerner did not think Professor Spengler's judgement about the present population being the optimum one was invalidated by bringing in the word 'dynamic'. That was only relevant if an increase in population brought into existence capital that would otherwise not be there. There was no reason for depending on population changes to increase the level of activity. Therefore it followed that, if American population were already greater than the optimum, it would be foolish to increase its size further.

THE DISCUSSION ON DR. LANGROD'S PAPER

Fifth and Sixth Sessions, Monday, 5 September 1955

Professor Timlin opened the discussion on Dr. Langrod's paper. She said that this paper had been prepared explicitly from the social rather than from the economic viewpoint, and social factors had so far been under-emphasized in the discussions. This would be remedied during the day, but she had decided, herself, to begin by referring to the economic effects of migration in receiving countries.

In the first place, the postwar movement of immigrants into the receiving countries had followed the dislocations both of the war and of the depression of the 1930's. War depression had affected the economies of immigration countries differently, and the differences were both of degree and of kind. Seen against this background, the building of models to explain this period appeared to be a fruitless pastime. Since 1930 we seemed to have experienced something quite different from Professor Thomas's 20-year cycle. For example, residential and non-residential building first fell because of the stagnation of the 1930's, and then was held to a minimum during the war by strict controls. After the war some fifteen years of pent-up demands were released, more or less suddenly, depending on the methods of relaxing controls in the various countries. The effects of this were increased by the large savings made during the war, by artificially low rates of interest, and by the ease of obtaining loanable funds.

At the end of the war the structure of demand had changed on both the home and export markets, which made the capital and labour structures inherited from the depression and from the war less appropriate. Structures consequently changed, not only because the 20-year and other cycles had been interrupted, but also because of changes in resource utilization, and because new products and new techniques of production came into use. The economic impact of the inflow of immigrants must be seen against the need to adapt capital and labour structures on a large scale.

Since these, however, were essentially dynamic problems, Professor Timlin thought we needed to remember Alfred Marshall's dictum that elasticity of supply is a function of time. That was to say, the technical combinations that could be used within a short time to get a given product might be fairly rigid. If some factors of production were relatively scarcer than others, importing these scarce goods or services might reduce the need for technical substitution and increase the elasticity of supply of both old and new products. This was more than a matter of eliminating or reducing 'bottlenecks'. It was a question of increasing the total speed of adaptation in the face of extraordinary changes, some temporary and some permanent, in the structure of demand. For the relatively young economy, subject to strong influences from relatively more developed economies, the rate of such adaptation might be of special importance. Professor Timlin suggested that much of the material about immigration policies in Dr. Langrod's paper must be seen against these special conditions, which differed from country to country. Otherwise many policy details might seem incomprehensible.

Professor Timlin pointed out that Canadian policy had been very self-consciously selective in this respect, but she was going to content herself with giving three examples. First, in construction industry, the internal mobility of labour had been provided by Canada's many young workers. But the rapid expansion of construction depended largely on the importation of *skilled* labour of various types. The importance of this immigration was well illustrated by statistics given in the publications of the Central Mortgage and Housing Corporation, which administered Canadian housing legislation. Second, the speed of development of oil resources in Alberta had been accelerated by importing managers and skilled labour from the United States. Third, the growing urbanization that had accompanied growing industrialization and the growth of service industries had imposed a new structure of demand on much of Canadian agriculture. The coming of Dutch agricultural immigrants had been of peculiar importance. For it filled the vacuum left by the departure of farmers' sons for the towns and by the retirement of older farmers, by introducing a *new* agricultural element specially skilled in growing the products required by the new concentrations of urban population.

Professor Spengler asked whether a selective immigration policy led to disproportions in the emigrant country, creating a shortage of skilled labour, even though it tended to eliminate bottlenecks in the receiving country. Why could not countries bring in more young and less-skilled immigrants? In the United States only three to six months' training was needed, and there was no language problem. He wondered if we exaggerated the length of time required to learn non-professional work. Would it not lead to less dislocation in the losing country if younger migrants left and were trained in the receiving country? How practical was this idea?

Professor Timlin said it was easier for the United States than for a smaller country that was just becoming industrialized. Similarly, it was easier now for Canada than it would have been ten years ago. Then, real experts were often quite invaluable. In the United States, with more mechanization and a larger population, it was much easier to accept less skilled workers. For example, in 1945 it was fairly easy to absorb young migrants in the United States. In Canada young people came off farms in large numbers, with growing agricultural productivity between 1939 and 1945, and caused internal migration problems within Canada. This helped to condition the absorption of older immigrants.

Dr. Wander was surprised by Professor Spengler's remarks. In the United States she had been told that vocational training was now much more important than earlier. Training was thus tending to become a longer process. Admittedly there still were many jobs which did not need specific training, but the demand for skilled workers was nevertheless rising rather than falling.

In the United States vocational training was given a different meaning from that in Europe, for example in German apprenticeship. Apprentice training was not so important in the United States, but labourers there would 'shop around' and become trained in this way. Perhaps after several years they would have the same skill as apprentices.

Mr. Lannes said that Professor Spengler's proposition did not hold for farmers. Many receiving countries were only satisfied if immigrants were trained farmers.

Dr. Langrod said that selection constituted one of those factors which, because of its very important social implications, should not be considered from an exclusively economic point of view. He pointed out that the policy of strict professional selection of immigrants emerged before the Second World War. In France such selection had existed before 1939; similarly, Germany had admitted as seasonal immigrants only those who were highly skilled in farm work. Dr. Langrod did not share Professor Spengler's view on the training of new-comers. He mentioned in this connexion that proper professional selection helped to keep newcomers in the professions for which they were brought into the country, or at least delayed the natural and unavoidable participation of immigrants in the drift of rural population to the towns.

Professor Spengler said that, to judge his proposition, one had to divide up occupations. It was true that it now took longer to train for nursing or medicine. Similarly, for the farmer as against the agricultural worker, a college education was essential in the United States. But many other jobs now required less time for training. During the war, and in the 1930's, studies showed that a very short training time was needed in factories and in services. This was what he was thinking of. One could put young immigrants into this training system. This would not stop the movement out of some occupations, but he did think that many jobs took little time to learn.

Professor Parenti said that controlled emigration had important disturbing effects on an economy. With a free economy and free migration there could be no economic harm. Supply and demand worked simultaneously. If there was no job for him in the new land, a migrant could at worst go home again. He might suffer, but for the immigrant country all would be well, as it had been in the nineteenth century. Nor was there much trouble in the country with planned immigration and a completely planned economy. One could have a programme for training both natives and migrants. Trouble arose only where the economy was not completely controlled but there was nevertheless complete control over migration. Some sectors were controlled and one could foresee labour needs, as for example with builders in France, where the State financed part of the housing programme and knew the numbers and type of worker needed. In other sectors, things were difficult. Selection was unambiguously good only if immigration and capital movements were simultaneous.

What of the authority deciding to let migrants in ? How did it decide whom to let in ? Not on the basis of statistics, or on a logical forecast. Australia, France, etc., were countries with public planning authorities which, in theory, could foresee needs. But in practice there were difficulties. It was hard to distinguish the economic, social, and administrative aspects of migration selection. What were the mechanics of the process ? There was always a lag between the need for migrants coming into existence and the arrival of the necessary workers. One could take the case where turners were needed in engineering. First, one had to find whether the nation had more such men of its own, and this took time. If not, immigration was considered. But where could immigrants come from ? Even when they were found, there were still formalities. A total of, say, six months could easily have elapsed since the need for turners was discovered. Sometimes employers wanted to increase their production to meet increased demand and needed workers to do so. If it took six months to get this labour, would the increased demand still exist ? Because of such doubts, the demand for migrants tended to be lower than effective demand would warrant.

Going back to Professor Spengler's statement, one had to remember that civil servants were responsible for migration policy. They thought of their own country, but also of their own personal responsibility. If they had to decide how much manpower was needed and they exaggerated this need, they would be blamed. But if the civil servants brought in too few migrants, this might be very harmful but they would never be blamed for it. Therefore officials proceeded by under-estimating rather than correctly estimating requirements. Since trade unions were powerful, there was always hesitation, even in conditions of full employment, before allowing migrants in. There was never 100 per cent employment at home, and trade unions were hard to appease. This kind of problem seemed to Professor Parenti to be a permanent defect of planned migration.

Dr. Wander suggested that the answer to Professor Spengler might be that the young unskilled worker would be too young to migrate. Yet when he was old enough to migrate alone, say from 18 to 20 years old, he was usually already trained and no longer wanted unskilled work.

Father Ávila thought Professor Spengler's view interesting for the underdeveloped areas. They needed skilled workers, but they did not present economic and social conditions which were attractive enough to specialized workers. Professor Parenti had said young migrants were not wanted. Yet in underdeveloped areas the fact that young workers had no ingrained cultural tradition, as with older people, made them desirable. Dr. Wander had spoken of their age and of their family trees. Here, one had a problem. Father Ávila drew attention to the possibility of setting up training schools in emigrant countries. In Italy schools had been set up to train people who could later go to Brazil, and these schools had been jointly financed by Brazil and Italy. Dr. Langrod had shown the big difference between the results of migration to Canada, Australia, and the United States on the one hand, and to Argentina and Brazil on the other. There were two reasons. First, conditions in South America were very special. There was a high birth-rate, and much income went on training the young as well as to individual capitalists. There was little to finance immigration. Second, especially in Brazil, there was much internal migration which competed with foreign migration. In São Paulo and Rio, for example, 1000 people a day arrived from inland.

Mr. Jacobsen said that Professor Spengler had touched on one of the two main problems affecting migration from Europe. If this particular problem were not solved soon, migration might come to a standstill. The oversea countries needed skilled and semi-skilled workers. On the other hand, most of the workers available for migration from Europe were unskilled. For example, Latin America could not absorb unskilled labour from Europe because her standard of living was too low to attract it. Thus, when arranging migration from Italy to that area — a very important migratory flow — it was important to find skilled workers in Italy who wanted to migrate ; but Italy did not want to lose these workers. Canada and Australia did take unskilled workers, but Australia fixed the proportion of skilled to unskilled workers in its annual intake, and this proportion was about 15 per cent. Therefore, if Australia was to be able to absorb the 85 per cent of unskilled labour, the 15 per cent of skilled workers must be found. They were hard to find now, and it would soon be even harder to find them.

Mr. Jacobsen did not agree that six months' vocational training produced a skilled worker. In Australia, for example, training lasted seven years, three to five years in a school and more in a factory. This was necessary in order to obtain a trade certificate. Such training was not only a technical necessity but was also needed to meet the political requirements of trade unions. One could train semi-skilled workers quite fast by intensive methods, perhaps in six months. The experiment described by Father Ávila was one such, concerned mainly with constructional trades. Similar experiments were now being made in both Italy and Greece. If they succeeded, joint projects might be decided upon by the Italian Government and ICEM to train several thousand people per annum and produce semi-skilled workers. Training for fully-skilled trades was difficult, and to attempt it might wreck the scheme.

Commenting on Professor Parenti's statement, Mr. Jacobsen said that in Australia there were 60,000 vacancies in industry. But for the reasons given by Professor Parenti, no workers were available. Because of the fears mentioned by Professor Parenti, there was always this lag between demand and supply. The opposite was true in Canada, where, at one moment, the supply was greater than the demand. Severe winter weather led to bottlenecks and caused unemployment for three to four months. The Canadian Civil Service therefore decided that it dared not repeat the mistake, and was now much more cautious.

Father Ávila had spoken of investment. This was a problem not only for Latin America, but also for Australia. These two problems — standards of skill in the emigrants and adequate investment — were the two major ones threatening the scale of migration at present.

Professor Bachi agreed on the danger of civil servants determining the number of immigrants, when there was professional selection. In general, the danger was that they would under-estimate the number of migrants that could be absorbed. This depended largely, however, on public opinion towards migration. When public opinion was favourable, the 'too prudent' civil servant was in danger of criticism. This was exceptional, but in Palestine from 1922 to 1939 immigration was favoured by the mandate. People with £1000-worth of capital came in freely. Those wanting to be workers came in on the basis of a thorough inquiry into demand in each sector of the economy. Jews made these estimates, public opinion wanted immigration, and so they may have been over-optimistic estimates. But the British then 'vetted' them, perhaps like Professor Parenti's civil servants. So the net result in 1922–39 may have been that the number of migrants admitted was just about right, on economic grounds. There was only one major crisis, in 1925.

Professor Bachi said that Dr. Langrod had warned of the danger of sending townsmen to the country. In Israel this was not correct. Jews coming from abroad were overwhelmingly urban dwellers. Yet, in Israel the rural population had risen from zero in 1862 to 360,000 now.

Dr. Langrod said that this confirmed that conclusions drawn from the immigration experiences of Israel should not be applied to other countries. The ideological strength so characteristic in Israel's immigration did not appear everywhere.

Answering a question put to him by Dr. Jacobsen, Dr. Langrod explained that the failure of land settlement schemes in various South American countries, like Brazil or Venezuela, had been due mainly to insufficient preparation. Migration, and particularly land settlement, was a comprehensive enterprise which required that such problems as housing, communication, marketing, health, property rights, etc. should be planned and solved simultaneously. Unfortunately, in various past settlement schemes insufficient attention had been paid to all of these problems, and this had resulted in frequent failures and the waste of both human beings and material capital.

Professor Timlin stressed that much of what she had said related to conditions just after 1945. Capital imports and the immigration of skilled workers had allowed easier adaptation after the war. But even in construction work skills were changing. Contractors now built perhaps fifty houses at a time, using standard floor plans, more machines, and more semi-skilled and less skilled labour per building. In much of the rest of the economy there had been an increase in the degree of skill required, and workers must now be at least semi-skilled. In farming, for example, a worker was nowadays of little use if he did not know how to handle machines. In wheat farming, constant prices and rising costs had led to a search for economies in production. This had destroyed the demand for unskilled labour, since these economies had largely been achieved through mechanization. After 1945 Canada had to make large-scale adaptations of capital and labour structures inherited as a consequence of slump and war. Now there was a process of longer-run adaptation. This process was increasing the demand for semi-skilled labour as compared with both skilled and unskilled. Therefore she thought Canada would be able to take more immigrant semi-skilled workers as time went on, but there would be very little demand for the unskilled.

Professor Timlin also pointed out that one could not easily get a big immigrant inflow in any *one* year. It was even harder over, say, twenty-five years. For periods of economic recession might increase the opposition to immigration of people who had grown up in Canada. Migrants needed to go where they could be employed quickly and not where they would exacerbate an unsympathetic population. This raised a political question. There was probably always a struggle in the government between those who were backed by trade unions with short-term interests and those who took a longer view. Who won might depend largely on whether an election was imminent.

Professor Rubin suggested that, since in underdeveloped areas with high fertility rates much income was devoted to bringing up infants, one might consider their problem in the light of the present growing need for skilled workers. Immigration of skilled workers might be encouraged during a period in which one educated natives to reduce their birth-rate. India took this seriously, but she had not the same problem of immigration. A country like Brazil might, however, pursue this policy.

Professor Ellis said that both unskilled and skilled artisans were disappearing in the United States because of mechanization. This was significant not only because America was the biggest immigrant country, but also because similar techniques would become characteristic of other countries also as time went on. Labour was now much less used in all fields. Pick and shovel labour had gone; the skilled artisan had been transformed. Machines played a bigger part both in factories and in building. No more than three to six months were now needed to learn a job, though trade unions imposed a longer training period. There were still some skilled watchmakers, piano-tuners, and so on, but the increase in their numbers was small. Even here, new electronic devices regulated a watch in a few minutes. Some labour operations still took time, requiring experience rather than dexterity, as, for instance, with train drivers and pilots. He thought Professor Spengler was quite right so far as the United States was concerned.

Professor Lerner said that he would agree with Professor Ellis, if this were purely an economic and social problem. For political reasons, however, people were forced to spend up to seven years 'pretending' to learn to produce things.

Dr. Wander agreed that the artisan had disappeared. But new skills were arising through technical development. She had watched brewing in the United States, with automatic checks on bottles passing. When the machinery was not working, however, there was much maintenance work. Machinery could replace unskilled labourers but not maintenance men. This was also true with cars, television sets, etc.

Professor Robertson, commenting on Professor Ellis's statement, said there was a demand for both real skill and for completely unskilled workers. On the other hand, Professor Ellis was right when he said that the present classifications were the result of organized labour. If the climate of opinion, at present in favour of retaining demarcation lines, changed, the selection of immigrants would be easier. It might be easier still if the standard of skill demanded of immigrants was not higher than local conditions made essential. In war-time South Africa, Italian prisoners of war were given considerable freedom. They were put on roads, in farming, and in building. The experience was that whether the Italian was officially a builder or not, he was good by South African standards. It was not possible to keep the Italians, but there was no doubt that, at that point, the Italians could have been easily assimilated with great benefit.

Professor Rubin said the dispute between Dr. Wander and Professor Ellis was on a question of fact, and we lacked data. He thought Professor Ellis was right that maintenance workers were small in number. But there was also the do-it-yourself movement. This ran into billions of dollars in the United States, in terms of materials sold, and covered skilled jobs such as painting, plumbing, etc.

Professor Ellis said that complicated repair work was either dealt with by replacement, or else sent to a skilled worker at a central plant. We did still need engineers, chemists, etc.

Dr. Wander felt that one should not trust statistics here, because it was hard to assess workers' knowledge and skill. But there were statistics showing that artisans had been replaced by the newer skills.

Professor Silcock agreed that we needed more statistics. But he still felt that, for international improvement, we might need more migration of semi-skilled labour, even though this might lower national income per head in the receiving countries.

Professor Lerner said that, even from a national point of view, the immigration of skilled workers might, though it reduced income per head, increase the incomes of the existing population by moving the income scale upwards.

Mr. Turvey suggested that it was in the interests of populations, before allowing immigration, to train their own skilled labour and then to import unskilled workers.

Professor Silcock thought the difficulty might be that it would be dearer, even if training was no dearer abroad, to train one's own workers rather than bring in migrants. In Asia, there were social and cultural difficulties in the way of training the indigenous population.

Mr. Jacobsen said he would ignore trends and assume that Professor Ellis was right. Was it not true that *at present* the degree of technical development outside the United States was still such that countries needed many skilled workers? Political circumstances were also important. In Australia welders were needed, but one could only be a welder after three to five years' training and three years' experience. One was not allowed to hold the torch otherwise. Yet so much training was not really needed.

Mr. Jacobsen felt that Professor Timlin was quite right about farming. A Greek peasant might go to Canada, but he needed *some* training to drive a tractor. So there was a need for semi-skilled workers. Professor Spengler had said one should give this in the receiving countries. Then migrants would be taught by the receiving countries' own technicians. ICEM thought so too. But this was impossible because of the reaction of trade unions and local workers — except in two or three countries. One must train migrants in the sending country. There was also the language problem. One tried to bring experts from the receiving country to give particular advice. Mr. Jacobsen said the Turvey solution was perhaps possible in Australia, Canada, and the United States but not in Latin America. One could not bring in unskilled Europeans to a country with such a low standard of living.

Professor Thomas gave his views on investment and migration since 1945. First, in 1945 the traditional capital exporters, especially Great Britain, were not able to resume their role. Second, the main source of capital was now the United States and she was an immigrant country. Third, nevertheless capital did flow from Europe to migrant countries on traditional lines. But it was only made possible through the receipt by Europe of large amounts of public capital from the United States. Britain got from the United States more than she needed to meet the deficit on her balance of payments, and was able not only to finance migration, but also to do indirectly what American private capital did not do. American private oversea investment since the war had been concentrated on oil, manufacturing, and smelting. Three-quarters of it had gone to countries where private investors could be certain that dollars would be sent back to the United States. Certainly American private capital had helped migration to Canada, but not to South America. Indirectly, however, American *public* capital exports had been of the greatest importance in maintaining what international migration there had been.

Europeans asked what would happen if this capital flow ended. There had been a gigantic and generous once-and-for-all recovery programme. As this slowed down, would its indirect benefits also diminish, and perhaps disappear ? Could Europe export enough capital to support migration, or was it possible that American private investors might change their policy ? Here, Professor Thomas was less certain. But he emphasized Mr. Jacobsen's point. Unless capital did flow in the right volume and the right directions, we should not achieve the migration flow that we wanted.

Professor Rubin said that no one could expect an expansion in private investment from the United States big enough to replace public investment. Whilst the American Government had tried to encourage private investment abroad, American investors were faced with big obstacles and risks and not much expansion was likely.

Dr. Edding wondered if capital flows were now so important, seeing that the nineteenth-century conditions for mass migration were definitely past. Skilled labour was now short everywhere, and it was mainly skilled labour — brain capital — which migrated. Why should this migration of brains and skill always be accompanied by other capital flows ? If it did, could Europe export such other capital ? Yes ; if growth continued in Europe as at present, most European countries could double their national product in twenty years or so, and treble it in thirty. Total population would remain relatively stagnant and ageing. The industrially developed European states could already export capital. What would induce them to risk investment overseas ? Why not concentrate their investment in the less-developed parts of Europe and so lessen the need for migration ? Economically it was not clear what advantages Europe would obtain from assisted migration to oversea countries. Migration within Europe was beneficial, but he was not convinced that it was in the interest of the losing countries to send migrants overseas. He thought, indeed, that up to now migration had been good for the migrants and for the receiving countries, in different degrees, and also for the sending countries. But what of the future ? Was it still advantageous for Europe to lose both migrants and capital ?

Dr. Edding said that his question implied no more than expression of his dissatisfaction with the usual reasoning in migration discussions. He could imagine that there were good arguments for increased European capital exports and for continued exports of skill and leadership. But he would feel much happier if these arguments were based on a dynamic economic analysis, and a more exact balancing of advantages and disadvantages to be expected for Europe in future years.

Professor Robinson wondered if one really should look to the receiving countries to see the benefits of migration. In the nineteenth century the main contribution of migration in Europe was probably not the relief of population pressure so much as the addition to food and raw material supplies. At present, food and raw material supplies were growing less rapidly than was manufacturing industry. The terms of trade were likely to give prosperity to primary countries and thus encourage migrants to go there to produce primary products, to the ultimate benefit of the manufacturing, sending countries, especially in Europe. Trade in manufactured goods was up 75 per cent on 1939; that in primary produce was up by 25 per cent. Was it not in the interests of both receiving and sending countries that migration should go on?

Dr. Hofstee thought it was still important for some parts of Europe to send out migrants, and he thought especially of farmers. In the Netherlands the problems of the peasant were very acute, and his position became relatively worse as wages in industry and agriculture rose higher and higher. The only solution was to have bigger farms. But to allow this, many farmers would have to leave. Besides, too many sons of farmers stayed on the farms, getting in the way; they had no education except in farming. Going into industry as unskilled workers was no· solution for them, because they considered it a step downward in the social scale. So their only possibility of getting a suitable living was to emigrate to countries like Canada, Australia, etc., with free land. The Netherlands could spare 40,000 young farmers now who would have to emigrate to remain farmers. But the major problem was to convince them of the need to migrate.

Mr. Jacobsen confirmed Dr. Hofstee's view. Dutch statistics showed that in 1950 there was an agricultural population surplus of 12,000 persons per year, plus a backlog of 2000 per year. There was also a reduction in vacancies in agriculture of 1000 per year. That gave a total of 15,000 people each year (plus their families) lost to agriculture.

In 1952 it was estimated that those in Greece who were engaged in agriculture worked only 56 per cent of possible working days. This under-employment was equivalent to at least 800,000 redundant workers in Greek agriculture alone. There had been no great change in this situation since 1952. Destitute persons 'with an income below 7 dollars a month', amounted to 25 per cent of the population. Theoretically they might find jobs in Greece, but that was not likely to be possible for some years. For the next few years emigration was essential. Mr. Jacobsen thought Dr. Edding might be partly justified in opposing migration from Germany and Austria, but not from Holland, Greece, or Italy. And even in Germany and Austria, were there not advantages in limited emigration from some sectors of the population, refugees and farmers for example ? Another consideration was how far did exports follow emigrants ? Perhaps, in part, German exports followed German migration, for instance to Australia. In fact German migration and German exports seemed to have gone up in the same proportion.

Mr. Phillips commented that the statistics for Latin America showed that in Argentina most migrants went into agriculture. Were we being too pessimistic about land settlement in South America, although it must be recognized that it called for considerable capital ? As regards non-agricultural activities, were we in danger of taking too narrow a view of the relation between capital and migration ? In practice, South America had taken large numbers of migrants since the war, but had not imported a commensurate amount of capital; real *per capita* income had risen, yet for the economy as a whole capital was the most vital need. It looked as if the immigrants were absorbed by a process of squeezing them to fit the existing stock of capital, or by making better use of it. European migrants in South America had exercised an important institutional influence. Further, they had on the whole a greater-than-average literacy and propensity to save, and their incentives were particularly strong when starting life in a new country. Moreover, they spread new techniques and skills by their example. The role of migration was limited by the need to protect the basic and long-term interests of the existing population, but it acted as a short cut to the mobilization of the resources of economic-ally underdeveloped areas. For it imported ready-made skills in the persons of human beings in whom considerable capital had been invested.

Professor Lerner said he wanted to question a basic premiss, namely, that some capital was essential to migration. He did not see why. It was pleasant, because the migrant's standard of living was higher. But people living in places where they were less productive wanted to become more productive, with a *given* amount of capital; and it was likely that they improved the conditions of people in the countries to which they went. The reason for assuming that capital was needed was partly that economists tended to assume that capital/labour ratios were more important than they really were. Also, it was usual to assume that a minimum standard of comfort had to be provided, and this might be an incorrect assumption. Professor Lerner felt that private investment needed making attractive to the *individual* investor and not to the country. This was the real reason for the lack of investment by private American investors since the war. Professor Thomas had said that the United States had helped migration by Marshall Aid, so that as the amount of aid fell, migration would fall too. But was it not possible for the United States to direct its money to help migrants more directly, and therefore more economically ?

Professor Timlin said that where there was strong internal migration within a country, new capital was produced by the ordinary investment process at home. Capital was also there to be taken over. Agricultural migrants could use capital left by people who had gone into industry;

those going to industry had capital provided by internal growth during the periods of high economic activity, when migration currents were strong.

Dr. Edding said Mr. Jacobsen was almost the only person at the Conference who could devote all his time to migration problems, and was therefore at a clear advantage so far as the possession of facts and figures was concerned. All that he had said sounded convincing. Dr. Edding said he himself was known as an advocate of migration as a normal function of the world economy in *normal* conditions (*i.e.* a reasonable degree of free factor movement). But conditions were not normal. Professor Robinson had said that the losing countries got a benefit from having more raw materials. But was trade free enough now to allow all to participate in these gains ? If the gains were shared, then not only the sender should raise capital, but there should be an international fund financed by all countries.

Professor Rubin said he would discuss the suggested contradiction between export/import policy and immigration. If trade were liberated and migration policies hardened, the two moves might defeat each other. Ideally, they must be treated as one problem, and this was not done. For example, Professor Röpke wanted completely free trade and completely free migration. This was an impossibility. On the notion of exports following immigrants, Professor Rubin said he had not studied this in detail, but the idea was very interesting. For instance, customs manifests in 1800 showed that German articles went to Philadelphia, where there was a German colony. Similarly, Polish ham worth 20 million dollars was currently imported into America. Despite political obstacles, there was a large and growing import of Polish ham. There was a Polish population in the United States, but the popularity of ham went beyond Poles because of propinquity. Not only did trade follow migrants, but others in the receiving country learnt to buy these goods too.

Mr. Turvey said that in so far as emigrants from European industry went where agricultural activity was increasing, this would help to improve the terms of trade for Europe and the losing country would benefit. This raised the question. How far should the process go ?

Professor Lerner replied that it should continue so long as it was beneficial for the emigrant country.

Dr. Edding said the question was not whether the senders would benefit at all, but whether they benefited enough to cancel out the fact that the cost of education went up. One wanted to see a clear balance of gain.

Dr. Zubrzycki said that, in discussing an agricultural increase in primary producing areas, one could see two lines of approach. First, one might have the emigration of whites to primary producing countries. This was largely impossible. Brazil, Argentina and West Africa were suggested as receivers of white agriculturalists. But whites could not go as workers, only as managers. Second, one might send whites to countries like Australia or Britain. In Britain the experience was that Poles when demobilized, being peasants, were expected to go into agriculture. This held good for two years, whilst the Poles were under obligation. After this the obligation ended, and most of the Poles left agriculture, except where they became farmers, as opposed to labourers. Therefore, could one have emigration of whites to Australia or Britain to work as agricultural labourers ?

Professor Silcock sensed some confusion over the need to import capital in order to get immigrants. Immigration might lead to growth and might cause labour shortage, so that capital was needed. Unless capital were imported, Professor Spengler's forces would operate and income per head would fall. Nevertheless, Professor Silcock did not see that it followed that immigration could not advantageously occur. If skilled workers came to underdeveloped areas to stimulate growth there, it seemed to him that the immigration could be frustrated by lack of capital. In some cases, however, as with refugees, it seemed possible that their fall in status might induce them to accumulate their own capital in an attempt to regain their old position. One needed to classify the possible circumstances.

Professor Silcock also wondered if the assimilation of migrants would be facilitated by providing a more normal sex ratio and cultural facilities, making them a self-contained community. It depended what one meant by assimilation. In South-East Asia there was a need to assimilate the Chinese migrants. Yet the Chinese fitted easily into their own separate villages, and this had not helped assimilation. Where there were few Chinese women, and few Chinese families, the migrants were fairly well assimilated. But a large immigration, to improve the sex ratio, tended to accentuate differences from the indigenous stock.

Professor Timlin, referring to Oriental immigration to Canada, said that the Chinese liked to bring their sons over to work, but were usually happier if they could leave their wives and daughters in China.

Professor Bachi said that Professor Silcock's ideas conflicted with those of Dr. Langrod, who had said that assimilation was hampered where workers had no families. He himself did not see why assimilation was hampered by bringing in workers without families.

Dr. Beijer said Dr. Langrod had said that the ideological background of migrants to Israel was the reason why as many as 35 per cent of migrants stayed on the land. This might be true, but there were also good communities and good organization.

Dr. Langrod drew attention to the role played by certain elements in shaping migratory movements. Up to 1914 this role was assumed mainly by the country of immigration, which was often the only one to decide about the source, composition, and extent of the movement. The role, if any, of the country of emigration was at that time usually limited to restricting emigration for military, and sometimes economic, reasons. In the period 1919–39 the interest of the country of emigration in encouraging or discouraging movement, as well as in securing acceptable conditions for migrants, grew. Migration more than ever before became a bilateral concern. Nowadays a 'third element' had emerged and become more and more important in influencing the movements : *the migrant himself.*

This should not be ignored, even in discussions of the economic aspects of migration. It should be remembered that even migration schemes agreed upon by the countries concerned could fail and, in fact, often did fail, because of the reaction of the human beings concerned. Migrants might not go to the country where they were wanted ; they might not wish to stay any longer in such countries. Prospective migrants might not want to move at all after they learned about the frustration of those who had emigrated before. In the past, migration had frequently resulted in human tragedies which were not publicized. The migration of Polish peasants to some South American countries was said to have cost between 80,000 and 100,000 victims. Recently a German professor, undoubtedly exaggerating, had declared that about 75 per cent of emigrants to-day were unhappy. But in general, migrants to-day, more than those of the past, were aware of what was due to them, and expected to be rewarded for moving by a substantial improvement in their position.

Part of the blame for the failure of migration schemes must be attributed to the various national immigration laws and regulations, which established unreasonable, lengthy, and costly administrative procedures, introduced scientifically unjustified discriminations, and often disregarded the legitimate interests of migrants. For example, certain countries wanted immigrants who were not accompanied by their families. This broke family groups and led to big return movements. Similarly, the advantages which countries could expect from mass immigration were seriously reduced when immigrants were rigidly admitted only to particular jobs which had to be arranged in advance. Mr. Lannes's study of immigration into France illustrated this. Dr. Langrod deprecated the numerous legal provisions in various countries which forbade aliens to change their employment freely, and sometimes even to change their residence. In the long run, such restrictions were unlikely to achieve their aim. Moreover, when immigrants did not enjoy the same rights as the local population, when they were subjected to special discriminatory measures, when they feared compulsory repatriation in time of economic crisis, when they were in danger of deportation if they became penniless, they continued to feel like aliens and their assimilation was seriously impeded.

Dr. Langrod felt that the continued enjoyment by immigrants of their old cultural pattern in the new country was important for assimilation. Of course, contact by newcomers with their national groups in that country, the existence of their own schools and newspapers, might delay the process of assimilation. In some countries, for example Brazil, legislation prohibited and restricted such things. Nevertheless, if the newcomers could maintain their old, traditional way of living this helped them to become more valuable citizens of the new country. In this respect the observations made by Stonequist in his *Marginal Man*, and by some other sociologists, seemed significant. They proved that in the United States criminality and insanity were much smaller in the first generation of immigrants, who still derived strength from whatever cultural pattern they brought from the old country, than in the second generation, where this old pattern had been abandoned but a new one had not been acquired. The third generation, which had become really American, which had lost any national inferiority complex, and which nevertheless showed a sentimental interest in the country of their ancestors, seemed to be the best one. The existence in the United States of ethnic groups bound by common traditions facilitated this process, such groups acting as 'shock-absorbers' and helping the new-comers to overcome the initial psychological and other difficulties of adjustment.

All this proved the importance of including social considerations in any formula for successful migration. In an age of social security, such security must be given to those who were in particular need of protection, namely immigrants. By providing it, failures would be prevented and migration might still play its role in the development of the various countries.

THE DISCUSSION ON DR. EDDING'S PAPER

Seventh and Eighth Sessions, Tuesday, 6 September 1955

Professor Parenti said that Dr. Edding's complex paper dealt with four main topics. These were, first, the character of traditional European migration and its connexion with economic development in Europe, as compared with other types of migration; second, the advantages of migration within an integrated economy in Europe; third, the difficulties of regaining the pre-war level of European migration; and fourth, suggestions for liberalizing the movement of European workers.

So far, said Professor Parenti, the Conference had mainly considered migration between continents. In the nineteenth century, in the new countries, one had a number of centres of development and many vacancies for labour which could not be filled from the 'empty spaces' surrounding these centres of development. In this instance, migration had furnished a way of filling the empty spaces. European manpower furnished workers for public utilities, like railways, and also labour for industry in the towns. In Europe, too, development had been centred in certain industrial areas, but these had densely populated rural areas near by. So, it was easy to get workers for urban industry. Intra-European migration was auxiliary, giving workers to the towns, and was often seasonal. Migration of the kind studied so far in the Conference, of the European-United States type, occurred in Europe only where the growth of a European population had lost strength. For example, in France gaps had been caused by the weakness of French rural population and these had been filled by migrants.

Professor Parenti said that Dr. Edding treated integration in terms of a special case, the East German migration to Western Germany. This postwar problem had been treated in detail by Dr. Wander. It was important, and he wanted to comment on it. First, in general, what lessons did it teach on the relation between migration and economic development? Second, how far could one generalize from it? He himself thought that the main point was that migration ought to increase the rate of economic progress, assisting changes in the structure of industrial economies. This meant changes in the distribution of their labour forces, and could be realized only within the limits imposed by the willingness of workers to move. If the necessary movement would have to be across frontiers, the East-West German experience was important. Germany had faced many difficulties in moving its labour from areas of lower to higher production.

Professor Parenti felt that the Conference should study the reasons why mobility in Germany and Europe should be stimulated. If the machinery had been adequate in the past, was it now? And if not, why not? If one assumed no restrictions on movement, then movement resulted from free choice. The migrant compared his own future livelihoods in two possible places. The present position was that if they were different, the difference must be big enough to offset the costs of transfer, both monetary and psychological. As an individual became better off, the greater were the 'psychological' costs of transfer and the lower his propensity to move. The situation was strongly influenced, too, by controls over the movement of migrants. If, as in moving from Italy to France, the worker was tied for some years to a given job, then his future in the receiving country was made less attractive. There was unfortunately a tendency for such controls to increase, and this weakened the tendency to free movement, because it meant a high 'cost' of moving. Some countries, like Italy, France, and Belgium, now gave financial help to migration. Governments might well agree to meet the costs of migration if only they thought of Europe as an integrated whole. Then all would be interested in the costs of migration being met. The High Authority of the Coal and Steel Community (Art. 69) already provided that if workers became redundant and had to move, the High Authority could contribute to the cost of moving. Perhaps, gradually, more of this kind of financial aid would come from growing integration.

Dr. Edding had said that, in future, the amount of intra-European migration was not likely to be as great as in the past. Professor Parenti agreed that its volume would not increase, but he nevertheless thought it unlikely that it would decrease. One reason why Dr. Edding took this view was that the demographic pattern in Europe was now much more balanced than in the past. But perhaps intra-European migration was little influenced by demographic factors. Again, the reduced demand for unskilled labour was given as a reason for less migration. But for forty years now migration had been mainly of skilled workers. Professor Parenti did not regard miners and farmers as unskilled labour, though they were, in fact, classified as such. A further reason was said to be that countries which had previously had surplus labour, like Italy and Greece, were now tending to work out plans to use their own. The result would apparently be to reduce migration. But then, at least in the Italian plan, the aim was to increase income per head by reducing drastically the amount of disguised unemployment. If progress in this direction were rapid, the release of under-employed agricultural workers would free much agricultural labour. This might well have to emigrate unless capital came in, which was not very likely in Italy.

Professor Parenti turned to Dr. Edding's final topic, the liberalization of European manpower. Organizations like OEEC and the High Authority for Coal and Steel had already tried to increase the possibilities of migration. Apart from such moves, however, Dr. Edding was apparently anxious to try other ways of obtaining greater movement. He suggested taking an area with active frontier migration and trying to allow completely free movement. Professor Parenti supported this idea, but he did not think Dr. Edding's suggestion would prove very fruitful. He himself wanted to see econometric models constructed to show the advantages of free migratory movements in terms of income per head. Professor Parenti said he was not keen on econometric models as guides to policy, but he felt that the question of their suitability might well provide a useful topic for discussion.

Professor Spengler thought the discussion would be easier if one distinguished between three stages. Stage One took things as they were now in Europe. Stage Two assumed completely free movement of labour, capital, and goods in Europe; in other words, complete industrial as well as geographical mobility. Europe with such completely free movement of goods and people would already have gone far towards complete integration. Perhaps it would have gone three-quarters or four-fifths of the way. Complete integration was Stage Three.

Professor Spengler therefore suggested freedom of movement as the main factor in bringing integration. So few barriers to integration would then be left that no serious obstacles would remain. This integration might well reduce migration overseas by leading to more movement within Europe. For instance, it might accelerate urbanization. But this was by the way. Professor Spengler said his main point was that obstacles to free movement of goods and people were obstacles to integration, and he felt that this meant that in twenty or thirty years the whole system would change, with a gain for everyone. Some people might suffer from adverse substitution effects, but the aggregate gain would more than compensate them. Free movement, then, was a 'way station' to integration.

Dr. Hofstee said Dr. Edding's main point was that the tendency to migrate was declining because of more equal real wages in all parts of Europe, and Professor Parenti had not denied that this was the case. Professor Parenti had indeed said that more migration was *needed*, but would there *be* migration ? Holland, for example, was overpopulated, but there was no intra-European migration to solve the problem. Therefore one had to take other measures, for example the geographical planning of economic and industrial development in Europe. In the Netherlands such measures had been taken on a smaller scale. The Netherlands had some overpopulated and some underdeveloped parts. Therefore the Dutch government was developing the latter areas by subsidizing rents, building factories, and so on in them. Did we need a similar general European plan for the location of industry ?

Professor Parenti said that Dr. Hofstee's ideas were correct for a restricted, depressed area. In Italy, however, the areas of unemployment and under-employment were too large to be dealt with in this way. The amount of movement might be reduced, but one could not avoid it altogether.

Dr. Hofstee said it was true that location policy was simplest when restricted to small areas. Nevertheless, the planning of economic development for Europe as a whole seemed possible. In southern Italy, for example, better roads would make it possible to set up new cities and towns with their own industry. For backward and overpopulated areas in Europe, then, planned location was a possibility — or, indeed, a real necessity.

Professor Thomas said we were concerned, in Europe, with a group of nations, and to be nations they must be definitive ; they must be separate. It followed that 'free' migration meant 'marginal' shifts. One implication of political independence was that a man should be allowed to choose where he worked. But because each country had its own government there were constraints. It was important that the individual should be able to choose what he wanted to do. If Dutch farmers preferred to farm in the United States they should be allowed to go to the United States, and not sent by planners to other parts of Holland to work in industry. This was true, too, of Italians. If they wished to emigrate, one should let them, since migrants would add more to the world's agricultural output overseas than in Europe, and this would improve Europe's terms of trade.

Dr. Edding, replying to Professor Thomas, said that if he had spoken of 'plans' he had not meant to imply any restrictions on free movement. There must be real freedom. For instance, foreign miners in the United Kingdom should not be compelled to remain miners. One could see that, throughout history, certain countries had attracted much labour. The danger was that a Europe without frontiers would experience the problems mentioned in Dr. Hofstee's paper. In the Netherlands there was no economic reason for migration. But people felt such a lack of 'elbow room', especially in Holland (strictly defined), that further agglomeration would create serious problems. This suggested two approaches to the question. First, was it economically profitable to allow such agglomeration? Second, one had the psychological problem of human reactions. It was not a question of limiting freedom, but of having counterbalancing attractions outside the attractive areas.

Dr. Hofstee agreed that one should not push people about, but one should also allow them freedom *not* to move. In Holland there was overpopulation in the rural areas of the east and south. There had always been internal migration to the western parts of the country, but many people did not wish to move. In general, *free* migration would never solve the problem of overpopulation completely. Therefore in overpopulated areas migration had to be combined with (planned) measures to stimulate economic development.

Professor Thomas said that Dr. Hofstee had said that he did not want to push anyone around. He was willing to let people stay where they wanted to be. But did this principle not imply that he must push business-men about?

Dr. Hofstee replied that businessmen were much easier to move.

Mr. Hague said that he sensed some confusion in the 'theological' debate between the 'planners' and those who wanted freedom in location decisions. He wanted to put the problem into a logical framework. One could distinguish three main situations in which location decisions had to be made: (1) the firm's private costs would be higher in the new location, so it did not move; (2) the firm's private costs would be lower in the new location, yet it still did not move; (3) workers would not move, even though employment conditions and wages were better in the location where the government wished them to be. In Case (1) one could either use force or 'bribery' to move the firm. Case (2) might arise from ignorance, from the importance of non-pecuniary factors, or from uncertainty about costs in the two locations in the future. The solution here was to spread more information and, perhaps, to cancel out psychic losses with monetary payments. In Case (3) one could do nothing — assuming that one dared not force workers to move by starving them out. However, even here, the 'elasticity of supply of mobile workers' was unlikely to be zero. One might therefore sometimes find it worth 'bribing' workers to move, so long as the social gain outweighed the social cost. These three cases covered migration within a country. For European migration one must add Case (4), where workers would move but another country would not let them in. This was where the case for planning was at its strongest, assuming that countries which refused to accept foreign workers did not object to the coming of foreign firms.

If one tried to plan location in Europe, how would one get on? The answer was: as at home. But how did one plan migration internally? Mr. Hague thought it was bad enough moving firms from London to South Wales. He was appalled at the idea of international civil servants moving firms from Lisbon to Lapland, or Birmingham to Bavaria. It would need almost superhuman officials. Quite apart from this, he had been a little alarmed when members of the Conference seemed to feel that they knew almost automatically into which of his four cases any firm would fit. But did we ? The obstacle to any planned location policy was that information about cost differences between various locations was so very scanty. This was true if one only considered private costs. If social costs were also considered, one had to abandon all hope of accuracy.

Apart from such 'irreducible ignorance' there was bound to be much more uncertainty in entrepreneurs' minds if they moved to another country than there was over moves within their own country. Political factors like the danger of expropriation by the foreign government and arbitrary changes in foreign exchange rates (unless all output were sold on the foreign country's internal market) would cause trouble. He was therefore not hopeful about a European location policy, quite apart from the difficulty of getting a number of separate nations to agree to plan together. Mr. Hague said his opposition to planned location was not on principle, but on the facts. It was doubtful if a location policy on a European scale could succeed now, or indeed for as long as full employment in most countries lasted.

Professor Spengler said the discussion was concerned with migration and integration. The best tactics were to begin a piecemeal attack on specific barriers to migration, and not to produce the grandiose plans of economists. Migration, as a way-station to integration, must be thought of in terms of local movements and small segments. The role of migration in fostering integration was in fact very limited.

Dr. Edding said he had gone into the question of Germany so deeply because the German Government took both the possible lines of action open to it. Industry was moved to overpopulated areas and people were moved to industry. He did not know enough about Italy, but one was given two very different views by the Italians. First, one was told that the labour surplus would soon end ; second, one was told the opposite. From the German point of view, immigration by Italians might be good. Labour was short in Germany, and there was cost inflation. In the short run it would undoubtedly be beneficial to import Italians ; in the long run social considerations arose. If more and more miners, rural workers, and domestic servants were nationals of another country, problems were created that could be avoided only if one could allow them to move into better jobs.

Professor Robinson said that as adviser on the Vanoni Plan for Italian development he had the impression that there were two Italys, each with a separate demographic trend. The North had approached some sort of equilibrium, but the South was far away from it. The Vanoni Plan assumed much internal migration. The population in the South would go on growing rapidly, and he thought it unlikely that the South could absorb its own natural increase. The Vanoni Plan was also based on the assumption that there would be the maximum amount of migration of Italians overseas that was politically possible. This was not an economic but a political problem. He agreed with Professor Parenti that development in the South would create as well as reduce unemployment. Rural under-employment could not go on for ever. The older people might submit, but the young were not content, and moved out. The young went to other, more prosperous, parts of Italy, and also overseas. He himself regarded migration and the Vanoni Plan more as a political than as an economic question.

Professor Parenti agreed that rural reform would increase unemployment. One farmer worked more productively than a whole group had done before, though perhaps more intensive cultivation would absorb some labour.

Professor Robinson suggested that land reclamation would give new opportunities for farming. He hoped for much development of secondary industry in villages. He was, however, convinced that Professor Parenti was right when he said that there would be a net move away from purely agricultural areas.

Dr. Langrod wondered whether emigration from Southern Italy had not done more harm than good. There could have been no real improvement in Italy in the numerous cases where, after the departure (*e.g.* to Argentina) of men not accompanied by their families, a valuable productive factor disappeared while the weaker factor remained on an uneconomically small plot of land. Again, if the whole family emigrated, but the land and property left behind was not used in a way which would improve the agricultural structure of the region, the country was still not helped. Had the position improved in recent times ? Was the property bought by an institution when the whole family emigrated, thus providing a link between emigration and the progress of land reform ?

Professor Parenti said Dr. Langrod was right about the situation in Italy before the war. Now there was a change, and almost all land that was vacant was sold. Before the war it was a social qualification to have land, and one handed it to the next generation. Now this force was not so active. Again, before the war an emigrant country would seek for labour and pay its fare under indenture. Now migrants tended to sell their land in order to pay their own fares. But who bought the land thus sold ? In general, the more active farmers, for in general those who had the most money were the most efficient. Professor Parenti said that land reform worked through an institution which took land from its owners and gave it to farm hands. Once the ownership had passed, the institution supervised and financed the farm, giving machinery, etc. There was a sort of compulsory co-operation with the new tenant to improve the farm.

Dr. Wander noted Professor Parenti's view that in the past demographic factors had not been of great importance to European migration, except in France. The postwar influx from Eastern Europe was a major exception. Ten million people had come since the end of the war, yet the age distribution of the population had not been improved by this influx. In the age groups 27–49 there was still an absolute deficit in Western Germany of 600,000 men. Again, social benefits reduced the propensity to migrate. Not only did these take the form of government aid ; there were also benefits paid by firms to their employees. In Germany many firms provided houses, old age pensions, etc., and all this helped to keep workers where they were.

Professor Rubin argued that the future volume of economic migration within Europe was not likely to be as high as before 1914. The Soviet bloc's 290 million population had been a potential source of migrants before 1914, but it was not now. This was a major point. On moves towards freer movement, Professor Rubin pointed out that in the Scandinavian area there was now a ' regional' labour market, which was a working model for the international transfer of labour, social security benefits, etc. Why could not other similar arrangements be made ?

Dr. Edding said Scandinavia had had this system for more than a year. He thought, however, there was so far much opposition in Norway, because skilled labour and qualified people had gone to Sweden. This would happen in Europe. The areas with high living standards would gain, and losing regions would be annoyed. Scandinavia would need to take the next step, for there were advantages to the 'losers' only if there was a complete 'circular flow' of incomes.

Professor Lindahl said there was free and considerable movement in some professions in Scandinavia. University and school teachers had freedom to move. In other professions there were legal restrictions. On the ordinary labour market Professor Lindahl doubted if there was much permanent migration. There were differences over social security and so on, so that he was not as optimistic as Dr. Edding.

Professor Parenti supported Dr. Edding. Apart from the professions, Scandinavian workers needed no permit, but, except for marginal movements, the only regional flow was from Norway to Sweden. In fact, this had existed before, but then one needed a permit. On European movement Professor Parenti said there were bilateral agreements on social security, for instance, between Italy and France, France and Belgium, and so on. At present, the convention of the High Authority for Coal and Steel was being ratified, so that, in the Community, bilateral agreements would be covered also by a multilateral one. Already the former covered about 80 per cent of European labour.

Professor Lerner said it had been suggested that more freedom of movement within Europe would lead to less movement to the United States. But was this so ? People protected from competition in Europe might move to America if restrictions on trade went. One had to remember Viner's argument that the removal of restrictions on trade in Europe would worsen the trade position. But this was an academic statement and one could not be sure how correct it was. Therefore, he accepted the idea that liberalization was an improvement, unless someone could prove the reverse.

Dr. Zubrzycki agreed with Professor Rubin that Eastern Europe was no longer a source of emigration. Dr. Edding had said that so long as Eastern Europe remained totalitarian there would be no free movement. However, if Eastern Europe were free, she would no longer be a potential source of migrants. There had been (*a*) a decline in fertility rates and population losses because of the war, (*b*) rapid industrialization, and (*c*) the disappearance of rural overpopulation, so that rural labour now appeared to be scarce.

Professor Spengler suggested that since most migrants were quite young they would accumulate social benefits in the new country. So the problems arising from difficulties in transferring social benefits from one country to another should not be very serious, on the face of it, in normal times. But this was all pure conjecture.

Professor Bachi stressed the need for fuller statistical research into migration. He suggested, for example, the use of more refined methods than those normally employed for treating the statistical data available about migration. He mentioned several methods, to be explained in a paper to be published later, which made it possible: (*a*) to calculate indices of 'preference' or 'dislike' by migrants for each of the possible *directions* of migratory traffic; and (*b*) to show the distribution of migrants by distances covered. Professor Bachi said his methods were based mainly on a comparison between the *actual* numbers of migrants, classified by place of origin and place of destination, and the *expected* numbers obtained on certain assumptions. His methods might lead to some synthetic measures of migratory traffic; for example, total kilometres covered by migrants, average distance covered by migrants as compared with expected distance, and so on.

Mr. Lannes said that European migration, in particular, depended on the working of the law of supply and demand on the international plane. Some countries had a surplus of labour; others lacked professional workers. Disequilibrium could be of two types: (*a*) there might be a *global* disequilibrium when the volume of aggregate demand was too small to employ the total population; (*b*) there might be a *quantitative* disequilibrium when the total demand and supply of labour was roughly equal, in total, but not in particular industries and occupations. Some degree of unemployment in certain professions could exist side by side with labour shortage in other sectors.

Type (*a*) resulted from the combined effects of two factors, (i) a demographic factor (increasing size of the working population), and (ii) the rapidity of economic development. Type (*b*) implied too little professional and geographical mobility of labour.

At the risk of over-simplification, one could say that in modern Europe the labour surpluses were of type (*a*) and the shortages of type (*b*) (except in Switzerland). There was also little proportion between the supplies of surplus labour in overpopulated countries and the number of jobs which these surplus workers might possibly fill in countries where labour shortage arose only, or mainly, from a lack of labour mobility. It followed that migration within Europe could do little to solve the problem posed by underdevelopment and unemployment in the Mediterranean lands.

The role of migration in a completely integrated economy, with no obstacles to the free movement of goods, capital, and labour, depended on whether economic development in the losing countries could be sufficiently stimulated to bring about a substantial reduction in unemployment. It also depended on whether the speed of development in countries with full employment could be so increased as to make substantial immigration imperative. Without this, free movement of labour in Europe would only reduce the standard of living in the wealthiest countries.

Mr. Turvey did not see how in type (*a*) one could talk of the demand for labour without mentioning real wages.

Mr. Lannes said he was not an economist. He meant that the available labour supply was greater or smaller than the number of jobs for it. He had meant no more. Perhaps one should not say supply and demand.

Mr. Turvey wondered if Mr. Lannes meant that an excess supply of labour implied that emigration was needed.

Mr. Lannes said this was not necessarily so.

Professor James said that when Mr. Lannes talked of an excess supply of labour, he talked of countries like Greece and Italy. Surely we, as economists, could agree that there was surplus labour in these countries.

Professor Hoffmann said there could be no absolute surplus ; all depended on social factors, like mobility, and so on.

Dr. Edding was not clear over the function of real wages. If labour were in surplus in Italy and short in Germany, could low wages in Italy create, in the real world of to-day, a move to Germany ? Was there any chance that one could induce German trade unions to allow in 300,000 Italians who would underbid them on the labour market ?

Professor Hoffmann said that trade unions did not like migration in all situations. Without migration from the East, German wages might be higher now and might have been for the past few years. In Europe as a whole, with the influx of foreign labour, wages would not be absolutely lower, but they would be less high than they might otherwise have been. The immigration of ten million Germans with not much capital was a specific case which was very interesting for itself.

Professor Hoffmann said that the German Government had a long-run road-building programme and there were discussions on how far Italian labour should be allowed to come in. The trade unions were not against it in present conditions, but they did not know how long the boom would last. So, at present, seasonal migration was preferred.

Professor Timlin said we had seen that, with free migration, the supply curve of labour was positively inclined. It might, however, be a negatively inclined curve in any individual country, so that wages would rise with strong trade unions. She thought of Professor Douglas's backward-sloping curve. This might not occur for the world, but it might in given countries.

Professor Rubin said that in Germany it was suggested that labour was exploited. Yet Israel did not do anything to discourage migration and keep up wages.

Professor Hoffmann said this was only relative exploitation. Without the movement from the East, wages would have gone up much more.

Professor Parenti said that this sounded right in theory, but might not migration into Germany have accelerated growth in the way Professor Spengler had suggested? *Professor Hoffmann* admitted that there were both aggregate and substitution problems.

Dr. Wander discussed the Schleswig-Holstein voluntary resettlement scheme, under which this area had been developed and work taken to the workers. Now the unemployed were few and mostly in the higher age groups. One might move entrepreneurs to use this idle labour force. But as labour became scarcer and wages higher, fewer 'competent' workers were available. Moreover, if Germany were reunited, Eastern Germany might take some migrants back and leave an even bigger labour shortage in Western Germany.

Professor Hoffmann said there was a similar feeling in Germany, the Netherlands, and Belgium to that in Britain. Should the immigrant, even if his productivity was lower, have the same wage rate, social security benefits, or houses as the native? These were the facts of 'adjustment'.

Professor Robinson felt one should look at the receiving countries on the basis of the Spengler analysis. Politically, the problem was whether one could persuade the receivers that there was a benefit to them as well as to the population exporters. All agreed that the countries of the world benefited in total by free migration movements. The exceptions were few. But when concrete proposals were made that a high-standard country should remove its barriers, there was hesitation. In Britain trade unions were worried in the way noted by Professor Spengler in his analysis of the United States. Sometimes migrants and home labour were complementary; but one could see why a coal-miner, who received a good wage, was wholly against migrants in the mines. Another factor which influenced public opinion was that Britain had a higher standard of living than the rest of Europe and social security payments were related to this. The welfare state, in Britain, gave education and health services, etc., which could be afforded by a rich nation but not by the average worker in Europe. Britain feared that any widespread migratory movement in Europe would lower living standards in some countries. One must therefore frankly admit the position of the receiving countries, who might have their standards reduced. As a European one had to admit that, in total, there would be a benefit to all. But this was not much help in a political decision about opening doors. Britain's problem was much like that of the United States.

Professor Thomas said that he did not agree. He did not accept the view that the United Kingdom and the United States were in real danger from a marginal shift of population. In the Empire movement was free; Jamaicans could and did come to Britain. There were difficulties, but when these people got jobs they were not a nuisance in the United Kingdom. They benefited the higher income groups. In the era of large-scale immigration in the United States the professional groups had not opposed the entry of foreign workers. It was only when immigration into the lower strata began to interfere with vertical mobility out of those strata that trouble began. The British creed was as important as the American, and Britain did not keep out members of the Commonwealth.

Professor Rubin was impressed with the statements of Professor Robinson and Professor Thomas. There seemed to be a divergence between them, but in reality there was not. In the early 1930's there were proposals to deport all the foreign-born from America to cure unemployment. This idea had gone, but it was necessary for the Government to plan. However, we should not give up our points of freedom. We needed a compromise which merged free capitalism with 'Vanoni' plans. Even now in the United States, with a high G.N.P., it was hard to convince Congress that it should double the migrant quota from a mere 150,000 to 300,000. Why should the inflow of immigrants lower living standards? But in a country smaller than the United Kingdom the position might be different.

Professor Robinson said he agreed with much of Professor Thomas's article of faith. But he was much more concerned with the humdrum problem of persuading people to remove obstacles to migration. No statement of faith would do this. One had to point to the aggregate gains from migration, which Professor Thomas emphasized, as well as the supposed losses of individuals. One should not ignore the strong resistance to removing obstacles to migration. These might well be ill-founded, but one did not remove them purely by argument.

Professor Lerner said he thought one should distinguish between ideal objectives and articles of faith. He had less faith than Professor Robinson that there was consistency between universal benefits and ideal aims. He had Professor Thomas's ideals, but he saw Professor Robinson's difficulties. Ideally wealth should be equally divided. One would therefore suggest that increasing wealth should be shared between the haves and have-nots. Yet this was too idealistic. If the migrants were paid their marginal product this could not harm other inhabitants as a whole. One could compensate the losers. But if one also gave social services, it might be that the natives were worse off. One might like to think that people could ignore this, but they would not. However, he would not like to discriminate against migrants by refusing them all social services. The resentment would be much too serious.

Professor Chandresekhar thought Professor Thomas was right. Dominion subjects were welcome in Britain. Yet intra-Dominion travel was not always easy. For instance, one could not go from Ceylon to Australia.

Mr. Turvey said he wished to dispute Professor Thomas's claim that immigration was desirable as a matter of human freedom. First, Professor Thomas wanted free immigration from the Commonwealth, but he did not want it elsewhere. He wanted 'Africa for the Africans'. This made for difficulties. These had perhaps been overstressed by Bauer, but *was* it desirable for there to be immigration into West Africa? Second, Mr. Turvey said he was prepared to be chauvinistic about the United Kingdom and to restrict entry from non-Commonwealth countries. Third, Mr. Turvey thought it quite likely that migration decisions taken by individuals might not be closely related to the general social gain. Economically one would approve of immigration if the migrant's real income was greater than in the country of origin. But in a particular country a migrant might have to pay more in tax, and this made it more difficult to see what would happen. The social and private benefits would differ.

Mr. Zubrzycki said he had benefited from the British creed of freedom, and resented Mr. Turvey's chauvinism.

Professor Lerner did not accept the chauvinist argument, though he thought it was important. One could not leave the chauvinist value judgement out of account, but the general weight of argument was against it. If one wanted to increase the *per capita* income of the world, one would restrict movement into countries with high incomes from those with lower ones. He suggested that the ultimate aim should be to limit migration in general terms, so that one could prevent fast-growing populations from bringing their own condition to other countries.

Mr. Turvey said that his chauvinism arose solely from his interest in his own standard of living. He would never suggest that refugees from persecution should be barred, but his point related to non-Commonwealth migrants moving for purely economic reasons.

Professor Robinson wondered how general Mr. Turvey's argument was. Mr. Turvey had talked of Africa. There, the deliberate policy had been to protect an under-educated people, and help them to govern themselves. Unless one thought that a single-race society was worse than a multi-race one, there was some justification for what Britain had done. One must recognize the risk that immigrant racial groups might entrench themselves and thereby prevent native improvement. One should not reject the idea of trying to develop Africa for the Africans. Perhaps the deliberate restriction of immigration had been wrong. But it was the result of a sincere desire to help the African.

Professor Thomas said that free migration was the British creed in the sense that one was a citizen of the 'United Kingdom and Colonies'. All shared the right to a job, to social services, and so on. Mr. Turvey's chauvinism was too half-hearted. To be consistent he should extend it to trade as well, regarding the United Kingdom as a wholly monopolistic concern. That idea would not be generally popular in Britain. Professor Thomas said his own statement of faith did include a little economics. He had put forward a theory of non-competing groups, but no one had taken it up. He viewed the idea of 'Africa for the Africans' with dismay, if it were taken literally. When the United Kingdom, faced with the enormous responsibility of its colonies, found that the colonies contained other people, say non-Africans born in Africa, what should it do ? Should it throw them out and try to stop others coming in ? Or should it try to set up a multi-racial society, even though this was very difficult ? It seemed much more realistic. 'Africa for the Africans' was a mere slogan. In the case of Jamaican migrants, the workers' productivity was greater in London than in Jamaica. When such labour came into a growing economy it fitted in and conferred benefits.

Professor Chandrasekhar wondered if there were not inconsistencies in British policy in Africa. In West Africa the British Government had only become concerned at a late stage. In other colonies the British were the founders. The climate prevented this in West Africa. Even to-day there was encouragement for British settlers to go to Rhodesia ; West Africa was a special case.

Professor Robinson thought it was not so simple as this. The climate in the Congo was much the same as in Nigeria. Yet the Congo had large estates, Belgian settlement, and other development. In any case, if there were inconsistencies why should one be surprised ? In East Africa there was at the moment determined opposition both to Britons and to others. Many of the apparent inconsistencies were the result of accidents of history. Yet in the last thirty years the governments concerned had tried to protect the African and not to improve the position of their own nationals.

Professor Robertson said that not to mislead would take too long, so he would merely confine himself to two points. He agreed that much of British policy depended on the accidents of history. For example, it had been impossible to settle closely in West Africa until after a change in the attitude to colonization had taken place in Britain. So Britain had protected African interests, and had slowed down, for example, the inflow of foreign entrepreneurs. This was now reinforced by a new feeling on the morals of colonial development which had grown up in Britain. Whilst the accidents of history and the facts of climate might be an explanation of different patterns of development in given areas, these were now due to an 'effort of will', and not to outside constraint. Africans could not now be exploited by European and Asian migration.

On 'Africa for the Africans' Professor Robertson said the key was to be found in the idea that this was a mere slogan which should never be taken literally. It was obviously quite as chauvinistic as our new slogan, 'England for the Turveys'. But the British had acquired many resources in the period of free-for-all in Africa. There was now a policy of protecting those who could not protect themselves, including the idea of areas reserved for Africans.

Professor Robinson thought there was a rate at which a country could satisfactorily absorb migrants, and that this was higher than the existing rate of immigration in Africa, both economically and culturally.

Dr. Edding replied to the discussion. He said that the liberalization of the movement of labour was the declared policy of European governments. But the practical details were left too much to civil servants, who treated people like goods and ignored both economics and sociology. We needed more research into qualitative changes in the demand for labour, labour mobility, assimilation conditions, and so on. This was very neglected territory compared with the movement of goods and money. We had only touched on the problems in this Conference, and there was great need for an effort to persuade both governments and electors of the great benefits to be gained from increased migration within Europe.

THE DISCUSSION ON PROFESSOR LERNER'S PAPER

Ninth and Tenth Sessions, Wednesday 7 September 1955

Mr. Turvey said that in general he agreed with Professor Lerner, so that his own contribution would be a critique rather than a criticism of Professor Lerner's paper. It was not possible to make any very general statement on this particular problem of the relation between demand, inflation, and migration. For example, if one had a bus service on which overtime was being worked, the employment of immigrants would allow a reduction in overtime working. The wage bill would fall, output would not be less, and with a suitable tax structure total incomes might fall. On the other hand, where firms making capital goods had long order books, an inflow of migrants would allow incomes to rise. Tax receipts would be up too, but there would be a net increase in income, so consumption expenditure might rise, while the increase in capital goods output would not be deflationary. Therefore one could make no general statement. But such a demand inflation, with effective demand greater than aggregate home output plus permissible import surplus, could be dealt with by an appropriate fiscal policy.

This led Mr. Turvey to the relationship between demand and cost inflation. What was common to them? Demand inflation meant that prices were pulled up; in cost inflation they were pushed up. Demand inflation occurred where there was an attempt to buy more than was being produced, or to produce more than could be produced. Cost inflation occurred where producers tried to raise real incomes, or to pre-

vent them from falling; they were trying to earn more than there was to
be earned. The common element was an endeavour to get more than
there was to be got.

Mr. Turvey said that Professor Lerner had claimed that, where cost
inflation was possible, migration might lead to three results. It might
lead to unemployment; and/or to prices rising continuously through
cost inflation; and/or to an unfavourable balance of payments. If the
problem was that real wages were too high, one could not deal with it
by ordinary fiscal policy.

Since Professor Lerner's model was not explicit, he would set it out
in a diagram dealing only with the real part of the model. One began in
equilibrium with full employment and a given price level. Workers

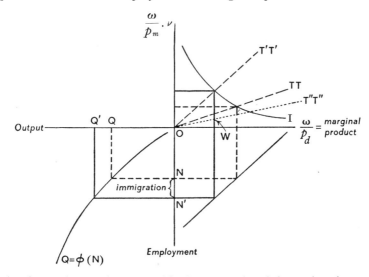

insisted on a given real wage, and both imported and domestic prices were
determinants of real wages. The wage in terms of domestic goods was
$\dfrac{\omega}{p_d}$; in terms of imports it was $\dfrac{\omega}{p_m}.\nu$. The real wages demanded were
given by the indifference curve I, in the north-east quadrant. The
marginal product of labour was a function of employment, N, as given
in the south-east quadrant. As employment rose, the marginal product
of labour fell, as the total function $Q = \phi(N)$, in the south-west quadrant,
also showed. The initial equilibrium was given by the dashed line.
Employment was full, at ON. The slope of the line TT showed the terms
of trade. The foreign trade position was such that real wages, the terms
of trade, and a total output of OQ allowed the balance of payments to
be in equilibrium initially.

Mr. Turvey assumed that NN′ migrants then arrived. The straight
line marginal productivity curve in the south-east quadrant showed that

the marginal product of labour would fall. To employ all the new labour, one needed a fall in real wages in terms of domestic goods. Thus if workers were to stay on the indifference curve I, their wage in terms of imports would have to rise, so the terms of trade would have to improve to T'T'. This, and the rise in output by QQ', would cause more imports to be demanded. On the other hand, the foreign demand for exports would fall, and there would therefore be a deficit in the balance of payments. If capital could be imported, all would be well. But if not, the terms of trade would actually have to become worse than before in order to offset the effect upon import demand of the rise in output. Say they had to worsen to T"T". Then real wages would have to be at W, below the level shown on the indifference curve, if there was to be full employment (ON' men employed). So, in order to avoid a balance of payments deficit, real wages would have to fall. If, as the indifference curve suggested they would, workers resisted this cut, the result would be a rise in money wages and cost inflation. This increase in money wage rates would cause an exchange depreciation and a further rise in import prices. The resulting unemployment could not be fought by fiscal measures, for the only result would be more inflation.

If the exchange rate were flexible, in the sense of always maintaining balance of payments equilibrium, one had three possibilities: (1) full employment (ON') and continuous inflation; (2) NN' unemployment and no inflation; (3) less than NN' unemployment and some inflation. Thus one reached the classical proposition that unemployment was caused by an excessively high real wage, and that fiscal policy would not cure unemployment except at the price of inflation. Professor Lerner had turned from a Keynesian into a classical economist.

Professor Lerner said this was a good exposition, and might even have cleared his own mind. It certainly drew attention to the fact that, initially, there was equilibrium both in the balance of payments and in the price level.

Mr. Hague said that his comments on Professor Lerner's paper were neither large-scale nor diagrammatic, but were intended to provide a basis for discussion. The problem faced was that resources were available in plenty, and yet these plentiful resources were not being used, because the real wage rate was too high. Did trade unions really behave like this, not in a country like Britain, but in countries of mass immigration? Professor Lerner's views were clearly coloured by experience in Israel, about which he himself knew nothing. Was Professor Lerner's assumption right for Israel? Was it right more generally? In Professor Lerner's model, prices were rising because of increasing costs and not because of excessive demand. Surely, in the Lerner model, prices rose not because costs did, but because the government allowed the supply of money to increase in order to keep the trade unions quiet. One had a government-perpetuated process and not an inherently self-perpetuating one. This led to the question, What sort of fiscal policy were receiving countries likely to pursue? Mr. Hague wondered if someone could provide the answer.

Professor Lerner had also assumed that the 'satisfactory' level of employment for the trade unions was low enough for there to be no problem with balance of payments. Yet if the level of money wages insisted on by trade unions led to a balance of payments deficit, one would have to put up with a 'less than satisfactory' level of employment. In the model, as in the real world, the balance of payments would have the last word.

Professor Rubin pointed out that inflation, being a self-perpetuating process, was affected by expectations that depended on memories of past inflations. But one need not have identically the same conditions. He also thought American experience showed that the high propensity to save on the part of immigrants to the United States, though anti-inflationary, was in conflict with the American tradition. On the other hand, the volume of immigrant remittances, in the form of savings sent to the old country, was a residual result of inflation in the receiving country which affected the country of emigration.

Professor Spengler said that the absence of a money illusion in Professor Lerner's model did not seem realistic but, even if it were introduced, it would not affect the outcome. The basic assumption was that the government would pursue a monetary and financial policy to keep the process in motion. Government action was crucial. Professor Lerner also implied that sellers could and would raise prices in anticipation of an increase in the cost of production. Could we examine that process? He was not sure whether sellers had this power; it seemed to suggest rather a mass response. It was also assumed that there were no groups which could be exploited to make up for the excess of the real wage of labour over its marginal product. In fact landlords, under rent restriction, or pensioners, could be made to foot the bill. The driving force of the whole process was government policy, and to understand why this was, one must go back to the social structure. One had to postulate a powerful trade union movement, which was a modern phenomenon. But was the trade union movement homogeneous, and would other groups acquiesce in its policy? It was not a self-perpetuating process on political grounds. It depended on the redistribution of power within society, on changing conditions of wage contracts, and also on government policy not bringing the inflationary movement to an end.

Professor Hoffmann said it was certain that mass immigration need not necessarily lead to inflation; the West German case supported this argument. Ten million migrants had come in during a few years, on top of a population of forty million, and these new potential workers had an occupation structure similar to that of the existing population. With such a sudden increase in the number of potential workers, only three results were theoretically possible. First, there might be an increased number of unemployed. This was the usual reaction. Second, if the amount of capital per man were to remain the same, there would have to be an increase in the capital stock. This was of great importance in the German case, because the propensity to save was very high there. Both the local population and immigrants wished to save in order to build houses. Fiscal measures were also used to increase the propensity to save. Third, the immigrants might, and this too had happened in Germany, go to agriculture and trade, where the amount of capital per man was low. This actually reduced capital stock per man throughout Germany, but after 1952 an increased capital stock per man was built up. In the long run, both the total capital stock and capital stock per man would increase, but at first the capital stock per man was not high by comparison with other countries, for example the United Kingdom and the United States.

Professor Timlin thought it a mistake in this discussion to bring in many empirical observations of events in North America. Professor Lerner's model fitted the Israel situation, where one had mass immigration taking place without much differentiation in the labour supply. Immigration into North America since the war, however, had brought labour into places where there were bottlenecks in the labour market. This had improved both the distribution of the labour force and the use of capital.

Professor Lerner answered criticisms of the one fundamental point about his model — the place of the government. Was the model descriptive of self-perpetuating inflation, or did it describe a government intervention? This was a terminological difference. Cost inflation would not continue if the government refused to increase the amount of money. But this did not imply a policy of intervention; it was not 'natural' for a government to hold the amount of money constant. Governments, not only in Israel, felt it important to keep down unemployment in order to be re-elected. It was 'natural' for them to provide more money if they could thereby prevent unemployment from becoming more severe.

Professor Robinson said that in one sense any economist must agree formally with Professor Lerner; in another sense, his paper was most misleading. It gave the impression that any volume of immigration could be absorbed, without inflation, if the right fiscal policy were adopted, and if 'realistic' levels of real wages, in terms of available resources, were accepted by all. This was grossly oversimplified. What about the proportion of real resources going into government expenditure? He was not sure whether Mr. Turvey was assuming that the level of real output per head was affected only by scale effects, and that the proportion of real national resources going to consumption was constant, or whether he was allowing for changes in the proportion of total resources available for consumption? It was very difficult to make the right assumption in this model. With mass immigration, one surely had to assume important repercussions on the proportion of national resources going into capital formation and into government expenditure. If one assumed that, then one was faced with a powerful inflationary process. Large-scale immigration would push up the ratio of gross capital formation to gross national product from, say 12 or 15 per cent to something like 20 or 25 per cent. It was also very likely that government expenditure would rise from, say, 15 to 20 per cent of gross national product. This would reduce consumption from about 70 to about 55 per cent of G.N.P. All agreed that inflation was very sensitive to changes in the consumption ratio. If the consumption ratio was pushed down farther than trade unions would accept, then, in the experience of the United Kingdom, one had inflationary pressures. The question was, what amount of reduction in real wages would trade unions accept ? And ought *any* level of real wages resulting from immigration to be accepted ? One variable in this model should surely be the volume of immigration. All immigration, on whatever scale, could, in terms of the model, but not in practice, be absorbed without danger of inflation. Professor Lerner was diverting our attention from something that was most important.

Mr. Turvey said that there were three determinants of the volume of consumption : (1) the amount of income consumers received ; (2) the amount they were *trying* to receive ; and (3) the size of gross national product, including any import surplus, minus government expenditure, imports and investment. A difference between any two of these would produce inflation. A divergence between (2) and (3) caused cost inflation. A divergence between (1) and (3) would produce demand inflation.

Professor Ellis felt that Professor Lerner's model was applicable to a wide range of countries. The situation in Argentina illustrated the model in operation, and if implicit wage increases were considered as well as explicit ones the applicability of the model could be further extended. He wondered whether Professor Lerner would consider cases where the increment to population came from an internal increase in population, and thus extend the applicability of the model. Since Mr. Borrie's paper showed that the Australian economy seemed to conform to Professor Lerner's expectations, he wondered if one could also extend the analysis to a large developing country with a small ratio of imports to national income ?

Professor Rubin said Mr. Turvey's model assumed a pure addition to the labour force. One could, however, introduce complications with immigration. One did not have a pure increment to the labour force ; consumers came in as well as producers, in the shape of members of migrants' families. Similarly, the age distribution of migrants and of the existing population would not be comparable.

Professor Lerner said that a natural increase in population was similar to a mass immigration of the Israel type, in that it was spread over the whole age distribution of the population.

Professor Lindahl said that *cost inflation* occurred when both demand and supply curves rose simultaneously. The increase in demand and in purchasing power came from the increase in incomes anticipated by the seller. A new equilibrium might in that case be established at a higher price level. *Demand inflation*, on the other hand, was characterized by an excess of demand over supply at the current price level. In this case the increased demand would induce producers to raise prices, and the result would be a further *shift* of demand and a new excess demand. The supply curve would shift too, and the process would be cumulative.

Professor Lerner said that he himself would say that demand increased because of the increased income of sellers. (He also pointed out that Professor Lindahl had assumed that the government provided extra money.) The supply curve would be vertical near full employment, so that demand could keep on rising, and the process would be cumulative.

Professor Lindahl said that cost and demand inflation had different implications for monetary policy. With demand inflation, monetary policy should decrease investment, decrease consumption, and eliminate excess demand. With cost inflation, if one tried to reduce demand by monetary policy, there would be unemployment, unless the supply curve returned to the original position.

Professor Lerner pointed out that cost inflation could occur before full employment was reached. In the case of cost inflation, one might restore equilibrium by lowering the supply curve back to its original position. In his paper, however, he was making the institutional assumption that one could not push down the supply curve, since the government was not prepared to accept the consequent unemployment.

Professor Lindahl said that migration to, say, Australia, would lead to inflation of both types. Migrants would demand the same real wages as in their home countries, but they would also increase the need for capital equipment and thereby cause demand inflation. In Germany, one had an exceptional case. There was no initial equilibrium, and one could fix wages and prices where one liked. Immigrants provided a large reserve of unemployed, depressing the wage level. Trade unions could not raise wages, and there was little investment demand resulting from immigration. At the same time, the economy was expanding. There was a large margin of profits, which were saved and therefore allowed capital formation to take place. As investment rose, more and more unemployed were taken from the reserve of unemployed. This, however, was a very exceptional case.

Professor Robinson suggested, and Professor Hoffman agreed, that the high capital formation in postwar Germany was made easier by low government expenditure, especially defence expenditure.

Professor James said that it was not merely immigration, as such, that provoked inflation. It was immigration which took place under three conditions: (1) a demand by the immigrants for a level of real wages which the receiving country could not support; (2) bottlenecks in the supply of capital, or in the import of foreign goods; (3) a policy of monetary expansion. In those conditions Professor Lerner's model applied, but it was not possible to apply his results to other forms of immigration. At the beginning of his paper Professor Lerner defined inflation as a cumulative process which was self-accelerating and self-perpetuating. But where the inflationary pressure was caused by immigration under the above conditions, was the inflation really self-perpetuating? He himself would not say yes. When one talked about a self-perpetuating process, one meant that the process induced events which reacted back on the initial cause. If inflation caused by immigration were self-perpetuating, immigration would lead to higher prices. This would lead to a new and greater influx of migrants, which again would lead to higher prices, and so on in a vicious circle. But inflation could not be self-perpetuating, leading to further immigration.

Professor Lerner said he was grateful to Professor James, who was right in saying that the process of inflation he himself had described was not limited to that caused by immigration. One could have vicious circles of varying kinds coming at different stages. Further immigration was not needed; the circle of cost inflation might have been caused by something else. Immigration was the initial cause, and not part of the later vicious circle. He wanted to join the first two of Professor James's conditions together. The necessary conditions for cost inflation were a supply of capital that was too small, and a government which provided the supply of money necessary for the process to continue.

Professor Robinson asked if Professor Lerner would add the condition that the proportion of capital formation to national income was not reduced.

Professor Lerner did not think one needed to make that assumption. Summing up the discussion thus far, Professor Lerner said he felt that whether one regarded his model of cost inflation as a general or a particular one depended on how much stress one put on the model and how much on the explanation. One part of the paper set out the model of cost inflation, while the other part showed how immigration could be the cause. Inflation was the result either of excess demand, or of a cost-inflationary push, which might be caused by immigration or by other changes in the economy. Immigration might lead to demand inflation, but only if there was also excessive government spending. Cost inflation could occur without excess demand. It was not true that *any* amount of immigration, however big, would be absorbed where one had a government policy of restraining demand inflation. But demand inflation did not help in absorbing immigrants, since it did not enable the government to obtain many resources from people who had had appreciable experience of inflation. In Israel, Professor Spengler's type of 'exploitation' of the fixed income groups would be impossible because of the universality of payments based on cost-of-living indices. Demand inflation was a more familiar concept than cost inflation, and there was therefore a danger that purely fiscal measures would be used against the latter, resulting in simultaneous inflation and depression.

If there were no expansion in employment and consumption, because the immigrants were unemployed, there would be no resulting inflation or balance of payments difficulties. If there were such an expansion, inflation and/or an unfavourable balance of payments would lead to the conditions required for cost inflation. But these two possibilities were not quite alternatives, as Mr. Turvey seemed to imply. They were the *results* of (*a*) an excess of the current wage over the marginal product of labour, which caused the inflation, (*b*) a rise in consumption, which created the unfavourable balance of payments. In both demand and cost inflation one tried to acquire more resources than were available, and this led to a continuing process of inflation. In Mr. Turvey's model it was the ratio of imported to domestic prices, rather than the terms of trade, that was the relevant variable.

The point raised by Professor Robinson, namely the possibility of limiting migration to ease the inflationary pressure, was left out of account because of Israeli conditions; but it was true that such immigration aided demand — as well as cost — inflation. Professor Robinson's description of the difficulty, however, was in terms of cost inflation — of the pressure to maintain real wages in the face of a falling marginal product of labour.

Professor Robinson did not think we could force our ideas into two such neat categories. With inflation caused by migrants, the volume of capital formation with a large population inflow was greater than in the absence of that inflow. Second, it was difficult to finance that volume of capital formation from the internal savings of the country. One had to depend on other sources. There was consequently a danger of a demand inflation, through too much expenditure, and a simultaneous cost inflation, because of the effect of demand inflation on prices. He did not believe one could separate the two ends of the argument.

Professor Lerner agreed that Professor Robinson had put his finger on the most difficult part of his model. He had found it hard to make this sharp distinction, because the two types of inflation did have so much in common. If higher wage demands were the result of rising prices caused by excess demand, one had demand inflation, and excess monetary demand could raise wages even in the absence of unions. Yet it sounded like cost inflation, since trade union demands were part of the mechanism of both types of inflation. But strong unions could raise wages, and cause cost inflation, where there was *no* excess demand.

Professor Robinson wondered what Professor Lerner meant in talking about the actions of unions. Was it a cost inflation when a union tried to restore a previous level of real wages? Was he talking in terms of real or of money wages?

Professor Lerner said that an attempt to restore real wages *was* cost inflation. It had exactly the same effects as a rise from the existing level. Cost inflation could arise from a system of wages pegged to a price index, as well as from wage increases obtained by negotiations. What was essential was that the increase in money supply needed to finance a cost inflation should not be confused with a demand inflation, since no one was trying to buy more than was being produced. The increase in the amount of money was undertaken by a government which was well aware of the danger of inflation. It did it to prevent unemployment becoming too severe.

Professor Parenti did not think Professor Lerner's model applied to any immigration country except Israel. The marginal product of labour was not reduced by immigration, except in Israel. Workers would not be hired if this happened. Professor Parenti thought the model interesting, and had the feeling that it fitted the pattern of the Italian economy, although Italy was a country of *emigration*. In the previous three years or so, Italy had experienced an increase in real wages, but an increase in productivity had followed after a short time. So there had not been inflation. The model was one with a more general application than merely to countries of immigration. If one applied the model in the hypothetical case of an immigration country, the model would not work if dynamic factors were introduced. Mr. Turvey had cited a case in which immigration brought about extreme inflationary pressure. If this example were considered dynamically one would find that, at each point when a migrant came in, capital goods produced by previous migrants were becoming available.

Professor Lerner said that the last point raised by Professor Parenti was especially interesting. It was exactly what was argued in Israel. In the long run, the accumulation of capital would solve the problem. Mr. Hague had asked him whether he meant by an import bottleneck the same thing as an unfavourable balance of payments. He did not. The bottleneck occurred when one would like an unfavourable balance but could not afford it. Such an import surplus would allow capital accumulation, which would ultimately come to the rescue; but not immediately. In the short run, capital produced in the past was not enough to make the existing real wage 'realistic'.

He was interested that the cost inflation description applied to Italy, and felt the applicability of the model was considerable. In future, there might be substantial immigration only if trade unions in receiving countries were persuaded to agree to it; and this was only possible if wage rates were guaranteed. Israel gave a preview of world problems in an exaggerated form. Professor Lerner said that if the United States was a melting-pot then Israel was a pressure cooker.

Professor Rubin wondered what a high-level immigration meant. High in relation to what? *Professor Lerner* replied that he meant high in relation to the existing population — 10 per cent *was* high.

Father Ávila thought the position in some South-American countries seemed to argue in favour of Professor Lerner's thesis. Professor Ellis had admitted the validity of Professor Lerner's model and had referred to the case of Argentina. The Brazilian case might be identified with it also. Nevertheless, in Brazil one had a simpler explanation of inflationary pressure.

Two features common to South American countries were that they engaged in monoculture, and they were countries where economic development was backed by and interrelated with political power. Therefore great exporters or industrial magnates could use inflation for their own ends. For example, one might have a situation were a coffee exporter sold a bale of coffee at 25 dollars (= 200 cruzeiros). If the price of coffee, fell to 15 dollars, this would equal 120 cruzeiros. Because of this, exporters would try to reduce the value of the cruzeiro until, for instance, one dollar equalled 12 cruzeiros. Exporters would then only have to face a 10 per cent instead of a 40 per cent loss. This showed that exporters were interested in influencing monetary policy, which was tantamount to 'socializing their losses'.

Father Ávila said he would like to raise a more general question. The discussion had been based on the decisive importance of economic factors; in this sense, migration was to the advantage of the receiving country, for example, if *per capita* income did not fall. These economic factors could not be decisive to new and vast countries. In Brazil the majority of the population lived on the coastline. Supposing that this population had attained a comfortable economic level, in the short run immigration could reduce its standard of living. In this case the native population would not be interested in immigration as well as in exploiting the resources inland. Nevertheless, Brazil had an international responsibility to put her resources at the disposal of the whole world. For him, said Father Ávila, economic criteria could not be decisive.

Professor Lerner said Father Avila's first point was that, instead of a cost inflation, one might have a simpler explanation in terms of the interest of magnates who controlled exports of a single product — an 'Exportocracy'. He did not think this was a good example — exporters of coffee would only benefit if there was no domestic inflation. In many countries the inflation resulting from deliberate devaluation might be delayed, and exporters would be able for a time to pass on their losses to the rest of the economy. But this was only a short-term possibility, if it were one at all. Professor Lerner sympathized completely with the moral issue. But he suspected that Brazil's resources could not be very valuable if it were so unprofitable to develop them. However, the urge to develop the land, rather than benefit the people, seemed to apply in southern Israel, and the position might be the same in Brazil.

Mr. Turvey said that if one had a deficit in the balance of payments, one might try to cure it by devaluation. The terms of trade would worsen and less goods would be available to the community as a whole, which would try to offset this by earning more. In this situation a cost inflation would, in the end, succeed in restoring the initial export surplus.

Professor Lerner did not see why the worsening of terms of trade should occur.

Mr. Turvey said that imports became more expensive, whilst export prices were unchanged, so the community had less to consume. The real wage available would therefore fall, and one would have cost inflation.

This would stop if home prices rose far enough, since real wages would be back where they started.

Professor Thomas suggested that one reason for the apparent unanimity in the discussion was that, on Professor Lerner's premises, it was difficult to find a flaw in his argument. In other words, it was hard to have a debate within the confines of his model. He wondered whether Professor Lerner would agree that this model was a first approximation — a static model. If one dealt in rates of change, then the result would be different. The nineteenth-century immigration waves were mostly induced by demand inflation; later they ran into cost inflation, which killed them in the twentieth century. Now, in Israel, and perhaps in Australia, one had a new problem. With strong trade union movements, one had mainly cost inflation. Inflation was often regarded as an evil, but, if one looked back over past upswings, it was precisely in those inflationary periods that there was rapid capital formation. Ploughed-back profits had added to capital equipment. We had a great deal to thank past inflations for.

Professor Thomas said he could not understand the sentence on page 61 of Professor Lerner's paper which referred to '. . . long-run and secondary disinflationary effects. . . .' *Professor Lerner* replied that he did not know whether one could defend this sentence. One could assume a demand inflation during which people came in with foreign capital. They did not spend it all on imports, which would have been all right, but on the limited supply of domestic products. This aggravated the demand inflation. But one could escape, because more imported goods were now available, and to the extent that natives or migrants bought imports this offset the inflation. However, if there was not infinite elasticity of substitution between domestic and imported goods, this friction would add to domestic inflationary pressure.

Professor Lerner said he wondered what happened if one made his model dynamic. It was possible that the argument would need to be fundamentally changed. But, in theory, static models normally came first, and he did not see why the basic argument should be affected by dynamic effects. He began from the premise that inflation was bad. Admittedly, it had been accompanied in the past by benefits. In comparison with severe depression, inflation seemed quite desirable, but this did not justify too much complacency about inflation at a time when there were no severe slumps. Secondly, exploitation of workers and consumers occurred during inflation, the proceeds being invested, with benefit for the future. But this was an expensive way of getting resources. Investment might sometimes be so important that inflation was a necessary evil, but this might not continue. In Israel one could not obtain resources from the public by inflation, so that one had only its evils and none of its benefits. And any attempt to protect the masses merely worsened the inflation.

Professor Lerner said that he thought more highly of the concept of cost inflation now in connexion with immigration than he had done when the day began. In the future, immigration would probably cause cost inflation, not demand inflation as in the nineteenth century. Immigrants would go only to places where arrangements were made to protect the existing workers and to maintain real wages, and governments would not try to prevent cost inflation by allowing mass unemployment. Another reason for the greater threat of cost inflation now was that demand inflations had been studied for a long time and economists' findings had percolated into public policy, so that governments seemed to know how to deal with them. But governments did not know how to deal with cost inflations, and they had no machinery for doing so. The future held the danger that cost inflation would henceforth be the more serious type. It was therefore most important that economists should be able to distinguish the two from one another.

Mr. Turvey said that Professor Lerner had drawn a sharp distinction between demand and cost inflation. Professor Robinson had suggested that they might coexist. He himself had shown, in the *Economic Journal* of September 1951, that one could fit all models into a common pattern, with one exception. One need only consider the markets for final goods and for labour, and the prices of both. The markets could be considered as cost- or demand-determined. Thus, for these two markets, one had four types of inflation; pure cost and pure demand inflation, with prices either 'pulled' or 'pushed' up; and two mixed types. Duesenberry, on the other hand, had a three-sector model which he claimed represented the United States economy. The prices of labour and of industrial goods were cost-determined. The prices of primary products were demand-determined. The correct reply to Professor Robinson was therefore that once one abandoned a simple model, one had this mixture. The same mixture of cost- and demand-determined prices would be found in any historical study of the real world. The nearest example of a pure cost inflation which he knew of was in the Icelandic case. Imports during the war came solely from the United States, and the exchange rate of the dollar was pegged at a constant level. Dollars were available from United States forces, and there was no shortage of imports. Prices went up, however, industrial earnings were pegged to the cost of living, and farmers' incomes rose in step. Hence, one had a pure cost inflation.

Professor Lerner said that when one started breaking down the analysis into segments, one could not have a pure cost inflation. Some prices would always be demand-determined; for example, those of 'Old Masters'. But one still had cost inflation, pure or not. What did one do? If cutting down effective demand prevented inflation, then it was demand inflation; if that was no use, it was cost inflation. There were great difficulties in knowing exactly where one was, since there was this range where one could not be certain. He would not like to try to draw a narrow and exact line, but for the purposes of the model one did not have a mixture.

Mr. Rahardt wondered if Professor Lerner would apply his model to Australian experience during the last seven years or so. During the years 1949–50, annual net immigration was between 1·7 and 2 per cent of the population. In 1951–2 there was inflation and unemployment, and immigration targets were cut, with the result that net immigration fell to 0·5 per cent of the population in 1953. The Government had said that this reduction was not a permanent policy, and in fact the immigration target was raised again as early as 1954. Net immigration for that year was 0·7 per cent, and would probably reach 1 per cent in 1955. This was a short-term cyclical movement in immigration and ICEM was interested in its causes, as, clearly, fluctuations of this nature made planning very difficult. Could Professor Lerner explain this cycle in terms of his cost inflation ?

Professor Lerner thought that the other elements leading to inflation in Australia were much more important than immigration, although immigration was blamed.

Professor Lindahl said that Australia had had demand inflation. Initially, this was used to bring about expansion, but one could not keep on with it, and migration was therefore slowed down to reduce the pace of development.

Professor Lerner said that, in a sense, inflations were always 'mixed'. The price of 'rent goods' was always demand-determined. But since demand and cost inflation needed different remedies, one had to know which predominated in order to prescribe a remedial policy.

Professor Lindahl said he could not accept a distinction which, he thought, depended on Professor Lerner's own judgement as to whether it was desirable or not to reduce effective demand. It was possible to give a general definition. One had demand inflation if there was a sellers' market characterized by excess demand. One could have this simultaneously with a cost inflation caused by a rising wage level. The two inflations could be mixed, and such a mixture was especially dangerous. If one had a sellers' market, this favoured strong action by trade unions, and an inflation of the mixed type might develop which could have been prevented by a restrictive policy. Professor Lerner was becoming too much interested in pure cost inflation. Israel was the only country with a pure cost inflation in an extreme form.

Professor Robinson said that this had been a difficult discussion, partly because of the characteristics of models. In a sense, everyone agreed with Professor Lerner that inflation was not a desirable thing. The question was how a country dealing with a large volume of immigration could handle it. Was there any sense in just dividing up inflations into two kinds ? Cost and demand inflations were so similar that one had no guide to action in this distinction. In deciding on action, one had to ask how one operated on demand. There were four ways. One could operate first on consumption by taxation ; second, on capital formation by interest rates, and by investment decisions on the part of the government ; third, on government expenditure ; and fourth, on the volume of immigration.

Israel did not wish to do the fourth, but that was a value judgement, albeit perhaps a justified one, which had not been adopted by all receiving countries. By which of these four methods should one operate ? Could one reduce consumption per head ? There were limits in practice, and one created a cost inflation after one had carried out a certain degree of cutting consumption. Should one cut down capital formation ? This depended on whether one believed that it was technically possible to reduce capital per head and yet maintain employment. In fact, a decision to reduce capital formation would be a decision to leave immigrants un-employed. If one operated on government expenditure, there were limits too. Dare one take in immigrants and not give them government ser-vices ? Finally, one could operate on the volume of immigration. Pro-fessor Robinson thought it was easier to think in broad terms if one brought in all these considerations. Moreover, he thought this was equally true in countries of emigration. If such a country had an economic structure adjusted to an outward flow of emigrants, the sudden creation of obstacles to emigration had exactly the same economic effects as did immigration into a country receiving immigrants.

Professor Bachi made two points. First, Professor Lerner had referred many times to experience in Israel. Did he not think that Israel's inflation had been partly due to other powerful causes than immigration, such as war, the establishment of the state, defence expenditure, the Arab boy-cott, etc.? Second, he wondered if Professor Lerner's model could be applied to Israel. In 1948–51 there had been much migration without cost inflation. Yet in 1951–53 there had been cost inflation but not much immigration.

Professor Lerner, closing the discussion, agreed with Professor Bachi that there were other causes, but he did not agree any more than he agreed that there were always other causes. With more capital and bigger foreign exchange reserves, even Israel could have avoided inflation. He did not think the second point invalidated his argument. In 1948–51 price controls prevented price increases, but in 1952 the new economic policy let prices rise, the accumulated liquidity being let out. The rises in wages then were the delayed effect of the previous inflation. The supply of money fell in real terms, and brought a buyers' market, turning the demand inflation into a cost inflation. Professor Rubin had spoken of the psychological effects of an inflation, thinking of countries where one was only at the beginning of inflation and people were not used to it. His idea that immigrants might save considerable amounts did not apply in a country where immigrants had all too often seen their savings liquidated by inflation.

Professor Spengler was right in saying that inflation required the absence of a money illusion, but for that very reason he was all the more wrong in supposing the possibility of alleviating the situation by 'exploiting' some groups.

Professor Lerner replied to Professor Lindahl that the distinction between cost inflation and demand inflation, so far as policy-making was concerned, might appear to be a case of 'implicit theorizing'. But this might be avoided by accepting Professor Lindahl's criteria of a sellers' market and a buyers' market as indicators of a demand and a cost inflation respectively.

Professor Robinson had given a useful list of means to deal with inflation, but he sometimes referred to cost inflation, sometimes to demand inflation, without saying explicitly what he meant. For example, taxation, investment, and government spending policy were methods of checking demand inflation, although demand inflation might, whilst being cured, be transformed into cost inflation. There was a limit to the volume of taxation which could be imposed without threatening cost inflation. On the other hand, the cutting down of immigration was primarily directed against whatever type of inflation immigration might be causing, whether cost or demand. Although, in the future, cost inflation would be more important, the danger of demand inflation would continue so long as governments ignored sound economic advice.

THE DISCUSSION ON PROFESSOR SILCOCK'S PAPER

Eleventh and Twelfth Sessions, Friday 9 September 1955

Professor Chandresekhar said that in studying Asian problems, the Conference would have to drop the mental framework which had been used for considering problems in Europe. In Asia social and non-economic factors were most important. Professor Silcock had begun his paper by facing the 'Malthusian dilemma'. Of the world's 2460 million people, about half lived in Asia. Demographic statistics for Asia were bad but, in the last twenty years, intelligent guesswork suggested that the rate of increase per annum had been 2·2 per cent in Ceylon, 1·3 per cent in India. China had no reliable figures, but the figure given was 3 per cent. There were each year 4·8 millions more Indians, 5·2 millions more Chinese, and 1 million more Japanese, out of a 26-million world population-rise each year. In other words, at the present rate, the population of Asia in the year 2000 would equal the entire population of the world at present. There was consequently a gigantic potential for migration in Asia. Only a few points would be considered.

Professor Chandresekhar said that migration between India and Pakistan was inter-provincial at first, and so reliable figures were very few. Since partition there had been the 1951 census, and the Indian and Pakistani censuses did not ask the same questions. The figure accepted by the two Governments was that 14 million people had moved. On Indian migration to Malaya and Ceylon, adequate material had been given by Professor Silcock. This movement began as indentured migration, but, because of the special demands of emigrants, a trickle of free migrants was allowed in to provide services for the indentured migrants. Professor Chandresekhar said that India had benefited from this, because these Indians began sending remittances back to India, a point which Professor Silcock had ignored. This was upsetting Ceylon's balance of payments. Similarly, the movement of South-Indian money-lenders to Ceylon, and their practices, had led to some anti-Indian feeling.

Professor Silcock felt that one should make the point that the contract under which the indentured labour had worked was for a specific period, and was enforced by penal rather than legal sanctions. In form, the contract was voluntarily negotiated, but there were objections to the ways in which the indentured labour was secured. Professor Silcock felt, however, that India had little to complain of in this respect, though China had much. The Indian Government took steps to end the practice very early, but on the China coast kidnapping, etc., went on for some time. Also, much of the misrepresentation in India was largely the work of Indian agents themselves, and they had been controlled. Professor Silcock said he thought he disagreed with Professor Chandresekhar about Ceylon's rate of population increase. The rate was now nearly 3 per cent per annum, after a rapid increase. Again, since the Indian death-rate would presumably fall in the future, as in other countries, one could expect a higher rate of population growth there — but probably not as high as 3 per cent.

Professor Chandresekhar said one could not rely on figures for particular years. There need be no regular rate of decline in death-rates, but only fluctuations.

Professor Silcock said he did not think the Conference should discuss migration within Asian countries so much as between them. However, he made an exception in the Indonesian case, because that had attracted much attention, and arose because of the emergence of independent states. Emigration from Asia to other countries had political importance, but no great demographic significance, so he had ignored it. Professor Silcock admitted that he might have thereby dodged some thorny questions of a political kind. He agreed that remittances from Malaya and Ceylon had made an appreciable difference in South India, and had had an even more important effect on the economy of China. The remittances were, however, more important factors in the economies of the receiving than of the sending countries.

Professor Thomas wondered if there were statistics of remittances, and how they were compiled.

Professor Chandresekhar said he did not know how reliable the statistics were, but they were taken regularly. The Government of India had given figures since 1919. They might mean anything, however, as they were not specifically itemized. Also, it was assumed that all Indians abroad were real emigrants.

Professor Thomas said that one large composite item, not broken down at all, was a very flimsy basis for any argument.

Professor Chandresekhar disagreed. He felt that, since few Indians in Ceylon and Burma were other than migrants, the figures there were quite accurate. He wondered whether, when specialists moved into other Asian countries, the attracting force was economic or non-economic. Did an Indian move because he would have higher real wages, or did he go to join his family, or to leave a little more space at home? Indians moving to South-East Asia had certain services to offer. In the liberal professions especially they were filling posts which natives could not fill. What did Professor Silcock mean when he discussed this in his paper? Professor Chandresekhar also felt that there was an omission in the paper. It was not of demographic significance, but it was important. Migrants from Asia to Western countries, for instance the Union of South Africa, Canada, and California, totalled about 6 millions. This was not important from India's point of view, but it led to problems in international relations.

Finally, Professor Chandresekhar wondered how migration should be organized. Should it be subject to governmental controls and not to individual initiative? In 1937 the movement of Indians overseas had been banned unless the receiving countries could guarantee immigrants the same status as in India. Some people felt that a small outlet had been blocked in this way. Should the government of any country take a strong stand against free movement, for example, by issuing passports slowly, or by refusing to allow migrants foreign currency? Since 1947 the American immigrant quota had been 140, and the Canadian 150, Indians per annum. This was a drop in the ocean, but if only Asian governments would use these quotas to the full it would be some slight help. Indian and other Asian governments had not taken a helpful attitude.

Professor Baudin said he had been very much struck from the beginning with a statement on page 252 of Professor Silcock's paper to the effect that, with the great expansion of education in Asia, a further increase in population could be expected. He did not agree. Education in under-developed countries could be said to contain three elements. First, there were spontaneous restrictions on population through empirical movement towards birth control. Second, there was education in the elements of hygiene, and at this stage perhaps Professor Silcock was right. But, finally, one came to stage three, where fuller education led to a knowledge of eugenics. There was a danger that Professor Silcock had given an oversimplified and distorted picture.

On page 255, when Professor Silcock spoke of Malayan and Indonesian migration, he was considering an unsolved problem. What was the origin of this movement? Surely the answer was that Malayans were migrants by character; there was a psychological factor.

On page 256 there was a discussion of the social structure of the migrant groups and of the receiving populations. One had the whole structure reduced into sections, each with different features. Professor Baudin suggested an 'ideal, abstract theory'. One might perhaps have migration statistics weighted in accordance with the kind of person migrating. Then one would have a better indication of the human value of migration than under the present system, where men were counted 'like sacks of potatoes'.

Professor Baudin wondered if it were possible to say that one had a spontaneous organization set up as a result of migration, for example a movement of the élite as well. Was there a tendency for a new structure to appear, with the tertiary sector following the primary and secondary ones? For example, one noted that Chinese migrants were merchants and Japanese migrants industrial managers. The 1947 movement in India and Pakistan had represented a structural disequilibrium. Would any spontaneous adaptation ever occur? Or would it be too long-term for us to consider? Forced migration had led to disequilibrium; could free migration? Finally, he thought the only generalization that could be made about 'categories' of migrants was that the problems in each country were in accordance with the characteristics of those countries.

Professor Robinson returned to the question of the dispersion of real incomes as a result of migration. He thought it worth coming back to the Spengler model as it had come out of the discussion. One had two types of migration. First, there were unskilled workers, who were complementary to the higher skills of the receiving country. Second, there was the migration of the more skilled workers, as in the American-East African model. Indian migration was of both kinds. Indentured labour, in the early stages, was relatively unskilled, and migration to Burma until 1939 was of that character. At the same time, however, India was importing the higher types of skill, and exporting to Burma small entrepreneurs and money-lenders. Even more in the case of East Africa, India sent migrants who were complementary to the African native unskilled labour, providing trades, small manufactures, and handicrafts. These movements were small, as indeed were all movements of skilled Indian population. In East Africa the total Indian population was equal to about two months' natural increase in India.

The immigration of specialists was apt to be temporary, since they created the people who would replace them. They were assimilated only over a short period. The native population developed new skills and was then anxious to dispense with the skilled immigrants. With independence, the Burmese were anxious to become their own skilled workers, and to dispense not only with British, but also with Indian, specialists. This made it clear that this form of migrant was more difficult to assimilate than unskilled labourers who were complementary to the local population, but who were later raised to higher social status. The important question was to which type Indian migrants would belong, because this would determine whether they could be assimilated.

Turning to long-term population pressures, Professor Robinson said he had the impression that demographers saw the problem in some such terms as this: The world had experienced dramatic revolutions in medical knowledge and skill; the first impact was on death-rates, first in Europe and America, and now in Asia; countries later adjusted their birth-rates *to* death-rates; the decline of death-rates leading to an increased expectation of life, and sooner or later to a downward adjustment of birth-rates in the kind of way Professor Baudin had described. These adjustments had been completed in Europe, where one had a new balance. During the period before the two rates became adjusted, however, the size of the population was carried upwards, but this phase was only temporary. In Asia the question was how quickly birth-rates would become adjusted to the decline in deaths. Asia seemed to have been moving towards this faster than did Europe, which took two centuries to make the adjustment. India was showing signs of a rather rapid adjustment in its thinking. There was the possibility of populations in Asia becoming relatively stable, after the inevitable lag had carried population to much higher levels. The crucial point was how far population would be carried in the period before stabilization could occur.

Professor Silcock said he agreed more with Professor Robinson than with Professor Baudin on the stage at which birth control techniques came in the process of transforming the population; it was at a later rather than an earlier stage. The first impact was on the death-rate. Because it needed no cultural changes, one could reduce the death-rate fairly rapidly. This led people to postpone marriage and to have fewer children. There was less desire to have children as 'an insurance against the future' if they had a good chance of survival. He agreed with Professor Robinson's interpretation of the view of demographers, but one had to prophesy a rapid growth in India for at least one or two generations. Even then, an adjustment might only take place if there were a rise in the standard of living, and that was not likely. Nevertheless, India's change in attitude was most encouraging, and he was optimistic enough to hope that the problem might be of relatively limited duration. He agreed with Professor Baudin that Malays always had been migrants, but was not so sure about using weighted indices. One had to concentrate on different sectors and their interaction. He could think of no concrete problem where the weighted index would be useful. On the question whether one had a spontaneous adjustment of the structure to migration, Professor Silcock thought that one should ask: Does a group of migrants bring equilibrium to the social structure, or vice versa? He suspected that the two interacted. Where certain skills were scarce, one had a movement of domestic skills to fill that gap, but also a likelihood of immigration. Sociological problems might arise, because the people in possession of the skills might resist immigration. This was the theoretical point on which we could gain most by discussion.

Dr. Edding noted that Professor Silcock expected even more rapid rates of natural increase in the near future. Could he give any estimate of how this increase would be composed ? For example, would the relative sizes of the 'active' and 'non-active' groups of the population change ? Professor Silcock had said that big efforts would be necessary to prevent a rapid decrease in living standards. Did he see any chance that production in the regions concerned could be increased in proportion to the rate of natural increase ? Finally, assuming considerable emigration from Asia, what would be the reaction of the fertility pattern ? Would emigration lead to an increase in the birth-rate ?

Professor Hoffmann said that if one assumed that Asian populations would increase considerably, the net national product must grow even faster if there was to be an increase in standards of living. If net national product was to grow more rapidly than population, one would need maximum savings ; and yet the countries were too poor to save much. He knew little of their capital-output ratios. What were the possible sources of capital ? This should be discussed before we came to the question of future development. These Asian countries were mainly agricultural, so that the primary need was to intensify agriculture. But how could the whole economy have more capital, if capital had to be found at home ? Industry did not exist on a large scale. How far was trade and agriculture a source of capital ? On the answer to this depended whether the Western world should send labour-saving or capital-saving devices to the East.

To Dr. Edding, *Professor Silcock* replied that the fall in death-rates was leading to a tendency for births to outrun deaths for a period, though there was this hope of equilibrium at a later stage. Nevertheless the present high proportion of children entailed heavy capital expenditure, for example on education. To Professor Hoffmann, he said that there was no chance of capital formation within Asia at a rate high enough to lead to any significant rise in productivity per head. A fall in productivity was much more likely. There might be changes in techniques, but even instruction was capital-consuming. This method was stressed both by the United Nations and also by China. But not enough thought had been given to how one could increase the Asian marginal propensity to save.

Professor Silcock said he would relate his analysis to that of Professor Spengler. Professor Spengler, basing his outlook on the idea of non-competing groups, took the view that the class structure was stronger than migration. He himself took a middle view. All technicians were opposed to the immigration of skilled workers, but there was an insuperable obstacle to reaching a higher level of technical skill.

The assimilation of specialists was difficult, but should we think in terms of organizing temporary specialist immigration with little adaptation of the migrant's skill, or should we do the opposite and try to overcome the difficulties of assimilation by special means ? Whatever else happened, he was sure Asia needed a substantial flow of capital from outside, but as much of this as possible should be in the form of technical assistance.

Professor Chandresekhar said he would answer Professor Baudin and

Dr. Edding. In Asia the main wish was to raise the standard of living from its very low level. Politicians both of the extreme right and of the extreme left were dedicating their policy to raising Asian standards of living, which, in comparison with any other country, seemed unbelievably low. In the past twenty years, birth- and death-rates had come down faster than was expected. In India, in 1901, the infant mortality rate had been 269 per thousand live births; now it was 116. In time, India would reach the English rate of 24 per thousand if medical improvements continued. Similarly, if improvement in public health systems went on, the death-rate would come down by 50 per cent. Everyone in India accepted this prolongation of human life as desirable. So, in forty years, the population of India might reach 800 million, and the net addition to the Indian population might even become 10 million per year, and still go on growing.

What could be done? Should one shoot all the doctors? It was clearly unthinkable that one should reverse progress. It was also unthinkable that the standard of living could be allowed to fall any more. The birth-rate was therefore the only line of attack; it was 34 to 35 per thousand at the moment. The idea of family planning always met with heated resistance. In 1950 India asked the World Health Organisation to do something about it. Could birth control be included in the WHO programme for India? But the Catholic Church objected. So India set up pilot projects. Most people said, however, that this was a waste of time, since emigration was so much easier. In fact, it was not practicable on a big enough scale. What was the attitude of people towards birth control, from the most illiterate level up to civil service level? In India 16 per cent of a sample group of mothers had expressed a desire to hear about methods of birth control, so the Government took steps to do something about it. The obstacles in the way of disseminating knowledge were enormous, since so many people could not read. So far, £1 million had been spent, without success. It was felt that one must have education before there was any chance of a decline in birth-rates. Now, the only ways of solving the problem that were being considered were internal and external migration. With internal migration there were huge sociological problems such as caste, occupational structure, homesickness, and so on. Asian external migration was discussed much less than the migration problems of Europe and America. Indeed, Indian and Japanese migration was hardly ever discussed at all.

Professor Lerner said he was especially interested in Professor Silcock's views on the migration of skilled workers, and the need to provide for increasing populations in areas where the source of capital was not obvious, but one needed a better use of existing resources. The migration of skilled workers to underdeveloped areas implied high rates of pay, compensation, etc., in order to attract them from elsewhere. This high pay would tend to be diminished as local inhabitants were trained, partly because of the greater supply of skilled labour, and partly through the 'dilution' of skilled labour. There was a tendency on the part of under-developed countries to anticipate the results of this development by trying to establish in advance the greater equality of income which would ultimately occur. This was the ideology of India. Yet this attempt to forestall the future had the effect of preventing change. The present application of an ideology interfered with its ultimate objectives. Everyone seemed to assume that the assimilation of skilled workers was desirable. He himself thought it unimportant. The skilled workers could leave again when high rewards were no longer forthcoming. This was a natural state of affairs and no harm was done if they were not assimilated.

Professor Rubin took up the same point as Professor Baudin. Professor Baudin thought the birth-rate would fall with the education that was now taking place. Yet Japan had had a greater expansion of education. Had the birth-rate of Japan declined so much?

Professor Silcock thought Japan illustrated the cycle very well. There was a marked decline in the birth-rate, particularly since the war.

Professor Rubin was still doubtful. In the case of a country like India, even a temporary period before adjustment was dangerous.

Professor Robinson agreed that there might be a great increase in population during the period of disequilibrium. The population might double itself before the adjustment was achieved. The interesting question was how long the adjustment would take.

Professor Ellis thought that in the preoccupation with *rates* of growth, one should not lose sight of the absolute population base on which these rates were acting. The size of the absolute base was very important, and also the fact of differences in the initial standard of living in various countries. A low rate of population growth in Japan or India was a more serious problem than in other countries with a small population base.

Professor Spengler returned to the problem of the period of disequilibrium. Japan in the mid-nineteenth century had a population of 30 million. It was expected to stabilize at 120 million. Now, when death-rates could fall so much faster, one needed a very rapid fall in birth-rates to achieve stability. He could take very little consolation from the adjustment process without knowing the parameters.

Dr. Zubrzycki thought there was some evidence to suggest that the time lag between a reduction in the death-rate and a fall in the birth-rate need not be very long. In the Soviet Union, the lag was very short. In 1938 the rate of increase was 21·5 per thousand; in 1952 it was 14·8 per thousand. This was a significant reduction, in a country where birth control was prohibited.

Professor Rubin said that taking these two years gave a false impression. There had been a huge loss of men during the war years.

Dr. Zubrzycki replied that other evidence from Eastern Europe also suggested a decline in fertility with economic development.

Father Ávila observed that participants tended to identify the reduction of death-rate in the nineteenth century in Europe with the same reduction that could now be observed in most Latin-American countries. But in Europe that reduction was made little by little, *pari passu* with medical progress, and accompanied by the industrial and technical progress which was necessary to absorb the increase of population. In Latin America, on the contrary, the reduction of death-rate was due to the introduction of the medical methods of Europe and America without any proportional improvement in the technical, economic, and social conditions. In this case, the reduction in the death-rate in underdeveloped areas could be, in a sense, an ephemeral phenomenon. Those who escaped from infant mortality were much more likely to be the victims of other diseases, and there might eventually be an increase in death-rates for higher age groups. In Brazil there was a need for much more economic and social progress in order to make the reduction in the death-rate genuine and permanent.

Professor Baudin confirmed the views of Father Ávila. There was a disparity in some countries between falling death-rates and relatively stable techniques. This disparity came from ideological movements in Latin America which hamstrung progress by preventing the import of foreign capital.

Professor Mahr doubted the possibility of creating outlets for large-scale Asian emigration. There was also the question of self-preservation. With present rates of increase of population in Asian countries as compared with the rest of the world, unlimited migration would lead to an Asiatic majority everywhere in, say, a hundred years. Was there any information about the attitude in China to birth control ?

Professor Chandresekhar said that the Chinese attitude on the population question seemed to be the same as that of the Marxists — the more the merrier. The Chinese could move 50 million people into Manchuria, so that their problem was not so severe. Malthus and Marx would not go together.

Professor Rubin felt the Chinese attitude on population was Communist rather than Marxist. Marx gave no data on this subject.

Dr. Edding stressed that it was not only a question of self-preservation for the Western world, but also a question of self-preservation for Asia. Unlimited migration would harm both of them. Who would pay the fares of a mass of unskilled migrants ? Was there an economic demand for such migrants in receiving countries ? Nor would the migration of skilled workers benefit Asian countries.

Professor Lerner said that Professor Chandresekhar could be interpreted as saying that other countries should admit large numbers of immigrants from India because India could not practise birth control. Yet such emigration would only have the effect of allowing a larger natural increase in India while the rest of the world had a lot more population too. The trouble in the world was that there was too much population altogether.

Professor Chandresekhar claimed that incoming populations, after about one generation, adopted the fertility pattern of the receiving country.

Report on the Proceedings

Professor Thomas returned to the question of factor scarcities. One of the biggest problems was the scarcity of entrepreneurial skills to use the country's assets. If one took an Asian country, with a prolific indigenous unskilled population and a skilled immigrant group of entrepreneurs, one could distinguish three cases. In Case 1, one had skilled entrepreneurs who were constant in number and subject to perfect competition; on the other hand, the indigenous population formed a non-competing group. If the indigenous population was increasing, one could have a high marginal productivity in the skilled entrepreneurial group, and real income per head there would be rising. In Case 2, one could introduce oligopoly into the entrepreneurial group. There would now be a stronger tendency for real income per head in that group to rise in relation to the *per capita* real income of the indigenous population, and, correspondingly, greater social tension. Case 3 was the best from the point of view of the local population. There was here a relative increase in the number of skilled entrepreneurs, with free competition, leading to the point where the non-competing groups broke down. The cost of acquiring skills would fall, the level of income of entrepreneurs would be reduced, and this would push the least efficient of them into the unskilled class, while the ablest of the unskilled workers would move upwards. If this analysis was sound, it seemed, on purely economic grounds at least, that from the point of view of the indigenous population it was best to encourage the immigration of skilled entrepreneurs, provided there was free competition. In Asian countries, however, the 'exploitation' of the indigenous population by immigrant entrepreneurs was such that they did not want any more to come in. This attitude was misconceived. One should not ask for a reduction in immigration of skilled entrepreneurs, but insist that the government ensured conditions of free competition.

Professor Robinson said Professor Thomas's analysis was interesting, but he was in danger of making the generality the exception, and vice versa. On the question of doubts as to whether the monopoly position of particular nationalities could be controlled, Professor Robinson quoted the Latin-American attitude to-day. Politically, one must always remember Professor Spengler's point that there would be benefit to the whole group of natives, and damage to small groups who competed with immigrants. Those in the most competitive position were often those who had the loudest voice in politics. Professor Robinson entirely agreed with what had been said about 'temporary' growth. During the period of disequilibrium, one could get huge increase. His real point was that long-term projections based on existing rates of growth were not profitable unless other considerations were brought in.

Professor Silcock said that the discussion so far had considered two different problems: (*a*) how much population pressure does Asia face, and how are we to deal with it? (*b*) questions concerned with the movement of entrepreneurs. So far as the first problem was concerned, he felt that one should emphasize Father Ávila's point on the difference between the fall in the death-rate in Europe, and a fall in underdeveloped countries. The relation between population increase and economic development was so very different in the two cases. The fall in the death-rate had been 'imported' to areas like Brazil, and was not the result of natural developments, though the fall in the European death-rate was itself not particularly 'natural'. Perhaps it was best to say that the fall in the death-rate in Europe was equilibrating and the fall in under-developed countries was disequilibrating. As a result, we had a situation where population was increasing rapidly in underdeveloped countries.

Professor Silcock did not think the increase was serious because of existing overpopulation. It was the *rate* of increase that was serious, because of the drain which it imposed on capital resources. The problem was aggravated in countries which were already overpopulated, because the capital/income ratio was unfavourable. On the other hand, where population was already very great, certain natural checks held its growth back. On the question of 'self-preservation' and Asian migration, he did not think it was justifiable to exclude Asians on the ground that if they came in, in time the majority of the world's population would be Asian. This implied the inferiority of Asians. However, it was natural for countries with a higher standard of living to object to immigration on a large scale which lowered standards of living. So, though this attitude was morally questionable, we must accept it as a fact.

So long as one had the great flood of people in underdeveloped countries, there would be opposition. Moreover, the cost of moving these people might well prove prohibitive in relation to existing capital. If one were moving them to areas with a large supply of capital, the difficulty was less serious, but if one were considering a move to Borneo, or Brazil, countries with little or no capital, there would be a considerable capital cost of movement, in providing social services, etc. This cost would be high in relation to the cost of financing development in the country where the potential migrants lived. Asia did need a supply of capital in the overpopulated countries, and the only long-run solution lay in a reasonably rapid increase of productivity. Then, Western capital was more likely to flow to the East, because the process might tend to become automatic.

This was connected with the immigration of skilled workers. The main hope of raising standards of living in Asia was to increase produc-tivity by improving techniques rather than by using more capital. There were considerable opportunities for increasing productivity with very little outlay of capital per head, but only if the necessary skills and training were undertaken. This would need a changed attitude. One wanted training and improved methods at all levels and not only at the highest levels. The Communist countries had tackled the problem of training and of using radically new methods at all levels, and might have succeeded for that reason.

Professor Silcock said it had been suggested that the educated middle classes in underdeveloped areas were opposed to the immigration of people in their own special classes, because their incomes would fall. Therefore trumped-up nationalistic reasons for keeping out people who might bring down their standard of living were invented. He felt that this interpretation was unfair to nationalists in these areas. As Professor Robinson had said, their opposition sprang from a reluctance to believe that monopoly could be prevented if the migration were large. People outside the areas found it difficult to appreciate that incoming migrants might develop a special 'group mind', delaying the pace of development by a desire to prolong their job and stay in the receiving country for a long period. Both nationalists on the one hand, and countries sending in technicians on the other, were likely to misjudge the importance of economic motives in distorting the attitudes of the migrant group.

There was, however, no effective opposition to education in underdeveloped areas. Indeed, there was great eagerness for technical education and training. But how could it be carried out, with the limited number of indigenous population capable of training others? If one brought in migrants at all levels to be temporary trainers of the indigenous population, one found it difficult for the migrants themselves to make the transition. The migrant was unlikely to understand fully the culture of the indigenous people, and his instruction would not be completely effective. On the other hand, if one sent natives away and trained them in foreign countries, they would need to be exceptionally able if they were to come home and apply the knowledge gained abroad, in a different cultural setting, to their own country.

On the whole, Professor Silcock thought the arguments in favour of having temporary migrants outweighed the arguments in favour of making migrants permanent. But, in either case, one needed to work out a detailed programme to meet particular needs. If one were importing capital and also entrepreneurs, the capital was intended to come permanently, and the entrepreneurs would cling to it and would resent the idea of handing it over to natives. One needed temporary migrants to run public investment and public works, as well as much technical assistance. Joint programmes should be worked out by the receiving and the sending countries, with finance arranged on an international basis. There were, moreover, drawbacks to having all temporary migrants brought in under a single administrative scheme. Salary scales would then depend on attracting specialists to an international organization. Many of the problems of specialist migration might be solved by bilateral agreements, for example between India and Japan and some of the other Asian countries.

Professor Bachi said he shared most of Professor Chandresekhar's views, but was not convinced by the argument which he brought to support these views. Professor Chandresekhar thought that since the fall in mortality rates was inevitable, and since birth control was not possible and internal migration in Asia would not work, Asian countries must have oversea migration. He was not convinced by Professor Chandresekhar's points about birth control. There had been disappointing results in the research in India, but it was too soon to draw final conclusions. The expense of birth control would not be so great as the expense of raising millions more children. Free emigration from countries with population pressure merely meant that they would bring their own problem with them.

Professor Chandresekhar had said that people going to other countries would learn birth control quickly. He was not convinced, though, in time, birth control could be enforced. When mortality was reduced, and more children kept alive, the number of children per family would increase. The indirect cost of compulsory education, which meant that the child could not work until the age of 14 or so, would bring great pressure on the economic resources of the family. But Professor Bachi did not see why these people should learn birth control any more quickly if they emigrated; they would not have sufficiently large cultural contacts. In Israel there was a very large oriental immigration, and these immigrants were living in the most favourable conditions from the point of view of making contact with other people. After a few years they should have learnt birth control, but they had not, although the infant mortality rate had dropped very much.

When speaking of internal migration within India, Professor Chandresekhar stressed the great difficulties of adjustment to conditions in other provinces. But this argument applied, *a fortiori*, to Indians leaving India. Father Ávila's suggestion that the decline in mortality in underdeveloped countries might be only temporary was not convincing. Mortality rates in fact did continue to decrease. We must base ourselves on statistics and facts, and not on arguments. In spite of the shortcomings of statistics, the available figures certainly did not bear out Father Ávila's argument.

Professor Spengler replied that Father Ávila really meant that the changes in death-rates were affected by economic influences. After a time, improvements in medicine could not contrive to diminish mortality if there were adverse economic effects. This was a sound generalization.

Professor Lerner said it was important to argue deductively here, although Professor Bachi said one should stick to statistics. Statistics showed that, when medical advances lowered infant mortality, this was not followed by higher mortality among older people. But this implied continuing economic development. Progress in medicine might result in the substitution of malnutrition for malaria.

Professor Timlin pointed to the dynamic problem for the receiving nations. In Canada the population was between 15 and 16 million. The rate of natural increase was currently about 2 per cent with fair prospects of continuing at that rate. Death-rates were falling continuously. Some

Canadians held that a rate of population increase per decade of about 25 per cent was the greatest the country could stand without social dislocations. She did not believe there was any magic about this particular figure. This limit would vary with circumstances; but there must be some rate, at any time, which would be the maximum tolerable one. It seemed likely that for some time Canada's yearly intake could not be much more than 200,000 without risk of serious dislocation. There was not the faintest chance that Canada could take enough migrants annually in the near future to make any real contribution to solving general world population problems, even if the migrants came from nations which assimilated with Canadians fairly quickly. There was a genuine dynamic problem in the receiving countries as well as in the countries of emigration.

Professor Bachi said he did not intend to say that Father Ávila's argument was the same as the nineteenth-century scientists' arguments. It was a good biological model, but was not confirmed by the statistics. For the time being, statistics did not confirm that the fall in mortality was provisional, though, of course, it might be.

Professor Mahr said he had suggested that Western countries should prohibit larger immigration in the interest of self-preservation. There was also little prospect that a lower standard of living (on account of large immigration from poor countries) would induce Europeans to have more children. As was shown by recent European experience, a sophisticated population would stick to birth control when the economic situation got worse. Hence the proportion of immigrants would increase rapidly. Dr. Edding had said that it would be in the interest of overpopulated countries if they were to prevent the emigration of the only people European countries wanted, namely, skilled workers. It was not a very strong argument. In European countries there were many profitable uses for unskilled labour. The real objection to Asian migrants was that there was no widespread desire to import vast amounts of cheap labour into European countries. They desired to keep up their standard of living.

Professor Silcock did not dispute that there could, with migration, be an Asian majority in time in European countries, but there was no reason to regard that as a disaster.

To Professor Chandresekhar, *Professor Lerner* said he did not think that overpopulation, resulting in bursting at the seams, was a cause of war. If peoples could not produce enough to feed themselves, they could not afford to produce the implements of modern war, though this was cold comfort. Many sentimental arguments had been used in the discussion. For example, to explain the resistance to birth control by saying that it was too expensive was unconvincing. It was cheap when compared with the expense of the alternatives. A cultural objection was at the root of the problem. Second, there had been objections to emigration by Indians. In some countries they had become money-lenders and indulged in sharp practices. Yet a few more Indian migrants would soon stop excessive earnings for money-lenders by bringing greater competition.

Third, the restrictions on emigration of unskilled people, who were not given all the privileges of citizenship in receiving countries, were again the result of sentimental feeling preventing an amelioration.

Father Ávila said that the only alternative to birth control was industrialization and the development of natural resources. One must decide which type of solution would bear fruit soonest, leaving out the sentimental arguments. If birth control were to be enforced, it would be a long time before the demographic changes in birth-rate could give economic results. If one compared this necessity for long waiting with the possibility of trying other solutions, industrialization might be much quicker. So far as the decline in death-rates was concerned, he had merely meant that there was a question not only of saving the lives of children, but also of saving the lives, in illness, of young people and of those in later life.

Professor Ellis said that the argument by which Professor Spengler and Professor Lerner had supported Father Ávila was correct, but too narrow. They were still talking in terms of mortality rates. Father Ávila was considering not only birth- and death-rates but, in addition, all the elements of economic welfare, including *per capita* income. The advances of medicine might leave a large population which, whilst not noticeably dead, yet suffered the illnesses that went with poverty, and whose productive efficiency was seriously impaired. This was a serious brake on the internal accumulation of capital.

Professor Chandresekhar said that Professor Bachi had given an objective summary of his thesis, but he himself had kept out, for brevity, the objectives of the Indian plan. The first aim was the improvement of agriculture, since one could not now afford the luxury of a desert. Industrialization came second, and this needed raw materials, 'know how', capital, and an internal market for cheap, semi-skilled labour. India had not got capital or 'know how'. Third came internal migration; fourth, external migration, and fifth, more birth control experiments.

To Professor Lerner, Professor Chandresekhar said that Asian emigrants did not wish to lower the standards of living in other countries, but to raise their own. War was not likely to happen, though over-populated countries could be a menace to international peace. It was not the man at the bottom, but the one a little higher up the ladder who would fight for another chance. There was a place for sentiment in human affairs, and one might well suggest the need for humanizing economics.

Professor Lerner felt it important to distinguish two interpretations of sentiment. He paid as much attention to Professor Chandresekhar's type of sentiment, meaning liberal ideas, as anyone. But his own interpretation of sentiment was quite different. He meant a point of view which overlooked the ultimate effects of a policy because it concentrated on immediate symptoms.

Professor Rubin said that through conquest by population we might eventually have an Asiatic or a Communist majority. It was the problem of a finite planet. What troubled him was that we had considered the problem of the Far East in isolation, as though one could solve it without solving Europe's problems. But might there not be competition between European and Asiatic migration ? Who would go to Brazil ? Italians or Indians ? There was no point in talking of one world; we had a free world, a Communist world, and an 'uncommitted' one. Could world migration be divorced from the world population problem ? The approach to-day had been on the lines of individual experiences. No one was looking at the problem in a total, international sense.

Mr. Meenan had been struck by the contrast between Indian and Irish experience. In the first half of the last century, Irish population had grown faster than the means of subsistence. Since the potato famine it had become smaller, and emigration was only one reason for that. Before 1840 marriages took place early and were very fertile, but since the famine the pendulum had swung the other way, with later marriage and low fertility. The rural population, in other words, did adapt itself to the situation in its own way.

Dr. Edding repeated his view that large-scale migration from the Asian countries was undesirable for both parties. He thought that speakers were mixing up free and assisted migration. Free migration was highly selective, and through it Asian countries would lose their most efficient workers. Assisted migration must surely be selective too. So, in fact, all migration was selective, and this seemed to be a law. So far as demand in the potential receiving countries was concerned, he stuck to the assumption that, for unskilled labour of the type available in South-East Asia, there was no demand in the rest of the world. Unskilled workers must nowadays have some skill in handling machinery, etc. He was convinced that the unskilled labourer from South-East Asia was not in demand in Europe, and workers with even the slightest experience of modern methods of production were needed urgently in Asia itself. In the future, with the large technological changes to be expected, conditions for development schemes and migration would perhaps be different.

Professor Bachi wondered if Professor Chandresekhar would agree that his criticism of internal migration would apply also to external migration. If there were barriers to migration, this could lead to war, but it worked the other way too, and some wars were the effect of the existence of national minorities.

Professor Chandresekhar said that internal migration did lead to some problems of assimilation. But there was no space for internal migration anyway, and the only internal migration in India was seasonal.

Professor Thomas was surprised that Professor Silcock should take it for granted that monopoly would prevail in the immigrant sector. He was not satisfied with this assertion, which needed an empirical foundation. Professor Silcock wanted a big inflow of capital to provide public utilities, and said one could not avoid monopoly in the skilled and entrepreneurial sector. Economic development would confer big monopoly gains on this group, and nothing could be done about it. Was it not more reasonable to say that, since there must be government intervention to encourage the capital flow, it was reasonable to suppose that the government of the receiving country would step in to ensure competition ?

Professor Robertson said he wanted to develop Professor Thomas's point, and at the same time redeem a promise to answer the question whether, though an inflow of skilled labour ought to benefit unskilled indigenous labourers, it might also delay their upward movement in industry. He felt diffident, because he could not provide material for the model-builders, and had no unambiguous answer to his own questions. In this field the easy answer was always wrong. He would not try to give a simple, comprehensive statement, but only make a few observations. Professor Silcock had suggested that the professional interests of migrants with skills might lead them to resist the idea of transferring these skills to competitors among the indigenous population. There was some evidence in South Africa which seemed to support this.

In two provinces of the Union no certificate of competency was issued to anyone but a white for a position of responsibility in a mine, by an Act of 1911. It was obvious that competence was necessary to responsibility. In the Cape, a certificate was granted to anyone who could prove his competence, but in the Transvaal and the Orange Free State only to whites. This was an absolute legislative barrier to the rise of the coloured worker. Did the immigrant raise this barrier to the rise of the non-white worker ? The answer was not clear. It was a legislative barrier, and South African governments had not shown themselves particularly anxious to protect recent white immigrants. By now, at least 70 per cent of white miners having these positions were Afrikaans-speaking. Skilled immigrants had succeeded in keeping out competition only from the black indigenous population, and not from the white indigenous population. In the Union, and in Southern Rhodesia, all trains were driven by whites. These used to be Irishmen or Scots, but were now African-born, Afrikaans-speaking whites. There was no barrier to skill being acquired by the white indigenous population. But further north, trains were driven by coloured men. Was this a difference of policy ? Or was it the consequence of smaller migration ?

The answer was not easy. It was, at any rate, far too simple to claim that immigration necessarily cut down the opportunity for indigenous populations to acquire skill. The social, economic, and political pattern formed during a period of extensive migration had imposed a barrier to the upward movement of indigenous workers. How far did these factors operate for present and future migration ? That depended on degrees of competitiveness and complementarity.

Recent experience, since 1945, showed that in conditions of near-full employment, and with assisted immigration, some benefits to indigenous workers were possible. Although the skilled group was now very large, technical education was as yet quite unable to provide an adequate supply of technicians. Hence, in the short run, immigrants seemed to be complementary with, rather than competitive to, indigenous workers; for the long run, the evidence was inconclusive. On the whole, in the long run, immigration seemed more likely than not to be in the interests of the indigenous population. In East and South Africa, the balance of advantage was in favour of permanent, and not temporary, immigration. The permanent migrant had a continuing interest in the new country. The other attitude was essentially the same as the much criticized one of the government of South Africa. It assumed that the interests of the different races and colours must always clash, and the races must there-force be kept apart. Yet such clashes of interest could only be worked out in a common society.

Professor Hoffmann said that, so far, there was general agreement that migration was desirable in principle. Whether it would raise specific problems depended on its magnitude. If we were to avoid unlimited migration from the East, there were only two possibilities. First, capital might move to labour, as in Italy, though free investment of capital was more successful if combined with necessary entrepreneurship. The other problem remained. The backward countries themselves must be developed. Agriculture should come first. To-day it had been argued that, with rising incomes in Asia, the propensity to consume would rise so fast as to rule out saving. But the possibility of compulsory saving, and of specific methods of encouraging free saving, were still to be considered. One needed to develop 'saving-mindedness'. If only one could develop savings and improve agriculture, the agricultural surplus would allow for capital formation. A market was surely still available for this surplus. Parallel with the development of agricultural productivity, there should be slow and systematic industrialization. If the process could be correctly synchronized it would create the chance to carry out internal capital formation, and that was the only chance to absorb more population increase. If a rice surplus could not be exported, what about other products? We often overestimated the importance of immediate industrialization as a factor in economic development.

Professor Silcock closed the discussion, saying that he did not wish to imply that we should take it for granted that monopoly would exist among immigrant entrepreneurs. But a tendency did exist, and it was as reasonable to expect monopoly as to accuse nationalists of putting development in jeopardy by resisting immigration. He was not saying that the acceptance of migration by nationalists was impossible, but that there were obstacles in the way. One needed the Asian countries to open their doors to migrants and to make adjustments in their own economies. Which was the best method: temporary or permanent migration? Temporary migration had advantages, but its problems were considerable, and temporary migration needed even more advance planning than permanent migration. Much preparation had to be done, and there was much to be said for bilateral negotiations and less for arranging migration through international agencies.

Professor Silcock stressed the difficulty of placing refugees. One should recognize that absolute standards for professional work differed over time. Methods were different from what they had been thirty years ago, and one should not expect to be able to transplant easily old ideas to a new country. Much preparatory study had to be done. Professor Silcock felt that the movement of temporary workers might, in future, replace permanently the movement of entrepreneurs bringing in their own capital. The development of public utilities required external aid, as did the training programme. What was needed was public capital for building up public utilities, not a large supply of capital for particular industries.

THE DISCUSSION ON PROFESSOR SAUVY'S PAPER

Thirteenth and Fourteenth Sessions, Saturday 10 September 1955

Father Ávila said the first point to settle was the meaning of 'assimilation'. It meant becoming similar to the native. The term had been taken over by biologists to mean the integration of an individual into the *milieu*, but this description did not cover its sociological meaning. Father Ávila said that Professor Sauvy had hesitated in his definitions. On page 299 he had defined 'assimilation' as occurring when the former immigrant could no longer be distinguished from natives, and was indeed no longer aware of his peculiar characteristics. On page 301 he had said that assimilation did not mean that all individuals born of migrants became identical with nationals. There was, however, no fundamental contradiction between these definitions. The first definition referred to the individual and the second to the group, though the individuals in the group might not themselves become assimilated as individuals.

He himself preferred the definition proposed by Professor Morini-Comby in Professor Baudin's book, *Traité d'économie politique*. This defined assimilation as an attitude of loyalty on the part of the immigrant, whereby his reactions manifested his spontaneous solidarity with the receiving country, and his free participation in the collective life of the receiving country. Starting from this, Father Ávila discussed assimilation. He considered it first in terms of the individual. The process of assimilation, he said, had several stages, installation, adaptation, assimilation. There was a voluntary element in assimilation, and the immigrant who wished to become assimilated did so much faster. Professor Sauvy regarded naturalization as an index of assimilation. Father Ávila agreed; but it was not 100 per cent indicative of assimilation. People who were entirely assimilated might not be naturalized, because the receiving country did not bestow all rights on migrants, and they could not, therefore, afford to lose all the rights of the old country. People might also become naturalized, in order to gain economic advantages, without being assimilated. In considering assimilation, the capacity of the receiving country was important. In Canada, Professor Timlin had suggested that there was an optimum annual rate of absorption; too many people could not be absorbed in a given period. The absorption capacity of a country might be defined in terms of an economic optimum. Social and psychological factors were also important, but economic troubles would be less acute if the annual entry were adapted to the country's absorption capacity.

Since this raised the concept of an economic optimum, one should be able to decide whether a population was too numerous or too small by calculating an index of resources available for home use and comparing this with the size of population. For Brazil, he himself had drawn two curves. The curve of economic development had a regression coefficient of 5·13; that of demographic increase a coefficient of 2·95. This showed that population in Brazil was not increasing as rapidly as the economy was expanding. On such a basis one should be able to estimate the correct rate of annual entry. If the annual rate of entry exceeded the absorption rate, one either had considerable repatriation of migrants, or many 'socially marginal' immigrants who were not integrated in the population, for instance criminals. The whole problem of psychological assimilation was less difficult if the immigrant could contribute towards the achievement of an optimum population. Immigration countries with low national incomes should apply a progressive immigration policy.

So far as the group was concerned, it was important to realize that in Latin America the rate of assimilation of the group depended largely on the capacities of the receiving country and on its 'social digestion'. In Brazil there were groups of immigrants who had been there for two generations and who were still not assimilated. Would they have done better in the United States, with its bold immigration policy? In Latin America one had a vicious circle. These countries could not allow a rate of immigration higher than that which they could assimilate; and yet a large volume of immigration was a force which increased assimilability. In Latin America, too, there was a fear of minority groups, which were looked on as artificial growths on the body politic. There was opposition to compact migrant groups. The existence of groups two or three generations old did not signify that they were not assimilated. The complete dissemination of the group was so rare as to be exceptional.

For instance, in the first phase of Jewish immigration into Israel there was great idealism and dissemination. Now, the groups going into Israel tended to retain their identity. Similarly with Italian and German immigration into Brazil, group migration had either improved the reception of new migrants, or led to assimilation. In Brazil there were two groups, one in the north and one in the south. In the south these were entirely homogeneous communities, with many Germans still speaking no Portuguese; yet they had been assimilated into the economy through establishing their position and becoming economically stable. The northern group had all the economic and social characteristics of the natives. They had been assimilated to the extent of losing all their individual features.

Father Ávila wondered if one had to assimilate migrants to the extent of lowering their standards of living. Surely one should not worry about complete assimilation, so long as people established their place in the economic life of the country. The countries of Latin America offered tremendous possibilities, provided that there was international co-operation, and that there was not too much nationalist sentimentality which so often only concealed economic selfishness.

Professor Baudin said assimilation was often described as a social problem. He did not like this definition, since it was too vague. It was a very complicated psychological problem, all the more so because it was often a problem of 'mass' psychology. There were very few general studies, only partial ones; the problem as a whole had not been tackled. Professor Sauvy had ignored psychological influences from the point of view of the emigration countries, yet psychological problems arose there too. Assimilation could be defined as a bilateral phenomenon, namely the clash of two national psychologies. It represented an adjustment to surroundings and also an absorption by the receiving country, depending on its attitude to migrants. Professor Baudin did not want to revert to the definition used by Professor Sauvy, though it did not satisfy him. Professor Sauvy regarded assimilation as a terminal point; he himself thought of it as a process with various stages.

The first stage was that of pre-assimilation. This first effort towards adaptation by the migrant was an effort of will power, in which he might be or might not be assisted by the receiving country. Physical adaptation to climate, for example, getting used to the tropics, had to occur in certain countries. There was always economic adaptation, to new housing, employment, etc. and psychological adaptation; habits, social life, etc. This stage was not difficult to understand, but it was difficult to apply principles to it in practice.

The second stage was the one of integration. This was much more interesting, though there was not yet complete fusion with the native element in the new country, or a complete rupture from the country of origin. Migrants were now no longer the same as people in the country they left. There were here two elements, one subjective and one objective. Subjectively, immigrants started to feel some solidarity with their new surroundings. Objective criteria showing this would be their knowledge of the local language, and naturalization. Father Ávila was right when he said that naturalization did not necessarily mean adaptation, being only a legal phenomenon. Willingness to do military service in the new country had often been regarded as a determining criterion by many countries. In the economic field, there were some very good indicators of assimilation. The family budget showed the degree to which the mentality of the migrant had been adapted to his new surroundings. At any rate for any given item — saving, for instance — it showed how far migrants felt like natives. But still, even in stage two, there were dissimilarities, for instance in language. The migrant still had a foreign accent. In stage three there was complete amalgamation and complete identification of the migrant with the native.

On the other side of the picture, one had to look at the capacity for absorption in the surroundings. From an economic point of view there could be the defence measures of the new surroundings; for example, hostility by local trade unions. Similarly, political factors, like fear that immigrants would take over the country, led to talk of undesirable aliens. Government policy might be based on the assumption that migrants would not be assimilated. One had often seen this fear in the governments of receiving countries, though it was not rational. For example, during mass immigration the Venezuelan Government's official immigration policy at the time of Juzman Blanco had been based on the fear that foreigners would become undesirables. German and French colonies were established to achieve a balance among the immigrants, so that neither nationality would become too powerful. The unity of such colonies differed. German colonies in the Rio Grande do Sul (Brazil) were quite coherent. In the French colonies in Argentina the settlers were much more separate, and the colonies less coherent.

The most important question in this context was: what are the determining factors in the process of assimilation ? The situation in this field was obscure, because of a lack of reliable statistics. Professor Baudin said he would like to enumerate the factors. (*a*) The ethnic element was essential; race was a fact. Demographic statistics in Latin America were no longer kept according to race, in order to avoid 'racial discrimination', according to the first Inter-American Demographic Congress in Mexico (October 1943). But now the statistics were chaotic. In any case the cataloguing of races was difficult, all the half shades being very difficult to classify. In Brazil the problem did not exist, because of an admirable process of assimilation. But in the Pacific states, Peru, Bolivia, and Ecuador, with their juxtaposition of races, there was still some antagonism and hostility. The decision to do away with racial statistics was bad for science. (*b*) The problem of different ideologies, languages, religions, habits, food, and clothing had to be studied as a factor in assimilation. (*c*) Professor Baudin suggested that there were different processes for the assimilation of the *élite* and the mass. The assimilation of the *élite* represented individual infiltration. The assimilation of the mass was a process concerning groups as a whole. From this difference resulted a problem of the concentration or dissemination of migrants. Some South-American governments had provided plots of land in different parts of the country in order to break the coherence of the groups, but there was also a spirit of coherence in the masses which should not be too much damaged. Polish immigrants to France had been disseminated to all parts of the country. They spoke no French, and suffered a high rate of mental disease, etc. The French Government later issued regulations to try to keep Poles near enough to each other to avoid these evils. In many cases it had been found that the *élite* assimilated much more quickly than the average citizen. This applied also to lower categories. (*d*) Another important factor was the migrant's generation. Assimilation was proportionate to one's generation. Second generation migrants assimilated much better than others. The maternal element was also important. In mixed marriages the process of assimilation was more rapid when the wife was a native. Sex proportions were therefore important. Male migrants sometimes assimilated much too well with native females. French and Polish girls in Argentina were assimilated quickly. It was very hard to classify the elements which came into play during assimilation, that was to say, according to groups and not according to nationalities, since it depended very much on individuals. In his attempts to get statistics which would throw light on this problem, Professor Baudin had been unsuccessful.

Professor Spengler felt that one should distinguish, in discussing assimilation, between (*a*) the community, and (*b*) the association based on contractual relationships. In studying assimilation, one might say that too high a rate of immigration undermined the community of a society. A much higher rate of migration could be absorbed if one were looking at a country only in terms of (*b*). In other words, one had two absorption rates, and (*b*) was much higher than (*a*), so that (*a*) was the limiting factor. In the United States one had cultural pluralism. Many cultures, like overlapping circles, surrounded a common core, which was the peculiarly American culture. This core had to be sufficient to sustain the immigration. For 'Gesellschaft', the community must have this underlying 'Gemeinschaft'. American culture was pluralistic because of its diverse ethnic origins, with the result that groups were assimilated rather than individuals, and there was little immigration of the *élite*. This pluralistic character would persist. Professor Spengler did not agree that assimilation was always to the good; a pluralistic society had its advantages. The minimum 'Gemeinschaft' was the only essential, so that one could build on it. The pluralistic character of American society seemed to make for progress, accelerating the rate of American development.

In answer to a question from Professor Robinson, Professor Spengler explained that by a pluralistic society he meant one in which a number of elements had been imperfectly fused. They shared in the common core, but beyond that they displayed distinct group characteristics. In America the imperfectness of the fusion process had been beneficial. Fusion was a dynamic element, leading to progress; with too little tension there would not be enough of a dynamic basis for progressive economic life. It followed that assimilation should not be pushed too far.

Professor Rubin did not agree. America's first problem was the assimilation of the native-born, for example French Canadians, negroes on the Southern border, and Puerto Ricans. The problem was first to assimilate all natives into the general pattern, and second to assimilate the foreign-born. Professor Spengler was clearly right to say that America was not homogeneous; there were tremendous differences. Each state had such different characteristics that there were in fact forty-eight different operating communities. Each state had its own laws, preventing foreign-born people from holding certain positions, and the geography of assimilation was likewise variable. There was a tendency for immigrants to concentrate in large cities; 90 per cent of foreign-born in 1950 were concentrated in about ten large cities. Within these cities the foreign quarters were even more clearly defined. One had Italian communities, foreign language newspapers, and so on.

The age distribution of immigrants also raised problems. Young children going to school had an easier time than the parents with problems like language. The adult education programme of 'citizenship preparation' was not a substitute for the normal education of children. Another factor was the occupations into which immigrants had gone. In New York City there was an extreme concentration of immigrants in the garment trades. But the children of Jewish and Italian migrants had not followed them there; Puerto Ricans were now going into the garment trade instead. This process of occupational limitation did not lead to assimilation; but political and cultural literacy was another problem. In the reverse direction, the United States had adopted many foreign words into its language. The immigrant had become assimilated, in part, by ceasing to use his native language. Assimilation of vices took place too; the second generation of migrants had a crime rate closely approximating that of the native crime rate.

Dr. Zubrzycki gave information about the absorption of Poles and other postwar immigrants into the United Kingdom. But first he made a general point. Assimilation, as a general term, was not sufficient to describe a process which required some kind of adjustment on society's part. He preferred to use the term 'adjustment' as a term to cover three processes. First, there was conflict (a feeling of alienation, personal disorganization, mental illness, suicide, etc.). Second, there was assimilation, a positive adjustment where the immigrant was so completely integrated that he lost the sense of separate identity. Third, between these two extreme cases, one had various states of accommodation — various kinds of half-way houses. The minority group would retain its cultural identity and might not be completely accepted, though it would be tolerated if it did not obtrude too much. Such a minority would associate only with itself and would not use the social and cultural amenities of the receiving society. Within this framework, Dr. Zubrzycki considered that the postwar immigrants to the United Kingdom (four-fifths of them Poles) had reached a state of accommodation, but were not assimilated in his sense. Assimilation occurred in mixed marriages, or with children who received education in Britain.

The main impetus to assimilation came from: (*a*) a predisposition to change on the part of refugees, which was not high in the case of political refugees. The nature of economic and political society affected this predisposition to change. There were also institutional factors. Refugees kept up their own political parties and social organizations; there were sixty to seventy refugee schools in the United Kingdom, and the Poles had their own churches and newspapers. The Polish daily paper in London had a circulation of 32,000 and a much bigger reading public.

(*b*) The attitude of the receiving people was important. The British Government had shown a reasonable attitude, sometimes acting in the opposite direction to public opinion. The Polish Resettlement Act aimed to absorb immigrants, though treating them as migrants did not help assimilation. Similarly, when certain trade unions were voting against immigrants and hampered their absorption in various trades, the Transport and General Workers' Union, under Arthur Deakin, opened the door to immigrants and set up special branches for immigrant groups, providing an institutional framework for their absorption. But this again did not speed up assimilation, as it provided no medium for contact between individuals. There was great danger of the extreme isolation of immigrant groups.

REFUGEE HOSPITALIZATION RATES IN THE UNITED KINGDOM PER 1000

Attitude of Surrounding Population	Mixing	Not Mixing
Friendly	2·02	4·55
Indifferent	3·03	6·58
Unfriendly	—	6·21

An inquiry into the mental health of refugees (the results of which are given in the above table) showed a difference in the incidence of mental disease between mixing and non-mixing immigrant groups. Mental disease was here taken as an index of maladjustment. Dr. Zubrzycki said he had established a correlation between the attitude of the population and the attitude of the refugee. The lowest index of hospitalization was for migrants mixing with a friendly surrounding population. The correlation was not perfect, as the sample was too small, but it did seem to illustrate the danger of complete isolation of immigrant groups. It might be noted that the corresponding hospitalization rate for all England was 0·5 per thousand.

Professor Timlin said the Canadian problem had to be seen against the peculiar regionalism of Canadian society. Immigrant settlers came into the West at the same time as settlers from the native stock came in, a different situation from that in other areas of Canada. The attitude towards immigrants was consequently different in the different areas, people being more hospitable in the West. In Ontario, for example, one had a large body of opinion which regarded the British as the only possible immigrants; and in French Canada one had, among certain sections of the population, the attitude that 'no immigrant is a good immigrant'.

Professor Timlin agreed that Canada's experience supported the Spengler thesis. One had in Canada, with this pluralism, a setting which allowed the immigrant to feel an 'identity with a difference'. For example, Ukrainians came in without an *élite*. In two generations they had developed a new intellectual tradition, and were more confident of their racial background. As they became more Canadian, they had more confidence in their own traditions as well. So the plural background gave not only a biological diversity but also a richer and more varied cultural background. Descendants of migrants were not afraid to be different, because they felt Canadian. It was found that different stocks were intermarrying more quickly than in earlier generations. Genetic assimilation might soften cultural differences a little, but these would remain to some extent. In the great depression, internal migration from West to East had modified attitudes, and the war had changed them further. A man's rights as a human being, and not as someone of a different nationality, were being recognized; facts were marching before the law. Large-scale deportation of immigrants had been abandoned because public attitudes had changed. Politically it was often very dangerous to throw out landed persons now, though there were still some areas of hostility to migrants. Professor Timlin thought it was good for a country working for cultural diversification to bring in some groups needing protection in the first generation — but one must have some balance between those who assimilated slowly and those who assimilated quickly. Moreover, situations changed. A certain *rapport* had, for example, grown up between Canada and the Netherlands, based on the fact that Canadians were the liberating troops after the war, and on the quality of Dutch immigrants since the war. This was making assimilation of the Dutch into the Canadian pattern of society progressively more easy.

Professor Bachi discussed assimilation in Israel. He said that Jewish immigration into Israel was very recent. The population had grown from 84,000 in 1922 to 1·5 million now. He could not agree with Professor Spengler on the criteria for distinguishing old from new stock. 75 per cent of the population was foreign-born in 1950, and this was relevant to the discussion of the optimum number of immigrants. The immigrants had brought in very different cultures, so that cultures were now incredibly mixed, but one could make four definite assertions.

(*a*) Immigrants had a common Jewish background.
(*b*) They were prompted to move by a common political factor — the Zionist attraction to Israel.
(*c*) They still showed solidarity in their struggle for independence.
(*d*) There was still agreement on immigration policy — it must be free.

There was a revival of old ties, and of the Hebrew language. These were common values. But, within this framework, many different cultures were represented. Professor Bachi had doubts on whether this would develop into a truly pluralistic society.

It was difficult to find jobs for all migrants, because of the abnormal occupational structure of the Jewish population all over the world. For example, there were very few farmers. Yet the Zionist movement aimed to build up a self-supporting population, with a balanced occupational structure. Changes of occupation were being made, with the aid of deliberate state policy. Housing, for instance, was offered to agricultural workers, and 56 per cent of migrants had adapted themselves to different occupations in Israel. The main increase had been in agriculture and building; the main decline was in commerce.

Professor Bachi said new immigrants disliked communal life. The settlements were built up partly of people from the same countries, whilst the rest were mixed. Distances were so small that there were few areas where immigrants were isolated. Family budgets, languages and social contacts had all been the subject of research. On language, Professor Bachi said that in the first place there had been a revival of Hebrew for ideological reasons at the end of the nineteenth century, assisted by orthodox religion. Now Hebrew was the main official language. In 1948 half a million people used Hebrew — 75 per cent of the population. The vast mass of immigrants had much less ideological preparation, but necessity now did what ideas would not do. Hebrew was now the *lingua franca*. Research showed that age at arrival influenced the use of Hebrew, as did the length of stay, education, occupation, and country of birth. Females used Hebrew less than males. Professor Bachi said studies of personal adjustment had been made only for small groups. Here ideological orientation was found to be important.

On intermarriage, Professor Bachi said there was a tendency in Israel for people to choose partners from their country of origin. The main influences were the size of the migrant's group and the type of group. There was a systematic decrease, according to the length of stay, in the tendency to marry someone from the same country. The barriers between, say, Central Europeans and others were now much less than before. They might be integrated into a European core with the other countries round it. Professor Bachi said there was great opportunity in Israel for studying the stages of assimilation. He hoped he had been able to correct the negative conclusions of Professor Baudin in the morning session.

Professor Parenti emphasized the contradictory policy of immigration countries. They stressed the importance of assimilation, and yet kept tight control by means of labour permits, on the occupations open to migrants. European countries particularly did this with labour permits, which restricted migrants to occupations and/or locations. Permits were, first, temporary, with no certainty of renewal, and second, did not cover the migrant's dependants, so that children could not be integrated into the economy unless another permit were obtained. Third, controls over the migrant were not normally removed after a lapse of time. The exceptions were in the United Kingdom (after four years), Belgium (after ten years), France (after thirteen years), and, in the last month or two, Norway (after five years). This obviously hampered rapid assimilation, since the immigrant had no long-term prospects. Professor Parenti said that, comparing individual and group assimilation, there seemed to be difficulty for the Italian if he had to adapt himself in isolation. There was also difficulty in group immigration. It was hard for anyone to settle if all national groups were forcibly split up. This was particularly difficult with agricultural settlements.

M. Lannes said he agreed with Father Ávila that naturalization in no way indicated assimilation. Especially in countries where it was easily allowed, naturalization was a step towards assimilation; it marked a desire to be assimilated, since it expressed the wish to break deliberately and finally the political attachment to one's country of origin. But the desire to be assimilated, although a necessary condition, was not a sufficient condition for assimilation. On the other hand, he found it hard to believe that one often found immigrants who were fully assimilated but not naturalized. To the extent that naturalization depended on the wishes of the immigrant, which was usually the case, the fact of not having asked for it was a sign of non-assimilation.

There was, however, a tendency to confuse assimilation with adaptation. There were often occasions when there was satisfactory assimilation into an industrial or social *milieu*, but where total assimilation nevertheless did not occur because sentimental ties with the country of origin meant a refusal to break political ties.

In so far as racial factors constituted an obstacle to assimilation, this should be considered not in the narrow, anthropological sense, but in the larger sense of an ethnic factor. Migration from North Africa to France suggested that certain cultural factors (religion, morals, clothing, etc.) constituted as serious an obstacle to assimilation as racial characteristics in the strict sense.

Professor Silcock said the final stage of assimilation had three aspects. First, there had to be willingness to stay in the new territory and engage in the common life. Second, one needed group consciousness. Third, there must be indistinguishability. Willingness to remain permanently did not in itself constitute assimilation. There must be at least some measure of common consciousness. The amount of group consciousness depended on the functions of the community. If the community was under foreign rule the amount of common consciousness necessary to make self-government possible was very high indeed, though the colonizing power itself might provide the link, as the British had in Malaya. The degree to which group consciousness was necessary also depended on the attitude of the countries from which migrants came. Changes in the form of government, as in China, might affect the degree to which it was necessary for the Chinese to be integrated with the receiving community in order not to be a political danger. Since the various races, in Asia especially, were never likely to merge completely, absolute assimilation was not likely; one was not likely to reach an irreversible state.

Mr. Phillips said the discussion had illustrated that, in consideration of a desirable rate of immigration, one independent variable was the desire or reluctance of the receiving country to see changes in its population. UNESCO had stopped using the term 'assimilation' and now spoke about 'integration'. The assessment a country made of the strength of its community core was one basis for a decision on the number of immigrants to admit. Countries often refused to meet an economic need for more population by migration, because they were unwilling to alter the character of their populations. Techniques for promoting and speeding up the cultural integration of immigrants were being studied, and could affect the volume of movement. The capacity of individual migrants to be integrated had also to be considered. He referred to two UNESCO publications, *Flight and Resettlement* and *The Positive Contribution by Immigrants*. Professor Brinley Thomas, on behalf of the International Economic Association, had contributed to the latter study a paper which contained very interesting material.

Professor Chandresekhar said that, in considering cultural assimilation, one should remember that in certain ancient cultures, like India, China, and Russia, there had been many ethnic groups who had lived together side by side for centuries without any ostensible attempt or conscious aspiration to assimilate. The groups were mutually exclusive and showed no desire to merge. The presence of these diverse blocks was held to be a barrier to national unity, but experience showed that this was not so. The presence of these groups should be a symbol to countries which were trying hard to get assimilation. In the matter of cultural autonomy, the Indian Government was anxious to know whether to follow the American (melting-pot), or the Russian, model. In India, people preferred integration to assimilation.

Professor Robinson wondered if he could try to provoke the theorists. What was the relation between assimilation and the creation of some sort of economic structure? Professor Thomas had been holding out as an ideal the vertical mobility of all workers.

Professor Lerner said he had noted a movement towards a discussion of 'integration' rather than 'assimilation'. It had been suggested that assimilation was not complete while cultural differences remained. Yet complete economic fusion, with cultural separateness, was surely not incomplete assimilation. We should aim at a state where political and economic differences had gone but different cultures remained. Was it inevitable that old cultures must be lost if there was to be complete economic and political integration? Was this a sociological law?

Professor Brinley Thomas wondered if he could bring things into perspective. The nation, in principle, was represented by immobile factors of production in a certain area. If one had a 100 per cent turnover of units of population in a year, one had not got a nation; it was a contradiction in terms. The very idea of a nation presupposed a large degree of immobility. One had to accept the idea that one started from a common core, as Professor Spengler had said.

In Phase I there would be a host of immigrants coming into the country, and immigration would proceed up to a first critical limit, where migration was beginning to disrupt the core. Phase II, therefore, was one in which immigration slowed down, so that the nation could recover. The social tensions which had been generated would then act on economic growth. In Professor Spengler's model, economic growth was a function of tension, and, after a while, this tension acted on the core again. Finally, in Phase III, a choice had to be made between a lower rate of economic growth and less tension, or a higher rate of economic growth and more tension. In the nineteenth century America had a strong core to begin with, and a remarkable constitution that has withstood one and a half centuries of change. Phase I lasted a long time. The doors closed when the final wave of immigration, with unassimilable elements, reached the point where the country was threatened with social 'fragmentation'. No Latin-American countries had such a margin to play with — there was not much core. In the case of Israel, there was no core in Palestine itself at all.

Professor Thomas said Professor Robinson's point took him into different territory. The meaning of assimilation to an economist was the creation of a high degree of vertical mobility, to be achieved from one generation to another. By the third generation, immigrants to America were interchangeable with the native born. So one created what was, from some points of view, an ideal society. What did sociologists have to say on this?

Professor Rubin did not think there was any strong law of tensions. In the United States one sometimes had and sometimes did not have tension. In times of depression, foreign immigration became a disease; yet when there was a boom, America imported Mexicans in large numbers, despite the fact that Americans were not very fond of Mexicans. Professor Rubin also thought that Israel had seeds, even if it had no core.

Mr. Meenan suggested that where there was no economic tension, the pattern of development was very slow. The Irish position was that the natural increase was exported. For the people who were left there was a much higher standard of living than was justified by existing activity, and it was very difficult to push the economy into any new activity. Mr. Meenan pointed to the American constitution. The United States was predominantly a Protestant community, but the constitution did provide for the separation of the Church and the State; this removed one factor that might have caused tension.

Professor Hoffmann asked Professor Thomas if it was not necessary

470

to qualify the idea of tension ? Was he not assuming that tension was a positive factor, in that thriving competition was a motive force leading to economic growth ?

Professor Thomas said that by tension Professor Spengler meant sharp inter-group rivalry, a clash of interests between groups which were not well-integrated. On the other hand, he thought the concept was an unusual one. Tension as a result of economic growth was much more normal than this model, which regarded economic growth as a result of tension.

Professor Spengler said there must be a common core, with an essential harmony, to make the economic system work. The American population was of diverse origins, and the core itself was a changing thing ; each new group added to it. At the same time, one had something like integration. There were diverse cultures, partly integrated, and the basic conflict between them provided the competitive drive in the economy.

Professor Robinson said one could grant all this, but was it not true only because the system was integrated, allowing vertical mobility ? Would the kind of conflict which one found in parts of Africa lead to increased productivity ?

Professor Spengler said that certain intervening variables made the American case different from the African. The driving element was always present and one had the intervening variables to add to it. In the United States, integration rather than assimilation had generated pressures and had given rise to economic growth.

Professor Thomas suggested that one should make a distinction between (1) America, where the groups making up the society were all growing, and there was movement between them, so that the core was growing too ; (2) East Africa, with three 'nations' within one, the so-called 'nations' being in fact castes. Immigration was quite different in these two cases. In the United States one had increasing secular vertical mobility and no caste system. In East Africa there were three cores which did not cohere, and therefore there was no assimilation except within the individual 'nations' or castes. In the case of a country like the United Kingdom, wherever the freedom of movement hit a critical limit a crisis would be created for the nation. It was a matter of proportion. One should admit migrants only up to the point where migration had serious effects on the nation, on the core ; and this applied to all nations. Each nation would act in self-preservation and had a right to do so.

Professor Rubin suggested a model in terms of this analysis. In America, there was competition amongst the native-born, competition amongst the foreign-born, and also competition between the native-born and foreign-born groups. There was an attempt to keep one's old name and still be an American. In sport, in the arts and in the theatre, one could see competition between the groups, with migration in depression. The growth of the American economy depended on this double competition.

Professor Silcock wondered if the core was to be looked on as a group of people or an institutional structure. Was nationhood to include the type of core found in the American nation ? The core in the model must be that structure of relationships which was modified by bringing people in. If the core could only permit the entry of people with certain functions, there would not be much economic mobility. Hence the structure of the core might not be such as to foster mobility, and migration might not foster economic growth.

Professor Mahr stressed the importance of the availability of space in the United States at the time of large-scale immigration. Without space, America would not have experienced a very big growth in any of the other directions. Nowadays, technological resources and inventions were taking the place of space.

Dr. Langrod said that it was important to accept economic integration as a prerequisite of cultural integration. An immigrant who did not enjoy the economic opportunities and the social status which were given to natives could hardly be expected to become a really good citizen of a country. This applied also to the right to choose freely his place of residence and his occupation. One should follow Professor Parenti and recognize that the fear of becoming immobile within the receiving country, and the mental stress caused by the feeling of being discriminated against, increased the shock which any immigrant suffered for a quite lengthy period after his migration. Any such shock remained not without influence on the second generation, leading to an inferiority complex.

Dr. Langrod thought it important that public opinion in the immigration countries should be systematically influenced with a view to obtaining a better understanding of the purpose of migration and of the psychological needs and difficulties of new-comers. Unfortunately public opinion, and therefore also legislation, were often inspired not so much by professors as by grocers. To change this situation was therefore an important dynamic role of the professors.

Commenting on Professor Silcock's observations concerning the difficulties of assimilation of the Chinese in Malaya, Dr. Langrod said that where the wall between the local population and the newcomers was so high, a scheme for using the existing foreign ethnic groups and their old traditions to facilitate assimilation did not work. Assimilation needed an organized effort on the part of both groups. It needed time and, in certain countries, perhaps also the deliberate creation of a multiracial society. Dr. Langrod emphasized again that there could be no successful assimilations without economic and social integration.

Mr. Rahardt stressed the importance of vertical mobility. Many Dutch immigrants to Canada, who now owned their own farms, had entered the country as general labourers under a contract to work for two years on sugar beet farms. They had large families, who worked hard and saved hard. So, with the advantage of agrarian credits, they were to buy their own farms after the two-year contractual period. This principle of importing people to work in certain trades for a limited time was not necessarily indefensible.

Father Ávila closed the discussion. He replied to M. Lannes's criticism of his statement on naturalization. The contention that some assimilated people were not naturalized merely stated a fact. By naturalization a man did not merely acquire all the rights of the new country, and did not lose all the rights of his country of origin. There were also financial considerations. Father Ávila thought there was a need for negotiations between governments. He admitted that cultural factors did play a considerable role. One aspect of racial difference was that mixed marriages helped greatly towards assimilation. There was, however, a twofold obstacle; both individuals and also the country of immigration might be opposed to mixed marriages. Professor Spengler's model had been concerned with tension, introducing the idea of competition. He himself preferred to go back to sociological ideas of assimilation. Contact between cultures might be very valuable, and most fruitful for economic and cultural progress.

THE DISCUSSION ON PROFESSOR ELLIS'S PAPER

Fifteenth Session, Sunday Morning 11 September 1955

Professor Robertson said that the rather negative results, in terms of policy prescription, so far achieved at the Round Table, made this paper very important. We had already seen the lack of correspondence between the world's large supply of unskilled emigrants and its demand for skilled immigrants. The virtue of Professor Ellis's paper was that it really tried to deal with the fundamental issues. Nor did it avoid the problem of what constituted economic welfare. Professor Robertson suggested that we should provisionally accept Professor Ellis's definition and assume that our aim was to maximize *per capita* real income in each country, and yet not to lower incomes anywhere.

On the basis of static equilibrium analysis, it might be shown that an expansion of international trade would raise incomes more rapidly than would greater mobility of factors of production. But, since he stressed the importance of political interference with the movement of factors of production, Professor Ellis might have improved his exposition if he had not explicitly excluded the by-no-means-uncommon interference of governments with international trade in commodities. In fact, the argument ran here at rather different levels, owing to its compression. Part was concerned with the optimum distribution of resources in the world as a whole, an ideal case. Part dealt with what happened where governments interfered with this distribution — or with situations where one could not say what had happened to welfare because one country lost and another gained. Thus far, one was concerned with pure theory, though there was also a political judgement on likely developments in the real world. In the discussion, it would help to separate formal analysis from political assumptions.

Professor Robertson said he was glad to see the reference to 'Say's profound insight'. Say's much maligned law extended Adam Smith's realization that not merely was the division of labour fundamental to economic progress, but that it also could, and must, be a cumulative process. As a condition of this one should remember the important role which Adam Smith assigned to capital accumulation, so important a role, indeed, that Smith would not regard as productive a labourer who was not adding to real capital.

Professor Robertson said that Professor Ellis had noted how the standard of living in 'the West' was higher in the eighteenth century than it was now in the underdeveloped areas. We might well think better of Adam Smith's exhortations to parsimony as a means to rapid capital accumulation in backward areas. Could someone in the discussion examine the prospects and possibilities for capital formation in under-developed areas ?

Professor Robertson said that he did not regard Say's Law as 'mechanical.' It was an integral part of an analysis which needed the 'active entrepreneur' as an agent of the consumer, *anticipating* demand. Say had given a remarkable, though not systematic, analysis of the qualities of a good entrepreneur. One naturally wondered how far one could improve the supply of entrepreneurial ability in underdeveloped areas, in order to make the best use of capital from outside and to bring in new products. When one saw the ability and competitiveness of the new African entrepreneurs, fortified by the knowledge of modern industry, the task did not look impossible. But we had a very long way to go.

Professor Robertson said that everyone had assumed that the world did want economic progress. He was not sure whether, if Bentham's calculus could be established, a little stagnation might not be relished more than universal 'progress'.

Professor Ellis agreed that his static analysis might not have been sufficiently carefully formulated, and that one should certainly separate economic from political factors. One thing which he did not mean to do was to imply the Samuelson result that product mobility was a complete substitute for factor mobility. He thought Professor Samuelson had since modified his analysis and had shown that it was only a narrow model. He himself only wanted to say that, because of political barriers to the free movement of factors of production, the political gains from trade liberalization seemed to be all the bigger.

Professor Spengler wanted to make it clear that whilst migration had a function, that function was limited. For example, it was no solution for *severe* population pressure. So one must concentrate on the narrow field within which migration had a contribution to make. It could help to reduce disequilibrium in Europe and to solve the problems of countries like Canada. If one concentrated on such smaller problems, one might begin to see the very real contribution of migration to world economic welfare.

Professor Robinson said that Professor Ellis had rightly agreed that migration would be valuable if it moved people from over- to under-populated areas. But whilst the move might benefit the world as a whole, the underpopulated areas would resist it. Was the trend towards greater overpopulation ? Did economic progress imply increasing the pro-ductivity of men as compared with land ? Inventions tended to be either labour-saving or capital-saving. In the last fifty years, inventions had been labour-saving in relation to land, so that land was getting more and more scarce. Land-saving inventions were needed, which would increase output per acre with a given labour force ; such inventions were fertilizers, better seeds, etc. His own feeling was that land would become progressively more scarce, and that this growing scarcity would increase countries' reluctance to accept large-scale immigration.

When we suggested places where there was room for more migrants, did we take enough account of the effects of migration on the capacity of the indigenous population to use their land ? Even if economic development in East Africa led people to use land better, it would quickly make land more scarce. Some areas might be farmed more intensively and with greater productivity, but he did not believe that Africa would ever be settled as intensively as Europe.

Professor Robinson wondered how accurate Professor Ellis was when he talked of the relative costs of moving factors and products. He him-self was sceptical whether it ever paid to move labour. He had been trying to work out orders of magnitude, but was uncertain on the statis-tical form of Professor Ellis' argument. How much did it cost to move a worker ?

Mr. Rahardt said that I.C.E.M. calculated that it cost an average of 170 dollars to move one migrant from Europe to North America, and 350 dollars to Australia, with an extra 75 dollars added to cover the cost of inland transport and services at both ends.

Professor Robinson said that, in other words, the migration of a worker cost rather less than one year's product, ignoring capital investment in the receiving country in making this calculation. Besides, why add it in ? One would need resources for investment in the receiving country, but one would similarly release them in the sending country. He was not sure how much re-employment would cost. However if, through migra-tion, output in the new country was increased by, say, 10 to 15 per cent the cost of the migrant's movement would be repaid in, say, ten years. And in Canada and the United States productivity per man might be double what it was in his old environment. Movement to those countries could fairly quickly pay for itself.

Professor Robinson thought Professor Ellis might have stressed even more the 'migration of goods' as contrasted with the migration of people. However, he felt one should not say that, with free trade, it did not pay to move people, but only that there was less need to move people when one had free trade.

Professor Rubin agreed with Professor Spengler that migration would not solve the problems of Asia. Immigration could not be a unilateral solution. But the title of Professor Ellis's paper was misleading. There was no single solution to the problem of overpopulation. The whole problem should be seen as a world problem, to be looked at by a 'World Planning Commission' with a given aim (say, maximum *per capita* income). The Commission would need to examine both migration and trade as well as everything else. The problem was not soluble in terms of relations between two countries only. One needed a more general approach, and the mention of 'alternatives' suggested exclusion.

The paper suggested a piecemeal approach to the entire problem, and this meant that one must look at it on the largest possible scale. One must, however, remember that, in 1954, world trade equalled about 9 per cent of world income. Migration could never be of this size. Nevertheless, so far as it could be encouraged, migration was desirable. It could lead to both material and non-material gains.

Professor Silcock returned to the problem of the effect of development on the shortage of land. We had been asked to look at it in terms of land- and labour-saving devices. If one saved labour *vis-à-vis* land, that made land more scarce. But as incomes rose, the proportion of land-using goods consumed fell. So, with large-scale capital accumulation and rising incomes, the shortage of land might diminish. In fact, though capital was usually regarded as mobile, the really important factor was the mobility of capitalists. In the modern world, the need was to build up enterprise in different regions. If one got that, one might have capital drawn in because one could borrow money more easily with greater entrepreneurial ability. The real problem was to train entrepreneurs, and this need not mean scarcity of land. When one was considering the training of entrepreneurs, it was important to realize that enterprise did not merely mean the seizing of opportunities, hard work, and thrift. There must be a further factor. Hard work, thrift, and enterprise were found in China, but they did not lead to the building-up of large capital structures. Some of the ideas about accumulation were important, especially if one wanted to attract capital and not entrepreneurs. One needed to know about other factors affecting enterprise, and this was especially important in relation to migration.

Professor Robinson said Professor Silcock started from the claim that economic progress did not lead to a growing scarcity of land, because as incomes rose one had a smaller increase in the demand for land-using goods. In fact, in Europe one tended to use more land to get a given amount of goods than in Asia. Similarly, raw materials and textiles, which would be needed in larger amounts as income rose, all had high land-inputs. Again, water catchment requirements were very large in the United States. He very much doubted if one could double one's income and yet use only the same amount of land.

Professor Silcock said that he might have been reasoning on a fallacy. Yet the chief user of land was food production, and expenditure on food fell relatively with rising incomes.

Professor Lerner pointed out that one would still need more land per person, even though a rise in income meant that a smaller *percentage* of income was spent on land-using goods, even if food production really was the main consumer of land.

Professor Spengler said that the land input per unit of output had been reduced in some countries, though this had been partly offset by a change in the pattern of land use. On the other hand, world population was rising, and this was an important factor increasing the scarcity of land.

Professor Lerner said that the discussion had been on 'substitutes' for rather than 'alternatives' to migration. But the notion of substitutes raised the question of degree. How close substitutes were they? The elasticity of substitution between trade, capital movement and migration was not infinite and there was consequently still a place for migration, even with free trade and much capital movement. The problem really needed re-defining. First, for what purpose did one need migration? It was not practicable to use it to relieve population pressure. If one agreed on this, if one supposed that we stopped all population growth, and if development were defined as anything raising *per capita* income, the fact remained that one would still need population movement to equalize incomes in various countries. And one would have to move millions of people to do this — an impossible task. What Professor Ellis had in mind was moving people to raise *per capita* income in the receiving countries. This was a political issue of protecting the people in receiving areas.

Professor Thomas said he did not deny that, within a country, population moves could be a powerful force for relieving regional overpopulation, but in the present discussion we were concerned with migration between different national economies. In this sense, migration was a feeble method of overcoming population pressure, and this had always been so. The big transatlantic population movements in the nineteenth century had not done very much to alleviate population pressure in South and East Europe. So, when one considered migration as a means of international adjustment, one had to rule it out as a means of relieving the enormous population pressure in two-thirds of the world. On the other hand, this should not lead one to overlook the fact that internal development, so rightly stressed by Professor Ellis, ought to accompany any marginal adjustments such as the movement of capital or entrepreneurs. Nor should one forget that in some areas, for example New Zealand and

Latin America, there was more room for the nineteenth-century process than had so far been admitted.

Professor Thomas said he was at variance with Professor Ellis over the latter's statement that migration was ceasing to be a major factor in raising *per capita* incomes, because of economic and not because of legal factors. He himself would change the emphasis. Professor Ellis seemed to imply that the present legal system did not check migration, which was obviously not what he meant. There would clearly be a new inflow to the United States if the Immigration Act were repealed, and perhaps a very considerable movement from the less developed areas. Similarly, in South Africa would there not be more British migrants, given a different legal system? A change in attitudes, and a consequent change in laws, would lead to more fruitful marginal movements.

Mr. Turvey was still not convinced of the correctness of the arguments about land shortage, though he did not suggest that previous speakers were wrong. The income-elasticity of demand for primary products was less than one, but it had been said that the income-elasticity of demand for *some* highly land-using primary products might be greater than this. The pattern of consumers' expenditure depended on relative prices, so that the richer countries might spend more on land-intensive products.

Professor Robinson agreed with Mr. Turvey that the income-elasticity of demand for food was less than one. But he felt that for textiles, and so on, it was greater than one, especially in underdeveloped areas.

Mr. Turvey pointed out that Ricardo had said that some improvements would reduce rents. But labour-saving improvements would always make land more scarce. If one did have a relatively high income-elasticity of demand for agricultural products other than food, and most agricultural improvements were labour-saving, then the scarcity of land would be increased. The difficulty, from the point of view of migration, was that after a point land-saving developments became very expensive in terms of capital outlay, as, for example, with land reclamation. Did we not need specialist migration to deal with this?

Professor Hoffmann said that if the trend towards overpopulation in some areas continued, there would be a shift in the distribution of world production. Europe's share in world production, and presumably trade, would fall. Europeans might do better to sell their goods outside Europe because of the more rapid rise in incomes there. The volume of migration might be reduced, but not necessarily its quality, since there were much more attractive possibilities of earning big incomes outside Europe. This argument was supported by the socio-political point that the feeling of tradition was declining all over the world.

Professor Ellis said that all he knew about migration was what he had heard at the Conference, but he had found his thesis more plausible than he had hoped. In one respect he would like to qualify it. He was prompted by Dr. Hofstee's remarks to say that in special cases, like the Dutch one, there were potential migrants who could be spared and who could also help the receiving country. But, in support of his main idea, he had been struck by the contrast between the demand for immigrants in the receiving country and the supply of emigrants in the losing country. In general, these seemed to match badly. The receiving countries wanted skilled or semi-skilled workers — but so did the emigration countries.

In his paper he had ignored the effects of migration on techniques. This might be important, but he held to the general argument that transfers of technique were not intimately connected with capital movements. Another way in which he had been fortified was by Professor Lerner's views on inflation. Inflation was a besetting problem of developing countries. It was not so much an organic problem as the focal point for ultimate, 'real' institutional causes. For example, primitive tax systems led to inflation, because governments wanted large investments in public utilities which the tax system was unable to finance. He wished to emphasize how Professor Lerner had shown that the 'cost push' would arise where organized labour was strong, or where the government depended on the labour vote, even though trade unions were not strong, as in Argentina, and perhaps Brazil and Chile. The 'cost push' was even stronger where the budget was unbalanced because of large welfare spending, and where costs were increased by social security contributions from firms. This kind of factor was crucial for economic development in underdeveloped areas. Not only was there demand or cost inflation; one also had the distribution struggle mentioned by Father Ávila.

Professor Ellis said that he had not written more in his paper about the scarcity of land, because he felt it was a subject of such complexity that it would need an encyclopaedia to deal with it fully. He felt, however, that one must make Professor Robinson's distinction between land used for food and land used in other ways, for example through using up natural resources. So far as food was concerned, he did not see why our increasing ability to produce more food through technical advance need argue for migration. In fact, the new techniques affected the production of food in the more developed areas more markedly than in the less developed areas. With wasting resources, for example tin, the position was quite different.

Professor Timlin thought that, in discussing land shortage, one needed to do more than distinguish between land used for food and land used for textile fibres. One needed to take into account different types of food. Meat eating might be more important at higher incomes, and might lead to a more than proportionate change in the demand for land. Therefore one needed to base one's argument on statistical investigations of the consumption patterns for both food and textiles.

She herself did not believe that labour-saving improvements were necessarily rent-raising. There might be a change in techniques rather than a shift between the use of labour and land. One might come to use more capital and less labour per acre. This would raise family incomes because of greater investment incomes, but did not necessarily change land rents. Nor did increased farm output necessarily imply labour-saving or capital-using methods. Farm practices were subject to change. In Canada, one could use more fertilizer. It was a question of the relative values of inputs and outputs; one looked for bigger outputs from given inputs.

Mr. Turvey doubted whether Professor Timlin was right in saying that the introduction of labour-saving devices did not raise rents.

Professor Timlin said she was thinking of a bigger acreage per worker.

Mr. Turvey replied that one would not substitute capital for labour unless this led to lower costs. So, given that the price of the product remained constant, rents would rise. In practice, however, the price of the product might fall, and perhaps rents too. Since the war, with given wheat prices, one tended to economize on labour and use more capital. One might then have the same output per acre but not per man.

Professor Lerner thought that if the price of wheat did not fall, the demand for land might rise and thus keep up rents.

Professor Lindahl noted that in his paper Professor Ellis had spoken at one point of country A having lower wages than country B, and also a lower rate of interest. This seemed strange in terms of static analysis. Lower wages usually meant high interest rates. However, Professor Ellis's situation might be possible if one brought in land. For example, a country might have low wages but lack natural resources, so that its capitalists might therefore send their money to the United States, say, to get a better return on their money investments. But Professor Ellis went on to say that movement of capital might seem better than migration if one merely concentrated attention on the prices of capital and labour in A and B, especially if the country with low wages exported capital to a country like the United States. Professor Lindahl said he would suggest putting the proposition the other way round. One should assume that the country with the lower wages had the higher rate of interest. This would make the remaining argument easier too. A country like Japan had too much labour but was short of land and capital. This required either emigration or the sending of American capital to Japan.

Mr. Turvey commented that Professor Lindahl was assuming only one rate of interest for both lenders and borrowers. An efficient economic system would ensure this. In fact, rates to lenders and borrowers could differ, so that, for example, a West African might find it better to export his capital, because he thereby got a higher rate.

Professor Ellis said he did not see why, if one argued in real terms, all factors could not be abundant in relation to demand.

Mr. Turvey said that the idea of net advantage depended on relative factor endowment.

Professor Silcock thought it was clear what Professor Ellis meant. If capital were relatively more scarce than labour, then one needed migration to a country.

INDEX OF SUBJECTS

1. Numbers in *italics* refer to papers on the subject concerned.
2. Where references to *emigration, immigration,* or *migration* are shown separately under a country's main entry, they are usually further sub-divided into four groups labelled *causes and effects, policy, quality,* and *volume and direction.* This is intended as a rough classification and should not be interpreted too rigidly.

Absorption, 114-15, 117, 125, 128-9, 191, 198, *303-12*, 397-412, 460, 462-3, *see also* assimilation

adaptation, 299, 300, 398

Africa :
  British policy, 424-6
  emigration, 319-20, 322-4, 329-33, 338-41
  employment ratio, 356
  for the Africans, 424-5
  immigration, 117, 177, 179, 382, 388
  incomes, 351
  population, 176-8
  recruiting of labour, 179
  sex ratio, 177
  see also East, North, South *and* West Africa, *and the separate countries*

ages :
  of migrants, 25 n., 68-70, 79-81, 92, 119-23, 136-42, 203-5, 286-7, 323-6, 342-3, 384, 399, 401, 431, 464
  of population, 67, 142-3, 204-5, 241-242, 244, 324-6, 384, 386, 419, 431

aggregative effects of migration, 20-4, 28, 31, 381-3, 386-7, 392-3, 422

aggregative mode, 18-22

agriculture :
  development and structure, 124, 128, 133-4, 149, 175, 317, 326-30, 399, 409, 455, 458
  employment, 126, 180, 207, 276, 286-287, 329, 332-3, 383
  finance, 14, 128, 328, 355, 380
  migration, 45-6, 78-9, 95, 118, 124-8, 136-7, 146, 197-8, 216-17, 286-7, 332-3, 353, 380, 385, 387, 392, 398-9, 407, 415, 475
  movement into, 124, 216-17, 328, 330-331, 402, 408, 467
    out of, 127, 158, 192, 199, 221, 235-237, 409-10, 418

agriculture—*cont.*
  overpopulated, 45, 118, 125-6, 197-8, 221, 226, 341, 355, 407, 414, 418
  technical change, 127, 235, 353-4, 392
  training, 127, 288-9, 306, 399, 405
  workers needed, 127, 222-3, 306
    position of, 45-6, 284, 289-90, 386, 396, 472-3
  see also land settlement *and various countries*

air transport, 67, 113-14

Algeria, 219, 221, 319, 372

America :
  emigrants, 164, 320, 332-3, 339-40
  population, 25-6, 315
  see also Central America, Latin America, North America, South America *and individual countries*

Apartheid, 183-4

Arabs, 275, 278, 318-20, 326

Argentina :
  agriculture, 118 n., 305, 306 n., 408
  assimilation, 307, 463
  capital, 45 n., 47, 373
  construction, 6
  growth, 40
  immigration :
    causes and effects, 373, 401
    policy, 307, 310
    quality, 32, 34, 121
    sources and volume, 25, 26 n., 27, 37, 47-8, 89, 92 n., 120, 227, 312, 314, 409
  inflation, 431, 435-6
  internal migration, 401
  population, 25-6, 47
  public expenditure, 359
  repatriation, 310
  wage demands, 359
  see also South *and* Latin America

Asia :
  births, 340-1, 447, 453

Index of Subjects

Brazil—*contd.*
births, 401, 403
capital, 45 n., 47-8, 355
coffee, 188-91
economic development, 40, 188, 190-191, 460
foreign trade, 188, 191, 436
immigration :
causes and effects, 20 n., 25-6, 40, 47-8, 186-92, 348, 355, 361, 400, 436
policy, 401
quality and conditions, 32, 50 n., 121, 409
sources and volume, 25-7, 37, 89, 120, 185-7, 227, 312, 314
income, 348
inflation, 435-6
internal migration, 192, 400
population, 25-6, 47, 460
protectionism, 190, 193
repatriation, 310
terms of trade, 189-90
wages, 188-9
Britain, *65-76*
African polity, 175-6, 180, 424-6
agriculture, 410
assimilation, 422, 465
capital and investment, 3-9, 12-13, 66, 68, 71
construction, 6, 9
emigration,
causes and effects, 6, 65-6, 68-76, 360, 366, 390-1
policy, 71
quality, 41, 65-70, 73, 75, 136-7, 177
volume and direction, 4, 6, 12, 27 n., 37, 46, 65-8, 71-2, 137, 151, 154-5, 161, 163-4, 169, 175, 262, 274-6, 320
employment, 6, 70-1, 203
foreign trade, 9, 15, 70, 102
immigration :
causes and effects, 74-6, 82, 423
policy, 74, 81, 203, 422-3, 465, 468
quality, 41, 73-5, 81, 240
volume and direction, 67-9, 71-6, 80, 88-9, 169, 240, 312, 423, 425, 465
internal mobility, 71, 75
labour mobility, 376-7
migration finance, 405-6
population, 39 n., 65-6, 69-71, 75, 240
productivity, 75
refugees, 74, 465

Britain—*contd.*
resettlement, 68, 73, 465
terms of trade, 71, 365-8, 370
trade unions, 422, 465
building, *see* construction
Bulgaria, 225-237
Burma, 254-5, 261-2, 264, 444
business cycles, 66, 365, 375

Canada, *146-62*
agriculture, 146-9, 158, 385, 398-9, 407
assimilation, 152-3, 306-9, 399, 465-6
births, 26, 157
capital, 12-14, 45 n., 47-8, 71, 158, 368-70
Catholic Church, 152-3
Citizen Department, 156, 158, 160-2, 309 n.
construction, 6, 148
deaths, 157, 453
economy contrasted with U.S., 370
emigration :
causes and effects, 28, 147, 153, 159-60, 385
policy, 385
quality, 28-9, 153
volume and direction, 28 n., 36-7, 47, 147
foreign trade, 102, 159-60
immigration :
causes and effects, 26, 28, 40, 45 n., 46-8, 71-2, 103, 105, 147, 153, 156, 158-60, 305-6, 348, 361, 368, 370, 398-9, 401-2, 454
policy and requirements, 76, 146-156, 158, 160-2, 304, 307, 309 n., 385, 398-9, 403, 443
quality and conditions, 28-9, 32, 119, 121, 146, 153-8, 307, 398, 403, 410
volume and direction, 4, 12, 26 n., 27, 28 n., 65-6, 89, 120, 147, 153-6, 203, 227, 312, 314, 384-5, 398, 410, 443, 466
income, 158, 348
internal mobility, 398-9, 466, 472-3
labour force, 29 n., 156, 159-60, 306, 402, 472-3
marriages, 157
non-government agencies, 310-11
pluralism, 466
population, 20 n., 25-7, 47, 147-50, 153, 156, 353, 453-4
prices, 367-8
sterling crisis, 153

497

INDEX OF PERSONS

Entries in the Index in **black type** indicate the papers or the discussion on the papers of the persons concerned. Entries in *italics* indicate contributions to the discussions.

Index of Persons

Nathan, R., 264 n.
Nurkse, R., 354

Ohlin, B., 35 n., 42
O'Leary, P. J., 8-10, 374
Oudegeest, J. J., 96 n.

Pant, P., 284 n., 293 n.
Parenti, G., 85-95, *383, 389, 392, 399-400*, 402, *412-15, 418-19, 422, 435, 467-8, 472*
Parsons, Talcott, 40 n.
Pearl, R., 23, 153
Perlman, S., 36 n.
Petersen, W., 96 n.
Phelps Brown, E. H., 36 n.
Phillips, P. D., 44 n., 47 n., *373, 408, 469*
Pigou, A. C., 389
Plummer, A., 20 n.
Plunkett, Sir Horace, 80
Prebisch, P., 358
Prokopovicz, S. N., 46 n.
Purcell, V. W. W., 261 n.

Rahardt, E., *438-9, 472-3, 475*
Rao, V. K. R. V., 283 n.
Reed, L. J., 153
Reid, E. B., 156 n.
Rhodes, C. J., 177
Ricardo, D., 478
Riemersma, J. C., 10 n.
Robertson, Sir Dennis, 375
Robertson, H. M., 173-84, 176 n., 178 n., 179 n., *366, 379, 386, 391, 404, 425-6, 457-8, 473-4*
Robinson, E. A. G., 45 n., *368-70, 377-83, 386, 387-8, 390-4*, 395, *396, 407*, 409, *417-18, 422-6, 430-4*, 438, *439-40*, 441 445 *448* 452, 463, *469*, 470, *471, 475-8*, 479
Rogoff, N., 31 n., 34 n.
Röpke, W., 409
Rothbarth, E., 36 n., 382
Rubin, E., 25 n., 27 n., 48 n., 49, 49 n., 133-45, *366, 372, 375, 377-8, 380, 385-6, 390, 396, 403-4, 406, 409, 419*, 420, *422-3, 429, 431, 435*, 440, *448-9, 455-6, 464, 470*, 471, *476*
Ruppin, A., 314 n.

Samuelson, M. C., 40 n.
Samuelson, P. A., 43 n., 474
Sastri, Rt. Hon. V. S. Srinivasa, 262 n.

Sauvy, A., 20 n., 297-302, 305 n., **459-473**
Saxon, E. A., 172 n.
Say, J. B., 357, 474
Schechtman, J. B., 226 n., 283 n.
Schneiter, P., 124
Schumann, C. G. W., 175 n., 181 n.
Schumpeter, J., 350-1, 354
Silcock, T. H., 251-72, 361, *367, 373-4, 378-80, 387, 390, 394, 405, 410, 441-59, 468-9, 472, 476-7, 480*
Singer, H. W., 253 n.
Skaug, A., 45 n.
Smith, Adam, 474
Smith, T. E., 261 n.
Smith, T. L., 50 n.
Smuts, J. C., 182
Snell, G. D., 39 n.
Spengler, J. J., 17-51, 352, 359, *367-8, 376, 379*, **381-97**, *398-9*, 400-1, 404-5, 410, *414, 420*, 422, *429*, 433, 440, 444, 446, *448*, 450, *453*, 455, *463*, 464, 466, 470, *471*, 473, *474-5*, 476, *477*
Spiegel, H. W., 20 n., 41 n., 44 n., 45 n., 190
Srinivasa, *see* Sastri
Steigenga, W., 96 n.
Stonequist, E. V., 412
Strijdom, J. G., 183
Sunarti, W., 282 n.
Sundbärg, G., 4
Sundoro, 273 n.
Svennilson, I., 46 n.

Taeuber, I., 255 n.
Taft, D. R., 35 n.
Taussig, F. W., 31, 35 n., 36 n.
Theal, G. M., 174
Thomas, Brinley, ix-xiii, **3-16**, 21, 27 n., 28 n., 33 n., 34 n., 36 n., 37 n., 38 n., 45 n., 46 n., 47 n., 48-9, 48 n., 49 n., 51 n., 66 n., **365-81**, 382, *390-1, 393-4*, 395, *396, 405-6*, 408, *415-16, 423-5, 437, 442-3, 450, 456-7, 469-71, 477-8*
Thomas, Dorothy S., 46 n., 51 n.
Thompson, L. M., 179 n.
Thompson, W. S., 26 n., 35 n., 47
Thorndike, E. L., 50 n.
Timlin, M. F., 20 n., 28 n., 50 n., 146-162, *367-8, 370, 372*, 378, *384-5, 389, 397-9, 403*, 405, *408-10, 421, 430, 453-4*, 460, *465-6, 479-80*
Toynbee, A. J., 38 n.
Truesdell, L. E., 28 n., 153 n.
Tucker, J., 298, 392

Index of Persons

THE END

PRINTED BY R. & R. CLARK, LTD., EDINBURGH